PERFORMING ARTS SERIES

General Editor

FARLEY P. RICHMOND

VOLUME IX

Semiosis in Hindustani Music

Semiosis in Hindustani Music

José Luiz Martinez

MOTILAL BANARSIDASS PUBLISHERS
PRIVATE LIMITED • DELHI

First Indian Edition: Delhi, 2001

First Published in 1997 by International Semiotics Institute, Imatra, Finland

ISBN: 81-208-1801-6

Also available at:

MOTILAL BANARSIDASS

236, 9th Main III Block, Jayanagar, Bangalore 560 011
41 U.A. Bungalow Road, Jawahar Nagar, Delhi 110 007
8 Mahalaxmi Chamber, Warden Road, Mumbai 400 026
120 Royapettah High Road, Mylapore, Chennai 600 004
Sanas Plaza, 1302 Baji Rao Road, Pune 411 002
8 Camac Street, Kolkata 700 017
Ashok Rajpath, Patna 800 004
Chowk, Varanasi 221 001

Printed in India

BY JAINENDRA PRAKASH JAIN AT SHRI JAINENDRA PRESS, A-45 NARAINA, PHASE-I, NEW DELHI 110 028 AND PUBLISHED BY NARENDRA PRAKASH JAIN FOR MOTILAL BANARSIDASS PUBLISHERS PRIVATE LIMITED, BUNGALOW ROAD, DELHI 110 007

Contents

III Hindustani Classical Music and the Rasa Theory: A Semiotic Interpretation

Musical Examples

Tables

Figures

Foreword

It is a pleasure and an honor to introduce to Indian readers the work of the Brazilian scholar and composer Dr. José Luiz Martinez. The present volume—*Semiosis In Hindustani Music*—is the fruit not only of his studies in musicology and semiotics at the University of Helsinki, under the distinguished guidance of Professor Eero Tarasti, but also of his practical training in dhrupad (with Ustad Zia Fariduddin Dagar) and tabla (with Probir Mittra). To this unusual international mixture of South American, Northern European, and South Asian ideas, we must add Martinez's virtuoso command of the writings of the North American thinker Charles Sanders Peirce (1839-1914), one of the great pioneers in the discipline of semiotics.

Like most other successful studies, this work has a beginning, a middle, and an end. From the perspective of Indian musicians and music-lovers, the beginning will be the object of Martinez's study—the classical music of North India, as it is known today through practice and as supported by the śāstric tradition of Sanskrit musical treatises. The middle will be Martinez's examination of this great tradition, as seen through the lens of Peirce's provocative ideas on perception and the artistic experience-issues that have preoccupied Indian thinkers from ancient times, but none more significantly than Abhinavagupta, whose ideas receive detailed attention in this study. The end will be the theory of *rasa*, arguably India's major contribution to aesthetic theory and the philosophy of music.

As I wrote a few years ago when reviewing the Finnish edition of this work for the *Journal of the American Oriental Society*, '...some of the greatest advances in scholarship have arisen when an author demonstrates connections between seemingly unrelated fields. Martinez has an impressive command of these diverse fields of inquiry and makes a persuasive case for viewing and understanding the value systems of ancient and modern Indian music through the prism of Peirce's ideas. [...] Martinez is probably the only scholar in the world with this particular combination of interests and expertise, but there is nothing narrow about his scholarship. Anyone concerned with issues of signification and meaning - in Indian music, in Western music, or in other world musics - will find something to ponder here.' (Vol. 119, n. 1, 1999)

Musicologists will find that Martinez has drawn on both Western and Indian sources in his lively account of the evolution of the rāga system and the explanations offered by various śāstric authors for the meanings and special connotations of important rāgas. In the process he touches upon many controversial issues, and, while it is foolish to expect any author to say the last word on how and why rāgas mean what they do, Martinez provides a rich storehouse of information and interpretation that will help readers examine their own listening experience and their own reactions to rāgas.

Finally, I find it significant that this study is informed, not only by the literary and historical perspectives of a musicologist, but also by the musical instincts of a composer and performer. Indian thinkers have consistently held that theory is barren without practice, and of course they are correct. I invite Indian rasikas to consider the insights that can be gleaned from the present volume, and to take pleasure and pride in seeing how radiantly their musical tradition shines when reflected from an outside observer's perspective—a perspective that is at once thoughtful, perceptive, and informed.

LEWIS ROWELL, PH.D.
Professor of Music, Ethno-
musicology, and Indian Studies
Indiana University, U.S.A.

Preface

This study is the product of twelve years of passion for the music of India. It started with an instrument, the tablā, and the more I learned about Indian music, the more I come to appreciate how wonderful and multifaceted its universe is. But my passion for Indian music has never been monogamous. In addition to several other musics (including my own), I have long been interested in semiotics, and from my first readings, I realized that semiotics can help composers, musicians, listeners, critics, and others to understand aspects of music that have not been adequately investigated by the traditional disciplines of musicology. Curiously, the idea of analyzing Indian music via semiotics appeared to me very early—long before the present study, which necessarily was prefaced by wanderings and wonderings in the labyrinths of Indian music, formal semiotics and musical semiotics. I have walked the main avenues, discussed the itinerary with my guides and fellow travelers, investigated patiently the paths and narrow lanes, asking for directions here and there, and possibly opening some new passages myself (whether they are dead ends or useful routes is for the reader and the test of time to decide). Yet the maze of Indian music and musical semiotics is vast, its boundaries are vague, and several labyrinths are interconnected, with labyrinths within labyrinths...and obviously, at the core of the labyrinth is a sphinx. I have not met her yet, but parts of her riddle are scattered here and there along the walls. Most of the walls are made of mirrors, however, and the wanderers face only themselves when they try to connect the parts of the enigma.

In view of its large proportions, I have, on one hand, set some limits to this study, and on the other, provided a map, which can be used in future explorations. Out of the complex mass of Indian music, I have chosen the classical tradition of North Indian music; and for its cartography, the theory of general semiotics as conceived by the American polymath and philosopher Charles Sanders Peirce. The map I have drawn is undoubtedly provisional, to be criticized, updated and corrected whenever necessary.

The central question of this study is not so much *what* does music mean, but rather *how*. In technical terms, it is a study of semiosis in Hindustani music. Semiosis, as defined by Peirce, is the process by which all forms of signification occur. This includes not only communication, and its most outstanding case, that of verbal languages, but all kinds of perception, reasoning, structuring, reproduction, evolution and so on. Semiosis is carried out by signs, which stand for an object or groups of objects, and are to be interpreted by some kind of mind. True, questions of musical signification are as old as music itself. However, the importance of thinking of music as sign and music-making (in all possible senses) as semiosis, is that a whole universe of new understandings of musical matters becomes clear in the light of their interrelations. Music is a sign of itself, and the various ways of organizing musical material can be viewed as forms of semiosis. Music, however conceived, has the power of reference, and the objects it signifies range from pure musical materiality, to entities (such as things, real or imaginary beings, persons, and so on) and all forms of individual and cultural representations (again signs), from emotions to political ideas. However, music could not exist if no one interpreted it. Interpretation, interpretant, and interpreter are used throughout this study in their semiotic technical sense. Sign interpretation consists in the process of producing or modifying an idea that the sign represents in reference to its object; such production is semiosis itself. Musical interpretation involves perception and cognition and all forms of aesthetic enjoyment. It is also the mental and physical aspects of musical learning and performance. Musical interpretation is certainly the basis of all music criticism and scholarship, and composition would be impossible without it. Hence, musical semiosis, in general terms, is a composite of significations, and its actuality depends necessarily on interpretation.

Therefore, my purpose is to translate into scientific language, to discuss and analyze, the modes of semiosis as present in the world of Hindustani music. Some of my conclusions might be read as having a broader scope than North Indian music, in reference not only to Karnatic music, but also to other musical systems in time and space. This work is divided into three sections. In the first, I discuss some approaches to the study of musical meaning according to the views of ethnomusicology, musicology and musical semiotics. The last chapter of that section devises a classification of musical studies according to Peirce's architecture of sciences. In the second section I propose a possible Peircean semiotic theory of music as applied to forms of early and later, but mainly contemporary Hindustani music. The essential elements of Peircean phenomenology and semiotics are discussed in the first two chapters, with a view to their application to music. Then follows the semiotic theory of music itself, divided into intrinsic musical signification, musical reference and musical interpretation. In the third section, the classical Indian theory of aesthetics, or the theory of *rasa* (essence, feeling), is explained, and its connections with Indian music are studied in a historical sequence, from early to present-day Hindustani music. Finally, I present a semiotic analysis of aesthetic musical experience according to rasa theory.

To read this study, a basic acquaintance with both Hindustani music and Peircean semiotics is desirable. I see no need here for a broad exposition of the fundamentals of Hindustani music theory, for there are excellent works on this subject, in English and in other languages.[1] The semiotics of Peirce, however, is another matter, for most of his writings are still unpublished manuscripts.[2] In this sense, I have provided explanations as broad as I thought necessary for the comprehension of my musical interpretations. The semiotic side of this study is essential, and the reader will not follow my analysis of Hindustani music if the semiotic parts are disregarded.

The international conventions for transliteration of Sanskrit and Hindi words have been followed, and the key is displayed in Table 1. Even so, absolute consistency between Sanskrit and Hindi (and occasionally Persian) is not possible. I have adopted the spelling form for contemporary Hindi words when the subject is discussed in this context, but kept the Sanskrit forms otherwise. Thus, hiṇḍol is used in the former case, but hiṇḍola in the later. I briefly define every musical term upon its first occurrence. These first appearances are italicized, with consequent instances of the same word typed in normal characters. I have kept the words *rāga* and *tāla* in their Sanskrit form throughout the text. Names of *rāgas* and *tālas* are always in lower case, and the spellings of proper names vary according to the context or source. The words *god* and *goddess* have been kept in lower case, without any implied ideological or religious assumption. The spelling and rules above may appear differently in quotations. Finally, the codes for musical notation, both *sargam* and staff, are given in Table 2. In the transnotations and transcriptions in the musical examples presented on staves, the note ṣaḍja is represented as C. Yet it must be made clear that pitch in Indian music is never absolute, nor are the pitch sets organized according to equal temperament. Most of the examples are prescriptive transnotations rather than descriptive transcriptions.

---

[1] Refer to the following bibliographies: Powers (1965), Bernett (1970), Nijenhuis (1977), Jairazbhoy (1993). In addition, in the last years significant books and articles have also appeared.

[2] Ways to access Peirce's writings on semiotics can be examined in Fisch, Ketner and Kloesel (1979). A number of fundamental publications have appeared more recently, the most reliable being the *Writings of Charles Peirce: A Chronological Edition*, Fisch et al. (eds.), of which five volumes have been published (1982-).

Acknowledgments

Because this is a study of Indian music, my gratitude must go first to Śrī Gaṇeśa, the elephant-headed, scribe and knowledgeable guru, not only for removing obstacles, but also for imposing them—the only way to compel us to find solutions in all spheres of life. In this project, I have had the assistance and company of several friends, musicians, teachers, scholars, and institutions in Brazil, Finland and India. To all of them, my heartfelt thanks.

First of all, I am deeply indebted to Eero Tarasti, who has offered his essential support in the artistic, intellectual, scientific and practical aspects of this work, as well as his friendship and faith in my project. Lewis Rowell has always been for me a model of high standards of scholarship in Indian musicology, and I am grateful for many of his suggestions in the course of this research. I am also obliged to Wim van der Meer, who offered valuable ideas and criticisms on the drafts of this work. My. thanks to Alfonso Padilla and Maritza Núñez, for their friendship and support during my stay in Finland. Alfonso Padilla also read and discussed parts of this study, for which I am indebted. My thanks to Lúcia Santaella, who gave me a solid grounding in Peircean semiotics, years ago in Brazil.

I am deeply indebted to Ustād Zia Fariduddin Dagar, who opened for me the doors of the venerable tradition of dhrupad singing, accepting me as his student, and introducing me into the current life of music in India. I am obliged to Probir Kumar Mittra, not only for his clear and enthusiastic instruction on the tablā, according to the gharānā of Lucknow, but also for his sincere friendship. I am thankful to Late Prem Lata Sharma, for clarifications of rasa theory. In my first period of residence in India (1994-1995), I enjoyed the camaraderie and intellectual company of Bernard and Andréine Bel in New Delhi, without which my studies would not have borne the fruit it did. Francoise 'Nalini' Delvoye kindly volunteered to help with my translations of compositions in Braj, and she facilitated access to her unpublished dissertation on Tānsen. I am thankful to Sharbari Mukherjee, from the Sangeet Natak Akademi in New Delhi, for kind help and friendly sharing of ideas on Indian music. Mohan Lal Sar introduced me not only to the Hindi language, but also to various aspects of Indian culture.

I also wish to thank several people who have helped this work in different ways: Asko Parpola, Timo Riiho, Edward Henry, Ulrik Volgsten, Paul Forsell and Richard Littlefield. This book was developed and written in Finland, between 1992-1997. The staff at the Department of Musicology of the University of Helsinki consistently provided a warm and helpful environment which facilitated the human, practical and technical sides in the development of this work. I would like to thank particularly Irma Vierimaa, Timo Laitakari and Kalev Tiits. My parents kept me supplied with the latest semiotic publications from Brazil.

A community of inquirers, constituted by the members of the Musical Signification Project, directed by Eero Tarasti, especially in their meetings in Helsinki and Imatra, provided the necessary field of discussions and interchange which characterize the sincere pursuit of science.

This project would not have been possible without the financial support of the Fundação CAPES, Comissão de Aperfeiçoamento de Pessoal de Nível Superior (Foundation for High-Level Personnel Development), Ministry of Education, Brazil. I am also indebted to the Niilo Helanderin Säätiö and the University of Helsinki, for providing support for the printing of the first edition of this document, published by the International Semiotics Institute in May 1997. I also wish to thank N.P. Jain, who accepted this work to be printed in India by Motilal Banarsidass, the distinguished indological publishers.

It is an honor to have this book printed now in India, who has been giving me opportunity to delight with her culture and to work for my own improvement, by means of contemplating and studying her music, dance, poetry and philosophy. Thank you very much.

São Paulo, **José Luiz Martinez**
December 5, 2000

Abbreviations

NŚ - *Nāṭyaśāstra,* Bharata, [c. 200 A.D.] (1967).

D - *Dattilam,* Dattila, [c. 200 A.D.] (1988).

BD - *Bṛhaddeśī,* Mataṅga, [c. 800 A.D.] (1992, 1994).

DL - *Dhvanyāloka,* Ānandavardhana [c. 9th cent.] (1982).

SR - *Saṅgītaratnākara,* Śārṅgadeva [1240 A.D.] (1978-1989).

SŚ - *Saṅgītaśiromaṇi,* [1428 A.D.] (1992).

RV - *Rāgavibodha,* Somanātha [1609 A.D.] (in Nijenhuis 1976).

SD - *Saṅgītadarpaṇa,* Dāmodara [c. 1625 A.D.] (1930).

KPM - *Hindusthānī Saṅgīta Paddhati Krāmika Pustaka Mālikā,* 6 vols., Bhātkhaṇḍe, (1939, 1990-1993).

SA - *Saṅgītāñjali,* 6 vols., O. Ṭhākur (1955-75).

RN - *Rāganidhi,* 4 vols., S.B. Rao (1965).

RVJ - *Rāga Vijñāna,* 7 vols., V. Paṭvardhan, (1982).

CP - *Collected Papers,* C. Peirce (1938-1956).

W - *Writings of Charles Peirce,* C. Peirce (1982-).

L75 - Manuscript L75, C. Peirce (1902).

Upaniṣads: *The Principal Upaniṣads,* S. Radhakrishnan (1994).

Table 1
Transliteration of the devanāgarī script

			Velar	Palatal	Retroflex	Dental	Labial
Vowels	simple	short	अ - a	इ - i	ऋ - ṛ	ऌ - ḷ	उ - u
		long	आ - ā	ई - ī	ॠ - ṝ		ऊ - ū
	diphtongs	short		ए - e			ओ - o
		long		ऐ - ai			औ - au
Consonants	stops	voiceless unaspirated	क - ka	च - ca	ट - ṭa	त - ta	प - pa
		voiceless aspirated	ख - kha	छ - cha	ठ - ṭha	थ - tha	फ - pha
		voiced unaspirated	ग - ga	ज - ja	ड - ḍa	द - da	ब - ba
		voiced aspirated.	घ - gha	झ - jha	ढ - ḍha	ध - dha	भ - bha
	nasals		ङ - ṅa	ञ - ñ	ण - ṇa	न - na	म - ma
	semivowels			य - ya	र - ra	ल - la	व - va
	sibilants			श - śa	ष - ṣa	स - sa	
	voiced glottal fricative		ह - ha				
	flaps	voiced unaspirated			ड़ - ḍa		
		voiced aspirated			ढ़ - ḍha		
Visarga			: - ḥ				
Anusvāra			- ṁ				
Candrabindu			ँ - m̐				
Persian, Arabic, and English sounds							
			क़ - qa	ख़ - kha	ग़ - ga	ज़ - za	फ़ - fa

Table 2a

Musical Notation: sargam

S - ṣaḍja (sa)
R̲ - komala ṛṣabha (komal re)
R - śuddha ṛṣabha (re)
G̲ - komala gāndhāra (komal ga)
G - śuddha gāndhāra (ga)
M - śuddha madhyama (ma)
M̄ - tīvra madhyama (tīvra ma)
P - pañcama (pa)
D̲ - komala dhaivata (komal dha)
D - śuddha dhaivata (dha)
N̲ - komala niṣāda (komal ni)
N - śuddha niṣāda

M- - note prolongation
N̲/S, D\P - ascending or descending glissando (mīṅḍ)
G̲~ - oscillation (andolan)
°R̲ - grace note (kan)

Table 2b
Musical Notation: staff

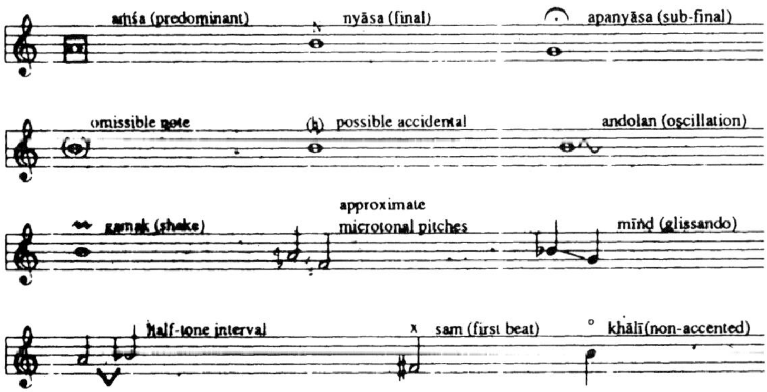

SEMIOSIS IN HINDUSTANI MUSIC

Gītam (vocal music) came from the *Sāmaveda* and was collected by Brahmā. Śiva, the Omniscient god, husband of Pārvatī, is propitiated by gītam; Kṛṣṇa, the lord of Gopīs,though infinite, was captivated by the sound of the bamboo flute. If Brahmā is devoted to sāmagīti (performing the hymns of the *Sāmaveda*), and Sarasvatī is attached to the vīṇā, then what can we say of other creatures, such as the yakṣas and gandharvas, the gods and demons, and human beings? An infant, crying in cradle, as yet unable to enjoy objects, on tasting the nectar of a song, feels boundless joy. Even the fawn, which feeds on grass and roams the forest, when attracted by the hunter's song, is willing to sacrifice its life. Who indeed can describe the grandeur of melody? Surely it is the only means of realizing the four primary values of human life: righteousness (dharma), wealth (artha), enjoyment (kāma) and emancipation (mokṣa)

Śārṅgadeva's *Saṅgītaratnākara* 1.1.25c-30

The Signification of Indian Music

> The song should be sustained in the throat; its meaning must be shown by the hands; the mood [*bhāva*] must be shown by the glances; time [tāla] is marked by the feet. For wherever the hands move, there the glances follow; where the glances go, the mind follows; where the mind goes, the mood follows; where the mood goes, there is the flavour [*rasa*]. (Nandikeśvara 1970: 35)

Music in India, since the earliest treatises (NŚ and BD),[1] has been seen as acoustical forms that signify a variety of natural and cultural elements (and their interrelations), which are not merely to be recognized by the listener, but ultimately to be enjoyed as refined feeling, or *rasa*. The quote above, from *The Mirror of Gesture*, Nandikeśvara's Sanskrit treatise on dramatic performance, locates music as the starting point of signification in the process of aesthetic enjoyment. The Sanskrit word for music – *saṅgīta* – encompasses song (*gīta*), instrumental music (*vādya*) and dance (*nṛtta*). Gīta has precedence over the other two; and it is certainly an independent art, for meaningless syllables can be used for singing. Three significant elements interact during a performance: (1) the music; (2) representation of the bhāva, or mental states (which encompass the represented dramatic circumstances and their conventions, viewed as generalized emotions); and (3) rasa, or essence, interpreted by the spectator. Thus, according to Indian aestheticians, music, bhāva and rasa are the basic components of signification, interacting in the universe of the performers' and listeners' interlinked minds.

Indian philosophers dealt with the issue of signification much earlier than the classical aestheticians did. The compound *namarupa*, concept and form, in the philosophy of the *Upaniṣads*, represents the empirical world, and Brahman is the transcendence of that world. The *Bṛhadāraṇyakaupaniṣad* adds a third element to the nāmarūpa dyad, that of *karma*, or action: 'Verily, this (world) is a triad of nāma, rūpa and karma' (1.6.1). Concept, form and action are not isolated elements, however, and they are viewed as a triadic unity: 'These three together are

[1] Except for D, which is mostly concerned with musical matters.

one; this self, though one, is this triad' (ibid. 1.6.3). Thus, not only is the world characterized as nāma, rūpa and karma, but so are individual beings. Later, Buddhism took nāma in the broader sense of mind,[2] and rūpa as representing the human body (Hiriyanna 1993: 139).

These concepts have an eminently semiotic character, but this is not the place for deep discussion of such a broad subject. I instead refer to nāma, rūpa and karma as ideas that can generate a fruitful understanding of music. Music is at once form and concept, rūpa and nāma. Music, as rūpa, has its own peculiarities of quality, existence and form; but it also represents a diversity of other forms and concepts, or nāma (purely musical concepts or otherwise). Music, as a compound of nāmarūpa, is to be interpreted by the listener, and this is the means by which to access its meaning, another sense of nāma. 'Form is a manifestation to the senses, a concrete presentation of something abstract, and an appearance of something that cannot be perceived directly but can only be inferred. Form is a sign and a way to knowledge' (Rowell 1992: 226). Rowell is keen on identifying rūpa as the mediation through which nāma is realized: 'the aim of perception is to see and hear through phenomena' (ibid.). Rūpa, in one sense, can be understood as sign, and music is certainly sign. Its mode of action (its karma) is that of providing access to ideas, or the universe of nāma. In another sense, music is also nāma, because it depends on the web of significations engendered by the human mind. In fact, signification is the central mode of existence of music, a fact of which Indian scholars have been aware for millennia.

Contemporary Hindustani music is basically a system of rāgas, individual musical entities whose ancestors date back at least 20 centuries. Rāgas, which can be thought of as musical organisms, are forms that signify a wide variety of ideas. These include musical concepts, natural phenomena of the Indian subcontinent (such as the monsoon rains), the multiplicity of Indian cultural manifestations, philosophical and religious beliefs, categories of feeling, and so on. The associations are complex, and a single rāga can refer to several elements. For instance, rāga miyāṁ kī malhār refers specifically to the rainy season in India. This season is marked by the refreshment that follows the heat of summer, and the correspondent feeling, expressed by bird songs and human contentment. But gladness is not the rāga's meaning, for miyāṁ kī malhār signifies a serious mood. A pleasant season does not necessarily make everybody happy. Those who are separated from loved ones may feel gloomy, a feeling that includes both lovers' feelings and religious longing. In addition, this rāga indicates the composer, Tānsen, who supposedly created miyāṁ kī malhār in the 16th century.[3] This rāga has particular musical structures, such as a pitch set including a minor third, and the

---

[2] The later, classical Indian philosophical systems referred to mind by the term *manas*.

[3] Miyāṁ (master) is one of the titles of Tānsen.

conjunct use of minor and major seventh. Miyāṁ kī malhār is also characterized by certain melodic motifs. All of the foregoing are issues of signification, which includes the way a rāga is structured, performed, perceived, enjoyed, and conceptualized in music theory. The objective of the present study is to understand this universe of signs, their modes of being, their action and multiplication in the hands, voices, and minds of musicians, listeners and music scholars. Therefore, this is a study of musical semiotics. The framework adopted is the general theory of semiotics as conceived by Charles Sanders Peirce (1839-1914) and his interpreters.

According to Peirce, a sign is something that stands for its object to an interpretant.[4] This triadic relationship is a dynamic model of signification, where representation is understood as the action of signs, or semiosis. If music is considered as sign, the first question likely to be asked is, What does it represent? This issue, which is dealt with extensively in the Indian tradition, will be clarified in sections 2 and 3. In the quote at the beginning of this introduction, music is situated in the context of actual semiosis. A song is performed in accordance with its structural features of rāga and tāla. It is reinterpreted by a dancer, and the ideas represented by both art forms are perceived, judged and enjoyed by the spectator's mind. Several treatises on Indian music emphasize the power of music to affect the mind. The meanings and moods alluded to by Nandikeśvara are objects represented by musical resources in a variety of modes. Thus, complementing the question of what, there is the issue of how music refers to its objects. Clearly, whatever music refers to, it only makes sense to an interpreting mind. Thus, the listener's mind 'follows' the musical sign, and this produces another sign or interpretant, which is refined by the musical connoisseur's mind as the essence of music, or rasa.

The comprehension of musical semiosis in Hindustani music inheres in questions such as: What is the character of the musical sign? What are its objects and how is reference achieved? And more specifically, how are musical signs perceived, interpreted, generated, and theorized in the tradition of North Indian music? The use of semiotics to understand such broad aspects of music in India is not an extraneous undertaking, though superficially the world-view of Peirce and that of Indian art and philosophy constitute two seemingly distinct universes.

Peirce's work is defined by Santaella as a dialogue of one man with twenty-five centuries of Western philosophy (1983: 27). However, all that tradition has not been isolated from the rest of the world, and there are many links connecting the traditions of South Asia with those of the Western world, the Indo-European trunk of languages being one of the most widely recognized of such links. The differences are also great, certainly, but the use of semiotics to study Hindustani music need not

[4] See 2.2 for a complete overview of Peirce's conception of sign and semiosis.

imply the dominance of one culture over another. Besides, the semiotics of Peirce is not totally foreign to the study of Indian society and culture. Milton Singer (1984) is a pioneer in this area, having developed a semiotic anthropology. Peirce, in Singer's work, far from clashing with the Indian mind-set, helps one to understand better a culture rich in significations, as well as full of ambiguities and overlapping categories. Singer even thinks that 'Peirce's world view is much closer to the Indian than to the Western' (1984: 184). Peirce was not an indologist, however, and the points of contact referred to by Singer are the result of independent developments of traditions that shared ideas and sources in both the remote and the more recent past. In fact, Peirce's dialogue with Western thought was a critical one; but his criticism, far from being enclosed within itself, generated a vast edifice of scientific philosophy.

It seems to me that it does not matter whether Peirce was born in this or that part of the planet, for the system of logic called semiotics is largely the heritage of human thought in several different places, and that thought has been accumulated, criticized and refined for thousands of years. Semiotics does not belong to one man or culture. It is the transitory result of a web of inquiry that has been woven by innumerable minds in time and space, and that will be continued by other minds in the future. Because of its great generality and capacity for theoretical translation, the system that Peirce achieved, around the beginning of this century, seems to be the one most apt to bring understanding on a diversity of problems of signification. Thus, the application of Peirce's semiotic to Hindustani music is not a colonialist incursion, but a scientific view of problems of musical signification, drawn broadly in Indian terms. What matters is the capacity of the theory to bring better understanding and an integrated view of the complexity of Hindustani musical phenomena and musical thought. Conversely, by means of semiotic study, Indian musical thought and aesthetics are brought forward, into the contemporary world, thereby conveying – as a semiotic nāmarūpa and karma triad – its rich heritage, and contributing its part to discussions of the semiotic web.

I

ON MUSICOLOGY, ETHNOMUSICOLOGY, MUSIC SEMIOTICS AND EPISTEMOLOGY

1.1 (Ethno)Musicology and Musical Meaning

John Blacking, in his now-classic *How Musical Is Man?*, introduces his basic premise, which emphasizes the anthropological side of all music. He writes: 'The Venda taught me that music can never be a thing in itself, and that all music is folk music, in the sense that music cannot be transmitted or having meaning without associations between people' (Blacking 1973: x). In addition to the necessary cultural dependence of music on those who practice it, Blacking advances the idea that music is supposed to represent or transmit something between people. He also states that music in itself has no reality, hence it follows that reference is the natural state of music, and that the idea of 'pure' or absolute music does not correspond to the totality of facts. His position is opposed to that of the early structuralists. Indeed, Blacking argues for studies based on the non-isolation of music from its social functions. He criticizes comparative approaches in this way: 'Distinctions between the surface complexity of different musical styles and techniques do not tell us anything useful about the expressive purposes and power of the music, or about the intellectual organization involved in its creation' (ibid.). Yet music, if it depends on the web of cultural facts and functions as Blacking claims, also has within itself signs of its creative principles and signifying design. If music is indeed 'expressive', then it can communicate and convey meaning. Part of those functions are to be found in the musical patterns, forms and structures themselves, as well as in their relations with individuals and their culture, and in the way those individuals conceive music.

Blacking recognizes that music is shaped by both human nature and culture, concluding that musical patterns cannot be defined by arbitrary principles. 'Music is too deeply concerned with human feelings and experiences in society, and its patterns are too often generated by surprising outbursts of unconscious cerebration, for it to be subject to arbitrary rules, like the rules of games' (1973: x). The human unconscious probably determines some musical aspects as much as it does the constitution of the body, shaping factually the music that human beings make or can make: 'Many, if not all, of music's essential processes may be found in the constitution of the human body and in patterns of interaction of human bodies in society. Thus all music is structurally, as well as functionally, folk music' (Blacking 1973: x-xi). As much as the unconscious can be understood as a system of signs (according to psychoanalysis), human corporeal movements also establish a sort of dynamic language, determining musical possibilities in vocal or instrumental music; although the limits of musical virtuosity have always been surpassed by astonishing performers. Bodily movements not only determine musical possibilities, but conversely, music also signifies its causal, physical origin. Further, in the same way as music is generated by 'outbursts of unconscious cerebration', it also influences and shapes the quality of feelings of the musicians' and listeners' consciousness. The core of the problem is, therefore, to understand what kind of relations exist between music, facts of culture and nature, and the people who make music, as well as how such relations occur. Therefore, it is necessary to search for an integrated approach to comprehend these features of musical signification and their relationships.

Blacking's view was preceded by that of Allan Merriam, who wrote: 'music cannot be defined as a phenomenon of sound alone, for it involves the behavior of individuals and groups of individuals, and its particular organization demands the social concurrence of people who decide what it can and cannot be' (Merriam 1964: 27). Like Blacking, Merriam also denies real status to pure music, but the behaviorist framework offers little to the understanding of music, for it is largely limited to the problem of functionalism. The dynamics of interaction between music and human beings in the context of a culture is not merely a question of learned responses determined by cultural patterns and physiological structures of the human body. This is not to deny that dyadic forms of relationship exist in music, but rather to contend that this is a partial view of musical phenomena. Music engages in the universe of culture as systems of signs (as do the other arts, myths, philosophies and sciences). All musical phenomena have significance in themselves, besides having a great variety of dynamical relations; but, as signs, they also take part in processes of interpretation and reinterpretation performed by the human mind and body.

Musicology and/or Ethnomusicology

Indian music, in its classical form in both North and South India, plus all the other rich universes of tribal, folk and film music, was for decades considered the province of ethnomusicology,[5] as was all non-Western art music. This ethnocentric view has been contested by most leading ethnomusicologists in the second half of this century. Because the present study focuses on the (mainly classical) music of North India, it is appropriate to reflect briefly on some conceptions of ethnomusicology as a science, and later to examine some ethnomusicological views of musical signification.

---

[5] Some authors, such as Powers (1970, 1976, 1980a) and Rowell (1992), have dealt with Indian music rather in the context of indology and musical analysis, their work being unrelated to ethnomusicological methods. In fact, non-ethnographic approaches are not uncommon in studies of Indian music. Yet Neuman (1990: 27) and similarly Henry (1988), for instance, base their studies on the ideas of Merriam, Hood and Nettl.

Bruno Nettl, in *The Study of Ethnomusicology* (1983), instituted the basic tenets and ideas of the field as it is currently practiced. His book considers what the community of ethnomusicologists has being doing, and how they regard their field. Nettl lists three activities that can direct the work of ethnomusicologists: 'a) comparative study (of musical systems and cultures); b) the study of music in or as culture, or perhaps music in its cultural context; and c) the historical study of Oriental and "primitive" music' (1983: 3). The main activity of comparative study consists in the search for universals. The second activity – the study of music in culture – focuses on the description of 'all factors which generate the pattern of sound produced by a single composer or society' (cf. Blacking in Nettl, ibid.). Finally, Nettl refers to an ethnomusicological version of historical musicology, whose business is 'the establishment of laws governing musical development and change' (1983: 3).

The first paradigm of ethnomusicology – comparative musicology – concerns the search for universals. It is, at the same time, a classificatory and synthetic approach. By studying the musics of the world, scholars were, on the one hand, trying to understand musical differences and similarities, and eventually to establish classifications of musical systems and concepts. On the other, by extracting (or abstracting) the most recurrent elements, they hoped to discover universal features, the bases of all human music. This line of work went on mainly during the first decades of the 20th century, finally proving to be unfruitful. For comparative musicologists either did not realize or refused to accept the inherent epistemic limit to their approach: that absolute universality cannot be attained.

The study of music in its cultural context, the second of Nettl's paradigms of ethnomusicology, realizes that music is not a universal language. Musical diversity reflects cultural diversity. Nettl describes Merriam's anthropological approach to music as two successive steps of a growing theory: 'Studying music in culture would imply a holistic view of culture as an organic unit, and descriptively assigning to music a unitary role, ascertained in field research. The "music as culture" approach moves one step further in that direction, implying that one takes up a theory of the nature of the culture and applies it to music' (Nettl 1983: 131-32). On one hand, the scope of this paradigm is broader than that of the first, in the sense that not only is the musical material studied, but also its relationships with people and its cultural traits. On the other hand, and contrary to the comparative musicological approach, the study of music *in* or *as* culture focuses on a single cultural unity. What is lost in breadth is gained in depth. Yet in response to Blacking's claim above, that all factors must be known, one may ask if it is possible to know everything about a musical culture. It turns out to be impossible to attain absolute, complete knowledge of the latter, given the complexity of human societies and the web of relationships between a society's musical and cultural elements.

To consider merely what might possibly be known about a musical culture, it is necessary to include cultural history in the equation, which brings up Nettl's third type of ethnomusicology. Perhaps as wrong as the idea that music is a universal language, is to think that music in non-Western cultures does not change. Such misguided thinking, even if corrected today, has left an indelible mark on ethnomusicological studies. Nettl writes: 'A very great deal of ethnomusicological literature is concerned somehow with the fact that things do happen and that, in one way or another, happening implies change. If indeed one can distinguish, in their attitude toward change, between the historical musicologist and the ethnomusicologist, it may be this: historical musicologists wish to know what actually happened; ethnomusicologists, what (typically or normally) "happens" ' (1983: 172).

In the context of more developed ethnomusicological views, it became clear that the distinction – between a musical science dealing purely with Western art music, and another concerned with all the other musics in the world – was unconvincing. For Blacking 'Ethnomusicology is not only an area of study concerned with exotic music, nor a musicology of the ethnic – it is a discipline that holds out hope for a deeper understanding of all music. If some music can be analyzed and understood as tonal expressions of human experience in the context of different kinds of social and cultural organization, I see no reason why all music should not be analyzed in the same way' (1973: 31). Every people's music deserves study, including that of the West. Thus it too can be the subject of ethnomusicological inquiry. Similar ideas, voiced by other scholars, along with traditional musicology's limited concern solely with Western art music, led to confusion in both disciplines. Ethnomusicology, at first restricted to the study of non-Western music traditions, extended its boundaries into the field of Western traditional musicology. Charles Seeger, as early as 1960, wrote about this situation in the following terms:

> Two meanings of the term 'ethnomusicology' are current. One equates the prefix 'ethno-' with the adjective 'ethnic,' meaning 'barbarous, non-Christian, exotic'; the other, with the prefix 'ethno-' as in ethnology. The former implies that the study now known as 'ethnomusicology' is limited to musics *other* than the student's *own*; the latter, that is limited to the cultural functions of music. Both of these meanings lead to unacceptable situations when applied to a musicological discipline *as a whole:* the first, because, in accord with it, if the study of a student's own music is to be known as musicology the same music studied by another student who does not carry its tradition, must be known as 'ethnomusicology'; the second, because no relatively independent academic discipline can be expected to confine itself to the view of a thing *in a context* to the exclusion of the view of the *thing in itself*. (Seeger 1977: 116)

Therefore, discussing the controversies between ethnomusicology and musicology, Seeger reaffirms the importance of also studying music in itself, even in the context of ethnomusicology. Consequently, he proposes a unified field theory (1977: 102-138), which I will reflect on later in this chapter.

Concept, Behavior and Music

The anthropological model of music, as conceived by Merriam, served as the point of departure for some later studies of music in or as culture. It thus deserves a closer examination. Merriam divides musical studies into three analytical levels: conceptualization about music, behavior in relation to music, and musical sound itself. The requirements for applying his model are these: the ethnomusicologist must consider both the folk and analytical evaluations, the cultural and social background, the relevant aspects of the social sciences and the humanities, and the symbolic, aesthetic, formal, psychological, and physical aspects of music (1964: 32). Furthermore, in Merriam's view, concept, behavior and musical sound operate as a dynamical system:

> we hear a song; it is made of sound ordered in certain ways. Human beings produce this song and in so doing they behave, not only when actually singing the song but also in their way of life, either as musicians or as people listening to music and responding to it. Since they are musicians or non-specialists responding to music, they conceptualize the musical facts of life [...] then they accept or reject the product because it does or does not accord with what they have learned to be proper music sound, thus inevitably affecting concept, behavior and sound again. (Merriam 1964: 34)

This model, however, exhibits a circularity which suggests that music-making takes place in a closed system. There is a logic in this model that unites the triad of musical concepts, actions and sounds, but it is more likely that the three components (and probably others) participate simultaneously and in a less deterministic away.

Merriam's first category of conceptualization precedes the actions that generate musical sounds: 'In order to act in a music system, the individual must first conceptualize what kind of behavior will produce the requisite sound' (1964: 33). In this way, Merriam avoids a strict behaviorist understanding of music, locating mental activities before behavior properly, and he concludes that: 'Without concepts about music, behavior cannot occur, and without behavior, music sound cannot be produced. It is at this level that the values about music are found, and it is precisely these values that filter upward through the system to effect the final product' (ibid.). Concepts cover a broad area of music-making, all the way from the delimitation of sound in terms of what musical sound is and is not, to musical micro- and macro-organization. It is doubtful, however, that musical concepts would necessarily precede music-making, unless in a restricted and questionable academic situation.

Secondly, Merriam discusses musical behavior: 'Music (...) cannot have an existence of its own divorced from the behavior which produces it' (1964: 7). It is certain that music only exists when practiced and performed. Merriam emphasizes this dimension, not as pure brute action, but as conditioned action based on habit. Further, he writes: 'we must also understand how and why the behavior which produces it as it is, and how and why the concepts which underlie that behavior are ordered in such a way as to produce the particularly desired form of organized sound' (ibid.). He identifies three species of behavior: physical, cultural and verbal (Merriam 1964: 33), but the answer to the above questions, it seems to me, is unlikely to be merely a matter of learned responses, which, in the last analysis, are forms of action and reaction. In an actual performance, for instance, music is part of an interplay of interpretations between musicians, listeners and the cultural environment.

Finally, Merriam engages with the notion of music in itself. 'This sound has structure, and it may be a system, but it cannot exist independently of human beings; music sound must be regarded as the product of behavior that produces it' (Merriam 1964: 32). In this respect, he was followed by Blacking, and scholars of other orientations, such as Molino. Blacking writes: 'We can no longer study music as a thing in itself when research in ethnomusicology makes it clear that musical things are not always strictly musical, and that the expression of tonal relationships in patterns of sound may be secondary to extramusical relationships which the tones represent' (1973: 25). Molino, in his famous 1975 article, wrote that 'pure or strict music is not an essential first datum; it is an artifact, the result of an arbitrary process of subdivision within the total social fact, a process that isolates a domain on the basis of which it is impossible – and would be meaningless – to reconstitute the whole' (1990: 119). Thus, all those scholars unearthed semiotic issues, especially that of musical reference to extramusical objects. Yet none of the cited authors realized that signification forms the basis of musical conceptualization, of the use of music in cultural contexts, and of mental or physical musical behavior (to put it in Merriam's terms); and certainly pure music should also be included, the latter being one particular form of semiosis (see Martinez 1996a: 70-72).

Symbolic Behavior

Musical meaning is an issue frequently raised by ethnomusicologists. Merriam, besides his regard of musical meaning as behavior, also takes up the question of communication in music. 'On a simple level, it can perhaps be said that music communicates within a given music community, but if this is true, it is equally true that there is little understanding of how this communication is carried on. The most obvious possibility is that communication is effectuated through the investiture of music with symbolic meanings which are tacitly agreed upon by the members of the community' (Merriam 1964: 10). Indeed, music cannot be disregarded as a means of communication. Sound is a very effective medium for warnings, and acoustic perception is a sense necessary for survival in a number of animal species. It is not improbable that music and verbal language evolved from those purely functional sound utterances. More to the point, Merriam identifies the chief problem of musical signification: 'we do not know what precisely music communicates, or how it communicates it. Communication also involves both understanding and receptivity to understanding. To view music as a communicative device is clearly one of the purposes of ethnomusicology, though it has been little investigated' (Merriam 1964: 13). The belated advances in this area of study are evident when, almost twenty years later, Nettl is still exposing the difficulties in finding answers for the basic questions of signification in music.

> The stately theme near the end of "The Moldau" by Smetana clearly represents the river flowing past the ancient Bohemian castle, Vysehrad. The marching band in the parade sends shivers up some spines. The sound of jazz used to remind people that they could break the routine, do the (at least slightly) illicit. Three kinds of musical symbol. Is it really the music that creates these effects, capable of meaning something other than itself? How, and to whom? Must the creator mean what the listener perceives? On the whole, ethnomusicology has eschewed the philosophical issues, but it has sometimes been concerned with defining symbol and symbolized when a society does not articulate such definition or provides no consensus. (Nettl 1983: 205)

Music can surely signify all those things. Music as sign or flow of signs, as soon as it reaches an interpreting mind, engages in semiosis; signs are translated into other signs; signs act and react with other thought signs. This process is not limited to the atomic level outlined here; rather, it spreads in one's mind, culture, and beyond. Properly answering Nettl's questions would lead, eventually, to a whole theory of musical semiotics. Yet even here some distinctions can be drawn briefly and some light shed on the issues. One of the most crucial questions is the 'how'. This question demands to be addressed by an adequate theory of meaning. Yet most studies that try to understand musical meaning adopt (or adapt) tools from linguistics, or linguistics as applied to anthropology.

For Merriam, musical meaning can be understood as a form of behavior. His response to questions about meaning in music results from his theory of symbolic behavior: 'music does seem to function as a "symbolic" part of life, at least in the sense that it does represent other things' (Merriam 1964: 234). He goes on to describe four kinds of representation. But before examining those, it will be useful to understand his basic semiotic concepts.

Drawing from the theories of S. Langer, Leslie White and C. Morris, Merriam works basically with two concepts, icons and symbols: 'a symbol in the first instance seems to be the sign of a sign; if the characterizing sign itself exhibits the properties of what it denotes, then it is an *icon*; if the properties are not in themselves found in the characterizing sign, then it is a symbol' (Merriam 1964: 232). On the one hand, his set of definitions is crude and consequently inaccurate; on the other, it lacks at least one important sign-object relation, that of factual reference, or index. Although Merriam quotes a definition of index according to Morris (1964: 231-32), he surprisingly does not use this concept in explaining musical behavior, an important aspect of which is indexical.

Merriam proposes four ways in which musical meaning takes shape, in his view, all of them symbolic: (1) music (or rather art) is symbolic in its conveyance of direct meanings; (2) music is 'the symbolic reflection of affective or cultural meaning;' (3) music reflects other cultural behavior; organization, and values; (4) music may symbolize, 'the deep symbolism of universal principles,' human behavior in general (1964: 258). Nettl criticizes Merriam's approach: 'Merriam includes a chapter on "music as symbolic behavior" but finds himself able to draw on only a small amount of literature, devoting himself to relatively general studies of symbolism in philosophy' (1983: 204). In fact, the application of semiotic concepts to music is not simply a matter of using or creating the appropriate terminology. Semiotic concepts are usually of such a high level of generality and abstraction that their application to music requires an intermediate theory, namely, a semiotic theory of music.

Merriam finds the first mode of musical symbolism to be of little use in understanding musical meaning. 'The first of these is perhaps closest to a "level of signing;" in this case, art is symbolic in its conveyance of direct meanings. This level is most easily expressed through arts other than music; [...] it is difficult to see how music sound itself can ever be a direct representation of anything' (1964: 234). To the first level, Merriam attributes 'the signing or symboling evident in song texts' (1964: 258). This is above all an issue of iconicity. In regard to Morris's argument that Western program music is essentially iconic, however, Merriam contends, 'It can be recalled, however, that an icon, by definition, exhibits in itself the properties an object must have to be denoted by it, and in these terms it is difficult to see how music can be iconic' (1964: 235). There are two mistakes in Merriam's view of iconism in music. The first, a theoretical one, concerns the concept of direct representation. For Peirce, semiosis can never be direct, since it is by nature a mediation, a sign representing its object to an interpretant. The second mistake concerns icons in music. It is by inherent properties that an icon represents its object, that is, by means of a relation of similarity between sign and object. Morris's suggestion is certainly accurate: not only is program music essentially iconic, but so is the baroque *Affektenlehre*, most speculative music (e.g., music of the spheres) and even the metalanguage of Western 20th-century music, such as some compositions by Charles Ives, Stravinsky, and Luciano Berio (see Martinez 1996a: 69-83).

Iconic musical representation, although a widespread form of musical representation, seems constantly to elude music scholars. Nettl stated: 'There is no intrinsic relationship between ascending melodic contour and going to heaven, but if this is the way a group of people agree to represent the Ascension, then a symbol has been created' (1983: 209). I would rather say that this is a case of iconic representation. Firstly, because in both cases there is an idea of movement, or perhaps virtual movement. Secondly, an ascending melodic phrase implies necessarily the use of pitches of progressively higher frequencies. Not only is there a rise in the number of vibrations per second, but also a rise in physical tension, say, in the singing of such a phrase. Thus, the iconic relation in this case is one of similar qualities of movement. Both ascending melody and going to heaven are seen as upward movements. It is true that this kind of representation has some features of conventionality (an iconic legisign), but the basis of it is still iconic, and not purely conventional as Nettl implies.

Merriam is rather confusing as to his second level. To him art and music 'are symbolic in that they are reflective of emotion and meaning; we can refer to this as "affective" or "cultural meaning"' (Merriam 1964: 237). That music can arouse emotional states in the listeners is a quite acceptable idea, even though Merriam does not say how. To qualify it as 'reflective' suggests, on the one hand, that music is a kind of iconic representation of emotional states. That is true in the case of some affective musical procedures (e.g., certain musical *Figuren* of the baroque period), but emotion can also be represented by musical symbols. On the other hand, 'reflective' can imply an indexical reference that takes music as the expression of the composer's or performer's emotional state, which is a controversial line of thought. What 'cultural meanings' consist of is much less evident, and possibly more pertinent to Merriam's next level: 'the ways in which music reflects other cultural behavior, organization and values'. Merriam's chief examples are musical distinctions between children's and adult's songs, sex roles, clans, and so on. Most of these examples constitute musical symbols, but it should be clear that they can also function as indices, from the listener's point of view.

The basic problem with Merriam's theory of musical symbolism is that the concept of symbol is used to qualify many different instances of semiosis, and quite imprecisely at that. This mistake is often made by other authors, as in the following quote from Nettl, who wrongly identifies as symbolic a very interesting and meaningful instance of indexical representation: 'Most of the world's societies find themselves in the twentieth century participating in two or more musics that can be rather easily distinguished, and the idea that each music functions as a symbol of particular aspects of a culture is a convenient approach to the study of one aspect of musical symbolism' (1983: 208). 'Symbol', however, is the least appropriate term for dealing with such kinds of representation, which are clearly indexical. A musical style or tradition represents aspects of its cultural environment on the basis of factual relation. For instance, the different tribal musics, several folk musics, film music and the two systems of classical music in India refer indexically to geographically, socially and culturally distinct milieus, to which they relate factually.

The fourth of Merriam's levels of musical signification, as pointed out by Nettl, is formulated as a question: 'instead of looking at music as indicative of behavior in a particular culture, we search for broad principles of universal application. That is, does music as such symbolize human behavior? Can we find underlying expressions, of whatever nature, about man and his behavior through symbolic expression in music symbols?' (Merriam 1964: 253) The essential issue is not if music can represent human behavior, which it obviously does by means of several distinct forms of representation, and not only symbolically. The point in Merriam's inquiry is whether anthropological universals can be found in musical representation. The answer to this question relies firstly on the debatable value in finding universals; secondly, it depends on a thoroughly developed semiotic theory of music, one applicable to all musical cultures. Both ideas show strong evidence of badly oriented epistemological approaches: the validity of extending the goals of comparative musicology to the semiotic view of music is as dubious as the idea of applying a consistent semiotic method to the study of all musical cultures; for a theory is also shaped by its subject matter, and only relative universality can be attained.

Unitarian Field Theory

A different paradigm is found in the work of Charles Seeger. Ignoring any possible differences between musicology and ethnomusicology, as referred to above, Seeger set up a broad conception of the study of music, entitled *Toward a Unitarian Field Theory for Musicology*[6] (1977: 102-138). He thinks of the field of musicology as five (with one more to be added later) interrelated universes:

> musicology is (1) a speech study, systematic as well historical, critical as well as scientific or scientistic; whose field is (2) the total music of man, both in itself and in its relationships to what is not itself; whose cultivation is (3) by individual students who can view its field as musicians as well as in the terms devised by nonmusical specialists of whose fields some aspects of music are data; whose aim is to contribute to the understanding of man, in terms both (4) of human culture and (5) of his relationships with the physical universe. (Seeger 1977: 108)

Seeger's universes are not isolated spheres of activity; each of them can be studied in relation to the others. In such a relationship, these five universes 'each includes all the others' (Seeger 1977: 109). They can be represented as circles, in which the first letter of the word gives the key to that element in the diagram: S – speech, M – music, I – individual student, C – culture, P – physical universe.

[6] First published in 1970.

Figure 1
Seeger's Unified Field Theory
(adapted from Seeger 1977: 109)

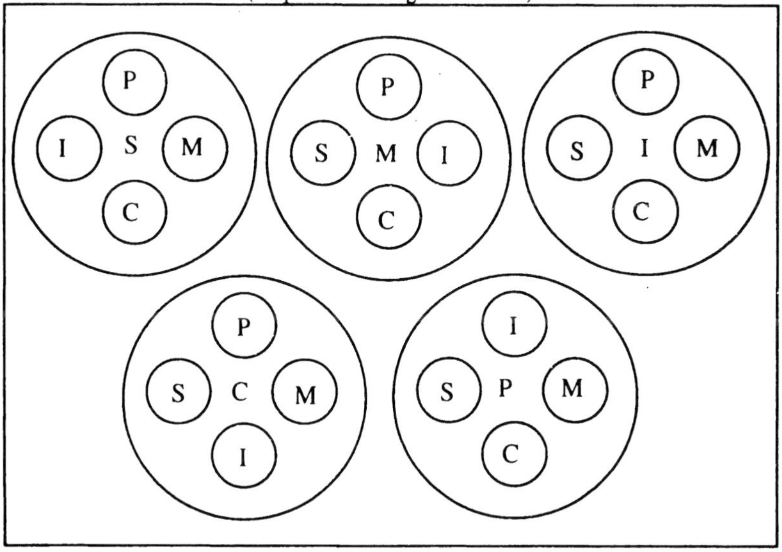

In this system, Seeger studies the relations of each universe to the other four. First, he considers the relations of speech with the others, in accordance with his concern about the role of verbal language in musicology. 'Inclusion S is representational, symbolic, semantic. By naming the other four – and itself – by relating the names (endosemantically), by relating the relationships among the names and the relationships among the named, and by relating the lot to ourselves, it includes the other four in the sense that it includes speech knowledge of them [...]' (Seeger 1977: 109). Verbal language is, indeed, the communication system most used by musicologists and ethnomusicologists, but it is not the only one. Visual systems and images are frequently employed, such as scores, graphs, tables, diagrams, drawings, photography, film and video. Musical recordings are particularly non-verbal. Furthermore, computational models and electronic communication via computer networks, encompassing all forms of musical representation referred to here, have come into increasing use as tools and media for scientific discussions on music. Verbal language certainly takes part simultaneously in some of these media, but from that fact it does not follow that verbal communication is necessarily the basis of all forms of communication (consider, for instance, musical graphs and recordings). Taking musicology as primarily a speech discipline, Seeger seems to reduce all other representational media to verbal language. Even if it is taken in the broader sense of any process of communicating ideas, not necessarily by verbal language (which then equates speech to semiosis), there remains a linguistic bias in the use of the word *speech*, which does not correspond to the facts. Namely, all thought is not fundamentally verbal thought, and musical thought is an exemplary case.

Seeger's Unitary Field Theory, although semiotic in many senses, has its limitations, especially concerning musical semiosis proper. He wrote: 'Inclusion M is presentational, embodied, semiotic but not symbolic. Music does not "mean" what is not music; it identifies itself with it. As I have put it elsewhere, "It does not say so; it does so." It cannot particularize or generalize. It can affirm but it cannot deny' (1977: 109). Seeger attributes a semiotic status to music, but his following statements are only valid as far as music is taken as referring to absolute or pure music. Indeed, at one level, music presents itself rather than representing an object. Yet an instance of pure music does not imply the absence of semiosis. This is merely the semiosis of pure icons, in which sign and object identify with each other, as I have argued above. Further, Seeger plainly dismisses any capacity of music to function as symbol. This position is difficult to maintain, because there is plenty of evidence to the contrary – from national anthems to leitmotifs (see Martinez 1991: 139-72) and complex aesthetic reference systems, such as the idea of rāga in Indian classical music (explained in sections 2 and 3). These examples are all musical representations based on general conceptions not related to their objects by means of similarity or as matters of fact. They are conventions, in the strict sense of the word 'symbol'. Music is not merely an issue of acoustic materiality.

The universe of the individual human being is represented by Seeger as Inclusion I, which 'is experiential, solipsistic, aesthetic. It is the individual man who senses P, carries C, makes S and M' (Seeger 1977: 109). How human beings are able to perceive the world, participate as members of a culture, make music and produce speech is the real riddle for which there is no other answer but semiosis, the aesthetic and the experiential included. Individuals are semiotic, that is, constant producers, consumers, interpreters of signs, even to the extent of being signs themselves. The problem of the self, viewed from a semiotic perspective, leads also to relevant and innovative conclusions (see Singer 1984: 159). According to Peirce, semiosis is the process by which individual minds establish relations among the physical, cultural, linguistic and musical universes.

The individual universe is obviously related to the cultural one:

> Inclusion C is axiological, consensual, valual. The other four are products of traditions that are members of the bundle of traditions that make up the variant ways of collective living that we call 'cultures.' Cultures, too, exemplify world views. In them are embedded the dearest values of their carriers. They are impressed upon the soft wax of the growing child's individuality and, thus inherited, are cultivated and transmitted to future generations. (Seeger 1977: 109-110)

The idea of culture as a bundle of traditions is relevant and can be extended semiotically to the individual, who is a collection of habits, as Peirce writes (CP 6.228). Yet the relations between the individual and her/his culture sounds somehow too deterministic in Seeger's statement above. Traditions and habits do change, in both the individual and in a culture. Besides, what are traditions but networks of signs – whose action may develop as contemplative, causative and interpretive – usually combined in a variety of ways.

Finally, Seeger explains the physical universe. 'Inclusion P is phenomenological, existential, factual. The other four universes are phenomena in it' (1977: 110). This is the only universe which Seeger thinks is not necessarily related to a universe of values, the sixth concept in his system. A universe of value is deduced 'out of four of our original universes, S, M, I, and C, all of which are valuative, that is, value-giving with respect to P, which – except for some religious teaching by which we, as musicologists, are not necessarily bound – is neither valuative nor value-giving. Thus, SMIC=V and can be related as follows' (1977: 118):

Figure 2
Universe of Value
(adapted from Seeger 1977: 118)

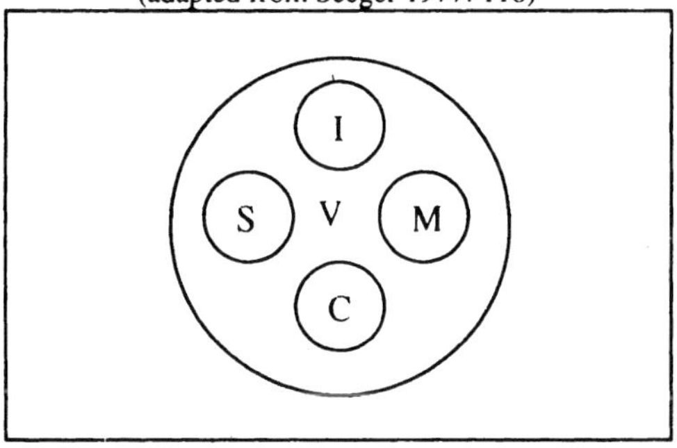

Thus, from this diagram Seeger draws individual values, cultural values, speech values and musical values. These result from relationships with facts: 'we relate facts to ourselves and ourselves to facts variously, and [...] it is this two-way relating that we call "valuation" – a function whose end products we generalize as the structural concept "value" ' (Seeger 1977: 118-19). Yet the fundamental question is how individuals relate to facts. Once again the answer is, by means of semiosis: the sign is the link between facts (object) and values or judgments (interpretants). It seems to me that Seeger's field theory, based on interrelated universes, could support broader conceptions of each universe if semiosis were taken into account.

1.2 Some Theories of Musical Semiotics

The last 25 years have seen a steady increase in musical studies based on semiotic theories. Combining different methods and approaches, these investigations have been directed toward a wide variety of musics and musical experiences. I shall not review in this chapter the major trends and achievements of such studies. Other authors have done so, in essays of varying scope, to which the reader is hereby directed: Hatten (1980), Lidov (1986), Hatten and Henrotte (1988), Monelle (1992), Dougherty (1994).

My focus here is on musical applications of the semiotic theory of Charles S. Peirce as made by selected scholars. I limit myself to these musical applications and not others because my interest lies in ideas that relate to the development of a semiotic theory of music on a Peircean basis. Thus, I do not deal with certain important lines of research, such as linguistics, structuralism, narratology, and cognitive sciences, which have generated a number of semiotic studies pertaining to music.

Before dealing with the ideas I have chosen to reflect on in this chapter, it is necessary to mention a few studies directly concerned with issues of signification in Indian music, though not all of them are engaged in musical semiotics. From the point of view of linguistics, Chandola has written on aspects of Indian music (1988), but his approach seems more effective in explaining drumming than in interpreting the melodic features of Hịndustani rāgas. In this sense, Nylund's article (1983) brings some interesting revelations on the structures of some rāgas. Yet both Chandola's and Nylund's views are limited by their theoretical bases, which cannot account for the openness and dynamism of rāga and tāla in Indian music. Other studies have tentatively approached aspects of Hindustani music or its aesthetics from a more or less definite semiotic standpoint, but the results in such cases are even less substantial than the two works mentioned above. They could nevertheless be taken as steps, on different paths, all of which lead to the understanding of signification in Indian music (see Erdman 1982, Montaut 1987, Goswami 1995). Much more fruitful have been purely musicological and indological approaches, which have provided an entire field of research to be explored in connection with semiosis in Hindustani and Karnatic music.

An empirical approach to the problem of rasa was developed in two experiments by Deva and Virmani (1968) and Deva (1981: 138-222). Those studies, aimed at the evaluation of psychological responses to

Hindustani music, were drawn from behaviorist experimental methods. Deva claims that pure music is fundamentally non-referential (1981: 139), which is a limited view of signification (see 2.3.2). He assumes that rasa theory cannot be applied *in toto* to pure music, and he proceeds by investigating the stimulus-response relation of a few rāgas. The technique for measurement was the semantic differential scale (Osgood, Souci and Tannenbaum), applied first to 37 respondents, and in the second experiment to 228. The tests consisted in playing recordings of short pieces of instrumental music, which the listeners were asked to score in a multiple choice format, according to bipolar adjectives. The results were compared to the traditional conception of the rāga. Besides the small sample of subjects tested, Deva's experiments are questionable in terms of the criteria adopted, which severely limits the accuracy, and hence the value, of the results. Furthermore, it is doubtful whether stimulus-response approaches such as this could shed any light on musical signification, when a diversity of cultural representations interact with educational and subjective factors during an actual instance of listening. Deva's studies ignore the fact that musical meaning is not merely a question of dyadic relations between music and listener. Musical meaning depends largely on several forms of semiosis, including musical reference to a variety of objects and referential interaction on many levels. Consider, for example, the cultural semiotic body of a rāga, the composition presented, the way it is performed, the communication situation of a concert, the sensitivity and cognitive capacities of a listener, and so on, all of which are interpretative processes. By ignoring semiosis in its complexity, statistical experiments can only produce doubtful results.

In examining the Peircean ideas presented below, I will make use of a number of concepts not introduced previously in this study. To do so, I must presuppose that the reader of this chapter is acquainted with the fundamentals of Peirce's semiotics, my own view of which can be found in chapters 2.1 and 2.2.

Early approaches and their developments

Since Molino defends the idea that the 'musical fact is a total social fact' (1990: 115), the need for appropriate theoretical foundations, in view of the comprehension of music in its entirety, evolved as the so-called 'semiology of music'. Molino argues for the study of music from a multicultural perspective, not as a pure phenomenon that is arbitrarily separated from its relationships with culture, but as signification or symbolic activity. In this connection, Molino refers to Peirce's trichotomy icon/index/symbol, emphasizing that music is simultaneously all three kinds of sign (1990: 125-26), but he does not proceed by basing his argument on Peirce's theory. Eschewing a mathematical scheme of communication, Molino instead presents a system of three dimensions, the tripartite model, by which studies of musical signification can be evaluated: the poietic, esthesic, and neutral dimensions.

The poietic dimension refers to strategies of musical creation or production: '*In the first place it is a product* and not simply a transmission, as people are in the habit of saying when they use the misleading model of communication. Music is thus closely connected with technique, both vocal and instrumental, both of the body and of the object. That product is a creation and as such not to be reduced to a purely intellectual or theoretical explanation' (Molino 1990: 129). The esthesic dimension refers to the perception of the musical fact: '*The musical object is received by the listener*, by the participant in the ceremony of the concert-goer – and also, of course, by the producer himself. As Valéry pointed out, however, there is no guarantee of a direct correspondence between the effect produced by a work of art and the intentions of its creator' (1990: 130). The neutral dimension refers to the music itself, for 'the symbolic phenomenon is also an object – matter subject to form' (1990: 130), which Molino takes pains not to separate arbitrarily from the total social fact. The tripartite model was adopted by Nattiez, who developed his well known musical semiology on a taxonomic-empiricist basis (see Nattiez 1975, 1990). Though later altered and expanded by Nattiez himself, it was roundly criticized by a number of scholars (see Hatten 1980, Dougherty 1994). There is no need to go through all the issues involved in that criticism, but it is useful to recall Hatten's critique of Nattiez's tripartite model of musical analysis:

> The levels of the tripartition contain seeds of useful distinctions, but Nattiez prescribes an order in their discovery, and an isolation in their designation, that cannot be defended. The many factors involved both interpenetrate and divide along different lines: the poietic cannot comprise at the same time the production end, the composer, and 'history' any more than the esthesic can encompass equally the perception end, the listener (every), and aesthetics and meaning. Nor can the objectivity of a neutral level necessarily lead us to great discoveries. (Hatten 1980: 152)

The neutral level, taken by Nattiez as the conceptual dimension that makes possible musical analysis, has generated some of the most heated disputes about the methods of musical semiology. Dougherty writes that 'the task of the neutral level (*niveau neutre*) is nevertheless to cleanse itself of any *poiétique* and *esthésique* taints that could sully its objectivity' (1994: 167). And Hatten challenges its very existence:

> The reason a neutral level does not exist, either theoretically or methodologically as Nattiez has framed it, is the reason science differs from art. Nature is not a message organized for our senses (in spite of superstitions); rather, our senses are organized to help us survive in our environment. Music, however, as a human form of organization, rests upon the possibility of an interpretative act. Therefore, a true semiology of music must disclaim a methodological 'purity' that would restrict the hypothesis-stimulating information issuing from the complex interplay of

all parts of the communication model, at every stage of our analysis. (1980: 153)

Nattiez acknowledged the ideas of his critics, but his response and reworking of musical semiology was reformulated not to change substantially his theory, but so as to clear up misunderstandings (1990: xii). On the other hand, Nattiez has tentatively approached Peirce's semiotics by way of his own system, developed from Molino's tripartition. As early as 1975, Nattiez mentions Peirce's idea of sign (apud Granger), and the notion of interpretant (1975: 56-61). Peirce appears only briefly in that study and in *Music and Discourse*, and yet Nattiez claims that his (later) 'book is, in a sense, both a defense and an illustration of the Peircean concept of the sign' (1990: 8). This statement and the few others in support of Nattiez's argument have been sufficiently criticized by Dougherty (1994: 169-72). Moreover, any reader minimally acquainted with Peircean semiotics will realize how far from the truth Nattiez's claim is. In fact, it does not collaborate in any sense with the development of musical semiotics as a whole. Nattiez's *Music and Discourse* should be rather taken as an extension of his earlier work, the basic rationale of which remains unaltered.

Another paradigm that appeared in the early seventies, though based on different theoretical assumptions from those of the taxonomic-empiricists, was the musical semiotics of Boiles (1973). From the very beginning, Boiles makes it clear that the essential problem of musical signification lies in the understanding of musical semiosis. Drawn from Morris's theory of signs, Boiles's *Semiotics of Ethnomusicology* is divided into three fields: syntactic, semantic and pragmatic. The syntactic dimension deals with 'the kinds of relationship concerning the signs, the combination of which is done according to the rules of formation and transformation' (1973: 35). The task of musical semantics is 'to discover which aspects of music constitute the signifiers and which are the designata of the signs' (1973: 36). Finally, pragmatics 'is the dimension of semiotics that studies the way in which signs are connected to their interpreters. Pragmatics studies the processes of recognition of a sign, the habits that make the interpreter perceive that a signifier designates certain objects or situations' (1973: 177-78). This system seems to me more pertinent to musical analysis than Molino's tripartite model. However, the syntactic, semantic, and pragmatic domains are not as capacious as one would wish, since the model has a behaviorist bias. Although Morris borrowed some concepts from Peirce, he transformed them into a system that was philosophically quite different, for Morris's theory of signs is based on behavioralist foundations.

Another theory derived from Morris's semiotics is the well known *Music and Meaning* by Wilson Coker, defined as a gestural semiotic theory of music and musical experience (1972: xi). According to Coker, 'A *musical gesture* is a complex stimulus to the response of the composer, performer, and listener as well as to further musical development: it comprises a recognizable formal unity and consists of a selection and organization of sonic and rhythmic properties in sonorous motion' (1972: 18). A musical gesture can refer to both purely musical and non-musical objects, including events and actions. Musical gestures are obviously signs, but Coker has a particularized understanding of them: 'musical gestures tend to be much more a doing of something than a saying of things about something. *Gestures are performatives*' (1972: 19). Thus, for Coker, the essence of musical signification is not representation, but action and reaction, which implies that music conveys meaning by patterns of sound stimuli and their corresponding responses.

Coker divides musical meaning into two kinds, *congeneric* and *extrageneric*. This division of inner and outer musical meaning has been adopted by many later music semioticians, though they often use different terminology. According to Coker, both congeneric and extrageneric signification depend on iconic situations, especially in the former case. Congeneric musical meaning occurs when 'someone interprets one part of a musical work as a sign of another part of that same work or a diverse musical work;' on the other hand, extrageneric musical meaning occurs when 'someone interprets a musical work or a portion of it as a sign of some non-musical object, including sounds not then organized as parts of the musical work' (1972: 61). Coker develops this scheme according to the triad of icons, indices, and logical or syntactical signs.

Towards a Peircean Semiotic Theory of Music

As seen above, only traces of Peircean semiotics can be found in music-analytic approaches derived from Morris's theories. Peirce, however, has a much more comprehensive theory to offer. Some of the earliest attempts at applying Peircean semiotics to music were made by the Brazilian composer Oliveira (1979), as well as by Moraes (1983) and Fisher (1985). Oliveira combines several different semiotic concepts, taken from various sources, with those of Peirce. Oliveira does not seek to elaborate a semiotic theory of music, but rather to explore in a provisional way some semiotic aspects of Beethoven's music. Thus, Oliveira tends to view musical signification mainly in terms of the purely musical, while only hinting at other issues of reference, such as musical metalanguage, ethnic allusions, iconicity, and emotional responses. Though he does not say so, Moraes was clearly influenced by Peirce's universal categories in his three 'manners of listening:' to listen with the body, with the emotions, and with the intellect (1983: 63-70). Fisher's article, on the other hand, is much more specific in its use of Peircean semiotics. As simple and unpretentious as it is, Fisher's study presents relevant arguments for a theory of musical semiotics founded upon a clear comprehension of the concepts and possibilities of Peirce's theory of signs. The application of Peirce's three trichotomies of signs to music has also been explored by Karbusicky (1987) and Tarasti (1987). Santaella (1988), in her Peircean classification of the main semiotic systems of thought and language, has mentioned music as an iconic matrix, whereas visual and verbal signs stand for indexical and symbolic paradigms. Those three broad domains relate, respectively, to the ideas of firstness, secondness and thirdness.

The triad of icon/index/symbol is certainly the most widely-known and applied of Peirce's concepts.[7] It has long been used by several music semioticians, but only in a restricted sense. Such limitation not only overlooks the great usefulness of the Peircean triad as tools for musical analysis, but in some cases even diverges from the original concepts. On the other hand, little effort has been made to understand Peirce's classification of signs in terms of sign-action, or semiosis, which is its true foundation. Inattention in this area has resulted in serious problems in the interpretation of semiotic concepts with regard to musical issues. Lidov, for one, has effectively employed some of Peirce's semiotic concepts, yet in some cases his views are disputable. Concerning whether musical signification is iconic or indexical, Lidov writes: 'I reject (as he [Peirce] does) any sharp, unqualified opposition between relations of similarity and relations of real connection. The general rule (so very well illustrated by photographs and seismographs) is that significant similarities have real causes and that real connections transfers features of similarity. To take an example from esthetics, catharsis, a real effect, depends on mimesis, a similarity' (Lidov 1987: 73). However, not all similarities are necessarily based on real connections. Furthermore, the examples adduced by Lidov are cases of complex signs, in which not only icons and indices play an active role in sign interpretation, but the representation is also determined by legisigns and symbols, as in the case of photographs. These cannot be taken as merely a compound of icons and indices, for the photographer's intentions – by framing the images in a certain way or from a certain vantage point, by freezing an action into a timeless instant, and several other issues – convey a whole web of technical and ideological factors that cannot be reduced to the icon-index pair (see Machado 1984). Peirce's trichotomies are essential to the building of a semiotic theory of music, but they must be understood in their proper theoretical context. Cases of actual signification are mostly complex signs, and to analyze them accurately requires the use of Peirce's ten classes of signs (CP 2.254-63). According to the logic of relatives, these evolve from the combination of the three trichotomies and their nine kinds of sign: (1) qualisign, sinsign, legisign; (2) icon, index, symbol; (3) rheme, dicent and argument (CP 2.243-52).

---

[7] Elsewhere I have explored the problem of reference in music, according to a division of iconic, indexical and symbolic semiosis (see Martinez 1991).

The place of Peirce in Tarasti's semiotic theory of music

Tarasti, as early as 1987, envisioned the use of the nine kinds of signs in terms of a spatial relation on three axes, each referring to one of the trichotomies of signs (see Figure 3):

> In the lowest musical dimension (that of a musical work), a composition consists in a chain of icons, indexes, and symbols which may alternate in any possible order. Similarly, any musical unity or member in the syntagm has its own legisigns, which have served as models or types for its creation, for its particular shape as a sinsign, and for its qualisign, i.e., its concrete, aural qualities (which depend in large part on how the piece is performed). These sign relations serve as the organs of a musical 'being,' the feelers or tentacles with which it orients itself and reacts to its environment. It receives 'nourishment' through them. (1994a: 55)

Figure 3
Tarasti's three dimensional model
(adapted from Tarasti 1987: 446)

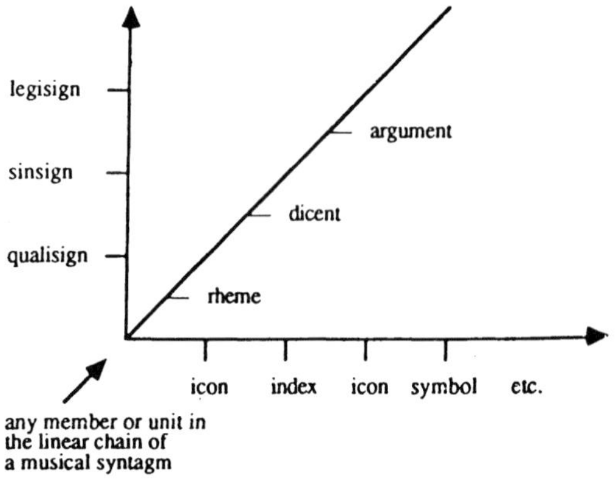

Most striking in Tarasti's three-dimensional model, is the fact that the lowest musical dimension is not that of signs in themselves (qualisign, sinsign, legisign), but that of the sign in relation to its objects, that is, the icon/index/symbol trichotomy. Tarasti equates this axis with the temporal development of music, by viewing the composition as a syntagmatic chain, of icons, indices and symbols, which may appear in any order. This is, therefore, not a general model of musical signification, but a possible diagram for musical reference. Tarasti sees the axis referring to signs in relation to interpretant as playing a role only in musical reception. Moreover, some questions arise concerning the relationship of the three axes. If icons, indices and symbols can appear in any order in the syntagmatic chain, could not the same be possible on the other two axes? Do either of the other two axes correspond to a paradigmatic axis?

It is true that, among the three axes, any combination of signs is possible. Yet one must not forget that there is a logical relation between the three trichotomies. Peirce understood as much, realizing that not all combinatorial possibilities are valid, but that only ten of those relations, the ten classes of signs, are significant. In the logic of relatives, which is the basis of Peirce's reasoning, it is rather the trichotomy of signs in themselves that constitutes the lowest level of signification. In fact, the 'syntagm' itself is a kind of legisign, and as Tarasti recognizes, all nine kinds of sign may take part in the musical structures (1994a: 57). It seems to me that semiosis, musical or otherwise, is not limited to three dimensions, but instead takes place in many dimensions. Furthermore, there is little sense in discussing species of sign if one does not take semiosis into account. Signs of any kind are what they are depending on the point of view of the analysis. Thus, a particular sign, its object and interpretant, as well as their subdivisions, require careful consideration, as does the network of surrounding semiosis, in order to achieve accurate and meaningful analyses from the semiotic tools developed by Peirce.

According to Tarasti, musical rhemes, dicents and arguments are signs related to musical perception: 'one could say that, in music, signs in relation to their interpretants concern those sign processes that take place in the mind of the listener, whereby he or she interprets the musical experience' (1994a: 55). Yet this is only one form of sign interpretation and there would be no music if interpretation were restricted to musical perception. Musical interpretation is basic to all actualized forms of musical semiosis, and in addition to the fundamental empirical act of perception, one must consider performance, composition, several forms of musical scholarship, and even educational and performing institutions as musical interpretants. And all of them are also signs. The same argument might be lodged against Tarasti's view of the trichotomy of signs in themselves as being restricted to the dimension of musical composition: 'Signs in themselves form a dimension of musical creation in the proper sense: musical signs take form on the basis of other, previously known sign complexes, and thus serve as a rule (or legisign) for the production of subsequent signs (sinsigns or single signs) and again for qualisigns' (ibid.). Issues of musical creation cannot be relegated solely to the layer of signification concerned with signs in themselves. All kinds of signs, all modes of semiosis bear upon the act of composing or improvising music. Such an act is fundamentally one of sign-interpretation or semiosis, and it is not primarily directed to the reception of music, but to musical interpretation in the sense of the causation of musical phenomena.

It seems to me that what is essential to a semiotic theory of music is not the varieties of sign, but rather semiosis itself; the trichotomies and sign classes are but a classification of possible forms of signification. In fact, all kinds of signs manifest themselves in the musical materiality of sound, and in the minds of listeners, performers, composers and scholars. Besides, signs are usually composite forms; for instance, a musical symbol is necessarily a legisign, and when manifested in a piece of music (as sinsign), it acquires an actuality that can function as index, and it has qualitative aspects (qualisign), which can also promote iconic forms of reference. In relation to an interpreter, potential or actual, this symbol might signify nothing but a possibility of meaning (rheme), which refers at least to its material qualities. Or the symbol might give some positive information about its object (dicent), or trigger a series of inferences (arguments), musical or otherwise. Thus all nine kinds of sign are potentially or actually present in the music itself, in the referential aspect of music, and in the interpreter's mind, be s/he a listener, performer, composer, critic, or computer program.

A semiotic theory of music must translate the actual forms of musical semiosis into a diagram that provides an understanding of musical signs and their processes. Such a theory should conceptualize the kinds of distinctions and semiotic analysis that eventually collaborate in the creation, performance and criticism of music. The classification of signs is therefore an instrument for the understanding of all forms of semiosis.

In Tarasti's theory, musical semiosis is conceived as discourse. According to him, musical discourse can be understood as a chain of communication, in which ideological and technological models determine the structures of communication, represented by 'stylistic structures insofar as a composer follows certain "automatisms" of stylistic norms' (1994a: 18), that is, the general system according to which a piece of music is organized. It is however in the domain of structures of signification that a composition acquires individual aesthetic values: 'in a musical work the structures of communication provide the area in which the composer's fantasy can move in a relatively free manner and thereby produce some unique signification' (ibid.). Tarasti further indicates that the structures of communication often constrain the composer's creativity.[8] Thus, in the structures of communication is the set of possibilities of a certain reference model, which is both technico-musical and cultural. Creativity consists in the ways the composer either follows or breaks the 'rules' of this universe of communication. It is this activity that results in a musical work's structures of signification, where 'the true aesthetic moment of music is to be found' (ibid.). This model, while interesting and significant in regard to musical creativity, can be understood as an extension of the linguistic concepts of *langue* and *parole*. The former is the general referential system of a language or musical style; the latter refers to the particular utterances of an individual speaker or composer.

Tarasti makes use of several different theories in formulating his view of musical semiosis (1994a: 289), sometimes combining them, as in his concepts of interoceptive and exteroceptive signification. He divides sign relations in music according to inner and outer signification, which echoes the Greimassian distinction between interoceptive and

[8] Personal communication.

exteroceptive signs: 'I will call exteroceptive those signs that direct our attention to the relation between the musical and the external world; inner signs, which refer to relations within the musical work, will be called interoceptive' (Tarasti 1994a: 57). Tarasti develops this distinction extensively, devising an interoceptive iconicity ('the paradigmatic aspect of music'), interoceptive indexicality ('the syntagmatic aspect'), and interoceptive symbolicity, which are 'abstract sign relations that allude to certain musical situations and their resolutions' (1994a: 57-58). The question of whether a musical sign refers to the music itself or to some external element is, above all, a question of reference. To answer this question, one must determine the nature of the object for which the signs stands. The nature of the object of a musical sign is such that it can be understood as musical or non-musical. If a sign is taken as representing a non-musical object, or something considered as such, then an instance of exteroceptive signification has taken place. But if the object of a musical sign is a musical feature, then the semiosis is interoceptive. The objects of musical signs may indeed be divided into musical and non-musical, but this is a controversial distinction. For instance, a musical sign refers to its object, but it may happen that the object is another musical sign, and even from a different work, as in the case of a musical quotation which refers to a piece by another composer. Should this be considered a case of interoceptive or exteroceptive reference? The fact is that the two domains overlap each other.

One hypothesis offered by Tarasti deserves careful investigation. He proposes that 'the more music functions as an outer sign the less we experience its functioning as an inner sign' (1994a: 57). It seems to me that the basic presupposition of this hypothesis is the view of musical signification in which, on the one hand, music is seen as – above all – signifying itself; and on the other, music may refer to something else, but only by sacrificing its independence as an autonomous language. An analysis of this hypothesis must take into account a third dimension of musical signification, namely, interpretation. Musical semiosis is not merely a matter of inner or outer signification, a distinction which comes mainly from the linguistic, dyadic conception of the sign as *signifiant* and *signifié*. For Peirce, semiosis is a triadic relation, the relata of which are sign, object and interpretant. If a listener relates music to a non-musical object, then its interpretant might be something other than purely musical ideas. Nevertheless, it was through the mediation of the sign – that is, the musical structures and their inner signification – that a non-musical object appeared. The reverse process would be impossible, for an object cannot be interpreted, in the sense of being recognized, without the mediation of a sign. Thus, semiosis can be limited to the musical aspects of a composition, but this does not preclude reference to other kinds of objects. The listener's attention can be distracted from the music itself, toward something 'external', but it is more likely that the two references, musical and non-musical, will overlap each other, without any decrease in the cognition of purely musical ideas. Moreover, non-pure musical reference need not be compulsory, since it depends largely on the capacity of the interpreter to distinguish between musical and non-musical objects. The division of musical signification into inner or outer reference, as proposed by Tarasti, seems highly problematic to me, because these are not mutually exclusive domains. It is perfectly possible to blend musical interpretants with those resulting from a non-musical reference. The combination of those two domains is likely to produce a richer aesthetic experience than that in which the two cases are conceptualized separately.

Another pertinent and interesting issue concerns how musical signs that refer to non-musical objects interact with signs that refer to the music itself (Tarasti 1994a: 57). In his analysis of Musorgsky's *Pictures at an Exhibition* (1994a: 209-41), Tarasti demonstrates 'the way a composer transforms external icons, indexes, and symbols into internal ones' (1994a: 209). Such an understanding of musical semiosis has the value of not separating musical reference from musical structures, which have semiotic status and aesthetic value in themselves. In other words, that music has the power to represent non-musical objects does not imply a lack of musical coherence, for musical signs, whether they are considered internal or external, are always – in their materiality – the same signs. There is no actual separation in the musical materiality of the signs; they only offer different possibilities of interpretation, as representing different objects. In fact, it partly depends on the interpreter (the listener or analyst) as to how the interpretants of musical signs are actualized. The signs are the same, but the object may be the music itself or some conception of the 'Great Gate of Kiev', as in the Musorgsky movement with that title. At the level of interpretant, music can be understood as a compound of signs operating merely at the structural level of a certain musical system, or as referring to non-musical objects, such as the watercolors of Victor Hartmann, the visual models upon which Musorgsky constructed the *Pictures*. Also, since the music merely hints at those visual images (usually unknown by the listeners), it is through the development of semiosis in the listener's imagination – the interaction of her/his inner universe of signs with the music – that Musorgsky's *Pictures at an Exhibition* acquires the fantastic aesthetic impression that it potentially has.

A fundamental theoretical and philosophical basis for the comprehension of Peircean semiotics – the phenomenological or universal categories of firstness, secondness, thirdness – has often been mentioned in musical studies, but only recently has it received sustained attention from scholars (Oliveira 1979; Moraes 1983; Santaella 1987; Martinez 1991: 31-37; Monelle 1991: 100; Hatten 1994a, 1994b; Tarasti 1994a, 1994b, 1994c; Mosley 1995). Those categories are still much misunderstood, but their analytical power should be recognized by music semioticians. Tarasti applies the universal categories to cognitive processes in musicology, illustrating his initial contact with and progressive modeling of a work by the Czech composer, Bohuslav Martinu (Tarasti 1994b: 338-41). The apprehension of music as firstness is not as common as one would suspect. What Peirce meant by a consciousness in firstness[9] is a totality of feeling irrespective of time and space (unless in the sense of *hic et nunc*), of analysis, or of any sense of polarity, such as the idea of ego and non-ego. Firstness, in the case of musical listening or appreciation, is when the consciousness of the listener completely blends with the qualities of the music. It is a pure quality of feeling that requires the listener to focus on that which is merely present to the ears. Tarasti wonders 'whether any art historian, aesthetician or musicologist of our post-modern time can still experience something as a First' (1994b: 338). Indeed, the human mind is deeply involved in webs of signification (thirdness), and in several levels of contact with reality in which one's individuality is constantly forced to act mentally and physically (secondness). Hence, to listen to music as firstness requires a naive mental disposition that is commonly found among children, artists and mystics, but that is hardly possible for a mind laden with significations during most of its conscious time. Anyone capable of truly experiencing firstness will have a great advantage, not only by being able to experience the music itself, but also because of the capacity to gain insights that are only possible when the mind is freed from the constraints of overly formalized, logical thought. And these insights may well lead to new forms of knowledge.

Peirce realized that the categories manifest themselves in all kinds of thought, including that of reason. In this respect, firstness, secondness and thirdness stand for abduction (the formulation of hypotheses), induction and deduction. That is to say, in relation to the three forms of inference (all of them thirdnesses), abduction is a first, induction is a second, and deduction is a third. Combining the two sets of concepts, the categories and the three modes of inference, Tarasti constructs an interesting model of musicological cognition (1994b: 341). I would classify Tarasti's model (see Figure 4) as an instance of musical-intelligence interpretation, in which perception is implicit (see 2.3.3). The first contact with Martinu's music (or any other music), as far as it is unprejudiced by other forms of consciousness, leads the listener to the appreciation of its musical qualities as they are. In a leap to thirdness – not a genuine thirdness, but one still close to the qualities experienced – the listener would formulate hypotheses that have only the potential of being true. Tarasti calls this the first model. At a second stage, the individuality and background experience of the listener interacts with the music itself, and a consciousness of the music as an existent or object takes shape in the listener's mind. Another incursion into thirdness, now by means of inductive inference, checks empirically to see how close the hypothesis of

[9] The categories were conceived by Peirce as having much broader consequences than their manifestation in the human mind (see 2.1). This is, thus, a particular instance, and not their essential case.

the first model accords with the reality of the music. For Tarasti, this is the second model of a musicologist. Finally, with Martinu's music taken as sign, by a form of listening characterized as genuine thirdness, the third model is reached, and a theory is laid out by means of deductions. In applying the Peircean categories, one must remember that firstness is included in secondness, and both firstness and secondness are part of thirdness. If music itself is viewed through the categories, its musical materiality corresponds to firstness, its existence in time and space to secondness, and its signification to thirdness. Thus, when Tarasti writes that the listener always returns to the 'empirical level', he implies that the pure qualities of musical materiality are present in all instances of secondness and thirdness, as the musicologist's cognition develops.

Figure 4
Tarasti's model of musicological cognition
(adapted from Tarasti 1994b: 341)

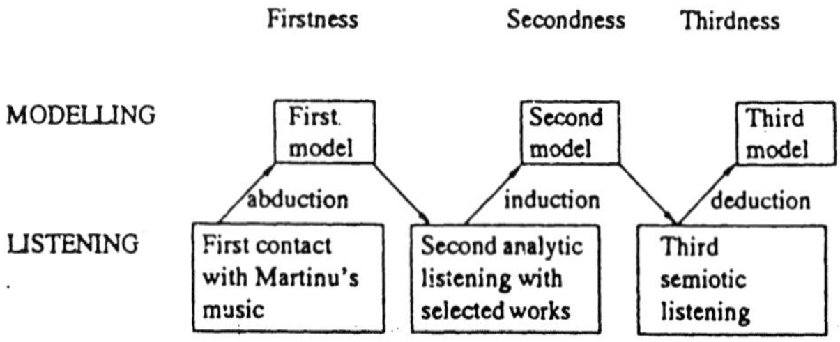

Monelle's view of Peircean concepts applied to music

As significant and pertinent as Peirce's categories and theory of signs are, music semioticians have often misinterpreted his concepts. Such misinterpretations must be rectified, and the understanding of his semiotic theory, by music scholars, must be raised to the high level found in Peirce's own writings and in the interpretations of his ideas by expert Peirce scholars. The imprecision with which Peircean semiotics has been treated by some music semioticians is exemplified in the following statement by Monelle, concerning the three trichotomies: 'The icon/index/symbol division was, in effect, the division according to interpretant, for Peirce attributes it to the "manner of relating to the object" (though Karbusicky calls it the "object-trichotomy"). If one considers the object, signs are classed as rheme, dicent and argument (oddly, this is the "interpretant-trichotomy" for Karbusicky); having regard to the representamen, the classes are qualisign, sinsign and legisign' (1991: 99). Karbusicky's 'odd' view[10] is in fact the correct one

[10] See Karbusicky 1987: 25.

of Peirce's trichotomies. By 1897-98 Peirce wrote: 'Signs are divisible by three trichotomies; first, according as the sign in itself is a mere quality, is an actual existent, or is a general law; secondly, according as the relation of the sign to its object consists in the sign's having some character in itself, or in some existential relation to that object, or in its relation to an interpretant; thirdly, according as its Interpretant represents it as a sign of possibility or as a sign of fact or a sign of reason' (CP 2.243). Thus, qualisign, sinsign, and legisign are the first trichotomy, which refers to the sign in itself (see CP 2.244-6); icon, index, and symbol are the second trichotomy (CP 2.247-9), which refers to the relation of the sign to its object; and rheme, dicent, and argument are the third trichotomy (CP 2.250-52), which refers to the relation of the sign with its interpretant. Peirce expanded the trichotomies to ten in 1908 (CP 8.344), incorporating the above three basic trichotomies, which are accurate enough for most semiotic issues in music. Monelle's mistake, unhappily, has not been corrected in his later work (1992: 195-200).

Monelle's misunderstanding of the Peircean trichotomies, while easily confusing, can be corrected quickly by a comparison his ideas to Peirce's own writings and to those of Peirce scholars. Monelle's views on iconism (1992: 200-209), however, require a more detailed critique. Firstly, take Monelle's description of an icon as having 'certain properties in common with its object' (1992: 200). This is a very restrictive view that does not do justice to the amplitude, significance and consequence of the Peircean idea of icon and iconic sign, and thus leads to mistaken arguments. The characterization of iconism as shared properties between sign and object is far from accurate. Peirce writes: 'An Icon is a sign which refers to the Object that it denotes merely by virtue of characters of its own, and which it possesses, just the same, whether any such Object actually exists or not' (CP 2.247). This definition, in its abstractness, makes clear that the sharing of properties is but one of the possible traits of iconicity. A frequently employed definition of the icon is based on similarity. Although less abstract, it is still representative of the wide scope of iconicity in Peirce's semiotics: 'A sign may serve as a sign simply because it happens to resemble its object. This resemblance will, then, constitute its internal meaning. But it cannot be said to have any external meaning, since it does not profess to represent anything; for if it did, that would be a manner of signifying its object, not consisting in merely resembling it' (CP 8.119). Monelle's argument that a drawing of a horse 'has nothing in common with the horse' is specious, for a drawing is an iconic sign in respect to some kind of isomorphism (such as a silhouette). What is implied here is a relation of resemblance and not contiguity. In this sense, 'An icon is a sign which would possess the character which renders it significant, even though its object had no existence; such as a lead-pencil streak as representing a geometrical line' (CP 2.304). Monelle goes on to write, erroneously, that 'Sign and object cannot have all properties in common; this would imply a relation of identity rather than a sign function' (1992: 201). The possibility of sign and object resembling each other to the point of identity is a real possibility which frequently manifests in music, when a composition or performance refers to its object as exactly the same acoustic phenomenon. This is the very basis of the idea of absolute music (see Martinez 1996a: 70-72). In fact, everything can be an icon, since everything is at least similar to itself (see Ransdell 1966: 150; 1986: 687).

Peirce's reference to a geometrical line leads to my second criticism of Monelle's 'radical modification of the idea of iconism', which concerns his view of diagrams: 'Peirce's classification of a logical diagram as an iconic symbol [sic] is obviously absurd, thinks Eco' (Monelle 1992: 200, 201). One must understand that Peirce classified several levels of iconicity according to the mode of firstness, or the way an icon resembles its object; for instance, hypoicons comprise images, diagrams and metaphors (CP 2.277). From a rigorously logical point of view, diagrams are iconic legisigns: 'An Iconic Legisign [e.g., a diagram, apart from its factual individuality] is any general law or type, in so far as it requires each instance of it to embody a definite quality which renders it fit to call up in the mind the idea of a like object' (CP 2.258). Therefore, a diagram is a composite sign wherein the relation of similarity with its object is rooted in formal principles, which are not arbitrary, but based on qualitative features that are similar to the objects' qualities in some respect, such as qualities of appearance or likeness in forms, functions, parts, and so on. There is nothing absurd in the notion of a diagram as an iconic legisign; rather, it is a fundamental mode of reasoning (see CP 3.363, 2.279-82).

According to Monelle, music is more likely to signify indexically than iconically. He states: 'The musical work, in its most typical form, is a rhematic indexical legisign; the actual performance, or a copy of the score, is a rhematic indexical sinsign' (1991: 107; 1992: 219). General statements such as these are of little use in comprehending musical semiosis. It is necessary to present clearly what is implied and in what context music (all the musics in time and space?) can be characterized as rhematic indexical legisign. Musical signs are complex entities, and their interpretation depends on several factors, which, if not clarified, turns classification into a frivolous use of semiotic terminology. Indexicality in music is certainly rich and manifold. The simple fact that music has its mode of being in actualization by performance implies an extensive network of indexical relations. Music can function as an index of its culture, historical period, musical style, individual composer, performer, her/his instrument, and so on. And at a level that is low in information, music can be interpreted as an index of itself, that is to say, as an index of its own acoustical qualities. This last possibility seems to be what Monelle implies by music as rhematic indexical legisign. Yet musical indices abound, for the very reason that, in most musical systems, music is understood as organized sound,[11] and thus it depends on legisigns that, when actualized as sinsigns, are prone to generate a diversity of possible indices.

Discussing the question of index in the context of feeling, Monelle concludes: 'Music and the passions are both the "work of nature". Music is a sign of natural order of which it is essentially a part; emotional life also partakes of that order. The relation of music and feeling is metonymic rather than metaphoric, indexical rather than iconic' (1992: 213). The issue of feelings in music has, for millenia, been the focus of philosophical and aesthetic investigations in several cultures. Obviously, there is no simple answer to the question of how music relates to feelings, moods, affections, emotions, and the like. However, if there is a science that can bring understanding on such matters, it is certainly musical semiotics. The view that music *represents* feelings or emotions seems to be the most pertinent one. In this connection, one finds different modes of representation by which composers and performers, in clearly-defined cultural and historical contexts, signify feelings and emotions. One finds iconic, indexical and symbolic approaches to accomplishing such signification. The baroque theory of affects, or *Affektenlehre*, seems to be a clear case of iconic representation of emotions, based on the scientific view of that period (cf. Descartes's *The Passions of the Soul*), and I have explored such means as a kind of diagrammatic reference (Martinez 1991: 92-97, 196-98; 1996a: 74-76). However, the *Affektenlehre* was a localized concept, and other musics, musicians and composers have employed different semiotic resources in representing feeling and emotion. Monelle's conception of indexicality in this regard is a behaviorist one, in its being limited to the dyadic act of listening, in disregard of how musical factors possibly convey such feelings, and above all, in not acknowledging the essential question of interpretants – how and why one listener can be indifferent to a piece of music that brings another to tears.

A model of growth in a musical style

In 1989 Hatten presented a paper at the C.S. Peirce Sesquicentennial International Congress at Harvard (1994b), in which he develops a model of musical style-growth based on the universal categories and the type/token distinction. According to Hatten, the idea of growth is suggested by the sequential disposition of the categories: 'by mediation (Thirdness) of the oppositions (Secondness) that emerge from novel tokens (Firstness)' (1994b: 352). It should be noted, however, that the categories are inclusive rather than sequential (see 2.1). Of course, ideas of temporality can be viewed by means of the categories. Peirce relates firstness to the present, secondness to the past, and thirdness to the future

[11] But not in all systems, e.g., not in some of Cage's compositions.

(CP 1.343, 8.330). Thus, it seems to me that growth is above all a feature of thirdness, which internalizes firsts and seconds. Unclear in Hatten's model is the association of 'novel tokens' with firstness (see Figure 5). Peirce conceives the idea of type/token as corresponding to two kinds of signs in the first trichotomy, legisign and sinsign. A type is a legisign, a general habit (or rule), whose mode of being as a sign is that of determining replicas, sinsigns or tokens. In this sense, tokens are seconds, individual existents, whose significance arises from the interpretation habit that forms the basis of the legisign. Tokens necessarily embody qualities (or qualisigns), but their essential semiotic feature is that of particularized existence. The imprecision occurs when Hatten refers to 'novel tokens'. On the one hand, if tokens are understood as replicas they cannot be related to firstness as easily as Hatten suggests, because they presuppose types, forms of thirdness, which regulate the appearance of tokens. On the other hand, if novel tokens are conceived merely as individual existents, or as simple sinsigns, although necessarily incorporating qualities, they are above all seconds.

As useful and powerful as the concepts of the Peircean categories are, it is desirable for analysts to state clearly on what scale and from what point of view the categories are invoked. The fact that Peirce thought the categories to be universal, implies a first rank of generality, which is not clear when music semioticians use the categories. There is a principle of firstness and secondness in the universe that is neither mental nor cognitive. Thus, application of the categories to music usually refers to instances of firstness, secondness and thirdness in musical semiosis; that is, to composite or degenerated forms of thirdness, loosely referred to as the all-encompassing first, second and third. In this sense, it is clearer and more accurate to deal with the sign classes, which were the tools developed by Peirce for the understanding of the finer distinctions of thirdness, or semiosis.

Figure 5

Hatten's model of growth in a musical style

(adapted from Hatten 1994b: 352)

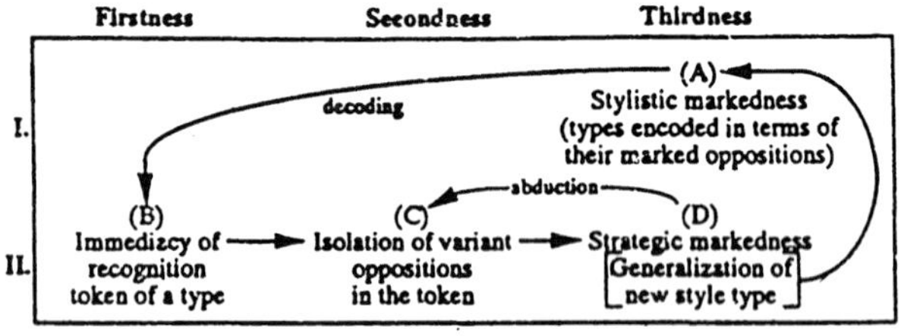

The type/token distinction proves to be quite useful. Hatten has demonstrated, in his analysis of chords used by Beethoven, how the interplay of types and tokens in terms of triads, their doublings and inversions generate new types, thus promoting stylistic growth (1994b:

354-56). It is remarkable that Hatten's most fruitful findings are derived from the type/token distinction and not from the universal categories. In fact, the growth of a musical style evolves in the field of thirdness. Thus, the phases described by Hatten in his model (Figure 5) as first and second are rather instances of degenerated thirdness, that is, the firstness of a thirdness, and the secondness of a thirdness. This much is clear when the process of growth is described in terms of interpretants (a third element in semiosis): 'a correlation at the level of style is "immediately" understood as the type for a token in a given work, but then "dynamically" interpreted in terms of its unique, differential features; these in turn may lead to a "final" interpretant based on their establishment as a new expressive type, and "ultimately" the new type may become a part of the style itself' (Hatten 1994b: 353). I will not discuss Hatten's use of the concepts of immediate, dynamical and final in the context of interpretation, suggesting Peirce's main division of the interpretant, which has a very specific sense in the context of semiosis (see 2.2), for Hatten has put those terms quotation marks, implying perhaps that he is using the terms loosely. Nevertheless, his model would gain in precision if, instead of the universal categories or the classes of interpretants, the sign classes were used. Thus, the immediacy of recognition of a sign is an instance of semiosis in which not types or tokens are understood, but rather qualisigns, which signify mere potentialities for the interpretant (rheme). Yet if the interpreter actually recognizes a token of a type, then the semiosis is not at this quasi-immediate level, but in a much higher formalized class, that of a dicent indexical legisign (CP 2.260). In this case, the recognition of type by means of its token implies the interpretant recognizing the legisign which determines the token. Thus, the sign in itself is an index of its own interpreting rule, or legisign; more precisely, it is a dicent sinsign. Simultaneously, the sign is an iconic legisign, which makes it able to convey information about its object. In more concrete terms, if a certain disposition of the notes F, Ab and C is understood as an occurrence (dicent sinsign) of the tonic F-minor triad, it functions that way because the given disposition of notes is in fact an iconic legisign of that triad, that is, the notes actually heard stand for the same acoustic relations as the concept of F minor. The meaning of this sign in the context referred to by Hatten, however, is not the qualities of that chord nor its aspects as an existent, but rather its character as a replica of a legisign, thus an index of its own type, which conveys definite information (dicent). Therefore, the recognition of a token of a type is a case of semiosis based on a dicent indexical legisign, which cannot be simply related to firstness, as Hatten suggests.

Looking at the other three phases of Hatten's model, one finds that the extra level of thirdness, which he calls upon to explain 'stylistic markedness' and 'strategic markedness' (1994b: 357), refers merely to different classes of signs (legisign and argument, respectively), both thirdnesses. To bring coherence to his model, and at the same time to keep it simple, the reference to firstness and secondness should be dropped, because all the processes of growth, in the context described by Hatten, evolve in thirdness. If real chance were involved in the growth of style, say in contemporary Western music or in improvisational forms, then firstness would truly have a place, but one cannot refer to mere chance in terms of type and token. As an alternative to the sign classes, instead of referring to the phases of stylistic growth as categories, they could be related to modes of inference, as Hatten suggests, such as the use of abduction in defining part of the style-growth process.

Peirce's categories can be very effective in dealing with musical phenomena, as long as they are set in the correct perspective. At the end of Hatten's paper is an example of how the categories can be used meaningfully in regard to aesthetic experience. He writes on 'the Firstness of art to be mediated by Thirdness, via Secondness' (1994b: 356-57). In the development of Hatten's theory of style growth, as presented in his *Musical Meaning in Beethoven* (1994a), he recognizes that his earlier model of development of a type from a token is basically operating as thirdness. Furthermore, Hatten provides valuable insights about the development of new musical entities (1994a: 261-68), but now with clear indications as to the point of view from which one is using the terms firstness, secondness and thirdness.

The flourishing of a Peircean semiotic theory of music

The essence of musical signification is not merely an issue of sign categories, but rather the understanding of musical semiosis, of which the kinds and classes of signs are analytical tools. Therefore, the general issue of musical semiosis is the point of departure for musical analysis. Yet few analysts have proceeded from the realization that, to achieve consistent results, the use of Peirce's trichotomies must be rooted in the understanding of musical semiosis as a whole. Semiosis in music appears in a variety of forms. Thus, not only are perception and cognition of musical pieces instances of semiosis, but so is the evolution of a musical style (Hatten), as well as the very process of musicological and semiotic research (Tarasti). In most applications of Peirce to music, although they discuss some aspects of musical semiosis, the various theories and approaches have no connection with the systemic idea and dynamic conception of semiosis as conceived by Peirce. That is to say, Peirce offers a rich theory of semiotics that has been underexplored by music semioticians. Musical semiotics indeed covers a broad field, and specialization is necessary in order to attain some level of conceptual depth. Yet it seems to me that not only does Peirce need to be better understood by music analysts (including myself), but also that a general architecture of musical semiosis should be elaborated (see 1.3 and 2.3). A general framework for musical semiotics should not be taken as a rigid model, but as a map to be revised and updated according to the development and findings of the community of inquirers (including not only scholars, but musicians, performers, listeners, producers, instrument makers, engineers, programmers, and the like).

That Peirce's semiotics seems the most effective and pertinent theory on which to base studies of musical signification is confirmed by the applications referred to above. Dependable scientific results are likely to be found in the work of more than one researcher. The capacity and validity of a theory can be proved by similar results achieved by scientists working independently. Interestingly, Dougherty has investigated, in a way compatible with mine, the problem of musical semiosis as applied to some case studies (Dougherty 1992, 1993). In his paper for the Second International Congress on Musical Semiotics, 'What Is a Musical Sign?: A Guess at the Riddle' (1992), Dougherty analyzes a passage from Beethoven's Piano Sonata Op. 2, no. 3, in terms of its components of triadic relation (sign, object and interpretant), its subdivisions (immediate and dynamical objects), and its immediate, dynamical and final interpretants – which are essential to explaining musical semiosis effectively. In the concluding paragraph of his paper, Dougherty writes: 'a triadic conception of the sign – securely founded on Peirce's general theory of the signs – provides sufficiently solid foundation from which musical semeioticians can erect a sturdy and substantial semeiotic perspective that embraces the realities of musical experience' (1992: 18). Dougherty's use of the specifically Peircean terms, *semeiotic* and *semeioticians*, indicates a rigorous adoption of Peirce's theory of signs, one based on deep understanding of that theory. This, however, should not be read as promoting a dogmatic view of Peirce's writings, which runs contrary to his episteme.

To judge by the many works applying Peirce's concepts to music, the semiotic study of music on a Peircean basis seems to be flowering. The use of Peircean semiotics to understand music, in all its variety and complexity, is not merely the future-hope of scholars, but a reality of the present. No single inquirer can unveil the secrets of music, that most ancient of cultural phenomena. As some philosophers and epistemologists believe (Peirce among them), the work of science involves a community of inquirers, who critically and constructively develop ideas (always submitted to the test of time) and who gain a more and more precise understanding of the subject of their research. And that subject matter itself is dynamic, as are all things in the universe.

1.3 The Place of Music in Peirce's Classification of the Sciences

> While Art ciphers, the sciences decipher. (Santaella 1992: 130)

Before introducing a Peircean semiotic theory of music as applied to Hindustani music, it will be useful to situate music studies in Peirce's broad classification of the sciences. To do so is not merely an exercise in taxonomy, but rather to understand how music studies relate to and depend on principles operative in the more general sciences, as well as those that are somehow complementary to musical research. This line of questioning leads one to interdisciplinarity, which seems to be the very mode of being of musical studies. Lucia Santaella wisely points out that 'it is in [Peirce's] cartography of sciences that more sophisticated and complex ways can be found by which to start thinking of interdisciplinarity in less blind flights [of fancy]' (1992: 105). Given the all-encompassing scope of Peirce's scientific 'architecture', it is also necessary to present an overview of his philosophy of science, not only to clarify his epistemology, but also to set parameters for the development, in section 2, of a theory of musical semiotics.

Peirce's philosophy of science

There exists a traditional view of science that considers it to be systematic knowledge. Charles S. Peirce – polymath, logician, philosopher, father of pragmatism and semiotics – denies this view. For him, it is the philosopher, rather than science itself, who has a system, one that encompasses all valuable knowledge. Peirce writes, 'it is not knowing, but the love of learning, that characterizes the scientific man' (CP 1.44). Peirce defines science as a living activity, a definition that rids itself of the myth of absolute knowledge and absolute truth, by focusing on the way science relates to truth. Peirce expresses this view in his theory of fallibilism (a paper written in 1897; see CP 1.8-14 and CP 1.141-75), which I will refer to shortly. Fallibilism must be understood in the proper context and in relation to his other theories, especially pragmatism and semiotics.

Science is an activity, a way of life. 'If a man burns to learn and sets himself to comparing his ideas with experimental results in order that he may correct those ideas, every scientific man will recognize him as a brother, no matter how small his knowledge may be' (CP 1.44). The hallmark of the scientific way of life is not the amount of knowledge gained, academic posts, or titles, but the sincere pursuit of truth. Everyone can be a scientist in this sense, but only the scientist who cooperates with a community of scientists can cause a field to advance:

> Science is to mean for us a mode of life whose single animating purpose is to find out the real truth, which pursues this purpose by a well-considered method, founded on thorough acquaintance with such scientific results already ascertained by others as may be available, and which seeks cooperation in the hope that the truth may be found, if not by any of the actual inquiries, yet ultimately by those who come after them and who shall make use of their results. (CP 7.55)

The notion of a community of researchers is indeed basic to Peirce's conception of science, but truth, the scientist's ultimate goal, is fundamental. What is truth? In so far as science, for Peirce, is not static, truth is not an absolute idea. It is a process wherein states of satisfaction and dissatisfaction constantly change places, in the activity of unceasing inquiry. Peirce's conception of truth is a pragmatic one: 'Truth is that concordance of an abstract statement with the ideal limit towards which endless investigation would tend to bring scientific belief, which concordance the abstract statement may possess by virtue of the confession of its inaccuracy and one-sidedness, and this confession is an essential ingredient of truth' (CP 5.565). Therefore, truth is essentially fallible and dependent on infinite inquiry. There is an important parallelism between this epistemological concept and the process of signification – semiosis, or the action of signs. Semiosis was conceived by Peirce as the triadic relation of a sign that stands for its object to an interpretant, which is another sign that is further interpreted, and so on. Signs tend to multiply, not chaotically, but in a particular direction; they are goal-oriented. Truth takes part in scientific inquiry in a way similar to the tendency of signs to spread and develop: signs are interpreted as more-refined signs, in procreative chains, which occasionally may end, but are quite often infinite. In fact, the parallelism mentioned above, between Peirce's epistemology and semiosis, is no mere coincidence, for semiotics forms the basis of Peirce's thought. The mere dissemination of signs does not assure the certainty of truth, but the purposiveness or goal-directedness of inquiry, and of semiosis in general, does provide that assurance. Peirce, speaking of this tendency of inquiry to progress toward the right answers, refers to the idea of self-correction:

> Thus it is that inquiry of every type, fully carried out, has the vital power of self-correction and of growth. This is a property so deeply saturating its inmost nature that it may truly be said that there is but one thing needful for learning the truth, and that is a hearty and active desire to learn what is true. If you really want to learn the truth, you will, by

however devious a path, be surely led into the way of truth, at last. No matter how erroneous your ideas of the method may be at first, you will be forced at length to correct them so long as your activity is moved by that sincere desire. (CP 5.582)

Self-correction is a force that counterbalances the other epistemic concept fundamental to Peirce's thought: the theory of fallibilism. He writes: 'there are three things to which we can never hope to attain by reasoning, namely, absolute certainty, absolute exactitude, absolute universality' (CP 1.141). Therefore, every theory, and even every inference, that is not fallibilistic is dogmatic. In addition to the uncertainty of inductive inferences, Peirce emphasizes that the action of chance in nature (the only explanation for its overwhelming diversity) is the cause of innumerable eventualities, errors, exceptions, anomalies and the like, which challenge every dogmatic assertion. In essence, fallibilism itself was not a novelty in Western philosophy, as Peirce recognized (CP 1.152). On its importance, he wrote: 'after all there is a difference between something and nothing' (CP 1.153). This thought has been emphasized by contemporary epistemologists. Feyerabend, for instance, writes that 'no single theory ever agrees with all the known facts in its domain' (1975: 55), and he goes on to draw important epistemic conclusions from that situation, such as the fact that any theory must have counterinductive arguments (1975: 65-66). Above all, the road of inquiry must not be blocked (CP 1.135).

Yet Peirce, above all a logician, does not discount the role of reason in the search for truth. On the contrary, 'if exactitude, certitude, and universality are not to be attained by reasoning, there is certainly no other means by which they can be reached' (CP 1.142). In this way, Peirce denies the validity of intuition, direct experience, or any other kind of knowledge by mere acquaintance. Peirce fought against 'the doctrine that we can break out of the miasma of our language or system of signs and have direct intuitive knowledge of objects' (Bernstein 1964: 166). That is to say, Peirce argued against Cartesian thought (still a mainstay of the late 19th-century), which he believed to be 'the cancer of modern philosophy' (Bernstein 1964: 165). He inferred that the only path to truth is that of reason, since direct experience of things is not knowledge; it assures nothing; it is just what it is – mere appearance (CP 1.145).

Peirce's Classification of the Sciences

Peirce began working on his classification of sciences in 1866, but did not fashion a satisfactory model until 1903. For almost forty years, he made successive attempts in which, little by little (in a pedestrian manner[12]), he sketched out the most important interrelations among the sciences. Peirce's notion of science, as a living activity practiced by human beings,

---

[12] 'Pedestrianism' is how Peirce desribed his step by step, 'slow and sure' method of working out his ideas (see Brent 1993: 43).

must be the starting point for understanding his classification. In contrast to Auguste Comte, Peirce strove for a natural classification of sciences. In other words, he tried to organize the sciences according to how they are really practiced, instead of collecting ideas on 'dead' or only theoretically possible modes of inquiry. Thus, Peirce refused to accept ad hoc definitions: 'A description of a natural class must be founded upon samples of it or typical examples' (CP 1.224). As for the categorization of the sciences, abstract arrangements do not have the usefulness that a natural classification offers: 'The purpose of Peirce's classification was "to embody the chief facts of relationship between the sciences so far as they present themselves to scientific and observational study" (1334.9-10, 1905). This could only be attained with a natural classification' (Kent 1987: 85). Peirce did not seek merely to categorize the sciences according to this or that scheme, but rather to build a system of relationships. That system was to constitute a hierarchical network that would make clear where the basic principles of any science come from, and what concepts a particular science confers upon later, more specific areas of study. In this way, important epistemological issues would become clear, such as to what degree a science can answer its basic questions, how it might be improved, and so on.

In 1889, Peirce arranged the sciences according to their abstractness – the level of organization of their objects of investigation. According to Kent: 'Sciences at the top of the scale provide regulating principles for those below, while the more specialized sciences provide data and problems for those above' (1987: 93). This feature reflects a dynamic view in which sciences exchange ideas at distinct levels of abstraction. Peirce distinguished and organized his classification in terms of his universal categories: firstness, secondness and thirdness.[13] He had a double purpose in doing so: at the same time as the classification laid out the categories, those categories were themselves accounted for, which proved that, since the ideas of firstness, secondness and thirdness are elements also present in the sciences, they are even more likely to be truly universal categories. In 1897, Peirce presented the first-rank level: 'The first major division in the classification of ideas concerns qualities of feelings and sensible qualities; the second, ideas of common life and experience; and the third [...] concerns the sciences' (Kent 1987: 104). This gives the basis for the numbering system, in which all the sciences start with the number three. Indeed, science can only be Thirdness, the classification numbering being consistent with that of the universal categories.

In 1903 Peirce achieved what Kent has called 'the perennial version' of sciences classification, having reproduced the scheme in all his following papers on logic (Kent 1987: 121), an indicator that Peirce had achieved a satisfactory level. A brief description of Peirce's science classification[14] is

[13] See 2.1 for a detailed explanation of Peirce's universal categories.

[14] Further details are addressed in Peirce's writings (CP 1.180-283, L75) and by Kent (1987).

necessary here, so as to situate music in it, but only the sections relevant to understanding semiotics and music will be expanded upon. First, science divides itself into three main branches, which are distinguished by their fundamental purpose:

3. SCIENCES:
    - 3.1 Heuretic sciences
    - 3.2 Sciences of review
    - 3.3 Practical sciences

The heuretical science, or the science of discovery, inquires exclusively into new truth. Its purpose is discovery in itself. The second branch, sciences of review, concerns itself with assimilating, criticizing and turning the discoveries of the first-branch sciences into available and intelligible information. Finally, practical sciences 'seek to satisfy human desires' (Kent 1987: 131). Each of these three main branches divides into three classes: mathematics, philosophy and the special sciences, or idioscopy (see Table 3). In this way, Peirce conceived of interrelationships among the classes of sciences according to their main branch. For example, heuretic mathematics relates to mathematical review and practical mathematics; and the same is true of philosophy and the special sciences.

In the heuretical sciences, mathematics corresponds to the first class. 'Observations in this case are of the creations of the imagination (usually diagrams and most likely mental diagrams in the form of lines or an array of letters) that instance hypotheses' (Kent 1987: 132). Mathematics inquires into the validity of those hypotheses, without any concern for actual occurrences of them. Therefore, mathematics is the most independent member of the heuretical branch, lending its principles to all subsequent sciences. Peirce also saw divisions to exist in mathematics, ranging from pure deductive logic to topical geometry.

Philosophy, or cenoscopy, is the second class. 'The task of philosophy is to develop an understanding of the "*omne* of being and of non-being and of its principal parts" (339.268r, 1905)' (Kent 1987: 146). The subject matter of philosophy is commonly-perceived phenomena. Positive universal truth is sought without any special instrument but only by means of usual experience acknowledged by everyone. Philosophy divides itself into three orders: phenomenology, normative sciences and metaphysics.

Phenomenology, or phaneroscopy, 'studies the phaneron as it immediately presents itself. It provides the observational groundwork for the rest of philosophy, endeavoring to determine the universal indecomposable elements in whatever appears before the mind' (Kent 1987: 133). Peirce considered the phaneron, anything that appears to the mind, as unrestricted; that is, it could be a real thing or not. The basic concepts in Peirce's phaneroscopy are the universal categories of firstness, secondness and thirdness. The phaneron can be qualified according to how the categories appear in it.

Table 3
Peirce's Scheme for the Classification of the Sciences

3. SCIENCE	
3.1 Heuretical Sciences	
3.1.1 Mathematics	
3.1.2 Philosophy	
3.1.2.1 Phenomenology	
3.1.2.2 Normative sciences	
3.1.2.2.1 Aesthetics	
3.1.2.2.2 Ethics	
3.1.2.2.3 Logic or Semeiotic	
3.1.2.2.3.1 Speculative grammar	
3.1.2.2.3.2 Critic	
3.1.2.2.3.3 Methodeutic	
3.1.2.3 Metaphysics	
3.1.3 Special sciences	
Physics	Psychics
3.1.3.1 Nomological sciences	Nomological sciences
3.1.3.2 Classificatory sciences	Classificatory sciences
3.1.3.3 Explanatory sciences	Explanatory sciences
3.2 Sciences of Review	
3.2.1 Mathematics	
3.2.2 Philosophy	
3.2.3 Special sciences	
Physics	Psychics
3.1.3.1 Nomological sciences	Nomological sciences
3.1.3.2 Classificatory sciences	Classificatory sciences
3.1.3.3 Explanatory sciences	Explanatory sciences
3.3 Practical Sciences	
3.3.1 Mathematics	
3.3.2 Philosophy	
3.3.3 Special sciences	
Physics	Psychics
3.1.3.1 Nomological sciences	Nomological sciences
3.1.3.2 Classificatory sciences	Classificatory sciences
3.1.3.3 Explanatory sciences	Explanatory sciences

The normative sciences, or the 'study of the phenomenon insofar as we can act upon it and it upon us' (Kent 1987: 133), can be divided into three families, according to their object of study: aesthetic, ethics, and logic, or semeiotic. This classification represents a major achievement in Peirce's philosophical system, which can be mentioned here only in passing. In 1902, he wrote to William James, explaining the development and unity of his thought:

> But I seem to myself to be the sole depository at present of the completely developed system, which all hangs together and cannot receive any proper presentation in fragments. My own view in 1877 was crude. Even when I gave my Cambridge lectures I had not really got to the bottom of it or seen the unity of the whole thing. It was not until after that that I obtained the proof that logic must be founded on ethics, of

> which it is a higher development. Even then, I was for some time so stupid as not to see that ethics rests in the same manner on a foundation of esthetics. (CP 8.255)

In brief, here is Peirce's view of these three sciences: 'Esthetics is the science of ideals, or of that which is objectively admirable without any ulterior reason. [...] Ethics, or the science of right and wrong, must appeal to Esthetics for aid in determining the ***summum bonum.*** It is the theory of self-controlled, or deliberate, conduct. Logic is the theory of self-controlled, or deliberate, thought; and as such, must appeal to ethics for its principles' (CP 1.191). Kent elucidates: '*Aesthetics* inquires into the deliberate formation of habits of feeling that are consistent with the aesthetic ideal. [...] *Ethics* inquires into the theory of the formation of habits of action that are consistent with the deliberately adopted aim. [...] *Logic* studies the deliberate formation of habits of thought that are consistent with the logical end' (1987: 133-34). Thus, in addition to those three sciences being defined by their ultimate goal, Peirce also explains how they interrelate, according to the principle of hierarchical dependence: aesthetics gives its principles to ethics, which in turn provides the principles for logic. The normative sciences are also regulated by the more general ideas handed down from the higher sciences, mathematics and phenomenology .

Logic is of special importance to the present study. Hence it is very important to realize that, by 'logic', Peirce did not mean simply deductive, classical logic; rather, he enlarged substantially the very concept of this science. He wrote that, of 'All thought being performed by means of signs, logic may be regarded as the science of the general laws of signs' (CP 1.191). Thus, logic is just a synonym for semiotics, or 'semeiotic', as he preferred (CP 1.444, 4.9, 8.377). Logic, or semeiotic, 'has three branches: 1, Speculative Grammar, or the general theory of the nature and meanings of signs, whether they be icons, indices, or symbols; 2, Critic, which classifies arguments and determines the validity and degree of force of each kind; 3, Methodeutic, which studies the methods that ought to be pursued in the investigation, in the exposition, and in the application of truth. Each division depends on that which precedes it' (CP 1.191). Peirce also called the third division of logic *rhetorica speculativa* (CP 2.93). Considering himself mainly as a logician, Peirce developed this science to a very high level. What was then known as logic, Peirce called critical logic, or logic in the narrow sense (CP 2.93); i.e., 'the science of the necessary conditions of the attainment of truth' (CP 1.444). Logic, in its broad sense,

> is the science of the necessary laws of thought, or, still better (thought always taking place by means of signs), it is general ***semeiotic***,[15] treating not merely of truth, but also of the general conditions of signs being signs (which Duns Scotus calls ***grammatica speculativa***), also of the laws of the evolution of thought, which since it coincides with the study of the

[15] My emphasis.

> necessary conditions of the transmission of meaning by signs from mind to mind, and from one state of mind to another, ought, for the sake of taking advantage of an old association of terms, be called ***rhetorica speculativa.*** (CP 1.444)

The third order of philosophy is metaphysics, which, 'using the principles of logic, inquires into what is real (and not figment) as far as can be ascertained from ordinary experience' (Kent 1987: 133). Metaphysics divides itself into three families: ontology, physical metaphysics and religious metaphysics.

The third class of heuretic sciences concerns the special sciences, or idioscopy. 'Observations are of previously unknown phenomena. By means of special training, special instruments or special circumstances, they inquire into individual experiential events and infer truth that is usually only plausible but, nonetheless, worth testing. In doing so they assume the truth of propositions that are outside the scope of their own investigations' (Kent 1987: 132). Therefore, the special sciences investigate particular classes of phenomena, which are not perceived normally, but require special means of doing so, such as laboratory equipment, analytical devices or processes, fieldwork, and the like. Particularized training is implicit, since most of the special instruments or circumstances necessary for the practice of such sciences demand the skill required to handle and interpret the information that they acquire.

In 1898, Peirce asserted that 'all knowledge has two elements: one element is determined by the object; the other is a mode of thought. He thought this distinction prominent in the special sciences: physics is considered as the science of things as such, and psychics as the science of things governed by the intellect' (Kent 1987: 107). Therefore, he divided the special sciences into two parallel groups, according to the nature of the objects investigated: physical sciences and psychical sciences. Physiognosy, or physical science, studies the material nature of phenomena; this includes sciences such as physics, chemistry, biology and cosmography. Psychognosis, or psychical science, studies the mind of humans and other forms of intelligence.

Psychics must be understood broadly, as should most of Peirce's classifications. He included in this group such sciences as psychology, ethnology, and history. Santaella writes that 'all psychical science is, in a certain way, interpretation of signs, interpretation of interpretation. It is not possible to avoid this, since the objects of those sciences in themselves are processes of semiosis' (1992: 142). Thus, the principles offered by semiotics are fundamental to the understanding of psychic sciences. Moreover, there is probably some overlapping between the psychical and physical sciences. Peirce, especially in his metaphysics, suggested that some physical processes can be semiotic in nature. In 1891, he wrote: 'The one intelligible theory of the universe is that of objective idealism, that matter is effete mind, inveterate habits becoming physical laws' (CP

6.25). But this topic must be left here, because it lies far beyond the scope of this chapter.[16]

For Peirce, physical and psychical sciences do not stand in a relation of dependency. Thus, he viewed them as parallel groups, although he concluded that physical studies come before psychical studies, as much as the survival instinct precedes that of reproduction (Kent 1987: 108). Physical and psychical sciences are also related to the two universal principles of efficient causation and final causation: dynamic action and sign action (semiosis). Each one of the groups can be divided into three subgroups (see CP 1.188-189):

> *Nomological* division studies the ubiquitous phenomena of the psychical and physical universes, ascertains their general laws, and measures the quantities involved.
>
> *Classificatory* division describes and classifies the various kinds among the objects studied and endeavours to explain them by means of the general laws.
>
> *Descriptive* and *explanatory* division studies and minutely describes individual events which it subsequently seeks to explain using the findings of the nomological and classificatory sciences. (Kent 1987: 134)

Now that the sciences have been viewed in terms of their definitions, goals and dependencies, it is necessary to explain how Peirce devised their multidimensional relationships. All divisions pertaining to the branch of heuretical sciences (sciences of discovery) expand into the review and practical sciences. Inasmuch as the sciences relate vertically according to principles of dependence and exchange of data, the same sorts of interrelation obtain between each level, in breadth and depth; i.e., the heuretical, review and practical sciences interrelate simultaneously, and in several dimensions. Peirce proposed the use of diagrams illustrating these interrelations as multidimensional ladders or waves (see Kent 1987). Finally, the scheme is conceived as dynamic, in that the position of different sciences will change according to new paradigms as they appear.

The Science of Music

While working on his classification of the sciences, Peirce left some clues about how music might relate to other studies. In 1892, Peirce thought that the psychical sciences should be divided into four groups; one of them would be practical psychics. It is in this last category where Peirce put music, along with political economy, ethics,[17] poetry, games, etc. In 1895, among classificatory psychics he included ethnological psychics, to which one could properly append classical ethnomusicology as a specific study of the 'manners & customs' of different societies. In the same work,

---

[16] See Peirce's *The Architecture of Theories*, CP 6.7-34, 1992: 285-97; see also the following papers of that series.

[17] At that time, Peirce did not consider ethics to be one of the normative sciences, but rather a practical science.

descriptive psychics is mentioned as including the history of art and literature. It is not a great stretch to think of the history of music as also belonging to descriptive psychics.

Another of Peirce's classifications, again made in 1895, re-classifies the practical sciences as arts. In this case, he concluded that arts 'depend on both psychical and physical knowledge; some almost entirely psychical such as rhetoric, ethics, religion, jurisprudence; others almost entirely physical – glassblowing, horology; still others require both – painting, music, etc.' (in Kent 1987: 99). When Peirce classifies music alongside glassblowing and painting, it becomes clear that he means not only the study of music or musicology, but the practice of music as well. That is a good point to question: is music a science, or is it a practical craft? In light of his remarks on music as an art that is dependent on both physics and psychics, it seems that Peirce conceived of music-making as a special kind of practical science. In fact, music is simultaneously an art, the practice of that art, and a science, a situation which can be understood with the help of the universal categories. Music is an art – its aspect of firstness – because music concerns mainly aesthetic purpose, which is admirability in itself. Music as craftsmanship – secondness – refers to its praxis, for music actually exists only when it is performed. Music is a science – thirdness – inasmuch it concerns learning, musical knowledge and its continuous development, and the existence of a community of musicians, listeners and scholars. There are obviously several kinds of relations among these three features of music. As early as 1884, Adler related musicology to musical practice: 'Musicology originated simultaneously with the art of organizing tones' (1981: 5). However, the various forms of musical study – ethnological, historical or systematic musicology (historical or systematic, according to Adler's scheme, 1981: 14-15), the practical side of music, and so on – would be located on different levels in Peirce's classification.

The most general division obtains in heuretical studies on music. To gain new understanding of music is the goal of disciplines such as musicology, ethnomusicology and, above all, music semiotics. They therefore have the status of heuretical sciences. As sciences of review – where new information attained by the heuretic sciences is digested, criticized and organized systematically, giving feedback data to the sciences of discovery – one could list subjects such as music encyclopedias, archives, critiques of performances and compositions, book reviews, articles, textbooks for musical education, etc. The practical side of musical science appears in performance, conducting, composition, music education, fieldwork, the production of concerts and other events, and so on.

In considering the special scientific cases, Peirce noted that music depends on both physical and psychical sciences. There are, indeed, many disciplines that bear upon musical studies, such as physics (acoustics, wave forms, the acoustical properties and mechanical behavior of materials such as wood, wire, metal), the physiology of hearing and of muscular movements, neurophysiology, etc. In psychics, music is connected with neurology, psychology, sociology, anthropology, ethnology, history, etc. Musical aesthetics seems to constitute an applied field of general aesthetics, as well as being a special psychic science. Specific studies such as harmony, organology (the study of musical instruments), music history, and musical forms are combinations of physic and psychic sciences.

In Peirce's general scheme of classification, where the main areas of inquiry are arranged, simultaneously, according to a hierarchical and dynamic diagram, musical studies appear only on the level of the special sciences. Hence musical studies depend on principles established by all the higher, more general sciences, from mathematics to the normative sciences, including metaphysics. It is nothing new to relate music and mathematics. Yet because Peirce thinks of the latter in such broad terms, music's dependence on mathematics does not only concern numerical features, but also matters of finite and infinite collections, pure deduction, and so on, theories of which Western contemporary composers often make practical use.

Musical studies certainly depend on philosophy, and philosophers of all periods and cultures have had something to say about music. Nevertheless, for Peirce, philosophy concerns itself with commonly perceived phenomena. Thus, acoustic phenomena are also subject matter for philosophical studies. Yet once philosophy starts with phenomenology, the study of the *phaneron* (a phenomenon as present immediately to a consciousness), then all musical studies inherit phenomenological propositions. An examination of Peirce's classification of sciences makes it clear that Peirce's universal categories and their degenerated forms are basic tools for the study of music (see 2.1).

Although they remain inadequately studied, it is essential to understand the normative sciences, which are Peirce's second division of philosophy. The normative sciences – aesthetic, ethics and semeiotic – form the core of philosophy, because they approach phenomena in their relationship to a possible mind. By means of the normative sciences, one also arrives at the most significant group of basic, general laws of music. In the triad of normative sciences, aesthetics relates to firstness, ethics to secondness, and semiotics to thirdness. The concept of firstness is especially relevant to understanding aesthetic goals and, consequently, the goal of music. Parret (1994: 218), discussing Peirce's aesthetics...' mentions the paradox of firstness, which is simultaneously first (a quality) and last (as an ultimate ideal). The presentation and enjoyment of qualities are considered to be the aesthetic object; at the other extreme, firstness aids in defining the *summum bonum*, the highest ideal, which, for Peirce, is also an immediate feeling that is adopted for no reason other than its fineness. That is to say, it is an admirable thing or idea, the admirability of which depends on nothing other than itself. It seems that Peirce's conception of the *summum bonum* can also be applied to music. The most abstract and general value-principle of music is that it is admirable in itself; music is a phenomenon that is relished for no reason other than musical qualities, or better, admirable acoustic qualities. This notion leads straightway to ideas of pure or absolute music. Nevertheless, all other conceptions of music inherit this principle, as far as any music can also be perceived and enjoyed as pure sound qualities. Ethics receives its basic principles from aesthetics. Thus, in this respect, action must be based on admirable – hence, controlled – acts, which leads one again to the *summum bonum*. This situation applies to music in regard to correct acts, both mental and physical. The former regulates all musical studies; the latter, musical practice and performance. The principles of logic, or semiotics, come from ethics and aesthetics. In turn, logic bestows its rules on all the special sciences. Its precedence over the special sciences makes clear that semiotics is relevant to all following studies. Therefore, concerning music, one can conceive of a semiotics of musical systems, of musical forms, of music history (the deciphering and interpretation of indices), of social facts about music, etc. Semiotics exerts a strong influence on subjects like musical aesthetics, perception and composition.

It is important now to make a distinction between formal and applied semiotics. Formal, or pure, semiotics is a highly abstract and theoretical domain. It is strictly one of the heuretical sciences, as explained above. Applied, or descriptive, semiotics concerns practical fields, and pertains to issues in specific disciplines or other areas of application (Houser 1990: 208). Therefore, logic (semiotics), as a normative heuretical science, is a formal semiotics, which gives its principles and analytical tools to all applied semiotics, such as that of music. Applied semiotics, belonging to any possible field, is a special science.

As noted above, semiotics divides itself into three sub-fields: Speculative Grammar, Critic and Methodeutic (or Speculative Rhetoric). According to Houser, the scholar who studies speculative grammar deals with the intrinsic nature of signs and semiosis (sign-action). S/he examines relations among signs, the nature of the correlates taking part in semiosis, Peirce's sign trichotomies, and his ten or – broadly speaking – sixty-six classes of sign (see 2.2). The study of critic deals with signs in relation to their objects, and especially the condition of signs' references in relation to their signified objects. Consequently, critic deals with truth and the concept of truth. It encompasses the study of reasoning, or the three kinds of arguments (abduction, induction and deduction). Methodeutic studies signs in relation to their interpretants. Thus, semiosis is focused on the interpretant level, and how interpretants themselves can become signs during semiotic processes (Houser 1990: 210-11).

The main problem in establishing a Peircean semiotic theory of music concerns how to apply broad and general formal semiotic concepts to the specific subject matter, which is music. It seems to me that, between formal semiotics and music, there must be an intermediate theory of musical semiotics. Just as Peirce divided formal semiotics into three areas, musical studies can also be understood as three interrelated fields, not as broad and abstract as speculative grammar, critic and methodeutic are, but still showing a concern for the following: (1) 'the general conditions of signs being signs' (CP 1.444), that is, the intrinsic nature of semiosis, or the study of signs and their systems of inner relationship; (2) 'the theory of the general conditions of the reference of Symbols and other Signs to their professed Objects' (CP 2.93), that is, the relation of signs to their objects; and (3) 'the necessary conditions of the transmission of meaning by signs from mind to mind, and from one state of mind to another' (CP 1.444), that is, the relation of signs to their interpretants, interpreters and systems of interpretation. On the microscopic level, the same division represents the basic relations of Peirce's model of semiosis: (1) the sign in itself, (2) the sign related to its possible objects, (3) the sign related to its possible interpretants. The three relata are interdependent in the following way: **{3[2(1)]}**.

A semiotic theory of music has to investigate these three areas equally, if it is to understand musical phenomena from a broad perspective. Each field interacts with the other two, both in a relation of logical dependence and material actualization, inevitably constituting triadic unity. Thus, any narrow or overly specialized inquiry risks separating essential features of musical semiosis, which only recovers its integrity when its links to other fields are clearly pointed out. Since the scientific foundation of semiotics is Peirce's phaneroscopy (or phenomenology), it follows that previous study of musical phaneron is a necessary step towards a Peircean semiotics of music. Hence, the three relevant fields of musical inquiry are these: (first) Intrinsic Musical Semiosis, or the study of the general conditions of musical signs, i.e., their qualities and properties, their occurrences, and the frameworks that determine their actualization; (second) Musical Reference, or the study of the conditions of musical signs referring to their objects, i.e., the nature of objects in music and how the reference is accomplished; (third) Musical Interpretation, or the study of the conditions of musical semiosis in actuality, i.e., the cognition of musical signs, and the forms of efficient and final causation in music. I will not expand on this subject here, but refer the reader to section 2.3 (below).

II

A PEIRCEAN SEMIOTIC THEORY OF MUSIC, AS APPLIED TO HINDUSTANI CLASSICAL MUSIC

2.1 Music and Peirce's Phaneroscopy

In Peirce's architecture of sciences, the first division of philosophy corresponds to phaneroscopy, or phenomenology, which is the science that gives general principles to the other two parts of philosophy: the normative sciences, viz. aesthetics, ethics, semiotics; and metaphysics. In 1905, Peirce wrote that 'Phaneroscopy is the description of the ***phaneron***, and by the ***phaneron*** I mean the collective total of all that is in any way or in any sense present to the mind, quite regardless of whether it corresponds to any real thing or not' (CP 1.284). This science has no concern with truth (CP 2.120), for it deals with phenomena as appearance. Moreover, when it is in the mind that phenomena appear, it should be noted that, for Peirce, mind is not limited to human thought; for instance, the cosmos and its evolution is an instance of mind (see CP 6.33, 6.101 [g]). The study of phaneroscopy is essential for the comprehension of semiotics, for the latter is based completely on the principles laid by the former. Therefore, it is valid to start the study of acoustical or musical phenomena by means of phaneroscopy, taking the precedence of this science as a necessary ground on which to build a semiotic theory of music.

The task of phaneroscopy is to determine the universal, undiluted elements of whatever appears to the mind (Kent 1987: 133). Those are the Universal Categories, a subject that several Western philosophers have investigated (Aristotle, Kant, Hegel). Peirce writes, 'The business of phenomenology is to draw up a catalogue of categories and prove its sufficiency and freedom from redundancies, to make out the characteristics of each category, and to show the relations of each to the others' (CP 5.43). The researcher must be prepared for such an enterprise:

> The faculties which we must endeavor to gather for this work are three. The first and foremost is that rare faculty, the faculty of seeing what stares one in the face, just as it presents itself, unreplaced by any interpretation, unsophisticated by any allowance for this or for that supposed modifying circumstance. This is the faculty of the artist who sees for example the apparent colors of nature as they appear. . . . The second faculty we must strive to arm ourselves with is a resolute discrimination which fastens itself like a bulldog upon the particular feature that we are studying, follows it wherever it may lurk, and detects it beneath all its disguises. The third faculty we shall need is the generalizing power of the mathematician who produces the abstract formula that comprehends the very essence of the feature under

> examination purified from all admixture of extraneous and irrelevant accompaniments. (CP 5.42)

Thus, for the inquirer of phaneroscopy, there is no need of special instruments to mediate the investigation, for the object of study is phenomena as such.[1] The necessary powers are those of seeing, attention and generalization. In this way, turning to experience rather than the work of previous philosophers (see MS L75, draft A, 21-29), Peirce demonstrated, in his work of 1867, *On a New List of Categories* (CP 1.545-59, W 2.49-59, 1992:1-10), that there are no more than three universal categories, termed in that article: quality, relation, and representation. A similar conclusion was reached in his study on the logic of relatives (CP 3.63). In purely logical terms, the components of phenomena can be thought as valency: 'If, then, there be any formal division of elements of the phaneron, there must be a division according to valency; and we may expect medads, monads, dyads, triads, tetrads, etc.' (CP 1.292). Peirce realizes that some of these are insignificant. For instance, a medad (from μηδέν, nothing) 'would be a flash of mental "heat-lightning", absolutely instantaneous, thunderless, unremembered, and altogether without effect' (ibid.). On the other hand, he inferred that 'A thorough study of the logic of relatives confirms the conclusions which I had reached before going far in that study. It shows that logical terms are either monads, dyads, or polyads, and that these last do not introduce any radically different elements from those that are found in triads. I therefore divide all objects into monads, dyads, and triads' (CP 1.293). These are the basis of his universal categories, which he also called the 'cenopythagorean categories', for they relate the variety of phenomena that can appear to any mind to the ordinal numerals: first, second, and third (CP 2.87).

It was not without careful and diligent efforts to refute his own categories[2] that Peirce eventually accepted their validity. The ubiquitous elements in the universe, therefore, are these:

> Firstness is the mode of being of that which is such as it is, positively and without reference to anything else.
>
> Secondness is the mode of being of that which is such as it is, with respect to a second but regardless of any third.
>
> Thirdness is the mode of being of that which is such as it is, in bringing a second and third into relation to each other. (CP 8.328)

Peirce developed these ideas in a very broad sense, to the point of building a whole philosophical architecture on the categories, their 'deep and massive' foundations, the first attempt at which was the project of a

---

[1] An inquiry with the use of instruments is the subject of the special sciences; see Peirce's classification of sciences in 1.3.

[2] A work which served only to confirm their universality; see MS L75, draft A, 21-29; and CP 8.328.

book he never completed: *A Guess at the Riddle* (in Peirce 1992:245-279)[3]. In this work, Peirce describes the categories as 'thin skeletons of thought' (1992: 247, CP 1.355). In fact, firstness, secondness, and thirdness (or simply, first, second and third), whenever they appear in the writings of Peirce, either literally or merely implied, have a deep conceptual meaning: 'A thing considered in itself is a unit. A thing considered as a correlate or dependent, or as an effect, is second to something else. A thing which in anyway brings one thing into relation with another is a third or medium between the two' (1992: 280). In simple terms, the categories can be explained as follows: 'First is the beginning, that which is fresh, original, spontaneous, free. Second is that which is determined, terminated, ended, correlative, object, necessitated, reacting. Third is the medium, becoming, developing, bringing about' (ibid.). Indeed, either as deep foundations or as skeletons of thought, Peirce, by 1902, had refined his categories to the point of conceiving them as a heuretic science, a phaneroscopy or a phenomenology, which gives general principles to all sciences situated in his classification (see Table 3, in 1.3). The categories define the order of sciences; for instance, the normative sciences, the second branch of philosophy, is divided into: (1) aesthetics, (2) ethics, and (3) semiotics. The categories are the very logic that supports Peircean semiotics.

The categories perfuse everything, and therefore, they are elements of an infinitude of phenomena, among them, acoustic phenomena. It is not necessary to argue that those are fundamental phenomena in music, but there are phenomena of a non-acoustic nature in music, which are relevant for any study of musical semiosis. Acoustic phenomena, in general, are in nature. Actually, prior to their acoustic character, they are undulatory phenomena, determined by physical parameters such as intensity, frequency, and duration. Between the lengthy astronomical cycles and the highest cosmic frequencies, only a relatively low range of oscillations can be considered acoustic. On the other hand, the perception of sound phenomena is conditioned by the limits of audibility, which in the human species were probably established by the contingencies of survival (which also depends on the other senses). It was necessary to have enough sensitivity to perceive sounds implying imminent danger, as well as those which indicate possible sources of food, for instance, in the case of a hunt. On the other hand, those very limits preserve the hearing sense of continuous and irrelevant sounds, such as normal atmospheric noises, which are largely beyond the limits of human audibility.

Even circumscribed within such limits, sounds can manifest themselves in an infinite variety. Pierre Schaeffer (1952, 1988), a pioneer in electro-acoustic music, studied the characteristics of sound in a system of three axes, formed by the parameters of frequency, intensity, and duration, which can be projected spatially (Figure 6). Frequency or pitch can be

[3] Scattered through the *Collected Papers*: CP 1.354, 1.1-2, 1.355-68, 1.373-75, 1.379-383, 1.385-416.

measured either in octaves or in oscillations per seconds (hertz); intensity in decibels; and time in seconds. According to Schaeffer, the plane resulting from the pitch and intensity axis is the harmonic or timbral plane. In this plane, the criteria are the thickness of a sound (ranging from a single fundamental frequency with a clear pitch to a complexity of frequencies which results in noise), the richness and the color a sound (depending on its structure of partials). The plane formed by the axis of intensity and time is the dynamic plane; it determines the criteria of attack, sustain, behavior, and decay — all of which form what is called the 'envelope' of a sound. Finally, between the axis of pitch and duration there is the melodic plane, or the plane of tessituras, which has a single defining criterion, that of melodic direction.

Figure 6

Schaeffer's Classification of Sound Characters

(adapted from Schaeffer 1952: fig.36, facing page 225)

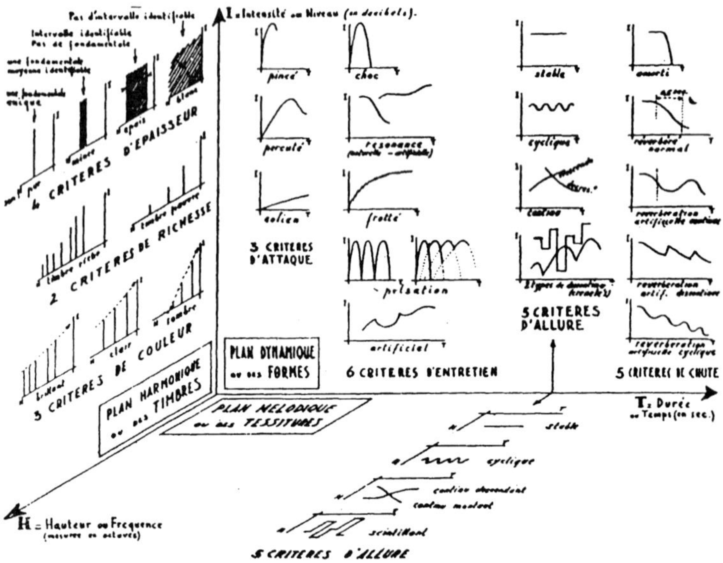

As simple and out-of-date as this classification of musical sounds is, it constitutes an interesting diagram by which to think the variety of possible sounds. In the space formed by the three planes, it is easy to imagine the manifold possibilities in which acoustical phenomena can be present to a mind. Besides all kinds of natural sounds, human beings have used their own body and created instruments to produce new sounds. But only the development of electronic synthesizers made it feasible for all the potentiality of sound characters to be controlled so as to generate absolutely any sound. In this universe of acoustical possibilities, and aside from all the rationalization employed up to here to describe it, as well as any cause or reason for the existence of a particular sound, every sound is a quality in itself, a sheer possibility. And this brings the idea of firstness:

> The idea of First is predominant in the ideas of freshness, life, freedom. . . . Freedom can only manifest itself in unlimited and uncontrolled variety and multiplicity; and thus the first becomes predominant in the ideas of measureless variety and multiplicity. . . . In the idea of being, Firstness is predominant, not necessarily on account of the abstractness of that idea, but on account of its self-containedness. It is not in being separated from qualities that Firstness is most predominant, but in being something peculiar and idiosyncratic. The first is predominant in feeling, as distinct from objective perception, will, and thought. (CP 1.302)

As seen above, sounds can be explained by a number of acoustical laws, and the perception of sounds is limited by some natural constraints. However, the multiplicity and uncontrolled variety of sounds, as an aspect of firstness, does not relate to any law or biological constraint. Acoustic firstness consists in taking a sound as what it is without reference to anything else. This is not an abstract statement, for it can be experienced by anyone with or without appreciative interest in sounds in general. The fact is that, in the jungle or in the wilderness of a metropolis, a great diversity of sounds present themselves, whether or not a mind is there to perceive them. The reason for this diversity is the idiosyncratic character of any sound. Peirce writes: 'the world is full of this element of irresponsible, free Originality. Why should the middle part of the spectrum look green rather than violet? There is no conceivable reason for it nor compulsion in it' (CP 2.85). In terms of possibilities, any combination of frequency, intensity, and duration is a particular acoustic quality; and in its qualitative nature, its firstness, a sound is what it is despite of any cause that produces it or any acoustic law that could explain it. Being present in a consciousness, a sound, as such, is no more than the consciousness of its quality as immediately present:

> The sense-quality is a feeling. Even if you say it is a ***slumbering*** feeling, that does not make it less intense; perhaps the reverse. For it is the absence of ***reaction*** – of feeling ***another*** – that constitutes slumber, not the absence of the immediate feeling that is all that it is in its immediacy. Imagine a magenta color. Now imagine that all the rest of your consciousness – memory, thought, everything except this feeling of magenta – is utterly wiped out, and with that is erased all possibility of comparing the magenta with anything else or of estimating it as more or less bright. That is what you must think the pure sense-quality to be. Such a definite potentiality can emerge from the indefinite potentiality only by its own vital Firstness and spontaneity. Here is this magenta color. What originally made such a quality of feeling possible? Evidently nothing but itself. It is a First. (CP 6.198)

A sound quality is a first, and the quality of feeling of a sound is a monadic state of mind; anything other than its acoustic quality is disregarded. Thus, concerning the universe of musical phenomena, listening to what is presented to the mind merely as it is, is listening to sounds as firsts. In the West, John Cage is the composer who developed a whole philosophy of music on the idea of letting sounds be what they are, without any purpose and without any distinction between the musician's or listener's ego and the sounds. Cage said: 'What I try to approach is the sound in itself, as it is' (Cage & Charles 1981: 78). As a composer, he thought that 'sounds should be honored rather than enslaved' (in Kostelanetz 1988: 232). However, in his approach to sounds as they are, Cage naturally found that sounds which *are not music* are better than sounds which *are music* (ibid. 227). He was, of course, referring to the traditional distinction between musical sound and noise, and his opting for the later. A conception like this is usually not considered musical in most of the traditional cultures in the world (Cage's *4'33"* is 'anti-music' for Ritwik Sanyal, 1987: 39-40), but its mode of musical appreciation has profound implications in the state of affairs in which world music finds itself nowadays; for it would be much more difficult for the common listener to enjoy another culture's music if s/he could not listen to it at least as firstness, as sound qualities to be appreciated in themselves.

As soon as an acoustic quality is recognized as embodied in place and time, and or related to some object of existence, its monadic character is put in relation to other qualities, and the idea of secondness comes forth. In fact, a sound does not exist by itself, but it would not exist at all if deprived of qualities (see CP 1.527). Materialized sound is sound produced, and as such it is part of a universe of action and reaction, an existing entity manifesting dyadically in the world. If the consciousness of a quality, in its firstness, is disturbed by another quality that appears and conflicts in that mind with its former monadic state, what results is a dual state that Peirce called secondness. 'The phenomenon of surprise in itself is highly instructive in reference to this category because of the emphasis it puts upon a mode of consciousness which can be detected in all perception, namely, a double consciousness at once of an ego and a non-ego, directly acting upon each other' (CP 5.52). As soon as the consciousness of ego (the former quality) and non-ego (the invading quality) arises, the experience itself is divided into two moments, because something happened. Thus, if firstness brings the idea of the immediate present, secondness brings that of the past. The category of secondness, therefore, encompasses the ideas of binarity, action and reaction, existence, experience, past, struggle, brute force, etc. (see CP 1.325). Peirce wrote to William James on June 8, 1903:

> The practical exigencies of life render Secondness the most prominent of the three [categories]. This is not a conception, nor is it a peculiar quality. It is an experience. It comes out most fully in the shock of reaction between ego and non-ego. It is there the double consciousness of effort and resistance. That is something which cannot properly be conceived. For to conceive it is to generalize it; and to generalize it is to miss altogether the ***here***ness and ***now***ness which is its essence. (CP 8.266)

Secondness, in its purity, is a matter of *hic et nunc*, as Peirce often writes. Examples of secondness among acoustic phenomena are easily found and belong to the experience of all listeners, for sounds are constantly invading the ears. Human hearing is designed in such a way that it cannot be shut off, and all kinds of sounds *insist* on appearing to the listener. This insistence is another element of secondness, because sounds are in the world independently of our will. They have concrete existence.

In view of the ideas involved in the concept of secondness, some interesting considerations can be made in relation to functional music. Functionality was certainly an important step on the long journey that was probably taken by the human beings, a journey which led them from the field of mere acoustic possibilities to that of a musical art. Produced by the voice, by other parts of the body, or by the very tools used for work, sound, unified by rhythm, harmonically shapes the labor. At the same time as sound coordinates the work, the activity in itself determines the acoustic event. A lullaby has its particular qualities, which are irreconcilable with those of a war or hunting call, or those of a vigorous work song related to heavy physical work, or the repetitive and plaintive singing that typically accompanies the work of Indian village women toiling at the millstones. In this sense, action and reaction is a central process in functional music, and secondness is the category that manifests in this circumstance. All true functional music is indelibly marked as such by secondness. This category could even be thought as the preponderant element in this kind of music, but to the extent that every work song has a purpose, which implies a striving to reach certain goals (even if that goal is merely to distract the mind during dull work), those elements of secondness become part of a whole that is directed by thirdness.

The acoustic phaneron enters into thirdness whenever its features of quality and existence are related to a third element constituting a genuine triad. For instance, if the tranquillity of a grove is broken by a terrible roar, then consciousness changes from firstness to secondness. But if the roar produces in that consciousness the recognition of danger, which is based on anterior experience that relates the sound of a roar with the idea of a predator, and which urges one to action in accordance with a previously learned habit (escaping or fighting), then thirdness is actually present. In this case, a genuine triadic relation is established. Peirce gives another example: 'I tell my dog to go upstairs and fetch me my book, which he does. Here is a fact about three things, myself, the dog, and the book, which is no mere sum of facts relating to pairs, nor even a pairing of such pairs.' Therefore, 'Just as a real pairedness consists in a fact being true of A which would be nonsense if B were not there, so we now meet with a Rational Threeness which consists in A and B being really paired by virtue of a third object, C' (CP 2.86).

Thirdness is not limited to the idea of purpose, though. Peirce pointed out that 'Some of the ideas of prominent Thirdness which, owing to their great importance in philosophy and in science, require attentive study are generality, infinity, continuity, diffusion, growth, and intelligence' (1.340). To the degree that firstness is related to the present, and secondness to the past, thirdness relates to the future (see CP 1.26, 2.86, 8.330). In the example above, the roar interpreted as a sign of danger implies some definite attitude toward the future, or at least the prevision of what that future could be in the face of that circumstance. Moreover, thirdness implies habit or law:

> We have here a first, a second, and a third. The first is a positive qualitative possibility, in itself nothing more. The second is an existent thing without any mode of being less than existence, but determined by that first. A third has a mode of being which consists in the Secondnesses that it determines, the mode of being of a law, or concept. Do not confound this with the ideal being of a quality in itself. A quality is something capable of being completely embodied. A law never can be embodied in its character as a law except by determining a habit. A quality is how something may or might have been. A law is how an endless future must continue to be. (CP 1.536)

Further, concerning the aspects of the idea of law among the categories, Peirce is keen in making distinctions such as this: 'Law as an active force is second, but order and legislation are third' (CP 1.337). The manifestation of sound phenomena does not *result* from the action of an acoustic law, because law, as an intelligible principle, consists in more than mere secondness (see CP 8.330). However, those features of acoustic phenomena that will persistently appear, such as the velocity of sound in the atmosphere being approximately 330 m/s., or the ratio of partials in a string being 1:2:3:4:5 etc., irrespective of the particular quality or causal existence of a sound – all these are instances of thirdness. Beyond the laws of physics, and in many cases, as a reflection of those laws, thirdness characterizes all systems and musical traditions, as long as the acoustic elements are controlled and submitted to rules of organization, or 'enslaved' by those rules, as Cage suggested.

Finally, if a sound is intelligible to a consciousness because it has a purpose or some kind of signification, this implies one of the most consequential instances of thirdness, that of meaning, or representation. 'In its genuine form, Thirdness is the triadic relation existing between a sign, its object, and the interpreting thought, itself a sign, considered as constituting the mode of being of a sign. A sign mediates between the ***interpretant*** sign and its object' (CP 8.332). An acoustic phenomenon is a sign if it stands for something to a third element, such as an action or a thought. In this sense, a sound, besides its particular quality, or dynamical existence, represents some sort of signification for a mind. Musical signs represent a diversity of objects and generate different interpretations according to the culture in which they are dealt with. In fact, a culture can be considered a sort of collective mind, a web of semiotic systems, and the ways in which music is perceived, practiced, and conceptualized are all instances of thirdness, which connect triadically the sounds, the objects they stand for, and this collective mind. Defining and conceptualizing the nature, mode of action, and meaning of each of those three elements is, of course, the subject matter of musical semiotics, as applied to a particular culture.

Figure 7
The Logic of the Categories

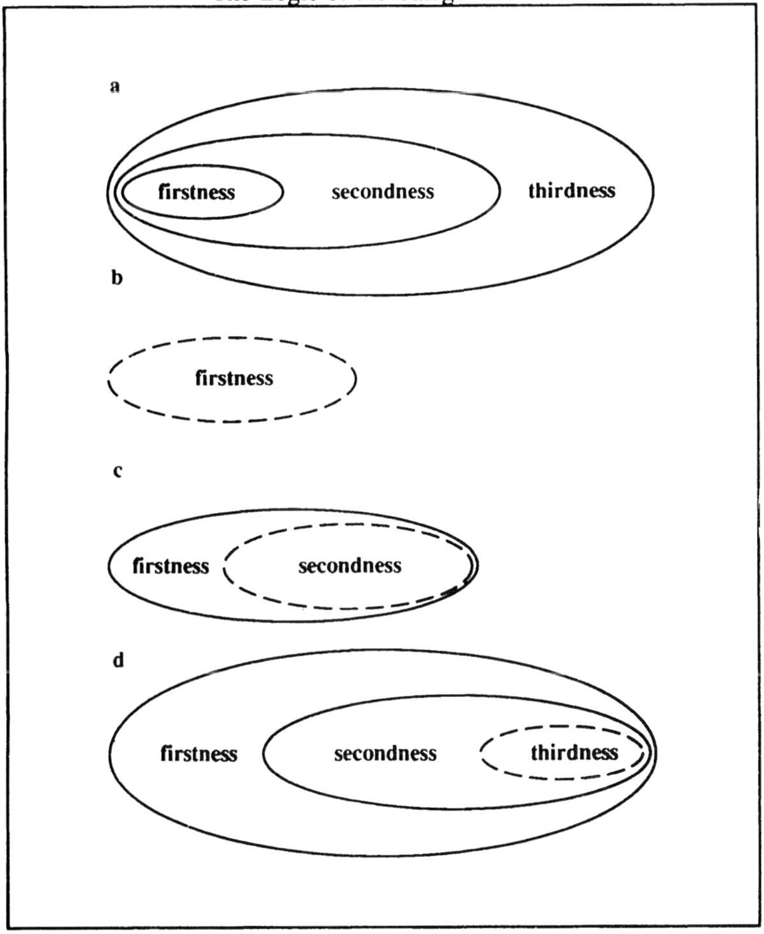

Before entering into the study of musical semiotics proper, it is important to bear in mind that the universal categories are not isolated spheres. It should be clear that only a monad can be absolutely independent, and so it is firstness. Secondness, however, being a dyad, cannot exist without firstness, but it precludes thirdness. Thus every secondness includes firstnesses as a part of it. Thirdness, as a triad, encompasses and depends on both secondness and firstness. 'The category of first can be prescinded from second and third, and second can be prescinded from third. But second cannot be prescinded from first, nor third from second' (CP 1.353). The diagrams in Figure 7 represent the interdependency of the categories. In Figure 7a, firstness, secondness, and thirdness are delineated in terms of necessity. In Figure 7b, firstness is presented as potentiality, represented by the oval with a broken cut, according to the convention for modalities in Peirce's existential graphs (see CP 4.514-17, 2.382, 2.323; Roberts 1973: 80-86). In 7c, secondness is a potentiality; and in 7d it is a thirdness.

The categories can also be present, in a particular instance of phenomena, in different degrees and measures. Peirce developed his phaneroscopy to the point of identifying the degenerated categories, which are one in relation to secondness and two in relation to thirdness, besides the three genuine forms (see CP 1.521-539; 5.66-72). Basically, the firstness of a secondness is a degenerated second; and the firstness of a thirdness, and the secondness of a thirdness, are the two degenerated thirds.

Being universal, the categories are found in a variety of forms and points of view in relation to acoustic or musical phenomena. Firstness, secondness, and thirdness can organize multiple systems of musical classification, but a study of this kind would necessarily imply other sciences, such as aesthetics, ethics, and semiotics. Even when not intended to make explicitly a phaneroscopic classification, one can recognize the elements of firstness, secondness, and thirdness in the work of many authors, when they express their thoughts in a *comprehensive* way (in both senses of comprehension, as thoroughness and inclusiveness). Such is, for instance, the case of Pierre Boulez, when he defines music as 'at the same time an art, a science, and a craft' (1986: 32). Indeed, music, as a *first*, is an art, because it is concerned with the aesthetic ideal, that of being admirable in itself. Then, music, as a *second*, is a craft, in the very sense of its praxis, because music only exists in actuality when it is performed. Finally, music, as a *third*, is a science, for it implies learning and development, both in aid of understanding music better, and of making and composing better music. In fact, 'a category is an element of phenomena of the first rank of generality' (CP 5.53), and thus they not only manifest in all levels of semiotic analysis, but they are the underlying structure, the 'thin skeletons of thought' which support the study of signification.

2.2 The Concept of Musical Sign and Semiosis

From the phenomenological categories of Peirce one can infer that every musical *phaneron* can present itself as mere acoustical qualities (firstness), as particular existents (secondness), or as habits, laws, or signs (thirdness). The very idea of semiosis, the triadic nature of the action of a sign, is a genuine triadic process, in which three relata take part. Peirce clearly distinguishes semiosis from dyadic relations:

> It is important to understand what I mean by ***semiosis***. All dynamical action, or action of brute force, physical or psychical, either takes place between two subjects [whether they react equally upon each other, or one is agent and the other patient, entirely or partially] or at any rate is a resultant of such actions between pairs. But by 'semiosis' I mean, on the contrary, an action, or influence, which is, or involves, a coöperation of ***three*** subjects, such as a sign, its object, and its interpretant, this tri-relative influence not being in any way resolvable into actions between pairs. Σημειωσισ in Greek of the Roman period, as early as Cicero's time, if I remember rightly, meant the action of almost any kind of sign; and my definition confers on anything that so acts the title of a 'sign'. (CP 5.484)

Semiosis, the cooperation of three elements (or relata), being defined by Peirce as action (see also CP 5.473), implies necessarily a dynamical model. 'A sign stands for something to the idea which it produces, or modifies' (CP 1.339); or, 'I define a Sign as anything which on the one hand is so determined by an Object and on the other hand so determines an idea in a person's mind, that this latter determination, which I term the Interpretant of the sign, is thereby mediately determined by that Object' (CP 8.343). All these definitions (and many others that Peirce presented in his writings), although differing in minor details, or representing several angles from which to approach the idea of semiosis, emphasize *action*, as the essential character of semiosis. Peirce, never repeating himself, presents his conception of sign and semiosis at various levels of abstraction (see Santaella 1995: 21-22, 83-85). The idea of sign, on one hand, can be described abstractly by this formula: the sign, or representamen, is a first that is determined by a second, its object, to a third, its interpretant. On the other hand, it can center on the idea of a person as a concrete recipient of an interpretant. The following quote seems to be an intermediate explanation, which is adequate for musical studies:

> a sign endeavours to represent, in part at least, an Object, which is therefore in a sense the cause, or determinant, of the sign even if the sign represents its object falsely. But to say that it represents its Object implies that it affects a mind, and so affects it as, in some respect, to determine in that mind something that is mediately due to the Object. That determination of which the immediate cause, or determinant, is the Sign, and of which the mediate cause is the Object may be termed the ***Interpretant***. (CP 6.347)

All three terms can take part in semiosis in the most varied ways possible. They can be a quality, an existing thing or person, or a sign; they can be something false or a sheer fantasy. Even when real things or persons are part of a semiosis triad, what is usually dealt with is their semiotic forms, that is, signs of those things and persons. The most common semiotic situation is that of all relata being signs. The triadic structure of semiosis can be thought of as a signification unit, but all three relata can, individually, be multiple or compound entities as well. In that case, the object of a sign, for instance, can be composed of several elements assembled into one complex object (CP 2.230). This is also true of the sign and the interpretant. Thus, a musician is a sign, and the community s/he belongs to can also be viewed as a sign, as well as her/his culture. Each case, although constituted by multiple elements, can be conceived as a single sign. To do so can be advantageous in some cases, but in other situations the sign might be better understood in terms of its component parts.

The idea of semiosis does not relate only to the signs produced and interpreted by human beings, but extends to life and mankind itself. Peirce goes even further, identifying the individual with her/his systems of signification (language):

> the fact that every thought is a sign, taken in conjunction with the fact that life is a train of thought, proves that man is a sign; so, that every thought is an external sign, proves that man is an external sign. That is to say, the man and the external sign are identical, in the same sense in which the words homo and man are identical. Thus my language is the sum total of myself; for the man is the thought. (CP 5.314)

First, it is important to make clear that Peirce is not reducing semiosis to the verbal mode, for the language that makes up man might well be the most abstract mathematical reasoning, or the melodic phrases extemporized by an Indian musician. Thus, 'man is thought' need not necessarily be restricted to linguistic thought. A person's thought is obviously clear in the significations s/he perceives, reacts to, and creates. And this includes all musics. But Peirce implied much more than that. In fact, Peirce extended semiosis beyond culture: 'the entire universe – not merely the universe of existents, but all that wider universe, embracing the universe of existents as a part, the universe which we are all accustomed to refer to as "the truth" – that all this universe is perfused with signs, if it is not composed exclusively of signs' (CP 5.448). This last statement, however, must again be correctly understood, for though everything can be a sign, everything is not only a sign. Max Fisch, writing on the generality of Peirce's theory of signs, states: 'whatever else anything may be, it is also a sign' (1986: 357). Peirce[4] does not deny the material existence of things; this is clear in his conception of firstness and secondness, which are prerequisites of thirdness. Ransdell writes that 'no sign is ever nothing but a sign since, in Peirce's view, it could not stand in the triadic representation relation if it did not also stand in a dyadic relationship, which in turn presupposes that it bears a monadic property' (1986: 683). In fact, in regard to Peirce's semiotics, both strict materialism and idealism are incomplete views of how things (or matter) and thought (or signs) relate to each other.

The triadic nature of semiosis, which is essentially dynamic, could be understood as a chain or chains of signs, since semiosis is a continuous process of interpretation. The logical distinctions between sign, object and interpretant do not negate the idea of semiosis as a process. Signification is not merely the single instance of an interpretant of the triadic relation, as one might be led to believe by from the short descriptions above. The instance of a single interpretant, a link in the chain, is further interpreted as another sign, and so on. Furthermore, the idea of semiosis as a chain of sign interpretations is also limited, because it is too linear. A better image of semiosis is that of a web, as many semioticians say.

It seems that Śāriṅgadeva, a celebrated Indian music scholar of the 13th century, was conscious of the sign-web that spreads everywhere when he wrote on *nāda* (sound): 'Nāda manifests the letters (of the alphabet), letters constitute the word, and words make a sentence; so, the entire business of life is carried on, through language; and therefore, the whole phenomenon (i.e., the world) is based on nāda' (SR 1.2.2). Nāda, is the object of the letters, their signs; and letters, (or more precisely syllables in the case of Sanskrit), in a sense, are also objects of words,[5] and so forth. Although in the semiotic chain in the quote above Śāriṅgadeva emphasizes verbal language, that is not the exclusive interpretation, for the concern of Indian scholars with nāda, the pervasive sound, is broader than its associations with systems of speech, for nāda has deep connections with Indian cosmogony and cosmology. Notice that, in the end, it is on nāda that the chain closes, the cycle indicating the supremacy of sound itself, rather than language. I am not denying that nāda is important in relation to verbal language. Any brief consideration of Vedic culture will show how speech (*vāc*) and the power of words (*brahman*), as understood in the *Ṛgveda*, are important in this respect. Yet, I want to emphasize the idea of nāda as a semiotic entity, for it promotes meaning, not only in terms of verbal language and music, but also as the fundamental element in the universe. Moreover, music is an excellent semiotic system to

---

[4] Who graduated as a chemist and worked as a physist most of his professional life (see Brent 1993).

[5] They are the immediate object of a word, as I will explain later.

represent and signify the pervasive nature of nāda in the cosmos (see 2.3.2).

Continuity and growth are other essential features of semiosis. In fact, if semiosis can be considered infinite from the interpretant point of view, it is equally so from the object side. This is specially true in the case of genuine representamens, signs whose character is that of law or habit. Both the object and interpretant of a genuine sign are generalities, which implies that they are above all signs themselves. Thus, on one hand, the genuine sign is infinitely distant from its first object, and on the other, infinitely distant from its last interpretant. Semiosis, therefore, is not merely the figure of a triangle connecting the three relata, which is a misleading diagram, for a triangle is a closed system. Semiosis is the continuity of the action of signs, an interpretation generating another one, and this should not be conceptualized as a linear process, but rather as a network of relationships, ever expanding and in constant mutation. This expansion is goal-oriented, for the interpretant of a sign is a better developed sign (see CP 2.228, 5.594). Peirce addressed the issue of truth in this semiotic context, as a transitory conception of something, which tends to improve constantly, the passage from a state of unsatisfactory understanding of something to that of a satisfactory one (see CP 5.358-87, 5.555 ff., 6.485). The question of Truth, however, is far beyond the limits of this chapter, and it is time now to return to musical matters.

Anything, acoustical or not, if related in some way to any kind of musical semiosis, can be a musical sign. The first rank of musical signs is acoustical phenomena, of course, but there are other possibilities such as scores, recordings, musical instruments, musical cultures, and so on. The present study concerns mainly this first class, acoustical phenomena, though not in total isolation from the others. The nature of musical signs, as acoustic phenomena, is temporal. It follows that, in any consideration of musical signs, the time dimension is implicit. There are no *static* musical signs. Besides this concrete sense, the dynamic character of music, from the semiotic point of view, is evident when one realizes that a musical sign can bear a wide diversity of objects and interpretants. In this sense, music is a very flexible sign system.

There are many different kinds of representation, and their classification depends on the structure of the sign and the nature of its action. In 1903 Peirce conceived the classification of signs as three trichotomies, based on the relations between the three semiosis relata: the sign in itself; the sign related to its object; and the sign related to its interpretant.

> Signs are divisible by three trichotomies; first, according as the sign in itself is a mere quality, is an actual existent, or is a general law; secondly, according as the relation of the sign to its object consists in the sign's having some character in itself, or in some existential relation to that object, or in its relation to an interpretant; thirdly, according as its Interpretant represents it as a sign of possibility or as a sign of fact or a sign of reason. (CP 2.243)

Thus, each trichotomy encompasses three kinds of sign (CP 2.244-252), which are submitted to the logical architecture of firstness, secondness, and thirdness (see Table 4).

Table 4
Peirce's Basic Trichotomies

	Firstness	**Secondness**	**Thirdness**
The Sign in Itself (firstness)	Qualisign	Sinsign	Legisign
The Sign Related to its Object (Secondness)	Icon	Index	Symbol
The Sign Related to its Interpretant (Thirdness)	Rheme	Dicent	Argument

Some simple Indian musical examples can be used to explain the three basic trichotomies. Concerning the sign related to itself: **Qualisign**, 'a quality which is a Sign' (CP 2.244), could be, say, the peculiar timbre of a *tambūrā*.[6] **Sinsign** is 'an actual existent thing or event which is a sign,' which can only exist by means of its qualities, so 'it involves a qualisign, or rather, several qualisigns' (CP 2.245); e.g., a live performance of Tānsen's rāga myiāṁ kī toḍī. **Legisign** is 'a law that is a Sign'. Peirce says that 'every conventional sign is a legisign [but not conversely];' besides, a 'legisign signifies through an instance of its application, which may be termed a Replica of it' (CP 2.246). Thus, a musical legisign is any structure as a law or convention; e.g., the *kāyadā*, a *tablā*[7] solo form. Concerning the sign related to its object: An **icon** is 'a sign which refers to the Object that it denotes merely by virtue of characteristics of its own, and which it possesses, just the same, whether any such Object actually exists or not' (CP 2.247). Thus an icon represents its object by the fact that the sign has qualitative or formal likeness to the object, e.g., the heavy *pakhāvaj*[8] drum strokes in a composition, representing the steps of Gaṇeśa, the elephant-headed god. **Index** is 'a sign which refers to the Object that it denotes by virtue of being really affected by that Object' (CP 2.248). An index represents its object by means of dynamic relations with it; e.g., a *nagasvaram*[9] solo, as a sign of South Indian music. The **symbol** is 'a sign which refers to the Object that it denotes by virtue of a law, usually an association of general ideas, which operates to cause the Symbol to be interpreted as referring to that Object' (CP 2.249). Thus, being the symbol a general type or law, the symbol is necessarily a

6 A long-necked, fretless, drone lute.
7 A pair of Hindustani drums.
8 A double-faced Hindustani barrel drum.
9 A South Indian double-reed aerophone.

legisign acting through a replica; e.g., a national anthem, such as Rabindranath Tagore's song *Janaganamana;* or a certain *śahnāī*[10] melody, in rāga sohanī, played at weddings in the Indian state of Maharashtra (see RN 4.148). Concerning the relations of sign to interpretant: **Rheme** is 'a Sign which, for its Interpretant, is a Sign of qualitative Possibility, that is, is understood as representing such and such a kind of possible Object' (CP 2.250); e.g., an accompanist drummer, trying to figure out what tāla should be played from the very first beats, when the soloist starts singing or playing the metered section in a performance. A **dicent** is 'a Sign, which, for its Interpretant, is a Sign of actual existence' (CP 2.251), that is, a factual sign to its interpretant; e.g., recognition of a certain composition at a concert. Finally, an **argument** is 'a Sign which is understood to represent its Object in its character as Sign' (CP 2.252); this could be the thoughts of a music connoisseur who is following the development of a rāga performed by a great musician.

Upon the basic trichotomies follows the logical combination of these nine kinds of sign, establishing ten sign classes: (1) qualisign , e.g., 'a feeling of "red" ' (CP 2.254); (2) iconic sinsign, e.g., 'an individual diagram' (CP 2.255); (3) rhematic indexical sinsign, e.g., 'a spontaneous cry' (CP 2.256); (4) dicent sinsign, e.g., 'a weathercock' (CP 2.257); (5) iconic legisign, e.g., 'a diagram, apart from its factual individuality' (CP 2.258); 6. rhematic indexical legisign, e.g., 'a demonstrative pronoun' (CP 2.259); (7) dicent indexical legisign, e.g., 'a street cry' (CP 2.260); (8) rhematic symbol or symbolic rheme, e.g., 'a common noun' (CP 2.261); (9) dicent symbol, or an ordinary proposition (CP 2.262); (10) argument (CP 2.263). The logical structure of the classes of signs is displayed in Table 5 (see also CP 2.264, 8.341; and Ransdell 1986: 685-91). There should be no difficulty in finding musical examples for the ten classes of signs. Yet this is not necessary here, and as I emphasized in 1.2, musical semiotics is not merely a matter of sign classification, but rather the in-depth study of musical semiosis. Classification, however important, is just one part of such an investigation.

Therefore, to achieve more accurate semiotic analysis, it is necessary to take semiosis into more precise account. Peirce divided the concepts of object and interpretant (which increased sign classification to ten distinct trichotomies, left by Peirce to future explorers; see CP 8.344). These finer divisions of object and interpretant are necessary in musical analysis since they reveal important features of semiosis. Instead of the traditional triangular scheme of the sign, which does not correspond to a dynamic conception of semiosis (see Ketner 1988), consider instead the semiotic triple fork of Figure 8a, 'an emblem of fertility', in Peirce's words (CP 4.310). Furthermore, the divisions and subdivisions of object and interpretant are represented in Figure 8b, and are explained in the rest of this chapter.

---

[10] A Hindustani double-reed aerophone.

Table 5
The Ten Classes of Signs

1. Qualisigns – icons – rhemes		
2. Sinsigns	2.1 iconic signs – rhemes	
	2.2 indexes (and replicas of legisigns)	2.2.1 rhemes
		2.2.2 dicents
3. Legisigns	3.1 iconic signs – rhemes	
	3.2 indexical signs	3.2.1 rhemes
		3.2.2 dicents
	3.3 symbols	3.3.1 rhemes
		3.3.2 dicents
		3.3.3 arguments

Figure 8a
Sign diagram

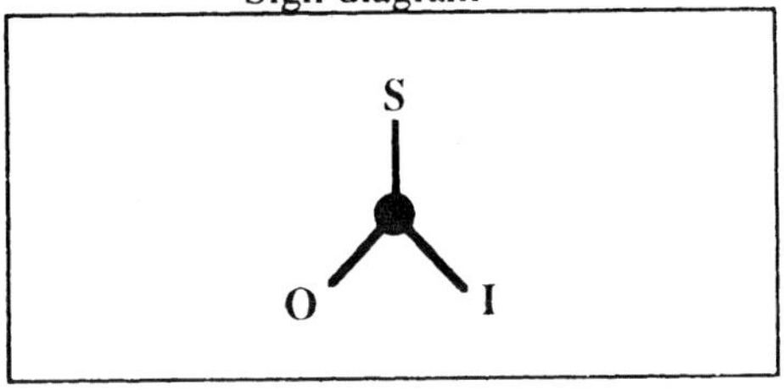

Figure 8b
Sign diagram, object and interpretant divisions

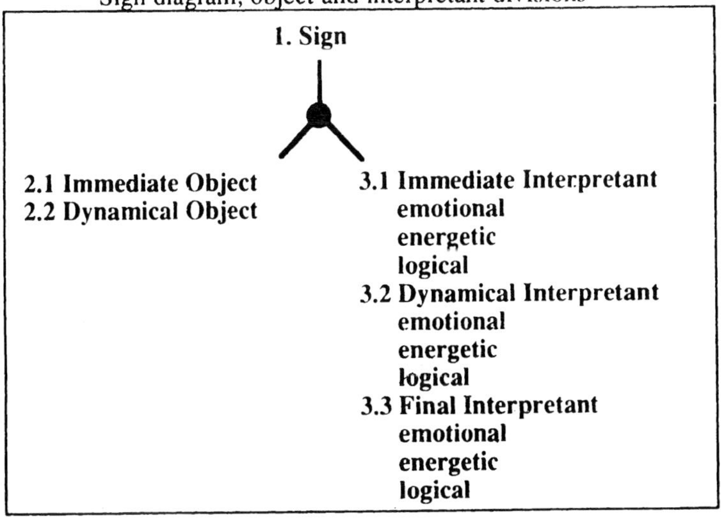

Any instance of semiosis would imply a network of relationships composed of many forks such as that of Figure 8. In that case, the denominations of sign, object and interpretant are relative to the levels of representation, according to a certain adopted point of view. Basically, the interpretant (which is also a sign) exists at a higher logical level than the sign, but, in reference to the object (reference which is mediated by the sign), the interpretant is not at a higher level than the sign (Ransdell 1986: 679). Thus, the diagram above should be seem as the projection of a multidimensional graph, where, from the point of view of the sign, the interpretant is situated in a plane of a higher logical level, but from the point of view of the object, sign and interpretant are on the same plane. However, a sign cannot refer directly to an object. The reference is in fact mediated by another sign, which Peirce called the 'immediate object', in contradistinction to the dynamical object, which is the object proper. They all occupy different logical levels in the representation. It would be impossible to represent graphically such relations, which are never absolute, but always relative to each other and to the analyst's point of view. Yet, a drastic reduction to a single plane could show a few of those relationships.

Figure 9
Levels of Representation

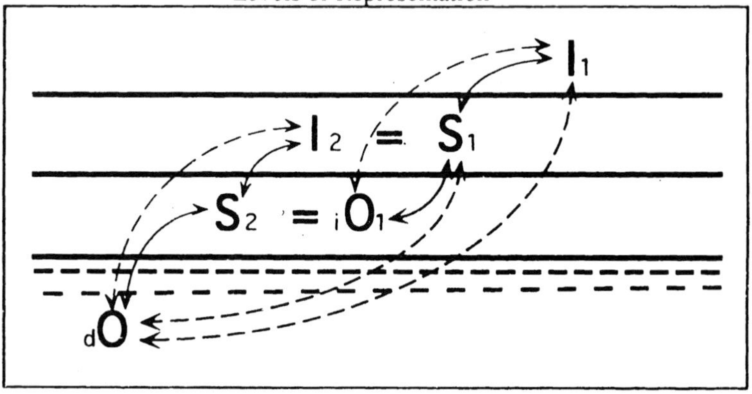

In Figure 9 each logical level is separated by a horizontal line. The focus of this semiosis system is the sign S_1, which determines an interpretant I_1, kept, in this case, at the most simple instance of sign interpretation. The double arrows represent, on one hand, determination; and on the other, reference. A continuous arrow is an instance of efficient causation, whereas a dashed arrow represents mediation. S_1 refers to a dynamic object $_dO$, not directly, but mediated by another sign, S_2. This sign is what Peirce called the immediate object, 'which is the Object as the

Sign itself represents it, and whose Being is thus dependent upon the Representation of it in the Sign' (CP 4.536).[11]

From I_1's point of view, the immediate object can be said to be the object as represented *in* the sign. It is the inner part of the sign and it is conditioned by the representation. The dynamical object is the object in itself, and it determines the sign. Peirce wrote:

> As to the Object, that may mean the Object as cognized in the Sign and therefore an Idea, or it may be the Object as it is regardless of any particular aspect of it, the Object in such relations as unlimited and final study would show it to be. The former I call the Immediate Object, the latter the Dynamical Object. For the latter is the Object that Dynamical Science (or what at this day would be called 'Objective' science,) can investigate. (CP 8.183)

Musically, the immediate object of a composition (as sound construct) or of a musical performance (as sound constructed at the moment of performing) will be those very acoustic qualities, the musical materiality. The dynamical object of the same kinds of sign will depend on each particular case. For example, take the famous song *Vande Mātaram* as a sign: its acoustic features are the immediate object. If, for a certain listener, only those acoustic features are meaningful, then there is an identity between the immediate object and the dynamical object. The sign is a pure icon, a case of absolute music. However, if the cultural context of India is taken as the dynamical object of the sign, from this point of view, the *Vande Mātaram* is an index of India, and one would simply say 'It is Indian music.' Further, if one takes into account the political situation in India at the beginning of the twentieth century, when the song was often performed, with a political tinge, at the conclusion of classical music recitals, then the *Vande Mātaram* represents the struggle for independence. In that case, the dynamical object is the idea of 'independence' related to the sign's immediate object (the same acoustic features of the above-mentioned cases) on the basis of habit. The sign is a symbol.

The interpretant was divided by Peirce into three concepts: immediate, dynamical, and final. The interpretant, in general, is a process, a web of sign translations. But important features are revealed through division and subdivision. Similarly to the distinction between immediate and dynamical object, 'It is likewise requisite to distinguish the Immediate Interpretant, i.e. the Interpretant represented or signified in the Sign, from the Dynamic Interpretant, or effect actually produced on the mind by the Sign' (CP 8.343). As the immediate object, the immediate interpretant is part of the sign. According to Ransdell (1986: 682), it is 'the range – always vaguely circumscribed – of the interpretant-generating power of the sign at a given time.' Thus, the immediate interpretant of a sign consists of the cluster of sign-interpretation

[11] There are further divisions of the immediate object; see CP 8.349 and Santaella 1995: 56-58.

possibilities that can be actualized as a dynamical interpretant. This range of possible interpretants can be classified, according to another of Peirce's divisions, into (1) emotional, (2) energetic, and (3) logical interpretants (CP 5.475-76). The emotional immediate interpretant would be the potentiality for conveying 'qualities of feelings or appearances.' The immediate interpretant, in its energetic capacity, would convey 'actual experiences'. Finally, the logical immediate interpretants would be 'those which are interpretable in thoughts or other signs of the same kind in infinite series' (CP 8.339). As emotional, energetic and logical interpretants conform to the logic of the categories, they can be represented by the diagram of Figure 10. In 3a, they are represented in terms of necessity; that is, a logical interpretant necessarily implies an energetic and emotional one; and in 3b, in terms of potentiality.

Figure 10
The Immediate Interpretant

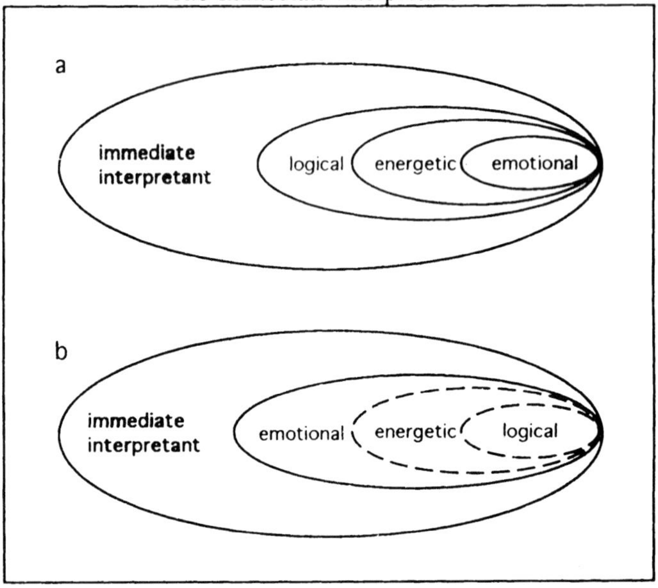

The immediate interpretant, as stated above, is part of the sign, in the sense that it represents the potentialities of the sign's interpretation. Whenever one of such interpretations is actualized, a dynamical interpretant is determined. A diagram of this stage of semiosis would imply other dimensions than those of the sign. An attempt to represent this graphically is presented in Figure 11, where the logical levels of the sign, including its immediate object and immediate interpretant, constitute the Sign Plane. The dynamical interpretant of that plane, being another sign, is represented as another plane, the Dynamical Interpretant Plane, which again is submitted to a drastic reduction to two dimensions in this diagram. The dynamical interpretant $_dI_1$ is, on one hand, linked to the sign, S_1; and on the other, it refers, through the mediation of S_1, to the dynamical object, $_dO$. Here is the triad - sign, object, interpretant - surrounded by a web of internal components and their relations, and the diagram of Figure 11 certainly does not cover all the possibilities.

Figure 11
The Determination of a Dynamical Interpretant

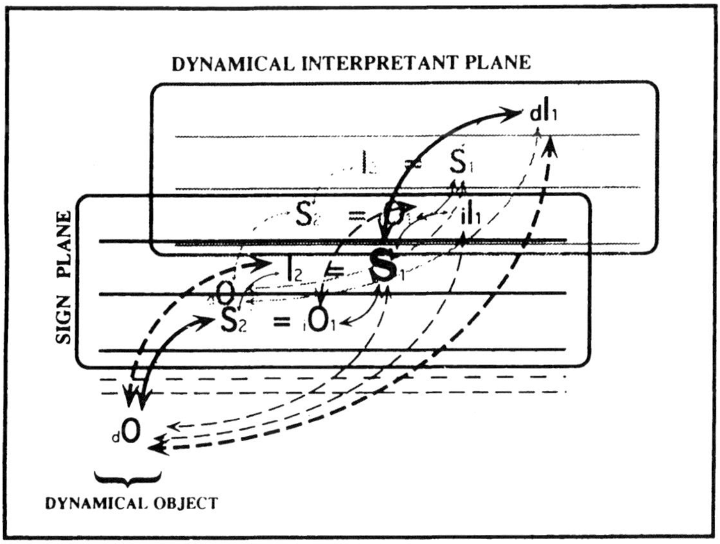

Music offers a wide range of possible interpretants. The action of a musical sign determines a dynamical interpretant, 'the actual effect produced upon a given interpreter on a given occasion in a given stage of his consideration of the sign. This again may be 1st a feeling merely, or 2nd an action, or 3rd a habit' (Peirce MS. 339d: 546–47, in Johansen 1985: 247). On emotional and energetic interpretants, Peirce wrote:

> There is almost always a feeling which we come to interpret as evidence that we comprehend the proper effect of the sign, although the foundation of truth in this is frequently very slight. This 'emotional interpretant', as I call it, may amount to much more than that feeling of recognition; and in some cases, it is the only proper significate effect that the sign produces. Thus, the performance of a piece of concerted music is a sign. It conveys, and is intended to convey, the composer's musical ideas; but these usually consist merely in a series of feelings. If a sign produces any further proper significate effect, it will do so through the mediation of the emotional interpretant, and such further effect will always involve an effort. I call it the energetic interpretant. The effort may be a muscular one, as it is in the case of the command to ground

> arms; but it is much more usually an exertion upon the Inner World, a mental effort. It never can be the meaning of an intellectual concept, since it is a single act, [while] such a concept is of a general nature. (CP 5.475)

Peirce mentions, as an illustration, the capacity of music to generate an emotional interpretant. Yet, it is clear that quality of feelings are not the only interpretant that music can engender; music can also have energetic and logical interpretants. However, the category of qualities, or firstnesses, be the sign a piece of music or Einstein's theory of relativity, will always be its first dynamical interpretant. Whereas the quality of feeling induced by a scientific theory is not essential to its understanding, musical qualities of feeling are the very ground upon which musical listening is built. It should be clear that quality of feeling is not what is commonly called emotion, thus *emotional* interpretant is a technical term in Peircean semiotics.

The logical interpretant is defined as follows:

> In advance of ascertaining the nature of this effect, it will be convenient to adopt a designation for it, and I will call it the ***logical interpretant***, without as yet determining whether this term shall extend to anything beside the meaning of a general concept, though certainly closely related to that, or not. Shall we say that this effect may be a thought, that is to say, a mental sign? No doubt, it may be so; only, if this sign be of an intellectual kind – as it would have to be – it must itself have a logical interpretant. (CP 5.476)

Music, being the presentation of acoustic qualities, embodied in existents, and organized by rules or habits of structure-making, is a semiotic system able to generate interpretants of all three kinds. A logical interpretant presupposes a sign bearing intellectual concepts or general ideas (CP 5.482). There are several features of musical structure that a listener can consider to be intellectual concepts. After all, the melodic or harmonic relations, the rhythmic flow, the musical forms, the rules of improvisation and development are all musical laws, to which even musical styles and aesthetic canons could be added. Naturally, a logical interpretant, as a sign, belongs to the class of arguments. Otherwise, it would be a change of habit: 'It can be proved that the only mental effect that can be so produced and that is not a sign but is of a general application is a ***habit-change***; meaning by a habit-change a modification of a person's tendencies toward action, resulting from previous experiences or from previous exertions of his will or acts, or from a complexus of both kinds of cause' (CP 5.476). However, logical interpretants are not assured, even when the immediate interpretant of the sign can afford a habit-change.

> It is not to be supposed that upon every presentation of a sign capable of producing a logical interpretant, such interpretant is actually produced. The occasion may either be too early or too late. If it is too early, the semiosis will not be carried so far, the other interpretants sufficing for the rude functions for which the sign is used. On the other hand, the

> occasion will come too late if the interpreter be already familiar with the logical interpretant, since then it will be recalled to his mind by a process which affords no hint of how it was originally produced. (CP 5.489)

The logical interpretant of a musical sign would manifest too early if the listener did not have familiarity with the musical codes. The dynamical interpretant, therefore, will be restricted to the emotional or energetic interpretants. Conversely, the logical interpretant can manifest too late for the listener who is conscious of the musical processes, codes, and rules, because the structural processes that organize the musical system of that particular piece of music are already current in the mind of the listener. In this case, therefore, there is no change of habit.

Thus, an actual listener could dynamically interpret a musical sign as (first) pure sound qualities (or qualities of feeling), as (second) inner action (mental or psychosomatic) or body movement (applause, work or dance), or as (third) intellectual construction (analysis or any kind of rational listening). All these possible interpretants are part of a musical sign, such as the *Vande Mātaram*, for instance. For a listener who ignores anything about this song, its emotional interpretant would be the qualities of feeling determined merely by the musical materiality of the sign, that is, its immediate object. In that case, the song is a qualisign, and the interpretant is a rheme, just a possibility of interpretation. Another case would be that of a listener who experienced the struggle for India's independence. In that case, a performance or recording of this song, itself a sinsign, would be interpreted as an index or symbol, and the dynamical interpretant could arouse a response so strong as to make the listener shed tears. Yet, perhaps, her/his grandchild might instead dance innocently to the *Vande Mātaram*. Both cases represent energetic interpretants. Conversely, a scholar might instead analyze the musical materials of the song, identifying the rāga and tāla used, how well the lyrics are set to the musical structure, etc. The logical interpretant could even induce a change in the mental habits of this scholar if the sign proves that some of her/his conceptions do not correspond to the actual state of the musical legisigns; that is, a mistaken or old-fashioned concept may be corrected or improved.

Before I proceed to the final interpretant, let me introduce here the concepts of utterer and interpreter. Dines Johansen, in his application of Peircean semiotics to the interpretation of linguistic texts, defines these two concepts as 'positions within the dialogical framework of semiosis of speech' (1985: 259). A dialogic analysis of music can consider implications not only between composers, conductors, performers, and listeners but also between scores and performers, recordings and listeners; for Peirce conceived the utterer and interpreter as broader categories than the simple idea of persons (see Johansen 1985: 258). In this context, the semiotic pyramid (1985: 266, actually a hexahedron) and the analytical approach proposed by Johansen could have great value for studies of certain musical situations. However, a few points must be made clear beforehand. The utterer and the interpreter are not simply the musician(s) and the listeners; and, above all, these concepts must not be understood as engaged in the simplistic communication scheme of sender-message-receiver. The utterer and interpreter, caught up in the web of semiosis, may even be difficult to locate in some circumstances, for they are thoughts among thoughts among thoughts. . . . Besides, in many musical situations their positions are irrelevant. It seems to me that the most consequential instance for the application of a dialogical semiotics to music is that of song. The interaction of lyrics and melody often presents cases in which a distinct utterer (actual or fictional) addresses an interpreter by a particular mode of semiosis. Another typical case in Indian music is the interaction between musicians, such as the question/answer procedure (*javāb/savāl*), often performed with the intention of dispute.

The term final interpretant refers to 'the manner in which the Sign tends to represent itself to be related to its Object' (CP 4.536; also 8.314-15). Ransdell considers the final interpretant as 'the totality of all that the sign-powers of a given sign would have manifested when it had shown all that it could be – all it could *do* – as a sign' (1986: 682). The final interpretant, or normal interpretant (in the mathematical sense of 'normal'), therefore, constitutes the actualization of the entire scope of significations of a sign; and as such, it is not an unitary entity, but a teleological continuum. Figure 12 is intended to represent graphically this idea.

In a letter to Lady Welby, Peirce explains the final interpretant in the following words: 'we must also note that there is certainly a third kind of Interpretant, which I call the Final Interpretant, because it is that which would finally be decided to be the true interpretation if consideration of the matter were carried so far that an ultimate opinion were reached' (CP 8.184). The real accomplishment or completion of a final interpretant, especially in music, would be very occasional, since sign development can be infinite. It would be better to think of final musical interpretants as a continuous process of interpretation fulfillment. That is, if signification is, in the immediate interpretant, at a potential level and, in the dynamical interpretant, at an actual level, it is in the final interpretant that the sign manifests its tendency to grow, or better, its teleology. Consider the web of signs that promote the idea of rāga as a flavor to be tasted by the mind (by means of rasa theory, explained in section 3). Consider the possibility that the multitude of existing musical phenomena, all musics of all cultures, are simultaneously unfolding and converging upon a tomorrow that will never come. Only examples of such magnitude can account for final interpretants in music.

Figure 12
The Final Interpretant

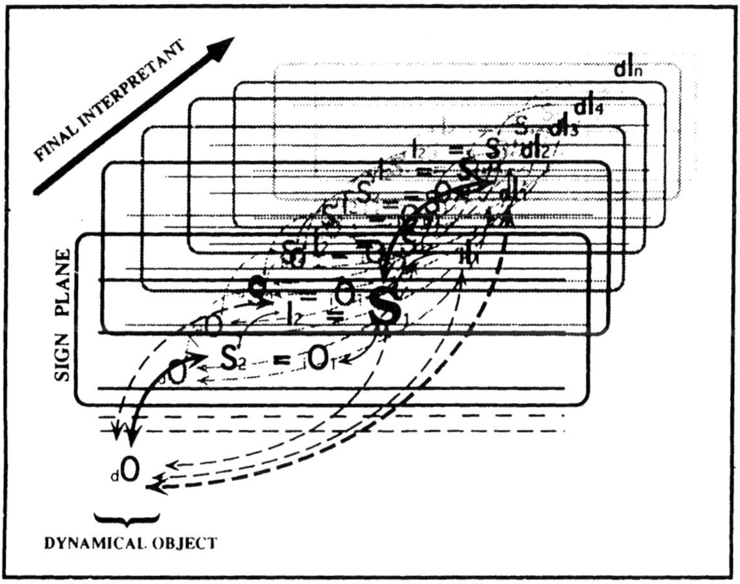

2.3 Fields of Musical Semiotic Inquiry

In structuring a semiotic theory of music in Peircean terms, it seems necessary to define fields of inquiry. The study of musical semiosis, which supports a great many layers of signification, will become clearer if distinct fields are selected from the total complex of a particular case. This must be understood as merely an analytical aid, since any isolation of the fields necessarily results in a distorted image of the totality.

From the Peircean conception of sign action as a triadic process, musical signification studies can be broadly divided according to the relations between the three relata, that is, between sign, object, and interpretant. The essential issues of musical semiosis can be found in the following relations: (1) the musical sign in relation to itself, (2) the musical sign in relation to its possible objects, and (3) the musical sign in relation to its interpretants. This division is supported by the logic of semiosis, which at its most fundamental level reflects the universal categories. Thus, a sign is a first because it is the foremost entity apprehended in any circumstance. There would be no semiosis without this level of appearance. In its closest relation with reality, a sign would extend itself to the point of merely conveying qualities (CP 8.332), that is, firstnesses. Thus, the study of the musical sign in itself does not represent an arbitrary separation of reality, but rather the most immediate reality possible. Next, a sign is also a second in any instance of actual embodiment. This aspect of the sign is clear when the interpreter is surprised by the occurrence of a sign, but secondness is present constantly in the process of semiosis. Finally, as thirdness, a sign is rarely interpreted in music as a terminal unit. Rather, semiosis tends to generate semiosis indefinitely.

The musical sign in relation to its possible objects brings up the questions usually dealt with by musical semioticians: the nature of objects in music, and how musical signs represent those objects. The simplest division is that of musical objects and non-musical objects. This actually refers to the dynamical object of a musical sign, whose immediate object is musical materiality as acoustic phenomena. However, the great volume of musical signs indicates a variety of possible immediate objects. For instance, if a musician or a musician's instrument is a musical sign, then what would be the nature of its immediate object? Would it be the material properties of the instrument, the musician's body – or perhaps the musical capacities of the instrument and the sum total of the musician's thought, as Peirce characterizes the man-sign (CP 5.314). It seems to me that everything depends on the analyst's point of view, and the relativity of semiosis is such that any slight fluctuation in the approach to an actual case will produce significantly different results. Hence, the need to distinguish fields of inquiry. Furthermore, a musical sign does not effectively work as a sign if it does not determine an interpretant.

In fact, it is at the interpretant level that musical semiosis works, for it necessarily encompasses the former aspects. Thus, all forms of musical activity are in fact systems that generate musical interpretants. There is no sense in discussing signs in themselves or signs in relations to their objects if the interpretant is not considered, at least as a logical consequence of one of the particularized levels. It must be clear, however, that interpretants are not necessarily logical; they can also be energetic and emotional interpretants. The last two classes are highly relevant to musical semiosis. Musical interpretants can also be seen as a continuum that ranges from the emotional to the logical. Further, to the extent that a musical interpretant depends on the former levels, it also determines the nature of musical signs and what they represent in a musical system. And this is obviously not an isolated system, but one that is intermingled in the semiotic web of a culture, as cause and consequence of historical interrelationships, preferences, chance happenings, and so on.

Therefore, the three fields of inquiry are: (first) Intrinsic Musical Semiosis, (second) Musical Reference, (third) Musical Interpretation. According to the logic of the categories, they relate to each other as represented in Figure 7a (2.1). Intrinsic musical semiosis is part of musical reference, which in turn is part of musical interpretation. In this study, and without starting a discussion of what music is, I will give preference to signs whose immediate objects are of an acoustic nature. Yet, this is not an exclusionary postulate. It might be profitable, in certain cases of analysis, to consider other kind of musical signs, such as treatises, musical instruments, recordings (in themselves), musicians, musical communities, and so forth.

Intrinsic Musical Semiosis, or the study of the musical sign in itself, deals with internal musical signification. It constitutes the semiotics of musical materiality. Acoustics and the several music theories (according to the various musical systems) may be supplemented here by semiotic analysis. This field could study issues such as musical qualities or **qualisigns** (timbre, melodic, rhythmic, formal qualities, etc.); individualities or sinsigns (works, performed music, and the broad field of replicas or actualizations of legisigns); and habits, laws or legisigns (musical systems, genres, forms, improvisation or development rules, imitation, variation, recurrence, etc.). In this field, the immediate and dynamical objects of a musical sign are always of an acoustic nature. There is a material identity between the two relata.

Musical Reference, or the study of musical signs related to their possible objects, deals with the signification of a broad class of objects.

Acoustical immediate objects can be related to both sonorous dynamical objects or non-acoustic dynamic objects. This field would investigate questions such as how a musical sign refers to an object, the possible relations between a dynamical object and the immediate object as represented in the sign, the possible dynamical objects represented by music and their modes of being.

These issues can be organized according to different perspectives. Reference is indeed a broad field. As early as 1897 ('On a New List of Categories'), Peirce stated that there are three kinds of representation:

> First. Those whose relation to their objects is a mere community in some quality, and these representations may be termed likenesses [later called icons].
>
> Second. Those whose relation to their objects consists in a correspondence in fact, and these may be termed indices. [. . .]
>
> Third. Those the ground of whose relation to their objects is an imputed character, which are the same as general signs, and these may be termed symbols. (CP 1.558)

Later (1903), the three kinds of representations were conceived as the second of three basic trichotomies, set according to the relation of the sign to its object. It is an icon if the sign has some character in itself; an index, if it is in some existential relation to the object; or a symbol, if in its relation to an interpretant it operates on a conventional basis. From this point of view, musical representations emerge firstly as sheer acoustic reference (the question of pure musical icons) and reference by quality and formal likenesses (musical hypoicons, or iconic signs); then as existents or signs of existents (index and indexical signs); finally as habitual or conventional reference (symbols).[12]

Musical Interpretation, or the study of the musical sign related to its interpretants, deals with the action of musical signs in an existing or potential mind. The basic questions in this field are the nature of the musical interpretant (emotional, energetic, logical); how the sign determines the interpretant (rheme, dicent, argument); the understanding of the sign and the dialogical process that can happen in a single mind (especially in the case of logical interpretants), or among several minds. Issues of Musical interpretation can be divided into three sub-fields: (first) musical perception; (second) performance (or modes of playing, singing, or conducting), and (a double third) musical intelligence (analysis, criticism, teaching, theorizing and, of course, musical semiotics) and composition (as intellectual elaboration based on all three fields). Interpretation here should be understood according to Peirce's semiotics, that is, in terms of questions regarding the third element of semiosis - the interpretant. It seems to me that perception is the first category of interpretation, although there are crucial elements of

[12] See Martinez 1991 and 1996a for previous considerations on this field.

secondness (as well as thirdness) in every act of listening. But this opens another level of sub-division, which will be dealt with later (see 2.3.3). Performance is a second sub-field since it emerges from the action of playing or singing. But it is not pure secondness, for it consists in learned and finely controlled psychomotor action. Musical intelligence is obviously a third form of musical interpretant, as an activity based on analysis, inferences, generalizations, and the dissemination of this knowledge. Composition must be as well, since it presupposes all the musical activities that come before.

At first, it seems possible to apply this framework to every kind of musical phenomenon or musical system, since Peirce's semiotic theory was conceived to be applied to every kind of sign. But, of course, each musical system will determine its own semiotic theory, which will be a theoretical translation rather than a rigid model intended to govern all types of music. In fact, each actual application will generate a particular theory, for the object determines the sign. It is of the greatest importance to notice that this possible semiotic architecture constitutes an interrelated, flexible structure. There is no isolation between the fields, which could also be organized in different ways. Actually, it is undesirable to think about one field without referring to the other two. As stated above, even when a layer of semiosis is selected for analysis, the other layers are necessarily implied. In the analysis of any of the three fields, all signs of the three basic trichotomies, and the ten classes of signs derived from them, can be used. Thus there is no strict correspondence between the three trichotomies and the three fields of inquiry. This division into three fields and the ten classes of signs may be sufficient for musical studies. Nevertheless, Peirce's later ten trichotomies could expand musical semiotics to hitherto unthought-of limits.

2.3.1 Intrinsic Musical Semiosis in Hindustani Music

> There is no gīta (song, music) without nāda, there are no svaras (musical notes) without nāda, there is no nṛtta (dance) without nāda, hence the world is of the essence of nāda. (BD 1.2.18)

2.3.1.1 Musical qualities

The most basic layer of musical signification is that of acoustic qualities, which, as a representamen, is designated by Peirce as qualisign. A qualisign is necessarily an icon in relation to its dynamic object, and a rheme to its final interpretant. A qualisign 'has no identity. It is the mere quality of an appearance and is not exactly the same throughout a second. Instead of identity, it has ***great similarity***, and cannot differ much without being called quite another qualisign' (CP 8.334). Peirce refers here to a pure qualisign; however, musical qualisigns are usually embodied in sinsigns, which can be replicas of legisigns, and from this point of view, they are not as close to firstness as a pure qualisign is. There is no doubt, however, that acoustic qualisigns do exist, be they considered as music or not by the interpreter, and if the listener is able to pay attention to the sounds as what they are, s/he is listening merely to qualisigns.

In fact, what I call *musical materiality* is, first of all, a matter of qualisigns. Its nature is that of pure acoustic qualities. Irrespective of its causative origins, its position in time and space, music, in its first-most instance of semiosis, presents only qualities. Yet, the complexity of musical systems usually leads the interpretant beyond qualisigns, outshining their suchness. A listener must have a specially receptive disposition or capacity, in order to be able to immerse her or himself in this universe of pure acoustic qualities. Qualisigns manifest musically as timbre, intensity, quality of pitch and duration, before any intellectual apprehension of the sign, and before any analysis. Musical movement and texture are also rich in qualisigns. In this way, 'it is sheer quality that functions as a sign, and so it does because it addresses someone and produces in the mind of this individual something like an indivisible and vague feeling' (Santaella 1983: 85). But quality of feeling, as the interpretant generated by musical qualisigns, is already an instance of emotional interpretant, and thus an issue germane to the field of musical interpretation (see 2.3.3). Musical qualisigns, as I envision them here, refer to the phenomenal suchness of musical materiality – music in itself, in its utterly concrete conception. This is certainly the most universal element of music. Musical materiality is of course virtual materiality, those kinds of qualities arising from a particular combination of frequency, intensity, and duration.

Anāhatanāda and firstness

Some issues in Indian philosophy are prominently semiotic and at the same time deeply related to Indian music; they deserve some thought at this point. Such is the case with two forms of sounds, or nāda: *anāhatanāda* and *āhatanāda*. The latter refers to the common conception of sound, as produced by physical impact (āhata); the former is the unstruck sound (anāhata), which permeates the whole universe, being its creative force. Besides the metaphysical questions that are at the very center of any discussion of anāhatanāda, there is an apparent feature of firstness in this kind of vibration, for firstness is the consideration of anything in its pure qualitative aspect. Any sound, therefore, is an unstruck sound, if perceived not as a product of any physical vibration of matter, but merely as pure quality, in its presentness, a sound in itself. Of course, any kind of āhatanāda can be perceived in this mode, and the traditional view is that anāhatanāda cannot be perceived except by supranormal means. Rowell writes:

> If there is a central core to the idea of sound as developed in the systematic Indian philosophies, it is that sound is a quality, inhering in the substratum of *ākāśa* [ether or atmosphere] which pervades both the outer spaces of the world and the inner spaces of the body. It is one, universal, eternal, causal (but not caused), permeating both personal and transpersonal consciousness, and manifested along the human pathway from inner to outer space. (1992: 41)

The anāhatanāda that perfuses the universe, including all living beings, if not directly perceptible, can be represented by its audible counterpart, āhatanāda, specially when the latter is produced by the human voice. Both forms of nāda, in fact, are thought to be closely related (I would say iconically related; see 2.3.2). In the same way Śārṅgadeva linked nāda with all the levels of speech (SR 1.2.2), he also recognized the function of nāda as 'the very essence of vocal music' (SR 1.2.1), as well as instrumental music and dance. In this respect, Śārṅgadeva was following Mataṅga, the author of the ninth-century music treatise the *Bṛhaddeśī*, who stated that notes, songs, and dance depend on sound (BD 1.2.18).

Musically, nāda is the continuum out of which *svara* (note) emerges. The agent mediating the organization of the scale is the controversial *śruti* (hearing, listening), a discrete element, of which a collection, 22 in number, organizes the basic tunings of early Indian music.[13] Mataṅga writes: 'That which is heard (is known as) śruti' (BD 1.3.anu.1). Śruti can be only one or an infinite number. If one, Mataṅga actually refers to the idea of nāda; if many, he is recognizing that the set of 22 is arbitrary, and an infinity of pitch positions can be placed in the continuum of nāda. He inquires: 'how many rows of waves do not take effect, being born of the multitude of water disturbed by strong-blowing winds' (BD 1.3.27); so are the śrutis. Coming before its role as the discrete pitch element organizing the choices of tones, śruti is the quality of frequency itself. Thus, what is implied here is not the acoustical parameters that organize the pitch sets of Indian music, for those are a matter of legisigns. Rather, I call attention to pitches as qualities, irrespective of their organization.

Besides the quality of pitch, timbre is another topic the most preeminent scholars have dealt with since the period of early Indian music. The timbre of the human voice, more than the timbre of instruments, was considered in detail, with respect to what voice qualities are desirable or undesirable in a singer. The first scholar to present the merits and faults in the qualities of a singer's voice was Bharata, in the *Nāṭyaśāstra* (a theory of dramaturgy, composed by 200 A.D.):

> The six qualities of voice are that it should be loud, compact, smooth, sweet, careful, and distinctly related to the three voice-registers. That which is heard from a distance, is called loud (*śrāvaka*). The loud voice which is sweet but not diffused, is called compact (*ghana*). The voice which being loud does not become harsh, is smooth (*snigdha*). If at the highest point of the voice-registers there occurs no discordance, then the voice is called sweet (*madhura*). The voice which does not lapse into excess or deficiency, is called careful (*avadhānavān*). The voice which striking the head, the throat [and the chest] becomes sweet with reference to three places, always providing sweetness to the three voice-registers, is considered distinctly related to voice-registers (*tristhānaśobhī*). (NŚ 32.514-18)

The first quality Bharata considers is that of loudness, a parameter rarely specified in the literature of Indian music. In terms of performance practice, loudness, intensity, or dynamics is left entirely to the performer's discretion. In this sense, and not being formalized, it is one of the most purely qualitative aspects of Indian music. Bharata then considers the other qualities, which are in general timbral, but may also be phraseological. Among those, smoothness and sweetness are the most highly esteemed qualities. These are iconically described with reference to the flowing qualities of particular substances, for snigdha also translates as 'viscous' or 'oily', and madhura, as 'syrup' or 'treacle'. Finally, the viscosity of a voice should be splendid in the three registers

13 For the relation between śruti and svara, see: NŚ 28.4; D 8-15; BD 1.3.24, 1.3.44-52; SR 1.4.8-46b; Jairazbhoy 1975; Rowell 1992: 144-49; Widdess 1995 passim.

(tristhānaśobhī). The flaws Bharata indicates should be avoided by a singer also explain, from the negative side, the ideal qualities of a voice:

> The five faults of a singer are that his voice may be *Kapila* (unsteady), *Sandaṣṭa* (bitten), *Kākī* (crow-like), and *Tumbakī* (nasal). When the voice is unnatural, and there is a gurgling sound, it is called Kapila. The voice of one who has phlegm in the throat, is also called Kapila. When there is irregular excess or want of volume in voice, it is called unsteady. A lean voice is also given this name. A voice produced by [unduly] using the teeth, is called Sandaṣṭa by good masters. The voice which in its enunciation does not properly touch its proper voice-register, and which is harsh, is called Kākī. The voice connected with the nose is called Tumbakī. (NŚ 32.519-23)

The qualities to be avoided are those which result in a discontinuous and harsh timbre, lacking the rich viscosity that a good voice should have in Indian music. Thus, the 'ideal vocal sound should be full and concentrated, oily smooth, and honey sweet' (Rowell 1992: 309). Later authors kept the essence of these choices. For Tumburu, a scholar of whom there is no extant work, śruti is also a quality of timbre. Mataṅga quotes the view of this author: 'The high voice that is *rūkṣa* (dry) is known as *vātaja* by the wise. The deep, full and clear voice should be known as *pittaja* (born of *pitta*). The creamy, soft and sweet voice is *kaphaja* (born of *kapha*). That (voice) which combines the qualities of the three (types of voice) should be known as born of *sannipāta* (admixture)' (BD 1.3.anu.4). Tumburu seems to have based this classification on the three humors of ayurvedic medicine: *vāyu*, pitta and kapha. The balance of those three humors is a necessary condition for health. The voice is vātaja when born of vāyu, the windy humor. Pitta is the bilious humor, whose attribute is heat. Kapha is phlegm and is supposed to be cold. Although Bharata states that a voice gurgling with phlegm is a *doṣa* (defect) rather than a *guṇa* (merit), it seems that what Tumburu had in mind was rather the creamy and smooth qualities of the humors.

Śārṅgadeva, similarly to Tumburu, also classified voices according to the humors, now denominated: *khāhula* (arising from kapha), which is creamy, sweet and soft; *nārāṭa* (arising from pitta), being full, deep and clear; *bombaka* (arising from vāyu), which is hollow, harsh and gross; and four other kinds of combined voices (*miśra*) (SR 3.39-67). In addition, he raised to fifteen the excellences of a voice: *mṛṣṭa* (pleasing), madhura (sweet), *cehāla* (that which is present in female voices and among boys, up till the breaking of the voice), *tristhānaka* (fine in the three registers), *sukhāvaha* (comforting), *komala* (soft, tender), *gāḍha* (dense or deep), *śrāvaka* (resonant), *karuṇa* (pathetic), ghana (dense, powerful), snigdha (creamy), *ślakṣṇa* (continuous as the flow of oil), *raktimān* (charming), and *chavimān* (lustrous, faultless). Continuity and easy flow are thus still appreciated qualities, to which good resonance can be added. In fact, defining the musical note, Śārṅgadeva uses the same attributes: 'Immediately consequent upon śruti, creamy and resonating, the sound that delights the listeners' minds by itself is called svara' (SR 1.3.24c-25b). As Rowell has pointed out (1992: 311), the quality of musical sound is at least as important as the quantities that define the pitch of svaras. In face of the long list of musical qualities provided by Śārṅgadeva, based on scholarship already older than a millennium at his time, it is clear that great attention to acoustic qualisigns has always been a concern in Indian music.

2.3.1.2 Musical existents and replicas

A qualisign, in fact, cannot act as a sign unless embodied (but Peirce makes clear that 'the embodiment has nothing to do with its character as a sign'; CP 2.244). Conversely, existents necessarily have qualities, for they could not exist without any character. Strictly speaking, all existents are unique entities, and so are musical signs (as acoustic phenomena). Any musical performance is singular, for its characters – qualisigns – are always peculiar at the absolute level of an occurrence. Even a musical recording, whenever played, will sound somehow different, because sound-system devices always have different constructions and responses, each room has its peculiar reverberating properties, and so on. The degree of singularity of musical signs of course varies. A live performance is much less fixed than a recording, and an improvised piece is less determined than the performance of a composed score. In sum, there is always a component of singularity in a musical event, and this is a feature of sinsigns:

> A ***Sinsign*** (where the syllable ***sin*** is taken as meaning "being only once," as in ***single***, ***simple***, Latin ***semel***, etc.) is an actual existent thing or event which is a sign. It can only be so through its qualities; so that it involves a qualisign, or rather, several qualisigns. But these qualisigns are of a peculiar kind and only form a sign through being actually embodied. (CP 2.245)

A sinsign, however, does not signify by means of its qualities. It is rather its occurrence in time and space which grounds the representation. There are two kinds of sinsigns in music. First come those occurrences that are considered musical signs independently of any musical system, such as a single musical entity that appears by chance in music.[14] An example of this kind of sinsign is the train shriek that once disturbed a concert of Ustād Bade Ghulam Ali Khan, who immediately incorporated the pitch of the sound into the performance (see Wade 1984: 234). Secondly, there are replicas of musical legisigns, that is, events that are materializations of some musical rule or habit. These are the majority of sinsigns in music. They can also be thought of as tokens of musical types, the latter being the structures organizing all levels of a musical system.

---

[14] And certainly this is the basic material of 'chance music'

Although the distinction type/token is often used by Peirce (see CP 4.537), I will instead use the terms sinsign and legisign, for they are more consistent with all the other kinds of signs used in this study, whereas type/token (and *tone*) are used in a more specific context in Peirce's writings. The term 'replica' (CP 2.246), a sinsign or a token, is also a technical designation in Peircean semiotics, and so it should be understood here.

Indian music, and improvised music in general, is made by sinsigns that are very flexible in relation to the legisigns of which they are replicas. However, being replicas, they are not totally independent and they conform to the habits the system imposes on them. A rāga is always performed differently by musicians, even though all those performances are considered sinsigns of the same rāga, inasmuch as they are rendered correctly. Indeed, even the same musician, whenever s/he plays or sing a rāga, will not perform it exactly the same way. Likewise, the performance of a musical form or genre is a sinsign, a singular materialization of the genre, which is the general, determining rule. Thus, the unique *khayāl* created at each performance (Wade 1984: 11) is a sinsign of the idea of khayāl as a genre and form, that is, a legisign. Even a composition, which is the closest structure in Hindustani music to a fixed form, has its variations as actualized sinsigns. For an interesting example of how varied the conception of the same piece of music can be, when considered by different musicians, one can compare three transcriptions of the dhrupad *Jagata Jananī* in rāga bhairavī: as presented by Wade, from a recording by Ustāds Moinuddin and Aminuddin Dagar (1987: 165-68); the version of N.C. Bural, according to Widdess (1995: 183); or that of Ustād Zia Fariduddin Dagar (Ex. 12 in 2.3.2). On closer levels, the phrases, the motifs, the way each svara is approached, developed, ornamented and concluded are all sinsigns of different levels of singularity; all of them conform to some established habit of musical performance, whether conceptualized in music theory or not.

Hindustani music is highly structured in several respects, but it is interesting that at the surface level of performance there are so many elements left totally to the capacity of the musician in giving body, clothing and accessories to musical legisigns. A single svara is never a pure tone in Indian music. Each performed note is peculiar at its microscopic level. In *dhrupad*, a traditional vocal musical form and genre, there are two terms, *āghāt* and *anuraṇa*, which conceptualize the way a svara is set forth and developed. Widdess explains: 'āghāt is the onset of a pitch, whether by direct attack, or by indirect approach; anuraṇana is its "resonance" – its prolongation and/or inflection up or down' (1994: 62). A svara can be approached by a *mīṇḍ* (glide), or with a *kaṇ* (a barely audible appoggiatura); then the svara can be inflected in many different ways, and so on. Thus, in Indian music, each note is clearly singular, although conforming to the pitch set of a certain rāga.

It is at this surface layer that sinsigns are mostly active, and their variety and richness of appearance is certainly one of the charms of Hindustani music. It is true that these fine elements of musical appearance are all replicas, and the ways a musician presents, ornaments, and develops them are also the result, in some measure, of the style of the tradition to which s/he belongs, that is, the musician's *gharānā*.[15] At any rate, pure structure was never attractive enough to sustain Indian music, and Bharata states that 'A song without any *alaṁkāra* will be like a night without the moon, a river without water, a creeper without a flower and a woman without any ornament' (NŚ 29.75). Indeed, alaṁkāra, or ornamentation, has been an essential aspect of Indian music since the early stages. By the time of Śārṅgadeva, there were already fifteen varieties of shakes or *gamaks* (SR 87-97b). Some of these are still current in contemporary musical practice, such as several of the ten *svara-lakṣaṇas* (note features) employed in the Dagar tradition of dhrupad singing:

> In *bīṇ*-playing [*rudra-vīṇā* [16]] the tender feelings of the notes are pronounced by plucking the wires on the fret. The vocalists produce this effect on the vocal cords by sensitive modulation called *kampita*. When such a modulation is of a swinging or wavy nature by the ascent and descent of notes, it is *āndolita*.
>
> In *lahak*, the Dagars make notes travel in a lashing manner, with some breath-force. In gamak, the notes spring with a modulating force and are articulated with rounded lips. In *hudak*, the articulation is heavy and the notes are pulled upwards with extra breath force, creating a humming sound. (Sanyal 1986: 46-47)

Another level of sinsigns (and their correspondent legisigns) is that of improvisation techniques used in the main vocal genres in Hindustani music. In *laykārī* (rhythmic manipulations), for instance, the dhrupad singer improvises with the words of the *bandiś* (composed song), setting a selection of lyrics to rhythmic and melodic variations created at the moment of the performance. Some performers use composed forms of laykārī, such as *dugun* (double speed), *tīgun* (triple speed or triplets), *caugun* (quadruple speed), and so on, as well as several other forms of cross-rhythms; but the best singers rather do laykārī spontaneously, thus presenting asymmetrical and rich rhythmic and melodic variations (see Widdess 1994: 68). In this case, each occurrence of a laykārī may be thought as a sinsign, of which rāga, tāla and bandiś are legisigns. Similarly, there is the actualization of improvisation techniques such as the *tān* (fast melodic figure), *boltān* (a tān sung to the lyrics), *bolbāṅṭ* (rhythmic variation), and *sargam* (improvisations with note syllables: sa,

---

[15] For the concept of gharānā, see Wade 1984, Deshpande 1987, Neuman 1990, and A.D. Sharma 1993.

[16] North Indian fretted stick zither, with gourd resonators at each end of the shaft, on which four strings are plucked and stopped by the musician; also called bīṇ.

re, ga, ma, pa, dha, ni), used currently in khayāl; or the *bolbanāo* (melodic variations meant to highlight the meaning of the lyric's words) employed in ṭhumrī – these are all forms of sinsigns in Hindustani music. Certainly, what is referred to here in terms of vocal music also have counterparts in instrumental music, be it melodic or percussive.

2.3.1.3 Musical legisigns

The normative aspects of music can be understood by the concept of legisign, a sign which is a general type or law. Peirce wrote:

> A ***Legisign*** is a law that is a Sign. This law is usually established by men. Every conventional sign is a legisign [but not conversely]. It is not a single object, but a general type which, it has been agreed, shall be significant. Every legisign signifies through an instance of its application, which may be termed a ***Replica*** of it. Thus, the word "the" will usually occur from fifteen to twenty-five times on a page. It is in all these occurrences one and the same word, the same legisign. Each single instance of it is a Replica. The Replica is a Sinsign. Thus, every Legisign requires Sinsigns. But these are not ordinary Sinsigns, such as are peculiar occurrences that are regarded as significant. Nor would the Replica be significant if it were not for the law which renders it so. (CP 2.246)

Every musical system is composed by sets of musical laws, habits or procedures, which usually were established through the development of a tradition, such as Hindustani, Karnatic, or Western classical music. A musical system can also be the invention of an individual, such as Arnold Schoenberg's dodecaphonism; or the rāga vedī kī lalit, composed by Dilip Chandra Vedi (see Meer 1980: 176, 246-7); or the system may be a result of technological advances (electronic music). In any case, there must be sinsigns working as replicas of those musical systems which they manifest. Conversely, musical legisigns define the features of their replicas, such as the pitch set and melodic motifs that characterize the performance of a rāga. Further, musical legisigns determine their interpretants, that is, how the musical sign should be understood by the interpreter. This determination can be actual or potential (CP 8.177). For example, in the same performance, a competent listener will identify the music played as a replica of a particular rāga, but a listener unable to interpret that legisign will perhaps be limited to appreciating the performance's qualisigns or sinsigns, not as replicas, however, but merely as occurrences.

There are several levels of legisigns in Hindustani music, which should be studied in at least three fields: tāla, rāga, and musical forms. It is obvious that these fields are not isolated from each other, but much to the contrary. Tāla, rāga, and musical forms are strongly interdependent. On the other hand, they are not frozen and immutable structures, they are full of life. This should be understood in two senses. First, life in Indian music is related to the fact that it has been continuously evolving for millennia; second, the legisigns of Indian music allow great scope for variety in their replicas. Rowell has described these features in terms of organic unity:

> As far back as we can trace it, the organic unity of the music of India has been assured by several of its inherent properties: by the stability, continuity, and generative potential of the idea of rāga, which must also include those melody types from which rāgas arose; by the rhythmic unity and many of the formal tactics in the domain of tāla [...]; by the relationship of ornamental variations to a prior model; and above all by the general orientation toward process which we have noted in both the anthropomorphic and organic paradigms. (1992: 234-35)

The organic unity of Indian music is an issue of intrinsic musical semiosis, as far as it is concerned with their musical structures, such as tāla, rāga, improvisation techniques, and forms. The anthropomorphic and organic paradigms mentioned by Rowell above, if taken as objects of musical representations, are rather a study of musical reference (see 2.3.2). From an abstract point of view, however, they bring the idea of life and its generative power, which are features of legisigns. Still, the generative power of legisigns are not chaotic. Short writes:

> legisigns only exist *in order* to be used – that is, to signify through replication – and that presupposes the existence of creatures prone to interpret those replicas according to the rules associated with the legisigns replicated. Conversely, the interpretation of something as the replica of a legisign presupposes that it was produced *in order* to be interpreted *as* a replica of that legisign. (1982: 292)

Therefore, legisigns are telic representamens, that is, they are goal-oriented. Legisigns are created and replicated with a purpose, and the purpose of musical legisigns is to generate music and musical meaning. This can be manifold. Among other things, a rāga can signify its own structure, and Powers has explored this level in *The Structure of Musical Meaning* (1976); it can also signify the product of a culture, as ethnomusicologists usually conceive it; or it can signify a particular effect on a mind: 'That which colors or delights the mind [...] is known by the wise as rāga,' as Mataṅga wrote more than one thousand years ago (BD 3.263).[17] In all these modes there are aesthetical values that make Indian music something admirable and worthy of listening to. That is to say, all modes of musical semiosis are also aesthetical.

Tāla

Every level of temporal and metrical organization in Hindustani music is a legisign. Thus, *mātrā*, as a division of time based on a regular pulse, is a legisign, as is the concept of laya and tempo, such as *vilambit* (slow), *madhya* (middle), *drut* (fast), and their combinations. The *vibhāg*, a

---

[17] What are those 'colors or delights' is the subject of section 3.

group of mātrās, several of which partly define a particular tāla, is a legisign; and so is the *ṭhekā*, the sequence of drum strokes (*bols*) representing a tāla. Essential to the teleological aspect of rhythmic organization in Hindustani music are the concepts of *sam* (together, jointly) – which is the first mātrā of a tāla – and *khālī* (empty) – the contrasting section to the *tālī* (clap) vibhāgs, for they determine the *āvart* (one complete cycle) and the metrical character of a tāla. All these levels of legisigns are simultaneously present in any particular tāla, such as cāutāl or ektāl (see Ex. 1). Thus, the several layers of legisigns in a tāla – mātrā, vibhāg, āvart, ṭhekā, tālī, khālī, sam – manifest simultaneously in a performance as solo drumming, vocal, or instrumental composition. The actualization of a tāla is a set of sinsigns, and each tāla has its character or qualisigns.

Example 1

Structure of cāutāl and ektāl

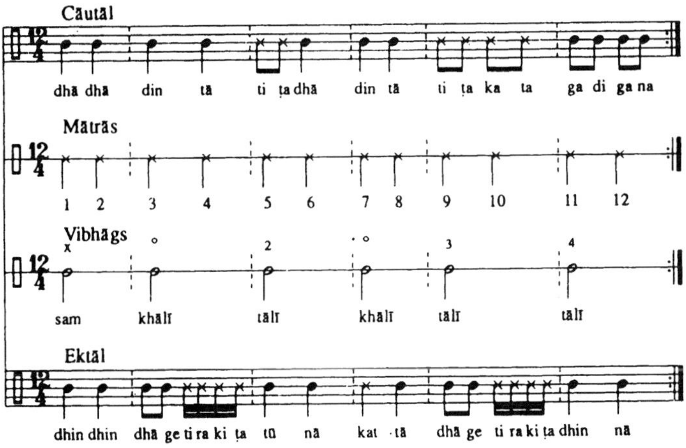

The idea of sam, in particular, deserves closer attention, for, as Saxena writes, 'the Sama not only initiates, but consummates the cycle' (1979: 67). Thus, the sam has, above all, a telic function. It is not simply the first mātrā of a tāla; it is also a focal point, a clear goal in the metric development of any measured performance. Although during the performance the sam appears cyclically, the best aesthetic effect is drawn when it is not emphasized mechanically at every āvart, but rather treated elusively, by means of several procedures and cadential sequences, such as the *tihāī* (a melodic phrase or drumming pattern composed of three sections whose last note falls on the sam).

A replica of a sam can, obviously, signify as an index, that is, indicating the first mātrā of the tāla by its occurrence. But this is not its main function. The sam is above all a legisign. On one hand, it organizes the tāla, determining its extension; and, on the other, the sam establishes a dynamical directionality, promoted by the agogic goal which the sam itself is. Certainly, these functions only actualize by replication. The sinsigns which materialize the tāla and its sam can be set in such a way as to emphasize this goal-directedness: 'the centrality of the sama can be heightened by making it appear as the natural culmination of a pattern that seems clearly to move towards it' (Saxena 1973: 14), as in the case of *āmad* (literally, 'approach', thus a phrase leading to the sam) and tihāīs. These forms can also create different levels of expectation, heightened either by disappointment or fulfillment. Thus, a tihāī may have in its structure cross-rhythms in relation to the tāla, but when the last stroke or note eventually ends clearly on sam, the tension arising from those rhythmic phasings is resolved. Ex. 2 presents a *cakkradār tihāī*, which is a wheel-like tihāī (in Yādav 1992:3. 164). Each of the three phrases is composed of an introductory motif, **dhātirakiṭa dhagena**, and a small tihāī made by a triple sequence of the motif: **dingadi nāgina dhā**. The last stroke **dhā** falls precisely on the sam, after two āvarts of tīntāl (a sixteen-beat tāla). The composition is set to *āṛīlaya*, triple meter.

Example 2
A cakkradār tihāī in tīntāl

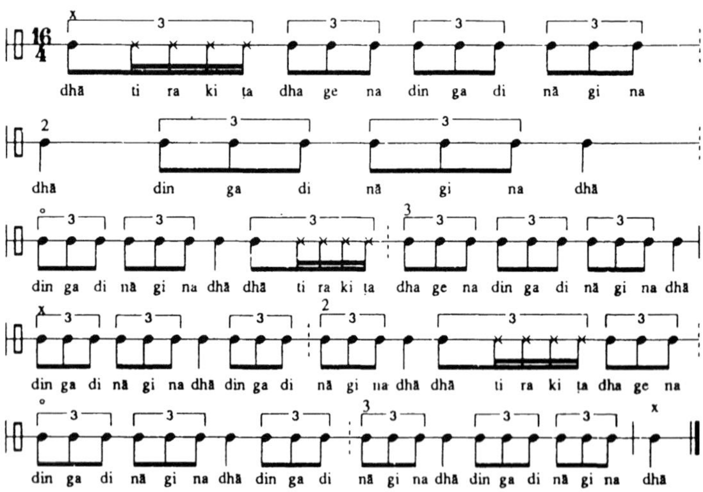

Another musical resource that plays into the telic nature of the sam, is the technique of *anāgat-atīt*. The final resolution of a phrase can be anticipated (anāgat) or delayed (atīt) so that an entirely different aesthetic quality arises in its relation to the sam. Saxena explains: an 'ideal emphasis on the Sama also occurs in terms of atīt-anāgat patterns. These are marked not by withholding the Sama-stroke entirely, but by making it fall purposely a little after or before the fixed location of the Sama-beat. In so far as the Sama, as played here, is in both cases "displaced" from its place in the cycle, these patterns are classed as *viṣam* [odd]' (1979: 85). In Ex. 3 (from Yādav 1992: 3.185), an anāgat tihāī in tīntāl, composed by three phrases of **kradhā ṭeṭe dhāge ṭeṭe dhā**, ends on the 16th beat, that is, one mātrā too early. In Ex. 4 (from Yādav 1992: 3.184), an atīt tihāī, at the end of a *tukṛa* piece, composed by three times **tiṭakata gadigana dhā**, ends one mātrā too late, that is, one beat after the sam. In his aesthetic of Hindustani rhythm, Saxena described these patterns as 'rhythm in a spirit of abandon' (1979: 63).

Example 3

Anāgat tihāī in tīntāl

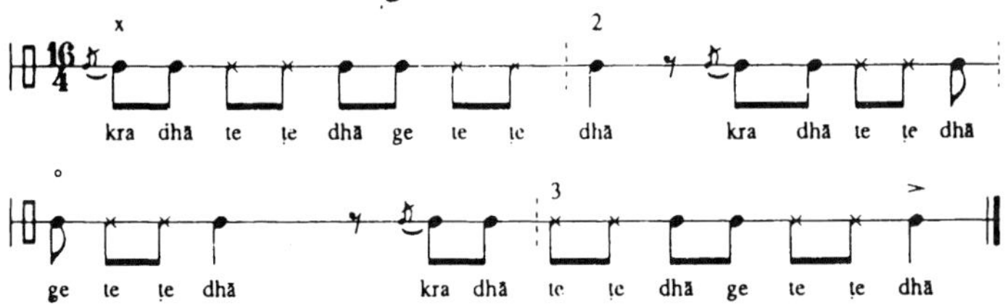

Example 4

Atīt tihāī in tīntāl

Rāga

Since the very first writings on Indian music by Western authors, there has been a preoccupation with understanding and explaining the concept of rāga. Jones, as early as 1784, translated rāga simply as mode (1990:

142). Willard, in 1834, recognized that a rāga has features of both mode and tune (1990: 64-66), and this is a view which has been refined by many authors. Stern wrote, in 1933, that 'The rāga is more fixed than the mode, and less fixed than the melody, beyond the mode and short of melody, and richer both than a given mode or a given melody. It is a mode with added multiple specialties' (in Gangoly 1989: 6). This notion was taken up by Powers, with the formulation: 'A rāga is not a tune, nor is it a "modal" scale, but rather a continuum with scale and tune as its extremes. Many rāgas can share the same intervallic structure, that is the same scale type (*mela*, *ṭhāṭ*); at the same time, any number of compositions or improvisations can be in the same rāga' (1980a: 98). Powers' definition has been accepted by several authors, among them Rowell (1992: 166) and Widdess (1995: 30). However, this model brings with it an idea of linearity – a continuum with two clear extremes – which does not cover other important features of the concept of rāga.

Another approach is the understanding of rāga as melodic type. Popley, around 1921, was perhaps the first to present this idea (see Gangoly 1989: 6). A similar conception would render it as ' "melody-mould," a "melody-type," or a "musical pattern" ' (Gangoly 1989: 4). In this formulation, rāga is seen as a type (that is, as a legisign), which presupposes that a rāga actualizes by means of tokens (or replicas). Powers described the type/token relationship of a rāga in these terms:

> If a rāga as a whole is a melodic type. then any particular manifestation of that type, whether precomposed or improvised, is a 'token' of a 'type'. Any 'token' of a given rāga – call it a tune – can be heard as series of connected motives and phrases, many (not necessarily all) of which will individually more or less strongly resemble many of the individual motives and phrases heard in any other tune in the same rāga (not necessarily coming in the same order). All mutually similar motives or phrases in different 'tokens' of a melodic type – a single rāga – may in turn be considered 'tokens' of a 'motivic type' or 'phrase type' proper of that rāga. (Powers 1976: 314)

Powers' clearly views rāga as a legisign which actualizes in the form of sinsigns. Saxena, who previously defined rāga as a type (1973: 7), later argued that a rāga can be understood as a matrix but not as a melodic type. He writes: 'A type is the concept of a class. It certainly covers or is applicable to all things of the same kind; but it obviously does not make or enter into the substance of these things' (1992: 10). This might be correct, as far as linguistic types or legisigns are concerned. Yet in music and other arts (including poetry), a type and its replica or token do participate in the presented materiality. At the core of this issue lies a confusion between the several overlapping kinds of signs. A rāga is at the same time a legisign, its replica or sinsigns, and their qualisigns. Its abstract character as a type does not have materiality, but a sign could not exist if it did not materialize in any way. This need not be a physical materialization, for a sign can actualize in someone's imagination. Saxena continues: 'a rāga may be said to be a matrix in the sense of being a ground-mass which is at once the necessary and pervasive condition, the material, and the regulative and individuating principle, of musical creation' (ibid.). If matrix is taken in the sense of ground-mass, it does include materiality in its generative power; however, in logical terms, the idea of promoting individuality is not consistent with that of mass. Besides, 'mass' connotes the idea of indistinct matter, and a rāga is a very clear set of legisigns. In fact, the definition of rāga as matrix still confuses the logical levels which characterize a rāga. Further, a possible and common understanding of matrix is as a 'mold'. In this case, it would signify the same range of meanings as type. The only difference I see between characterizing a rāga as matrix instead of type is the emphasis on the generative power that matrix implies (from the Latin, *māter*, mother). But it is necessary to distinguish the several logical constitutive parts of a rāga. This is clearly done when thinking of it in terms of semiosis, where the rāga's materiality is conceived as qualisign, and its individuality is the result of the action of sinsigns, which are replicas of the higher, regulative levels: the rāga as legisign. Moreover, the triad of qualisign, sinsign, and legisign makes explicit the structure of musical meaning and its interrelations.

The materiality that embodies a rāga when performed constitutes several layers of melodic legisigns that are actualized as sinsigns. The intervallic structure, the motifs and phrases, ornamentation, and so on are all constitutive legisigns of distinct levels of abstraction. The descriptions of rāgas, as presented by scholars such as V.N. Bhātkhaṇḍe (KPM), V.R. Paṭvardhan (RVJ) and O. Ṭhākur (SA), frequently use some of these legisigns to define the features of a particular rāga. Bhātkhaṇḍe developed the widely known system of ten ṭhāṭs, scale types, according to which rāgas are classified (see KPM 1.67-68; Nayar 1989: 141-46; Wade 1987: 80-81). The other two authors, however, prefer to deal individually with each rāga, recognizing the relationships among rāgas not solely in terms of an abstract parent scale. Another parameter, specially useful for classification of rāgas, is the concept of *jāti* (class), comprising *auḍava* (pentatonic), *ṣāḍava* (hexatonic) and *sampūrṇa* (heptatonic), plus their combinations in terms of *āroha* (ascent) and *avaroha* (descent). There are also other parameters, such as the definition of predominant degrees: *vādī* (speaker) and *samvādī* (co-speaker). The nomenclature and validity of these concepts are disputed by some scholars. Ṭhākur, for instance, refers to the modal functions as defined in classical Sanskrit treatises: *aṁśa* (predominant), *graha* (initial), *nyāsa* (final), *apanyāsa* (sub-final), and so forth. However they are denominated, it is important to conceive not too rigidly the emphasis that one or two pitches may have in a rāga, as Meer points out (1980: 4). Indeed, the individuality of rāgas is manifested by more musically specific legisigns. Those are the melodic motifs and phrases of various lengths and tessiturae, ranging in importance from fundamental to peripheral.

Melodic motives and phrases are not clearly classified in Hindustani music. A set of overlapping concepts includes the following: *pakaḍ* (catch phrase, distinctive melodic phrase that characterize a rāga), *calan* (a sketch demonstrating the main melodic patterns of a rāga), *mukhya svarūp* (brief outline of the melodic structure of a rāga), *mukhya aṅg* (principal component), *sargam* (a short composition without lyrics), *vistār* (elaboration, extension), and others. Most of these terms are thought as representing the essential features of particular rāgas, whereas vistār, for instance, refers to melodic development in general. All of them are legisigns of several levels, and the way they constitute the melodic habits, which conjointly form a rāga, can be seen in the following examples.

A transnotation of Bhātkhaṇḍe's descriptions of rāga mālkauṅs is presented in Ex. 5 (KPM 3.701-02). First of all, for this author, this rāga belongs to the ṭhāṭ of bhairavī, of which R̲ and P are omitted. The āroha/avaroha svarūp of the rāga shows that the ascent of the rāga should begin with the minor seventh N̲, and indicates also some resting degrees in both phases. The pakaḍ displays some of the essential motifs that characterize mālkauṅs. A sargam, a short composition in tīntāl, illustrates some more melodic movements. This sargam is, to some extent, more a didactic piece than a rāga description. Finally, Bhātkhaṇḍe gives a series of 15 svaravistārs (KPM 3.782-83), which progressively illustrate the melodic developments that can be performed in this rāga.

The āroha and avaroha of the same rāga given by Paṭvardhan has more details on the treatment of svaras (Ex. 6, RVJ 3.207). Two of them are ornamented in āroha; G̲ and D̲ are preceded by a kaṇ, a light touch, of M and N̲, respectively. The general aspect of the mukhya aṅg is different from Bhātkhaṇḍe's pakaḍ, but presents equally some of the essential motifs of mālkauṅs: the motif S M G̲, often performed with a mīṇḍ between S and M. This is only indirectly apparent in Bhātkhaṇḍe's pakaḍ, in which the first svara is M. Besides, there is also the cadence G̲MG̲S. Both Bhātkhaṇḍe and Paṭvardhan mention M as vādī and Ṡ as samvādī.

Example 5

Rāga mālkauṅs according to Bhātkhaṇḍe

Sargam

Svaravistārs

Example 6

Rāga mālkauṅs according to Paṭvardhan

In Ex. 7 are the features of mālkauṅs according to Ṭhākur (SA 3.129). In the mukhya aṅg, the motif SMG is very clear, and one more bit of information is given: G should be performed with an *āndolan*, G~. This oscillation is typical of mālkauṅs in slow-tempo movements. In terms of mālkauṅs' modal functions, for Ṭhākur, M is aṁśa, and also graha in the case of an *ālāp* (unmetered, progressive exposition of a rāga); N is graha when initiating a tān; and the final tone, or nyāsa, should also be M.

Example 7

Rāga mālkauṅs according to Ṭhākur

In describing mālkauṅs each author proposed a set of legisigns of varying scope. Bhātkhaṇḍe's ṭhāṭs are abstract to the point of being inconsistent in many cases with the rāgas they should classify (see Jairazbhoy 1971: 48). The āroha and avaroha scales are also general legisigns in defining a rāga. More concrete motifs and phrases appear in the pakaḍ, mukhya aṅg, calan, and the like, which are supposed to represent the essential character of a rāga. All these forms are, in some respect, legisigns of a rāga. But the descriptions they offer are always partial. It is rather when performed extensively, when a body of sinsigns materialize and develop the rāga legisigns, that the real character of the rāga appears. Some musicians were specially concerned with creating condensed forms that would unmistakably incorporate the overall legisign that a rāga is. Such is the case of Dilip C. Vedi, whose calans are short ālāp forms with two sections: *sthāyī* (permanent) and *antarā* (intermediate). Bor writes: 'D.C. Vedi makes a conscious effort to create an image of the rāga that is original, aesthetically pleasing and as complete and informative as possible. In a few ascending and descending phrases he is able to show three main aspects of rāga performance: how to begin, how to progress and how to end' (1984: 21). A calan is not a fixed composition. Vedi would sing a slightly different calan each time a calan was needed. In any case, each replica of the calan presented the essential features of the rāga. Therefore, a calan is a sign of a rāga, a representation of its legisigns in several layers, and as such, it is a symbol (see 2.3.2). The object it stands for is precisely a rāga in the broad sense. A calan composed by Vedi for rāga mālkauṅs is presented in Ex. 8.[18]

Example 8

A calan composed by Vedi for rāga mālkauṅs

The various melodic legisigns that constitute a rāga could be classified in terms of their importance in defining the core of a particular rāga. This is the view of S.S. Rao: 'First, there are some catch-phrases (pakaḍ) which define the core of a rāga and, secondly, there are complementary phrases constituting a periphery of the rāga-structure. The core phrases are among the essentials of rāga with almost definite structure and their presence is imperative, while the structure of the complementary phrases depend upon imagination, skill and style of the performer' (Rao 1992: 71). However, this dichotomic view seems inaccurate to me. In fact, there

[18] My transcription from a private tape, recorded by B. Bel and W. van der Meer.

are more than two levels of phrase organization in a rāga. A performer can create shades, mixing pakaḍs with other motives, in a graded scale of central and peripheral motives. Another factor which multiplies the melodic complexity of rāgas is the influence of the motives of other related rāgas, creating shades or shadows (*chāyā*), inserted in the performance of one rāga. Besides, not all rāgas have specific core motifs or phrases. Some rāgas are more flexible in this sense, say, being closer to the scale end than to the tune end of Powers' continuum, such as rāga haṅsadhvāni.

The complex compound of legisigns that ground a rāga, however dissociated in the analyst's or teacher's mind, must result effectively in a general principle that characterizes its individuality. After all, a rāga is not a bunch of disconnected motives and phrases, but an organic structure. This unity must be clear in any replication, that is, performance, of a rāga. In this sense, an individual rāga may be understood as a complex legisign, of a higher level than its constitutive, lower-level legisigns, and whose object is the *rāgabhāva*: 'Every rāga represents a musical entity, a tonal complex, pervaded by its own atmosphere. This is called rāgabhāva by the musicians' (Meer 1980: 110). The word *bhāva* (being, existence) refers to the character or quality of something. Bhāva is derived from the Sanskrit root *bhū*, become, arise, happen. Therefore, rāgabhāva is the manifested essence of a rāga. The semiotic status of the idea of rāgabhāva is that of a purely musical object, or the immediate object itself of a rāga.

Another semiotic question related to the rāgabhāva is the individuality of a particular rāga. The rāgabhāva of mālkauṅs is definitely distinct from the rāgabhāva of bhairav; and even rāga caṅdrakauṅs, which is close to mālkauṅs in many respects, has own specific rāgabhāva. The issue of musical individuality in Indian music is very peculiar, for the replicas of a rāga are variable within the boundaries of an individual rāga, but defined by its 'grammatical character', as Saxena writes. Thus, 'a rāga is limitless in spite of its being possessed of a specific individuality' (Saxena 1992: 10). The more legisigns two rāgas share, as a general pitch set, the more will be the need for specific motifs or other features to identify and distinguish one rāga from another. Thus, the degree of definition of dozens of rāgas in the music of North India will vary according to the number of rāgas set to the same, or similar, musical configurations.

In performance practice, the aim of the musician is to manifest the rāgabhāva. This is accomplished by the series of presented sinsigns, but a musician does not emphasize continuously the motifs and phrases that make evident the rāgabhāva. Such a performance would soon become too repetitive. A resource for enriching the replication of the legisigns of a rāga is the performance of phrases that are not central to the character of a rāga, although being correct sinsigns. Sometimes those neutral passages may even suggest another, related rāga, for the central motifs which differentiate them are still not clearly presented. The technique of elusive performance of a rāga is known in Hindustani music as *tirobhāv* (disappearance), as opposed to *āvirbhāv* (emergence), the clear presentation of the features of a rāga.[19] These procedures evoke the teleological aspect of a rāga in a way similar to that discussed above, in relation to the sam of a tāla. Indeed, the actions of legisigns which characterize a rāga are not pointless, but directed to the idea of signifying the rāgabhāva.

The aspect of individuality of rāgas, and of their dynamical and flexible mode of actualization, certainly brings forth the idea of rāga as living beings. Saxena, in view of these facts, conceived the idea of rāgas as 'euphorganisms,' that is, organic musical individuals (1973: 7-8). The life of rāgas are patent in several senses. First, since the first description of them by Mataṅga in the 9th century (BD), rāgas have been multiplying generation after generation. New rāgas were created, or transformed from folk and tribal tunes into the classical systems. At the same time, other rāgas became old and obsolete, though they were recognized by the scholars as parents and grandparents of the new, younger rāgas. Not surprisingly, between the 16th and 18th centuries, rāgas were classified in families, with a patriarchal leading male rāga, his wives and sons (see 3.3.4). Rāgas were combined with each other, and a number of subvarieties exists. Other new rāgas arose as offspring of the 'musical immigrants,' Persian modes transformed in rāgas, specially during the Mughal era. Rāgas have traveled from one tradition to another, in both directions: Karnatic rāgas were accepted and became popular in North India; conversely, Hindustani rāgas found a place in the South. In all those innovations, transformations, and mutations, life is the most remarkable characteristic of the development of Indian music structure.

Indeed, life is a distinctive feature of legisigns in general. Short stated: 'There are signs throughout nature, but there are legisigns only where there is life, and legisigns always exist in order to serve the purposes of living things. Conventional legisigns, created and manipulated by individuals in ways that constantly produce new meanings, are distinctive – perhaps constitutive – of the form of consciousness found in human life' (1982: 298-99). Rāgas were certainly created by human beings, and in this respect they reflect the luxuriant variety of life and culture in India. The semiosis of life and the semiosis of culture certainly depend on legisigns, their actualization as sinsigns, which present a richness of qualities. In another sense, however, it is not surprising that rāgas were considered to be individuals or deities. This personification reflects the amazing forms of life that rāgas are. Not only do they have their own

---

19 Examples of tirobhāv and āvirbhāv phrases in Powers 1980a: 111 (rāga pūriyā); Meer 1980: 111 (rāga lalita).

characters, but they also relate to each other, as a society of musical beings.

The interrelation of rāgas prompted scholars, since the early periods, to design classification systems, which have succeeded in different degrees. This is still a concern of many musicologists today, but the web of rāga legisigns is so entangled that a satisfactory classification has still not appeared. For Powers, the 'North Indian rāga system is a system of melodic types grouped in fields, and [...] the meaningfulness of a named rāga can be said to be based on the multiple relationships of its motives and phrases with those of other rāgas' (1976: 330). Powers' view of the interrelation of the several rāgas is clearly from a purely musical-meaning perspective; that is, he studies the musical sign in itself. However, rāgas are not only purely musical structures, for they are also representamens which cover a great scope of non-musical objects. This has been recognized by Indian authors since the earliest treatises. Thus, any comprehensive view of rāgas must take in account those other levels of musical semiosis, be they called musical reference or musical aesthetics. But this is the subject of the next chapter and the following section.

Form

An important field of legisigns in music is that of forms, genres, and styles. An exhaustive semiotic study of these issues is beyond the scope of this section. In Hindustani music, there are at least three fundamental vocal forms: dhrupad, khayāl, and ṭhumrī.[20] Each of these comprises some related minor forms, such as *dhamār*, *tarānā*, *tappā*, and so on. Instrumental music usually follows the structure of one of the vocal music forms, but it has its own particularities. Moreover, there is a rich area of studies in drumming, both on pakhāvaj and tablā.[21]

The first formal structure to be considered is the ālāp, which can be unmetered in dhrupad, or metered in the vilambit khayāl (also called *bolālāp*).[22] The distinction between the two forms of ālāp is exposed as early as the SR: '*Ālapti* is the vocalization of rāga which is considered to be (the process of) manifesting it. That is said to be qualified by *rāga[ālapti]* and *rūpaka[ālapti]*' (SR 3.189c-190b). Rāgālapti is the improvisation rendered independently of a composition (rūpaka), that is, without lyrics and free from the bounds of tāla. Conversely, rūpakālapti is the improvisation based on the framework of tāla, presenting and developing a composition. Each kind has internal divisions, which can still be found in contemporary forms, although not strictly corresponding

---

20 There are several studies of varying depth on these forms. For dhrupad, see Meer 1980: 30-49; Srivastava 1980; Perera 1994; on khayāl, see Meer 1980: 50-70; Wade 1971 and 1984; for ṭhumrī see Manuel 1989.

21 For studies on tablā drumming see Kippen 1988, 1992a and 1992b.

22 Except for a very short unmetered introduction, preceding the bolālāp of a khayāl.

to Śārṅgadeva's. Besides those formal legisigns of ālāp, the quotation above brings once more the important issue of actualizing a rāga. To perform an ālāp is to replicate rāga legisigns, in such way as to manifest the rāga. Saxena says: 'The true aesthetic warrant of ālāpa, I believe, is its unmatched power to produce such effects as those of grandeur, serenity, seamlessness and infinity; and to evoke an intense yet identifiable rāga-atmosphere' (1992: 6). Indeed, the progressive exposition of a rāga during the performance of ālāp, instills, by means of continuous and constantly evolving melodic movements, the rāga's essence or rāgabhāva.

The legisigns of musical compositions embed the structures of, and at the same time define, tāla and rāga. Thus, on one hand, a bandiś (structure), as a composition, is arranged according to a particular tāla and rāga, to which the lyrics are set. An instrumental composition, or *gat*, is similarly organized. On the other hand, all compositions in the same rāga are legisigns, which establish the very rāga they represent. Saxena writes: 'A good composition (or bandiś), be it a Khayāl or Dhruvapada one, projects the rāga as a single and easily identifiable wholeness' (1992: 11). Most of the compositions feature two sections:[23] sthāyī and antarā. They constitute not only divisions of the lyrics (in vocal music), but configure different stages of the rāga presentation in a metered form. In the sthāyī, the very first phrase is an important legisign. It is called *mukhṛā* (diminutive of face), and signify the essential features of the rāga, as well as representing the essence of the bandiś itself. Usually the mukhṛā has the length of one āvart, having a cyclic designed melody. The phrases of the sthāyī, including the mukhṛā, are composed around the *pūrvāṅga*, the lower tetrachord. The antarā, conversely, represents a contrast and is developed in the *uttarāṅga*, the higher tetrachord, defining the high tonic, Ṡ. In Hindustani music, being actually assembled at the very time of performance, the function of a bandiś's sthāyī and antarā is not that of constituting the whole. They rather serve as fixed components with which the musician plays, creating improvised variations according to the rāga, tāla and the elements of the composition. Deshpande defines this relation as the variable and the constant parts of musical form (1987: 33). The mukhṛā is the basic constant component that is alternated with variable improvised phrases.

Finally, the improvisation techniques of each form are also legisigns, in the sense of being habits of musical development, which actualize in sinsigns, as discussed above. Hindustani musical forms and genres constitute, in fact, a broad field of studies, of which some important forms, such as the dhrupad, have been poorly investigated.

---

23 A dhrupad can have up to four sections.

2.3.2 Musical Reference

> Mālavakaiśika is derived from kaiśiki jāti, has ṣaḍja for its initial, fundamental and the final notes, and takes the weak dhaivata and *kākalī*:[1] Its *mūrcchana*[2] is ṣaḍja, it (is embellished by) *prasanna-madhya alaṅkāra*[3] in the ascending *varṇa*[4] and is employed in the sentiments of valour, wrath, bewilderment and love in separation, and is sung in the last quarter of the day in winter to the endearment of Viṣṇu. (SR 2.70d-73a)

The main question orienting the inquiry of this chapter is the means by which a musical sign refers to its dynamical object. The subject is organized according to the triad of icon, index, symbol. However, the diversity of the modes of reference in music requires a more specific categorization than the general ideas represented by the most well known of the Peircean trichotomies. Thus, I will make use of internal divisions in the concept of iconic sign (which Peirce also called hypoicons); similarly, I propose a division for the several kinds of indices, a distinction which Peirce suggested but did not develop to the same extent as he did the iconic signs. Symbols may also be distinguished among themselves, but this seems to be less important in music than is the finer division of icons and indices. An equivalent logical basis for these subdivisions of the second trichotomy can be found in the architecture of the ten classes of signs. Probably, these divisions would not be necessary here if, instead of my employing the triad of icon, index, and symbol, the ten classes were used. For instance, the three levels of hypoicons – images, diagrams, and metaphors – are all iconic legisigns, which, when materialized, constitute iconic and indexical sinsigns. However, since the second trichotomy is much better known than the ten classes of signs, it might, at this stage, be clearer to proceed to the analysis, by exploring the heuristic capacity the second trichotomy can offer.

Another question in the field of musical reference is that concerning the nature of objects to which music refer. Yet it seems useless to me, to list objects represented in music. A general tendency in musical semiotics is to divide dynamical objects into those that are musical and those that

[1] A major seventh. Corresponds to the śuddh N in contemporary Hindustani music.
[2] A rotation of the basic scale.
[3] A kind of ornament.
[4] Melodic movement in this context.

are non-musical (or extra-musical). Yet this division also seems not very useful. It depends on what is considered music or not, which is a critical question in many cultures. Even if this distinction could be clearly established, the class of non-musical objects is very indefinite. Objects can certainly be divided according to whether they are acoustic or non-acoustic. But this seems to be a secondary problem, for the references and representations music produces are without doubt deeply rooted in a particular culture. This is a voluminous issue in any musical system. Thus, it will not the objective of this chapter to present an extensive study of dynamical objects in Hindustani music. I am rather concerned in presenting the semiotic tools used in Hindustani music, and thus the dynamical objects discussed here are merely illustrative. Dynamical objects referred to in Hindustani music will be discussed in the context of Indian aesthetics, or rasa theory (section 3).

The question of reference in music should be understood as a field that encompasses that of intrinsic musical semiosis. That is, in general terms, icons are also qualisigns; indices are sinsigns; and symbols are legisigns. Musical reference focuses on the relation between sign and dynamic object. Thus, musical signs, whether they are icons, indices, or symbols, relate to their dynamical object and final interpretant each in a particular way. Peirce wrote:

> A regular progression of one, two, three may be remarked in the three orders of signs, Icon, Index, Symbol. The Icon has no dynamical connection with the object it represents; it simply happens that its qualities resemble those of that object, and excite analogous sensations in the mind for which it is a likeness. But it really stands unconnected with them. The index is physically connected with its object; they make an organic pair, but the interpreting mind has nothing to do with this connection, except remarking it, after it is established. The symbol is connected with its object by virtue of the idea of the symbol-using mind, without which no such connection would exist. (CP 2.299)

Furthermore, it is necessary to make clear that the three modes of representation are not isolated fields. Ransdell warned that 'It is of the first importance for understanding Peirce's icon-index-symbol trichotomy to bear in mind [...] that the entity functioning as sign is capable of bearing and usually does bear all three semiotic functions at once' (1977: 174). Thus, a logical hierarchy grounds the interdependence of the trichotomy. Namely, the icon (as a First) is the most independent. The index comprehends the icon; that is, every index has an icon or icons as part of it. The symbol comprehends the index, and consequently, the icon too. Although they are clearly distinct in their mode of referring to an object, icon, index, and symbol are concepts that have all derived from the relations between sign and dynamic object. This is the grounding of the second trichotomy. One could take these words of Peirce as highly relevant to music: 'the most perfect of signs are those in which the iconic, indicative, and symbolic characters are blended as equally as possible' (CP 4.448).

2.3.2.1 Icons and iconic signs in music

The representation of possible acoustic or non-acoustic objects in music, referred to only by (in some respect) similar properties shared between them, occurs by means of the action of icons. According to Peirce's concept of icon, this kind of sign refers to the object that it denotes merely by virtue of attributes the sign possess, be they whatever kind of qualities, existents, shapes, forms, habits, laws, and the like:

> An ***Icon*** is a sign which refers to the Object that it denotes merely by virtue of characters of its own, and which it possesses, just the same, whether any such Object actually exists or not. It is true that unless there really is such an Object, the Icon does not act as a sign; but this has nothing to do with its character as a sign. Anything whatever, be it quality, existent individual, or law, is an Icon of anything, in so far as it is like that thing and used as a sign of it. (CP 2.247)

The notion of icon, though simple, has far-reaching significance. J. Ransdell writes: 'An *icon* is any possible qualitative content of consciousness – what Peirce calls a "Firstness" – considered in respect to its possible function in cognition as the form (that is, quality or character) *of* an actual or possible object. An *iconic* sign ("hypoicon") is anything whatever which does or can function as a sign in virtue of its embodiment of some icon proper' (1979: 55). Peirce's notion of the icon has two important and intermingled sides: that of pure icon, and that of iconic signs. The pure icon (or qualisign) is the kind of representamen which is closest to the category of firstness. The action of a pure icon is characterized by identity among the three relata – sign, object and interpretant united by a quality or a pure form. The universe is full of possibilities that can work as pure icons. Besides, everything can be an iconic sign, as Ransdell explains: 'everything whatsoever, insofar as it is like anything else, is a potential iconic sign. And this means that everything is a potential iconic sign, since everything is always at least like itself' (Ransdell 1966: 150). Further, an iconic sign embodies a pure icon: 'in every case of an iconic sign relation there will be a point of formal identity – i.e. there will be a pure icon in common to the terms of the sign relation – which constitutes the similarity or "iconicity" which grounds that relation' (Ransdell 1966: 149). What might at first sound tautological here has deep meaning in music and leads to a bifurcation: on the one hand, music as a pure, non-referential language of sounds; and, on the other, the enormous power of musical mimicry.

Pure music as the semiosis of icons

> No pure Icons represent anything but Forms; no pure Forms are represented by anything but Icons. (CP 4.544)

Before any kind of imitation or other mode of reference, music has a special autonomous property. Although musical signification can be accomplished formally by several semiotic means, it is always the material, acoustic features that set up the initial level of semiosis. The first kind of reference submits to the icon and generates only icons.

The controversial question of musical autonomy can be understood as the action of the icon. The object of a musical sign, at least its immediate object, firstly concerns sound qualities. Peirce said that 'a pure icon does not draw any distinction between itself and its object. It represents whatever it may represent, and whatever it is like, it in so far is. It is an affair of suchness only' (CP 5.74). Music may represent something other than its own materiality, by several modes of reference. Yet a musical sign could also be just those sound qualities, and that is enough to give birth to a musical interpretant. In that case, there is no distinction between sign and object. The musical sign will not lack musical status or cognitive coherence if its signification (interpretant) relates only to sound qualities. Such a condition is proper of music.

It is not necessary, for instance, to know the structural, cultural or aesthetic meanings implied in a dhamār composed in rāga bahār, such as *Horī khelata sirī Mohana* (KPM 4.644), to listen to and enjoy a performance of this composition. Musical semiosis will take place even without that knowledge. In the same way, it is possible to listen to, as pure music, a recording of an Inuit vocal play, without any knowledge of its ethnic contexts or its aesthetic or functional purposes. It will always be music. One could claim, of course, that that is a kind of surface listening, but this is not the question here. Furthermore, having open ears to enjoy pure acoustic qualities, pure flow of sounds, is not so facile or natural. It requires high mental availability and freedom from prejudices.

Thus, the contention here is that, since any kind of musical sign is preliminarily an icon, then nothing more than its own acoustic qualities are necessary for the accomplishment of musical meaning, or better, musical semiosis. The first instance of musical representation is at the pure icon level: music as icon of itself, which, from this point of view, is just 'an affair of suchness'.

This is true of all musics, but music as 'suchness' leads most directly to the idea of absolute music. One can trace aspects of this idea in Europe throughout the centuries: Aristoxenus (4th century BC), Charles Burney (18th century), Eduard Hanslick (19th century), and in the 20th century, conceptions of music ranging from those of Igor Stravinsky and Pierre Boulez to those of John Cage. There would be little significance in dealing with those authors in the context of Hindustani music, since their ideas and theories refer necessarily to musical conceptions and to a cultural milieu very alien to the Indian ones. Surprisingly, some Indian scholars (see Deshpande 1987, Goswami 1995) seem to be influenced by the very Western, music-specific aesthetics of Hanslick,[5] for instance,

[5] Who wrote the famous book, *The Beautiful in Music*, first published in 1854, in reference to 19th-century European tonal music, opposing in particular the operatic ideas of Richard Wagner.

which they apply to Indian music unaware of the referential universe Hanslick's ideas come from.

In this respect, it would be better to refer to some contemporary Western composers, who have a much broader musical view. Boulez, for instance, writes: 'Music is an art that has no "meaning": hence the primary importance of structures that are properly speaking linguistic, given the impossibility of the musical vocabulary assuming a simply communicative function' (1986: 32). It is clear that Boulez has a linguistic paradigm in mind, and what he means by 'meaning' is far more restricted than the Peircean idea of semiosis, which encompasses the action of icons as well as those of indices and symbols. Of course, even absolute music can generate interpretants, which range from emotional to logical. Thus, there is always meaning in music, from a Peircean point of view. Still, Boulez's statement that in music ' "word" and idea are identical' (ibid.) nears the semiotic formulation of pure icon as an entity wherein the relation between sign and object is based on total identity, and music under this point of view is absolute music.

Another instance of a musical conception based on the semiosis of pure icons is that of John Cage. Notice how technically different are the actual musical systems (sets of legisigns) dealt with by those composers: the integral serialism of Boulez, and the aleatorism of Cage. Yet, Cage seems to value as highly the importance of pure icons in music as does Boulez, although Cage does not direct his ideas to syntactic structures: 'In my opinion, listening is listening to each sound. If you listen to the relationship, you lose those sounds' (Cage in Kostelanetz 1988: 200). That is probably the most radical conception of absolute music. It concerns not primarily musical constructs but, rather, *sounds*. In his *Silence*, Cage stated that 'To obtain the value of a sound, a movement [i.e., in dance], measure from zero. (*Pay attention to what it is, just as it is.*)' (1961: 96, my emphasis). Anything that is just what it is can only be a quality (free, a mere possibility); thus, it is a qualisign and, in relation to its dynamical object, a pure icon. It is paradigmatic that chance, an important element in Cage's compositions, is a distinctive feature of firstness. In this sense, Cage's famous silent composition, *4'33''*, is not a conceptual piece but a physical work (cf. Cage in Kostelanetz 1988: 206). What is sought in *4'33''* is the materiality of every possible sound as an aesthetic entity, admirable in itself. Moreover, Cage's ideas, far from pertaining only to his musical thought, have important consequences:

> If I want 'life as art', I risk falling into aestheticism, because I would appear to be trying to impose something, a certain idea of life. It appears to me that music – such as I envision it, at least – imposes nothing. It can effectively change our manner of seeing, making us view everything around us as art. But that is not the goal! Sounds have no goal! They are, and that's all. They live. Music is this life of sounds, this participation of sounds in life, which may become – but not voluntarily – a participation of life in sounds. In itself, music does not obligate us to anything. (Cage & Charles 1981: 87)

Cage's conception of music is broad enough to encompass every kind of acoustic semiosis as focused on the qualitative feature of its materiality. The greatness of this point of view is its ultimate refusal of any kind of musical ethnocentrism or musical prejudice. If every acoustic event can be music, then, consequently, all musics are music, and all are respectable and worth listening to. It is simply up to the listeners to be permeable enough (at least) to pure icons. Absolute music, however, is restricted almost totally to Western culture, though one finds other occurrences, as in shakuhachi flute-playing in the Zen school of Fuke (see Gutzwiller 1984: 57-58) and in Hindustani solo drumming.

Any genre of Hindustani music can be listened to as pure music, but the musical sign in India is so saturated with significations, which unfold in the listener's mind, generating interpretant after interpretant, that it is not generally very prone to semiosis at the pure icon level. Nonetheless, there are some interesting instances which might be considered here. One of these is an aspect of the ancient Vedic chants. Buitenen writes:

> The sacred quality of the Veda prevents it from being considered, in the Indian tradition, as literature. To the ritualists, even the poetry of the *Ṛg-veda* and the *Atharva-veda* was reduced to mere recitation, where sound was more important than meaning. The veda is considered mantra: lines that at particular sacrifices have to be recited in this way or that by certain priests whose hereditary business it is to know which lines to recite and when – and not to know what they mean. (in Dimock et al. 1974: 47)

Aside from the functional aspect of the Vedic ritual, which introduces other modes of semiosis, there is a component of pure icon in the idea of mantra. In the same way, Buitenen considers that, in a sense, Vedas are not literature, for the sounds of the words are more important than their meaning; it is also true that sound in itself is the most significative element in Vedic chant, when the priest concentrates merely on reciting them.

Gāndharva, the sacred store of early Indian music, as understood by Lath (1978, 1988a), is closely related to the pure icon aspect of Vedic chant. The *Dattilam*, a concise treatise on svara, tāla and forms (*gītakas* and *gītis*), written by Dattila no later than the 2nd century A.D., can be considered a dissertation on pure (absolute) music. In it one finds only technical discussions of music. Except for a few references to the attainment of religious merit by the practice of music, there is no concern with musical structures as related to the hours of the day, seasons, folk-tunes, deities, rasa, and other topics which abound in the NŚ, and in later treatises such as the BD and SR. Even the song text is treated in the D from a purely acoustical perspective. Lath writes: '*Pada* in language is understood as a meaningful syllable or string of syllables. But in gāndharva many strings of syllables were used which had no meaning: such as "*diṅgle*", *jhaṇtum*", "*titijhala*", "*kucajhala*", etc. (which are analogous to our "*nom-tom*")' (1988a: 68). In fact, the use of meaningless syllables in contemporary vocal music narrows the modes of semiosis, which could be that of pure music in the ālāp, if the listener dissociates the existential references and the several kinds signification most of the rāgas convey. However, the concept of gāndharva does preclude meaning that is not purely musical. For example, the 18 jātis are defined in the D solely in terms of their inner acoustic relations (D 48-90a), whereas in the NŚ several kinds of acoustic and non-acoustic reference are attached to them (see 3.3.1).

In contemporary Hindustani music, the most outstanding form of pure music is drumming, either on the pakhāvaj or on the tablā. Aside from some very special forms of composition that can refer to dynamic objects other than musical materiality (such as the *paran*), most solo drumming presents only the qualities of the strokes used on those instruments, the textures and metric organization of the tālas, and the mathematical order of the compositions as well as their forms of variation and development. Saxena is keen on identifying this musical purity in drumming: 'If rhythm neither represents nor expresses life-content, how is it at all significant? My ready answer is that it charms us by its very "look," like beautiful objects of nature which are not ordinarily said to symbolize, express or embody anything' (1979: 17). What Saxena mentions here can be understood in semiotic terms as reference, or representation, which signifies the apparent qualities and forms presented by the percussionist. That is, the musical sign stands for nothing more than the very sounds which constitute the sign itself. As such, there is identity between sign and object, and thus this is the purest form of iconic representation, or better, an icon proper. The interpretant of the icon is necessarily a rheme, 'a sign which is understood to represent its object in its characters merely' (CP 2.252).

Iconic Signs in Music

Iconic signs appear in complex and variegated forms in music. Thus, to employ iconicity properly as an analytic tool, one should consider the divisions of the concept of icon: pure, actual, and hypoicons (see Santaella 1989; and 1991: 136-37). Besides pure and actual icons, hypoicons in music are extremely important. An iconic sign or a hypoicon 'represents its object mainly by its similarity, no matter what its mode of being' (CP 2.276). Music can represent many phenomena iconically; and every musical culture in the world has made use of this mode of representation. Music can imitate other sounds; music can represent several types of movement and forms. And this capacity of music asks for detailed divisions:

> Hypoicons may be roughly divided according to the mode of Firstness of which they partake. Those which partake of simple qualities, or First Firstnesses, are ***images***; those which represent the relations, mainly dyadic, or so regarded, of the parts of one thing by analogous relations in their own parts, are ***diagrams***; those which represent the representative

> character of a representamen by representing a parallelism in something else, are ***metaphors***. (CP 2.277)

Images, diagrams, and metaphors can also be referred to as hypoicons of first, second, and third level, respectively. A musical image represents its object by likeness to that object's appearance qualities. Musical mimicry, in the sense of musical onomatopoeias, are images, as are recordings, electronic synthesis and samplings. Concerning diagrams: melodies, rhythmic patterns, forms or acoustic structures (especially their features of motion) can refer to other, similar forms, whether sonorous or not. Music as diagram can represent elements of the cosmos, of the environment, or of human psychophysiology. Finally, musical metaphors are complex imputations of related significations, whose more familiar idea is that of musical metalanguage. The subject may be summarized as follows:

Musical Hypoicons:
- Image
- Diagram
    - Representation by likenesses on movement qualities
    - Representation by likenesses on formal qualities
- Metaphor
    - Paraphrase
    - Quotation
    - Allegorical Reference.

Musical Images

The most elementary mode of musical representation is grounded on likeness in *acoustic qualities* between sign and object. Musical images necessarily imply a sound or sound complex, which, by resemblance with another acoustical form, becomes an iconic sign of the latter. In most cultures the musical universe is usually more or less distinct from the non-musical sonorous universe, and this is also true in India. Iconic representations (images) of the first universe in relation to the second will always be imitations or reproductions of 'non-musical' acoustic qualities by means of musical devices. Images include sounds of nature, such as bird calls, rain, thunder, and sounds produced by man, in rural, urban, domestic or industrial environments.

Hindustani music abounds in images, which usually reinforce an idea expressed by the lyrics. These signs can last as short as a few mātrās and rarely extend to a complete āvart. They also vary in their degree of fidelity in relation to the referred-to objects, sometimes being closer to a diagram than a proper image, or combining the two kinds of representation. Musical images are often not taken seriously in Hindustani music, as is the case with modulations of the bāyāṇ that mimic something in a tablā solo: 'Kanthe Maharaj, according to his disciple Shital Prasad Misra, used modulations as a kind of deliberate musical joke: imitating the roaring of lions' (Kippen 1988: 95). Yet, when appropriate to the aesthetic context of a bandiś, an image can be very effective in enhancing the listener's interpretants, as in the khayāl *Jhanana jhanana* (RVJ 1.10-11), in rāga chāyānaṭ. In this piece, the jingling of a lady's ankle bells (*bichuvā*) is represented onomatopoeically by the lyrics (jhanana) and the music. This is accomplished by repetitive svaras, over which the text is set syllabically, by the interval of a fourth between the first and second words, and by some simple, progressive melodic motifs in thirds (Ex. 9). The song refers to a bride who is about to leave her parents' house on the day of her marriage. Done worshipping, she now prays on the ornamented square of flour (*caukā*), where the wedding ceremonies take place. The lyrics translate as follows:[6]

Jhanana jhanana, tinkle the ankle bells,
I have left my house to meet my beloved.
I come out of my dwelling to do pūjā,
In the *caukā* [ceremonial square] – says Inayat –
Again and again, I was the only woman.

Example 9

Khayāl *Jhanana jhanana* (RVJ 1.10-11)

6 My translation.

A culturally important element in the rainy season is the call of the cuckoos, which are considered a symbol of love. Many compositions in rāgas related to the rains present images of bird song. Often the melodic mimicry is set exactly to the Braj word for the black cuckoo: *koyala*, or its bird-song onomatopoeia, *kūka kūka*. Several instances of these images are shown in Ex. 10 (RVJ 4.41-42, 4.47-48; KPM 4.589-91, 6.277-78, 6.290-91), all related to rāgas of the malhār group.

Example 10

Images of bird song (cuckoo)

These examples, though presenting different musical images of bird song, nevertheless refer to their object fittingly. Such congruence is due, of course, to the image *modus operandi*. Although conventional in some respects, the imitations do have melodic and rhythmic features that are in common with real bird calls. Moreover, this kind of musical representation can also be regarded as homage to the primeval music teachers of human beings – birds. Indeed, according to the ornitho-musicological view: 'birds evolved elaborate musical utterances long before the appearance of man, who may be supposed to have derived his primitive music under the instigation or, at any rate, influence of their song' (Sebeok 1981: 222). This contention is reasonable, not only because 'man and bird share certain requisite physiological foundations: both sense the world most consequentially by optical means, and both address it most saliently by acoustic means' (ibid.), but also because human beings and some bird species have the capacity for acoustic mimicry, that is, the ability to apprehend and reproduce iconic signs.

Besides these images inserted in compositions, there is a whole field of iconic representations actualized by musicians when they are developing a rāga. 'Thunder and lightning in a monsoon song will be expressed through heavy gamakas, uneasiness by a *murkī*.[7] It is however difficult to go much further as most of the feelings in the text are embodied in the expressive qualities of the voice' (Meer 1980: 91). Indeed, the capacity for vocal flexibility in Hindustani music is such that a variety of iconic and diagrammatical representations are possible. But this is found at the performing level, rather than in the compositions. Some genres were specially prone to using iconic signs, produced by vocal effects and ornaments. In the bandiś ṭhumrī of Lucknow (as performed at the end of 19th and beginning of the 20th century), besides the techniques of bolbāṅṭ and bolbanāo, there were the '*nakhrā* ("blandishments, coquetries") in which the singer employed histrionic gestures (often stylized into mimetic *abhināya*), sobbing-like vocal effects, and dramatic changes of vocal dynamics' (Manuel 1986: 478). Certainly the kind of images produced by the nakhrā depended also on the context for their efficiency as representations.

In fact, there is an important point to be made clear in this respect. No iconic sign, being merely analogous to its object, can unmistakenly assert the reference. The interpretation is rather a *possibility* of reference, subject to the interpreter's capacity or will to understand it as such. Ransdell writes:

> an object is not an actual iconic sign of anything until it has been referred to that thing *as* an iconic sign of it. *A*'s resemblance to *B* does not make *A* an actual iconic sign of *B*, though it does make it a potential iconic sign of *B*. To say that *A* is a potential iconic sign of *B* is simply to say that *A* could legitimately function as an actual sign of *B*, the legitimacy being grounded in the form (quality, character) which *A* and *B* both exhibit. (1979: 56)

Indeed, iconic signs have great potential for reference, but this does not mean something is necessarily an iconic sign of such and such an object to which it happens to be similar. Moreover, Ransdell continues, 'this is independent of any causal relation in which *A* might or might not stand to *B* ' (ibid.). That is, any sinsign can potentially refer to something else iconically, although the existential or causal relation grounding that sign as a sinsign becomes irrelevant.

Musical images do not only concern nature or events of social life. The mechanical world is also represented as iconic musical signs; for example,

---

[7] A short grace note, acciaccatura.

the sounds of a locomotive. Saxena informs us that a 'drummer can produce some patterns of syllables that resemble everyday sounds and familiar happenings, such as the movement and noise of a train as it steams out and gathers speed' (1992: 16). During my period of tablā training with Probir Mittra in New Delhi, he demonstrated a few times this kind of composition.[8] The representation is very accurate: the music moves in a slow tempo at the beginning, referring to the start of a journey, accelerates as the train speeds up, slows down at the end – all of which are diagrams. Yet the composition goes even further, and uses images: strokes and motifs that are images of the sounds a locomotive makes when the tracks are on solid ground, represented by series of closed strokes (**dhereketẹ dhereketẹ**); and the different resonance when the train crosses over a bridge, represented by open – resonating – strokes (**dhīnṛadhīn- dhīnṛadhīn-**), and so on. Mittra was emphatic, however, in stating that this kind of piece was used by his Ustād (Afaq Husain Khan, 1930-1990) only as light entertainment for the lay public who could not appreciate the pure music of a tablā solo. In fact, as Saxena concludes, 'whenever this is attempted, those who look at rhythm as an art only feel amused' (ibid.). It seems, however, that more and more this is becoming a standard item on percussion concerts in India, for drummers as famous as Zakir Husain, when performing for large audiences, often resort to compositions presenting images and diagrams of non-acoustical objects.

Musical diagrams

Diagrams are used widely in music. Highly flexible as representamens, diagrams do not resemble their objects as directly as Images do. Diagrammatic representation is instead a kind of structural analogy: 'although there be no sensuous resemblance between it and its object, but only an analogy between the relations of the parts of each' (CP 2.279). In this kind of iconic representation it is not similarity of qualities of appearance that grounds the representation. Thus, a musical diagram of a river does not present the sounds of running water. Since the reference is made by structural analogy of movements, shapes or forms, what would be represented by a musical diagram of a river is the undulations of waves, in the form of matching melodic patterns. The waves of a river and the undulations of a melodic line have isomorphic movements, the shifting of water and the succession of pitches thus present the same dynamical configuration. Therefore, the dynamical object and the immediate object of a diagrammatic sign correspond in some respect.

Musical diagrams are apt to represent a much wider variety of objects than images do. The onomatopoeic nature of images limits its objects to the same sensory domain. That is, musical images can only refer to acoustic features of phenomena. Conversely, diagrams can refer to any

[8] My recording on April 24, 1995, in New Delhi.

aspect of their objects. Here, I shall consider two paradigmatic cases of representation: by *movement likeness* and by *formal likeness*. Qualities of movement are present in a variety of instances in Hindustani music. Formal likenesses concern basically the ideas of speculative music.

In the application of music to Sanskrit drama, as prescribed by Bharata in the NŚ, there is frequent resort to diagrams, both in the *dhruvās*, songs to be performed during a scene, and in instrumental music, including drumming. In chapter 32, on dhruvās, one reads about songs that signify different kinds of movement:

> In the case of chariots, horses, elephants, deer, birds, palanquins and aerial cars, the experts should make Dhruvās with a view to their movement and progress. In the case of chariots, arrows, horses, elephants, heavenly cars, swings and birds as vehicles, the expert should compose the Dhruvās with words and syllables that can be uttered quickly. In the case of bulls, elephants, lions and bears, the Dhruvā should be made up of heavy syllables that can be uttered with force. In the case of crows, monkeys, swans, and peacocks, the Dhruvās should be made up of light syllables with swift movement, and of heavy syllables, with their slowness. This being the case, one should apply swift [Dhruvās] after knowing the states [*bhāvas*] [connected with them]. (NŚ 32.428-31)

The movement of animals, vehicles, and devices such as arrows and flying chariots should be represented by a dhruvā with features diagrammatically similar to the qualities of movements of the represented objects. This is accomplished by the slow flow of notes and heavy attacks, or by light and swift notes, and so on. Those forms of signs should also be in accord with the mood of the scene in question. In the chapter on drumming, Bharata indicates how to represent the movement of vehicles, be they earthly ones, such as chariots and boats, or celestial vehicles: 'In the case of movements of boats, chariots and aerial cars, and moving heavenly bodies, the playing of drums should be by running the fingers [on the face of the drums] or by striking on the *Catuṣka* [9] by the two hands alternatively' (NŚ 33.232). This technique suggests that a sort of roll should be played on the drums. In this case, the roll refers to the continuity of movement of the signified objects on an iconic basis. It seems that all these forms of iconic signs were very important in the classical Sanskrit drama, for the play was quite conventional in its dramatic means. The hierarchy of characters was clearly signified with musical symbols, which should announce their entrance on stage; but iconic musical signs were very important as well, for instance, in referring to the character's gait. Thus, the walking style of characters, which accorded with their social status and physical condition, was similarly represented by the stage music (see NŚ 33.130-69).

---

[9] A kind of early Indian drum.

Another interesting passage in the NŚ prescribes the use of instruments to represent iconically a dramatic situation of great noise, or conversely, a quiet domestic scene:

> In a festival, a royal procession, and a Maṅgala ceremony, on an auspicious and happy occasion, at the time of marriage and of birth of sons, etc., in a battle where many fighters assemble, and during such acts, all the musical instruments should be played. A small number of instruments are to be played during ordinary [lit., 'natural'] household affairs. During expeditionary marches and performances of plays, all the instruments should be played. (NŚ 33.19-21)

The musical parameter involved here is that of intensity. Thus, the representation of scenes that naturally would be noisy requires maximum power from the orchestra; conversely, quiet scenes should be illustrated by few instruments. All those musical signs, frequently used in the classical Sanskrit play, probably influenced Indian court and temple music, whose early forms are directly related to the drama. This is evident as late as the SR, in which some melodic patterns are classified clearly according to iconic references. *Sthāya* is the term Śārṅgadeva uses to designate these melodic patterns: 'Sthāya is an organic component of rāga' (SR 3.97c).

The verses on sthāya in the SR classify melodic phrases, 96 in number, to be used in the development of a rāga. Several species of sthāyas present interesting iconic signs. The sthāya called *dhāla* presents notes in 'a rolling movement like that of a pearl' (SR 3.113ab). *Gati* are sthāyas with majestic movements, resembling the gait of an 'intoxicated elephant' (3.129c-130a). *Lalita* 'is sportive' (3.147b). *Lulita*, rolled, is characterized by 'softness and a swinging movement' (3.147cd). *Vaha* is the pattern in which the notes tremble, as someone oppressed by a burden (*vahantaḥ*) (3.152ab). *Taraṅgita* is the sthāya, the svaras of which 'move like the waves of the Ganges' (3.153cd). *Salambita* is the pattern played in such a way as 'to sound like the swirling of water in a half-filled jar' (3.154). *Troṭita* is the sthāya performed by the player's touching slightly the octave of a note and then leaving it quickly, as if touching a flame and instinctively jerking back the hand (3.155d-156b). *Pratigrāhyollāsita* is the pattern in which notes are thrown up and caught back again, as if one were playing with a ball (3.157c-158b). *Vakra* is a twisted pattern (3.171d).

It seems that most of these sthāyas were melodic and rhythmic diagrams of the suggested movements. Sadly, Śārṅgadeva does not give notated musical examples of them, which would permit verification of their semiotic nature. Further, it is debatable whether those sthāyas were thought of as representations, or if the iconic view is rather a descriptive or didactic resource. The musical signs referred to in the NŚ were no doubt representations that were intended to be used as such on the stage (and thus always were legisigns), but at the time of Śārṅgadeva, the tradition of Sanskrit drama was almost extinct, and music was much more independent than before. This does not mean that music was conceptualized as pure and absolute, but much to the contrary, as proves the evidence of dozens of treatises. Some of the semiotic resources employed in the music of the first and early second millennia are still found in contemporary Hindustani music.

One example of this, in the ancient art of drumming, is the paran. Originally a pakhāvaj compositional form, later incorporated into the tablā repertoire as well (specially in the accompaniment of *kathak* dance), the paran often makes use of iconic signs. Parans are usually named after gods – so one hears of Śiva paran, Kṛṣṇa paran, Gaṇeśa paran – but there also other titles, such as *megh* [cloud] paran. A megh paran recited by the pakhāvaj player Manik Munde[10] represented the lightning and thunder of a storm by sequences of 'bolting' strokes that iconically resemble (as diagram and partly as image) those phenomena. A paran dedicated to Gaṇeśa, played on the tablā by Probir Mittra, represents the heavy and low-sounding steps of the elephant-headed god, with drum strokes that are similarly grave and slow, as can be seen in the first three strokes in Ex. 11.[11] Besides, some of the names and attributes of Gaṇeśa are verbally included in the composition, and the musician converts the syllables into drum strokes: **gaṅ gaṅ Gaṇapati gaja mukha maṅgala** ('Oh, Gaṇapati, Auspicious Elephant-Headed One'). This kind of composition is used by kathak dancers and accompanists as the very first item of a performance, a propitiatory prayer or *vandana*. Note that although the animal is huge and heavy, the gait of an elephant is seen in India as graceful and well-balanced, and so it stands for similar qualities in drumming and dance.

Sanyal employs this kind of analogy to compare the general pace of a dhrupad and dhamār: 'whereas dhrupad compositions have the gait of an elephant (*hāthī ki cāl*), dhamār compositions resemble the gait of a camel (*uṇt ki cāl*)' (1993: 31). Dhrupad is a living musical form in which one can find many musical structures as described in the old *śāstras* (treatises). Sanyal claims that some of the ornaments employed in the Dagar tradition of dhrupad are directly related to the forms described in the SR (1986: 46). Ornaments and patterns of melodic development of dhrupad are described in iconic terms, just as the sthāyas of the SR. Most of those are applied in the ālāp, as Saxena explains:

> For production of effects, certain ways of singing individual notes and traversing their linkages are employed. Thus, the device commonly known as gamak suggests depth and power; and *dyut*, āndolan, *ḍagar*, and *anuranātmaka* produce, respectively, the effects of a twinkle, oscillation or swing, an ascending meander, and a kind of nasal resonance which can be so regulated as to sound very similar to the tinkling temple-

10 My recording on March 8, 1996, in the Netherlands.

11 Composition taught by Probir Mittra in April 1995, New Delhi.

bells as they sway and appear to draw near and to recede in alternation. (Saxena 1992: 6)

Example 11

Gaṇeśa Paran (tīntāl), oral tradition, according to Probir Mittra

Although Saxena emphatically states that the singer is not intending to represent anything when using those vocal techniques, the passage below, presented in the same article, seems to contradict his remark:

> Some have wondered if music can ever provide a perception similar to that of 'a wave moving across the sea'. But the kind of passage we call ḍagar in the language of ālāpa is a clear, if gentle, meander; and earlier stages of ālāpa on the *Vicitra Vīṇā* [12] abound in suggestions of a mighty billow arising from and receding into the depths of the melody; and enabling us to glimpse at the same time the points of its upsurge and subsidence. (Saxena 1992: 13)

The diagram of a meander (ḍagar) or wave can in fact be represented by the melodic undulations of the ālāp expansion, or rāgavistār. On the vicitra vīṇā, this diagram is even visible in the movements of the left hand, which delineate the melodic phrases with a wooden or glass cylinder moving smoothly on the strings. As discussed above, iconic representations can refer to anything, as long as the sign has similarities with the object. It does not matter if the musician intends such representation or not, and the listener can interpret the sign in a variety of ways. The same phrase could refer to a wave, a meander, or the delicate movements of a charming lady. But a musical sign is always engaged in a web of significations which direct the interpretants in a certain direction. Thus, the tāns performed in a rāga associated with the

[12] A plucked lute, the strings of which are stopped with a block of wood or glass.

rains are more likely to be interpreted by the listeners as thunder and lightning than anything else with similar qualities. In fact, as Peirce says, icons assert nothing (CP 2.291), even though they are powerfully suggestive representamens.

Ustād Bade Gulam Ali Khan (1903-1968) was a khayāl and ṭhumrī singer famous for making use of references to emphasize the rāgas and compositions he performed. B.R. Deodhar describes several instances of musical representations that Gulam Ali Khan used to create and intentionally perform:

> The time was two o'clock in the afternoon during the heavy July downpour of Bombay and the place, Bombay's Marine Drive. The rough sea was dashing against the parapet walls and gigantic water spouts rose thirty or forty feet high. Khansaheb remembered the rāga Miyāṁ Mālhar and said 'Deodsahaab, this is a wonderful time and a wonderful place for practice. Come'. And Khansaheb started. As wave after wave dashed against the wall and jumped up high overhead, Khansaheb's tana-s leapt up with equal force and speed and descended with the down-rushing masses of water. Waves went up in single jets but broke into cascades while coming down. Khansaheb's tana-s traced the same pattern. If the force of the tana did not match the force of the wave Khansaheb, with an impatient gesture, started all over again. This went on for quite three quarters of an hour. (Deodhar in Deshpande 1987: 55-56)

The diagrammatic reference is very clear, the shape of the tāns were representing the way the waves rose up and broke down with violence. By the same means, Bade Gulam Ali Khan signified the flight of birds, in their diversity of forms, and even the charming movements of a young woman walking in the streets, who the singer had followed and attentively observed, later representing the lady's movements in a ṭhumrī: 'Khansaheb began to sing a ṭhumrī. He elaborated it in such a manner that the loveliness of the girl was entirely reflected in that piece' (Deodhar in Deshpande 1987: 56). However, Deshpande criticizes heavily the procedure: 'This weakness for pictorial representation is part of the larger philosophy of what may be termed "spectacularism." [...] What is one trying to accomplish here? Is music basically capable of representation beyond pointing to surface similarities? Is not the function of music confused here with that of other arts?' (Deshpande 1987: 59). Its true that a sort of *spectacularism* exists in Hindustani music, but this should not be equated to whatever forms of musical representation that abound especially in vocal music. They are not necessarily gimmicks or facile effects to win over a lay audiences, but rather genuine and ancient semiotic forms which enhance and sometimes constitute the very essence of aesthetic utterance. Bade Ghulam Ali Khan explains his style: 'all the objects in this world are full of beauty and I strive to give expression in musical form to everything that attracts my attention' (in Deshpande 1987: 55). Khan's justification is a perfectly acceptable aesthetic conception, and it seems to me that there is no historical or technical reason to defend a view of absolute music in Hindustani music.

An example of how diagrams can be an important resource in serious music can be found in the dhrupad *Jagata jananī*. The latter is a composition attributed to Baijū Bavare (15-16th century) in rāga bhairavī, transcribed in Ex. 12, according to the oral tradition of Ustād Zia Fariduddin Dagar.

The bandiś is a prayer to Sarasvatī, the goddess of the arts and knowledge. Two outstanding iconic signs refer to the attribute of Sarasvatī in removing the sorrows and granting the desires of her devotees. These are represented by the melodic direction of the phrases set to the verses: *dukha haranī* (who takes away our pain), and *johī johī māṅgata* (lit. [faithfully] longing for boons). In the first case, a descending melody represents the unburdening of pain or sorrow, and eventual pacification when the tonic is reached. This is found in the last āvart of both sthāyī and āntara (Ex. 12 a). The rising of the melody in the beginning of the āntara represents the progressive bestowal of boons to the persistent and deferential devotee. In b, the melodic line rises starting from a **G̱** to the motif **ṠṞ̇Ṡ**, in the *tar saptak*.[13] The second time the phrase is rendered (Ex. 12 c), higher pitches are presented **ṘĠ̱Ṟ̇Ṡ**, and a **Ṙ** is even introduced, which is a svara that does not pertain to the basic pitch set of bhairavī (but that may be inserted at appropriate moments in this rāga, as are other chromatic notes). This motif may represent the highest boons which Sarasvatī can concede. Thus, the relief of pain as descending and the granting of requests as ascending phrases are diagrams, which have a certain degree of abstraction, for they refer to the dynamism of ideas rather than actual movements.

The poem translates as follows:[14]

Mother of the world, with resplendent face,
Mother Sarasvatī, who bestows knowledge,
Who is compassionate, who takes away our pain.
Those who faithfully look for gain,
Receive the good fruits [they asked for],
[It is you] who fulfill the desires of our mind,
Who takes away our pain.

---

13 High octave.
14 My translation.

Example 12

Dhrupad *Jagata jananī* – Baijū Bavare (16th. century)
According to Ustād Zia Fariduddin Dagar

Nādabrahman – iconic representation of the cosmos

> *Dhvani* [sound] is the ultimate origin;[15] dhvani is the cause of everything. The whole world of immobile and mobile (beings) is encompassed by dhvani. (BD 1.1.12)

> It is curious how certain facts escape us because they are so pervading and ubiquitous: just as the ancients imagined the music of the spheres was not heard because it was heard all the time. (CP 1.159)

Mataṅga's and Peirce's remarks bring the study of diagrams to one of the most ambitious musical signification projects: that in which the universe and its *formal relations* are represented by means of acoustical iconic signs. Almost every musical culture has contributed to this idea, and music is often practiced as representations of physical or metaphysical laws of the universe. Several cultures regard the very beginning of the cosmos as involving some kind of musical activity. In India, the concept of nāda is of the utmost philosophical importance; and the Chinese *lü*, 12 bamboo tubes tuned in a cycle of perfect fifths, are said to express musical and cosmological relations. In the West, from Pythagoras onwards, musicians, philosophers, and astronomers have conceived the cosmos musically and have created music meant to mirror the harmony of the spheres, or celestial bodies (see Martinez 1996a: 77-80).

In the Indian tradition, as mentioned previously, nāda, especially as non-struck sound, constitutes the cosmos. It follows that the production of sound, particularly by means of vocal utterance, not only represents this vibrational essence, but also pārtakes of its power. In the *Chāndogyaupaniṣad*, a distillation of the essential things in the universe reveals that the ultimate essence of the cosmos is the Vedic chant:

> *Om*. One should meditate on this syllable, the *udgītha*, for one sings the loud chant beginning with oṁ. Of this (follows) the explanation. The essence of these beings is the earth; the essence of the earth is the water. The essence of water is plants; the essence of plants is a person. The essence of a person is speech. The essence of speech is the *Ṛk* (hymn). The essence of the *Ṛk* is the *Sāman* (chant). The essence of the Sāman is the udgītha. That is the quintessence of the essences, the Supreme, the highest, the eighth, namely the udgīta. (1-3)

The universe, in this view, is made of compounds which are contained in each other, in a progressive scale that leads from dense matter to the subtle element of sound. Thus, earth stands for matter, as the grossest element. Water, the next level, permits, in combination with earth, the existence of the vegetable kingdom. Human beings belong to the next level, and their essence is speech: *puruṣasya vāg rasaḥ*. The essence of language is, however, the Vedic chant, of which the udgīta, the singing of

[15] *Dhvaniyoniḥ*, 'dhvani is the yoni,' lit., 'sound is the vagina'.

the syllable om, is the subtlest, perfusing everything. Two points are remarkable in this passage. First, the idea of essence, recurrent in this text, and which is referred to by the word *rasa*, has important consequences for Indian classical aesthetics (see section 3). Second, the reference to speech (*Vāc*, a Vedic goddess), as the essence of mankind, emphasizes the semiotic aspect of culture. Indeed, if there is a civilization to be credited with the invention of semiotics, it is certainly that of India (see Piatigorsky & Zilberman 1976, Small 1987, Srivastava & Kapoor 1988).

Further, sound as an essential element in the universe, represented by the syllable ॐ (oṁ), is explained in the *Māṇḍūkyaupaniṣad* as connecting to the idea of Brahman: 'Oṁ, this syllable is all this. An explanation of that (is the following). All that is the past, the present and the future, all this is the syllable oṁ. And whatever else there is beyond the threefold time, that too is only the syllable oṁ. All this is, verily, Brahman. This self is Brahman' (1-2). Thus, oṁ, which can be equated to nāda, perfuses everything. That is the meaning of the first sentence in the quote. Since oṁ, constitutes everything in the past, present and future, whether they are gods or humans, visible things in the world or beyond time and space; therefore, the concepts of nāda and Brahman are interlaced, a point greatly emphasized by music scholars.

In the BD, Mataṅga equates sound with the gods of *trimurti* (Brahmā, Viṣṇu, and Śiva or Maheśvara) and Śakti (the goddess, or female principle of energy): 'Brahmā is known to be of the form of nāda (*nāda-rūpa*), Janārdana (Viṣṇu) is of the form of nāda, Parā Śakti is of the form of nāda (and) Maheśvara is of the form of nāda' (BD 1.19) Later, Śārṁgadeva subsumes all the deities and the cosmos under the compound word *nāda-brahman:* 'that incomparable bliss which is immanent in all creatures as intelligence and is manifest in the phenomenon of this universe' (SR 1.3.1). This is a magnificent view of the cosmos as vibration, a space for the manifestation of qualities, of which sound is prominent. If, on one hand, sound is the essence of the conception of nāda-brahman, on the other, it also means Brahman manifested as nāda. In this sense, it implies several interconnected levels of semiosis: the qualitative aspect of sound, the causal aspect of existence, and intelligence, or the argument which the universe is. Thus, from a broader point of view, a gradation of firstness, secondness and thirdness is inherent in the conception of nāda-brahman.

The capacity of music to represent the universe understood as nāda-brahman lies, certainly, in the controlled forms of sound, which can be thought of as an iconic sign of the cosmos. Thus, the formal relations of the universe are the dynamical objects to which the formal aspects of music refer. It is clear, however, that vocal music has a special place in this form of semiosis, the justification of which is based on one more iconic sign: breath, as the principle of life that permeates the cosmos. In the *Bṛhadāraṇyakaupaniṣad*, the unity of breath – *prāṇa* – and chanting is exposed: 'And this is also the udgītha. The vital breath, verily, is *ut*, for by vital breath is this whole (world) upheld. Song, verily, is speech. This is udgītha, for it is *ut* and *gītha*'' (1.3.23). Prāṇa in not merely the medium of singing, but the vital energy that holds together the universe. In the *Chāndogyaupaniṣad*, prāṇa is equated to the sun: 'This (breath) in the mouth and that (sun) are alike. This is warm. That is warm. This, they call sound and that, they call sound as reflecting sound' (1.3.2). Thus, there is a unity in Vedic philosophy among the concepts of nāda, oṁ, prāṇa, the cosmos and/or Brahman.

Singing, therefore, is an activity conceived as reflecting deeply the Indian cosmology: 'When he [the priest] began his recitation by intoning the sacred syllable oṁ, he symbolically inhaled the whole world of phenomena, and with the mantras that he uttered, he exhaled vital substance that became one with the universal continuum of spiritual energy' (Rowell 1992: 17). The basic form of semiosis implied here is diagrammatical representation. The two phases of breathing, a whole science in itself (*prāṇāyāma*), is defined in yoga as *pūraka* (filling) and *recaka* (emptying). Inhaling prāṇa, the singer becomes the whole universe, or Brahman; and exhaling prāṇa, the act of universal creation is performed. Thus, the activity of singing, as manipulation of sound and breath, is 'both an act of worship and an affirmation of universal process' (Rowell 1992: 41). Although the diagrammatic reference is outstanding, singing, according to the Indian conception, is a complex sign, in which several levels of representations are superposed. There is the pure icon feature, the sounds in themselves. There is the iconicity of absorbing the universe and creating it again by the breathing process. Yet, because the sounds are part of the universe (even its innermost essence), there is also an indexical representation. Finally, as a cultural paradigm, breathing, singing, and the Vedas are symbols of their own capacity of representation, interpretation, and procreation.

Not only does vocal music have such semiotic status. Instrumental music, too, can represent cosmic relations. In the NŚ, three instruments are indicated for the performance of gāndharva, the sacred form of music: the human throat, the vīṇā and the *vaṁśa* (flute) (NŚ 20.10). Vīṇā represented several kinds of string instruments in early śāstra.[16] Conversely, vīṇā also stands for the vocal tract, as Bharata states in this verse: 'notes, *grāmas* [tuning sets], alaṁkāras, varṇas, voice-registers, *jātis* [modal types] and overlapping notes are available in the vīṇā of the human throat' (NŚ 28.15).

The vīṇā, with its lattice of parallel strings and transverse frets, is also an iconic sign for the cosmic loom *played* by the *puruṣa*, the primeval

[16] Two forms of vīṇā are played nowadays, the rudra-vīṇā in North India, and the Sarasvatī-vīṇā in the South.

being. A description of this apparatus and its weaver in the *Ṛgveda* recalls the figure of a cosmic musician: 'Puruṣa stretches the warp and draws the woof; he spreads it out upon this dome of the sky. These are the pegs that are fastened in place; they made the melodies into shuttles for weaving' (10.130.2). The analogy with the vīṇā is clear: the warp corresponds to the strings, which are stretched by pegs; the woof corresponds to melodies woven on the frets. The shuttle could be the musician's plectrum. From a broader point of view, the structures and development forms of Indian music are also diagrams of the cosmic loom, as Gottlieb writes:

> The symbolism of the shuttle has particular significance for Indian music even today. Just as the shuttle is used for passing the threads of the woof between those of the warp, melodies are woven through the 'fixed' threads of a rāga. The shuttle is symbolic of the very process of improvisation which characterizes the form of the ālāp. And the procedure outlined for the alternation of the kāydā and vistār phrases also relates to this symbolism of the shuttle. Just as the separate strands of the warp and the woof are intertwined, so the separate entities of music are combined; the 'fixed' entities represent the warp, the 'improvised,' the woof. (1981: 30)

According to this diagram (rather than symbol), the fixed elements of rāga and tāla (legisigns) are the warp, and the flexible actualization of those (sinsigns), in the form of expansion, are the shuttle and woof. The combination of both contrasting ideas generates the fabric of music, an iconic sign of the cosmic loom, and a sacrifice in the same sense of the Vedic chant. The musician stands in the same position as the weaver, puruṣa. It is no wonder that music is considered in India as a means to reach *mokṣa*, ultimate freedom: 'He, who thoroughly knows the art of vīṇā playing, and is an expert in the subject of śruti and jāti, and who knows the time as well, that person is without effort on the way to mokṣa' (SD 1.32).

The diagrammatic thinking of Indian philosophies has a capacity for encompassing phenomena of different magnitudes. The cosmological level is represented by the anthropomorphic forms and processes. Indeed, as Rowell writes, 'Just as all forms are ultimately one, so do all processes manifest one process – the world process of continuous creations and dissolution, as proclaimed in Hindu scriptures' (1992: 242). In fact, iconic semiosis is more than an artistic device. As C. W. Spinks states, 'The icon goes beyond the pattern of constructing similarities to engender the basic features of form, predication, judgment, and inference' (1991: 62). In this sense, the extraordinary views of Indian cosmology do not represent just mythological and religious forms, which are usually understood as products of a culture. Advances in contemporary physics have generated interpretations of the cosmos which are amazingly similar to some of the ancient Indian conceptions, such as the interchangeable nature of matter and energy, time and space, and the vibrational nature of the cosmos (see

Prigogine & Stengers 1984). In this sense, iconic thinking, whether in science or in traditional cultures, constitutes the basis for discoveries (see Holyoak & Thagard 1995). The heuristic power of icons was very clear for Peirce:

> all deductive reasoning, even simple syllogism, involves an element of observation; namely, deduction consists in constructing an *icon* or *diagram* the relations of whose parts shall present a complete analogy with those parts of the object of reasoning, of experimenting upon this image in the imagination, and of observing the result so as to discover unnoticed and hidden relations among the parts (CP 3.363, my emphasis).

Peirce goes further in his view of the universe as mind and thought, and connects the universe to the arts: 'The Universe as an argument is necessarily a great work of art, a great poem – for every fine argument is a poem and a symphony – just as every true poem is a sound argument' (CP 5.119). When music is equated with an argument (as a class of signs), as well as with the universe, it is true that the level of iconic signs has been incorporated into higher forms of semiosis. This, however, does not diminish the importance of icons. What is implied in an argument is a complex of sign relations, and certainly a mathematical argument is based on a framework of iconic signs as much as a musical composition is. Yet, the performing of music gives movement and aural forms to icons, which, if seen as representing cosmic relations, constitute a truly dynamical model of the universe.

Metaphors in music

The third kind of musical hypoicon is the *metaphor*. For Peirce, metaphors are iconic signs that 'represent the representative character of a representamen by representing a parallelism in something else' (CP 2.277). Metaphors are, therefore, the result of a double process: (1) the representation of the representative character of a sign; and (2) the interaction of this first representation with another sign. These processes can occur in a variety of distinct combinations, thereby setting up many sub-levels of metaphorical iconic signs. The contention here is that there are three kinds of metaphors relevant to music: *Paraphrases*, *Quotations* and *Allegorical References*; all of them in the realm of musical metalanguage. The determining factor is the representative character of the representamen as being an icon or hypoicon, an index or indexical sign, or a symbol.

Musical Paraphrases, due to their semiotic configuration, can be taken as a first kind of metaphor. An iconic representation (image or diagram) interacts only with the materiality of the new disposition. Paraphrase, as the imitation of a pre-existing model or piece, is a traditional technique of music making. The process of emulating, in a new piece of music, a pre-existing work has been for centuries a traditional discipline for learning music and composition. The whole universe of Indian music can be said to be derived from the imitation of the musical forms presented by the master to the disciple. Some musical compositions are more specific iconic signs, though, as is the *lakṣaṇ gīt* (characteristic song).

Lakṣaṇ gīts are compositions designed to aid in the learning of a rāga. They present, verbally and musically, the main features of a rāga that a student should learn. This kind of song can be considered a paraphrase, because it represents the proper rāga to which the composition belongs – in a slightly different context, that of a learning and training process. It is also a form of scholarship, a practical demonstration of the features of a rāga. Even when a teacher does not make use of lakṣaṇ gīts, paraphrasing is the traditional teaching method of imparting musical knowledge, for Indian music spreads mostly by means of imitation.

Musical *Quotation* can be classified as metaphoric representation of a second kind. When a recognizable fragment of a rāga or of a particular piece is grafted onto a performance or composition, the result is an interaction of meanings. Because the quotation refers to the existential individuality of the quoted work, the character of the representation is indexical. There are two instances of quotations in Hindustani music. First is the quotation properly understood, which can be a piece of folk music, or a popular movie-song inserted in the performance of a rāga. Secondly, one rāga can refer to another, by a particular melodic motif that belongs simultaneously to both rāgas. This is technically known as chāyā, the shadow or tinge of one rāga manifesting in another.

A chāyā is produced whenever a typical motif or phrase of one rāga appears in the performance of another, related rāga. If a chāyā of an unrelated rāga appears, then, obviously, the musician has made a mistake. Powers explains that 'there need be neither a change of register nor a change of scale type for the chāyā of an extraneous rāga to be evoked. A characteristic motif from the other rāga, or even an emphasis on one of its modal degrees (if that contrasts with those of the established raga) is sufficient' (1980b: 432). Therefore, the phenomenon of chāyā is natural to Hindustani music, because many rāgas are interrelated in one way or another, constituting families. Only the pure rāgas do not have melodic material in common with the other pure rāgas. However, some rāgas are composed precisely by a mixture of two or more rāgas, which are called *sankīrṇa* rāgas. O. Ṭhākur describes the various chāyās present in māru bihāg:

> This rāga has obtained a widespread currency these days. Going S R Ṇ S G/M and then back to G is quite like bihāg; but if one makes a pause on M it [bihāg] is suppressed and the chāyā of nand is shown. Having shown its chāyā to that extent, then do P M M G- S and again bihāg is manifested. And from then doing S- G M̄ P ᴳM̄ P, at that point comes a view of suhāg.

In the uttarang, show the chāyā of nand [with] PDNP, DM, PG for the bihāg component. Then couple this with the kalyāṇ motif MG GR-S. From these gestures collectively a complete form of the rāga [māru bihāg] stands forth.

Remember that showing any one component repeatedly in the whole structure of this rāga will be a mistake. The rāga arises from the mingling of the components indicated above. Therefore when singing this mixed [sankīrṇa] rāga one has to develop it keeping in mind the varying movements of its assorted components. (SA 5.15)[17]

Example 13

Chāyās in marū bihāg

The examples of chāyās present in marū bihāg are transcribed into staff notation in Ex. 13. In fact, they are not undesirable motifs for the performance of this rāga, for marū bihāg has the character of a mixed rāga. The situation is different, however, when a serious rāga, such as darbārī kānhḍā, is performed. The chāyā of rāga miyāṁ kī malhār may appear with the motif GMRS, but a difference in the ornamentation of G distinguishes them: a heavy āndol should be performed on G in darbārī, whereas a lighter one is usually employed in miyāṁ kī malhār. Besides, two other rāgas have the same pitch set as darbārī: āsāvarī (jaunpurī) and aḍāṇā. One must avoid the chāyās of those rāgas in darbārī, for they represent distinct musical entities. The āroha in darbārī is SRG~~MPD~NṠ while that in āsāvarī is SRMPD~, NṠ, omitting D. The avaroha in darbārī is ṠD~N\P, whereas āsāvarī descends as ṘNDP or ṠNDP. Aḍāṇā ascends as SRMPD, NṠ and descends as

[17] Translation according to Powers, 1980b: 432.

ṠD̲N̲P, G̲MRS (see Ex. 14). Darbārī and aḍāṇā are also distinct in tessitura and tempo, which – in general terms – are low and grave for the former, and high and fast for the latter. Besides, chāyās of rāga sārang can appear in darbārī with the motifs MR and N̲P (see SA 5.122). A recognizable fragment of a rāga is certainly a legisign. However, as it appears in the performance of another rāga, the function this sign exerts is indexical, and, in itself, the chāyā is an iconic sinsign. The metaphor appears via the parallelism of this iconic sign of another rāga with the proper sinsigns and legisigns of the main rāga performed. The question of chāyā may be also understood as a case of cross-reference.

Example 14

Rāgas darbārī, āsāvarī (jaunpurī) and aḍāṇā

A musical form that is related to this issue, and may deliberately use chāyās, is the *rāgamālā*, the garland of rāgas. It consists in the sequential presentation of several rāgas in the same piece of music. Rāgamālā phrases are usually not long, and the musician has to make use of calans and other characteristic legisigns of the presented rāgas. Rāgamālās are performed frequently by instrumentalists. Since the performance involves several rāgas in a row, the individual feature of each presented rāga is outstanding; hence this is also an instance of metaphorical reference.

The third kind of musical metaphor is the *Allegorical Reference*. Here the representative character of the represented sign is symbolic. Musically, the allegorical reference takes a typical feature of a certain genre or form, usually in a too-obvious or even distorted way, and forces that feature to interact with other signs. An allegorical reference is not a textual quotation. It sets up a kind of metonymic reference by the precise use of particular musical patterns consecrated by habit or convention. This kind of musical metaphor is usually found as instances of parody and pastiche. Actually, Hindustani classical music rarely makes use of this semiotic device, which is not uncommon in Western classical music (see

Martinez 1996a: 82). A case of allegorical reference occurs, for instance, when a musician imitates the style of another in an exaggerated or ironic way. In contemporary music, however, this is certainly never presented in public performances, and thus has little significance as a mode of semiosis in Hindustani music.

There is another case, that can be understood as allegorical reference, and which is related in some respects to quotation as well. As more and more Indian music is performed abroad, occasionally musicians decide to insert a well-known Western composition or tune into the performance of a rāga, usually during a rāgamālā, perhaps as homage to a culture that has so warmly welcomed Indian classical music. It is known that Ustād Ali Akbar Khan sometimes plays on the *sārod*[18] tunes such as *Greensleeves*, or J.S. Bach's *Bourrée* (from the Lute Suite in E minor).[19] Although this could at first be considered a plain case of quotation, the issue is more complex than that.

Very well-known Western tunes can indeed refer to classical Western music, as a general idea, even in an extrinsic context. It happens, however, that when a musician quotes such a composition within the framework of Hindustani music, some alterations are unavoidable. Indian music operates as a system of modal structures. *Greensleeves*, in its multiple forms and arrangements, although not strictly a tonal piece, can be successfully performed in the space of modal music. However, Indian music is always rendered along with a continuous drone, provided by a tambūrā or other special instruments. Thus, when performed by an Indian ensemble, *Greensleeves* is necessarily superposed over a drone, which is not original, and rendered by instruments that will give completely new forms of attack and ornamentation to the notes. In fact, even if a version of *Greensleeves* is fully structured as a piece of modal music, its performance by an Indian ensemble will in some way transform the original (at least at the surface level), thus signifying an allegorical reference, rather than a plain quotation.

The metaphorical character is more accentuated when the inserted piece is not structured according to its original musical system. That is the case with the *Bourrée* (Ex. 15), a clearly tonal piece, involving harmonic cadences and several modulations, including the typical tonal gambit of minor/major, which are inconsistent with the strict modality of Indian music. The tonal structure of the *Bourrée* is supported by a fragile two-voice polyphony (the last four bars can be considered as having three voices), which breaks down when the bass voice is suppressed, since only the higher voice is performed in the structure of a rāga. Therefore, all the harmonic features of the piece are necessarily transformed when the *Bourrée* is played as a monodic tune against a

---

[18] A plucked fretless lute.

[19] Unhappily, there is no commercial recording of those rāgamālās.

constant drone. In Ex. 16,[20] Ustād Ali Akbar Khan plays the first phrase of Bach's piece in the context of rāga pīlū, whose svaras and motifs can easily accommodate the minor melodic scale of the *Bourrée*. However, besides being played monodically and with a small change in the original melody, the piece is inserted in the rhythmic structure of rūpak, and thus the original quadratic grouping interacts with the seven-beat pattern of the tāla. The two joined musical structures, the Hindustani corpus and the *Bourrée*, in their similarities and contrasts, produce an amalgam of peculiar qualitative features, an amalgam which operates semiotically as a metaphor of the third kind.

Example 15

J.S. Bach's *Bourrée*, Lute Suite in E minor (BWV 996)

[20] Part of a live recording at McGill University, Montreal, December 1978, in which Ali Akbar Khan performs a rāgamālā as a development of rāga bhūp mānḍ. The tablā is played by Zakir Husain. The recording was kindly offered to me by John Campana, of the University of Toronto.

Example 16

Bach's *Bourrée*, as performed by Ustād Ali Akbar Khan

2.3.2.2 Index and indexical reference

> [...] it would be difficult if not impossible, to instance an absolutely pure index, or to find any sign absolutely devoid of the indexical quality (CP 2.306).

In music, the dynamic relations between sign, object, and interpretant can manifest a diversity of indexical references. All musics, being existents, are part of a context and thus can signify as indices. Every work, genre, style, and musical system interacts dynamically with a universe of relations: individual, social, cultural, etc. According to Peirce, an '***Index*** is a sign which refers to the Object that it denotes by virtue of being really affected by that Object' (CP 2.248). It is by dyadic relations, or dynamic connection, that sign and object interact, operating indexically. Compositions, styles, genres, and systems take part in causal processes, those by which composers, musicians, listeners, musical schools, social processes, and technical resources (e.g., musical instruments) interact with the acoustic elements that constitute a sinsign, an actual piece of music. All music refers to these features. They are indices merely by the fact that their individuality points to a particular context, historical and geographical, from which they emanate, as cause or consequence.

Pieces of music are indices even when not interpreted as such. The effective connection sign-object enables indexical reference to take place independently of an interpretant. Conversely, the object of an index is a *sine qua non* element: 'An index is a sign which would, at once, lose the character which makes it a sign if its object were removed, but would not lose that character if there were no interpretant. Such, for instance, is a piece of mould with a bullet-hole in it as sign of a shot; for without the shot there would have been no hole; but there is a hole there, whether anybody has the sense to attribute it to a shot or not' (CP 2.304). Indeed, without Japanese culture, there would be no Japanese music. But even if a listener ignores the *gagaku*, or is unable to consider it as music, that musical genre still works as an index of its culture, to which it is factually associated.

The most outstanding feature of Hindustani music in this sense, is its connection with a civilization that exists in time and space. This is certainly obvious to most listeners, and may even be irrelevant for an Indian one. But when the distinction is that of Karnatic or Hindustani music, each of them, respectively, works as indices of their cultures. Musicians are also indices of their culture, and some world-renowned names refer unmistakably to Hindustani music: Pāṇdit Ravi Shankar, Ustād Ali Akbar Khan, Chatur Lal, Ustād Alla Rakha, Zakir Husain, Ustād Bismillah Khan, among others. Because they were the first musicians to become famous outside India, their quantity of indexical reference is heavier than that of others. Individuals and their music always refer to their cultural and historical context. Thus, Tyāgarāja (1767-1847) is factually connected with Karnatic devotional music, and he is an index of that tradition (but his compositions will instead function as indexical signs). The same is valid for Jayadeva (12th century) as representing the Sanskrit forms of Vaiṣṇava poetry and music; or Tānsen (1492-1589), standing for the court music of Emperor Akbar. The excellence of Tānsen is referred to in the memoirs of Emperor Jahāngīr, in these terms: 'Of these poets the chief was Tānsen Kalāwant, who was without a rival in my father's services (in fact, there has been no singer like him in any time or age)' (in Delvoye 1994b: 2). Indeed, Tānsen has been an outstanding index of the high level of music practiced in Akbar's court. His personality and compositions, for more than four hundred years, have been praised to the point that they have truly become symbols of excellence in Hindustani music.

If individual musicians are indices by their mere existence, groups of musicians can also generate this type of semiosis. In fact, 'indices refer to individuals, single units, single collections of units, or single continua' (CP 2.306). The gharānās of Hindustani music constitute a special case in this respect. Each gharānā represents a school, a line of musical conception and interpretation. A gharānā depends on the continuity of the *guru-śiṣya* (master-disciple) tradition. According to Deshpande, 'A musical tradition is not called a "gharānā" unless it exists for at least three generations' (1987: 12). Musically, gharānās can be defined in the following terms: firstly, 'Each gharānā has an artistic discipline of his own in addition to a discipline common to all gharānās. In musical parlance the gharānās follow certain kāyadā-s (laws);' and secondly, 'Each gharānā takes its origin from the quality of the voice of its founder' (Deshpande 1987: 13). The gharānā is not a simple concept, though; and the contradictions of the system have been discussed by Neuman (1990: 145-167). The point here is that a musician, as an individual who belongs to a gharānā, represents that tradition and style by a factual connection, and the music s/he makes is an index of that gharānā.

The variety of indices requires a comprehensive division. Peirce distinguished indices into genuine and degenerate: 'If the Secondness is an existential relation, the Index is ***genuine***. If Secondness is a reference, the Index is ***degenerate***'(CP 2.283). Musically, genuine indices are any and all musical existents: works, styles, genres, systems, instruments, performance styles, etc. Degenerate indexical signs gather every kind of reference since, representing some object, they refer to this object in some way. Peirce writes: '***Subindices*** or ***Hyposemes*** are signs which are rendered such principally by an actual connection with their objects. Thus a proper name, personal demonstrative, or relative pronoun or the letter attached to a diagram, denotes what it does owing to a real connection with its object but none of these is an Index, since it is not an individual' (CP 2.284). In the same way as iconic signs may be divided into three levels of hypoicons, indexical signs or hyposemes can be distinguished from each other. The contention here is that the mode of representation of indexical signs sets up subdivisions in three levels.

Indexical signs of the first level are significant by virtue of their inner qualities: 'In so far as the Index is affected by the Object, it necessarily has some Quality in common with the Object, and it is in respect to these that it refers to the Object' (CP 2.248). That is the case of a musical image, in itself a hypoicon, but it has also a kind of effective connection with its object, its indexical feature. Musical recordings (phonographic, magnetic, or digital) are typical cases. There were dyadic relations between the original sounds and the microphone membrane that picked them up and encoded them as electric impulses or bytes. The same happens with musical imitations in general. Peirce was conscious of this indexical feature of iconic signs:

> We say that the portrait of a person we have not seen is ***convincing***. So far as, on the ground merely of what I see in it, I am led to form an idea of the person it represents, it is an Icon. But, in fact, it is not a pure Icon, because I am greatly influenced by knowing that it is an ***effect***, through the artist, caused by the original's appearance, and is thus in a genuine Obsistent relation to that original. Besides, I know that portraits have but the slightest resemblance to their originals, except in certain conventional respects, and after a conventional scale of values, etc. (CP 2.92)

Thus, the motif which recalls a *kokil*, the Indian cuckoo, is an iconic sign in a bandiś. When performed, it will act as a dicent sinsign pointing to that species of bird (*Cuculus indicus*). Notice that it is not the resemblance of the kokil motif itself which operates as an indexical sign, but the association of ideas developed in the listener's mind, connecting the real bird-song (previously heard in a forest, on a recording or even imagined) with the represented one. In this sense, the interpretant of an indexical sign is not assured, but a mere potentiality, or a rheme. The closer a singer renders the motif to an actual bird-song, the more indexical the sign will be. It is possible to extend indexical signs of the first level to other types of hypoicons such as diagrams and metaphors.

Indexical signs of the second level are representations of existents. Peirce suggested that: 'Any individual is a degenerate Index of its own characters' (CP 2.283). Therefore, signs of the production conditions of a musical work, the relations with its dynamical universe and its semiotic body (immediate interpretant), are objects of indexical signs of this level. Notice that it is not the genuine index that is meant here, but representations of it. Functional music works evidently as indexical signs. Thus, as much as a *bhajan* refers to the devotional context, *horī* songs bring the festival of Holī, the celebration of life and the approach of spring to the mind of interpreters. The functional aspect of Indian music seems to have been recognized for a long time. For instance, one finds petition songs performed in the early second millennium: 'When the song contains words of request, asking a special favour from the kings, people call it a *sāpekṣa-jhombaḍa*' (SŚ 13.286). Such a composition would be an indexical sign of certain concrete situations. In this connection, eulogies are also indexical; for example, the dhrupad addressed to Emperor Akbar in rāga śrī, presented in Ex. 17 (KPM 3.378). The text can be translated as follows:[21]

A powerful man has come,
The great ruler Akbar has arrived.
On the seven islands,
[In] the eight directions,
He is a lord of men,
In each house,
Everyone shivers with fear of him.

Rāgas of all periods present a huge store of indexical references. Early Indian music rāgas often refer to regions such as these: rāga vaṅgāla (Bengal), takka (the city of Taxila), karṇāṭa or karṇāṭī (Karṇāṭaka), bhoṭṭa (Tibet) and tribes such as śaka (the Śakas), pulindī or pulindika (the Pulindas), bhairava (Bhairavas), mālava or mālavaśrī (Mālavas, a martial tribe, formerly in Pañjāb). Later texts also mention these kinds of rāgas: hijeja, hejjuji, hijāja (Persian city, Hijāz), vṛndābanī-sāraṅga (Vṛndāban), and the like. Seasons and festivals are often referred to by rāgas: vasanta (spring), megha (cloud) and malhāra (the rainy season), hiṇḍola (the swing festival), etc. Persons and musicians are obviously indexical references in these rāgas: bāhādurī-toḍī (Sultan Bāz Bahadur [1556-1570], of Mālwā), mīrā kī malhār (Mīrā Bāī [1500-1550], the Vaiṣṇava Rajput poet), sūradāsī malhāra (Sūrdās, 15th century poet), etc. Some of these rāgas may have a factual connection to the object to which they refer, whereas others are rather dubious as historical facts. But this

[21] My translation.

is not the point here, for an indexical sign can refer to a non-existent object, a fantastic or mythical creature, or whatever.

Example 17
Dhrupad addressed to Emperor Akbar (KPM 3.378)

A special case in Hindustani music is the rāgas and compositions attributed to Tānsen. Gangoly writes: 'It is well known that Tān Sen was the first to introduce the E-flat (Komala gāndhāra) and both varieties of Niṣāda (B flat and sharp [sic]) into the rāga mallār which came to be known as "Mīyān-kī-mallār." Similarly he is the inventor of a new type of Toḍī known as Mīyān-kī-toḍī. The modified forms of Kānarā known as Darbārī Kānarā are attributed to him' (1989: 53). Although many compositions and rāgas attributed to Tānsen are of questionable authenticity, there is no doubt that the musician did live during the time of Akbar and that he produced remarkable music. Even if apocryphal, they are indexical references to the legendary composer.

Indexical signs of the third level are based on conventions. They therefore involve legisigns. For Peirce 'any mere land-mark by which a particular thing may be recognized because it is as a matter of fact associated with that thing, a proper name without signification, a pointing finger, is a degenerate index' (CP 5.75). The musical symbol can also lead the interpreter's attention to the represented object. In most cases, musical legisigns semiotically act as proper names, representing their objects by convention, that is, as symbols. But the very fact that they have been associated with such and such objects enables indexical references. Every occurrence (replica) of a symbol is also an index.

Any legisign involves sinsigns in which the general aspect of a law is actualized. These very sinsigns operate as indexical signs of the former legisign. Thus, the svaras presented in one rāga point to the pitch set that makes up the general idea of that rāga. In the same way, notes with special function, such as the vādī and saṁvādī, can signify as indices to rāgas. The emphasized degrees differentiate rāgas that have the same scalar configuration; for instance, mārvā and pūriyā, both of which employ SR̲GM̄DN. But, in mārvā vādī there is R̲, and in saṁvādī is D; whereas in pūriyā, vādī is G; and saṁvādī is N. In the same sense, the occurrence of a sam indicates the first mātrā of a tāla. Melodic motifs refer indexically the rāga to which they belong; thus, the question of chāyā appears here in a different light. A chāyā also signifies as an index of the rāga or rāgas to which it belongs.

Indexical signs are essential to musical practice. Their reference gives to the musicians several kinds of rhythmic and melodic clues that enable the performance to be realized with perfection. Musicians also communicate by the exchange of indexical signs while they are playing, without recourse to verbal language. Thus a tablā player will figure out the tāla in which a composition is set merely by interpreting the indices of the mukhṛā that the piece offers. The soloist does not need to tell the tabliyā what tāla is to be performed. Similarly, the soloist will insinuate change of tempo, important cadences, and so on to the other musicians, so they can play accordingly. The action of indices in the interaction of musicians on stage may be extended to the audience. The indexical signs will show the way the mental interpretation of a rāga or a drumming composition should be understood.

2.3.2.3 Symbols in Music

> The necessary and true symbol is immortal. And man must also be so, provided he is vivified by the truth. (CP 7.593)

The use of the word 'symbol' is critical, for different schools of thought have attributed several conceptions to this term. Peirce even states that 'The word ***Symbol*** has so many meanings that it would be an injury to the language to add a new one.' Peirce, however, understood the notion of symbol in terms of its original Greek etymology: 'I do not think that the signification I attach to it, that of a conventional sign, or one depending upon habit (acquired or inborn), is so much a new meaning as a return to the original meaning' (CP 2.297). Hence, for Peirce, 'A symbol is a representamen whose special significance or fitness to represent just what it does represent lies in nothing but the very fact of there being a habit, disposition, or other effective general rule that it will be so interpreted' (CP 4.447). A symbol can be understood as convention or law, but a more precise Peircean formulation places its mode of action, or semiosis, as the way it determines an interpretant, that is, 'if the grounding lies *only* in the fact that the sign *will be* represented in its interpretant as a sign of that object, regardless of any likeness or existential relation that it may have to that object, then the sign is a "symbol" and is necessarily a legisign' (Ransdell 1986: 686). Thus, symbol is a sign that represents its objects by the fact that it will be interpreted as a sign of that object. Every symbol is inevitably a legisign.

If an acoustic phenomenon refers to a certain object, or to a general group of objects (which can be qualities, existents, ideas or signs of all those), it does so only because there is an interpretation habit that set up such a significative relation for a group of minds or interpreters so enabled, and that sound disposition is therefore a musical symbol. By the action of the symbol musical representation constitutes itself in full. In this case, the role of the interpretant is essential, because there is no symbolic semiosis without integrated participation of the three members of sign action: sign, object, and interpretant.

A sequence of notes played on a bugle at a military headquarters is a symbol, because in the mind of each person of that community it has been established as a general rule of interpretation relating those sounds with a particular object (a thing, an order, or other signs). The action of this representamen is not related to the timbre of the brass instrument, nor to the melody in itself, nor to the act of playing (the player does not want to call attention to her or himself). The bugle call means the same thing to all interpreters that follow the same regulation. But the lack of interpreters disarticulates the symbol: a bugle call would not be able to signify its original meaning to the community of a Buddhist monastery in Daramshala. The symbol is intrinsically formal and denotes general ideas. The reveille call does not refer to a particular dawn but to each and every dawn. Any occurrence of the reveille call is a materialization of the general rule, or a replica of the symbol, which relates that sound with day-break and the military-life context surrounding that circumstance. The symbol would not be annihilated if the bugle were destroyed in battle, its player killed, and dawn were to arrive without the performance of the proper call. That symbol would continue to exist in the regulations and minds of soldiers and officers.

An interesting musical symbol of ancient India is the *pañcamahāśabda*, the five great sounds. Those were sounds representing five kinds of music: the metal of bells or cymbals, vocal music, drumming, the sound of a vīṇā, and the *śaṅkh*, the conch shell horn. The five great sounds were an insignia, according to Shakuntala: 'The military commanders and chiefs who had won laurels on the battlefield were rewarded with titles and distinctions and were given the right to appear in public with a special band in attendance known as Pañcamahāśabda – comprised of five primary musical instruments' (1968: 11). Besides, military orders and messages were transmitted on the battlefields of ancient India by means of musical symbols, played with the śaṅkh and drums. The *Mahābhārata* contains plenty of references to instruments used for this purpose.

Several musical conceptions base their aesthetic grounding on symbolic representation. In a broad sense, the purpose of promoting reference by music is, in itself, a mode of symbolic semiosis. A programmed musical intention, when directed to an enabled community of interpreters, acts as a symbol. Peirce says that 'The being of a symbol consists in the real fact that something surely will be experienced if certain conditions be satisfied. Namely, it will influence the thought and conduct of its interpreter' (CP 4.447). Music that, by tradition, or the conception of a composer, makes use of this kind of representation, does so in order to represent something, and to be interpreted as such. The symbol only exists as a representational purpose, thus the action of symbols is intrinsically teleological.

Several layers of semiosis are implied in 'normal' symbol usage. This is because, on one hand, a symbol actualizes by the replicas it determines, which are sinsigns of several kinds; and, on the other, the replicas themselves exhibit their qualities of appearance. The identification of these levels of semiosis gives clues as to what constitutes the species of symbols; which are three, one genuine and two degenerate:

> A Symbol is a law, or regularity of the indefinite future. Its Interpretant must be of the same description; and so must be also the complete immediate Object, or meaning. But a law necessarily governs, or 'is embodied in' individuals, and prescribes some of their qualities. Consequently, a constituent of a Symbol may be an Index, and a constituent may be an Icon. A man walking with a child points his arm up into the air and says, 'There is a balloon.' The pointing arm is an essential part of the symbol without which the latter would convey no information. But if the child asks, 'What is a balloon,' and the man replies, 'It is something like a great big soap bubble,' he makes the image a part of the symbol. Thus, while the complete object of a symbol, that is to say, its meaning, is of the nature of a law, it must ***denote*** an individual, and must ***signify*** a character. A ***genuine*** symbol is a symbol that has a general meaning. There are two kinds of degenerate symbols, the ***Singular Symbol*** whose Object is an existent individual, and which signifies only such characters as that individual may realize; and the ***Abstract Symbol***, whose only Object is a character. (CP 2.293)

The two kinds of degenerated symbols may arise from special instances of semiosis. Both, index or icon, can constitute and work as degenerated symbols. The grounding of these symbols relates to what Peirce called an indirect interpretant (CP 2.294). That is, an index may be indirectly interpreted as a singular symbol, and an icon may be indirectly interpreted as an abstract symbol.

Singular symbols denote individual objects. Their law of interpretation is not general but particular. National anthems are singular symbols, as are jingles and musical introductions associated with, say, particular goods or people. Singularity is a essential feature of these symbols owing to their representative intention. No company would use a jingle to advertise its product if the jingle did not refer specifically to its own brand. Calans and chāyās are singular symbols, as far as they signify a particular rāga. An abstract symbol focuses representation on a particular character or quality, which is its object. Iconic signs can indirectly be interpreted as abstract symbols. The timbre of an instrument can be taken as a symbol; for instance, the sound of a śahnāī as auspicious.

The necessary condition that characterizes a genuine symbol is generality. The symbol denotes a general idea; its object is also general. The interpretant of a symbol can be a rheme, dicent or argument, depending on the context. Military calls are genuine symbols, as are special tunes and anthems. Songs such as the *Vande Mātaram*, or Mahātma Gandhi's favorite bhajan, *Raghupati Rāghava Rāja Rāma*, are genuine symbols, the former denoting a patriotic idea and the latter Gandhi's conception of the unity of Muslim and Hindu India.

Above all, rāgas are genuine symbols. They are general ideas on how sounds should be related to each other in a musical performance, which, in a global perspective, will be interpreted as the rāgabhāva of a rāga. Rāgas represent a complex of other aesthetic ideas, such as a class of feeling, or an abstract and ideal image of a festival, or perhaps the spectacle of rising or setting sun, with all possible associations it could evoke in the mind of an interpreter. Rāgas, though used by musicians and interpreted by listeners, are independent of the individual existence of those persons. As much as a word, a symbol 'lives in the minds of those who use it. Even if they are all asleep, it exists in their memory' (CP 2.301). Beyond a persons' memory, symbols have a life of their own in a culture. As much as people *are born* into an existing culture and are compelled to learn its rules and languages, Indian musicians and listeners have to learn how to utter and understand rāgas that are currently in use. All this characterize genuine symbols.

I have discussed, in the preceding chapter, how rāgas can be considered legisigns that actualize in the form of sinsigns. Rāgas, however, are more than legisigns, for they refer to ideas, or the general association of ideas, and they are capable of generating interpretants that range from the pure technical aspects of a rāga, its existential facts, to – and above all – their aesthetic program. Since the earliest written evidence, the *jātis*, *grāmarāgas* and *deśīrāgas*[22] described in the śāstras

[22] Early prototypes of rāgas; see the definitions in 3.3.1 for jātis, 3.3.2 for grāmarāgas, and 3.3.3 for the deśīrāgas.

have been said to represent something. In the NŚ jātis represent certain dramatic situations or character types of the Sanskrit theater. In a more abstract sense, jātis represent rasas, feelings organized in eight or nine categories (see 3.1, 3.2 and 3.3.1). Both dramatic types of scenes and characters are general ideas, and the reference to them signified by the jātis is certainly symbolic.

Later treatises extended these references to the grāmarāgas and deśīrāgas. As the theatrical tradition was declining, the musical structures became more and more independent of dramatic references, but not less significant. Deśīrāgas, being essentially regional rāgas adapted to the classical system, originally signified the character of the area or the people to which they referred. It is clear, however, that musicians and scholars transformed drastically both the musical structures and the ideas those structures used to stand for. That is, the meaning of regional rāgas were certainly allegorical references, which later became so formalized as to be understood simply as symbols. Hence, in the BD, one reads about rāga pārvatī, which is referred to as 'born in the mountainous region' (4.B.13). Pārvatī is a *bhāśā*, or a musical 'dialect', and is related to rāga hiṇḍola. Thus, pārvatī was probably a tune performed in the hills, that is, some form of folk music, which was adapted by the classical musicians as a rāga. It was associated with another, older rāga – hiṇḍola – in terms of its musical structure. Hiṇḍola, in turn, was an old and well established grāmarāga, and its interpretant should be the idea of the union of lovers, or *sambhoga* (BD 3.anu.198). The bhāśā pārvatī supposedly refers to the same range of meanings as hiṇḍola does, although the BD does not say so explicitly. Sanskrit treatises, however, were written in a synthetic style, and if pārvatī is related to hiṇḍola musically, it is probably aesthetically related as well. Thus, in the development of this musical structure, there was initially an indexical reference, the bhāśā pārvatī, recalling in the mind of musicians and listeners a relationship of contiguity with certain tunes sung in mountainous regions. This relationship was transformed more and more, however; the original folk melody was altered in some respects, and the reference tended toward a general idea of love according to a – perhaps – idyllic construal of love, in the simple manner of mountain people.

The word pārvatī conveys yet another meaning: it is one of the names of the goddess, the spouse of Śiva, both of whom dwell in the Himalayas (except for their times of residence in Kaśī). In the BD, there is no mention of the goddess being linked to the musical form of pārvatī, in spite of the fact other rāgas are explicitly connected to deities; for instance, piñjarī, which 'is sung by Umādevī' (BD 4.B.12). In any case, the signification of pārvatī as love in union is perfectly related to the mythological aspect of Śiva and Parvatī. Again, the lack of explanations in the BD can be attributed to the obvious character of this information for the readers Mataṅga had in mind.

Rāgas were later broadly associated with deities, specially in the SR. After the 13th century, rāgas were more and more conceived as individuals with divine or human characters. They were also consistently attributed to a certain period of the day, or a particular season of the year, in which they should be performed in order to achieve their fullest significations. The way treatises conveyed the aesthetic information of rāgas was by poems, called *dhyāna*, themselves symbols, intended to determine the interpretation habits that musicians, connoisseurs and general listeners should have in order to fully appreciate a performance of classical music (see 3.3.4). Not surprisingly, those poems were translated into miniature paintings, perhaps as an aid to illiterate music lovers, who could not have access to the Sanskrit treatises.

The objects rāgas represent in contemporary Hindustani music are, in general, much more diffuse than in the established, previous systems. In a certain way, categories of feeling overlap with indexical references, and are influenced by other systems of representation, such as the lyrics, the genres, and the way a rāga is actually performed. Making use of a Peircean metaphor for consciousness (CP 7.547 ff.), I could say that contemporary rāgas are symbols that float on the surface of the bottomless lake which the history of Indian music is. It cannot be denied that the representations that rāgas signify are based on an enormous body of significations, which has been evolving and mutating for millennia (the mass of water that constitutes the lake). This encompasses the musical structures and the objects represented by rāgas. The objects themselves are complex signs, which can only be understood with a deep knowledge of Indian culture.

The mutation and evolution of rāgas and their objects are typical features of the semiosis web which they constitute. Particularly, since rāgas are symbols, they have the power to multiply themselves, which is nothing but the function of dynamical interpretants, signs generating other signs, each new sign-generation tending to be better developed representations. Peirce wrote: 'every symbol is a living thing, in a very strict sense that is no mere figure of speech. The body of a symbol changes slowly, but its meaning inevitably grows, incorporates new elements and throws off old ones' (CP 2.222). The older signs may lose their signification, become obsolete, and even die. Rāgas, as euphorganisms, have demonstrated this dynamical living process, the evidence of which is clear in the way new rāgas constantly appear historically in the treatises, and in the struggle of music scholars to keep the old traditions registered, if not alive, while not disregarding the new forms that were in current practice.

The conception of rāgas as symbols (and their constitutive legisigns) should not suggest that they are, in a certain period of time, very strict ideas of musical habits. If, on one hand, the performance of most Hindustani rāgas is conducted by 'a general consensus shared by established practitioners;' on the other, 'variant versions, both of familiar and slightly esoteric rāgas, do exist and are widely acknowledged. The variants most likely to be accepted as legitimate alternates are those codified in the pedagogical traditions of established gharānās' (Manuel 1990: 20). The relative latitude of interpretation of a rāga in a certain generation is one of the factors that promotes the maturation and growth of rāgas' legisigns and their meanings. In fact, as Manuel maintains, when considering the scope of variations the replicas of a rāga can possibly afford, it is important to be 'able to accommodate change and evolution. Much of the vitality of Indian music derives from its dynamic versatility and its ability to grow and change' (1990: 22). That is, in turn, proper of symbols. T. Short writes: 'Symbols, in contrast to other legisigns, exhibit greater variation in the rules by which their replicas are to be interpreted. [...] Dynamic interpretants of the symbol – that is, actual habits of interpretation – vary from person to person and vary with one person from time to time' (1988: 85). Thus, what Peirce writes below on symbols, represents quite well how rāgas evolve, in several senses:

> Symbols grow. They come into being by development out of other signs, particularly from icons, or from mixed signs partaking of the nature of icons and symbols. We think only in signs. These mental signs are of mixed nature; the symbol-parts of them are called concepts. If a man makes a new symbol, it is by thoughts involving concepts. So it is only out of symbols that a new symbol can grow. ***Omne symbolum de symbolo.*** A symbol, once in being, spreads among the peoples. In use and in experience, its meaning grows. Such words as ***force, law, wealth, marriage,*** bear for us very different meanings from those they bore to our barbarous ancestors. The symbol may, with Emerson's sphinx, say to man,
>
> Of thine eye I am eyebeam. CP 2.302

Indeed, rāgas spread in use. Their way of existence is that of being performed. Even if in the past rāgas were kept carefully locked among a small group of musicians and transmitted from generation to generation as family properties, they must have been performed to exist. They have thus attracted the attention of other musicians, and there are plenty of anecdotes on the several means musicians have used to acquire the knowledge of rāgas belonging to traditions other than their own. The musical ideas that contained valuable qualities, that is, rāgas which were charming and capable of being admired, certainly survived, being learned by musicians who cared to keep them alive. Thus, rāgas have spread 'among the peoples'.

But rāgas also grow in their meanings. This is because, as symbols, they represent a purpose. When a rāga is performed and interpreted it intends to bring a certain idea to the mind, and this could be the rāgabhāva or the rasa or whatever meaning associated with that rāga. Good musicians are never satisfied with their work and always strive to play or sing better and better. Thus, a rāgas grow in meaning, for the way of presenting their constitutive legisigns, in the variety of forms and details which their replicas can assume, improve during the course of a musician's life, and a more general improvement will occur over several generations of musicians. But improvement, here, is not confined to making it better, but also to finding new possibilities and combinations of musical elements, which, in a sense, is a growth of meaning, although the rāga still represents the same individual rāgabhāva.

Furthermore, a rāga grows in the scope of aesthetic representations it can signify. Contemporary Indian musicians commonly refer to a variety of meanings when they explain the *mood* of a rāga. In some respect, they are not being imprecise. For instance, there are several shades of the idea of love, in a continuum from the erotic love to the sacred, which can simply be referred to, in Indian classical aesthetics, as *śṛṅgāra*. But *love*, as understood in the NŚ, for instance, is distinct from that conceived by Bhoja centuries later, and the Vaiṣṇava poets later added the devotional idea of love. None of those conceptions, nor the rāgas that represent them, are the best or the ultimate interpretation of love. The symbol, represented by the idea of śṛṅgāra, has seen its meanings grow, and they continue to grow. It is a symbol which is immortal, not in the sense that its meaning is fixed forever, but that its capacity to generate interpretations is infinite. Rāgas also have great scope of interpretations, and their continuously evolving life of more than two millennia indicates that they might also be immortal. Indeed, an Indian sphinx would say: 'Rāga is the eyebeam of Indian music.'

2.3.3 Musical Interpretation

> From the nightingales of the garden of music we hear that in the past every Raga or Ragini produced a particular effect. Even today people say that when Raga Bhairon was sung an oil press moved without any aid whatsoever; the Malkaus stopped the flow of water and the Hindol moved a swing. Similarly the Deepak Raga caused a fire, even the lamps burnt without being lit by anyone. The beasts and birds became senseless when the Shri Raga was sung, why speak of the soft-hearted human beings! And similarly, the Megh Raga brought about a downpour. (Imam [1856], 1959: 6)

The field of musical interpretation constitutes a group of interrelated disciplines, the subject matter of which is musical semiosis as it happens in real time. The point in grouping the study of musical perception, performance, intelligence and composition in Hindustani music under the heading of sign interpretation is precisely to expose their fundamental semiotic character, instead of attempting an exhaustive investigation of these topics. Concerning relations among the three fields of semiotic inquiry, it should be clear that musical interpretants depend on the musical signs themselves and how they refer to their objects; that is, intrinsic musical semiosis and musical reference are encompassed by musical interpretants. The relationship among the fields of inquiry can be expressed logically by this formula: {3[2(1)]}. Therefore, to understand the field of musical interpretation requires considering that of musical reference, which necessarily includes the field of intrinsic musical semiosis.

Perception, performance, intelligence and composition are complex forms of musical interpretants because they are the actual result of semiosis. This is obviously clear in the case of perception. A musical sign reaches the hearing sense and is interpreted as another sign in the mind of the listener, which is further interpreted, and so on. The other three areas of musical interpretants result not from a single instance of perception, but from a cultural-dialogical process of semiosis. Perception starts the process that leads to the causation of musical signs, that is, the performed music, the treatise or conference, and compositions. In the case of Indian music, musical interpretants constitute a millenary web, which has been spun continuously by listeners, musicians, scholars and composers since Vedic culture and even earlier.

The study of musical interpretants implies the understanding of mind and consciousness on a semiotic basis. It would be interesting to compare Indian philosophical conceptions of mind, consciousness, perception, causation, and so on, with the semiotic views of Peirce. But this would lie far beyond the scope of this work. Thus I limit myself here to considerations about Hindustani music by means of a semiotic interpretation. Peirce presents an enticing view on the issue of mind, consciousness, cognition and causation.

To Peirce, mind, phenomenally understood, cannot be merely consciousness, for consciousness is rather feeling in general (CP 7.365). Peirce also recognized that unconscious mind exists (CP 7.364). What truly characterizes mind is final causation: 'The psychologists say that consciousness is the essential attribute of mind; and that purpose is only a special modification. I hold that purpose, or rather, final causation, of which purpose is the conscious modification, is the essential subject of psychologists' own studies; and that consciousness is a special, and not a universal, accompaniment of mind' (CP 7.366). Final causation and its complementary efficient causation are vital processes in the generation of interpretants. These two concepts refer to the possible modes of action in the universe. Dyadic action, or efficient causation, constitutes the forms of brute force. It is by efficient causation that a pair of *mañjīrā*[1] struck together vibrate and produce sound (āhatanāda). Triadic action, or final causation, in turn, implies intelligent or significant action. Thus the mañjīrā is not merely struck, but the musician plays the instrument on time, according to the tāla, with the purpose of performing a certain piece of music. Final causation is actually the essential attribute of mind. Santaella writes, 'Wherever there is law, regularity, real potentiality, there is mind, reason, rationality, and they do not necessarily suppose consciousness, but only knowledge embodied in some form' (1994b: 406). This does not mean that consciousness is unimportant. What Peirce says is that consciousness is a special attribute of mind. Consciousness is a significant feature of musical interpretants, and it can be studied by means of the phaneroscopic categories:

> It seems, then, that the true categories of consciousness are: first, feeling, the consciousness which can be included with an instant of time, passive consciousness of quality, without recognition or analysis; second, consciousness of an interruption into the field of consciousness, sense of resistance, of an external fact, of another something; third, synthetic consciousness, binding time together, sense of learning, thought. (CP 1.377)

Those are the general interpretants a musical sign can produce in perception. Further, all three categories are fundamental in musical semiosis, as I have argued since the beginning of this section.

---

[1] A Hindustani idiophone made up of a pair of small cymbals.

Resuming the problem of mind, final causation implies a telic process, of which semiosis is the essential form. Final causation is a concept that shapes several fundamental issues of Peirce's philosophy, for it is the primary law: 'The hypothesis suggested by the present writer is that all laws are results of evolution; that underlying all other laws is the only tendency which can grow by its own virtue, the tendency of all things to take habits;' and concerning mind he writes that 'this same tendency is the one sole fundamental law of mind' (CP 6.101). That is why Peirce says that man is a bundle of habits (CP 6.228). Among them are habits of thought, but there are several meanings implied by the word thought. Thought in general is the result of final causation, triadic action or semiosis, and thus Peirce writes that 'just as we say that a body is in motion, and not that motion is in a body, we ought to say that we are in thought and not that thoughts are in us' (CP 5.289 n.). At the same time as man is in thought, in another sense, man also is a thought. Peirce writes that 'life is but a sequence of inferences or a train of thought. At any instant then man is a thought, and as thought is a species of symbol, the general answer to the question what is man? is that he is a symbol' (CP 7.583). In other words, man is sign, and its way of being is semiosis. Therefore, in Peircean semiotics, the human mind is not an isolated individuality that interprets an external world, for both are of a sign-character. Santaella writes: 'The sign is not something inert, standing by for an individual ego which will implant meaning in it. We are also signs, and hence, we are apt to interact with the interpretive potential of signs, actualizing them' (Santaella 1992: 196).

Thus, as far as music is sign and musical activities are forms of semiosis, listeners, musicians, scholars and composers are also signs, and their particular sign-character influences the way music is interpreted and created. A listener (or musician, scholar, etc.) can only interpret Indian music as an interaction of the bundle of habits s/he is with the bundle of habits that music is. Furthermore, there is a general mind in Hindustani music, composed by the society of musicians and listeners and the signs they have created and transformed. Again the semiotic web, but the weavers and the web itself are often not clearly distinguishable from each other.

2.3.3.1 Perception

Musical perception is the starting point in the process of actual interpretant generation, which is musical semiosis. Perception and cognition are certainly essential in the process of forming a musical mind, which depends necessarily on manifold kinds of external inputs. Thus, a theoretical case of purely internal, mental semiosis cannot be equated, in terms of power of generation and growth of meaning, to that of dialogical semiosis, or semiosis among several minds. The act of perception lies between phenomenology and semiotics. Firstness can be a preponderant category if the interpreter is able to keep her/his mind at this level. But listening usually leads to genuine semiosis. There is an important element of secondness in perception, namely, the otherness of sounds, the conflict generated by them in any actual instance of perception, because acoustic phenomena intrude on the listener's ears independently of her/his will. Still, perception is not merely dyadic, for cognition and reasoning have also been recognized as fundamental. Indeed,

> for Peirce there is no, and there cannot be, any separation between perception and cognition. According to him, every logical thought, every cognition, begins with perception and results in deliberate action. Further, cognition and perception are not disconnected from the languages [2] by which man thinks, feels, acts and communicates. Hence, Peircean perception theory is closely related to his sign theory, which, in turn, is based on a three-relata logic, highly rigorous; that [logic] splits neither mental processes, nor even sensory ones, from the languages in which they are expressed. (Santaella 1993a: 16)

Therefore, musical semiosis, in a broad sense, originates in perception, for it is with the participation of a mind, which perceives and deliberately acts mentally and physically, that music is realized, enjoyed, conceived, transformed, performed, taught, and composed. In fact, the idea of *mind* is behind all semiosis, and Peirce did not restrict mind to human reasoning: 'Thought is not necessarily connected with a brain. It appears in the work of bees, of crystals, and throughout the purely physical world' (CP 4.551). This conception, which is highly important in Peirce's philosophical system, may be seen as lying beyond the concerns of a semiotic theory of music. Yet in view of the worldwide role of technology in contemporary music, Peirce's expansive concept of mind may be crucial when cybernetic issues are discussed. Concerning Hindustani music, artificial intelligence has already proved useful in the study of improvisation in tablā solos (see Bel 1992; Kippen 1992a, 1992b), and the influence of electronic and digital media on Indian music will certainly extend the importance of this question in the near future.

A Peircean – that is, semiotic – view of perception should not be confused with the several psychological theories. In fact, Peirce found

---

[2] What Santaella means here by *language* is certainly not exclusively verbal language, but any system of signs, including music.

himself at odds with the psychologists of his time, and he proposed meaningful reorientation in *The Philosophy of Mind*, 1902 (CP 7.362-87). On the other hand, Peirce's theory of perception, as connected to semiosis and, consequently, with reasoning, should not lead one to think that he was a rationalist. For him, 'perception also involves non-cognitive processes, as well as unconscious elements. Actually, the majority of the perceptive process is irremediably beyond our control. We only get control over perception when the percept is interpreted' (Santaella 1993a: 17). Besides, the relation between the percepts as acknowledged by a mind and the objects they represent is not one of identity:

> that which appears immediately in perception cannot *in general* be identified with the object itself toward which perception is directed since the entity which appears immediately sometimes fails to be consistent in character with what the object is otherwise known or found out to be. Hence, that which appears is called an 'idea' ('representation,' 'sign'), and it is supposed that our perceptual knowledge of an object is always mediated through an appearance or idea of it. A three-term distinction is thereby set up, consisting of the knowing mind, known object, and intervening or mediating idea through or by means of which the knowing mind is put in connection with the known object. (Ransdell 1979: 52-53)

Thus, the triadic nature of semiosis takes place in perception; a sign is the mediating element relating an object to a perceiving mind and the interpretants it generates. According to Peirce there is, on the one hand, no direct or intuitive knowledge of the object. Objects present themselves to a cognizing mind by means of percepts. On the other hand, whatever appears to a mind is represented as perceptive judgments, which are to be further interpreted. The perceptive judgments can not be equated to percepts, for they are fallible and only validated in relation to other judgments and interpretations. Peirce's theory of perception, which is definitely non-Cartesian (see Bernstein 1964: 165-68), has already been investigated by some Peircean scholars,[3] and thus what follows is merely a schematic view of studies in musical perception.

The starting point in perception is certainly an external object, that is, the dynamical object of perceptive semiosis. What is presented to a mind is not the reality of that object, but some manifestation of it, the percept. This can be more or less distant from an *ultimate reality*, but in any case it is external and compulsive. The sound of a mosquito can be conceptualized as the result of its wings vibrating the air, waves of which reach someone's ears. The mosquito sound is, however, independent of the listener's will, and exists even if s/he does not believe in mosquitoes, as Peirce would say. 'I am forced to confess that it appears. Not only does it appear, but it disturbs me, more or less. I cannot think the appearance is not there, nor dismiss it as I would a fancy. I can only get rid of it by

---

[3] See Bernstein 1964, Ransdell 1979, Santaella 1993a.

an exertion of physical force' (CP 7.620).[4] Thus the percept can only be firstness and secondness; it 'is absolutely dumb. It acts upon us, it forces itself upon us; but it does not address the reason, nor appeal to anything for support' (CP 7.622).

The percept can be directly experienced, but cannot be known directly, that is, intuitively (see Bernstein 1964: 170); for 'Direct experience is neither certain nor uncertain, because it affirms nothing -- it just ***is***' (CP 1.145). Thus direct experience cannot be knowledge. I have contended that direct experience of sounds is musically important, but the fact is that when an acoustic percept reaches the ear it is immediately translated into what Peirce called a 'percipuum', which is already a form of mediation. The percipuum can be understood as an iconic image of the percept, but it is not a genuine sign. The percipuum is as compulsive as the percept. Yet it is not identical with it, for the percipuum bears already the constraints and biases that the particular sense of hearing (or any other sense) imposes:[5] certain frequencies are less perceivable than others, etc. Further, 'we perceive what we are adjusted for interpreting' (CP 5.185). Thus, the percipuum, as thin as it may be, is a layer of mediation. Peirce writes:

> We know nothing about the percept otherwise than by testimony of the perceptual judgment, excepting that we feel the blow of it, the reaction of it against us, and we see the contents of it arranged into an object, in its totality [...]. But the moment we fix our minds upon it and think the least thing about the percept, it is the perceptual judgment that tells us what we so 'perceive.' For this and other reasons, I propose to consider the percept as it is immediately interpreted in the perceptual judgment, under the name of the 'percipuum'. (CP 7.643)

But, if the percept is the dynamical object of a perceptive semiosis, then the percipuum constitutes the object as represented in the sign, that is, the immediate object (Santaella 1993a: 97). Of course, the sign in this case is the perceptual judgment. In spite of the dumbness of the percept, that is, its firstness and secondness, the percipuum allows the possibility of thirdness, or semiosis. The percipuum is in itself a form of interpretation, probably iconic in nature, but it cannot be equated to the percept, for perceptual illusions prove this clearly. This leads the discussion to matters of perceptual judgment, as Peirce writes: 'The percept is not the only thing that we ordinarily say we "perceive", and when I professed to believe only what I perceived, of course I did not mean percepts, since percepts are not subjects of belief or disbelief. I meant perceptual judgments. Given a percept, this percept does not describe itself; for description involves analysis, while the percept is whole and undivided' (CP 7.626). Thus, confronted with an insistent

4 In the original text, Peirce refers to a chair (CP 7.619). I have introduced the sound of a mosquito as an acoustic example. At any rate, the point under discussion is the same for whatever existent.

5 See Santaella 1993a: 98-99.

buzzing sound, the listener would think that a mosquito is around, even if in the dark s/he can not see the insect. Thus, the idea of a mosquito is a judgment about the percept in the way it manifests to the sense of hearing, or percipuum.

The perceptual judgment has some apparently contradictory features. On one hand, it is indubitable; on the other, it is fallible. It is indubitable because of the compulsive character of percepts, which force themselves upon the perceiving mind. An individual could not survive if its perceptual judgments were constantly doubted (Santaella 1993a: 67). Perceptual judgments are nonetheless extremely fallible. What sounds like a mosquito can in reality be the distant sound of an electric saw. The reason for the mistake may lie in the iconic character of the percipuum.[6] Further, being a sign or representation, the perceptual judgment is open to a variety of possible interpretations.

Thus, according to Peirce, perception partakes of the triadic nature of semiosis, although constituting a particular kind of semiosis. The dynamical object is perceived by a consciousness as a sign, the perceptual judgment, which is a form of hypothetical inference (abduction). This representamen starts the web of semiosis, determining interpretants which are set in relation to other signs, perceived or resident in the memory. But this does not mean that only rational thoughts emerge from perception. Rather, it consists in a composite of the three categories: 'There is in all perception a consciousness of immediate quality, a dyadic element of compulsion where we are conscious of something forced upon us, and a judgment factor' (Bernstein 1964: 180). All these elements are important in musical perception.

As the perceptual judgment of a musical event is interpreted, due to the tendency of the sign in expanding and generating meaning, it is possible to expect dynamical interpretants, which are divided into three categories: emotional, energetic and logical (see CP 5.475-76). Each of these can be further divided, and a more precise classification, based on a recurrence of the categories, gives the following list of interpretants that musical perception can determine:

1. Emotive listening:
    - 1.1 quality of feeling
    - 1.2 sensation
    - 1.3 emotion
2. Energetic listening:
    - 2.1 mental effort
    - 2.2 instinctive movement

---

[6] The percipuum, however, is not an iconic sign. It is merely the percept as presented to a consciousness in the actuality of perception. It could be called a quasi-sign. Peirce conceives the percipuum as 'what forces itself upon your acknowledgment, without any why or wherefore' (CP 7.643).

2.3 applause, work, dance

3. Rational listening:

3.1 abduction
3.2 induction
3.3 deduction

A classification of kinds of listeners presented in the NŚ comes closer to the general division of emotive, energetic and rational listening. Bharata writes: 'Masters [of musical art] like a harmonious closure (sama), the scholars distinct [enunciation of] words (*pada*) of the song, the women a sweetness [of voice in singers] and the rest [of the audience] a full-throated singing [lit., crying aloud]' (NŚ 33.227). The sweetness[7] of a musical sign concerns the mode of emotive listening. The mostly physical aspect of a performance, referred to by Bharata as 'full-throated singing', suggests a similar bodily appreciation, and corresponds to energetic listening. And the balance and structure of a musical legisign attracts the experts, for they are engaged in rational listening. This scheme is not exhaustive, however, for emotional, energetic and rational forms have their own internal sub-divisions. Moreover, they overlap each other, for rationality necessarily includes some forms of physical and emotional reaction.

Emotive listening encompasses at least three distinct levels: quality of feeling, sensation and emotion. The first level, quality of feeling, is the psychical manifestation of firstness. Peirce writes that 'feeling is simply a quality of immediate consciousness' (CP 1.307). A quality of feeling has no parts (CP 1.318), and each quality is unique; but on the other hand, 'qualities of feeling show myriad-fold variety' (CP 5.44). This mode of interpretant seems to be so important in music, that it warrants quoting a long excursion on the topic:

> A quality of feeling, say for example of [a] certain purple color, might be imagined to constitute the whole of some being's experience without any sense of beginning, ending, or continuance, without any self-consciousness distinct from the feeling of the color, without comparison with other feelings; and still it might be the very color we see. This is a conclusion which anybody can reach by comparing his different states of feeling; but we cannot actually observe a quality of feeling in its purity; it is always mixed with other elements which modify it greatly. Were a feeling thus to usurp the whole consciousness, it would necessarily be perfectly simple; for the perception of different elements in it is a comparison of feelings. Moreover, with us every feeling has its degree of vividness, which does not affect its quality, but is apparently the degree of disturbance it produces. It is necessary to speak vaguely, because it is not settled precisely what vividness consists in. But [were] the feeling uncomplicated by anything else, no particular degree of vividness would attach to it. The quality of feeling would then be the whole feeling.

[7] Sweetness can refer to the singer's voice quality, as Ghosh interprets in his translation, but I would rather consider the sweetness of the music itself.

> Qualities, then, constitute the first category. A quality of feeling is perfectly simple, in itself; though a quality thought over and thus mixed with other elements, may be compared with others and analyzed. A quality of feeling, in itself, is no object and is attached to no object. It is a mere tone of consciousness. But qualities of feeling may be attached to objects. A quality of feeling, in itself, has no generality; but it is susceptible of generalization without losing its character; and indeed all the qualities of feeling we are able to recognize are more or less generalized. (CP 7.530)

Every rāga has its quality of feeling, but such a generalization does not do justice to the distinctive quality of feeling of a particular performance. Such a feeling, in the moment of its experience, and if the listener permits her/his consciousness to be totally filled with it, has a great degree of vividness and a powerful aesthetic effect. In terms of class of signs, the quality of feeling of a rāga is a qualisign; in relation to the object it is a pure icon; and, at most, it is a rheme for the interpretant. Nevertheless, a quality of feeling cannot be enjoyed without the mediation of the hearing sense and perceptive semiosis (unless it is as purely mental, musical feeling, such as the present state of the mind itself, or a feeling emerging from the memory). Thus, the level of sensation, although a second in the logic of categories, precedes in time the quality of feeling. Peirce distinguishes between feeling and sensation:

> meaning by sensation the initiation of a state of feeling; – for by feeling I mean nothing but sensation minus the attribution of it to any particular subject. In my use of words, when an ear-splitting, soul-bursting locomotive whistle starts, there is a sensation, which ceases when the screech has been going on for any considerable fraction of a minute; and at the instant it stops there is a second sensation. Between them there is a state of feeling. (CP 1.332)

A sensation does not necessarily lose its sense of externality, becoming merely a quality of feeling, if the listener keeps on relating to the outward aspects of a musical performance. This can indeed be an obstacle to aesthetic enjoyment, according to Indian aestheticians (see 3.2, 3.4). However, transient sensations take place constantly in the act of listening to music, and they are the first impressions made by indexical signs, which are essential for the apprehension of higher forms of musical semiosis, such as rational listening. Thus, sensations can bring about forms of dicent signs.

The next level of an emotive interpretant is not characterized by the peculiarity of a quality of feeling, or the externality of a sensation. Emotion is the result of a complex input of sensations and qualities processed by the interpreter's mind:

> Now, when our nervous system is excited in a complicated way, there being a relation between the elements of the excitation, the result is a single harmonious disturbance which I call an emotion. Thus, the various sounds made by the instruments of an orchestra strike upon the ear, and the result is a peculiar musical emotion, quite distinct from the sounds

> themselves. This emotion is essentially the same thing as an hypothetic inference, and every hypothetic inference involves the formation of such an emotion. (CP 2.643)

Thus, the musical emotion Peirce uses as illustration consists in a representation that is still not understood in terms of its component parts, as a rational listener, by means of analysis, would understand it. It comes close to it, however, for it is already a form of inference. Peirce writes:

> The indescribable, the ineffable, the incomprehensible, commonly excite emotion; but nothing is so chilling as a scientific explanation. Thus an emotion is always a simple predicate substituted by an operation of the mind for a highly complicated predicate. Now if we consider that a very complex predicate demands explanation by means of an hypothesis, that that hypothesis must be a simpler predicate substituted for that complex one; and that when we have an emotion, an hypothesis, strictly speaking, is hardly possible – the analogy of the parts played by emotion and hypothesis is very striking. (CP 5.292)

The most common form of musical emotion is that usually understood as the play of expectation and fulfillment. In Hindustani music this is an important form of emotional interpretant, for the performance of a rāga is always improvised. The interpreter is less prepared for what comes next than if he or she were listening to the performance of a fixed score. According to Deshpande:

> Creation of 'suspense' or 'tension' is tantamount to creation of 'expectation'. The singer stimulates expectation and then fulfills it with 'resolution'. But sometimes it is artistically necessary not to resolve the tension immediately after it has been created. An occasional non-fulfillment of an expectation increases the sense of wonderment and heightens the already accumulated suspense. As note after note falls on the ear the intelligent listener goes on guessing what is coming next. When he has formed an expectation of a certain possible svara or svara-combination he gets a pleasant jolt when an entirely unexpected phrase or grace emanates from the singer. [...] It will thus be seen that both fulfillment and non-fulfillment of expectation have room in a musical design. Only one has to use these imaginatively. (1987: 36)

Deshpande's view (as well as Ranade's, see 1951:135-6) is very similar to that in Meyer's classic *Emotion and Meaning in Music*. Meyer wrote: 'the customary or expected progression of sounds can be considered as a norm, which from a stylistic point of view it is; and alteration in the expected progression can be considered as a deviation. Hence deviations can be regarded as emotional or affective stimuli' (1956: 32). Semiotically, the gambit of fulfillment and non-fulfillment of expectation in Hindustani music is an interplay of musical legisigns and their actual, performed sinsigns. The legisigns are previously known, either consciously or instinctively, by the listener, who, in face of the replicas actually presented by the musicians, experiences the musical emotion in terms of a confluence of the sinsigns in relation to the legisigns that characterize a rāga. An important element in a bandiś is the mukhṛā, the first phrase of a composition, which when performed brings stability and affirmation of the rāgabhāva and the sam of the tāla. The improvisation develops between the presentations of the mukhṛā (and/or other segments of the bandiś); each sequence of improvised music may conform in several degrees to the legisigns of the rāga. According to Deshpande, 'the two elements, tension and resolution, make themselves felt in every cycle. In other words, the very texture of music is made up of the tension-resolution duality' (1987: 34). Expectation and fulfillment can be extended with the play of tirobhāv and āvirbhāv (see 2.3.1), but at the emotional level, there is no analysis of the presented phrases, but only hypothetical inferences (or abductions, the first kind of arguments), of which predicates are the musical emotions. This can proceed to rational listening if the interpreter is able to identify, classify and understand the musical structures presented by the musicians; to do so involves the ability to anticipate possible segments of musical material, even to the point where the listener is apt to perform the same elements. But instead of a rational mode of listening, the musical emotion can also be subject to an overwhelming quality of feeling, or manifest as energetic interpretants.

The second class of interpretants generated by musical perception consists in energetic reactions to the act of listening. Such reactions range from mental effort, such as the component of volition in the hypothetical inference of an emotion, to bodily reactions, which can be instinctive or organized and codified. The apprehension of a musical sign, besides its mental aspects, can produce psychomotor reactions of an involuntary nature: 'Considerable excitements expend themselves out of the spinal nerves, either in contractions of voluntary muscles, attended mostly with a sober activity of mind, or in glandular secretions, actions on involuntary muscles, probably through the sympathetic nerves, and these cases are apt to be accompanied by emotional excitement of the soul' (CP 7.396). The last point made by Peirce is important, for whatever form of interpretant is generated by music, there always will be some kind of quality of feeling as component(s) of a complex entity. Energetic interpretants of a psychosomatic or psychomotor nature can be forms of rheme or dicent signs.

Finally, energetic interpretants can appear in the form of conventional signs, which presupposes previously learned forms of semiosis. The most known of those is the applause, as the audience's sign of appreciation for the musicians. In Hindustani music, listeners also react verbally, with conventional phrases such as *Vāh!, Vāh!* (Splendid!); or *Kyā bāt!* (How good!). In the Indian concert milieu, verbal manifestations of the audience are usually understood as an instinctive outburst of musical appreciation, uttered especially when the performers present sinsigns that characterize the rāgabhāva, for instance, or exceptionally admirable phrases, brilliant sequences of improvisation, and the like. The conventionality of verbal statements is also manifested in popular concerts, when at every instance of musical virtuosity someone in the audience says 'vāh,!', even if the phrase is not particularly laudable from the experts' point of view. This is a form of logical interpretant, although the argumental sign is a very simple one, not related necessarily with musical legisigns; for applause can instead be a consequent sign of social conventions and habits, such as the norms of concert customs.

Energetic listening can also evolve as bodily interpretants. They are organized forms of corporeal movement in response to music. There are basically two forms, the labor performed in conjunction with functional music (such as work songs), and dance. In the first case, the functionality of music does not necessarily find its outlet in physical work. A devotional song also has functional aspects, the bodily manifestations of which can be seen in a performance of *qawwālī*,[8] for instance (see Qureshi 1986). But energetic interpretants can be as sophisticated as dance. The energetic interpretant (of both musicians and dancers) is possibly one of the semiotic boundaries that connects music and dance, but the subject requires a much more thorough investigation than is possible here. The art of choreography, for instance, could be studied in the same three semiotic fields of intrinsic signification, reference and interpretants; to which the relations with music, stage design, costumes, makeup, literary texts (if any) should be added – all of which constitutes a complex case of intersemiosis.

Rational listening distinguishes itself from the categories of emotion and energetic physical reactions, for it involves thought on musical habits or laws. In this category cognition is predominant, and it should be understood here in semiotic terms: 'A ***Sign*** is a representamen of which some interpretant is a cognition of a mind' (CP 2.242). Although the concept of sign can be extended as far as an action, experience, or even quality of feeling (CP 8.332), what is implied in rational listening is genuine thirdness, when all three relata of semiosis are of the nature of thought. This last is of three kinds: (1) thought as possibility or vague idea; (2) thought in its aspect of secondness, acknowledging the general traits of experience or information; and (3) informing thought, the processing of information and giving body to ideas (CP 1.537). Mere attentive listening to music, even if not determining logical interpretants, is a form of potential thought. When musical information is discriminated by the listener into general features (musical habits or legisigns), a second level of musical thinking is reached, which is essential for the next level. Informative musical thinking is the synthetic processing of musical habits, which gives body to and conceptualizes musical ideas. Peirce refers to cognition as the third kind of thought, but it is clear, as for the idea of

[8] A devotional form of Sufi music, often of an ecstatic nature.

sign, that he extended his conception of cognition to other modes of semiosis as well:

> But by far the most confused of the three members of the division, in its ordinary statement, is Cognition. In the first place every kind of consciousness enters into cognition. Feelings, in the sense in which they alone can be admitted as a great branch of mental phenomena, form the warp and woof of cognition, and even in the objectionable sense of pleasure and pain, they are constituents of cognition. The will, in the form of attention, constantly enters, and the sense of reality or objectivity, which is what we have found ought to take the place of will, in the division of consciousness, is even more essential yet, if possible. But that element of cognition which is neither feeling nor the polar sense, is the consciousness of a process, and this in the form of the sense of learning, of acquiring, of mental growth is eminently characteristic of cognition. This is a kind of consciousness which cannot be immediate, because it covers a time, and that not merely because it continues through every instant of that time, but because it cannot be contracted into an instant. It differs from immediate consciousness, as a melody does from one prolonged note. Neither can the consciousness of the two sides of an instant, of a sudden occurrence, in its individual reality, possibly embrace the consciousness of a process. This is the consciousness that binds our life together. It is the consciousness of synthesis. (CP 1.381)

Thus cognition, though encompassing qualities of feeling, and the will in the form of attention, is above all consciousness of a process, and this cannot be reduced to the categories of firstness and secondness, because it is genuine thirdness. The importance of this conception for musical studies is that musical cognition is essentially the logical apprehension of musical interpretants, which is based on attention, and includes quality of feelings.

Cognition, in terms of interpretants determined by a musical sign, can be understood according to the third trichotomy of signs, concerning 'the extent to which the sign limits what its actual interpretant *can* be' (Ransdell 1986: 689). Peirce writes: 'a Rheme is a sign which is understood to represent its object in its characters merely; that a Dicisign is a sign which is understood to represent its object in respect to actual existence; and that an Argument is a Sign which is understood to represent its Object in its character as Sign' (CP 2.252).

If a musical sign is understood in such a way that there is no identification of the object (be it acoustic or non-acoustic), then the sign is a rheme, and it only presents features of timbre, frequency, duration, and intensity qualities, as well as the more elaborate qualities of melody, rhythm, and so on. This is the case, for instance, with a melodic motif that can represent several related rāgas; but as for the svaras, how their relative direction and ornaments are presented, they do not include any peculiar element that could make clear which particular rāga is being performed. It may also be that the interpreter is unable to recognize the motif, and thus the notes can only convey their material characteristics to her or him. The motif is a qualisign or an iconic sinsign at most, and the interpretant is a rheme. A rheme, as an interpretant, can only be contemplated (CP 8.338); and this is certainly an important kind of musical semiosis, for the contemplation of musical characters is a basic form of musical perception, that of quality of feelings.

If the sign limits reference in such a way that some kind identification of the object is included for interpretation, then the sign is a dicent. In the case of a motif, it can be structured so that a recognition of the rāga is possible, but even then some latitude is still possible. Say that G~MRS is heard by an interpreter who has somehow learned that this motif is usually performed in rāgas of the kānhḍā group. In that case, the sign has acted as dicent, permitting identification of possible objects: rāga darbārī kānhḍā and aḍāṇā; but the motif is also used in rāgas miyāṁ kī malhār and bahār. Thus more musical material is necessary for specifying the exact rāga. A dicent can be merely contemplated, but it can also be urged upon the interpreter by insistence (CP 8.338). That is how an attentive listener, even one ignorant of the theory of Hindustani music, can, after repeatedly listening to one of those rāgas, relate the motif G~MRS to the general legisign which the rāga is.

Finally, if the musical sign allows no latitude, for it specifies the interpretant as the logical consequence of a general rule, then the sign is an argument. This is the case when a key phrase is presented, such as the pakaḍ, mukhya aṅg or calan of a rāga; or when the performance of a rāga has developed for some time, and the combination of several musical elements makes explicit what rāga is being performed. This kind of musical inference is commonly practiced by Indian audiences, for usually the rāgas to be performed are not announced, nor their names printed in a program. In fact, musicians commonly decide what rāga they will play or sing first just some minutes before sitting on the stage, and the following rāgas are selected on the spot, at the moment of beginning the performance.[9] The recognition of a rāga as a form of argument can be submitted to the listener in the same way as any logical inference is. The typical legisigns of a rāga are the major premise, the performed motifs are the minor premise, and the naming of a rāga is the conclusive predicate. But this introduces the subject of the several kinds of arguments. Before this, however, it is necessary to state that an argument can not only be submitted to the interpretant; it can also be urged upon the latter by insistence or by being an object of contemplation (CP 8.338). Thus, it is once more evident that musical perception, even in its rational form, does not exclude the category of feeling.

Arguments can be of three kinds – abduction, induction and deduction – which relate, respectively, to the categories. By 1902 Peirce had refined his classification of arguments, which can be understood as follows:

---

[9] Personal communication from Ustād Zia Fariduddin Dagar.

> Deduction is reasoning which professes to pursue such a method that if the premisses are true the conclusion will in every case be true. Probable deduction is, strictly speaking, necessary; only, it is necessary reasoning concerning probabilities. Induction is reasoning which professes to pursue such a method that, being persisted in, each special application of it (when it is applicable) must at least indefinitely approximate to the truth about the subject in hand, in the long run. Abduction is reasoning which professes to be such that in case there is any ascertainable truth concerning the matter in hand, the general method of this reasoning, though not necessarily each special application of it, must eventually approximate to the truth. (L75 Draft A, 35)

In the classification of arguments, Peirce intended not merely to arrange and describe the kinds of inference, but also to demonstrate their operation in regard to scientific inquiry. In 1903, he wrote: 'Abduction is the process of forming an explanatory hypothesis. It is the only logical operation which introduces any new idea; for induction does nothing but determine a value, and deduction merely evolves the necessary consequences of a pure hypothesis' (CP 5.171). Abduction (which Peirce previously called 'hypothetical inference', or 'retroduction') is a method essential for the discovery of new ideas; it 'is an argument which presents facts in its Premiss which present a similarity to the fact stated in the Conclusion, but which could perfectly well be true without the latter being so, much more without its being recognized; so that we are not led to assert the Conclusion positively but are only inclined toward admitting it as representing a fact of which the facts of the Premiss constitute an ***Icon***' (CP 2.96). Thus, in ascertaining the identity of a rāga being performed, the first inference may be abductive, in the sense that the motif G̲~MRS is iconically similar to a characteristic motif of some rāgas, such as darbārī, etc. As soon as a hypothesis is adopted, the other two methods of inquiry come into play for testing the hypothesis and determining the rāga.

For instance, suppose an abduction suggests that the rāga being performed is darbārī kānhḍā. A deduction can provide information about the essential elements of darbārī kānhḍā, to which the performance should conform. Thus, motifs such as S^{N}Ḏ̣~~^{S}Ṉ̣^{N}S, Ḏ̣~~Ṉ̣P̣, S, RSR ^{M}G̲~~M- RS (SA 5.121; see Ex. 18) should necessarily appear if the rāga is darbārī kānhḍā. Fittingly, G̲~MRS is one of those, but further inquiry is necessary. This can be tested by series of inductions, where samples of the performance are compared with the major premiss. But if the motif ṂP̣Ṉ̣ḌṆ- SRS appears, it is obvious that the rāga cannot be darbārī; but it could be miyāṁ kī malhār, for the latter has both N̲ and N, besides the śuddh D (see Ex. 19, SA 5.60). Each of the three kinds of inference, therefore, has a special function in the inquiry: 'Deduction proves that something must be; Induction shows that something actually is operative; Abduction merely suggests that something may be' (CP 5.171). This method can be applied recurrently, up to the point where the listener is convinced he knows which rāga is actually being performed. The experimental face of cyclic application of deductions and inductions should not diminish the importance of abduction: 'Its only justification is that from its suggestion deduction can draw a prediction which can be tested by induction, and that, if we are ever to learn anything or to understand phenomena at all, it must be by abduction that this is to be brought about' (CP 5.17). Therefore, rational listening, dealing essentially with logical interpretants, can induce a change of habits (of thought or action), as previously explained (see 2.2).

Example 18

Rāga darbārī kānhḍā mukhya aṅg

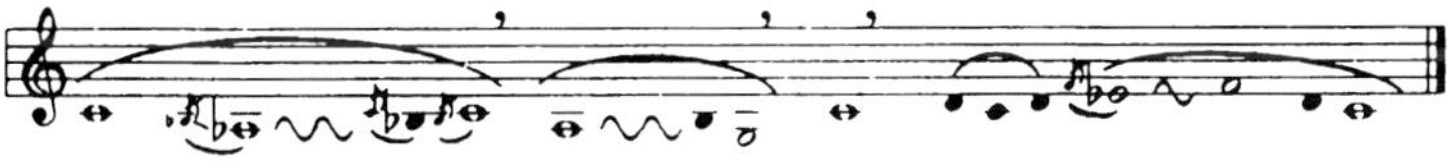

Example 19

Rāga miyāṁ kī malhār mukhya aṅg

The examples given thus far should not suggest that rational listening involves only the interpretation of intrinsic musical signification. Reference can also determine rhemes, dicent and arguments. For instance, a tān performed in the development of a khayāl may be simply a character of melodic movement and ornamentation, thus, a rheme for the interpretant. But if this tān has a timbral and melodic character such that the listener can recognize the voice of a certain singer, then it is a dicent sign to the interpretant. Moreover, if that tān, which has a particular shape, is being performed in the rāga megh malhār by Ustād Bade Gulam Ali Khan (who is known for his musical references), and is understood by the listener as an iconic sign representing lightning, then it is as an argument that it has connected the sign and its object with a style of musical performance.

Finally, all modes of musical perception may be involved aesthetically in an actual instance. Those, in turn, depend on intrinsic and referential musical signification, as in this description offered by Saxena:

> Profundity, as experienced by the singer of ālāpa and his listeners, derives from the following factors: a tranquil and regulated build-up of the melodic fabric, which captures attention partly by virtue of the very attitudes it requires us to adopt, that is, not merely sympathetic attention to the present music for its own sake, but the patience to wait for what is

> to come next, and a creative imaginativeness to bridge the many intervals of literal silence that punctuate the course of singing, an act which is helped by our knowledge of the rāga-form; abundant moments of manifestly absorbed, and not merely tuneful, singing; the seemingly exhaustless potential of the rāga to admit newer and newer effects of depth, height and beauty; and the melodic atmosphere which, once it has established itself, appears to be all around us, and steep us in a feeling of happy subservience. Phenomenologically, profundity is here a sheer immensity of satisfied feeling, which comes as a sequel to a blend of some purely musical values in what meets the ear, and in the discriminating but non-analytical attention of the listeners. (1992: 7)

Saxena selects the quality of feeling of profundity as the interpretant of the ālāp of an unspecified rāga. Sign, object and interpretant seem here to partake of similar qualities, which suggests that the semiosis takes place on an iconic basis. The sign in itself, 'tranquil and regulated', as ālāps in all rāgas usually are (at least in the stage of vilambit ālāp), refers to profundity by the features it possesses. The interpreters also adopted a similar attitude, that of patiently awaiting the musical development. The interpretation of an ālāp as the quality of feeling of profundity, implies an energetic mode of attention, or mental effort; which rationally develops as discrimination based on knowledge of rāga legisigns, not in the sense of analytical reasoning, but as aesthetic enjoyment. That is the rational interpretation of the sign as a character of profundity, hence, a rheme. Emotional, energetic and rational listening blend together in the act of perception of an ālāp. Consequently, by the combination of different kinds of interpretants, it is possible to comprehend the complexity of aesthetic experience, and I do not exclude the higher forms of inference from it; for even a mathematical demonstration has its quality of feelings, and so does musical reasoning. But when I mention aesthetic enjoyment, as above, another question of perception in Hindustani music arises; namely, the issue of rasa, the essence, taste or feeling of a musical performance. The semiotic nature of rasa in music requires wide-ranging considerations of the theory of rasa itself, the musical signs (i.e., rāgas) and their evolution, and will be the subject matter of section 3 (below).

2.3.3.2 Performance

A necessary (and, in relation to perception, complementary) form of musical interpretant is undoubtedly performance, the physical actualization of musical signs. The modulation of sound waves, either by controlling the vocal chords and breath or by putting an object (such as a string) into vibration, is dyadic action that is accomplished by physical force. But musical performance, obviously, is not pure brute force, because there is necessarily an intelligent principle guiding the way psychomotor and muscular efforts produce sounds of a certain kind and having particular characteristics. Performance is thus a combination of dyadic and triadic action, both of which were recognized and studied by

Peirce. 'There is dyadic action, which is mechanical or dynamic; and there is triadic action which is intelligent or signic. Dyadic action was equated with efficient causation and triadic action with final causation' (Santaella 1994b: 403). The origin of this distinction is as old as Aristotle. Peirce gave it new signification in the light of semiotic, pragmaticism, and other branches of his studies (see CP 6.66 ff.; 6.101).

Efficient causation 'is a compulsion determined by the particular condition of things, and is a compulsion acting to make that situation begin to change in a perfectly determinate way; and what the general character of the result may be in no way concerns the efficient causation' (CP 1.212). Thus, efficient causation in musical performance concerns strictly the mechanical aspects of vocal or instrumental technique. The hitting of the right-hand forefinger on the tight skin of the tablā produces vibrations on the skin, which will be transmitted to the air and appear as a sound for the listener. It is, as I have limited the situation here, merely an affair of secondness.

Final (or ideal) causation is that 'mode of bringing facts about according to which a general description or result is made to come about, quite irrespective of any compulsion for it to come about in this or that particular way; although the means may be adapted to the end. The general result may be brought about at one time in one way, and at another time in another way' (CP 1.211). The most familiar case of final causation is purpose, a conscious form of final causation (CP 7.366). The tablā player has a purpose in mind when s/he hits the instrument in a particular way. Firstly, there is the intention of producing sounds of a certain general character, say the clearly pitched **nā**, and to do so requires that the forefinger strike a spot near the rim (the *kinār*) of the instrument, while the third finger keeps contact with another point of the skin (at the edge of the *siyāhī*, the black spot), thereby dampening certain partials; the fourth finger keeps the balance of the movement by holding to the rim, on yet a third spot. Notice that various musicians may use slightly different techniques for this articulation (moving the finger itself or rotating the wrist); even musicians of the same gharānā might have different opinions as to exactly how the sound of a **nā** is produced. What matters concerning final causation is the general qualities which characterize **nā** as a particular articulation of the instrument. Secondly, it is by a rational interaction, in face of the effects produced by efficient causation, that a musician develops her/his technique to bring the efficient causation into conformance with the intent of the final causation, by producing sounds of certain pitch, duration, timbre, intensity, and so on that serve particular musical purposes. Thus, thirdly, the musician produces an act of dyadic action, in order to generate sounds of a recognized and codified character, at a certain moment in the performance, according to the legisigns that represent habits of rāga, tāla, musical form and style.

The generality of final causation in musical performance may be studied as a classification of kinds of performance and kinds of performers. This is not a new issue in Indian music śāstra. Śārṅgadeva, for instance, divided vocalists in five classes:

> Five types of vocalists are recognized by the vocal experts viz. *śikṣākāra* [educator], *anukāra* [imitator], *rasika* [aesthete], *rañjaka* [entertainer] and *bhāvaka* [inspirer of emotion]. One who is capable of imparting flawless instructions is considered by the wise to be śikṣākāra (the educator). The imitator of another's style is called anukāra (the imitator). One who gets absorbed in aesthetic delight (rasa) is rasika (the aesthete), and one who entertains the listeners is rañjaka (entertaining), and one who is extremely expressive in the delineation of the song is known as bhāvaka (the inspirer of emotion). (SR 3.19c-22b)

The subject has also been taken up by contemporary authors. Deshpande proposed the theory that performers may be classified into svara-oriented and laya-oriented, which is to be understood as a continuum. He gives as examples of the two extremes the Kirana and Agra gharānās; respectively representing, on one hand, a style of performance emphasizing intonation, melody, ornaments, and perfect tunefulness; on the other, rhythmic play, well proportioned form, and impeccable fidelity to tāla (1987: 41-45). The balanced combination of the two extremes corresponds to what Deshpande calls the 'gharānās of the golden mean' (1987: 46-52).[10] This is represented by the Alladiya or Jaipur style: 'this gharānā has devoted conscious thought to the achievement of a fusion of svara and laya. It never considered either the svara or the laya as its only, or even prominent medium' (1987: 47). The gharānā of Gwalior is also pointed out by that author as blending the two tendencies, and a number of other schools are situated at some point of the continuum (1987: 68).

This theory is presented by Deshpande as hypothetical (1987: 69). Comparing his theory with the (later) study of Wade on khayāl, it appears that some of Deshpande's generalizations might be sustained. About the Kirana singers Wade writes, 'the general emphasis on melody – whether in terms of form or style – is the shared feature, and that is played out in ways that may be shared (ālāp, mīṇḍ, kān, and other means of vocal expressiveness) or individual' (1984: 226). In the Agra gharānā, Wade also found strong rhythmic elements that may be attributed to the closeness of the Agra khayāl style to the dhrupad: 'emphasis on laya is a prime factor in this, and it is maintained in the following ways: (1) boltān; (2) bolbāṇṭ; (3) use of a large proportion of text provided by the *cīz*;[11] (4) and a variety of ways in approaching sam, including (a) tihāī

[10] Notice that Deshpande was himself a singer of the Jaipur style (Wade 1984: 161, A. Sharma 1993:118).

[11] The lyrics of a khayāl, or a khayāl piece.

and (b) atīt-anāgat approaches; (5) *nom-tom*[12] and nom-tom like rhythmic emphasis; and (6) a lively relationship between the singer and tablā player' (1984: 129). Even so, the parameters of svara and laya, although important in Hindustani music, cannot account for all the subtleties of performance styles in Indian music. Indeed, there are musical aspects like tempo; general features of form; the use of text; techniques such as sargam, bolbāṇṭ, boltān; the use of ornaments such as mīṇḍ, gamak, kān, vibrato; the use of dynamics, and so on – all of which characterize the gharānās in general, as well as the particular style of each singer in a gharānā. All those musical elements depend on a combination of melodic and rhythmic factors. The classification presented by Deshpande certainly has general value, but further inquiry is necessary to establish a more accurate classification and understanding of styles of performance in Hindustani music.

Combining the classes presented by Śārṅgadeva and Deshpande, one arrives at a no-less hypothetical classification of Hindustani music performance. The latter is divided into three genera: (1) according to intrinsic musical features; (2) according to functional character; and (3) according to the representational purposes of a performance. Each genus divides into three species. Both layers, of course, relate to the universal categories of Peirce, and do not represent any sort of ranking in terms of artistic value.

Musical performance:

1. According to the musical features of performance:
    - 1.1 svara-oriented
    - 1.2 laya-oriented
    - 1.3 balanced performance
2. Functional features of performance:
    - 2.1 emotional
    - 2.2 imitator
    - 2.3 entertainer
3. Representational features of performance:
    - 3.1 aesthete
    - 3.2 referential
    - 3.3 educational

Svara-oriented performance is a first in the system of musical features of a performance, because it mainly relates to qualities of feeling signified by the musician by means of delicate ornamentation (kāns, mīṇḍs) and melodious phrases. Thus, Deshpande writes about the

[12] Improvisational technique typical of the dhrupad ālāp in which meanigless syllables (including nom and tom) are used for rhythmic play.

sweetness and delight of Abdul Karim Khan's (1872-1936) voice when singing ālāp (1987: 41), and Wade adds the more technical descriptor of 'pliant' to the list (1984: 197). The melodious tendency can be attributed in general to the Kirana gharānā. Laya-oriented performance is a second because by emphasizing rhythmical features the musician gives motion and energy to the performance. An example of a laya-oriented singer is Faiyaz Husain Khan (1886-1950), whose sense of rhythm, laykārī, sam, bolbāṇṭ, etc. always found favor with the critics (see Wade 1984:108-09). The rhythmic activity is a highlighted feature of the Agra gharānā. The combination of both principles, svara and laya, is placed as a third species of musical performance, for the idea of synthesis is necessarily related to thirdness. Alladiya Khan (c. 1855-1946), for example, cultivated a sweet, mellow, elastic voice, and was equally able to perform intricate rhythmic patterns in the form of tāns and boltāns (Wade 1984:171). Deshpande classifies the style of the gharānā of Gwalior also as a balanced one. The gharānās of Patiala and Indore are placed in an intermediate position, between a svara-oriented and a balanced style (1987: 67-68). In another essay, Deshpande tries to extend his classification to dhrupad *bānīs*[13] (1987: 135-44), but this is an issue even less studied than the khayāl styles. The counter-argument to this kind of classification is the fact that gharānās have become less and less distinguishable. The style of contemporary singers has absorbed elements, not only from several gharānās, but also from other genres, as witnessed by the widespread use of ṭhumrī ornamentation in khayāl (Meer 1980: 188).

The second genus is related to the functional features of performance: the emotional, the imitative, and the entertaining musician. All three species come from Śārṅgadeva's classification: bhāvaka is the emotional musician, one who can strongly affect an audience, by means of his expressiveness; the anukāra is the imitator, one who is able to perform accurately another's style; and the rañjaka is the entertainer. The emotional musician uses musical resources and textual significations (in the case of vocal music) to arouse emotion in the audience. A prime example are the singers of ṭhumrī of the early 20th century, remnants of whose style may still be found among some contemporary singers. The species of musical imitators does not refer to the normal imitative process by which the learning of Indian music takes place (paraphrasing). Probably, Śārṅgadeva meant something more specific. Still, nothing seems to indicate that imitators were kinds of courtly parody makers (working by means of allegorical references), for such activity would have been as far removed from the classical music sphere then as it is today, belonging more properly to the theater world. Imitators could have been minor musicians who never developed a musical personality of their own, or who out of sheer admiration performed according to

---

[13] Lit., sound, voice. Thus the term bānī refers to the schools of dhrupad and their features.

someone's style. Nowadays, it is not necessarily derogatory to refer to someone as being an imitator. Thus, D.C. Vedi has stated that Kumar Gandharva (1924-1992) was a follower of O. Ṭhākur to the point of being an imitator (in Meer 1980: 163). In fact, Kumar Gandharva was a disciple of B.R. Deodhar (b. 1901). Both Ṭhākur and Deodhar, in turn, were disciples of V.D. Paluskar (1872-1931). Therefore, there was no direct teaching link between Ṭhākur and Gandharva, and if the latter's style reflects Ṭhākur's, Vedi's assertion is justifiable.

Finally, the entertainer is the musician that most pleases lay audiences. S/he not only makes use of musical resources such as displays of virtuosity, but also theatrical techniques, such as facial expressions, glances, hand gestures and costumes.

The third genus refers to the representational features of performance, Śārṅgadeva's two other kinds of singers are situated here. I propose one extra specie: the rasika or aesthete. This kind of performer both leads the audience to, and becomes personally involved in, the highest aesthetic experience, or rasa. The question of whether a performer can really experience rasa when playing or singing is complex, and deserves further research. Here I merely argue for a species of referential musicians that concerns performers who engage in forms musical reference of either an acoustic or non-acoustic nature. The educator, or śikṣākāra, is certainly a third species, for her/his main purpose is to spread musical knowledge.

The outstanding example of an aesthete/performer is O. Ṭhākur, a scholar devoted to the study of rasa and other aesthetic features of rāgas (see SA). Ṭhākur was also an educator, who would inform audiences about the aesthetic character of the rāgas he was to perform (according to Rao 1992: 38). Another singer who is especially concerned with the question of rasa is Kishore Amonkar (b. 1932). The typical referential performer is Ustād Bade Gulam Ali Khan, but other names may be included, such as Ustād Ali Akbar Khan, known for his musical metaphors (see 2.3.2). It bears repeating here, that the aesthetic value of musical reference is an important mode of signification in Hindustani music; my position on this matter thus disagrees with that of scholars who hold an absolutist view of Indian music. Finally, in relation to the performer who is an educator, one distinction is crucial. Virtually all performers are also teachers, but by 'educator' I mean the singer or player who tends to educate when performing. In this sense, V.D. Paluskar was a typical educational performer. Powers writes that Paluskar 'was a convinced nationalist and was able to link Hindustani music, as an indigenous high art neither stifled nor adulterated by European rule, with the nationalist movement. He helped make Hindustani music respectable by enabling students of middle-class families to perform publicly under the auspices of [Paluskar's] music school' (1980a: 89). In regard to the political posture of Paluskar, it is known that he used to sing the patriotic song *Vande Mātaram* at the end of concerts. Hence he can also be classified as a referential performer. In sum, the genera and species of performance discussed here frequently appear simultaneously on different levels in the styles of various musicians, and do not represent absolute boundaries. Overlapping of genera and species is more likely to appear according to the logic of the Peircean categories.

There should be a subfield of musical performance that also inquires into the creative process involved in Hindustani music improvisation. I can merely hint at this topic in this space. Among the very few studies on Hindustani music improvisation, the work of Kippen on tablā drumming stands out. In his training with Ustād Afaq Husain Khan, Kippen realized 'the near absence of any verbalized rules on how to improvise successfully; rather I was taught by example and, through trial and error, I absorbed the rules for improvisation as an *intuitive* system in much the same way as a child absorbs the rules for speaking a natural language' (1992a: 75). Kippen realized (after Blacking) that the comparing of tablā drumming with the functioning of verbal languages is a limited means of understanding improvisation (1992a: 72, 96). However, whether *intuition* can constitute a system of improvisation is an equally important question. Peirce criticizes several aspects of the problem of intuition in the article *Questions Concerning Certain Faculties Claimed for Man* (published in 1868; see CP 5.213-63 or W2:193-211). It seems to me that if there is any system of improvisation in the mind of performers, then it would rather be a system of trained instincts, in the broad, Peircean conception of ***instinct*** (see CP 2.3, 2.170, 5.533, 6.476).

Kippen pursued his studies by means of an ingenious method of interactive computational musicology (1992a, 1992b). Employing software created by the programmer B. Bel (1992) – the Bol Processor (BP, latest version 2.5) and Question-Answer Validated Analytical Inference Device (QAVAID) – Kippen was able to determine Chomskyan generative grammars for tablā improvisations, making clear several strategies used by master drummers in their performances. The method has its shortcomings (as the authors have keenly pointed out), one of which is the inability to deal with musical ambiguities; for instance, in the segmentation of motifs (1992a: 94). The fact is that the inference of generative grammars takes place necessarily by means of induction and deduction, which in their rigidity cannot cope with the overlapping categories and multiple validations of Indian musical thought, but only with the latter's formalized aspects. There must be some latitude for musical inferences, and that is the fundamental role of abduction, the only form of reasoning that allows for the freshness and vitality of new ideas and new combinations of the same. Forms of abductive inference have been recently investigated in artificial intelligence (see Thagard 1988: 51-73), and this could be the next step in computational musicology as well.

There seems to be an interplay of musical interpretants coordinating the output of actual music during the performance of a rāga (in the several musical forms and genres) or a pure tāla (the drumming forms). As seen in 2.3.1, musical legisigns determine musical elements and forms, but their actualization as replicas leaves much room for variants. The actual choices made by the musicians can be understood as instinctually trained inferences, as an aspect of final causation determining the efficient causation of playing or singing. The improvisational inferences are abductive, inductive and deductive (see Tarasti 1994c: 77), of which a balanced combination is essential for the production of creative and significant music. Notice that the mental processes of performing are not only a matter of instinctual inferences about purely musical signs, for reference can be equally important. Hence iconic and indexical signs, as well as symbols, are combined with musical legisigns in the musicians' semiotic loom. Saxena gives an example that may illustrate the point:

> Now, imagine a devotee hallowing the morn with svaras of rāga Bhairav, which is meant for this particular part of the day. Steadying himself with the utterance of the tonic, he sets out to develop the singing in such a way that he may be able to saturate himself with images and attitudes that suit the hour – the rising sun, yearning in prayer and the concomitant chastening of self, pouring *arghya* (sacred water) on the idol, and detachment from the things of the world. A brief but immaculate touch on the tonic, followed at once by komal re (D flat) prolonged firmly and sweetly, attunes the mind with the sunrise outside, by suggesting emergence. The same note (D flat) touched while descending from ga (E) provides, in a manner, a clear euphonic transcript of the downward angle of arghya being poured on the idol. As attunement grows through the aid of svaras (or notes), detachment deepens and the singer cooperates by articulating the sa (tonic) merely ideally and lingering on the re (D flat) – now faintly, though of course sweetly – the note suggesting transcendence. The re thus becomes an aid to devotion and to elevation of the self. (1992: 9)

The singer, in this case, is making use of iconic signs, such as an ascending motif that refers to the rising sun or to spiritual detachment, or a descending motif that suggests the pouring of sacred water on the divine image. The statue, although not specified by Saxena, can be reasonably inferred as representing Śiva, for that is the deity which rāga bhairav symbolizes. At any rate, the performance follows the legisigns that characterize this particular rāga, the sinsigns of which are modulated by icons, indices and symbols.

Creative and significant musical improvisation does not appear in a vacuum. A musical idea comes from other musical ideas. A musical idea can be any form of musical sign that takes part in a dynamical process of musical semiosis. In the domain of performance, ideas are signs that function in the musician's mind in view of musical final causation. According to Peirce, an idea is characterized by three elements: 'The first is its intrinsic quality as a feeling. The second is the energy with which it affects other ideas, an energy which is infinite in the here-and-nowness of immediate sensation, finite and relative in the recency of the past. The third element is the tendency of an idea to bring along other ideas with it' (CP 6.135). All of these elements have consequences for musical improvisation. The quality of an interval, for instance, may suggest a whole sequence of variations in sargam, bolbāṇṭ or tāns; or the resonance of a stroke may configure some patterns in a tablā solo. Secondly, a musical idea – according to its relative amount of energy – interacts with other ideas previously presented, and this can suggest for the musician still newer possibilities. Thirdly, a musical idea attracts other, similar or contiguous ideas, and may even constitute a mold or pattern in which other musical ideas of a less general level may be developed.

How musical ideas are manipulated by the musician seems to be a matter of the three kinds of arguments. It is obvious that the articulation of musical legisigns and their actualization as sinsigns is largely the result of deductive and inductive inferences. Thus, one can develop generative grammars that represent rules of transformation and development of musical materials, as Kippen and Bel have done. However, the flexibility and vitality of improvisation in Hindustani music implies that musicians make use not only of deductions and inductions, but also of another form of open reasoning, the abduction, in which the musical ideas appear as solutions not rigidly determined, but rather as hypothetical possibilities. These are not merely a question of chance, although chance may play a part in the abductive process. Abduction is a paradoxical type of inference: 'abduction is a mental process which partakes of the nature of laws, consequently inserting itself into the territory of thirdness. However, although it is a logical inference which has a "perfectly definite logical form", and although it reaches a conclusion, therefore becoming a type of argument, abduction "is very slightly hampered by logical rules" and it asserts its "conclusion only problematically or conjecturally" (CP 5.188-205; see also 7.219 and MS 962)' (Santaella 1991: 126). Therefore, abduction is a form guessing, which is highly fallible and illogical on one hand, but on the other, it is truly a form of argument, capable of unveiling new solutions. Moreover, the conclusion of an abduction can be tested afterwards; and if the hypothesis proves to be true, it will certainly modify the terms of previous deductive/inductive syllogisms.

The role of abduction in musical reasoning is to generate musical ideas,[14] not in a mechanical way, as the early computational models of musical inference, but as a musical instinct that produces original sinsigns out of the complexity of possible forms afforded by a rāga or tāla. Abduction works between the boundaries of crystallized musical forms and the limits of musical variations (those acceptable in the case of the rāga or tāla being performed), the musical genre, the particular style of the musician, and so on. The performing syllogism for the musician is highly complex, and even more so for Hindustani music, whose very

[14] Musical abduction concerns not only the singing and playing of the soloist, but also the role of accompanists: the drummer and the saraṅgī player in khayāl or ṭhumrī; or the second singer, rudra-vīṇā, violinist, harmonium player, etc., according to the genre.

boundaries are not strictly demarcated (which, of course, does not mean that anything goes). In India, musicians are identified as conservative or as more inclined to be inventive, depending on how they actualize rāga legisigns: 'certain artists may prefer a strict, narrow, highly structured approach to rāga interpretation, whereas others may feel more at ease adopting a somewhat liberal attitude toward detail, confident that they can accurately present the image of a given rāga while adhering in a slightly less dogmatic manner to the conventions articulated by purists' (Manuel 1990: 22). How a musician performs less dogmatically, yet still without singing or playing unacceptable musical forms (according to the current tradition), can be explained as the product of instinctual guesses provided by abduction. Those guesses are not so different from those which are used to put forward hypotheses leading to new scientific theories. Peirce writes:

> However man may have acquired his faculty of divining the ways of Nature, it has certainly not been by a self-controlled and critical logic. Even now he cannot give any exact reason for his best guesses. It appears to me that the clearest statement we can make of the logical situation – the freest from all questionable admixture – is to say that man has a certain Insight, not strong enough to be oftener right than wrong, but strong enough not to be overwhelmingly more often wrong than right, into the Thirdnesses, the general elements, of Nature. An Insight, I call it, because it is to be referred to the same general class of operations to which Perceptive Judgments belong. This Faculty is at the same time of the general nature of Instinct, resembling the instincts of the animals in its so far surpassing the general powers of our reason and for its directing us as if we were in possession of facts that are entirely beyond the reach of our senses. It resembles instinct too in its small liability to error; for though it goes wrong oftener than right, yet the relative frequency with which it is right is on the whole the most wonderful thing in our constitution. (CP 5.173)

The instincts of musical thought do not constitute exclusively a logic of musical creation, but also one of speculation, divination, insight. Being a form of inference related to the mode of operation of firstness, abduction 'is mental and at the same time sensuous. It is simultaneously thought and emotion. It is rational – or at least reasonable – but grants no satisfaction to reason. Last, but not least, it is inspiration, instinct; but at the same time, therein lies the only source of new ideas and discoveries' (Santaella 1991: 127). A closely related idea is the play of musement (see Sebeok 1981), which Peirce identified with aesthetic contemplation or 'distant castle-building (whether in Spain or within one's own moral training)' and which could be defined as pure play: 'Now, Play, we all know, is a lively exercise of one's powers. Pure Play has no rules, except this very law of liberty. It bloweth where it listeth. It has no purpose, unless recreation' (CP 6.458). Peirce refers to the power of imagination that, although not intending to fulfill serious purposes, is capable of generating new ideas by the very way thought is carried when relaxed from rigid forms of reasoning: 'There is no kind of reasoning that I should wish to discourage in Musement; and I should lament to find anybody confining it to a method of such moderate fertility as logical analysis' (CP 6.461). Thus, every form of inference can appear in the play of musement, but its non-tendentious character favors discovery and invention. Peirce counsels on how to play with musement in these terms: " 'Enter your skiff of Musement, push off into the lake of thought, and leave the breath of heaven to swell your sail. With your eyes open, awake to what is about or within you, and open conversation with yourself; for such is all meditation." It is, however, not a conversation in words alone, but is illustrated, like a lecture, with diagrams and with experiments' (CP 6.461). It is clear that abduction plays an important role in the musement, and conversely, abductive inferences are a form of musement.

When great musicians improvise, they are not merely following rules of musical forms, that is, conforming their performance to different layers of legisigns. Rather, the truly creative musician can play the game of musement in the universe of a rāga and tāla. Her or his voice (or instrument) is the skiff of musement, which sails in the lake of musical thought, the universe of a rāga. A conversation takes place with the listeners, the other travelers on the same journey.

2.3.3.3 Musical Intelligence

There are two recognized forms of musical intelligence in Indian music, both of which have been developing for millennia on the subcontinent. First, the performance-practice tradition, whose form of transmission is the oral instructions imparted by guru to disciple. In Sanskrit, this is called *guru śiṣya pāramparā*. Second, there is the written tradition, or śāstric, whose medium is the scripted form of treatises, the study of which is also frequently held on a guru-śiṣya basis. Thus, there is some overlapping in this two-fold division, a division further blurred by the fact that there have been (and still are) musicians who were also scholars. In fact, Indian intelligence often makes use of ambiguities on several levels, as Rowell has pointed out:

> Inquiry is open-ended in the Indian tradition, and the process of making categories is infinite – at least in theory. Every statement that can be made blurs a finer distinction, and ultimate truth or reality lies beyond the reach of human experience or inference – except perhaps in those moments of suprasensible illumination vouchsafed to the yogin. Indian musical thought has thus been channeled into elaborate taxonomic structures within which subcategories unfold in profusion, subcategories that often are not mutually exclusive and which thereby encourage a certain amount of ambiguity. (1992: 6)

The endless character of inquiry, as well as the distance of an ultimate truth or reality, are very semiotic concepts. Because the universe is continuously expanding and humankind is in a state of mutation – intellectually, psychologically, morally, and otherwise – there will always be something to study, and truth can only be a transitory state of satisfactory understanding. The exclusive means of knowing reality are signs and their action, and there seems always to be a layer of mediation between the cognizing mind and a 'reality out there'. This does not mean that immediate contact with brute reality is not possible, but that such contact is not knowledge, only experience. Probably this immediate contact with reality, a form of consciousness restricted to firstnesses and secondnesses, is exactly the kind of experience that yogis are familiar with (see Lannoy 1971: 273-74). To the extent that many of the philosophical ideas developed by Indian traditions are based on the idea of continuity, this can also be seen as the semiotic process of generating interpretants – interpretant being a sign that determines another, better developed sign, which in turn triggers another interpretant, and so on. The continuity of Indian music intelligence has similar features, both in the guru śiṣya oral tradition and the written śāstra scholarship. Thus, a guru is as much a semiotic mind and body as is a treatise.

A classification of subfields of musical intelligence can be based on the subject matter of musical investigation:

Musical intelligence:

1. musical aesthetics
    - 1.1 aesthetic perception
    - 1.2 aesthetic performance
    - 1.3 aesthetic theory (rasa theory)
2. musical pragmatics
    - 2.1 analysis
    - 2.2 musical education
    - 2.3 criticism
3. musical semiotics
    - 3.1 intrinsic musical signification
    - 3.2 musical reference
    - 3.3 musical interpretation

Musical aesthetics is obviously a first, because it is concerned with what is admirable in music. Its subdivisions include: 1.1 the study of aesthetic perception, 1.2 the means of signifying aesthetic qualities in musical performance, and 1.3 the theory of aesthetics, which in Indian tradition is called rasa theory. There follow, as seconds, 2.1 musical analysis, 2.2 education, and 2.3 criticism. They are all forms of study in which a relation with something else is implied; in analysis, the relation is with music in itself; in musical education, with ways of imparting musical knowledge; and in criticism, with the ways and values of music produced by accomplished performers. Finally, as thirds, there is musical semiotics, or musical scholarship in a broad sense. Musical semiotics goes even further, and encompasses 'non-semiotic' musical scholarship. All the other genera and their species of musical intelligence can be studied from a semiotic point of view.

Indian musical scholarship corresponds to several of the divisions above. Another possible classification, with more direct application to the history of Indian musical intelligence, refers to forms of thought used in the treatises. Rowell distinguishes two modes by which Indian thought has been organized (1992: 27-34): (1.) Systematic thinking, represented by the six orthodox schools of philosophy (*nyāya*, *vaiśeṣika*, *sāṅkhya*, *yoga*, *mimāṁsā*, *vedānta*; see Chatterjee & Datta 1984, Hiriyanna 1993), as well as the tantra and Kashmiri Śaivism (and I would add the materialist *cārvāka*; and the Jain and Buddhist philosophies); (2.) Symbolic thinking: represented by metaphors, tales, sayings, and the like that help students to understand Indian philosophies, music, arts, etc. I would instead refer to the second group as kinds of analogical thinking (if not iconic thinking), and even postulate another class, that of empirical (or indexical) thinking. Therefore, with a semiotic rearrangement, these classes are as follows: (1.) analogical thinking, (2.) empirical thinking and (3.) systematic thinking. They are obviously related to the three forms of arguments, which appear in the three forms of thought as mixed inferences with different weights of abduction, induction and deduction. In truth, analogical thinking is fundamental to all forms of reasoning. Peirce writes that 'the act of inference consists in the thought that the inferred conclusion is true because ***in any analogous case*** an analogous conclusion ***would be*** true' (CP 5.130). Empirical thinking is predominantly inductive. Because some terms in the classification above have strong connotations with different Indian and Western philosophical views, and do not constitute a Peircean triad, I must make clear that – in this section – analogical, empirical and systematic thinking are merely explanatory categories concerning forms of scholarship in Hindustani music.

Analogical thinking in Hindustani music intelligence, in which tales and metaphors are used instead of experimental or systematic reasoning, besides avoiding 'the dangers of overabstraction' (Rowell 1992: 23), constitutes a truly heuristic mode, a characteristic feature of iconic semiosis (see CP 3.363, 3.641; also Holyoak & Thagard 1995). An interesting example found in the NŚ is the description of how drums were conceived:

> During a break from studies, in the rainy season, Svāti once went to a lake to fetch water. After his having gone to the lake, Pākaśāsana (Indra), by [sending] great torrential rains, commenced to make the world one [vast] ocean. Then in this lake, torrents of water falling with the force of wind made clear sounds on the lotus leaves. Now the sage, hearing suddenly this sound produced by torrents of rain, considered it to be a wonder and observed it carefully. After observing the high, medium and low sounds produced on the lotus-leaves as deep, sweet and pleasing, he went back

to his hermitage. And after arriving there, he devised the *Mṛdaṅgas*, and then the *Puṣkaras* [like] *Paṇavas* and *Darduras* [with the help of] Vīśvakarman. On seeing the *Dundubhi* of gods, he made *Muraja, Āliṅgya, Ūrdhvaka* and *Āṅkika*. Then he who was a master of reasoning of the positive and the negative kind, covered these and Mṛdaṅga, Dardura and Paṇava with hide, and bound them with strings. He also made other drums such as *Jhallarī, Paṭaha*, etc., and covered them with hide.[15] (NŚ 33.5-13)

The description does not seem purely mythological, but a true case of iconic inference and insight, that is, an analogical abduction (see Thagard 1988: 60-63). The lotus leaves, an image of the tight skin of drums, hit by falling raindrops, function iconically as drums. The tale does not explain how Svāti created the several shapes that constitute the drum's shells, but as far as the essential principle of drumming is concerned, it was by means of diagrammatic reasoning. The text above even suggests that the principle of variation of pitch was discovered by Svāti's observation, for he probably inferred that differences in the diameter of the leaves produced sounds of high, medium and low frequencies. Another example of analogical thinking in Indian scholarship is the defining and explaining of concepts by means of drawing a parallel with some idea of common experience. For instance, take the way Mataṅga elucidates the concepts of vādī (sonance), saṁvādī (consonance), anuvādī (assonance), and vivādī (dissonance): 'Vādin is so because of *vadana* (speaking), like the master. The saṁvādin is so because of *saṁvadana* (supportive speaking), like the minister. The anuvādin is so because of *anuvadana* (following or obedient speaking) like the attendants. Vivādin is so because of *vivadana* (opposite speaking), like the enemy' (BD 1.4.anu.19). Thus the relative hierarchy of intervals and modal functions in a rāga are compared with the social intercourse of a king (or master) in relation to his subordinates and enemies. But the way Svāti operated in inferring how it would be possible to have instruments like drums, and Mataṅga in comparing social and political relations to musical functions, also involve an element of observation, which brings up the problem of empirical thinking.

Empirical thought as a form of scholarship should not be confused with any form of empiricist philosophy. To do so would be quite contrary to some Indian philosophies, specially in regard to the idea of *māyā*, sensory illusion or divine play. I am rather concerned with inductive reasoning in the description of musical elements and structures, as well as some forms of experimental methods. A classical example is the two vīṇās experiment described in the NŚ (28.24), intended to demonstrate the existence of 22 śrutis. It is a truly experimental

15 Among the several ancient drums, only the double faced, barrel shaped mṛdaṅga is still known and played. Puṣkara refers to several kinds of wooden drums; paṇava was a form of hour-glass drum; āliṅgya a small face drum with a body like a cow's tail; āṅkika a middle size drum with a body like the myrobalan (?); and the dundubhi an earthen kettle-drum.

approach, rather rare in Indian musicology. A much later scholar, Ahobala-paṇḍita (17th century), described in the treatise *Saṅgīta-pārijāta* the octave relation, as well as and the seven diatonic notes and their intervallic relations, in terms of string division and the position of nodes corresponding to the harmonic partials:

> The places (nodes) for each note are described on the Vīṇā, which generates the notes and which can be seen with the eyes. The node for the upper Sa or Octave stands at the mid-point of the open wire, and that for the Ma (the Fourth) should be taken mid-way between the two – the fundamental and its Octave. Dividing the wire-length into three equal parts the Pañcama (the Fifth) is obtained at the first division, near the top. The Gāndhāra (the Third) is obtained mid-way between the fundamental and its Fifth. The Re (Second) is to be placed at the first (of the three divisions) between Sa and Pa, while the Dha (the Sixth) is to be placed between the Fifth and the Octave. In turn, Niṣāda is at the end of the second (of the three divisions) between the Fifth and the Octave. (in Ranade 1951: 177-78)

Another aspect of empirical thinking concerns the way Indian music theory changed in respect of the constantly evolving musical practice. The growth in varieties of rāgas, for instance, implied the need for more precise forms of description and demonstration of the differences among several rāgas with similar features. This was probably the main function of the ālāp, as Widdess points out:

> The idea that ālāpa demonstrated and indeed embodied the lakṣaṇa or defined characteristics of a rāga, so clearly enunciated by Śārṅgadeva [SR 2.2.23-24], may have arisen as part of a single process along with the theoretical analysis and definition of rāga and the rapid expansion of the rāga system. The more numerous the rāgas in practical use, and the more subtle the structural and aesthetic distinctions between similar rāgas, the more the need would have arisen for a systematic method of demonstrating and developing a particular rāga, in such a way that its unique structural and aesthetic identity was established. (1995: 313)

The classification of rāgas evolved also according to the expansion of musical practice. The *grāma-jāti* system (see NŚ), in use from the early centuries A.D. to the 5th century, were supplanted by the *grāmarāgas*, which evolved from the seven primary grāmarāgas to a number of 33. But this system was not closed and some 100 other structures, the *bhāṣās*, or dialects, were related to the older grāmarāgas (see BD). Even the bhāṣās became aged, and by the late first and early second millennium another system was created by scholars, in order to cope with the new regional *deśīrāgas* (see SR). By this time, the cumulative material of musical scholarship was enormous, for the scholars did not abandon the earlier systems when describing current practice, but rather incorporated new information into the treatise, relating it to the oldest forms and structures, even if those parent and grandparent rāgas and jātis had been obsolete for hundreds of years. Little by little, more rāgas were created and classification systems were put in check. By the 15th and 16th centuries, a paradigmatic change had occurred. By means of analogical thinking, scholars started classifying rāgas into families, quite like the extended Indian family (see SD, and also 3.3.4). Those were known as the rāga-rāgiṇī systems. A male rāga headed a group of five or six wives, the rāgiṇīs. However, Hindustani music continued to develop progressively, and it was necessary to incorporate new rāgas into the systems. Thus, related to the wives, there appeared the rāga sons, and then the sons' wives. Finally, the continuous flow of new structures made the system itself obsolete, and scholars started looking for a new, more capacious system of rāga classification. The result was the mela systems of the 17th century (see RV), and the Hindustani ṭhāṭ system of the 19th-20th centuries (see KPM), both based on scale-type classification.[16] The aspect of empirical reasoning in all these systems relates to the fact that scholars were, in the course of centuries, forced to recognize that old systems had become incommensurable with current practice, and that either the system would have to be extended in some way, or another paradigm invented.

Some traits of systematic thinking in Indian musical scholarship can be equated to general aspects of Indian thought. Firstly, there is an authoritative character in scholarship, a deep sense of valuing traditions. Lannoy writes that 'It is virtually an axiom of Indian culture that the oldest is best' (1971: 272). The NŚ, as the oldest extant treatise, has an authority similar to that of the *Vedas*, even being qualified as the fifth *Veda*. Secondly, in its transition from a habit of thinking totally dependent on oral transmission to the written form of treatises, the early, very concise *sūtras* – written on palm leaves – were commented on and amplified with other leaves inserted into the batch, which in turn were commented on again, copied as a single unitary work, glossed again, and so on. Thus, on one hand, there is the encyclopedic character of treatises (many of them multi-authored and ascribed to quasi-mythical sages, such as Bharata); and on the other hand was the commentarial aspect of the writings. The latter became a literary genre of its own, the *bhāṣya*.

The importance given to the continuity of traditions is an indexical feature. For instance, a deśīrāga is explained in the SR as derived from a bhāṣa, which is related to a grāmarāga, and this, in turn, is connected with an ancient jāti, molded in one of the two grāmas, ṣaḍja or madhyama. Conversely, the continuous expansion of Indian musical intelligence is evident in a number of old treatises, in which invariably the author begins by explaining the grāmas and the jātis of Bharata's NŚ, as a way of connecting the oldest and incontestable tradition with current

[16] The linearity of my explanation here should not give the reader the idea that each musical system of rāga classification substituted for the earlier system in a diachronic way. Rather, some of the systems existed simultaneously, overlapping each other for centuries.

practice. Indian musical scholarship is also taxonomic and pluralistic; classifications are not mutually exclusive; and musical elements and structures are related to other aspects of reality and to metaphysical concepts (see Rowell 1992: 123-24). Finally, systematic musical thinking is not closed, but generative, permitting new ways of expansion and variation which appear in the next generation of scholars.

The advent of Islamic rule in North India did not essentially change the musical systems and scholarship. It is true that new forms, styles and instruments were introduced, but all those were assimilated into the mainstream of Indian music. In terms of musical intelligence, there is plenty of evidence of the interest which Muslim rulers took in Indian music. Gangoly writes that 'the Moghul patrons took care to ascertain accurately the fundamental principles of Indian musical science, before proceeding to help towards its further growth and enrichment. And for this purpose, more than one authoritative treatise in Sanskrit was translated into Persian as the basis of a scientific investigation' (1989: 141). It may be said that Persian 'ethnomusicologists' were at work in the Moghul courts, but in fact ethnomusicology in India is much older. There is evidence that the grāmarāgas were known in Central Asia by the 6th century (see Widdess 1995: 15-18), and this was certainly thanks to the spread of musical scholarship by musicians and travelers, such as the famous Husuan-tsang, a Chinese who traveled in India for 15 years in the 7th century collecting Buddhist sūtras. The most consequential ethnomusicologists were the Persians, who wrote a number of treatises, as well as translations of Sanskrit works:

> About 1375 the author of the *Farid-ul-Zamanfil Maarefat-i-Ilham*, a treatise on Persian-Arabian music, also wrote a work on Indian music entitled *Ghunyat-ul-Munya*. In it he cites Bharata's *Nāṭyaśāstra* and other, less known works on Indian music such as the *Saṁgīta Vinoda*, the *Saṁgīta Mudrā*, the *Ṣatanak* and the *Rāgārṇava*. Umar Sama Yahya, an Afghan who studied Indian music in India wrote (in Persian) the *Lahjat-i-Sikandar Shahi*, quoting from the *Saṁgītaratnākara*, the *Saṁgītamataṅga*, the *Nṛttasaṅgraha*, the *Udbharat* (=*Nāṭyaśāstra*), the *Sudhanidhisaṅgīta-samassya* and the *Saṅgīta-kalpataru*. (Nijenhuis 1974: 7)

Musical conferences were another scholarly practice that influenced systematic thought. Many treatises were composed as result of these conferences. The SŚ, for instance, was written in 1428 by a group of scholars invited to the court of Sultan Malika Śāhi. It is also known that Rājā Mān Singh Tomar, king of Gwalior (ruled 1486-1516), organized a musical conference, headed by Nāyak Bakhśū, which resulted in the composition of a treatise in Brajbhāṣā entitled *Mānkutūhal*, unfortunately no longer extant (Sarmadee 1984-5: 18). The musical conferences organized early in the present century by Bhātkhaṇḍe were very important in helping classical Indian music to survive in the context of new social and political realities. The conferences represent clearly the idea of semiosis as developing in a community of inquirers, an aspect of scientific thought valued by Peirce: 'Let us remember that science is a pursuit of living men, and that its most marked characteristic is that when it is genuine, it is in an incessant state of metabolism and growth' (CP 1.232). Musical scholarship is also a form of material evidence for the final interpretant of Indian music: the continuous and ever-growing *theoretical* semiosis about extinct and living practices of *musical* semiosis. Several features of Indian musical intelligence discussed above represent superbly the Peircean idea of the growth of symbols – an organic, overwhelming and never-ending growth, as the biological environment of the Indian subcontinent used to be, and still is, in some measure, in spite of all the destructive and centrifugal forces of contemporary life.

2.3.3.4 Composition

Composition in Hindustani contemporary music has a distinctive role, namely, that of providing a structure with fixed melodic line (and text, in the case of vocal music), arranged according to a particular tāla, to be developed and expanded by improvisational techniques. It is not certain, however, that composition has always been material for improvisation. Widdess argues that the early treatises, such as the NŚ and D, 'speak only of composed songs, with extended texts, elaborate modal, rhythmic and formal structures, and accompanying dances; their performances by ensembles of singers, instrumentalists and dancers can have left little room for soloistic improvisation as it is understood today' (1995: 96). Thus, it is possible that a gradual change took place, from the conception of music as being previously composed, to one in which music was understood as improvised (or spontaneously processed, as Widdess suggests, 1995: 95). The evidence of such a change is the technique of ālāp, described in the SR (2.2.23c-25b) as an improvisatory demonstration of the features of a rāga, to be performed prior to a composition. Since then, however, compositions are forms to be processed by the musicians into live music; but this does not diminish their importance. For centuries compositions were considered to be the property of the musicians and were transmitted only to those belonging to the same gharānā (see Kippen 1988: 121-23). Compilations of compositions were commissioned by the rulers and viewed as cultural treasures (see Delvoye 1990b: 99-100). A good composition is highly valued, and musicians are praised for the excellence of their repertoire (Neuman 1990: 83-84).

A semiotic classification of compositions may be set in three genera:

1. absolute music
2. functional music
3. representational music

Absolute music refers to compositions that do not point to dynamical objects other than the music itself. They are thus icons, properly speaking, or structures of musical legisigns. Functional pieces, for their dynamic action in relation to something else, constitute the second category. Finally, representational music is a broad area that includes musical metaphors and iconic, indexical and symbolic references to acoustic and non-acoustic phenomena. The three genera would certainly bear subdividing into more specific species, but this does not seem to be necessary concerning Hindustani music. This is because, on one hand, species of absolute music based on chance operations, a possible subdivision of absolute music, do not exist in India. On the other hand, except for the songs of Rabindranath Tagore, compositions are to be developed by the performers by means of improvisational techniques, and thus a more detailed account of semiotic features of compositions would demand relating several areas of inquiry.

Absolute forms of composed music in India are represented by instrumental pieces, of which drumming is an outstanding example. Indeed, most forms of pakhāvaj and tablā solo compositions do not refer to anything but the pure qualities and structure of the music. Another form of pure music is the gat, a fixed composition ranging from 2 to 16 āvarts of tāla. Gats are not referential, in as much as the rāga in which they are set is abstracted or indefinite in its symbolic import. For instance, a gat in rāga mālkauṅs will tend to signify a serious character (Ex. 20, acc. to Bhaṭṭ 1967:150), whereas another in rāga khamāj will be lighter (Ex. 21, acc. to Bhaṭṭ 1967:63-4). In this sense, they are as representational as the rāgas. Even though, since instrumental music tends to rely much more on technique and virtuosity than does vocal music, gats result in music which is more abstract than that of songs.

Functionality in contemporary Indian music is predominantly a feature of folk and tribal music. In the past there were some forms of functional music in the classical styles, for example, the sāpekṣa-jhombaḍa, used for presenting requests to a king (SŚ 13.286). Contemporary classical Hindustani music is still functional in particular cases. Compositions designed to be performed at dance recitals (such as the kathak style) are functional as far as they take part in efficient and final causation processes between the musicians and dancers. There is a special form of dialogical semiosis between the two parts, an interactive feature that qualifies dance compositions as a second class in the classification above. There are basically two forms of music for kathak: (1) rhythmic compositions in several special forms; and (2) song forms, such as bhajan, ṭhumrī and tarānā (see Saxena 1991b). Besides being in compositions conceived for dance, functionality is also present in devotional music: 'Music, as we are told, is not a matter of mere entertainment, but essentially a way to spiritual emancipation' (Saxena 1992: 4). Being a means to reach a particular aim, that is, an instrument for worship, devotional songs (or any composition viewed as such) is a form of functional music. Finally, there are compositions designed to spread musical education, the lakṣaṇ gīts. They are arranged so as to expose the main features of a rāga to the student, and this is reinforced by the lyrics, which describe the musical elements presented in the melodic line (see several lakṣaṇ gīts in the KPM and RVJ).

Example 20

Masitkhānī gat in rāga mālkauṅs

Example 21

Razākhānī gat in rāga khammāj

Most Hindustani musical compositions are representational. This is not merely a matter of a relationship between music and text, but complex interactions of meaning: the symbol which a rāga is, the indexical references that can appear as the name of a famous composer, or a regional musical feature present in the piece, the several iconic signs, from images and diagrams to metaphors, etc. Composition in Indian music has been recognized in the śāstric literature as a complex form of musical intelligence. Indeed, representation in Indian music is the norm. The fine *vāggeyakāra*, or composer, according to Śārṅgadeva, has to have the following aptitudes:

> The best vāggeyakāra is (possessed) of these excellences: a thorough knowledge of grammar, proficiency in lexicography, knowledge of prosody, proficiency in the use of (different) figures of speech, comprehension of aesthetic delight (rasa) as related to (different) emotive states of being (bhāva), intelligent familiarity with local custom, knowledge of many languages, proficiency in the scientific theories of fine arts, expert knowledge of the three musical arts (vocal, instrumental music, and dance), a lovely tone-quality, good knowledge of laya, tāla and *kalā*[17], discrimination of different intonations, a versatile genius, a beautiful musical rendering, acquaintance with regional (deśī) rāga-s, cleverness in conversation for victory in debates, freedom from like and dislike, aesthetic sensitivity, a sense of propriety in expression and new melodic forms, knowledge of another's mind, maturity in the understanding of different (varieties of) prabandha-s, the ability to compose songs at short notice, the expert knowledge of composing different verbal structures of particular melodic forms, maturity in producing gamaka-s (shakes and graces) pervading the three registers, proficiency in (the presentation of) different (forms of) ālāpa and attention. (SR 3.39)

The first point to notice is that the composer in early and later Indian music is above all a songwriter. This obvious conclusion recalls once again that vocal music is considered the basic form, and instrumental music and dance are derived from and dependent on it. The composer thus has to have poetic abilities and the capacity to relate the text and music in a creative and significant way, which is fundamentally an inter-semiotic task. It is clear that competence in understanding, dealing with, and representing several kinds of signs in music is called for in the demands for familiarity with local customs and regional music, and for the observation and knowledge of the varieties of human character. The composer must not only know music theory, but also be a good performer her or himself. The vāggeyakāra is also a scholar in the sense of being proficient in the theory of fine arts and good at defending her/his points in scholarly debate. Finally, the composer must be an aesthete, capable of fine aesthetic sensitivity; that is, not only experienced in the several qualities of feeling of music and poetry, but also able to discriminate among them. S/he has to be competent at representing the rasas appropriate to the particular aesthetic circumstances of the lyrics or playing in question, in relation to rāga, tāla and musical forms employed. For this, one must be free of likes and dislikes, for the vāggeyakāra is almost a scientist of musical creation. Any personal preferences would limit her/his capacity for musical composition and representation.

The quote above refers to the abilities of the excellent composer. The relative importance of musical and literary abilities of the vāggeyakāra can be seen in Śārṅgadeva's characterizations of average, bad, and unworthy composer. The average composer is adept at creating musical

[17] A time division equivalent to one mātrā.

structures, but not so good in regard to the literary merits of his songs. The bad composer is a good poet, but a poor musician. The unworthy composer is one who writes the verbal text, but sets it to melodies composed by others (SR 3.10-12b). Therefore, musical ability is the highest gift of a composer. Nevertheless, the best vāggeyakāra is one who is proficient in both arts, and knows how to relate them to each other.

A classical example of an expert vāggeyakāra is Jayadeva, who composed the *Gītagovinda* in the second half of the 12th century. This work is written in *prabhandas*, the first and early second millennium Sanskrit form of art song. A study of the relationship of the poems and rāgas of the *Gītagovinda* could shed light on aesthetic issues, such as the signification of rasa by the dual media of poetry and music. Jayadeva did not leave behind the musical notations for the songs, but only indicated the rāgas to which they are to be performed. The various editions differ in this respect, though there is agreement among them on some things. For instance, songs 3, 14, and 20 are always in rāga vasanta (Nijenhuis 1977: 12), the spring rāga. A brief consideration of those poems and their prescribed rāga shows the correspondence of text and music, both representing aspects of the sublime Indian spring. The lyrics of the 3rd song are directly related to spring and to joyful Kṛṣṇa roaming in the woods (Jayadeva 1977: 74-76). The poems of the 14th and 20th songs depict phases of the meeting of lovers. In the former, Kṛṣṇa meets another girlfriend; in the latter song, Rādhā eventually goes to join her beloved (Jayadeva 1977: 99-100, 115-18). The *Gītagovinda* songs are still performed in different styles in Orissa, Bengal, Bihar, Nepal and South India as well (Miller 1977: x-xii), and not necessarily to the rāgas prescribed by Jayadeva.

From the 13th century onwards, several composers worked in vernacular languages, rather than in Sanskrit. 'Āmīr Khusrau (1254-1325) is cited as the first to have composed in the earlier forms of Hindi (Buitenen in Dimock et al. 1974: 21), besides writing poems in Persian. A number of innovations are usually credited to Khusrau, such as the creation of new rāgas, the invention of qawwālī, khayāl and tarānā forms, and other innovations (see Gangoly 1989: 38; Desai 1979), but these are somewhat mythical accounts rather than historical facts (see Wade 1971: 38-49). Much more solid evidence is found in relation to later composers of dhrupad, indicating that many of them were truly vāggeyakāras. Baijū Bavare (15th or 16th century) was an early composer of dhrupad whose bandiśes are still performed. There is little biographical information on him (see Perera 1994: 46-54) but his dhrupads display evidence of a keen representational composer (see the dhrupad in rāga bhairavī, Ex. 12)

Nāyak Bakhśū, a composer and singer of the court of Rāja Mān Singh Tomar (king of Gwalior, ruled 1486-1516), was a prolific and successful composer, whose dhrupads were 'liked by the masses and admired by the elite,' according to Abū'l Fazl 'Allāmī, the writer of Emperor Akbar's chronicle (in Delvoye 1990b: 96). The compositions of Bakhśū were compiled in an anthology called *Sahasrasa* (*The Thousand Delights*), made up of 1004 ḍhrupads attributed to Bakhśū, in four rāgas, and 46 rāgiṇīs (see Bakhśū 1972). Most of his dhrupads center on themes of love and the poetic conventions of hero and heroine (the nāyaka-nāyikā bheda, see 3.3.4). Nāyak Bakhśū is also credited as a composer of rāgas, as stated by Nawāb Saif Khān 'Faqirullāh,' in his 1666 treatise *Rāg Darpaṇ:* 'Mixing Deśkār with Toḍī, he named it Bahādurī after the Sultān Bahādur of Gujarāt. Kānhrā is also his invention, a combination of Syām and Khambāichī. And so is his Kalyāṇ, an admixture of Hamīr, Kalyāṇ, and Jait-Kalyāṇ. This is now known as Nāyakī-Kalyāṇ, as Kānhrā has become Nāyakī-Kānhrā' (in Sarmadee 1984-5: 21).

The title of *nāyak* (lit., hero), attributed to Bakhśū, seems to be an equivalent to the Sanskrit term vāggeyakāra. According to Hakim M. Karam Imam, musicians can be divided into two classes: 'the one having theoretical knowledge only is called Paṇḍit. The one who is a master of theory and an expert exponent of both vocal and instrumental music and also a master of dancing, as well as being a composer, is called a Nāyak' (Imam 1959: 13). In this scheme, the scholar – or *paṇḍit* – and the composer/musician/dancer – or nāyak -- are separated, which suggests a specialization that does not exist in the concept of vāggeyakāra. Nowadays, the usage of the term paṇḍit or ustād includes not only the scholar, but also the musician and composer, whereas nāyak is not currently used.

A composer whose very name symbolizes excellence in Hindustani music is Tānsen. He was born in Behat, near Gwalior, around 1492, lived in Rāja Mān Singh Tomar's court up to 1518, and worked at several other courts until 1562, when he joined the court of Emperor Akbar (who was a music connoisseur and patron of the arts), where he served as musician and composer until his death in 1589 (Brahaspati 1979: 76-80). The compositions of Tānsen were not compiled into a single volume as were Bākhśū's. They are scattered in written and oral traditions, and many of them are still performed. However, the authenticity of those compositions, whether attributed to Tānsen or other great composers, is an issue of research (see Delvoye 1990a; 1993: 40). Tānsen's compositions were written in Braj (a dialect in the region of Mathura, Agra and Gwalior), the sonority of which is usually conceived by musicians to be well suited for musical purposes. Tānsen composed on a wide range of themes, notwithstanding the fact that the dhrupad was considered to be essentially a religious genre. According to Delvoye, Tānsen composed on Puranic themes and wrote in praise of gods, such as Gaṇeśa, Sarasvatī, Sūrya, Viṣṇu Nārāyaṇa and Śiva; he explored Kṛṣṇaite topics as well as the nāyaka-nāyikā bheda; the eulogy of kings was an unavoidable subject, for the court musicians and Tānsen wrote many dhrupads addressed to Akbar (see Ex. 17); music theory and terminology were also themes explored in his compositions, and those pieces evidence the great reverence shown music in India; the description of nature and its emotional appeal are often combined with hero-heroine and Kṛṣṇa themes; finally, Delvoye points to a less conventional category of introspective dhrupads – in one of them, for instance, Tānsen addresses his own mind (1994b: 3-8). Tānsen is also credited with composing new rāgas. The *Rāg Darpaṇ* by Faqirullāh states that 'Tānsen (may his soul rest in peace) mixed Malhār with Kānhrā; similarly he experimented with Kānhrā by mixing Kalyāṇ into it. With Āsāvarī he mixed Deva-Gandhar. Kānhrā he called Darbārī-Kānhrā, for it was his creation after reaching the Darbār (court) of the Arsh-Ashiyani (Akbar)' (in Sarmadee 1984-5: 21). Contemporary rāgas such as miyāṁ kī malhār, darbārī kānhḍā, miyāṁ kī toḍī are thought to be his creations, although a consistent link, based on musical evidence, has not yet been established by researchers.

A composer can also be responsible for the shaping and acceptance of a genre. That is probably the case with Nyamat Khan (1670-1748), a composer born into the family of Tānsen's daughter, and called Sadāraṅg ('ever buoyant') by his patron Muhammad Shah (ruled 1720-48). Sadāraṅg is credited with having transformed earlier forms of khayāl into the genre that is performed today, and with presenting it in a form acceptable to the court connoisseurs, although not singing khayāl himself at court (see Wade 1971: 71-77; A. Sharma 1993: 42-43). He was a prolific composer of dhrupads and khayāls, but the problem of authorship of the pieces signed 'Sadāraṅg' is similar to the difficulty one encounters with Tānsen's dhrupads.

The themes of khayāl are as wide-ranging, and include some similar categories, as those of dhrupads. Wade lists eight general topics for khayāls: (1) views of life, (2) a patron or king, (3) wedding, (4) religious themes (excepting the Kṛṣṇnaites, (5) Kṛṣṇaite themes, (6) the union of lovers (*sambhoga*), (7) the separation of lovers (*vipralambha*), (8) miscellaneous (1971: 121-35). Topics of union and separation of lovers are usually organized according to the literary conventions of nāyaka-nāyikā themes, and also occur in Kṛṣṇaite songs. Since the compositions can present a mixture of some of these categories, Meer instead prefers to classify the basic elements that might appear in a dhrupad or khayāl. Thus, he proposes five basic ideas: (1) social occasions (weddings, etc.), (2) the description of nature, (3) laudatory elements (praise to a king or deity), (4) love in union or separation, (5) ethical and didactic themes (on music, on priorities in life, on religious, philosophical and mystical ideas) (1980: 90).

Contemporary Hindustani composers have followed various paths, but basically have drawn from tradition. Bhātkhaṇḍe, besides his scholarly and didactic work, has also written compositions that have been analyzed in a lengthy study by Nayar (1989: 199-270). Bhātkhaṇḍe's compositions seem to be proper and well-crafted both poetically and musically. Whether they are spontaneously brilliant and widely accepted as great pieces of art, as were the old khayāls of Sadāraṅg, for instance, is a disputable matter. Yet, Bhātkhaṇḍe gives good advice on points a composer should observe in regard to rāga, tāla and text (KPM 5.49-50). He writes that good compositions must establish the svarūp of the rāga in their melodic lines. A composer should also take care to conform to the aṅgs (the typical motifs of a rāga), the musical phrases and the words. Special caution should be taken in using the *mukta svara* (the 'free note', which is an extraneous note inserted in a rāga), and in placing it in the proper part of a song. The relation between text and music is addressed with regard to a number of points: the number of words necessary to complete a poetic idea with respect to the melodic phrase; where to place pauses; what word should be prolonged in regard to the rāga, tāla and rasa of the composition; and the relationship of the verses to the tāla. Besides giving purely musical recommendations, such as how a composition presents the svarūp of the rāga, Bhātkhaṇḍe addresses a number of referential problems in the relation between text and music, which are demonstrated in his compositions (see Nayar 1989: 212-17).

Rabindranath Tagore (1861-1941), the Nobel Prize laureate in literature (1913), was also a great composer, writing more than 2000 songs on a great variety of themes. These are known as *Rabindrasangīt*, and they are considered as a separate genre, distinct from traditional Hindustani music. The fact that Tagore is a great poet should not suggest that poetry receives a higher place than music in his songs. Tagore gave great prominence to the music, and considering a publication of the songs without musical notation, he wrote: 'To set forth the music's vehicle and leave out the music itself is just like keeping the mouse and leaving out Gaṇapati himself' (in Strangways 1995: 97; see also Tagore 1991: 145-48).

The Rabindrasangīts reflected not only the classical styles but were also inspired by the folk music of Bengal and even by Irish, Scottish and English folk songs. Tagore was well acquainted with Western classical music, and also had contact with Persian, Japanese and Indonesian music. He was as progressive a composer as he was as a poet. According to Ray, Tagore urged the traditionalists 'not to concentrate on so called purity of grammar but to quest after the lost emotional fervour and aesthetic feeling associated with the essence of our rāgas and rāgiṇīs' (1992: 70). Thus, Tagore's compositions, although set to Hindustani rāgas and tālas, do not conform strictly to the musical canons, as dhrupads and khayāls are supposed to do. He was rather concerned with the expression which the songs signify. For this, he invented tālas, such as Jhampak (5 mātrās) and Navatāl (9 mātrās); he assimilated folk songs from several parts of India and from the West; and he dealt freely with the resources of classical Hindustani music. Tagore has therefore made use of various iconic and metaphorical references in his compositions, modeling and transforming the music he was acquainted with into his own pieces. According to Ray, Tagore's musical creativity can be understood according to the following principles:

> A Tagore-song is a lyrical-tonal entity, bearing the characteristics of Tagore's musico-artistic personality. Rhythmic feats (layakārī) are absent in his dhrupad- and dhamār-based compositions. Extempore tāns and ornamentations are taboo in khayāl-modeled compositions. Tagore exploited the essences of rāga-s and rāgiṇī-s in almost all his compositions, but avoided their conventional grammar. On the whole, the depth and serenity of classic air are inherent in his compositions but he did not yield to classicism in vogue. (1991: 112)

On one hand, Rabindrasangīts should not be embellished with the classical forms of development and ornamentation; on the other, they do not conform precisely to the rāga structures and genre forms. These compositions, therefore, adhere more to the Western idea of particular, individualized works, than to the traditional Indian improvisatory system.

Tagore also was a composer of drama. He wrote three *gīti-nāṭyas* (sung dramas), which were performed by the end of the 19th century. By the 1930s, he had conceived another form, the *nṛtya-nāṭya* (dance drama), based on several Indian theatrical forms (especially the kathakali), as well as Western and other Eastern drama traditions. In this form he composed nine works, the best known of which is *Chitrangada* (1936), based on an episode of the *Mahābhārata*. Tagore's expressed his political concerns in a number of songs, and in the national anthem of India, *Janaganamana*, which was composed in 1911 and sung in the National Congress on December 28, in Calcutta. There are several transcriptions of Tagore songs. The following piece, *Jadi tor dāk* (Ex. 22), imitates the style of Baul devotional singers of Bengal (thus, it is a musical paraphrase). The translation is by Tagore himself (in Strangways 1995: 93-94).

If no one responds to your call then go on alone.
And if there is no one to speak out, and if they turn their face and are afraid, then open your heart and speak only you[rself].
Speak alone, speak alone.
If everyone goes back and none accompanies you in the difficult path, then thread the thorns with bloody feet alone.
Tread alone, tread alone.
If there is no one to light the lamp, and if everyone shuts his door in the stormy dark night, then burn the ribs of your heart with the thunder fire and burn alone, burn alone.

Example 22
Tagore's *Jadi tor dāk*

If representation as creative force is present in Tagore's innovative songs, in the work of Vishnu Digambar Paluskar, another contemporary Hindustani composer, representation serves to make traditions stronger. That is the case with Paluskar's devotional compositions set to ṭhumrī rāgas. Powers explains: 'in a comparable stratagem of a purely musical sort, he took the beautiful and supple rāgas used for ṭhumrī (...), with their somewhat scandalous associations with singing-girls, and made tunes in them for the favourite devotional songs of the medieval Hindi poets, thus making those rāgas also respectable' (1980a: 89). Paluskar's procedure with ṭhumrī rāgas is certainly educational, if puritanical. Yet it can in no way be qualified as a 'stratagem of a purely musical sort,' as Powers writes. It is in fact a representational procedure, since the meaning of the rāgas under discussion, as either representing the traditional eroticism of ṭhumrīs or the devotional mood of bhajans, is without doubt an issue of reference and representation.

Composition is clearly related to the other three areas dealing with the study of musical interpretation. The most obvious relation is that between performance and composition. In the dhrupad tradition of the Dagar family, a student starts by first learning a composition in a certain rāga, and later the ālāp. According to Sanyal, 'by repeating the song, the intensity of the feeling-content is assimilated and taken care of. We were then trained to pick up cues from the original, beautiful phrase of the song-text and apply them in the improvisation of ālāp and in the rendering of the rāga. This is how the ālāp becomes meaningful with reference to the pada' (1995: 113-14). In this way, the signification of a composition is absorbed by the student and transferred to the general meaning of the rāga involved. Sanyal's argument is valid in so far as the lyrics of a composition match the general symbol represented by a rāga. The problem is that not all compositions reflect the significations of their rāga, and there might even be a conflict between text and music. Still, the bandiśes of the best composers usually represent an amalgam of literary and musical signs.

In the process of performance another intersemiosis occurs. Sanyal writes: 'My Ustad used to rightly say that rasa is inherent in the meaning of the pada but it is the singer who makes it come alive; it is possible only if the singer has the feeling within him' (1995: 116). If the meanings learned in the act of composition are to be expressed during the performance, such expression obviously depends on their previous perception. Thus, in real instances of musical semiosis, all four areas – perception, performance, intelligence and composition – are interrelated semiotically. And it would not be too redundant to repeat that musical interpretation, in turn, depends on musical reference and intrinsic musical signification. Thus completed is the diagram – a multidimensional labyrinth of musical semiosis.

III

HINDUSTANI CLASSICAL MUSIC AND THE RASA THEORY: A SEMIOTIC INTERPRETATION

3.1 The Rasa Theory

> If the poet is possessed of *śṛṅgārī* [aesthetic passion], the whole universe is full of rasa, and if he is devoid of that aesthetic sense, then, indeed, everything of the universe seems dry and insipid. (Bhoja in Prajñānānanda 1973: 237)

The word rasa (essence, sap, feeling) has been used in Sanskrit literature since the time of the *Vedas*, though its meaning has changed according to contexts, such as in Vedic ritual, in Upaniṣadic thought, and so on. Though rasa was certainly connected with aesthetic experience earlier on, the first available written information appeared at the beginning of the Christian era, in a treatise on drama and music called the *Nāṭyaśāstra* (NŚ). Rasa theory was widely discussed and further elaborated between the fifth and eleventh centuries. Before dealing with that, however, let me first examine briefly the notion of rasa in the *Ṛgveda* and in a few of the *Upaniṣads*.

Rasa, in its denotation as something liquid, is mentioned several times in the *Vedas*. In the *Ṛgveda*, *soma*, the intoxicating plant, essence of the Vedic ritual in the form of a specially prepared beverage (also a Vedic god to whom many hymns are addressed), is directly related to rasa (*Ṛgveda* 9.63). Rasa refers to milk or water in other verses of the *Ṛgveda* (5.44.13, 7.72.13). In the *Atharvaveda*, rasa denotes a kind of grain sap (3.31.10).

Less related to sacrificial rituals, rasa becomes the essential element, or prāṇa, in the *Upaniṣads*. In the *Bṛhadāraṇyakaupaniṣad*, one finds a cosmogony myth, in which gods and demons, the descendants of the original Prajāpati, struggle with each other for control of the *udgītha*, the Vedic chant. The demons prevailed over the gods when it was chanted as speech (generating evil as speaking what is improper), as life-breath (evil as smelling what is improper), by eye (evil as seeing what is improper), by ear (hearing what is improper), and by mind (evil as thinking what is improper). But the demons eventually lost out when the udgītha was chanted by the vital-breath in the mouth. At this point, the text reads: 'Here he is within the mouth. He (the vital-breath) is called *Ayāsya Āṅgirasa* for he is the essence of the limbs' (1.3.8-19).

Āṅgirasa – the essence of the parts of the body – is qualified as ayāsya (agile, dexterous) probably because it was able to defeat the demons. Hence one notes the power in vocal utterances, which constitutes the essence of all the parts of the body. It can also represent the superiority of chant over sacrifice, especially the horse sacrifice, the *aśvamedha*, which is mentioned in the previous section of that *Upaniṣad*. After defeating the demons, the Ayāsya Āṅgirasa brings forth the other parts of the body, which become the sun, the moon, and so on, and that vital breath saves them from death. Rasa in the *Taittirīryaupaniṣad* represents the ultimate reality, the essence of existence, the bliss of Brahman:

> Non-existent, verily, this (world) in the beginning. Therefrom, verily, was existence produced. That made itself a soul. Therefore it is called the well-made.
>
> Verily, what that well-made is – verily is the essence of existence [*raso vai saḥ*]. For, truly, on getting the essence, one becomes blissful. For who, indeed, could live, who breathe, if there where not this bliss in space?' (2.7)

The origin of the fundamental treatise of Indian dramaturgy, the *Nāṭyaśāstra*, was described in no less mythological terms, for it was Brahmā who combined the elements of the four *Vedas* in a new form: 'The recitative (*pāṭhya*) he took from the *Ṛgveda*, the song from the *Sāma* [*Veda*], the Histrionic Representation (abhinaya) from the *Yajur* [*Veda*] and Sentiments (rasa) from the *Atharvaveda*, [and] thus was created the *Nāṭyaveda* connected with the *Vedas* principal and subsidiary, by the holy Brahmā who is omniscient' (NŚ 17-18). According to Rowell, pāṭhya, or ritual recitation, is thus related to the *Ṛgveda*, the *Veda* of verses, in which 'the spoken word is a vehicle of elemental power' (1992: 15). Song, or gīta, is related to the *Sāmaveda*, the *Veda* of the hymns, thus 'song is rooted in the traditions of sacred chant' (ibid.). *Abhinaya*, meaningful gesture in theater performance, is related to the *Yajurveda*, the *Veda* of ceremonies; in this sense 'physical gesture is equated with ritual action' (ibid.). Finally, rasa, as emotion, is related to the *Atharvaveda*, the *Veda* of incantations, implying that 'emotion is communicated from person to person by suppressible means' (ibid.).

The meaning of the word rasa, as seen above, groups together related concepts, such as juice and the essence of something. The full scope of the word rasa is presented in the Monier-Williams' Sanskrit dictionary: 'the sap or juice of plants, juice of fruit, any liquid or fluid, the best or finest or prime part of anything, essence, marrow; elixir, potion; the seminal fluid of Śiva; charm, pleasure, delight; the taste or character of a work, the feeling or sentiment prevailing in it' (1994: 869). Therefore, rasa is not merely a kind of liquid, but something that has great semiotic potential to arouse delight in the interpreter.

According to P.L. Sharma, the word rasa 'has three primary associations of meaning, [1] Of being the object of perception by the sense of taste – "*Rasana*", [2] Of being the essence of anything or any being; the earth is known as "*Rasa*" as it holds the essence of life for all creatures – vegetable, human or animal, [3] Of being something liquid or dynamic, as opposed to being solid or static' (1970: 57). All of those associations, as I shall reveal later, are meaningful in connecting rasa with rāga. In the context of dramatic theory, the first two senses – taste and essence – are the most important. For rasa is that which the spectators relish, and at the same time it is the essence of a play.

It seems that the concept of rasa already had a well-developed aesthetic meaning some time before the NŚ.[1] In this treatise, however, it is clear that rasa refers to the context of Sanskrit drama of the classical period. According to K.C. Pandey, 'Rasa, the aesthetic object, is essentially a product of dramatic art and is not to be found in the creations of nature' (1950: 12). Rasa is neither a religious nor a metaphysical idea in the NŚ, but rather a technical term. Sanskrit theater was certainly a multimedia event, in which poetry, acting, music and dance functioned as complementary artistic languages that together constituted an integrated whole. It is precisely the idea of rasa that promotes this integration. The quality of feelings in a play perfuses all its elements, and finally leads to the goal, which receptive and learned spectators experience in their minds. Rowell gives a synthetic definition: 'By rasa we mean a transcendent mode of emotional awareness by which all aspects of a performance are integrated, an awareness that rises above the circumstances that awakened it (the poetical content, the stage spectacle, and the musical clues) and generalizes the individual emotional states of the spectators into a single emotional "field" ' (1992: 328). Besides the idea of integrating the elements of performance, Rowell refers to three other mental features crucial to rasa, as conceived by the Indian aestheticians (later commentators on the NŚ): detachment from the factual aspects of the performance, generalization of the emotions, and the unity of an ultimate feeling. According to Gerow, rasa has three critical functions: 'it distinguishes *nāṭya* [drama] from the poetry of which nāṭya is largely composed; it serves as an organic principle in terms of which the integrity of the drama can be understood; and [it] is also the result of the drama, its "end," understood as a state of awareness peculiar to the drama – distinct from normal worldly consciousness' (1977: 250). All points discussed by Rowell and Gerow are important to the field of interpretants, for through perception and cognition the spectator distills the rasa from its representational media.

[1] Rasa was probably developed as an aesthetic theory sometime before the *NŚ*, but there is no surviving evidence of its origin in this connection. See Masson & Patwardhan (1970: 1.1 and 1970: 2.2 n.8).

Bharata, in the NŚ, explains rasa by means of an analogy, in which the word rasa, in its sense of flavor, is referred to as the process by which a gourmet relishes well spiced food. The topic is introduced as if in a scene of a play. A group of sages, wishful of learning the art of drama, ask Bharata: 'What is it you call rasa?' The archetypal actor and director (*bharata*) answers his students:

> (It is called rasa) because it can be savored (*āsvādyatvāt*). How is rasa savored? As gourmets (*sumanas*) are able to savor the flavor of food prepared with many spices, and attain pleasure, [...] so sensitive spectators (sumanas) savor the primary emotions suggested (*abhivyañjita*) by the acting out of the various bhāvas [emotions] and presented with the appropriate modulation of the voice, movements of the body and display of involuntary reactions, and attain pleasure, [...] (NŚ 6.31)[2]

Although the explanation of rasa is given in gustatory terms, the main aesthetic senses, according to the NŚ, are above all sight and hearing (1.11). K.C. Pandey explains that touch, taste and smell are excluded from the aesthetic senses, because only the senses connected with the eye and ear 'can operate in relation to an object that is common to many. What is the object of touch or taste of one cannot be the object of the same senses of other persons. But the whole audience can have in common what is addressed to eyes or ears' (1950: 7). This is an ingenious explanation, as far as it concerns touch and taste. Yet, the absolute primacy of sight and hearing as aesthetic senses could be a later interpretation, perhaps introduced by Abhinavagupta in his commentary (Pandey 1950: 124-25). Taste, throughout the NŚ, is the metaphor for rasa. In the quote above there is another point, one of greater importance. Who is to relish a rasa? The word sumanas – meaning a good-minded, well-disposed or wise person – used in both sides of the analogy, suggests that great demands are made upon one who wants to be an enjoyer of rasa. As much as a gourmet, the spectator should have aesthetic sensibility, experience and knowledge, which can be thought of as related to the universal categories: aesthetic sensibility stands for firstness, experience for secondness, and knowledge for thirdness.

Moreover, Bharata's choice for taste as an analogy to the rasa experience is highly apt with respect to the immediacy of subject and object in aesthetical experience, another point of fundamental importance. 'In enjoyment of art the subject-object relationship is most intimate just as in the perception of "taste" the contact of subject and object is one of complete identification with or assimilation of the object by the subject' (P.L. Sharma 1970: 58).

An additional consequence of the idea of rasa as taste, concerns rasa as the synergetic result of a combination of distinct elements. Rasa is not a single, elementary flavor, but the refined combination of several ingredients submitted to a process. Its peculiar quality differs from the

---

2 According to the translation by Masson & Patwardhan 1970: 46.

taste of any one of the individual elements from which rasa can be experienced. P.L. Sharma writes: 'Just as the "taste" of a delicacy is not merely the sum-total of the taste of the ingredients, but is something quite new wherein the ingredients cannot be perceived separately, similarly the content of enjoyment of art is not the sum-total of the various components of artistic representation, but is quite different. This peculiarity is expressed by the analogy *pānakarasa-nyāya* – i.e. like the rasa or the taste of a *pānaka* or spiced sweet drink' (1970: 58). The pānakarasa (pānaka drink), which was probably an intoxicating liquor in classical India, has a flavor that is distinct from its components, but is at the same time the result of their combination in a synergetic process. P.L. Sharma's reference to the pānaka drink brings to mind the soma of vedic ritual. Both beverages are referred to as rasa, and both produce altered mental states in the one who tastes them. Rasa, as aesthetic experience, is also a special mental state, although it should not be equated with the alcoholic or hallucinogenic effects of pānaka or soma drinks. As for the synergy of rasa, it is not only the additive result of several forces, but an effect which exceeds that of the individual parts combined. Rasa is a state of consciousness, which exists on a different level than its components.

Bhāva, the object of rasa

The foregoing discussion leads to the complex issue of the components that provide the material basis for the rasa. To extend the gourmet analogy, I would say that only an accomplished chef knows how to combine the elements of a play into such a perfect blend that it can be relished as rasa. To describe this issue, Indian aestheticians use four keywords, all of them derived from the word *bhāva* (roughly translatable as 'emotion'). *Vibhāva* are the causes or determinants of an emotion, the consequences of which are called *anubhāva*. Besides this cause-effect relation, there are the subsidiary or transitory emotions, called *vyabhicāribhāvas*. The interaction of those three elements produces a major, permanent emotion, the *sthāyibhāva*. This last consists in eight fundamental emotions considered basic or instinctual to mankind. Abhinavagupta, in his commentary on the NŚ (the *Abhinavabhāratī*, circa the 10th century A.D.), explains the relation among the four concepts:

> Rasa, in this connexion, is just that reality (*artha*) by which the determinants, the consequents and the transitory feelings [,] after having reached a perfect combination (*samyag yoga*), relation (*saṁbandha*), conspiration (*aikāgrya*) – where they will be in turn in a leading or subordinate position – in the mind of the spectator, make the matter [one of] gustation [,] consisting of a form of consciousness free of obstacle and different from ordinary [conciousness]. (in Gnoli 1985: 78)

In the NŚ the relation between rasa and the several instances of bhāvas is explained, once again, by an iconic idea: 'Just as flavor (rasa) comes from a combination of many spices, herbs and other substances (*dravya*), so rasa (in a drama) comes from the combination (*upagama*) of many bhāvas' (NŚ 6.31).[3] The bhāvas that Bharata mentions cause rasa because of their connection with theater techniques: 'Those who stage dramas (*nāṭyayoktṛ*) should know that the bhāvas are so called because they give rise to (*bhāvayanti*) rasas that are related to the various kinds of acting' (NŚ 6.34).[4] Therefore, bhāva, by means of acting, gives rise to rasa. As a technical concept, bhāva refers to the emotions conveyed by acting as sign-representation.

The etymology of the word bhāva is explained at the beginning of chapter 7 of the NŚ. Bhāva is derived from the causative of the root *bhū*, to arise, to come into being. Both K.C. Pandey (1950: 18) and Gnoli (1985: XV n.1) mention the double sense of the word bhāva: (1) to cause to be, to bring about; (2) to pervade. The two meanings are relevant to the process of relishing rasa, for rasa is caused by bhāva, and this is an all-pervading experience. In the first case, that of bringing about, rasa is in the domain of the stage, either from the dramatist's, the director's, or the actor's point of view. By means of appropriate verbal language, the dramatist must make clear the mental states involved in any situation. The director provides music, costume, and other trappings for the performance. The actor contributes to the whole by means of his *abhinaya* (pantomime), vocal inflections, and expression of emotions. From the spectators' point of view, bhāva, as a perfume, impregnates their minds. Thus, the presentation and cognition of the bhāvas are the preconditions for experiencing rasa. In this connection, Bharata writes: 'rasas come from bhāvas, but bhāvas do not come from rasas' (NŚ 6.33).[5]

The issue of whether bhāva causes rasa, or vice versa, if rasa causes bhāva, was of some controversy among scholars. Between the fifth and ninth centuries, several Indian authors discussed this problem in their commentaries on the NŚ. Abhinavagupta makes clear that 'In the everyday world, there are no such things as vibhāvas and anubhāvas. They are merely causes and effects.' This is the view taken of drama in general; that is, the word bhāva and its derivations are above all theatrical conventions, technical terms. Abhinavagupta continues: 'Bhāvas give rise to rasas. And rasas give rise to bhāvas. That is, they create bhāvas. That is, they allow them to get the very name of bhāvas' (in Masson & Patwardhan 1970: 2.75 n.395). Here is the other side of the issue: Bhāvas are meant to convey rasa. Therefore, bhāva and rasa are, in a certain way, dependent on each other. Yet, from the spectators' point of view, that is, from her/his aesthetic experience, semiosis goes from bhāva to rasa, as Bharata says.

---

[3] Translation by Masson & Patwardhan 1970: 46.
[4] Translation by Masson & Patwardhan 1970: 47.
[5] Translation by Masson & Patwardhan 1970: 47.

Of the four instances of bhāva – vibhāva, anubhāva, vyabhicāribhāva and sthāyibhāva – the first three stand for cause, effect and collateral emotions in the theater. They do not refer to the emotions of everyday life. In this case, cause, effect, and concomitants are called the following in Sanskrit: *kāraṇa*, *kārya* and *sahacāri*. Vibhāva, anubhāva and vyabhicāribhāva are technical terms, meaning the *representation* of the causes, effects and transient feelings of a emotion in a play. According to K.C. Pandey: 'Thus, the word "Vibhāva" stands for the dramatic situation, which is not the cause but the medium, through which emotion arises in the actor. But emotion in the spectator is due to identification with the hero. Vibhāva is so called, because it arouses emotion in a manner quite different from that in which emotion arises in actual life (1950: 15). In the vibhāva, say the first meeting of the nāyaka (the leading character, hero) with the nāyikā (leading female character, heroine), the anubhāvas should appear as the consequence, as the effects of that emotion. Anubhāvas are of two kinds: voluntary, the movements the actors are to perform as a result of the vibhāva; and involuntary (*sātvikabhāvas*), which are reflexive bodily reactions. Bharata lists those movements and explains the context in which both kinds should be used.

To limit acting only to the representation of causes and effects, however, would result in a poor performance. There another factor, according to the Indian theory of drama, that leads to the accomplishment of a emotion to be digested by the minds of the spectators. That factor is the transient emotions or vyabhicāribhāvas. 'For, when a transient mental state is acted out in a befitting situation, there remains no doubt about the basic mental state, from which the transient one springs' (Pandey 1950: 19). Transient emotions, or 'complementary psychological states' (Ghosh 1967: XXXVI), are secondary feelings usually aroused in a certain dramatic situation. They reflect the character's state of mind, her/his apprehensions and expectations. Vyabhicāribhāvas also depend on the character types as defined in the NŚ; such as main or secondary, hero or villain, and so on.

The combination of vibhāva, anubhāva and vyabhicāribhāva leads to the main emotion in a play, the sthāyibhāva, or permanent emotion. Before dealing with this latter concept, however, it will be useful to list the complementary sentiments. They are thirty-three in the NŚ: world-weariness (*nirveda*), physical weakness (*glāni*), anxiety (*śaṅkā*), envy (*asūyā*), intoxication (*mada*), fatigue (*śrama*), laziness (*ālasya*), depression (*dainya*), worry (*cintā*), confusion (*moha*), remembrance (*smṛti*), peace of mind (*dhṛti*), shame (*vrīḍā*), rashness (*capalatā*), joy (*harṣa*), panic (*āvega*), lifelessness (*jaḍatā*), pride (*garva*), dejection (*viṣāda*), longing (*autsukya*), sleeping (*nidrā*), apoplexy (*apasmāra*), dreaming (*supta*), awakening (*vibodha*), resentment (*amarṣa*), dissimulation (*avahittha*), violence (*ugratā*), attentiveness (*mati*), sickness (*vyādhi*), insanity (*unmāda*), death (*maraṇa*), fright (*trāsa*), and perplexity (*vitarka*) (NŚ 6.18-21).[6] Abhinavagupta (in the *Abhinavabhāratī*), demonstrates their importance in relation to the permanent emotion, pointing out that they are like the jewelry of a play – the gems are the vyabhicāribhāvas, and the thread is the sthāyibhāva:

> Thus these transitory sentiments being, so to say, woven onto the thread of the permanent one, appear and disappear an infinite number of times. In some sense, they are like the beads of crystal, glass, magnet, topaz, emerald, sapphire, etc., which fill the thread on which they are threaded no matter if it is red, blue, etc. – such that they are set rather far apart from each other. Continuously changing their position, they do not leave, it is true, a trace of themselves on this thread, but, all the same, they nourish the ornamental composition which it makes; and, being themselves various, and varying in turn the permanent thread, they doubtless let it appear at intervals, in its nakedness, though, at the same time, they affect it by their polychrome reflections – the reflections, I mean, of the transitory jewels. It is for this very reason that these sentiments are called 'transitory'. (in Gnoli 1985: 75-76)

There are two fundamental ideas here. One is that the complementary sentiments, as colorful jewels, project their qualities onto the thread. This idea relates to the word rāga, not in its musical sense, but as affection, that is, an emotion that colors the mind. The other idea is that, even while the vyabhicāribhāvas are projecting their colors on the thread, they do not change its permanent nature. The white thread stands for the sthāyibhāva, the permanent emotion, which, however, is not merely a theatrical artifact. The sthāyibhāvas are deeply rooted in the nature of human mind. This is the point at which the Indian theory of aesthetic experience connects performance with perception.

It is precisely the sthāyibhāva that is the necessary condition for the relishing of a rasa, the level where inference is put aside and another state of consciousness is reached in the aesthetic experience. The word sthāyī means permanent, but also something inherent and enduring. It is a stable emotion in relation to the vyabhicāribhāvas, and it is inherent both in the work of art and in the performer's and perceiver's minds. The sthāyibhāvas listed in the NŚ are eight: 'love (*rati*), amusement (or laughter) (*hāsa*), sorrow (*śoka*), anger (*krodha*), dynamic energy (*utsāha*), fear (*bhaya*), disgust (*jugupsā*), and wonder (*vismaya*)' (NŚ 6.17).[7]

Different views exist concerning the inherent character of the sthāyibhāva. Its rationale is related to a philosophical concept, expressed by the words *vāsanā* or *saṁskāra*, which are essential ideas in several Indian systems of philosophy. Saṁskāra denotes the latent impressions every being accumulates and carries from birth to birth. According to

---

[6] Translation by Masson & Patwardhan 1970: 45.

[7] Translation by Masson & Patwardhan 1970: 44.

Saṁkhya-Yoga philosophy, for instance, *puruṣa* or the intelligence principle, of which consciousness is its very essence (Chatterjee & Datta 1984: 39), is from the 'beginning bound up with matter or *prakṛti* and its release from matter is dependent on its own exertions. *Citta* [mind, also *manas*] in its passage through time gathers up experiences in different lives. These stored up experiences, which must have their appropriate effects, are the vāsanās. The words vāsanā and saṁskāra evidently mean the same thing' (Chennakesavan 1991: 83). Thus, the traditional Indian interpretation conceives of the vestigial experiences, vāsanā or saṁskāra, as the result of cycles of births, or *saṁsāra*. According to Masson & Patwardhan, Abhinavagupta thought that 'in our beginningness (...) [in our] wanderings through the universe, we have had every conceivable experience, been open to every possible emotion. "Nothing human is foreign to us"[8] ' (1969: 48-49). Yet, there are other possible interpretations. Masson & Patwardhan consider saṁskāra, in a sense, as corresponding to Freud's idea of the unconscious (1969: 48). Thus, saṁskāra means the impressions of one's experiences of life, as fixed in the unconscious mind. The sthāyibhāva, on this view, corresponds to the conscious. In the aesthetic experience, the perception and inference of the several bhāvas leads to a cognizant state of mind that finds resonance with the latent impressions, the unconscious saṁskāra. This process arouses the sthāyibhāva, the stable consciousness of a general emotion. This is not an extraordinary process; every person should be able to experience a sthāyibhāva. Since all human beings in some way possess traces of all major human experiences, sthāyibhāvas are likely to develop as similar mental states in the spectators' minds. In the first section of the *Abhinavabhāratī*, one finds the rationale of Abhinavagupta demonstrating the universality of the sthāyibhāvas:

> The mental states of permanent nature are solely these nine. Indeed, every creature from its birth possesses these nine forms of consciousness. In fact, on the basis of the principle that all beings 'hate to be in contact with pain and are eager to taste pleasure', everyone is by nature pervaded by sexual desires [delight]; believes himself to be superior to others, whom he is thus led to deride [laugher]; grieves when he is forced to part with what he loves [sorrow]; gets angry at the causes of such separation [anger]; becomes frightened when he finds himself powerless [fear]; – but still is desirous of overcoming the danger which threatens him [heroism]; is attacked, when judging a thing to be displeasing, by the sense of revulsion directed just towards this ugly object [disgust]; wonders at the sight of extraordinary deeds done by himself or others [astonishment]; and, lastly, is desirous of abandoning certain things [serenity]. No living creature exists without the latent impression of these sentiments. (in Gnoli 1985: 74)

---

[8] Quote from Publius Terentius (*Heauton Timorumenos* 1.77): *Homo sum; humani nila me alienum puto* ('I am a man, I count nothing human foreign to me').

The way that Abhinavagupta argues all living beings have the nine[9] sthāyibhāvas brings up the idea of instincts, such as the pursuit of pleasure and avoidance of pain. Thus, all human beings wish the company of the beloved, the basis of rati; they take pleasure in mocking others, the basis of hāsa; everyone experiences sadness when their loved ones depart, or suffer a loss, the basis of śoka; and so on. According to Gnoli these states are 'inborn in man's heart. They permanently exist in the mind of every man, in the form of latent impressions (vāsanā) derived from actual experiences in the present life or from inherited instincts, and, as such, they are ready to emerge into his consciousness on any occasion' (1985: XV). Gnoli, though referring to the sthāyibhāva as instinct, does not discuss it extensively. Saxena has a point of disagreement in this regard: 'May we equate sthāyibhāva with instinct? No; it would be wrong to do so. For whereas a native capacity to deal, by instinct, with a situation in terms of some overt and relatively determined action is (in the main) conative in character, a sthāyibhāva is essentially an original tendency to feel. Yet, there is much that makes an instinct very similar to a sthāyibhāva' (Saxena 1989a: 9).

His point is that instinct cannot arise save as a physical action. Saxena's conclusion is that sthāyibhāva is 'an original (or natural) tendency to feel or to experience some emotion in a specific situation, that is, in a situation the character of which is clearly perceived. (...) The aesthetic transmutation of such a tendency into rasa would mean that it is activated in its (cognitive and) affective aspects without overtly dealing with any real situation' (1989a: 9). The last point is relevant, and perhaps, due the artificiality of drama, Saxena refuses the unrestricted relation between the ideas of sthāyibhāva and instinct. From a semiotic point of view, however, feelings do precede actions, and thus, there is no need for the strict separation of sthāyibhāva from instinctual responses. No spectator would kill the villain in a play. Raghavan also supports the idea of instinct as the basis for the aesthetic experience (1975: 17). Of importance to rasa theory, is that vāsanā or saṁskāra accounts for why spectators can enjoy an emotion as a general idea and not merely as a subjective experience, either because the spectators have lived it already, in the present or a past life, or because it is an inborn human instinct. In any case, it is a habit, an acquired tendency, which again compounds a triad, here comprised of the interrelated aspects of feeling, action and habit.

---

[9] Abhinavagupta introduces one more rasa to the list of eight found in the *NŚ*, *śānta*. Thus, the number *sthāyibhāvas* according to him is nine.

Navarasa, the Nine Rasas

> *For without rasa, there can be no meaning*. Rasa comes from a combination of the vibhāvas, the anubhāvas, and the vyabhicāribhāvas. (NŚ 6.31, my emphasis)[10]

Once the structure of aesthetic experience is laid out, it is possible to deal with its highest level, that of rasa. The rasas, in the NŚ, are eight: *śṛṅgāra* (erotic), *hāsya* (comic), *karuṇa* (pathetic), *raudra* (furious), *vīra* (heroic), *bhayānaka* (terrible), *bībhatsa* (odious) and *adbhuta* (wondrous) (NŚ 6.15).[11] Several other rasas were later proposed by Indian aestheticians, only one of which has been widely accepted: *śānta* (tranquillity), the rasa for which Abhinavagupta contended. In addition to the basic conception of rasa – as a process of relishing – there are some side issues on this topic that I will also consider in this section. Of concern here are the main and derived rasas, and the various kinds of the same rasa.

Although bhāva was discussed above, it is necessary to return to it for a while, in order to understand the distinction between sthāyibhāva and rasa. Abhinavagupta wrote: 'This Rasa differs from the permanent feelings, consists solely in this state of gustation and is not an objective thing (*siddhasvabhāva*), [...] [It] lasts exactly as long as the gustation and does not [exist at] any time separate from it' (in Gnoli 1985: 78). That is, rasa is not an object that exists independently of the aesthetic experience. Rasa arises from a distinctive form of perception, which is compared to the immediacy of tasting in the NŚ. The process of tasting a rasa will be studied in a special chapter in this section (see 3.4).

Yet, as unmaterial as it is, rasa is connected with and depends on the sthāyibhāva. A rasa cannot manifest spontaneously. Its enjoyment depends on the instinctual basis of a sthāyibhāva. About this conjunction, Raghavan writes: 'An emotion is recognized as Rasa if it is a sufficiently permanent, major instinct of man, if it is capable of being delineated and developed to its climax with its attendant and accessory feelings, and if there are men of that temperament to feel imaginative [and] emotional sympathy at the presentation of that Rasa' (Raghavan 1975: 17). Therefore, rasa depends on all its accessory bhāvas in order to be tasted, and this tasting requires imagination and understanding from the spectator. Moreover, 'when we experience rasa, it is always a specific rasa, and its distinctness arises from, and retains or evokes, the unique

---

[10] Translation by Masson & Patwardhan 1970: 46.

[11] The English translations for the Sanskrit names for *rasa* vary considerably. I have adopted the translations by Gnoli (1985: XVI), Saxena (1991a: 181) and Sinha (1986: 2.289-90) for the first seven *rasas*, but my preference is 'wondrous' and 'tranquility' for the last two. When quoting other authors, I have kept their translations, which may differ from those which I have adopted.

feel of the particular sthāyibhāva it builds upon' (Saxena 1989a: 7). There is a direct relation between each sthāyibhāva and each rasa:

Table 6
Nava Rasas and Sthāyibhāvas

Sthāyibhāva		⇨	**Rasa**	
Rati	love	⇨	**Śṛṅgāra**	Erotic
Hāsa	laughter	⇨	**Hāsya**	Comic
Śoka	sorrow	⇨	**Karuṇa**	Pathetic
Krodha	anger	⇨	**Raudra**	Furious
Utsāha	energy	⇨	**Vīra**	Heroic
Bhaya	fear	⇨	**Bhayānaka**	Terrible
Jugupsā	disgust	⇨	**Bībhatsa**	Odious
Vismaya	wonder	⇨	**Adbhuta**	Wondrous
Śāma or Tattvajñāna	peace or knowledge of the truth	⇨	**Śānta**	Tranquility

Bharata, in the NŚ, establishes groups and hierarchies among the rasas. Four rasas are considered major: the erotic, the furious, the heroic and the odious (NŚ 6.38). They give rise to the other four in the following way: 'The comic aesthetic experience comes from the erotic. The compassionate comes from the furious. The awesome aesthetic experience comes from the heroic and the terrifying from the disgusting' (NŚ 6.39).[12] The justification for these relations, from the point of view of the aesthetic experience, strikes one as feeble. Nevertheless, there seems to be some rationale behind it. The comic rasa that results from the erotic has its basis in parody: 'An imitation (*anukṛti*) of the erotic is known as the comic'. The relations between the furious rasa and the pathetic one, and between the heroic rasa and the wondrous one, are justified in terms of the results of an action (karma); e.g., a heroic acts leads to a wondrous feeling. Finally, the sight of the odious gives rises to the terrible (NŚ 6.40-1). Therefore, the first pair is grounded on an iconic relation (metaphor), and the other three are based on indexical relations. Later authors, when considering the śānta rasa in the context of these four groups of the NŚ, tend to take śānta separately, as an independent rasa.[13] One aesthetician, however, criticizes this scheme of main and derived rasas. Bhoja, in the *Śṛṅgāra Prakāśā*, states that there is no reason to hold

[12] Translation by Masson & Patwardhan 1970: 48.
[13] See the *Viṣṇudharmottarapurāṇa* 1.9-11.

a strict relation among the rasas as found in the NŚ. For instance, hāsya does not necessarily come from śṛṅgāra; karuṇa is sometimes the result of rati and not raudra; and so on (see Raghavan 1978: 424-25). Bhoja's negative criticism of the NŚ is not usual in Indian scholarship. Instead, Indian scholars tend to keep their comments in consonance with the oldest sources, rather than openly dispute the ideas of the great sage Bharata. Abhinavagupta, for instance, compromises with Bharata in respect of the same question.

If, on one hand, rasas can be grouped together, on the other, each rasa gives rise to a number of kinds. In chapter 6 of the NŚ, Bharata describes each of the rasas, and explains their typical vibhāva, anubhāva and vyabhicāribhāva. He also presents the varieties of each rasa in an uneven way, for his classifications are based on varying criteria. These last range from the peculiarities of each variety of rasa (on account of their qualities or firstness), theater techniques (performance or secondness), to determinants (vibhāva, plot of the play or thirdness). Some of the varieties represent the truly idiosyncratic qualities of a rasa; for instance, the two kinds of śṛṅgāra are divided into sambhoga and vipralambha. Others refer to the way a rasa can be represented in performance; śṛṅgāra may be signified by speech, costume or action. Finally, sub-species of rasa may be related to the dramatic situation, as are the three forms of karuṇa: *śukakṛta*, which results simply from any sort of sorrow; *dharmopaghātaja*, from a situation in which there is some kind of destruction of order; and *apacayodbhāva*, when a feeling of pathos results from a loss of wealth. This classification, however, is not mutually exclusive; in fact, a sub-species of rasa can, simultaneously, have its inherent quality, be acted in a certain way, and relate to the plot. The classification of the two kinds of śṛṅgāra was developed extensively and deserves special consideration. The following table provides information as found in the NŚ:

Table 7
Kinds of Rasas

Rasa	Varieties	
Śṛṅgāra	2	**sambhoga** (love in union) **vipralambha** (love in separation)
Śṛṅgāra	3	speech costume action

hāsya	6	**smita** (slight smile) **hasita** (smile) **vihasita** (gentle laughter) **uphasita** (laughter of ridicule) **aphasita** (uproarious laughter) **atihasita** (boisterous or convulsive laughter)
hāsya	3	body costume speech
karuṇa	3	**śukakṛta** (sorrow) **dharmopaghātaja** (destruction of order) **apacayodbhāva** (reduction of wealth)
raudra	3	body costume speech
vīra	3	**dānavīra** (munificence) **dharmavīra** (valor in following the right at all costs) **yuddhavīra** (martial heroism)
bhayānaka	3	**vyāja** (simulated fear) **vitrāsitaka** (dread born of shyness) **aparādha** (dread born of a grievous mistake)
bībhatsa	3	**kṣobhaja** (arises from the agitation of seeing blood, etc.) **udvegī** (arises from nausea, such as seeing faeces, worms, etc.) **śuddha** (unaffected [?])
adbhuta	2	**divya** (from seeing a divine or celestial event) **ānandaja** (born from the joy of achieving something special)

3.2 The Development of the Rasa Theory

The NŚ presents a very concise explanation of the concept of rasa. Bharata says merely that the experience of rasa comes from the combination of vibhāvas, anubhāvas and vyabhicāribhāvas (NŚ 6.31). Such a condensed explanation, which Gerow (1977: 250) designates *rasabīja* (seed of rasa), is characteristic of many old Sanskrit treatises, which were intended to record one area of knowledge – the oral and/or mental knowledge shared among a community of experts – rather than to lay out a subject matter in all its fullness. This is true at least for the oldest works, which were subsequently copied and furnished with commentaries and other addenda, in the attempt to preserve the bulk of intellectual information shared by a group of specialists, that is to say, by a guru and her/his disciples.

When later authors discussed the NŚ's seed-idea of rasa, in attempts to understand its ramifications, each commentary became a locus of scientific discussion, in which the original idea is quoted, and other authors' interpretations of it are shown and analyzed. Finally, the author criticizes his predecessors and puts forward his own views, trying always not to contradict the original source, in this case, Bharata's treatise.

It is not uncommon for authors to insert their own ideas, while claiming that they are Bharata's; for example, the śāntarasa is included among the eight original rasas in some redactions of the NŚ (Raghavan, 1975: 15). This procedure was not considered dishonest, but rather the natural development of discussions in a community of Indian scholars. Since śāntarasa had been accepted by the majority of scholars, it seemed reasonable to some of the scribes to add this rasa to the treatise. One must keep in mind that Sanskrit treatises had been copied by hand a number of times before they reached their final form; it is not unusual for a few versions to differ considerably from each other in some ways. The copying process promotes not only mistakes and corrupted text, but also a scholarly tradition in which a book, as a storehouse of knowledge, can be updated a number of times. As Rowell writes, 'the final form of a treatise as it has come down to us is sometimes more like a selection from an expandable data file than a unified dissertation' (1992: 22). The commentarial tradition (bhāṣya), which quoted extensively the original work, is an example of such an 'expandable' book.[14]

---

[14] See Buitenen in Dimock et alli 1974: 33-35.

Rasa, as aesthetic experience, is a concept that evolved from this long tradition of academic debate, in which scholars, from several different places in India, took part. One lineage of aestheticians flourished in Kashmir between the 9th and 11th centuries. The writings of Bhaṭṭa Lollaṭa, Śaṅkuka, Bhaṭṭa Nāyaka, Ānandavardhana and others display a great tradition of critical thinking on rasa, which culminates with the work of Abhinavagupta. The evolution of the concept shows a change, from Bharata's usual preoccupation with performance, to the experience of rasa from the spectators' point of view (as perception, cognition and enjoyment), reaching the highest point as a philosophical issue, in which the experience of rasa is considered akin to the final stages of yoga.

At first, as found in the NŚ, rasa concerns the practice of theater, the techniques for dramatic performance. The first commentators, Daṇḍin (court poet at Kanchi, during Pallava rule in the 7th century, in South India) and Bhaṭṭa Lollaṭa (Kashmir, early 9th century), held this view, which K.C. Pandey referred to as the traditional one (1950: 26). Both Daṇḍin and Bhaṭṭa Lollaṭa think of rasa as the sthāyibhāva raised to its peak by the combined effect of the vibhāvas, anubhāvas and vyabhicāribhāvas. Rasa, for Bhaṭṭa Lollaṭa, lies both in the actor's performance and in the represented character (Gnoli 1985: XVIII) as a matter of cause (bhāvas) and effect (rasa). Lollaṭa does not consider the spectators' perception in his account of the rasa process.

A scholar who opposed this traditional view was Śaṅkuka (9-10th century), to whom rasa comes rather from a process of imitation. He contends that the causes in a dramatic presentation are fictional, 'which through their resemblance with real causes suggest in the audience the model reality that lies behind them' (Gerow in Dimock at al. 1974: 222). Thus, a spectator realizes the sthāyibhāva presented in a play by means of inference. However, s/he deliberately ignores the fact that an actor is imitating characters and actions, and thus experiences rasa. The philosophical background of Śaṅkuka is the Nyāya system of logic, in which there are three methods of inference: (1) *pūrvavat* (induction of effect from cause); (2) *śeṣavat* (induction of cause from effect); and (3) *sāmānyatodṛṣṭa* (analogical reasoning). In the theater, each of these modes of inference, respectively, leads the spectator to realize: (1) the sthāyibhāva as an effect of the vibhāva, the dramatic situation; (2) the sthāyibhāva as causing the anubhāvas, the mental states displayed by the actors; and (3) vyabhicāribhāvas, collateral emotions related to the former two (Pandey 1950: 47-48).

According to Abhinavagupta's teacher, Bhaṭṭa Tauta, Śaṅkuka's theory is deficient in its assumption that rasa is nothing but the perception of an imitation. 'All that can be said, and this is in fact a presupposition that the audience takes to the theater, is that the actor, relying either on śāstra or his own past experiences, is able to convey by an entirely fictive non denotative, "generalized" set of words, gestures, and the like, (...) the understanding in the audience of love or sorrow' (Gerow in Dimock at al. 1974: 223). In this sense, the artificial or formal features of drama come to the fore of the discussion, for rasa, per se, is a mode of awareness that does not belong to the normal, daily sphere of emotions and cognition. Rasa is *alaukika*, non-worldly.

Bhaṭṭa Nāyaka (Kashmir, 9-10th century) criticizes both the traditional and Śaṅkuka's view of rasa theory in terms of Vedanta philosophy. He develops views about rasa that will later be accepted by Abhinavagupta, although from a different rationale. Bhaṭṭa Nāyaka refuses conceptions of rasa according to which it is perceived or produced. To him, rasa is a process of revelation (*bhāvanā*). "The specific task of this power, which as Nāyaka says, "has the faculty of suppressing the thick mental layer of mental stupor occupying our consciousness", is generalization or universalization of the things represented or described' (Gnoli 1985: XXI). Therefore, rasa, as bhāvanā or revelation, is a higher form of mental experience, achieved not as particular or personal feeling but as a universal one. But to Bhaṭṭa Nāyaka this is an experience rather than a cognition: 'Rása, the aesthetic experience revealed by the power of revelation (bhāvanā), is not noetic in character, is not a perception, but an experience, a fruition (bhoga)' (Gnoli 1985: XXIII). Therefore, rasa, in itself, is neither something apprehensible by the reason, nor merely related to the act of perception, but a purely mental experience.

The Dhvani Theory

It is time now to consider a monumental figure in Indian poetics: Ānandavardhana (Kashmir, first half of the 9th century). His theory of dhvani (resonance, suggestion) was commented on later by Abhinavagupta, and became part of his rasa theory. The theory of dhvani resulted from a scholarly inquiry into poetics as complex as the investigation of rasa in drama. It is, thus, a broad subject, to be merely touched on here. The focus of discussion was the comprehension of the aesthetic experience of poetry, and what distinguishes poetry from ordinary verbal constructions. Ānandavardhana wrote, in his *Dhvanyāloka* ([DL] 1.13): 'When the (directly expressive) word and the literal meaning both first subordinate themselves (to the suggested sense), the word subordinating its meaning and the literal meaning subordinating itself, and then reveal that (suggested) sense, that kind of poetry is called dhvani by the wise.'[15] Masson and Patwardhan give a thoughtful explanation of it:

> In fact, if we were to state what is the single most important characteristic feature of rasadhvani, we would say that it is the inability to lend itself to paraphrase. The reason this is so has to do with Ānanda's theory of the different functions that words fulfill in literature. (...) Ānanda inherited

[15] Translation by Masson & Patwardhan 1969: 76 n.2.

> from older works, two functions of words, *abhidhā* and *lakṣaṇā*. Abhidhā is denotation, the literal meaning of any utterance. Lakṣaṇā is more complex (it has often been misunderstood), but can be translated as secondary usage, including metaphorical usage. (...) Ānandavardhana revolutionized the field of poetics by adding a third function, hitherto completely unsuspected: *vyañjanā* or 'suggestiveness'. This *śabdavyāpāra* or 'linguistic function' is active in all three types of suggestion mentioned above. (...) Abhinava's major contribution to this notion was to show that rasa is not *niyata*, i.e., 'necessary', thus differing from *arthāpatti* [presumption] and from *anumāna*, which are logical processes. Direct statements 'produce' results. Thus the phrase *putras te jātaḥ*, 'A son has been born to you', 'produces' delight. This is not the case with aesthetical delight, which, according to Ānanda and Abhinava, can only be 'suggested'. (1969: 7)

A poem cannot be paraphrased (or translated) without losing its peculiar meaning, and this is a matter of suggestion, which differs from denotation, connotation or metaphor. For Ānandavardhana, the meaning of a poem is not only the information conveyed, it is quality of feeling as well. The suggestive power of language brings about rasa. 'Ānandavardhana did not confine himself to the words and sentences as indicators of meaning; he includes all contextual factors, the intonation, stress, gestures and even the pure sounds used in the utterance, as well as the literal sense, as indicators of the full meaning of an utterance. Not only the expressive symbols (*vācaka-s*), but the indicative signs (*bodhaka-s*) like gestures also form part of the language' (Raja 1977: 281-82). In fact, Ānanda's contextual poetry comes close to theater, in which the sounds of words in themselves (icons), indices pointing to the vibhāva, and all kinds of symbols display their possibilities of quality of feelings, which are relished by the reader/spectator and lead to the experience of rasa. Yet, symbols, in their conventional meaning, and indices, in their offering of evidence, are easier to grasp than the suggested qualisigns of dhvani. 'The suggested meaning is however completely unfixed (animate), since it depends on intangibles like the culture of the reader, the situation depicted, the person speaking, etc.' (Masson & Patwardhan 1970a: 17). The connection of the two theories, dhvani and rasa, is based eventually on the relation that each has to the object: 'what is suggested must be charming, and this charm must come only through rasa or emotion. The emotion is not something that can be expressed directly by the words, it can only be suggested' (Raja 1977: 285). The realization of this fact led Abhinavagupta to assert that 'the dhvani and the Rasa schools are indissolubly merged' (Gnoli 1985: XXXV).

Abhinavagupta

The confluence of all those theories reached its zenith in the work of Abhinavagupta. This encyclopedic thinker was born in Kashmir, about 960 A.D. (according to Pandey 1983: 56), into a learned brahmin family.

He was a Tantra yogī, an aesthetician and a philosopher, who wrote about 50 works, of which only two thirds have survived. Some scholars consider him a true polymath (see Raghavan 1981: 94-98). His teacher in dramaturgy was Bhaṭṭa Tauta, whose work on poetics is lost, as is Abhinava's commentary on it and, unhappily, the work of many other Kashmiri aestheticians. It is through the writings of Abhinavagupta that the ideas of Bhaṭṭa Lollaṭa, Śaṅkuka, Bhaṭṭa Tauta and Bhaṭṭa Nāyaka are known today. His main treatises on rasa theory are the *Abhinavabhāratī*, a commentary on the NŚ, and the *Locana*, a commentary on Ānandavardhana's DL. His contribution to the NŚ is the impeccable argument for the acceptance of the śāntarasa; and to the DL, the unification of dhvani and rasa theories. He wrote the *Tantrāloka*, an important work on śaiva tantrism. Also, he was not only a great scholar, but an accomplished practitioner of Tantra. According to Masson and Patwardhan, 'Tantric rituals affected Abhinava's views on the eventual goal of art, and led him to his transcendental theories on the aim of the aesthetic experience. The combination was unique in all of Indian history, and has produced one of the great monuments to the complexity and profundity of the human mind' (1969: 43). For Abhinavagupta, the final state of the enjoyment of rasa is that in which the spectator's consciousness is filled by light (*sattva*) and bliss (*ānanda*), a state similar to the consciousness of the supreme Brahman.

The influence of tantrism on rasa theory provides another set of ideas that hint at the real nature of the aesthetic experience of rasa. These ideas involve the Tantra conception of sexuality, not only as a religious metaphor, but also as ritual practice. In connection with rasa theory, Abhinavagupta frequently quotes verses from the *Vijñānabhairav*, a Tantra śaiva treatise, one of which reads: 'The pleasure that terminates in the infusion of power of bliss in a person on the achievement of a sexual intercourse – that pleasure is one's own pleasure on the realization of the essence of Brahman' (*Vijñānabhairav* 69, in Masson & Patwardhan 1969: 28). When quoting this passage, Abhinavagupta is not only referring to sexual practices, which are part of some Tantra yoga techniques; he is also comparing those with the idea of resonance in dhvani and the experience of rasa as bliss. Masson and Patwardhan explain: 'Here the comparison that Abhinava will make between sexual experiences and ecstatic experiences, is explicitly stated. Note that the commentary speaks of pleasure of knowing Brahman as being of the form of the resonance of a bell (*ghaṇtyanuraṇana*), a term that Ānanda applies to dhvani. He also speaks of sexual intercourse as the *abhivyaktikāraṇa* (i.e. that which manifests or suggests) bliss, again a term that Abhinava uses of rasa' (ibid.). Thus, several ideas are interrelated in connection with rasa: bliss, which can be aesthetic, sexual, religious, or all of them simultaneously; dhvani, or resonance, which can be a quality of feeling of poetry, but also the acoustic image of the supreme being. In fact, Brahman as the sound of a bell is an idea that has deep consequences for musical terms. Later musical treatises, such as the SR of Śārṅgadeva, develop fully the connections between musical sound and Indian cosmology (see 2.3.2, 3.3.4). Both complexes of theories and practices, namely, rasa and nāda, after all, converge in the direction of the highest of Indian concepts, that of Brahman.

Rasa Theory According to Abhinavagupta

The experience of rasa, whether in reference to poetry or theater or music, hinges on some prerequisites. A performance must be carried out flawlessly from both points of view: those of both stage and audience. Just as an actor is a person equipped with special training that makes possible the artistic performance of a play, the spectator who really aspires to relish rasa must be an experienced and sensitive connoisseur. The word Abhinavagupta employs for such a spectator is *sahṛdaya* (literally, possessing a heart, full of feeling, sensible, intelligent), for one must have not only a theoretical knowledge of art, but the iconic capacity to identify one's mind with that which is performed on the stage.

This is accomplished in steps. When watching a play or reading a poem, the sahṛdaya is not concerned with daily reality; rather, the consciousness of actual time and space fades away. By means of deep concentration and, initially, inference, s/he realizes the several elements represented, such as vibhāva, anubhāva, and so on. To acknowledge the sthāyibhāva, obstacles, both on stage and in the spectator's mind, must be overcome. For instance, the play must maintain consistency and veracity of plot, while the spectator must overcome the intrusion of personal desires or anxieties. Thus, on the one hand, the sahṛdaya transcends the inference level and the conventional aspects of the play; and, on the other, her/his personal life and feelings. In doing so, the sahṛdaya's mind becomes like a crystalline mirror, ready to take in and reflect all that is (re)presented in front of it. A pure stage of empathy with the play can now be achieved. Abhinavagupta writes in the *Locana:*

> The faculty of self-identification with the events represented [the Vibhāvas, etc.] demands that the mirror of the mind should be made completely clear, by means of completed acquaintance with and practice of poetry. The possessed of heart, those who possess the consent of their own hearts, are they who have this faculty. For it has been said: 'the tasting of that which finds the consent of the heart arouses the Rasa. The body is pervaded by it, as dry wood by fire.' (in Gnoli 1985: XLIII n.1)

Therefore, the one who is possessed of heart can completely identify her or himself with the circumstances represented, in such a way as to transcend the ego. S/he enjoys an exceptional sense of tranquillity. But there is yet another level to reach. All human beings have, in the deepest recesses of their minds, a bundle of instinctual and basic feelings – the latent impressions, dispositions or tendencies, called saṁskāra or vāsanā (the *raison d'être* of the nine general categories of rasa). The aesthetic experience, as reflected in the mirror of the mind, mingles with those latent impressions and eventually leads the sahṛdaya to 'experience sheer undifferentiated bliss (ānandaikaghana)[,] for we have come into direct contact with the deepest recesses of our own unconscious where the memory of a primeval unity between man and the universe is still strong' (Masson & Patwardhan 1969: VII-VIII). At this point, one is flooded by rasa 'as dry wood by fire', as Abhinavagupta puts it. This is similar to the bliss experienced by a yogī. The only difference is its impermanence in the field of art, because when the performance is over, the sahṛdaya returns to the real world. The aesthetic experience of rasa, or rasadhvani, is explained in the *Locana* by Abhinavagupta, in this condensed form:

> Now rasadhvani is something else altogether. It belongs only to the (suggestive) function in poetry. It is never included under worldly things and it is never even to be dreamed of as being revealed directly through words. No, quite the contrary, it is rasa, that is, it has a form that is capable of being relished (*rasanīya*) through the function of personal aesthetic relish (*carvaṇā*), which is bliss (*ānanda*) that arises in the sahṛdaya's delicate mind that has been colored (*anurāga*) by the appropriate latent impressions (*vāsanā*) that are deeply embedded from long before; appropriated that is, to the beautiful vibhāvas and anubhāvas, and beautiful, again, because of their appeal to the heart (*saṁvāda*), and which are conveyed by means of words. That alone is rasadhvani, and that alone, in the strict sense of the word, is the soul (of poetry). (In Masson & Patwardhan 1969: 50-51)

Śāntarasa – the Aesthetics of Tranquillity

Considering the features of Abhinavagupta conception of rasa and the experience thereof, it is not surprising that śāntarasa would have a special place for them in his system. The idea of śānta as a rasa appeared some centuries after the completion of the NŚ. In fact, in some versions of the NŚ, śānta is openly included among the other rasas, and śāma (peace) is mentioned as its sthāyibhāva. It was clear enough to several Indian aestheticians, however, that śānta did not originally belong there. Abhinavagupta had, therefore, to argue for its inclusion among the other eight rasas established by Bharata. Śāntarasa, which might be translated as 'the imaginative experience of tranquillity' (Masson & Patwardhan 1969. III), has its earliest mention in Udbhaṭa's *Kāvyālaṅkārasārasaṅgraha* (4.4). Masson and Patwardhan infer that śāntarasa was probably included among the eight rasas between the time of Ānandavardhana and Abhinavagupta. This means it appeared at some time during a period of about one hundred years (1969: 35). The scholars' opinions, at that time, can be grouped into three positions: those who accepted it without argument, those who refused, and those who argued for its inclusion. To argue for the inclusion of śāntarasa was difficult, for its opponents had strong points.

The biggest problem was that, from a strictly traditional point of view, śānta did not fit into the NŚ scheme. Each of Bharata's eight rasas has a fixed, corresponding sthāyibhāva. Further, the number of rasas and bhāvas (sthāyi plus vyabhicāribhāvas) adds to 49, which was considered a complete and auspicious number, any modification of which would destroy its harmony. On the other hand, some authors argued that śānta was contrary to the intrinsic nature of theater, that it cannot be represented: the sthāyibhāvas are 'love, energy, disgust, anger, mirth, amazement, fear and sorrow. Some add peace (śama), but it cannot be developed in plays' (Dhanañjaya's *Daśarūpaka* 4.35; in Masson & Patwardhan 1969: 149). The counter-arguments were also found in the NŚ. Bharata, in the chapter on successful dramatic performance, classifies spectators according to the traditionally Indian, four goals of life. He writes that young people enjoy watching plays in which there are representations of love affairs (*kāma*); others like some reference to religion and responsibility (*dharma*); business-oriented people prefer topics of wealth (*artha*); and people liberated of passion delight in plots relating to *mokṣa*, or ultimate freedom (NŚ 27.60). Abhinavagupta therefore thinks that, if mokṣa can be the subject of a play, then śānta must also be a rasa pertinent to theater. Another explanation for śānta, one not explicitly referred to in the NŚ, is that peacefulness is such a fundamental state of mind, in being connected to the highest aspiration in life (mokṣa), that it is not necessary to mention it. According to this view, śānta was presupposed by Bharata, and it should be assumed by the readers, as existing among the other eight rasas. Raghavan writes:

> So, if Bharata says that drama is of a varied nature in accordance with the varied nature of the world on the one hand and of the spectators on the other, if he says that one drama predominantly develops one Rasa whose appeal is only to those whose hearts are attuned to it and if he says that a certain drama may have its theme or purpose in Śama, it certainly means that Bharata has landed, though without expressly saying so, on Śānta Rasa. (1975: 17-18)

There was yet another matter to be settled before the complete acceptance of śāntarasa, and this concerned its sthāyibhāva. Because the aestheticians' normal practice was to introduce changes that did not contradict the oldest book on rasa, the search for śāntarasa's permanent emotion began with the text itself. Some authors claimed that the first of the vyabhicāribhāvas, nirveda, was the appropriate state of mind for conveying śānta. Nirveda has two meanings: disgust, in the ordinary sense of dislike; and religious detachment. The latter should be connected with śānta. Abhinavagupta writes, commenting on the NŚ: 'we ask you to tell us why the state of mind which is appropriated to the highest goal of man known as mokṣa cannot be raised to the status [of] a rasa? That state of mind just described is indeed the sthāyibhāva of śānta. But one must consider what its name is. Some say that it is complete detachment (nirveda – world-weariness) that is born from a knowledge of truth' (in Masson & Patwardhan 1969: 122-23). Others have suggested special terms such as *samyagjñana* (the realization of the self), by Rudraṭa; and *tṛṣṇākṣayasukha* (happiness which is the cessation of all desires), by Ānandavardhana (Raghavan 1975: 72-74). The expression used by Abhinavagupta is *tattvajñana*, the knowledge of truth. It is clear that all three of the possible sthāyis for śānta are based on philosophical concepts rather than those of dramaturgy. Another difficulty for Abhinavagupta was finding a play of high enough literary level to qualify as an example of śāntarasa. He argues that the *Mahābhārata* is such a work. In that play, the constant theme of greed and jealousy, which cause a war between two branches of the same royal family, would eventually arouse śānta in the readers, in the form of a peaceful consciousness of the impermanence and foolishness of material ambitions.

For Abhinavagupta, Śānta has a higher place than the other rasas. He writes: 'Because śānta is grounded on the highest goal of man, i.e. because it gives rise to mokṣa, it is the most important of all the rasas' (in Masson & Patwardhan 1969: 102-03). This is not only a statement of hierarchy, for Abhinavagupta believes śānta to be the foundation of all other rasas. He gives illustrations such as that of a white wall – representing the self in a state of quietness – on which the other rasas are projected, temporarily coloring the white, elemental basis, which returns to white after the performance; or that of the white thread and the jewels, mentioned before in relation to the bhāvas. A later inclusion in the NŚ reads: 'Various feelings, because of their particular respective causes, arise from śānta (a state of mental calm). But when these causes disappear, they melt back into śānta' (NŚ 6.87 in Masson & Patwardhan 1969: 140). It seems that the idea of śāntarasa becomes more and more philosophical than theatrical, or perhaps it is theater that is seen as a philosophy.

Indeed, Abhinavagupta was the first to assert that a particular rasa was a synthesis of all the others. Śānta, with all its philosophical relations with the self (*ātman*) in its purest state, peacefulness, light and wisdom, is the essential rasa of which the others are transformations. Above all, śānta was considered the fundamental rasa because it is the mental state proper of those who seek the highest of the four human goals, that is, mokṣa, which is freedom from saṁsāra. The other rasas are more connected with worldly aspirations (kāma, artha, dharma), whereas śānta is intrinsically non-worldly (alaukika). Although rasa in general is thought of as an alaukika experience, śānta is by nature the state of mind akin to a limitless and transcendent bliss. Certainly, the experience of such a state of mind is next to that of the mystic; and the spectator, or better, the sahṛdaya who relishes śāntarasa cannot but look at the world with transformed eyes after having that experience. 'The one thing śāntarasa does that no other rasa can [do], is that it disturbs us. If we really believe the message that any successful play dealing with śāntarasa tells us, we hear what Rilke said was the final lesson of all great literature: "You must change your life" ' (Masson & Patwardhan 1969: IX).

Śṛṅgārarasa – the Aesthetics of Love

Śṛṅgāra – love, sexual passion, desire or enjoyment – is a sentiment that had far-reaching consequences not for Indian arts and art theory but also on many of the mythological and philosophical texts. The word śṛṅgāra has some interesting semantic meanings that I believe can be related on a continuum linking archaic to highly developed thought – forms of thought which, in India, are frequently superposed. On one hand, there is sexuality as a natural power, worshipped in ancient India in forms that later would consolidate as the Śaiva mythology; on the other, one finds sexuality related to sophisticated philosophies and yoga techniques, Tantra being an outstanding case.

Besides the meanings referred to above, śṛṅgāra can be also translated as 'the horned' or 'the strong one'. The relation of horns with sexuality probably takes its significance from ideas that were surely important in a culture in which cattle breeding was (and still is) a source of life and wealth. A horn or tusk functions as an iconic sign for sexual arousal, and this could be a prototypical form of Śiva's liṅga.[16] There is evidence that some kind of sexual cult existed in Harappa (Parpola 1994: 218-21), and the protohistoric Indus Valley seal, which represents a horned deity or yogi with an erect penis, corroborates this hypothesis as well.

The power connected to a horn can refer to its use as a weapon, one often used by male animals fighting for leadership and for choice of females during the procreation season. Also, and from a economic point of view, it can refer to the power of a bull or stallion in bringing wealth to its owner or to a community dependent on animal breeding. In the Vedic *aśvameddha* ritual, the horse sacrifice,[17] the sexual power of a stallion is invoked when the animal is sacrificed and the queen is made 'to sleep' with the carcass, after priests have sung Vedic chants suggesting she is symbolically impregnated by the sacred animal: 'Come, lay thy seed well in the channel of the one who has opened her thighs. O thou, potent of manhood, set in motion the organ that is to women the nourisher of life. It darts into the sheath, their hidden lover, darkly buffeting, back and forth' (in Lannoy 1971: 116). The aśvameddha sacrifice intends to bring prosperity and political power to the king that performs it.

---

[16] The phallus, in which form Śiva is worshiped.

[17] Parpola argues that in pre-aryan cultures the sacrificed animal was a buffalo (1994: 219, 256). This is an interesting hypothesis, for the buffalo has actual horns, whereas the horse sacrifice might be a later aryan modification of the ritual.

However, the cult of eroticism was not restricted to phallic symbols; equally important was the worship of female deities, of which the concept of śakti is outstanding. In fact, according to the Kahādi school of Tantra, 'the supreme deity is an indissoluble unity of Śiva and Śakti' (Goudriaan 1979: 43), which has a special form of representation, the Ardhanārīśvara, the half male, half female deity. It is not surprising that śṛṅgāra was considered the principal rasa by some aestheticians, and the most developed system comes as the work of a king, the *Śṛṅgāra Prakaśā*, written by Bhoja.

Contemporary with Abhinavagupta, Bhoja developed rasa theory into an entirely different system, which was unusually irreconcilable with the NŚ on many points. The greatest king of the Paramāra dynasty of Mālavā, Bhoja started his reign about 1018 AD, and died in 1055. His capital, Dhārā (Madhya Pradesh), was not only his stronghold, but also is said to have had 84 or 104 temples[18] built by Bhoja, the same number of his royal titles and of books written by him. There is disagreement as to whether Bhoja really wrote all the works attributed to him (which range over an enormous variety of subjects), or if he was rather the patron of scholars who, upon completing their works, declined to take credit for authorship, in deference to their king (a common practice in Indian at that time). It is clear, however, that Bhoja was an expert in poetry, and that his chief work, *Śṛṅgāra Prakaśā*, a voluminous treatise on rasa, was certainly authored by him.

As the title suggests, śṛṅgāra is the main and only rasa for Bhoja. All other rasas belong to an intermediate state of mind in the process of aesthetic experience, which has śṛṅgāra as its goal. Indeed, one definition of the word śṛṅgāra is 'to climb a peak'. However, śṛṅgāra at this level denotes absolute, subjective, and objectless love (Raghavan 1978: 401). In Bhoja's system there are two conceptions of śṛṅgāra: a major one, corresponding to the finest aesthetic experience, also called *ahaṁkāra* (ego, individuality) or *abhimāna* (consciousness of self);[19] and a minor śṛṅgāra, which corresponds to the erotic rasa that in the NŚ comes from rati. Bhoja places the minor śṛṅgāra at the same level of the other rasas. Besides, for him, all bhāvas can be rasas themselves.

In the *Śṛṅgāra Prakaśā* Bhoja establishes detailed classifications of both major and minor śṛṅgāras. He divides the one major śṛṅgāra rasa into four, according to the four puruṣārthas: dharma-śṛṅgāra, artha-śṛṅgāra, kāma-śṛṅgāra and mokṣa-śṛṅgāra. In this way, at the same time Bhoja develops his philosophy of aesthetics. Linking love with the four aims of life, he refers to a typology of dramatic characters, describing

---

18 Most of them dedicated to Sarasvatī, the goddess of knowledge and arts.

19 Although Bhoja took those two terms from the Sāṅkhya system, they stand for different conceptions in relation to the aesthetic experience. *Ahaṁkāra* and *abhimāna* refer to levels of enjoyment, which begin with the consciousness of the self and eventualy transcends it, at the culmination of *śṛṅgāra* (see Venkatachakam in Chaitanya 1983: 103-04).

each of them in terms of nāyaka-nāyikā couples. It seems that major and minor conceptions of śṛṅgāra are mingled in this non-exclusive classification. Dharma-śṛṅgāra is the rasa of the character called dhīrodātta, artha-śṛṅgāra of dhīroddhata, kāma-śṛṅgāra of dhīrolalita, and mokṣa-śṛṅgāra of dhīraśānta (Raghavan 1978: 434). Each of them, therefore, refers to a character type with a particular orientation. Dhīrodātta is the hero who, above all else, pursues dharma, righteousness. Yudhisthira, for instance, as in the *Mahābhārata*. In the same way, dhīroddhata is the hero who seeks material gain; dhīrolalita is the amorous, playful hero, as the word lalita suggests; and dhīraśānta is the hero full of peacefulness and in search of liberation.

Śṛṅgāra, in its no-less religious sense of sexual passion or desire, belongs to the field of kāma-śṛṅgāra, which Bhoja divides preliminarily into two, after the NŚ (6.45): *sambhoga* (love in union), and *vipralambha* (love in separation). Further, Bhoja divides sambhoga śṛṅgāra into *sāmānya*, the union of animals and birds; and *viśeṣa*, the union of human beings, or *nāgarakas* (citizens). His classification of sambhoga and vipralambha śṛṅgāra, in all its minute sub-divisions, is very precise and detailed, an outstanding index of the great attention Indian culture has devoted to all the forms of love.

As usual in Sanskrit treatises, the classification of kāma-śṛṅgāra overlaps on many points. This should be kept in mind in connection with the several categories laid out below. Sambhoga śṛṅgāra – love in union – has four stages in its full development: *sattā*, *abhivyakti*, *anubandha* and *prakarṣa*, which represent levels of intimacy and the merging of the lovers' feelings for each other (see Table 8). Sattā, is 'the mere birth of Rati on the meeting of the two'. Abhivyakti is the stage in which clear signs of love appear in the play. Appropriate bhāvas, such as the usual emotions emerging in the lovers as they meet under the full moon or in a garden, and complementary feelings such as apprehension and the like are (re)presented to the reader or spectator. Anubandha is the 'continuation of the development of Rati in which the desired objects are sought after and the objects of dislike are [...] to be avoided.' Prakarṣa is 'the climax when Rati is said to be developed into the Śṛṅgāra-rasa' (Raghavan 1978: 65). These four degrees of relationship apply to each of the following varieties of sambhoga: (1) *saṁkṣipta*, brief or casual love; (2) *saṁkīrṇa*, mixed, in the sense of impure love, for instance an intercaste relationship; (3) *sampūrṇa*, full or accomplished love, also called *sampanna*; and finally, the highest premium of love, (4) *samyak*, united, going along together, or *samṛddha*, fortunate or plenteous love.

Table 8
Sambhoga śṛṅgāra

Levels ⇓	Kinds of sambhoga			
	1. Saṃkṣipta (brief)	2. Saṁkīrṇa (mixed)	3. Sampūrṇa (full)	4. Samyak (united)
1.	sattā – mere meeting			
2.	abhivyakti – appearance of bhāvas			
3.	anubhandha – development			
4.	prakarṣa – climax			

In terms of plot, Kāma-śṛṅgāra, in its form of vipralambha, can be approached in two ways, either as separation in itself, or separation as a process. The latter is the transformation of a state of separation into that of union (see Table 9). The richest scope of śṛṅgāra is that in which states of separation and union come in cycles of mutation. Again, Bhoja divides vipralambha śṛṅgāra into four kinds: (1) *prathamānurāga*, or *pūrvānurāga*, the 'promising to give and not really giving;' (2) *māna*, or belying love, 'where the lady is offended, jealous and angry;' (3) *pravāsa*, longing, 'the lover has gone on a long journey and the lady is suffering;' and (4) *karuṇa*, 'a case in which one of the two dies' (Raghavan 1978: 614). Concerning this last species, there are two important questions relating vipralambha-karuṇa and karuṇa proper: Are they are really distinct from each other? And, if so, how is it possible to know? Bhoja thinks they are definitely different feelings, which can be distinguished on four counts, in terms of origin, aim, object, and form. Raghavan explains: 'While the former proceeds from Rati or love alone, the latter develops from any kind of attachment, compassion, etc.; in the former, the end is reunion, whereas it is not so in the latter; the objects of the former are man and woman, of the latter anybody, and lastly the former is of the form of hope, the latter is destitute of any hope' (1975: 175).

Each of the four kinds of love in separation is able to come to an eventual union. This is technically designated by adding the suffix *anantara* (unbroken or adjoining) to the four terms for love in separation. In fact, each case produces a special kind of union. Pūrvānurāga-anantara is the union that comes from a mere promise of love. Its own nature calls for *pālana*, protection; and it is so tentative that is called *saṃkṣepa*, brief. Māna-anantara is much less innocent, and is the union that is consummated in spite of its impurity. It can refer to an adulterous relationship or to intercaste love, thus its nature is that of *kauṭilya*, crookedness. The result of such a relationship is *saṁkara*, mixed or impure love. Pravāsa-anantara is the state of union that follows a separation of lovers due to a long journey that one of them has taken. During the separation the lovers are in a way fasting, which explains the term *abhyavahāra* (eating), in the sense of breaking the fast. The end of this reunion is the satiation of the lovers' hunger, thus Bhoja calls it *sampūrṇa*, full. Karuṇa, the grief rasa, in relation to vipralambha śṛṅgāra, refers to the death of one of the two, and karuṇa-anantara is the fortunate reunion that occurs after the lovers' rebirth into another cycle of saṁsāra. Raghavan writes: 'When the dead are reborn and both unite, they enjoy fully. Their love cannot be shaken afterwards, for it has stood even the test of death. Hence, an ideal of love beyond this type of samyak in Karuṇānantara Sambhoga cannot be imagined' (Raghavan 1978: 621-23). Bhoja still designates for each kind of reunion 12 types of hero and heroine, according to their main *guṇa*, or mental disposition: *sattva* (lightness and pleasure), *rajas* (active and painful), and *tamas* (obstructive, heavy and dark). Thus, saṅkṣipta sambhoga, for instance, can be represented by four kinds of sāttvika hero – four rājasa heroes or four tāmasa heroes (Raghavan 1978: 65).

In Bhoja's detailed classification of śṛṅgārarasa something more than its divisions becomes clear, and that is the interchangeability of separation and union, a phenomenon which several authors have recognized. For instance, Abhinavagupta writes: 'Thus, in love in union, there is the fear of the possibility of separation, and in separation, there are the dreams of reunion. This is the very essence of love' (in Masson & Patwardhan 1970: 2.80 n.416). Furthermore, love has been considered as a kind of perversity by several Indian authors, which has been recognized as one of the finest elements in poetry and performing arts in India:

> (Love) is created by absence, and is highly nourished by it. In showing this, Bharata also showed that without absence, love in a play or in a poem would not be very appealing. This is why even in love in union poets show the perverseness (*vaiṣamya*) (of love), and how, because of the use of another woman's name, or because of jealousy, there are separations due to love-quarrels, precisely to remove the monotony of love in union which would otherwise be like tasting a single mass of sugar. As Vātsyāyana and others say: 'The ways of love are perverse' (*Kāmasūtra* 2.7.1). Bharata himself will say (that a woman's) persisting in perverse ways (leads to the highest pitch of love) (NŚ 22.207). (Abhinavagupta in Masson & Patwardhan 1970: 2.84 n.426)

Table 9

Bhoja's Classification of Śṛṅgāra Rasa

Vipralambha Śṛṅgāra - love in separation	⇨	**Sambhoga Śṛṅgāra - love in union**			
		Sambhoga (union after separation)	Prakṛtyartha (nature of the desire)	Upasargārtha (fate of the desire)	Nāyaka-nāyikā (theater characters)
1. Pūrvānurāga (the promissing of love)	⇨	Pūrvānurāgānantara (birth of love)	Pālana (protection)	Saṁkṣepa (brief)	4 kinds of sāttvika 4 kinds of rājasa 4 kinds of tāmasa
2. Māna (belying love)	⇨	Mānānantara (union in spite of)	Kauṭilya (crookedness)	Saṁkara (mixed, impure)	4 kinds of sāttvika 4 kinds of rājasa 4 kinds of tāmasa
3. Pravāsa (longing)	⇨	Pravāsānantara (reunion after separation)	Abhyavahāra (breakfast)	Sampūrṇa (complete)	4 kinds of sāttvika 4 kinds of rājasa 4 kinds of tāmasa
4. karuṇa (death)	⇨	Karūṇānantara (reunion after rebirth)	Anubhava (experiencing)	Samyak (fortunate)	4 kinds of sāttvika 4 kinds of rājasa 4 kinds of tāmasa

The Multiplication of Rasas

The evolution of rasa theory shows how different needs and purposes channeled its development in one or another direction. Arising from a somewhat technical conception of theater, Bharata's NŚ, the doctrines of Daṇḍin and Bhaṭṭa Lollaṭa, were concerned with practical matters of the aesthetic experience. Śaṅkuka, a younger contemporary of Lollaṭa, tried to use Nyāya's logic to study the spectator's point of view. He was criticized by Bhaṭṭa Nāyaka, which also disagreed with the theory of dhvani, proposed by Ānandavardhana. Nāyaka was under the influence of the Sāṅkhya and Vedanta systems. However, with the development of Śaiva philosophy, a new approach was proposed by Abhinavagupta. In fact, new needs appeared, often combining theatrical and literary requirements with religious needs. Thus, many writers proposed new rasas. (And I have already mentioned Abhinavagupta's argument for the inclusion of śānta, in the context of his relation to Tantric philosophy). Bhoja, besides his śṛṅgāra-based theory, proposed even more new rasas, as did other writers. Later, with the rise of the Bhakti devotional movement, a bhakti rasa was invented and a new theory was formulated, in which this was the supreme rasa.

The first new rasa to be added to the classical nine was *preyas*, which represented a form of non-sexual love. Preyas, as the tenth rasa, is mentioned for the first time in the *Kāvyālaṁkāra* of Rudraṭa (12.3). Possible translations for preyas include 'affection' or 'fondness', and its sthāyibhāva is *sneha*, 'friendship'. Later, other non-sexual affections also appeared as rasas. *Vātsalya*, parents' love for children, or elders for youngsters. *Prīti* implies feelings such as loyalty or devotion to a king by court poets, musicians, scholars, or the king's subjects; in a more general sense, prīti implies the sentiments connected with the relationship between leader and follower (Raghavan 1975: 119-21).

By the time of Abhinavagupta and later, Indian aestheticians had become more and more progressive, not limiting their theories strictly to the canons of the NŚ. A variety of new rasas appeared, in spite of the philosophical and aesthetical consistency which the main authors had striven for. The new rasas were not concerned with the main instincts of human beings, but represented any emotion that could be related to types of characters; these rasas were devised to support, in theory, the variety of plays, poems and songs, in a somewhat weaker way than before. Many of the newly proposed rasas were merely mentioned in the texts, without justification, and thus were rejected by the great aestheticians. In table 10, I have listed some of the new rasas and their authors (Raghavan 1975: 119-62).

Table 10
Additional rasas

Rasas		Scholar
Preyas	affection or fondness (non-sexual)	Daṇḍin, Rudraṭa, Bhoja, Bopadeva & Hemādri
Preman	non-sexual love	Bhoja, Kavikarṇapūra
Vātsalya	parental love	Bhoja, Viśvanātha, Haripāladeva, Bopadeva & Hemādri
Prīti	respectful affection	Daṇḍin
Laulya	lustfulness or greediness	others
Mṛgayā	hunt	Dhanaṁjaya
Akṣa	gambling	Dhanaṁjaya
Sneha	friendship	Rāmacandra, Guṇacandra, Bopadeva & Hemādri
Vyasana	vice	Rāmacandra, Guṇacandra
Duḥkha	uneasiness	Rāmacandra, Guṇacandra
Sukha	easiness or happiness	Rāmacandra, Guṇacandra
Udātta	elevated or mighty	Bhoja
Uddhata	arrogance	Bhoja
Śraddha	faith	others
Bhakti	religious devotion	Bopadeva & Hemādri, Madhusūdana
Madhura	sweetness, in the sense of religious devotion	Bopadeva & Hemādri
Sakhya	friendship, in the sense of religious devotion	Bopadeva & Hemādri
Dāsya	slavery or servitude	Bopadeva & Hemādri
Māyā	illusion, the world as perceived by the senses	Bhānudatta
Kārpaṇya	niggardliness	Bhānudatta
Vrīḍanaka	modesty	Anuyogadvāra-sūtra of the Jains
Citra	manifold, when incompatible rasas come together	Gaṅgādhara

The flood of new rasas brings to mind Raghavan's 'period of chaos' among Indian aestheticians (1975: 138). Actually, the profusion of rasas resulted from different understandings as to the foundation of rasa theory. A main reason for the wealth of new rasas was the view that any bhāva can become a rasa, and that sthāyibhāvas can also operate as vyabhicāribhāvas, as well as conversely. On the other hand, a much more detailed theory of drama required that each hero(ine) in a play should be distinguished by a particular rasa that expressed her/his personality. That is the case with Bhoja's invention of udāttta and uddhata rasas. But it is also true some authors diluted the concept of rasa to the point where any motif or idea could also be a rasa (Raghavan 1975: 126). It seems, however, that the multitude of additional rasas did not become established in the main course of the theory. Abhinavagupta examined and refuted many of them on the basis of his solid rationale for rasa theory. For him, there are only nine rasas, the eight found in the NŚ plus śānta. Abhinavagupta thinks that only those nine rasas are fit for representation, as Pandey explains: 'He admits [the] Rasas to be nine, not because this number was recognized in the literary circle to which he belonged, but because no other mental state admits of so interesting a presentation, nor is so closely connected with the objectives of human life'[20] (1950: 173-74). Indeed, his theory of rasa has become a standard in itself.

The last rasa to achieve some recognition, in synthetic and in one-rasa theory, was bhakti, mentioned above. The bhakti rasa reached a high level of development in the Vaiṣṇavas poets of Bengal. Bopadeva and Hemādri were the pioneers of a system later developed by aestheticians following the school of Caitanya (1486-1533), and Rūpa Gosvamin is one of its main scholars. Twelve rasas figure into their system. The object of this theory is not related to Sanskrit poetry or theater as understood by the classical writers, but rather to *sādhanā*, the realization of the supreme being in the form of Kṛṣṇa. This involves, besides the theoretical works, a huge amount of literature and song lyrics in several Indian languages, which combined amount to a body of work that cannot be underestimated.

The Vaiṣṇava poets base their theory on Bharata's. That is, the eight traditional rasas are accepted, as well as śānta. A few more special rasas are added. These theorists, however, established a totally different structure in order to fulfill their devotional aims. The rasas are classified into two groups: *mukhya* (primary) and *gauṇa* (secondary), 'according to their constant or transient nature in the hearts of their devotees' (Bhattacharya 1976: 152). The first group comprises five forms of śṛṅgāra, representing different attitudes of love for Kṛṣṇa: (1) śānta, for peace of mind and disregard for worldly desires is a requirement concerning the devotion of Kṛṣṇa (Bhattacharya 1976: 155-56); (2) *dāsya*, in the sense of servitude, implies the devotee's submission to the deity; (3)

[20] I.e., kāma, artha, dharma and mokṣa.

sakhya, friendship, such as that of Arjuna and Kṛṣṇa in the *Mahābhārata*; (4) vātsalya, the love of a devotee for Kṛṣṇa as father; and (5) madhura, the sweet feelings of the Gopīs, the milkmaid lovers of Kṛṣṇa. These five rasas are above all five forms of bhakti, implying a progressive scale in the realization of Kṛṣṇa.

The second group, the gauṇa rasas, are seven of Bharata's rasas (without śṛṅgāra): hāsya, adbhuta, vīra, karuṇa, bībhatsa, bhayānaka and raudra. They represent merely transitory feelings in relation to the primary bhakti rasas. According to Raghavan 'they are Rasas only when they involve Kṛṣṇa-rati' (1975: 145).

It is interesting to compare Abhinavagupta conception of śānta and the Vaiṣṇavas' bhakti. As Bhattacharya puts it, 'the Bengal Vaiṣṇavas may be represented as the advocates of a culture of feelings' (1976: 159-60). Their conception of bhaktirasa implies above all the development of a feeling of attachment (rati) to Kṛṣṇa. In no sense are the Vaiṣṇavas interested in getting rid of emotions, as the Abhinavagupta's conception of śāntarasa implies. Most of the other traditional means of divine realization, the goal of which is always mokṣa, take as a fundamental stage the control of feelings, that is, the acquisition of śānta. Yet, śānta in the bhaktirasa system is merely the initial focusing of attention in the direction of Kṛṣṇa. Bhakti is certainly one of the most popular forms of devotion, but in another sense, it can be easily connected to tantric traditions. It seems significant that the word bhakti also means sexual desire (Lannoy 1971: 25). This śṛṅgāra of a god is explicitly represented in many pieces of Indian art, and it constitutes a rich repertoire of classical songs, especially those telling of the amorous and positively erotic love of Kṛṣṇa and Rādhā, his favorite gopī lover.

3.3 Rasa in Hindustani Music

3.3.1 The Jāti System and Rasa

> When a note [representing a particular sentiment] is prominent (lit. strong) in a Jāti, the producers in regard to the production of such a sentiment should combine the song with it, i.e., should give it prominence there. [For example,] a song in the Erotic and the Comic sentiments should abound in many Madhyamas and Pañcamas, and in the Heroic, the Furious, and the Marvelous sentiments, songs should be made with many Ṣaḍjas and Ṛṣabhas. And the song in the Pathetic sentiment should be full of many Gāndhāras and Niṣādas. Similarly a song in the Odious and the Terrible sentiments should have many Dhaivatas. (NŚ 29.12-14)

It is the NŚ that presents the earliest extant information on how musical forms represent the categories of feeling and other dramatic elements. Yet, it seems that, during the first centuries A.D., rasa was related to musical structures only in the context of theater. There is no mention of rasa in the *Dattilam*, perhaps because this treatise is instead concerned with ritual music, or gāndharva (according to Lath 1978: 81-129). But in the NŚ, several musical topics were related to rasa, not merely the jātis, the mode classes of early Indian music, but also *alaṁkāras* (melodic configurations), *dhruvās* (a drama song form) and patterns of drumming. Besides, musical signs were thought also to represent standard elements in a dramatic performance, such as the entrance and exit of character types, the movement of vehicles and objects, and so on.

Although there is no space in this chapter for a detailed explanation of the jāti system (in use since early in the first millennium and likely declining after A.D. 500),[21] the following figure can remind the reader of its essential elements. The two basic pitch sets, *ṣaḍjagrāma* and *madhyamagrāma* (distinguished by particular configurations in terms of microtonal *śrutis*), are articulated by the ten modal functions, or *lakṣaṇas*, which results in the seven primary or śuddha jātis. From these, by means of scale rotations, one can derive the mūrcchanās and the other jātis (some of which also originated in regional music). Finally, from the 18 jātis the pentatonic and hexatonic forms can be obtained.

Figure 13

Jāti System -- a Generative Diagram

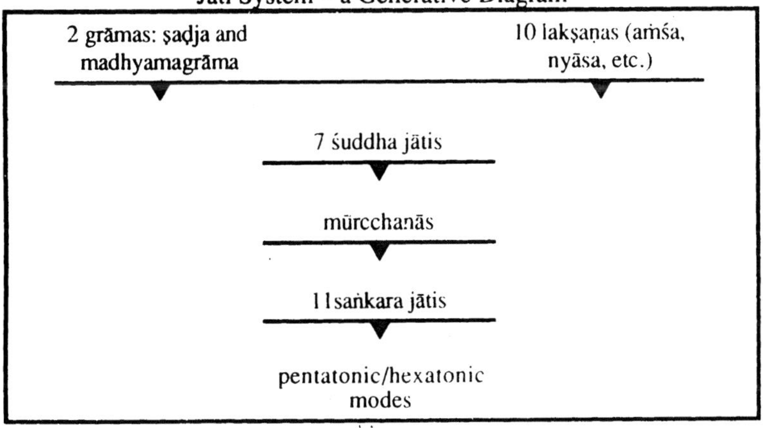

One of the most significant passages on musical aesthetics in the NŚ is the definition of aṁśa, the sonant note. It was a modal function actualized by an emphasized note in the melodic movements, which defined a complex of harmonic relations with the other functions (the lakṣaṇas, which define the characteristics of a jāti). Bharata explains the aṁśa in the following way:

> The aṁśa [is the note] on which [the song's] charm (*rāga*) depends, and from which the charm proceeds; it is the basis of the variation into low (*mandra*) and high (*tāra*) pitches depending on the [first] five notes, and in the combination of many notes it is perceived prominently (*atyartham*), and moreover other strong notes may be to it in [a] relation of consonance and dissonance, and it is related to the *graha*, *apanyāsa*, *vinyāsa*, *saṁnyāsa* and *nyāsa* [notes], and it lies scattered throughout the song. (NŚ 28.76-78)

The first point to note in this description is the direct relation connecting the *rāga* (charm) of a song with the aṁśa. Rāga is employed

[21] For a detailed description and analysis of the jāti system, refer to Rowell 1992: 144-179; Clough et al. 1993; and Widdess 1995.

here in its pre-musical sense, in which it denotes the aesthetical features of a song. It nevertheless seems to be the origin of the later concept of rāga as musical structure, which is, thus, deeply rooted in the issue of rasa expression. The relationship aṁśa to rasa is manifold: the charm does not only depend on the aṁśa, but also proceeds from it. Bharata is emphasizing the semiotic properties of musical movement and continuity, which, from an aesthetical point of view, refers to the perception and interpretation of a piece of music in terms of charm: fascination, delight and enchantment. Music, performer and listener are connected as such. Aṁśa is not merely a predominant svara in a jāti, but a focal point that organizes and gives individuality to the modal complex derived from the several possibilities that a jāti offers. The statement that aṁśa is the basis of variation of mandra and tāra registers suggests the aṁśa determines the range for melodic development, hence the mention of mandra and tāra not as registers but in the sense of the two modal functions of highest and lowest permitted notes. Moreover, the aṁśa is important for its relationship to the other functions: the graha (the initial), apanyāsa (a confinal), vinyāsa and saṁnyāsa (sectional finals) and nyāsa (the final). In relation to the 'strong notes', it must be in consonance (perfect fourth or fifth) or dissonance (other than a minor second or major seventh). In this way, aṁśa was not merely a frequently sung note in the mode, but its framework axis, keeping together the entire structure and giving it musical and aesthetical particularity.

A jāti represents a certain rasa according to the choice of aṁśa. This seems to be a matter of simple convention (i.e., the musical sign is a symbol), for Bharata announces in chapter 19 that madhyama and pañcama refer to śṛṅgāra and hāsya; ṣaḍja and ṛṣabha to vīra, raudra and adbhuta; gāndhara and niṣāda to karuṇa; and dhaivata to bībhatsa and bhayānaka (NŚ 19.38-40). However, at the beginning chapter 29, when the jātis are prescribed to represent rasas according to their aṁśa, the relations between signs and objects seem to be more complex. This could be attributed to the corruption of the text, but it seems to me rather to constitute a more detailed description, of which an abridgment was presented in 19.38-40. In fact, it is clear that not all jātis represent all rasas merely according to the rule above. Some of them are more flexible, and some represent a single rasa. In Table 11, the jātis with their possible aṁśas are related to the eight rasas according to the choice of particular aṁśas.

Table 11
Rasas and their musical structures according to Bharata

Jāti	Possible aṁśas	**Rasa**	Aṁśa
Ṣaḍjagrāma			
(NŚ 28.80-91)		(NŚ 29.1-5)	
śuddha jātis			
Ṣāḍjī	sa, ga, ma, pa, dha	vīra, raudra, adbhuta	sa
Ārṣabhī	re, dha, ni	vīra, raudra, adbhuta	re
Dhaivatī	dha, re	bībhatsa, bhayānaka	dha
Dhaivatī	dha, re	karuṇa	?
Naiṣādī	re, ga, ni	karuṇa	ni, (ga?)
saṅkara jātis			
Ṣaḍjodīcyavatī	sa, ma, dha, ni	śṛṅgāra, (hāsya?)	ma
Ṣaḍjakaiśikī	sa, ga, pa	karuṇa	ga
Ṣaḍjamadhyā	all svaras	śṛṅgāra, hāsya	ma, pa
Ṣaḍjamadhyā	all svaras	unmāda (madness)	?
Ṣaḍjamadhyā	all svaras	all rasas	all svaras
Madhyamagrāma			
(NŚ 28.80-91)		(NŚ 29.6-11)	
śuddha jātis			
Gāndhārī	re, ga, ma, pa, ni	karuṇa	ga, ni
Gāndhārī	re, ga, ma, pa, ni	śṛṅgāra, hāsya	ma, pa
Madhyama	sa, re, ma, pa, dha	śṛṅgāra, hāsya	ma, pa
Pañcamī	re, pa	śṛṅgāra, hāsya	(ma?), pa
saṅkara jātis			
Raktagāndharī	re, ga, ma, pa, ni	karuṇa	ga. ni
Gāndhārodīcyavā	sa, ma	vīra, raudra, adbhúta	sa
Madhyamodīcyavā	pa	śṛṅgāra, hāsya	pa
Gāndhārapañcamī	pa	?	?
Āndhrī	re, ga, pa, ni	vīra, raudra, adbhuta	(sa?), re
Nandayantī	pa	śṛṅgāra, hāsya	(ma?), pa
Karmāravī	re, pa, dha, ni	vīra, raudra, adbhuta	re
Kaiśikī	sa, ga, ma, pa, dha, ni	bībhatsa, raudra (?)	dha

Bharata starts with two saṅkara (composite) jātis: 'The ṣaḍjodīcyavatī and the ṣaḍjamadhyā should be applied in the erotic and the comic sentiments respectively because madhyama and pañcama are amplified in them' (NŚ 29.1). The amplification of svaras means assigning them to aṁśa. M and P are not to be used indiscriminately to represent śṛṅgāra and hāsya, but rather according to the jāti possibilities. In fact, ṣaḍodīcyavatī admits only S, M, D and N as aṁśas, but not P (NŚ 29.84-85). Ṣaḍjamadhyā concedes that all seven svaras are possible as aṁśas. But this still does not explain the word 'respectively', which seems to indicate that ṣaḍjodīcyavatī represents only śṛṅgāra. From this, one could further infer that M and P would represent, respectively, śṛṅgāra and hāsya; instead of both svaras representing indiscriminately both rasas. Yet, the following verses lend no support to this hypothesis.

Ṣaḍjamadhyā is an interesting case, for it can represent all the rasas. This flexibility comes from the fact that this is a jāti that bears all svaras as potential aṁśas. Therefore, ṣaḍjamadhyā has not only the potential to represent all the rasas, but also madness, which is not a rasa, but the vyabhicarībhāva unmāda. Bharata gives no explanation for this. It seems to me that if all svaras in ṣaḍjamadhyā are – at the same time – emphasized, or if the rules concerning the relations between the aṁśa and the other svaras are not followed properly, the result would be a state of melodic confusion, in which the destroyed hierarchical structure becomes an iconic sign of madness, as a mental state qualified by undifferentiated values and judgments. In fact, the *Sāhityadarpana*[22] states that unmāda is to be acted out as inopportune laughter or weeping, singing or talking incoherently, and so on (3.160 in Shukla 1994: 1.90).

More evidence that the relation aṁśa/rasa in the NŚ is not so simple as it is summarized in 19.38-40 (and 29.12-14 as well), is the prescription of naiṣādī and ṣaḍjakaiśikī for karuṇa. In this case, G and N seem not to be aṁśas with equivalent power to represent karuṇa. The text reads: 'The Naiṣādī with niṣāda as its aṁśa note, and the ṣaḍjakaiśikī with gāndhāra [as its aṁśa note] should be the jāti sung by expert singers in the Pathetic sentiment' (29.3). It is clear that ṣaḍjakaiśikī cannot have N as aṁśa (but only S, G and P), but why is not G mentioned as an aṁśa that would make karuṇa representable by naiṣādī? A possible explanation is that naiṣādī and ṣaḍjakaiśikī represent karuṇa not merely because their aṁśa are respectively N and G, but as higher musical signs, implying all the features that define those two jātis. Further, Bharata says dhaivatī can depict karuṇa, which would again require G or N as aṁśa, according to the general rule. But that jāti can only support D and R, which limits its representational possibilities to bībhatsa and bhayānaka for D; or vīra,

---

[22]*The Mirror of Composition*, a treatise on literary composition by Viśvanātha-kavirāja, 15th century A.D.

raudra and adbhuta for R (which Bharata explicitly does not mention); but never karuṇa. There seems to be no clear explanation for these details that contradict the general rule for aṁśa and rasa. Perhaps a more complex network of references for the jātis had already evolved from the general rasa/aṁśa rule stated in the NŚ, and was incorporated into the main text later.

Similar difficulties appear in the relation between rasa and jāti in the madhyamagrāma. M or P is the chosen aṁśas for representing śṛṅgāra and hāsya in pañcamī and nandayantī, as Bharata states; however, both jātis do not admit M as aṁśa. The same happens with āndhrī, when S is prescribed for vīra, raudra and adbhuta. One of the 18 jātis, gāndhārapañcamī, is not mentioned as representing any rasa in this section. Further, an inexplicable exception appears when the aṁśa D is prescribed for kaiśikī to represent raudra (which normally would need S or R): 'And in the Odious and the Furious sentiments the Kaiśikī with Dhaivata as their Aṁśa note, should be applied' (NŚ 29.10). Of course, all these inaccuracies can be attributed, if not to corrupted texts, to the extreme conciseness of the literary style typical of Sanskrit treatises. But it seems rather meaningful that Bharata prescribes for the kaiśikī jāti only bībhatsa and raudra rasas. Kaiśikī, with six possible aṁśas, could well represent śṛṅgāra and hāsya (for its M and P); karuṇa (for its G and N); vīra, raudra and adbhuta (for its S); and bībhatsa and bhayānaka (for its D). That is, literally all eight rasas, in almost the same way ṣaḍjamadhyā can represent all the rasas. Possibly the individuality of kaiśikī can be explained not merely by the relation aṁśa/rasa, which focuses its character so as to represent only bībhatsa and raudra, but also by more complex musical features.

A likely explanation for several of those inconsistencies could be that the system – which gives M and P as aṁśas for representing śṛṅgāra and hāsya; S and R for vīra, raudra and adbhuta; G and N for karuṇa; and D for bībhatsa and bhayānaka – concerns above all the śuddha jātis, or *svarajātis:* ṣaḍjī, ārṣabhī, gāndharī, madhyamā, pañcamī, dhaivatī and naiṣādī. Those are the least problematic in this sense. It could be that the composite, or saṅkara, jātis had a different rationale for representing rasas; for instance, concerning the jātis which seem to have a regional origin. Some of the saṅkara jātis have names indicating a certain geographical area in India, such as āndhrī – the region of Andhra in the Bay of Bengal; ṣaḍjodīcyavatī, gāndhārodīcyavā and madhyamodīcyavā – northern (udīcya) forms of ṣaḍjī, gāndhārī and madhyama, which can refer to the regions of Punjab, Indus Valley and Hindu Kush, according to Widdess (1995: 7); and karmāravī, for Karmāra. Rowell suggests that the inclusion of regional jātis was an early attempt to incorporate other musical traditions in the jāti system as laid out by Bharata (1992: 171), anticipating, in this way, the main issue of the *Bṛhaddeśī* (BD). If so, it is also possible that, in the NŚ, not only were the musical features of regional music absorbed, but some sort of aesthetic codification took place as well. This presumably differed from the aṁśa/rasa rule laid down in the NŚ, but it was accommodated by the scholars as best as possible. Another possibility, now grounded on indexical reference, would be the attribution of certain rasas to the circumstances related to the original melodic forms, or the general character of the people living in the area from which the jāti originates. For instance, Gangoly (1989: 72-73) mentions the āndhrī jāti as derived from the tribe of Andhras (Dravidians). In that case, the raudra and vīra rasas that Āndhrī represents would be connected to the fierceness of the original tribes, or the fierceness which the Indian scholars and musicians imagined the Āndhrīs to have.

If that hypothesis proves correct – that is, if the rule connecting aṁśas and rasas in a systematic way was first concerned with the śuddha jātis, and then forced to explain the other composite jātis at a later stage – then it should be possible to find a more accurate semiotic grounding for the established representations than simple convention. A first question concerns the groupings of rasas. Bharata, when explaining the rasas (NŚ 6.38), grouped śṛṅgāra with hāsya; raudra with karuṇa; vīra with adbhuta; and bībhatsa with bhayānaka. I tried to comprehend the rationale for those groups in chapter 3.1, above. From those four groups of rasa, only the pair śṛṅgāra-hāsya is consistently connected to the jātis. Karuṇa is treated separately from raudra, which joins vīra and adbhuta. The only obvious conclusion is that karuṇa has a special place in the Sanskrit musical drama, which can be validated by its further relation with vipralambha śṛṅgāra. Karuṇa, in its sense of compassion, is also said to be the rasa of poetic creation, in reference to the opening episode of the Rāmāyaṇa, when Vālmīki, deeply moved by the killing of copulating birds by a hunter, is inspired to write a poem (Vālmīki 1990: 9-11).

The second question is if there is any musical or cultural basis for the relations between rasa and aṁśa, other than those grounded on the symbol. In the jāti system, the melodic structures were based on the two grāmas, sa-grāma and ma-grāma, which constituted the two tuning sets that generate by rotation the 14 mūrchanās. From those pitch collections, the jātis emerged, featuring the ten modal functions (the aṁśa, nyāsa, etc.). The jātis, however, were not grounded on a tonic, as contemporary rāgas are to the svara S, but rather had their melodic development organized in a sort of plagal configuration, in which the relation S-M was stronger than that of S-P (see Rowell 1992: 156-57). M is also the only svara never dropped for the creation of hexatonic and pentatonic modes (see Widdess 1995: 52). Conversely, in three jātis the svaras S-P could be dropped to generate a pentatonic structure. Therefore, the melodic development of the jātis seems to have evolved around the pivotal tone M, which, however, was not a tonal center. This may explain why M is associated with śṛṅgāra, a rasa connected with the higher class of characters. M, in the *Nāradiyāśikṣā* (see Rowell 1992: 89), is associated with the celestial musicians, the Gandharvas, as well as with the highest caste, *brāhmaṇa* and the god of creation, Brahmā. P can also be explained as representing śṛṅgāra along the same lines, although not so distinctly (see Ex. 23 for the jātis representing śṛṅgāra). G and N, both connected to karuṇa, have their own peculiarity, that of being the two alterable svaras. However, *antara-ga* and *kākalī-ni* (svaras raised two śrutis from G and N) were instead regarded as transitional notes, and could not be selected as aṁśa. At any rate, G and N are the svaras that have the potentiality for alteration, which implies that they are conceived as being not as stable and pure as M, P and S. They are associated with the two lowest castes, *vaiśya* and *śūdra*. Karuṇa implies some sort of dissatisfaction, and this could be represented by the sensitivity and potential instability of G and N (see Ex. 24 for some jātis representing karuṇa). The connection of aṁśas S and R with vīra, raudra and adbhuta is less musical, but still an explanation is possible. R is a svara related to the *kṣatriya* caste (rulers and warriors, in a general sense), and the vīra and raudra rasas are thereby easily justified. Adbhuta, as the result of a heroic action, can also be connected to this group. The weakest point would be D, also a kṣatriya svara, but related to bībhatsa and bhayānaka. Such a relation is not clearly explainable, except from the victim's point of view. In most of the cases above, there is an iconic relation grounding the representation; for example, M, as the most stable svara, when chosen as aṁśa, refers to the rasa connected to characters of the highest caste. The evidence for this hypothesis, however, is clearly not very solid.

After the jātis, the next level in the constitution of an actual piece of music concerns the *varṇa*, patterns of melodic movement and their actual species, or *alaṁkāras*. Bharata says: 'When a regular (lit. having a characteristic) song (pada) adds [at least] two varṇas to it, then the varṇas give rise to rasas' (NŚ 29.21). Therefore, the expression of rasa, which is the result of a complete and complex musical structure in one of the song forms of early Indian music, does not depend solely on the choice of aṁśa but also on melodic configurations and embellishments. There are four varṇas (NŚ 29.17-18): *ārohin* (ascending), *avarohin* (descending), *sthāyin* (steady), and *saṁcārin* (mixed). From these basic possibilities emerges a number of combinations which constitute the 33 alaṁkāras, or ornaments. It seems meaningful that the number of alaṁkāras and that of vyabhicāribhāvas are the same. If the choice of aṁśa somehow determines the sthāyibhāva, then the alaṁkāras, in their complementary character, help establish the rasa in a song.

Example 23

Jātis representing śṛṅgāra (aṁśa M- P)

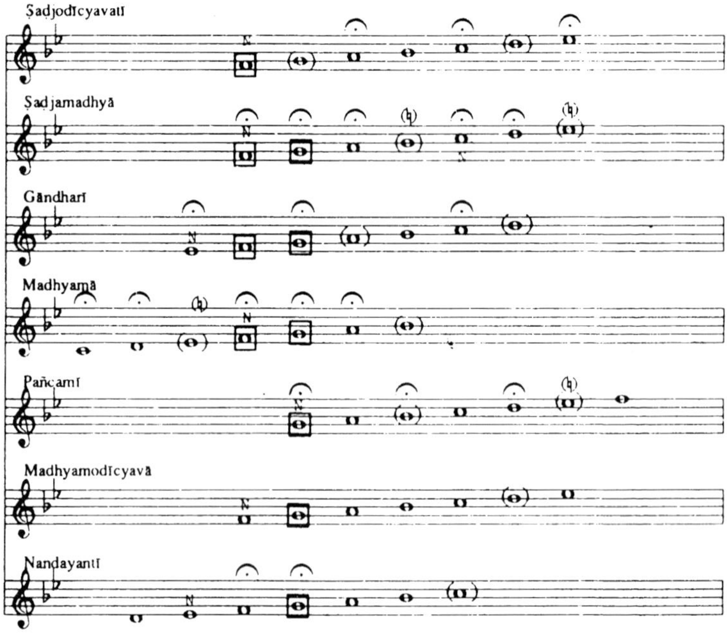

Example 24

Jātis representing karuṇa (aṁśa G- N)

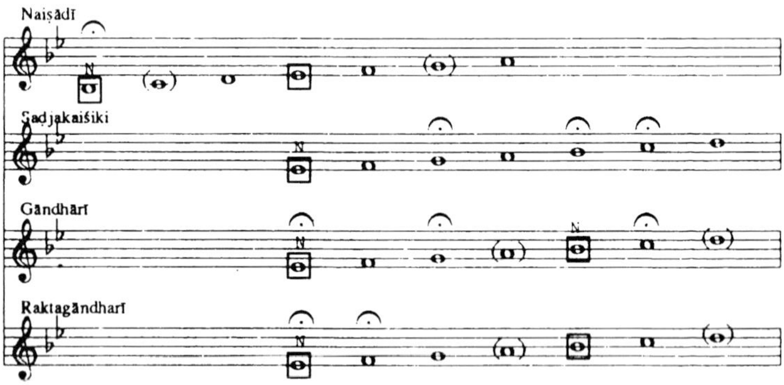

Prajñānānanda connects directly some of the alaṁkāras with śṛṅgāra: 'The sthāyī-varṇa is a symbol of peace and balance, and the alaṁkāras like *prasannādi, prasannānta, prasannādyanta, prasannamadhya, krama, recita, prastāra* and *prasāda* are included in it. The word "*prasāda*" means "calmness of mind," which originates from the basic sentiment, śṛṅgāra' (1973: 108). The melodic feature of these alaṁkāras is that it starts at one svara, progresses in a certain pattern upwards or downwards, and then returns to the same starting point. Thus, the peace and balance (in terms of symmetry) meant by the word *prasanna* or *prasāda* is represented iconically in the melodic pattern. However, the Sanskrit treatises do not relate those alaṁkāras with a specific rasa, such as śṛṅgāra. Both the NŚ and the BD are plainly technical in their description of the alaṁkāras. Moreover, the prefix prasanna (clear, bright, pure), in its musical sense, means merely having the lower svaras at the beginning (prasannādī), in the middle (prasannāmadhya), at the end (prasannānta), and at the beginning and the end (prasannādyanta). (see NŚ 29.17-86; BD anu.69). Peace and balance, as quoted above, seem to refer best to śānta than śṛṅgāra, except in Bhoja's conception of rasas. Finally, it is warned that excessive use of alaṁkāras is not desirable in the *dhruvās* (stage songs), for it obliterates the clear comprehension of the lyrics, thus decreasing the expressive power of a song (NŚ 29.37-39; BD 133-136). Explaining this question, Lath writes:

> Dhruvās were songs sung during the stage-acting of ancient plays and they formed an essential part of the plot. The poetical content of a dhruvā song was its mainstay and a clear enunciation of the words sung was of the greatest importance. Incorporation of melodic figures was secondary and subservient to the primary consideration of communicating the meaning of words. Certain alaṁkāras could so split the letters of a word that its meaning could be entirely lost to the audience. Such alaṁkāras were to be avoided when singing dhruvās. [...] In singing certain alaṁkāras, a syllable within a word was dragged [out] for so long that when the next syllable was pronounced, the link between the two was lost to the listener. This Bharata calls: *śrotṛvarṇaprakarṣaṇa* (NŚ 29.26). This was undesirable in dhruvās since it interfered with the goal of dramatic display: the arousal of rasa (*rasaniṣpatti*) in the spectator, mainly through the words of the play-write. Abhinava remarks that the aesthetic process consisting in the presentation of vibhāva etc. leading to *sādharaṇīkaraṇa* and the resulting relish of rasa, could only be initiated if meanings could be communicated. (Lath 1978: 19-20)

Therefore, on one hand the alaṁkāra is essential to unveiling and giving rise to rasa in a song (at least as the concept that relates to basic melodic movements); on the other, concerning the dhruvā, or theater song, alaṁkāras should be used carefully to preserve the intelligibility of the words. In this connection, Lath emphasizes the problem of preserving verbal meanings, which are surely important in a song; but there are other forms of purely musical signification that are influential in the expression of rasa. Moreover, Abhinavagupta possibly mean more than exclusively verbal communication when he relates the process of relishing rasa and meaning. This leads the discussion of rasa to the dhruvās, or plot songs, which are clearly prescribed in the NŚ to represent rasas and specific dramatic situations.

Dhruvā, Their Occasions and Rasas in a Play

The specifications for dhruvās in a play were necessary because most of the songs were not always previously composed and included in the dramatic text. The producer was responsible for composing the necessary dhruvās appropriate for the entrances and exits of characters, for emphasizing physical movements, and above all, for collaborating in the arousal of rasa. 'Dhruvās depending on the context and made to express sentiments [rasas] suited to the situation, embellish the drama just as the stars illumine the sky' (NŚ 32.383, 400). For this purpose, the utilization of dhruvās was regulated according to the dramatic themes, places, times, and seasons, the characters of the play and their status, and the manifestation of vibhāvas, anubhāvas and vyabhicāribhāvas.

The dhruvās were classified according to five causes, five occasions and six types. The causes are as follows: class (jāti), or the number of syllables in a metric line; occasion (*sthāna*); variety (*prakāra*), which depends on the number of syllables being odd or even; measure (*pramāṇa*) or tāla; and name (nāma) (NŚ 32.361). There are five dramatic occasions to which dhruvās are connected: entrance (*praveśa*), diversion (*ākṣepa*), departure (*niṣkrāma*), calming (*prāsādana*) and transition (*antara*) (NŚ 32.364). Finally, Bharata mentions the six types of dhruvās: *śīrṣaka*, a 'heady' or vehement song; *uddhatā*, or elevated song; *anubhanda*, a playful, free song; *vilambitā*, a slow song fit for the dramatic situation; *aḍḍitā*, a specially pleasing song expressing śṛṅgāra; and *apakṛṣṭā*, a song that draws away from the starting bhāvas (NŚ 32.384-389). Śīrṣaka and aḍḍitā dhruvās should be sung in connection with the entry *en scene* of gods and kings. For the appearance of goddesses and high-class female characters, again the aḍḍitā dhruvā, full of śṛṅgāra, is to be sung. The vilambitā dhruvā is reserved for the middle-class characters. Two extra types of dhruvās are assigned to inferior characters, the *natkuḍā* and *khañjaka*. They express mainly hāsya, but also the bhāvas of śoka and bhaya. These three are the only appropriate bhāvas for the inferior characters (NŚ 32.393-99).

Therefore, depending on the actual context of the play, a particular dhruvā should be sung, in a certain tempo and expressing a certain rasa. A very interesting passage in the NŚ reads:

> When one is captured, obstructed, fallen, attacked with illness, or is dead or in a swoon, there the Apakṛṣṭā Dhruvā in the Pathetic sentiment

should be sung. Where one is in [a state of] impatience, dissimulation, anxiety, lamentation, weariness, depression and despair, a Dhruvā in a slow tempo should be sung. In these States [bhāvas] and in pathetic reports the Dhruvā should be sung in a quick tempo furnished with a rapid movement. Where there is any sorrow from seeing before one's own eyes any one killed or wounded, the Dhruvās there should be in a slow tempo and in the Pathetic sentiment. In [the] case of seeing any calamity, of intolerance, seeing anything supernatural, being in despair, in carelessness and in anger, and in showing one's spirit, and in a direct report of anything in Furious, Heroic, Terrible and such other sentiments, and in agitation and in hurry, the Dhruvā should be sung in a quick tempo. In propitiating, requesting or recollecting anyone or in an exaggerated speech or in [the] meeting [of lovers] for the first time, in joy, in begging or in seeing anything strange in connection with love-making[,] the Dhruvā should be of the Prāsādikī class in a medium tempo. In physical distress and in anger and in aiming a missile [against any one] the Antarā Dhruvā should be made continuous. No Dhruvā should be sung when there is any entry of weeping or singing persons, and when there is any hurry in their coming or when they announce anything, or any calamity or surprise occurs [at the time]. (NŚ 32.373-82)

Tempo is a very important issue here. Slow (*vilambita*), middle (*madhya*) and fast (*druta*) tempos are referred to as representing sorrow, joy and agitation, respectively. The basis for these representations is mostly diagrammatic (iconic), but some instances above are difficult to explain. There is also instruction for a persistent performance of the Antarā Dhruvā, which probably creates a sort of continuous dramatic tension, in cases of anger and aiming a weapon. Conversely, Bharata also specifies the situations in which there should be no singing. The role of silence, as an element of astonishment, strengthens the idea of calamity, as well as reinforces the expression of any character who is weeping. If an actor is already singing, then there should be no other simultaneous song. The regulations for illustrating a dramatic scene with a certain kind of song are detailed. Bharata says: 'The wise should apply the Dhruvā after taking into consideration the theme (*vastu*), performance (*prayoga*), characters (*prakṛti*), in a play, sentiments [rasas], states [bhāvas], seasons, age, locality, time and mental condition (*avasthā*)' (NŚ 32.400). It is difficult, however, to find musical evidence to support the representations mentioned. Except for tempo, other features of dhruvās, such as tāla and formal structures, do not seem to bear any iconic or indexical representative function. Probably the lyrics were responsible for communicating most of the meaning implied in a dhruvā, but it is also clear that specific musical significations, such as proper tempo, were important in establishing the appropriate rasa.

Another significant passage relates the dhruvās and their occasions to time and rasa. In NŚ 32.422-23 one reads: 'The *Prāveśikī* Dhruvā is to be sung to indicate anything happening in the forenoon. And the *Naiṣkrāmikī* Dhruvā may serve [in general] for anything occurring throughout day and night. Gentle (*saumyā*) Dhruvās are to be sung to indicate the forenoon, and excited (*diptā*) Dhruvās are to be sung to indicate the noon, whereas pathetic Dhruvās are to be sung in [the] case of afternoon and evening.' This could be the origin of the later association of rāgas with the times of the day, still followed in the practice of contemporary Hindustani music. There seems to be nothing in the entrance and exit dhruvās that could support such references to time. However, when gentle songs are attributed to forenoon, excited ones to noon, and karuṇa songs to afternoon and evening there is some aesthetic consistency with the tradition of performing rāgas at their proper time of the day or night. The explanation is that a possible iconic reference connects the musical character of these three kinds of dhruvās with the increasing and decreasing pitch of energy in relation to the progression of the sun at forenoon, noon, afternoon and evening, in terms of its luminosity and heat.

Drumming and Rasas

The complexity of drumming, as described in the NŚ, seems to rival other subjects in importance. Indeed, drumming is still one of the main supports for contemporary Indian dance dramas, such as kathakali, odissi, kathak, and others. Drumming is considered to be the bedrock of the dramatic performance. Bharata writes that when drumming and singing are performed properly the production of a play is free from any hazards (NŚ 33.301). Drumming provides not only a counterpoint to the melodic structures, but it has also an equivalent expressive power. Rasa, movements, natural and celestial phenomena are represented by different combinations of drums and drum strokes.

The chapter dealing with drumming in the NŚ is very thorough. It begins with the mythic origin of drums, designed by a sage after he had listened to the sound of rain on lotus leaves (see 2.3.3). Then comes the description of the instruments (three of the main drums are called *puṣkaras:* mṛdaṅga, paṇava and dardura). A very important item is the set of strokes, represented by sixteen syllables, and their composite forms; the four *mārgas*, or combination of strokes on the several drums, stroke patterns, the three layas or tempos, and so on. Here I will only discuss the issues of signification related to drumming. The representative function of drumming makes clear that keeping tāla is not its main musical purpose. Tāla is maintained by all musicians as a foundational structure, and if its form must be heard aloud, then it is played by the idiophones.

The first instance of signification in drumming relates to the mārgas, or different ways of combining strokes on the several drums mentioned by Bharata. The instruments are the following: the mṛdaṅga (mid-sized, double-faced drum); the āliṅgya (small face, body like the tail a of cow, i.e., some sort of conic shape); the vāmaka and the ūrdhavaka (the biggest drums, shaped like barley [?]); the āṅkika (mid-sized drum, shaped like the myrobalan [?]); the paṇava (like a small damaru, i.e., a drum with a body shaped like an hourglass); the dardura was probably a tambourine-like instrument. The four mārgas are *aḍḍita*, *ālipta*, *vitasta* and *gomukha*. The aḍḍita mārga combines strokes of the āliṅgya and mṛdaṅga drums. The ālipta mārga combines strokes of the vāmaka and ūrdhavaka drums. The vitasta mārga combines strokes of the ūrdhvaka and the right face of the āṅkika. The gomukha mārga combines the strokes of all puṣkaras with those of āliṅgya (NŚ 33.44). What the result of these combinations sounds like is something difficult to assert. A low, middle and high pitch can be roughly attributed to the drums according to the relative size of their faces. For instance, probably the āliṅgya and the paṇava were the higher pitched drums; and vāmaka and ūrdhavaka the bass drums. The mṛdaṅga was a double-faced drum, probably shaped as it is still found in India nowadays. Therefore, one of its faces had a high-pitched sound and the other a low one. Another point of doubt concerns the number of instruments employed. The density of drumming in the four mārgas would depend largely on pitch and volume. The only possible conclusion is that āḍḍita mārga sounded somehow high and/or middle pitched, ālipta mārga certainly sounded low pitched, vitasta mārga sounded middle/low pitched, and the gomukha mārga was the heaviest combination, containing all possible registers.

The relations between the four mārgas and the rasas are organized according to the same grouping of rasas as prescribed for the jātis:

> In connection with the Erotic and the Comic sentiments, the instruments should be played in the Aḍḍita Mārga. In the Heroic, the Marvelous and the Furious Sentiments, they should be played in the Vitasta Mārga. The playing of instruments in the Pathetic sentiment should be in the Ālipta Mārga, and in the Odious and the Terrible sentiments this should be in the Gomukha Mārga. Instruments should be played in connection with a dance to suit the sentiments [rasas] and the states [bhāvas] and the Sattva [of characters] and their gestures, mode of walking and the location [of the scene]. (NŚ 33.52-54)

From this it is clear that a high/middle pitch combination of drum strokes refers to śṛṅgāra and hāsya rasas. Middle-/low-pitched strokes refer to vīra, adbhuta and raudra rasas. Karuna was represented by low-pitched strokes. The loudest combination of all drums represented bībhatsa and bhayānaka rasas. There seems to be a semiotic rationale behind these associations, mainly iconic, but it remains general and imprecise. Later, however, Bharata writes in a much more detailed way, relating rasas not only to the four mārgas, but also to drumming jātis and tempo. Often there are musical examples of sequence of strokes illustrating the several instances prescribed for the play. Thus, it seems the drumming jātis were types of compositions, of which examples were offered. If so, the jātis would instead be symbols, even thought they possess traces of iconic reference.

The first jāti described refers to śṛṅgāra in its form of united or accomplished love, sambhoga: 'The *Deśānurūpā* jāti played in the aḍḍita mārga, is used in the erotic sentiment involving the enjoyment of love (śṛṅgāra). It should be performed in a slow tempo. Mī mathi thamabhū tthi kimā will be the syllables in Deśānurūpā jāti. It is to be used in the best erotic sentiment of women' (NŚ 33.136-37). According to the several kinds of hand strokes (NŚ 33.42), the example offered seems to be based on a few left-hand strokes (i.e., bass sounds) and a majority of controlled or partially controlled right-hand strokes, such as **mī** and **ma**. This should sound be a light and bright drumming in a slow tempo, like smoldering fire, a frequent symbol of sexual desire in Hindu mythology (see O'Flaherty 1973: 90-110). The word deśānurūpā means 'suitable portion', which probably refers to a drumming pattern appropriate for the representation of this rasa.

Ālipta mārga should be used for expressing karuṇa. This calls for the use of the large drums: '*Deśād-apetarūpā* Jāti is played in Vāmaka and Ūrdhvaka in a quick tempo of Avakṛṣṭā Dhruvās. It is to be used in the Pathetic sentiment. [For] Ex.[,] Ghedrāṅ ghedrāṅ ghe gheru are the syllables in the Deśād-apetarūpā Jāti in playing [drums]' (NŚ 33.138-39). The strokes beginning with the letter **gha** and the combination of **da** with **ra** suggest heavy low sounds with appoggiaturas, which work well for representing karuṇa iconically as a heavy and downcast state of mind. But the quick tempo seems to contradict the common-sense idea of this rasa. In fact, to consider the jāti name, the word 'apeta' means 'free from', in contrast with the former jāti. Thus, deśād-apetarūpā jāti can be a non-iconic sign for karuṇa. A fast tempo relates more soundly to vīra. Yet vīra, adbhuta and raudra rasas have a special jāti called *paryāyā* (approaching): 'When the same set of Karaṇas played previously are followed in all three tempos, it is the *Paryāyā* Jāti. [For] Ex., ghodāṅ ghidiṅ gudugnoū played in the Vāmaka and Ūrdhvaka by the left hand should be applied in the Heroic, Marvelous and Furious sentiments' (NŚ 33.140-41). There is no doubt that the bass drums are appropriate for generating signs of those rasas. The three mentioned tempos are probably played in sequence, i.e., vilambita, madhya and druta, creating thus an iconic effect of something approaching. This kind of accelerating drumming pattern is still found in the kathakali of Kerala.

Finally, a particular combination of strokes is designated for śṛṅgāra: 'Two heavy syllables, two light syllables, one light syllable, three heavy syllables, and a light syllable such as siṅ māṅ ghaṭa ghendra gu du gheṅ gheṅ ghama tthi metchap constitute *Viṣkambhā* Jāti. It is to be applied in the Erotic sentiment of superior women' (NŚ 33.142-43). What are the light and heavy syllables in that sequence is not clear. Certainly the bols were corrupted in the process of copying the text over and over. There seems to be no iconic feature here, the representation instead being symbolic. The jāti name, viṣkambhā, means an interlude scene. Thus, the jāti bearing this name could be played in those parts of the drama, when the rasa referred to was śṛṅgāra.

Besides the rasas, considerable concern is dedicated to the representation of movements. This refers to the characters' gaits, according to their status or physical/psychical situation, as well as movements of vehicles and animals. Certain natural phenomena, such as storms, are also specified. 'Playing the drums in all Mārgas with *Karaṇas* of one syllable, and with the *Sama Pracāra* of hands, is called the *Paryastā* Jāti. Paryastā is to be used in the case of the quick movement of chariots, *Vimānas, Vidyādharas, Bhujaṅgas* (serpents), etc., in the sky, or in torrential rains' (NŚ 33.144-45). Paryastā, meaning spread-out or diffuse, can refer to a certain kind of roll, and the hand strokes defined as sama suggest an even sequence of attacks. In this case, the representation is certainly iconic. What is depicted could be both the sound of those objects (image) and their qualities of movement (diagram).

Bharata dedicates a special chapter solely to the posture and movements of characters. This is clearly related to drumming (NŚ 13.2). There are basically three tempos for the different gaits, according to their status: vilambita for the superior, madhya for the middling, druta and 'copious' for the inferior characters (NŚ 13.13). The passage quoted below follows this rule and specifies some details on how drumming is to accompany the characters' walking styles:

> *Pārṣṇi-samastā* Jāti should be played with Karaṇas tatthiṁ kaṭaṁ mamcchi and dhandrāṅ gudheṅ gu dhitaṅ, with the pressure of the *Pārṣṇi*. This is to be applied to the movement of [the] superior male character of calm type, and of the Dānavas. By [the] striking of all the Mṛdaṅgas with the movement of *Svastika* hands, one should play the *Duṣkara-karaṇā* Jāti in all their tempos. Duṣkara-karaṇā Jāti should include syllables like duṇā duṇo duṇā kiṁka dhima ghoṭeṅ madatthidugakiṭi ghoṅ. Duṣkara-karaṇā Jāti should be applied in case of movements of Daitya kings, chiefs, Nāgas (bhujaga), Rākṣasas, Piśācas, Gandharvas, and Guhyakas, etc. Light strokes on the face of Ūrdhvaka, Āṅkika and Dakṣiṇa in the Vitasta Mārga or striking of Dakṣiṇaka and Vāmaka after beginning with Āṅkika and árdhvaka [will constitute *Ūrdhva goṣṭhikā*.] Playing almost violently udhidhṛṁ dhṛṁ in the Vitasta Mārga will constitute Ūrdhva-goṣṭhikā Jāti. It is meant for the movement of heavenly characters. (NŚ 33.148-54)

The representational mode in most of these instances is iconic. The elevated and calm characters are accompanied by drumming jāti in which the same features are presented. The prescribed pressure of the pārṣṇi (heel, back) is probably an indication that the drum should be played with a glissando effect. On the other hand, demons – such as the daityas, rākṣasas, piśācas – snake demons (nāgas), and celestial musicians (gandharvas) are represented by all mṛdaṅgas playing simultaneously, thereby implying a great and powerful volume. In fact, not only kings, celestial beings and demons have their movements emphasized by drumming: 'The *Evaṁ-vādyā* Jāti should be played with syllables of the Gomukhī, and it should have all the strokes of Mṛdaṅga; and it should be applied in the pantomime of jugglery by persons with or without disguise, and it should include the syllables like gheṅṭāṇṭādo tadhitā gheṅ ghaṭatthi ghaṭa iṅghe. This should be applied in case of the movements of dwarfs, confused persons and lame men and those who have pain in their body and wood in their feet' (NŚ 33.157-59). A kind of roll is prescribed for terrified or flying persons: 'The *Saṁplavā Jāti* produced by using all the fingers and by all the strokes of the Mṛdaṅga, is to be applied to the movement of terrified persons and to any movement of them in the sky' (NŚ 33.166) – again an iconic representation. The subject of drumming deserves further inquiry, and its basic forms of representation are probably still used in the oldest classical traditions of dance dramas.

3.3.2 Grāmarāgas and Rasa

In addition to the jāti, another independent musical system appeared around A.D. 500. It was the *grāmarāga*, which was in use and in constant evolution up to the late first millennium. The grāmarāgas were originally a set of seven modes, the seven primary grāmarāgas. These last were first discussed in the *Nāradīyāśikṣā* (6th century), a dissertation on Sāmavedic recitation, and on the Kuḍumiyāmalai inscription (7-8th centuries), a rock carving on the wall of a cave temple in the state of Tamil Nadu. In the *Bṛhaddeśī*, written by Mataṅga around A.D. 800, there were already 26 secondary rāgas, which were related to the seven primary grāmarāgas, and more than 100 derivatives, called *bhāṣās* (dialects). It seems that the two systems – jātis and grāmarāgas – were in use simultaneously for some time. But the jātis crystallized, while the grāmarāgas remained open to multiplication and the absorption of regional tunes. Thus, the jāti system progressively became obsolete. Nevertheless, from the scholarly point of view, the authority of the jātis was not disputed, and most of the treatises continued to begin with an exposition of the śrutis, grāmas and jātis, even as late as the medieval and modern eras.

The grāmarāga system begins with the same two tuning sets, madhyamagrāma and ṣaḍjagrāma (see Figure 14), that were used for the jātis. However, instead of a cycle of rotations, the primary grāmarāgas are based on a few distinct pitch sets (see Ex. 25).[23] The use of altered G and N is essential in this respect. Grāmarāgas are also much more specific concerning the aṁśa and other modal functions. Only S, M and P can operate as aṁśas, and only M and P can be nyāsa (final). These features imply that other musical dimensions were necessary in order to distinguish some of them. The appearance of musical notation for the grāmarāgas on the Kuḍumiyāmalai inscription, in the BD, SR and later treatises, suggests that melodic contours and motifs began, at that time, to particularize the rāgas as musical entities that occupy a continuum, of which scale and tune are the extremes.

---

[23] See Rowell (1992: 173-75) and Widdess (1995: 59-78) for a detailed description and analysis.

Figure 14

Grāmarāga System – A Generative Diagram

ṣaḍjagrāma | madhyamagrāma | 10 lakṣaṇas

▼

7 primary grāmarāgas (madhyamagrāma, ṣaḍjagrāma, ṣāḍava, sādhārita, pañcama, kaiśikamadhyama, kaiśika; or the śuddha gīti)

▼

26 secondary grāmarāgas, classified in four styles or gītis (bhinna, gauḍa, rāgagīti or vesarā, sādhāraṇa)

▼

bhāṣās

▼

vibhāṣās

▼

antarabhāṣās

Example 25

The seven primary grāmarāgas

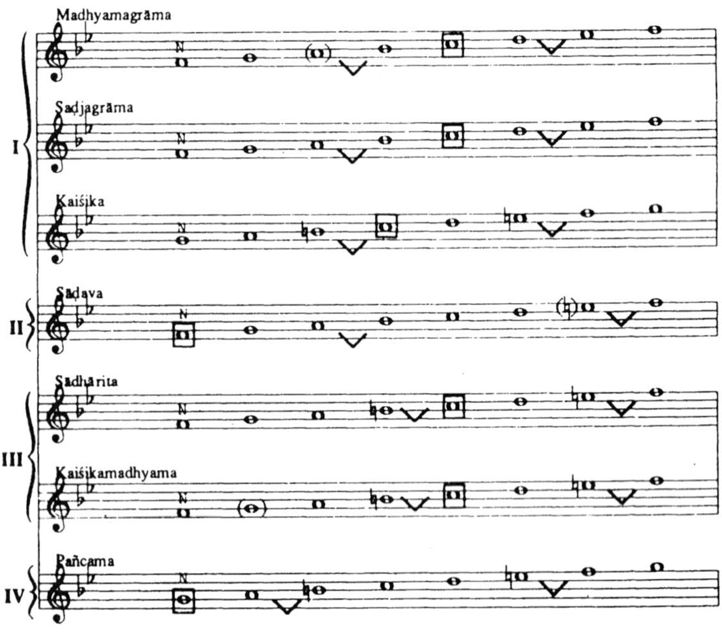

Although the grāmarāga and jāti were independent systems, they shared some theoretical concepts and terms. Widdess explains, for instance, that 'the two grāmas appear in both systems, but whereas in the jāti system they function as basic scales or tunings, in the grāmarāga system they are modes with distinctive melodic features' (1995: 64). Moreover, the theorists defined the grāmarāgas as being derived from certain jātis. This seems to be a feature of indexicality in Indian scholarship. All the subject matter of a new treatise should connect with and refer to the oldest and, hence, indisputable one, even if the older system no longer has any bearing on musical practice.

The bhāṣās are presented in the BD in the form of two quotations. The first and longest is by Yāṣṭika (BD 4.A.1-146), and the second by Śārdūla (BD 4.B.1-34).[24] Both writers suggest that the bhāṣās proceeded from two sources: from regional music, and from the combination and variation of the primary and secondary grāmarāgas. The former provenance is evident in the geographical references found in the names of many bhāṣās (see Widdess 1995: 28), and it is explicitly stated in the text. Those bhāṣās are often referred to as *deśī* or *deśa*, meaning place, country or region, in which mention is made of different peoples of North and South India. It is impossible to ascertain how close to the original folk tunes the regional bhāṣās were; most likely they were adapted and transformed in the process of integration with the classical music. Quite a few bhāṣās have no regional association, and they probably evolved directly from the grāmarāgas.

The bhāṣās and their derivatives (*vibhāṣās* and *antarabhāṣās*) constitute an important semiotic change in relation to the jāti system. Bhāṣās can support reproduction, one of the most remarkable features of legisigns. As early as the middle of the first millennium, the rāga system paralleled nature in its capacity for growth and renewal. Rāgas were born, reached their zenith in performance repertories, then became old and outmoded, and finally obsolete. This life cycle involved a substantial number of rāgas, which were characterized simultaneously as musical entities, having particular acoustical features, and as aesthetic entities, with their qualities of feeling, regional tinges, dramatic prescriptions; later, these aesthetic entities took on seasonal, temporal, religious, iconographic and poetic meanings.

Definition of Rāga

The concept of rāga as a musical entity appears for the first time in the BD. As see in the previous section (3.3.1), in the NŚ the word rāga refers merely to the charming quality of a song. The expression of rasa by the jātis, set in a conventional way, consists in the relation between a pitch-set

---

[24] Unfortunately, the original works of those authors are lost.

matrix offering several possibilities of modal organization (a jāti), and categories of feeling (rasa), both of which are general in nature. The grāmarāgas, however, are much more specific musical entities. They are individuals, which may procreate, but not generative modal matrices. Their scalar features alone do not reveal all of their musical essence. Grāmarāgas are located farther from the scale end of the scale-tune continuum than are the jātis. The fact that grāmarāgas are called rāgas is noteworthy, for they were conceived primarily to be interpreted as conveying an aesthetic quality of feeling or more conventional significations. In this sense, they are also more specific than the jātis, for they represent not only the rasas, but also other aesthetical, dramatic, temporal and religious referents.

The definition of rāga in the BD takes advantage of terms such as *rajyate* (delight), *rañjaka* (pleasing), *rañjana* (coloring). This is the earliest evidence for the oft-quoted definition of rāga as 'that which colors the minds' (Shankar 1969: 20). On the other hand, Mataṅga's definition specifies the materiality of the sign: dhvani (sound), svara, varṇa, aṁśa and other features common to the jātis. Mataṅga introduces the concept of rāga in the following context:

> That which colours or delights the mind of the good through a specific svara (interval) and varṇa (melodic movement) or through a type of dhvani (sound) is known by the wise as rāga. That which is a special dhvani, is bedecked with svara and varṇa and is colourful or delightful to the minds of the people, is said to be rāga. Lakṣaṇa (definition) is known to be two-fold[,] viz. general and particular. The general one is four-fold and the special [one] is (in the form of) aṁśa and the like. 'Rāga' is born from the act of coloring or delighting; this has been said to be the etymology. Thus is spoken of the etymology of the word rāga. (BD 3.263-66)

This is a rich excerpt, and it might be profitable to begin with the etymology of the word rāga. The term *rāga* points firstly to the aesthetic question, and can be translated variously as coloring, affection, feeling, passion, charm. The word comes from the roots *rāj* or *rāñj* and can also be understood as 'to be colored' (red in particular), 'affected with a strong feeling,' 'to be delighted with.' Therefore, semiosis is a key element in the process of singing (or playing), perceiving and interpreting a rāga. As I have argued before, semiosis is a process that encompasses aesthetic perception. It should be noted that the aesthetic property of 'coloring or delighting' the receptive listener's mind comes from the musical level of rāga. The arousal of aesthetic feelings does not depend primarily on the timbral qualities highlighted by the performer, the legisigns of a musical form, or the lyrics of a song. It is indeed rāga, as an individual musical (plastic) structure, as a semiotic entity (i.e., the sign) that essentially generates rasa. Finally, the term rāga encompasses two levels, the general and the particular. Both *sāmānya* (general) and *viśeṣa* (particular) are philosophical concepts, later developed in the Nyāya-Vaiśeṣika systems. Generality, or sāmānya, refers to 'those features common to all rāgas'. Particularity, or viśeṣa, concerns 'those features peculiar to individual rāgas' (Widdess 1995: 41). What are the four-fold aspects of generality is unclear. But, when mentioning sāmānya, Mataṅga seems to refer to the rāga system as such. Viśeṣa, or rāga as an individual musical entity, is the particular combination of attributes such as the aṁśa (predominant degree), other modal functions, and, more and more, melodic movements and motifs, of which the musical notations found in the BD are one of the earliest.

In the Sanskrit wording of the above definition there is a clear emphasis on the individuality of melodic characteristics, specified by the concept of viśeṣa. Thus, rāga is that which delights the mind by 'specific svara and varṇa' (*svaravarṇaviśeṣa*) or by 'a type of dhvani' (*dhvanibheda*) or by 'a special dhvani' (*dhvaniviśeṣa*). The *Nāradīyaśikṣā* defines rāga also as a distinct musical and aesthetic entity: 'They are called grāmarāgas on account of a particularity of musical pitch and aesthetic ethos (*svararāgaviśeṣeṇa grāmarāga iti smṛtāḥ*)' (in Widdess 1995: 41). Here, the compound svararāgaviśeṣa is even more specific in relating rāga, as an aesthetic entity, with particular melodic structures. That is, rāga as a symbol is identified with distinctive musical qualities and legisigns that refer to an object or a complex of objects, and that symbol intends to generate an interpretant, which actualizes when a rāga is performed (some of the rāga features becoming sinsigns).

In another chapter of the BD, the classification of notes in terms of sonance also gives rise to the idea of the individuality of rāgas. The division is fourfold and comprises the following: vādī (sonant), saṁvādī (consonant), anuvādī (assonant or neutral) and vivādī (dissonant). Vādī or vadana (speaking) is related to the qualitative aspect of a rāga, determined by the note functioning as aṁśa: 'Vadana is here intending to mean the exposition of rāga, not talking. What does it (vadana and the like) expound? It produces the *rāgatva* of a rāga. Those vādin svaras are only seven. That vādin should be understood as tenfold like the aṁśā' (BD 1.4.anu.20). The tenfold features are the modal functions previously related to the jātis, but still employed for the grāmarāgas. Aṁśa is the most important of them. It is interesting to notice that the exposition of a rāga is related to verbal communication, by the use of the word vadana, although clearly distinguished from talking. Remarks like this are certainly seeds of the Indian musical semiotics that appears in almost all saṅgīta śāstra. But the point I want to emphasize, in this quotation, is the expression *rāgasya rāgatvaṁ*, verbatim for 'the rāga-ness of a rāga', as translated by Rowell (1992: 158). A distinctive semiotic feature of a quality is its singularity, and the rāga-ness of a rāga represents the whole musical and aesthetical uniqueness that rāgas developed more and more in the history of Indian music:

> In sources such as MBD [Mataṅga's BD], NSHA [Nānyadeva's *Sarasvatīhṛdayālaṁkāra*], ŚSR [Śārṅgadeva's SR], rāgas are defined in terms of modal features such as Predominant, Final, strong and weak notes and so on, and increasingly in terms of aesthetic, extra-musical, or iconographic attributes. It is at this level that rāgas are distinguished from each other, not in terms of their basic pitch-set: the growth-point of the rāga-system is at the 'tune' end of the modal continuum, not the 'scale' end. The multiplication of grāmarāgas, bhāṣās and deśī-rāgas, distinguished and identified by subtle differences of modal dynamic and aesthetic, was accompanied, it seems, by a simplification of the scalar basis to a common pitch-set. (Widdess 1995: 246)

The rāga-ness of a rāga, being more dependent on musical elements which lead to plasticity than on the static character of scale types, certainly determined the way the performance of rāgas evolved, with improvisation always playing an important role in conjunction with composition. This plasticity is also an element of life, of which rāga legisigns partake so profoundly.

Grāmarāgas and Rasa

The primary grāmarāgas are mentioned briefly in the NŚ in connection with the sandhis, or junctures, of a play. The lines in question present an unexpected problem, because the reference system described in the treatise is that of the jātis, not the grāmarāgas. Possibly, the passage was a latter addition to the treatise, but whatever the case, it was acknowledged as meaningful and quoted subsequently. Mataṅga's version (BD 3.anu.171) reads differently from that of the NŚ and includes all seven grāmarāgas, as a possible index of the system's evolution. The NŚ prescribes that the grāmarāgas be played after the opening ritual of Pūrvaraṅga, that is, when the play starts, and thereafter at certain appointed times.

> Just as [a] well-built dwelling [or] house does not become beautiful without any colour, so without any song the drama does not attain [the capacity of giving] joy. The rule[s] regarding songs have been mentioned in connection with [the formalities of] the Pūrvaraṅga (preliminaries), and the worship of gods has also been mentioned there. Hence notes in the two grāmas[,] as well as the overlapping [note], should be applied to plays (lit. poetic compositions) which express the various states [bhāvas]. In the opening of the drama there should be the songs of the madhyamagrāma, ṣaḍja in the progression, the overlapping [*sādhārita*] in the development, pañcama(mī) in the pause, and kaiśika(kī) in the conclusion. These songs[,] depending on the junctures [*sandhi*] and metres, should be of suitable sentiments [rasas] and states [bhāvas]. (NŚ 32.482-86)

The term rāga is not specified here (in its later musical sense), but only in the first line above as an analogy stating that even a well structured play cannot express beauty without the inclusion of songs. Yet, the connection of rasas and bhāvas with the grāmarāgas is emphasized in almost every line of this passage. The two grāmas are mentioned, not as tuning sets, but as modes in their own right, that is, grāmarāgas. Madhyamagrāma should be sung at the opening (*mukha*) of the play. Ṣaḍjagrāma is prescribed for the *pratimukha*, or secondary plot. Sādharīta refers to the *garbha* (womb), or development of the story. Pañcama is recommended for the *vimarśa*, or crisis, and kaiśika for the *nirvahaṇa*, the denouement or conclusion. These are the oldest allusions in the technical literature to significations related to the primary grāmarāgas. It is clear that each grāmarāga refers to, at least, a general mood implicit in the several parts of the classical Sanskrit drama. The last three sections – garbha, vimarśa and nirvahaṇa – seem to carry increasingly high levels of aesthetic emotion. The references are, however, too feeble and general for one to draw conclusions about the particular mode of semiosis on which the primary grāmarāgas represent those five parts of the play.

The grāmarāgas are classified in the BD according to seven *gītis* (songs). More than mere songs, these are performing styles, defined by ornaments, relationships of melody, rhythm and text, and other features (see BD 3.274-89), as the word gīti suggests. The gītis are as follows: śuddhā or cokṣā (pure, comprising the primary grāmarāgas), bhinnakā (deviant or modified), gauḍikā (from eastern India), rāgagīti or vesarā (passion song or hybrid), sādhāraṇī (mixed), bhāṣā (language or dialect), and vibhāṣā (derived from bhāṣās). The last two were omitted from the SR, since they are not really styles but groups of rāgas derived from the main five gītis or adopted from regional music (SR 2.1.2c-7). Bhāṣās and vibhāṣās were subordinate in relation to the primary and secondary grāmarāgas, if not in actual practice, then at least theoretically. The dependence of bhāṣās on the grāmarāgas can be recognized as a feature betokening the later rāga-rāgiṇī systems. Indeed, the grāmarāgas have masculine names, whereas the bhāṣās have feminine ones (Gangoly 1989: 93; Widdess 1995: 76).

The authority of Bharata is not disputed as regards the rasa expressed by the primary grāmarāgas, classified in the śuddhā gīti. Rasa was still attributed according to the aṁśa rule stated for the jātis. The BD does not mention Madhyamagrāma and ṣaḍjagrāma – both with S as aṁśa – as being grāmarāgas, but other sources do. The SR refers to ṣaḍjagrāma as expressing vīra, raudra and adbhuta, in accordance with the rule concerning aṁśa and rasa (SR 2.2.27c-30b). Ṣāḍava, in the BD, signifies śṛṅgāra and hāsya, in conformity with M as its aṁśa (BD 3.anu.165). The text for Pañcama is missing from the BD. It probably expressed śṛṅgāra and hāsya, for P is its aṁśa. Sādhārita, Kaiśika-madhyama, and Kaiśika – all with S as aṁśa – refer to vīra, raudra, 'and the like' (BD 3.anu.167-9), implying also adbhuta, since this rasa is traditionally associated with the other two.

It is meaningful that in all primary grāmarāgas only five rasas are represented. Karuṇa, bībhatsa and bhayānaka are absent. It seems unlikely that these three rasas were unimportant, or perhaps obsolete by the time of the BD. The problem has two sides. On one hand, with regard to the rāgas classified in the five gītis, rasas related with śṛṅgāra and vīra are indeed prevalent. On the other, according to the BD text, there is a double scheme of reference to the meaning of the rāgas: (1) a category of context or application, which seems to be the current one, for the inclusion of the śāntarasa and other meanings; and (2) the category of 'rasa', comprising only the eight classical rasas, and following the NŚ rule, in which the aṁśa determines the rasa. There is frequent inconsistency between the two categories. For instance, gauḍakaiśika is prescribed to represent karuṇa. However, because this rāga has its aṁśa in S, the 'rasas' are vīra, raudra and adbhuta (BD 3.anu.188). It is not clear which prescription really prevailed. It seems, however, that the rule aṁśa/rasa, appropriate to the jāti system, was not effective regarding the grāmarāgas, which have only a single svara as possible aṁśa. Rowell, considering that five of the primary grāmarāgas have S as aṁśa, even asks 'what would be the emotional range of a system of seven diatonic scales of which five would be limited to the same rasas?' (1992: 332). Very few secondary grāmarāgas have G or D as aṁśa, and none has N, which limits the representation of karuṇa, bībhatsa and bhayānaka. Yet, three rāgas should be *applied* to the representation of karuṇa, none of them having G or N as aṁśa. Therefore, notwithstanding the new system, the scholars seem to have kept the NŚ rule out of reverence and respect for the authority of Bharata, in spite of the several resulting conflicts with other aesthetical attributes described by the BD and SR in regard to the secondary grāmarāgas and bhāṣās. In most cases, the readings of rāga descriptions, as concerning the NŚ rasa rule, seem to represent a category of merely theoretical value, a compromise between the jāti and the grāmarāga systems. The actual representations were mostly inconsistent with the jāti system. They included more rasas and other meanings besides those of the eight classical rasas of the NŚ, and were based on modes of semiosis different from the arbitrary aṁśa/rasa rule.

In relation to the jātis, the growth of meanings represented by the grāmarāgas is clear. Some of the grāmarāgas were not representing a rasa or a few rasas, but a specific dramatic situation. Those rāgas were thus much more distinctive signs. Some rāgas of the vesarā and sādhāraṇī groups are remarkable. Bhammāṇapañcama, for instance, 'is prescribed in (the situation of) travel on a path in summer, (by those) full of fatigue[,] and in (depiction of) forests' (BD 3.anu.207). This meaning is openly in conflict with the rasa attributed to the same rāga in terms of aṁśa: vīra, raudra and adbhuta. Such distinct meanings as a tiring journey or the depiction of forests could hardly be signified on the basis of iconic or even indexical semiosis, in light of the musical features of bhammāṇapañcama. The only possibility left is the representation grounded as a symbol, with or without the help of the lyrics. It is known that in the Sanskrit drama there were no stage settings which would provide visual information to reinforce the meanings. This is still a feature of the kathakali and other dance dramas of India. Thus, the importance of musical reference was certainly crucial. Besides the dramatic context, in the case of court or temple musical performance, the same rāga still refers to its conventional meanings, once the audience knows the meanings of the symbols. Another example of this kind is rāga sauvīra: 'Its application is prescribed in the context of entry and the like in the behavior of those who perform domestic sacrifices, who practice restraint and perform penance and in śānta rasa' (BD 3.anu.193). Again, on account of S being the aṁśa of this rāga, the rasas are 'vīra and the like', which match neither with śānta nor with the dramatic contexts mentioned in the quotation. Yet, not all grāmarāgas have a conflict between the application and the 'rasas'. Mālavapañcama, for instance, 'is prescribed in vipralambha śṛṅgāra [for] the entry of *kañcukin*' (attendant of the female apartments)' (BD 3.anu.194). Because P is its aṁśa, śṛṅgāra and hāsya are the rasas.

The attribution of rasas and other meanings to the grāmarāgas seems to follow no clear scheme. In each gīti there is a variety of significations, as well as across the gītis, if one traces the derivations, for instance, of pañcama (see Ex. 26), or kaiśika rāgas (see Ex. 27). Gangoly argues that rāgagītis were possibly distinct from the other gītis, in the sense that rāgagītis had the power to express rasa (1989: 19). This is not the case, however, for all rāgas described in the BD, no matter to which gīti they belong, are said to signify a certain rasa, or dramatic situation. The only exceptions are the bhāṣās mentioned by Yāṣṭika, who did not relate them to the rasas. From another point of view, rāgas referring to the same rasa do not necessarily relate musically. Bhinnatāna, gauḍakaiśika and rūpasādhāra, all standing for karuṇa, come from different gītis and have varying modal structures.[25] No rāga is attributed to bībhatsa, and a single one, unique in this respect, refers to bhayānaka: gauḍakaiśikamadhyama (BD 3.anu.189).

[25] See Widdess 1995: 290-99, table 9.5, for a classification and notation of grāmarāgas structures.

Example 26

Rāgas derived from pañcama and their meanings (BD)

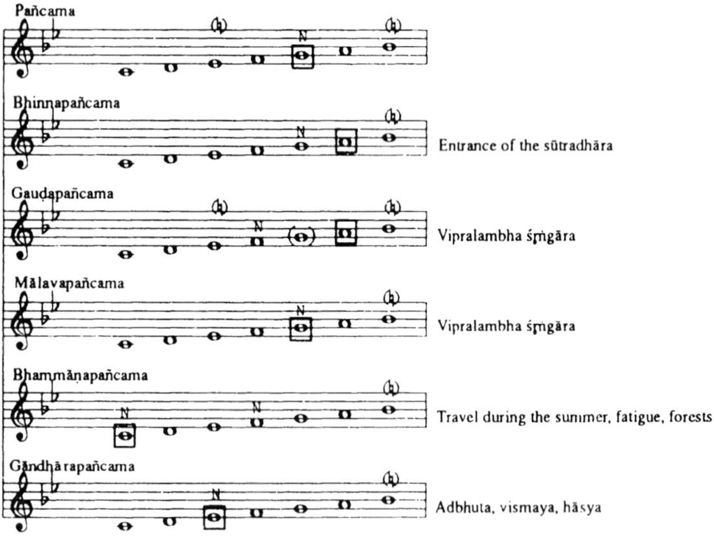

Only a few groups of rāgas, signifying the same or related meanings, can be connected on the strength of a common musical feature. The most consistent group of rāgas, according to the classification in the five gītis, is that of bhinnā gīti. Three out of five rāgas represent rasas related to vīra: bhinnaṣaḍja, bhinnakaiśikamadhyama and bhinnakaiśika. A pentatonic rāga, bhinnaṣaḍja, 'is prescribed in prāveśikī (dhruvās) related to the entry of the hero in a situation where he is inclined towards the use of all implements or tools (*upakaraṇa*), has an aversion to fighting which does not match his position (*vijātīya*) and proceeds [to go] hunting' (BD 3.anu.175). Its aṁśa is D, which matches somehow the application with the rasa bībhatsa (in the sense of disgust in an unequal or inappropriate fight), but conflicts with bhayānaka. Bhinnakaiśikamadhyama (BD 3.anu.179) and bhinnakaiśika (BD 3.anu.182) both represent dānavīra, munificent heroism, which in turn matches with their aṁśa S for vīra and perhaps adbhuta, but not for raudra. The other two rāgas in the bhinnā group are not related with vīra. Bhinnapañcama is prescribed for the entry of the *sūtradhāra*, or stage manager (BD 3.anu.177). Bhinnatāna, as mentioned above, 'is used in mature karuṇa' (BD 3.anu.184).

Example 27
Rāgas derived from kaiśika and their meanings (BD)

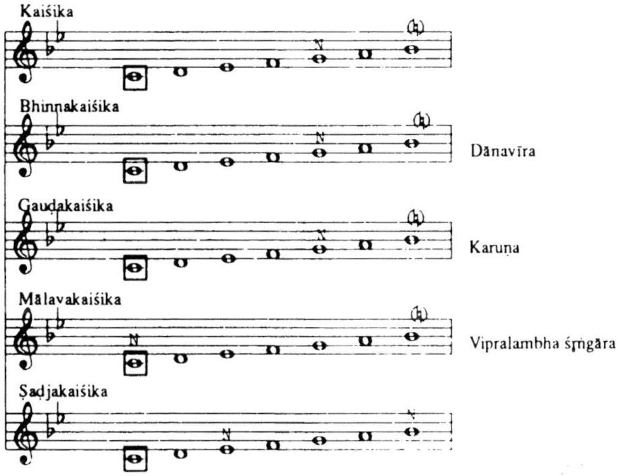

Another group of rāgas that exhibits some consistency in meaning is classified under the vesara or rāgagīti. Here, mālavapañcama, mālavakaiśika and ṭakkakaiśika should be applied to vipralambha śṛṅgāra, and hiṇḍola to sambhoga śṛṅgāra. There are also two rāgas representing śānta: vesaraṣaḍava and sauvīra. Considering these rāgas and rasas, one may doubt if vipralambha, sambhoga and śānta really make up a consistent group. There could be some relation between sambhoga and śānta rasas, but this is open to discussion. Vipralambha certainly does not link up with śānta. Vesara gīti is, therefore, not as uniform as it seems at first. Moreover, the other two rāgas in this group, ṭakka and boṭṭa, do not represent meanings related to vipralambha, sambhoga or śānta rasas.

Rāgas ṭakka (BD 3.anu.192) and ṭakkasaindhava (BD 3.anu.212), belonging to vesara and sādhāraṇī gītis respectively, stand for the same rasa, yuddhavīra (martial heroism). They have similar musical features, being clearly matched in this sense. Both have the svara S for aṁśa and nyāsa (thus compatible with the NŚ rule for vīra), r as a weak svara, and the possibility of using kākalī-ni. In the BD, Ṭakka is the only secondary grāmarāga associated with a deity (Lakṣmī). Two more musically related rāgas expressing the same meanings are pañcamaṣāḍava and revagupta, both in the sādhāraṇī gīti. They are the only rāgas to feature R as aṁśa, and both also have M as nyāsa. The description in the BD reads exactly the same for both: 'Its application is prescribed in the passionate performance of *cārīs, maṇḍalas* and (situations of) combat. Vīra and the like is the rasa' (BD 3.anu.210 and 211). *Cārīmaṇḍala* is a kind of dance sequence, composed by movements of the legs and feet, and does not necessarily refer to situations of combat in a dance-drama. Narta is another rāga in the same group, standing for the same significations, but having different musical features (BD 3.anu.203).

Some monotonal rāgas – that is, rāgas in which the functions of predominant (aṁśa) and final (nyāsa) are performed by the same svara – signify śṛṅgāra and śānta rasas: Ṣāḍava and pañcama (both śṛṅgāra) in the śuddha gīti; mālavapañcama, mālavakaiśika, ṭakkakaiśika (vipralambha śṛṅgāra), hiṇḍola (sambhoga śṛṅgāra), vesaraṣāḍava and sauvīra (śānta), in the vesara gīti. It seems remarkable that so many monotonal rāgas relate to some kind of śṛṅgāra or śānta. As I have explained in 3.1, two aestheticians considered these rasas to be of the highest importance: śānta for Abhinavagupta and śṛṅgāra for Bhoja. The concentration of the two main modal functions into the same degree is also a characteristic of the evolution of the rāga system, which later would result in the common-system tonic centered in s. The possible conclusion is that the confluence of meaning and musical structure displayed in those monotonal rāgas points (as an index) to the historical development of Indian music. On one hand, there was a tendency for some rāgas to have a single svara that combined in itself the most important modal functions; and on the other, one finds the same process at the aesthetical level, that is, rāgas representing rasas which became more important than other rasas. Of course, there are exceptions: the rāgas ṭakka, ṭakkakaiśika and śaka represent forms of vīra and are monotonal rāgas with s as aṁśa and nyāsa. Even so, there could be some consistency in this relation, for vīra (besides karuṇa) is probably the next rasa in importance.

Is there any evidence of indexical representation in terms of the ethnic character attributed to rāgas that have a deśī name? Some of the secondary grāmarāgas and many bhāṣās were named after a region or people in India. Ṭakka, for instance, refers to the ancient city of Taxila (Takṣaśilā), nowadays close to Islamabad in north Pakistan. Taxila was a center of learning during the early centuries BC. Alexander dominated that city by the 3rd century BC; it later became part of the Mauryan empire; and finally Taxila was conquered by the Scythians, known in India as Śakas, during the 1st century AD. Both ṭakka and śaka rāgas probably relate to the place and people of the Taxila area, and Widdess suggests that the music of that region influenced the grāmarāga system (1995: 24). In view of such historical complexity, it is hardly convincing to state that the rāgas ṭakka, ṭakkasaindhava and śaka could be an index of the music practiced there, or the vīra rasa attributed to them an indexical sign of the heroism of those ethnic groups or of the battles they fought. It is not impossible, however, that musicians and scholars could have made such references in an allegorical way, by actually absorbing (or not) the musical structures of those areas. Other rāgas, such as sauvīra (middle course of the Indus), boṭṭa (Tibet), and the gauḍa (eastern India) group, represent a variety of meanings not easily related to the places and people they are named after. Besides the names of the rāgas, there is no evidence for such a hypothesis.

Table 12 displays the primary and secondary grāmarāgas. The rāgas are classified in the five gītis, according to the BD. For each rāga, both aṁśa and nyāsa are given, thus clearly marking the monotonal and the bitonal rāgas. I present only the meanings related to the 'application' of the rāgas, since the 'rasas', according to the NŚ rule of aṁśa, were presumed to be merely theoretical. At any rate, the 'rasas' can be inferred by checking the aṁśa of each rāga.

Table 12

Grāmarāgas and their meanings according to the BD

The rāgas in the five main gītis and their meanings			
rāga	aṁśa	nyāsa	application
Śuddhā gīti:			
Madhyamagrāma	S	M	[vīra, raudra, adbhuta]
Ṣaḍjagrāma	S	M	[vīra, raudra, adbhuta]
Ṣāḍava	M		śṛṅgāra, hāsya
Sādhārita	S	M	vīra, raudra, adbhuta
Pañcama	P		[śṛṅgāra, hāsya]
Kaiśika-madhyama	S	M	vīra, raudra, adbhuta
Kaiśika	S	P	vīra, raudra, adbhuta
Bhinnā gīti:			
Bhinnaṣaḍja	D	M	vijātīya vīra (disgust for an unequal fight)
Bhinnapañcama	D	P	sūtradhāra entry
Bhinna-kaiśikamadhyama	S	M	dānavīra (heroism in charity)
Bhinnakaiśika	S	P	dānavīra
Bhinnatana	P	M	mature karuṇa
Gauḍī gīti:			
Gauḍapañcama	D	M	vipralambha
Gauḍa-kaiśikamadhyama	S	M	bhayānaka
Gauḍakaiśika	S	P	karuṇa

Vesarā or rāgagīti:			
Vesarāṣāḍava	M		śānta
Mālavapañcama	P		vipralambha
Mālavakaiśika	S		vipralambha
Ṭakkakaiśika	D		passionate acting/dance, love-lorn one (vipralambha)
Ṭakka	S		goddess Lakṣmī, yuddhavīra (battle-hero)
Hindola	S		sambhoga
Sauvīra	S		those who perform domestic sacrifices or penances, śānta
Boṭṭa	P	M	festivities, śānta
Sādhāraṇī gīti:			
Rūpasādhāra	S	M	vīra, karuṇa
Bhammāṇapañcama	S	M	travel in summer, fatigue, forests
Gāndhārapañcama	G		adbhuta vismaya hāsya
Ṣaḍjakaiśika	S	N	[not in the BD]
Ṭakkasaindhava	S		yuddhavīra
Narta	P	M	cārīmaṇḍala, combat
Śaka	S		vīra, adbhuta, hāsya
Kakubha	D	P	moderate karuṇa
Pañcamaṣāḍava	R	R/M	cārīmaṇḍala, combat
Revagupta	R	M	cārīmaṇḍala, combat

Bhāṣās

Bhāṣās described in the BD, in Yāṣṭika's section (75 in number), are classified as derivations of 15 grāmarāgas. They are also divided into four categories: *mūlā* (root or basic), *saṅkirna* (mixed), *deśajā* (regional) and *chāyāmātrāśrayā* (based on the shade or reflection of another rāga) (BD 4.A.1). These divisions are more than a simple classification: they reflect the means of evolution and growth of the rāga system. The existence of mūlā bhāṣās points that not all bhāṣās in fact derive from the grāmarāgas. Mūlā bhāṣās could be independent rāgas, perhaps belonging to traditions other than the grāmarāga system. Travaṇā and chevatī are said to be mūlās (BD 4.A.39, 43), among others. The other class, saṅkirna, comprising the bhāṣās that arise from the mixture of previously existing rāgas, relate to a process still in use in contemporary Hindustani music: the combination of structures of two rāgas, resulting in a new species. There are many references to the regional origins of bhāṣās, now textually attributed to such and such a region or people. For instance, the bhāṣā paurālī is related to the Nāga people (BD 4.A.109-10); drāviḍī certainly comes from the Drāviḍas (BD 4.A.136); several kinds of saindhavī refer to Sindhu (Sind, lower Indus basin), and so on. The indexical reference is, thus, surely active in those regional forms. Bhāṣās that are based on shades, such as śakamiśritā, are less independent than the other three classes. Śakamiśritā is a bhāṣā of kakubha, but has the chāyā (reflection) of śaka (BD 4.A.78-79). Thus, the character of śaka comes forth partially when that bhāṣā is performed.

Yāṣṭika almost makes no reference to rasas, except for a couple of rāgas: gāndhārī and bāṅgālī. Gāndhārī has N as aṁśa and S as nyāsa. It represents karuṇa (BD 4.A.123) and, although not referred to in the treatise as deśī, it is named after a region that is nowadays in northwest Pakistan. This is a mountainous area, matching accordingly the meaning of Śārdūla's description of gāndhārī: it is to be sung 'in (the context of) ascending the top of a mountain' (BD 4.B.19). In fact, Yāṣṭika describes three bhāṣās called gāndhārī. One is derived from bhinnaṣaḍja, another from gāndhārapañcama; the third gāndhārī, which express karuṇa, belongs to sauvīra. Śārdūla writes about two gāndhārīs, one in mālavapañcama with G as aṁśa, the other in bhinnaṣaḍja, with the same aṁśa. The latter 'is sung by those living in solitude' (BD 4.B.26). The descriptions of several kinds of gāndhārī refer certainly to different rāgas with the same name. Furthermore, it is clear that the meanings referred to by the different gāndhārīs are disconnected from the ones expressed by the grāmarāgas to which they are musically attached. The other bhāṣā related to rasa by Yāṣṭika is also regional. Bāṅgālī comes from Baṅgāla deśa, i.e., Bangladesh. However, the attribution of rasa is much less specific: 'This bhāṣā is full of rasa and it is also dear to the deity' (BD 4.A.111-12).

The bhāṣās found in Śārdūla's text (31 in number) have more remarks on their application than Yāṣṭika's. Yet direct references to rasas are limited to a few. Trāvaṇī, a pentatonic bhāṣā located in ṭakka, 'is (used) in the context of amorous women' (BD 4.B.3), which is an episode of śṛṅgāra. The same can be said about vibhāvinī, a deśa from mālavapañcama, 'sung in (the context of) hair-dressing (and) restrained union with an amorous woman' (BD 4.B.15). Besides the two that represent śṛṅgāra, there is the bhāṣā vegavatī, originating from the same grāmarāga as the former. It 'is sung in karuṇa in which dainya (depression or affliction) is profuse' (BD 4.B.16).

There are many bhāṣās that should be applied to very specific situations, such as the following: āndhrī, originally from the Āndhra region, is to be 'sung in (the context of) those who are corrupted by disease;' pañcamī, sung 'in (the context of) the song of (one with) a mature mind;' bāhyaṣāḍavā, 'sung on the occasion of *yajña*' (sacrifice); kausalī, also a deśa, 'sung in (the context of) the door-keepers;' or pārvatī, a deśa born from the mountains, 'sung in the assembly of kṣatrīyas' (BD 4.B.18-33). The bhāṣā pārvatī is not textually related to the goddess Pārvatī, wife of Śīva. None of these bhāṣās appears in Yaṣṭika's section. If one presupposes that Yaṣṭika's text was older than Śārdūla's, this could be evidence that the bhāṣās initially had very few attributed meanings, and later gained more and more significations. The richer scope of significations found in the SR is also evidence of this process of growth in the meanings of rāgas.

Besides the few cases pointed out above, it seems that the expression of rasa in the grāmarāga system was not related to internal musical features of the rāgas (neither to their modal structures, nor to the notated melodies), but was an attribute of their individuality as a whole. This again is a distinctive trait in relation to the jātis and a stable general characteristic concerning the later rāgas. In relation to the objects to which rāgas and bhāṣās refer, there is a downward turn of generality of the large-scale meaning of play junctures in relation to the primary grāmarāgas, to the several rasas and their subspecies in the secondary grāmarāgas, finally reaching some very specific dramatic elements in the bhāṣās. This scale of general to particular meanings attached to the levels of historical and musical development, in terms of primary and secondary grāmarāgas as well as bhāṣās, is also confirmed by other sources, such as Abhinavagupta's commentary on the NŚ (see Widdess 1995: 44).

As soon as the tradition of classical Sanskrit drama began to disappear, and the focus of musical practice became less associated with the constraints of theater music, it seems that the need for rāgas whose significations were closer to the tendency of deśī rāgas, in detriment to the already old grāmarāgas, caused the obsolescence of the latter by the early second millennium. The deśīrāga system, first recognized as legitimate by Mataṅga, was fully in use by the time of Śārṅgadeva, 400 years later. Indian music proceeded, nevertheless, by keeping the system open. As much as there was 'assimilation of a wide range of regional tastes and preferences' (Rowell 1992: 178), there was also the process of rāgas becoming obsolete, dying out, or being combined into new entities. Rāgas had their meanings transformed, along with their musical structures.

3.3.3 Deśīrāgas and Rasa

The grāmarāga system, with its capacity to absorb and incorporate new musical structures, evolved by taking in more and more regional forms, called deśī. Scholars differentiated between the expansion of the deśī rāgas, which happened during the second half of the first millennium, and that of the mārga – the right way, proper course (literally, 'road', 'path'). Mārga comprises not only the jātis and grāmarāgas but also all the other elements and structures, such as tāla and forms, that characterize learned music in opposition to popular music. In the BD one reads: 'That which is structured through ālāpa (melodic elaboration) etc. is called mārga, but the one devoid of ālāpa etc. is called deśī' (BD 1.1.16). Thus, Mataṅga considers deśī to be unelaborated music. It is devoid of the structures that govern mārga music, and comes about fortuitously in several places: 'In various regions (dhvani or manifested sound) spontaneously becomes pleasant to living beings and starting with them (it is also pleasant) to the people and kings. This dhvani that arises from region to region is called deśī (born in or proceeding from various deśas or regions)' (BD 1.1.1-2ab). Also: 'That which is sung by women, children, cowherds and kings out of their own will with love (and pleasure) in their own (respective) regions is called deśī (music)' (BD 1.1.14). However, the main purpose of the *Bṛhaddeśī* (*The Greatness of Deśī Music*) was to account for and codify the deśī traditions along with the mārga conventions. Unhappily, the chapter dealing with deśī rāgas in the BD was almost completely lost, save for a few verses. The main extant sources for deśī rāgas are the *Sarasvatīhṛdayālaṁkāra* or *Bharatabhāṣya* of Nānyadeva (1100 A.D.), and the SR, written by Śārṅgadeva (1210-1247 A.D.), who lived in the Yādava court at Devagiri (Deccan, nowadays Dautalabad). The latter shows that, by the beginning of the 13th century, much regional music had been collected; it was probably modified and harmonized to suit mārga standards and terminology. The names of many of the pieces refer to their places of origin. Moreover, in preference for performance the deśī rāgas had already supplanted several of the old-fashioned grāmarāgas. In fact, the definition of saṅgīta, presented in the first chapter of the SR, puts mārga and deśī music not as learned and cultivated in opposition to popular and simple, but in different terms, with mārga as mythological or sacred music in opposition to the secular deśī.

> Gītam (vocal melody), vādyam (playing on instruments) and nṛttam (dancing), all the three together are known as saṅgīta which is twofold, viz. mārga and deśī. That which was discovered by Brahmā and (first) practiced by Bharata and others in the audience of Śiva is known as mārga (saṅgīta), which definitely bestows prosperity; while the saṅgīta comprising gītam, vādyam and nṛttam, [which] entertains people according to their taste in the different regions, is known as deśī. (SR 1.1.21c.24b)

Mārga, as the music created and practiced by the gods and their followers, equates somehow with gāndharva, the celestial music. Deśī, now also classified as saṅgīta, and not merely dhvani, promotes mostly entertainment, but it is also a learned art. The absorption of deśī rāgas into mainstream music theory is clear in the descriptions of the rāgas presented in the SR, which align those deśī rāgas with their structurally and aesthetically correspondent grāmarāgas and bhāṣās. For some of the deśī rāgas, Śārṅgadeva offers notated examples of ālāpa (in chapter 6), which was an exclusive feature of mārga music during the time of the BD.

Rāgas and Rasa

The SR describes the grāmarāgas as having a wider variety of meanings than those found in the BD. The conflict between the rasas (according to the NŚ rule) and the dramatic application detected in the BD is still evident in some of the SR rāgas. Other rāgas in the SR seem to have incorporated the rasas and the drama-context meanings, as if now a far broader scope of signification was derivable from a single musical structure. Besides the rasas and dramatic application, most of the rāgas are associated with a deity and celestial bodies, such as the sun, the moon, planets and constellations. It is also prescribed that Rāgas be performed during a certain period of time or in a particular season. This is one of the first references to a tradition that is still followed in Hindustani music.

There are few instances of disagreement between the meanings ascribed to the grāmarāgas in the BD and in the SR. Rāga boṭṭa, for example, is related to śānta in the BD and represents śṛṅgāra and hāsya in the SR (2.52). Both sources mention festivities. Śārṅgadeva in general follows the information in the BD, and adds the rāgas and meanings that evolved during the nearly five centuries that intervened between the two works.[26] The SR is actually a great synthesis of the musical scholarship up to that time.

The classification system used in the SR is peculiar, for it has a double purpose: to distinguish ancient, well-known and current rāgas, and to explain their genealogy. Besides the division of grāmarāgas, bhāṣās,

---

[26] See Widdess (1995: 184-85) for a diagram of information transmission among the several treatises.

vibhāṣās and antarabhāṣās, there is a class of *uparāgas*, which comprises some of the BD grāmarāgas, and a class of *rāgas*, which includes new varieties. The deśī rāgas are classified as *rāgāṅga*, *bhāṣāṅga*, *kriyāṅga* and *upāṅga*. Rāgāṅgas are those deśī rāgas related to grāmarāgas. Bhāṣāṅgas evolved from the bhāṣās, vibhāṣās and antarabhāṣās. Kriyāṅga is a special class comprising only three rāgas. According to Shringy's and Sharma's commentary on the SR, kriyāṅgas are deśī rāgas 'related to specific emotive situations' ([SR] 1989: 15). Indeed, the definition of kriyāṅga in the BD (5.351) does mention rasas, but there is little evidence in the descriptions of rāgas in the SR that would support the preceding statement. Finally, upāṅgas are deśī rāgas that do not fit into any category or derive from the above three *aṅgas* (limbs).

In sum, it is possible to follow the evolution of rāgas and to assess their status in musical practice at the time of Śārṅgadeva. Seventeen of the grāmarāgas, classified as ancient, were probably obsolete at the time of classification. Some of the other grāmarāgas were still well known, and were related to deśī rāgas as their ancestors. Śārṅgadeva locates a few grāmarāgas among the deśī rāgas that were currently in use. This suggests that, besides being related to deśī rāgas, those grāmarāgas themselves were still in vogue. Bhinnaṣaḍja, for instance, was the progenitor of bhairava, a rāgāṅga which further gave rise to the upāṅga bhairavī. Bhinnaṣaḍja, as a grāmarāga, was certainly ancient, but was probably still performed at that time. Bhairava was already an old and well known deśī rāga, while bhairavī was younger. These three generations of rāgas display continuity in their musical and aesthetic features:

Bhinnaṣaḍja:

Born of ṣaḍjodicyav (jāti), bhinnaṣaḍja is devoid of ṛṣabha and pañcama, [it] has dhaivata as its fundamental and initial note and madhyama for its final note: it takes *uttarāyatta* and is embellished by *prasannānta* as beautified in the eirculatory (sañcārī) varṇa and employs kākalī and antara. Having Brahmā for its presiding deity, it is sung on the occasions of universal festivity in the first quarter of the day in the winter to (express) terror [bhayānaka] and disgust [bībhatsa]. (SR 2.79-81c)

Bhairava:

Bhairava, which is derived from it, has dhaivata for its fundamental tone, and madhyama for its final note, it is devoid of ṛṣabha and pañcama, and with equipoised notes, it is (sung in) a prayer. (SR 2.81d-82b)

Bhairavī:

Having dhaivata for its fundamental, final and initial notes and embellished by the high as well as the low gāndhāra, bhairavī, an upāṅga of bhairava, has the rest of the notes equipoised. (SR 2.140c-141b)

In the context of the early 13th century, to say that ṣaḍjodicyav was the jāti that gave birth to bhinnaṣaḍja would have been a redundant statement of historical priority. Yet, according to the protocols of Sanskrit scholarship, the link with the NŚ was theoretically necessary. Bhinnaṣaḍja is a pentatonic bitonal grāmarāga. It has D for aṁśa and M for nyāsa. R and P are omitted. These features are transmitted to bhairava, but bhairavī is a monotonal heptatonic rāga, and thus farther from bhinnaṣaḍja than bhairava. The bhinnaṣaḍja described in the BD has a specific dramatic application which is not mentioned in the SR; that application is in the context of vijātīya vīra, the hero disgusted by the prospect of an unequal fight. Here, it instead expresses the idea of 'universal festivity'. The rasas bhayānaka and bībhatsa come from the aṁśa D, and are in open conflict with the festive application. The two derived deśī rāgas gained much importance later on, and constituted two major rāgas in contemporary Hindustani music.

Originally, the deśī rāga bhairava was probably a song related to the mountain tribe of the Bhairavas (or Bhaīravas), and was later adapted to the deśī rāgas system (Prajñānānanda 1973: 135). Since bhairava is described as a pentatonic rāga in the SR, it is quite possible that this pentatonic feature is a musical index of the original melody played or sung by the Bhairavas. If this hypothesis is true, one can also say that bhairavī reflects a later development, into a heptatonic mode. Moreover, there seems to be some relation between the deity ascribed to bhinnaṣaḍja, Brahmā, the god of Vedic rituals, and the character of bhairava, to be 'sung in a prayer'. However, bhairava will be associated later with the Tantric conception of Śiva as Bhairava, the terrible deity.

Hiṇḍola is another grāmarāga (first mentioned in the BD) which can be traced continuously through the çenturies, up to the present time. This rāga, in the SR, is the source of a number of deśī rāgas, all of them related in terms of musical structure and signification. Hiṇḍola is a pentatonic monotonal rāga; S is the svara that bears all the important functions. R and D are the omitted svaras. As for its aṁśa S, the rasas of hiṇḍola are vīra, raudra and adbhuta. However, the dramatic application discloses its real character: 'employed in the context of enjoyment of erotic love [sambhoga] to the endearment of cupid [Kāma]' (SR 2.96a). Further, it is to be performed in spring, during the last quarter of the day. Hiṇḍola can be translated as 'swing', which has ties to a popular festival in India in which people play on swings and sing special songs (see Henry 1988: 99). It seems that at the time of Śārṅgadeva the hiṇḍola festival was held during the spring, but later, or in other areas, it was connected to the monsoon. The cheerfulness of both the festival and the rāga is clearly indicated by the association with Kāma, the god of sensual love, and sambhoga, the erotic rasa in its form of union. The lyrics of the song exemplifying hiṇḍola in the SR refer to Śiva and its mythological relation to Kāma: 'I bow down to Śiva who has satisfied the wishes (literally, the mind swans) of all people who have taken refuge in him, and who, accompanied by his consort, is the destroyer of the body of the cupid [Madana or Kāma]' (SR 2.96a ff.). The text can be understood in reference to the purāṇic mythology. The gods sent Kāma to arouse Śiva's desire for Pārvatī. Śiva, annoyed with Kāma for disturbing his yogic practices, burned up the god of love with his third eye. Kāma thus lost his body; the god of love himself became unable to enjoy sensual pleasures. He was nevertheless successful in his mission, and Pārvatī eventually became Śiva's wife or Śakti. In Example 57 (in chapter 3.4), the ***ākṣiptika*** (a kind of song used in the SR to illustrate rāgas) for hiṇḍola is transcribed into staff notation. The brackets mark melodic motifs that may characterize rāga hiṇḍola. No musical correspondence seems to ground the reference of hiṇḍola to śṛṅgāra on any basis other than indexical (for a possible connection with the folk festival) or symbolic.

Vasanta is the deśī rāga most closely connected to hiṇḍola. The rāga's name refers to spring, and therefore its relation with hiṇḍola is direct. The main difference is that vasanta is heptatonic. The text in the SR does not mention the rasa of vasanta, but it clearly should be śṛṅgāra. This is confirmed in later treatises such as the *Saṅgītaśiromaṇi* (SŚ 11.162-63). Two other bhāṣās are related to hiṇḍola: piñjarī and chevāṭī. Piñjarī gives rise to the bhāṣāṅga naṭṭa, and chevāṭī to the upāṅga vallātā. Chevāṭī expresses hāsya and is connected with festivities (SR 2.147b), whereas its offspring, vallātā, stands for śṛṅgāra. This pair of deśī rāgas refers to the same meanings of hiṇḍola. The diagram in Figure 15 represents the relations among these rāgas. The most remarkable feature is the unity of those rāgas in terms of aesthetical reference. Hiṇḍola, vasanta, chevāṭī and vallātā are all referred to as expressing śṛṅgāra or some meaning connected to festivities. Although the SR text does not indicate the rasas of piñjarī and naṭṭa, they are supposed to belong to the same context. In fact, the word naṭṭa is related to dance.

Figure 15

Hiṇḍola and Its Derived Rāgas

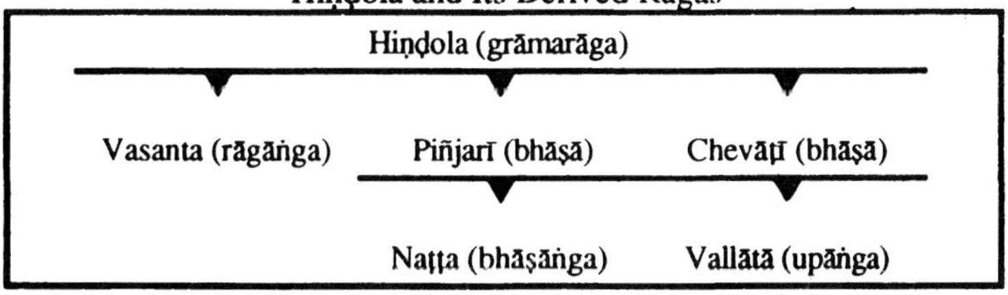

Another group of interesting rāgas, connected by meaning and somehow related to the hiṇḍola family, is that of śuddhapañcama (see Figure 16). It is a monotonal rāga again related to Kāma. Its description reads: 'it is to be sung in the first quarter of the summer day in (depicting) śṛṅgāra and hāsya, in the vimarśa (epitasis)' (SR 2.2.150). Śuddhapañcama's bhāṣā, dākṣiṇātyā, is to be used to depict 'the fond memory of the beloved' (152a), and its vibhāṣā, āndhālī, refers to 'the meeting of separated lovers' (153), that is, the rasa sambhoga that follows a state of vipralambha. Finally, from āndhālī emerges the upāṅga malhāra, which is a pentatonic deśī rāga (155). Malhāra is a word derived from *malahāraka*, the destroyer or purifier of the *malas*, dust or impurities, that is, the rains. The connection of rains and śṛṅgāra is based on the cultural fact that often, in the monsoon season, parted lovers met again when the husband returned to his village after a business trip, for it was not a good season for travel in old India. Therefore, sambhoga and śṛṅgāra are in general the rasas for such a situation. This is a standard theme in Indian literature, both vernacular and Sanskrit. Therefore, the reference here is indexical. Further, an upāṅga called malhārī is directly derived from śuddhapañcama and stands for śṛṅgāra as well (SR 2.2.154).

Figure 16

Śuddhapañcama and Its Derived Rāgas

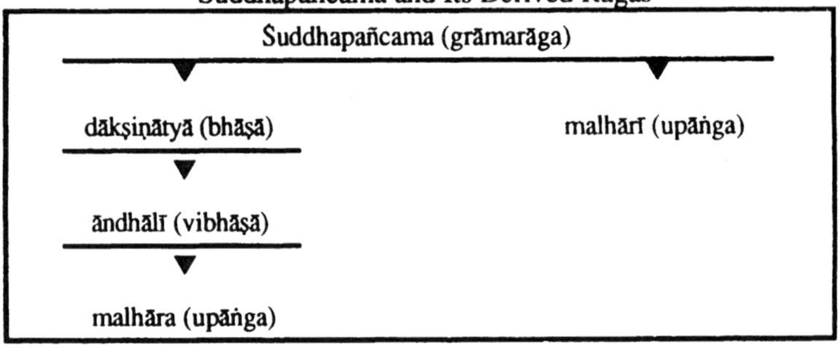

In the SR one finds another rāga connected to the rains, megharāga. Megha (cloud) is not related to any grāmarāga or bhāṣā and seems to be independent of that system. It is described as springing directly from one of the jātis, dhaivatī (SR 2.164c-165b). In fact, there is a reference to a megha gīti dating back to the time of the NŚ or perhaps earlier, in the Buddhist *Matsyajātaka* (see Prajñānānanda 1973: 137-38). This indicates that, side by side with the jāti system, other musical traditions probably existed, which were not recorded in writing down or whose texts have perhaps disappeared, almost without a trace. This subject, however, has received little investigation.

Other Meanings Referred to by Rāgas

Śārṅgadeva associates some celestial bodies with several of the grāmarāgas, which, among the bhāṣās, vibhāṣās, rāgāṅga, bhāṣāṅga, etc., are the musical entities most charged with meanings. The correlation in some cases is mingled with deities and mythological beings, for those are also related to the sun, the moon, the planets, and so on. Thus, Sūrya (Sun) and Soma (Moon) are Vedic deities. Dhruva (the polar star) is also another name for any of the *trimūrti* Gods: Brahmā, Viṣṇu and Śiva. Some groups of rāgas are specifically related to a certain celestial body. Three forms of kaiśikamadhyama are associated with Soma, two forms of pañcama to Sauri (Saturn), and two other pañcama with the couple Rāhu and Ketu (Dragon's head and tail). Another group could possibly arise from ṣāḍava rāgas. Śukra (Venus) is attributed to both vesaraṣāḍava and ṣāḍava rāgas (according to Nijenhuis 1974: 39). However, vesaraṣāḍava is associated with Jupiter in the SR's translation by Shringy and Sharma (2.48-50b).

Table 13

Celestial Bodies and Rāgas

Celestial bodies:	Grāmarāgas:	Rasas:
Guru or Bṛhaspati (Jupiter):	ṣaḍjagrāma	vīra, raudra. adbhuta
Dhruva (polar star):	madhyamagrāma	śṛṅgāra, hāsya
Soma (Moon):	śuddhakaiśikamadhyama	vīra, raudra, adbhuta
	bhinnakaiśikamadhyama	vīra, raudra, adbhuta
	gauḍakaiśikamadhyama	vīra, bhayānaka
Surya (Sun):	śuddhasādhārita	vīra, raudra
	rūpasādhāra	vīra, raudra, adbhuta, vīrakaruṇa
Śukra (Venus):	ṣāḍava	śṛṅgāra, hāsya
	vesaraṣāḍava (?)	śānta, śṛṅgāra, hāsya
Bhauma (Mars):	śuddhakaiśika	vīra, raudra, adbhuta
Sauri (Saturn or Viṣṇu):	gaudapañcama	bhayānaka, bībhatsa, vipralambha
	bhinnapañcama	bhayānaka, bībhatsa
Rāhu (Dragon's head):	gaṅdharapañcama	hāsya, vismaya, karuṇa
Ketu (Dragon's tail):	malavapañcama	hāsya, śṛṅgāra, vipralambha

Both ṣaḍjagrāma and madhyamagrāma are related to deities of cosmological ancestry; Bṛhaspati or Guru is the preceptor of Gods; and Dhruva, the polar star, has the attributes of constancy, permanency, eternity. Those musical structures, although referred to as grāmarāgas in this context, still bear the ancient idea of the two basic tuning sets from which all the jātis arise. These two rāgas, thus, are complex symbols referring to multiple objects. All forms of kaiśikamadhyama stand for vīra and have S as aṁśa and M as nyāsa. Soma, to which they are related, is the Vedic ritual drink and also the elixir of immortality, the drink of the gods. Indra, one of the main vedic deities, is the thunderbolt warrior, fed by Soma. Furthermore, all the Gods in the Hindu pantheon are heroes, and their particular weapons are clearly depicted in their iconography. Soma, as an intoxicating drink, may be also considered to have a stimulating effect which would arouse the vīra attitude, as suggested by the *Ṛgveda* hymn describing a person drunk with Soma (10.119.2-9). Rāhu is a demonic entity who stole Soma from the Gods; this can be viewed as an astonishing act, hence vismaya (wonder, sthāyibhāva of adbhuta) is represented by the rāga gāndhārapañcama. The other two rasas of this rāga, hāsya and karuṇa, may also be pertinent to the mythological episode (from different points of view), for as soon as Rāhu starts drinking Soma, causing a lunar eclipse, Viṣṇu punishes him by cutting his head off. Ketu is supposedly Rāhu's 'partner in crime'. Śukra is the name of a sage who taught the Daityas (demons), and the word is also related to kindness. The association with rāga vesaraṣāḍava that represents śānta is pertinent, with its ideas of the knowledge and kindness of a wise person. Finally, Sauri or Śani represents bad luck or an evil character, which matches the rasas bhayānaka and bībhatsa referred to by bhinnapañcama and gauḍapañcama. Both rāgas have D as aṁśa.

Therefore, the association of grāmarāgas with celestial bodies in the SR seems to be related to the dramatic character and rasas of both rāgas and mythological entities. In this case, there seems to be no diagrammatic representation of astronomical properties by iconic musical features of the rāgas. The performance times assigned to the rāgas are probably related to some kind of musical cosmology, although an objective rationale for doing so has not yet been discovered. Nijenhuis found that grāmarāgas in the SR relate to periods of time according to the five gītis in which they are classified: morning, śuddha and bhinna gītis; noon, gauḍa gīti; evening, vesara gīti; and for any time, the rāgas of sādhāraṇa gīti (1974: 36-37). The grouping of rāgas according to time can be traced back to the NŚ, which discusses the grāmarāgas appropriate to the sections of a play. On the one hand, this grouping developed into the seasonal rāgas (a cycle developing over a long span of time), and on the other, into the hours of the day (in the short span of time).

The grāmarāgas not connected to a celestial body in the SR refer to a deity. Among the trimūrti gods, Śiva is the patron of the largest number of rāgas. The explanation for Śiva's supremacy on this count is not only that Śārṅgadeva was devoted to Śiva (his personal Īśvara), to whom he addressed the opening propitiatory verses of the treatise, or that Śiva was the god of arts, but also that one finds a great variety of Śaiva mythological episodes and their rasas (see O'Flaherty 1973). The god of erotic love, Kāma, is associated with rāgas expressing śṛṅgāra, as mentioned above. And Yama, the god of death, is the patron of rāga kakubha, which should be sung in the autumn and which represents karuṇa (SR 2.109-10a). Thus, here is also an instance in which the character of the deity and the rāga share the same rasa.

The association of musical structures with deities on the basis of musical rasa and general temperament of the deity is extended in the SR to compositional forms such as the prabhandas. They are kinds of musical forms belonging to the nibaddha (composed), rather than anibaddha (improvised) division of songs. One of the most remarkable prabhandas is the *jhombaḍa*, **which** comes in a great variety of species, defined aesthetically as references to a rasa and deity:

> (The Jhombaḍa composed) with simile[,] metaphor and pun is (called) brahmā, with the sentiment of heroism combined with grace [*vīra-vilāsayoḥ*] (it is called) viṣṇu, with heroism [vīra] *cakreśvara*, with disgust [bībhatsa] *candikeśvara*, with marvel [adbhuta] *narsiṁha*, with terror [bhayānaka] *bhairava*, with mirth [hāsya] coupled with conjugal love [śṛṅgāra] *haṁsa*, with heroism in combination with terror [vīra-bhayānaka] *siṁha*, with conjugal love in separation [vipralambha] *sāraṅga*, with pathos combined with conjugal love [karuṇa-śṛṅgāra] it is known as *puśpasāra*, with wrath [raudra] *pracaṇḍa*, and with tranquillity [śānta] it is declared by the wise to be *nandīśa*. (SR 4.4.164-67)

The brahmā jhombaḍa seems to be related to Brahmā only in respect of being the first, the source of creation. Viṣṇu is the graceful hero incarnated as Kṛṣṇa in the *Mahābhārata*; and, cakreśvara, the lord of discus, refers to the same deity (the discus is one of Viṣṇu's weapons). Bībhatsa is related to the disgusting form of Śiva, as lord of caṇḍika, a terrible manifestation of the Devī, represented with twenty hands. Narasiṁha is the embodiment of Viṣṇu as a lion, who defeated an invincible demon king (hence adbhuta). Bhairava is the terrible form of Śiva, whose appearance would provoke bhayānaka. Haṁsa, the swan, is related to several deities, Kāma among them. Its connection with śṛṅgāra is multiple. Siṁha, the lion, is a symbol of heroism connected both with Viṣṇu and Durgā. Sāraṅga, the peacock, is the vehicle of Kāma. Puśpasāra, the nectar of a flower, can be related to karuṇa-śṛṅgāra in terms of poetic imagery. Pracaṇḍa, a Dānava demon, is described as fierce and violent. Finally, Nandīśa is the chief attendant of Śiva, depicted by the bull sculpture at all Śaiva temples, and iconically represents śānta. The religious and mythological references in this passage suggest a range of significations on which compositions could be based. Prabandhas were specified not only in their formal structure, including rāga and tāla, but also pada, the words to which the composer (vāggeyakāra) sets music. The combination of all elements should result meaningfully in rasa.

The SR reflects the expansion of musical meanings up to the time of Śārṅgadeva. Rāgas were not only related to the classical rasas, and their extensions, and to dramatic applications, but also to the universe of significations abounding in the several fields of Indian culture. In a lively semiosphere, rāgas slowly, but continuously, saw their meanings grown, sometimes even changing into different representations. Subsequent authors, after Śārṅgadeva, also had to revise their scholarly interpretations, introducing poetic descriptions to synthesize the aesthetic and anthropomorphic features of rāgas, out of which miniature painting finally materialized as visible music.

3.3.4 The Rāga-rāgiṇī Systems and Rasa

> Every branch of knowledge in this country has been embellished by poetical fables; and the inventive talents of the *Greeks* never suggested a more charming allegory than the lovely families of the six *Rāgas*, named, in the order of the seasons above exhibited, Bhairava, Mālava, Sri-Rāga, Hindola, or Vasanta, Dīpaca, and Mégha; each of whom is a genius, or a Demi-god, wedded to five *Rāginis*, or Nymphs, and father of *eight* little Genii, called his *Putras*, or Sons: the fancy of Shakespeare and the pencil of Albano might have been finely employed in giving speech and form to this assemblage of new aërial beings, who people the fairy-land of *Indian* imagination; nor have the *Hindoo* poets and painters lost the advantages, with which so beautiful a subject presented them. (Jones [1784] 1990: 146)

After the fourteenth century, the tendency to particularize meaning, as found in the grāmarāga and deśīrāga systems, triggered the rise and development of rāga personification. Each rāga was conceived as a being, divine or human, male or female, whose character represented the aesthetic form of a musical entity. The idea of personification was extended to the theoretical level, generating a system of rāga classification based on the extended Indian family: a male, patriarchal rāga, a number of female rāgiṇīs, their sons, and sometimes even the sons' wives. Some of the rāga-rāgiṇī families were clearly related to the Indian seasons, especially spring and the rainy season. If it is possible to trace the association of rāgas with seasons and hours of the day and night back to the seven primary grāmarāgas assigned to the sections of a play, as found in the NŚ and later treatises; in the same way, it is possible to follow the lines of aesthetic signification connecting the jātis and grāmarāgas prescribed to represent dramatic situations and characters in the classical Sanskrit theater with the later personification of rāgas. However, the very decline of that dramatic tradition may have influenced the way Indian music developed. Even codified as they were, jātis and grāmarāgas had to be representamens flexible enough to fit the dramatic needs of any play. Indian music, as described in the treatises of the mid second millennium, was much more independent of drama, and this may be the reason why rāgas and rāginīs became individualized as live beings.

From the time of Śārṅgadeva onwards, with the Islamic invasions in North India, a host of foreign influences gradually transformed Indian music. New rāgas, forms and instruments appeared. It is usually accepted that the distinction between the two classical traditions, South Indian music, or Karnatic, and North Indian music, or Hindustani, was born after the SR, although historical evidence seems to indicate that the situation was not as clear a dichotomy as is usually claimed, and that several musical traditions, distinct in various respects from each other, existed in both Muslim and Hindu states (see Brahaspati 1983; Widdess 1995: 28). In any case, there seems to be no essential change in the evolution of Indian music aesthetics that could be particularly related to that political situation. Sanskrit treatises were translated into Persian, and a number of new music treatises were ordered by the Islamic rulers, who were almost without exception patrons of music and art. The greatest of the Moghul patrons was Emperor Akbar, who reigned between 1556-1605, and in his court was the celebrated singer and composer Tānsen (1492-1589), to whom contemporary Hindustani music can be linked through history, and whose compositions are still performed.[27]

Treatises

From the 13th to the 17th centuries, a number of treatises presented various aesthetic concepts. The personification and deification of rāgas manifested clearly in the two systems of classification of rāgas of this period: the rāga-rāgiṇī (male and female musical entities) and mela (scale types). The personification of rāgas is actually the basis for the rāga-rāgiṇī classification, but it is also present in the mela systems. The earliest treatise classifying musical structures into male and female entities is the *Saṅgītamakaranda* , attributed to Nārada and written some time after the SR. In this work there are three categories of rāgas: *puṁliṅga-rāgāḥ* (male rāgas), *śtrī-rāgāḥ* (female rāgas), and *napuṁsaka-rāgāḥ* (neuter rāgas). The nine rasas are attributed to those groups in this way: vīra, raudra and adbhuta are represented by the male rāgas; śṛṅgāra, karuṇa and hāsya, by the female rāgas; bhayānaka, bībhatsa and śānta, by the neuter rāgas (Gangoly 1989: 22-23).

The oldest extant descriptions of rāgas in terms of personification or deification appear in the *Saṅgītopaniṣatsāroddhāra* , which was written in Guirat in 1350 by the Jain author Sudhākalaśa (Nijenhuis 1977: 15; Powers 1980: 79). This seems to be one of the few treatises dealing essentially with Tantric characterization of rāgas. Along with technical description of the musical features of the rāgas, extra-musical significations are designated by poems, called *dhyāna*, or contemplations. Sudhākalaśa's descriptions correspond to miniature paintings representing

[27] As noted in 2.3.3.4, compositions attributed to Tānsen cannot be authenticated beyond doubt.

rāgas, which were found on the back of pages in a *Kalpasūtra* manuscript (Nijenhuis 1977: 16; Ebelling 1973: 121, 150). The rāga paintings are multi-armed and multi-headed representations of deities, featuring typical emblems, and of animal vehicles. According to Gangoly (1989: 24-25), the first treatise to label female rāgas as rāgiṇīs was the *Pañcamasārasamhita*, dated 1362 A.D. In this text, the six main male rāgas are mallāra, mālava, śrī, vasanta, hiṇḍola, and karṇāṭa. Notably absent is rāga bhairava, which is invariably present in all later rāga-rāgiṇī systems, being the foremost rāga in some of them.

In 1428 Malik Shah, Sultan of Kaḍa (near Allahabad), organized a musical congress that resulted in the *Saṅgītaśiromaṇi*. The work is a compilation of previous treatises, drawing mainly from the SR. A system of rāga-rāgiṇī classification is also recorded there (see table 14). Another, more important compilation is the *Saṅgītarāja*, commissioned in 1453 by King Kumbhakarṇa of Mewar Rajasthan (Powers 1980a: 79). In this work, references to Mataṅga indicate that originally there were rāga dhyānas in the BD which did not survive. The *Saṅgītarāja's* dhyānas, according to Nijenhuis (1977: 18), resemble those of Sudhākalaśa, which suggests that the tradition of Tantric dhyānas flowered from the time of the BD up to the 15th century.

In the *Saṅgītadāmodara* (c. 1500), written by Śubhaṅkara in Orissa, the rāgas and rāgiṇīs are described with dhyānas, some of which were quoted later in the *Saṅgitadarpaṇa* (Nijenhuis 1977: 19). A treatise in which dhyānas are often illustrated by miniature paintings is Meṣakarṇa's *Rāgamālā*, dated 1509. In this work each rāga is related to five rāgiṇīs and eight putrās (table 14). The *Rasakaumudī* , written by Śrīkaṇṭha around 1575 in Gujarat, is peculiar in combining the system of melas (11 in this work) with rāga-rāgiṇī and their aesthetical descriptions. As the title suggests, the discussion of rasa is one of the subjects of this eclectic work. Śṛṅgāra is treated extensively, and there is even a chapter on eroticism (see P.L. Sharma 1963b). The tendency of combining aspects of what would later characterize the two traditions of Hindustani and Karnatic music is similarly found in the *Rāgamālā*, written by Puṇḍarīka Viṭṭhala in 1576 (Bengal). Viṭṭhāla applies Rāmāmātya's system of melas to Hindustani music (*Svaramelakalānidhi*, 1550, Vijayanagara), but he also classifies rāgas in terms of musical families (see table 14). These last are composed of male (*puruṣa*), female (*strī*) and sons (*putrā*) (Bhātkhaṇḍe 1990: 54; Nihenhuis 1977: 22; Powers 1980: 82). In Ex. 28 (after Bhātkhaṇḍe 1990: 53-55), I have transcribed the scales of rāga śuddhabhairava, its five rāgiṇīs and five putrās, according to Viṭṭhāla's *Rāgamālā*. The pitches on the staff are an approximation, as the interval in śrutis between each svara makes clear.

Example 28

Rāga śuddhabhairava, rāgiṇīs and putrās, according to Viṭṭhāla's *Rāgamālā*. (Figures represent interval in śrutīs.)

Rāga śuddhabhairava:

Rāgiṇīs:

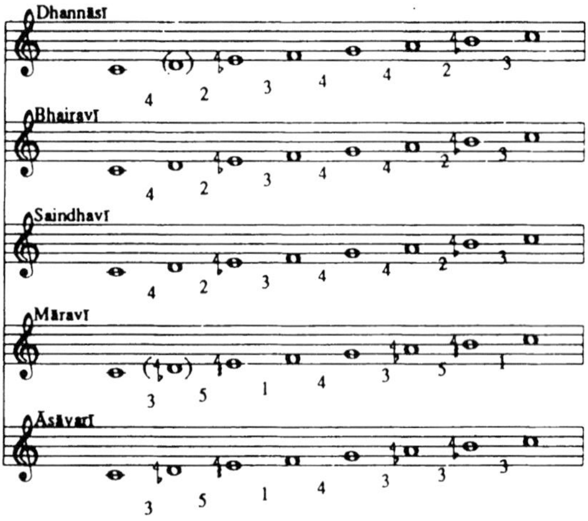

Putras:

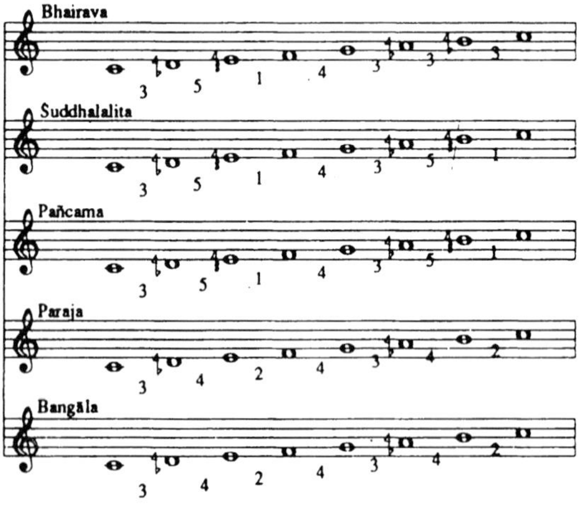

Table 14

Three Early Rāga-rāgiṇī Systems

	Saṅgītaśiromani (1428)	Rāgamālā (1509)	Meṣakarṇa	Rāgamālā (1576)	P. Viṭṭhala
	Rāgas and Rāgiṇīs	**Rāgas and Rāgiṇīs**	**Putrās**	**Rāgas and Rāgiṇīs**	**Putrās**
1.	**Śuddha bhairava**	**Bhairava**		**Śuddhabhairava**	
1.1	Śrīkaṇṭhī	Vangālī	Vangālā	Dhannāsī	Bhairava
1.2	Pulindī	Bhairavī	Pañcama	Bhairavī	Śuddhalalita
1.3	Māṅgalī	Velāvalī	Madhu	Saindhavī	Pañcama
1.4	Bhinnapañcamī	Punyakī	Harṣa	Māravī	Paraja
1.5	Śālavāhanikā	Snehakī	Deśākha	Āsāvarī	Bangāla
1.6	Ābhīrī	-	Lalita	-	-
1.7	-	-	Velāvala	-	-
1.8	-	-	Mādhava	-	-
2.	**Kolhāṭa** (or **koḍava**)	**Mālakauśika**		**Hiṇḍola**	
2.1	Kāmbhojī	Gauḍakrī	Māru	Bhūpalī	Vasanta
2.2	Bhinnapaurālī	Gandhāriṇī	Mevaḍa	Vasantī	Śuddhabaṅgāla
2.3	Paurālī	Mālaśrī	Varvali	Toḍī	Śyāma
2.4	Saindhavī	Śrīhaṭhī	Miṣūāṅga	Prathama-mañjarī	Sāmanta
2.5	Kacchellī	Dhanāśrī	Candrakāya	Turuṣkatoḍī	Kāmoda
2.6	Madhurī	-	Bhramara	-	-
2.7	-	-	Nananda	-	-
2.8	-	-	Kokkara	-	-
3.	**Dhvani**	**Hiṇḍola**		**Deśakāra**	
3.1	Kālindi	Bhūpālī	Mangala	Rāmakrī	Lalita
3.2	Khasikā	Devagirī	Candra-vimva	Bahulī	Vibhāsa
3.3	Cūtamañjarī	Vāsantī	Śubhrāṅga	Deśī	Sāranga
3.4	Vṛddhakaiśikī	Sindhurī	Ānanda	Jetaśrī	Trivaṇa
3.5	Saindhavī (1st)	Ābhirī	Vibhāṣa	Gurjarī	Kalyāṇa
3.6	Saindhavī (2nd)	-	Vardhana	-	-
3.7	-	-	Vinoda	-	-
3.8	-	-	Vasanta	-	-

4.	**Madhyama-ṣāḍava**	**Dīpaka**		**Śrī**	
4.1	Nādāntarī	Kāmodinī	Kamala	Gauḍī	Takka
4.2	Taraṅginī	Paṭamanjarī	Kusuma	Pāḍī	Devagāndhāra
4.3	Siṁhalī	Toḍī	Rāma	Guṇakarī	Mālava
4.4	Ambāhirī	Gujjarī	Kuntala	Śuddharāmakrī	Śuddhagauḍa
4.5	Saurāṣṭrī	Sāraṅgī	Kalinga	Guṇḍakrī	Karṇaṭa-bāngāla
4.6	Kauśalī	-	Vahula	-	-
4.7	-	-	Campaka	-	-
4.8	-	-	Hemala	-	-
5.	**Devāla**	**Śrī**		**Śuddhanaṭa**	
5.1	Gāndharī	Vairāṭī	Sindhavā	Mālavaśrī	Jijāvanta
5.2	Bhāvanī	Karṇāṭikā	Mālava	Deśākṣī	Sālanganāṭa
5.3	Nīlotpalī	Sāverī	Gouḍa	Devakrī	Karṇāta
5.4	Gorañjika	Gauḍī	Gambhīra	Madhumādavī	Chāyānaṭa
5.5	Cauhālī	Rāmagirī	Gunasāgara	Ahīrī	Hamīranaṭa
5.6	Utpalī	-	Vigaḍa	-	-
5.7	-	-	Kalyāna	-	-
5.8	-	-	Kurabha	-	-
6.	**Vibhasa**	**Megha**		**Naṭanārayṇa**	
6.1	Drāviḍī	Mallārī	Naṭa	Velāvalī	Malhara
6.2	Bṛhatī	Soraṭhī	Kanāra	Kāṁbojī	Gauḍa
6.3	Harṣāpurī	Suhāvī	Sāraṅga	Sāverī	Kedāra
6.4	Bhammāṇī	Āsāvarī	Kedāra	Suhavī	Śankarā-bharana
6.5	Saindhavī	Kokaṇī	Guṇḍa-mallāra	Sauraṣṭrī	Bihāgaḍa
6.6	Suravallī	-	Guṇḍa	-	-
6.7	-	-	Jalandhara	-	-
6.8	-	-	Śankara	-	-

Table 15
Three Schools of Rāga-rāgiṇī Systems According to Dāmodara's *Saṅgītadarpaṇa* (1625)

	Someśvara	**Hanumān**	**Rāgarṇava**
1.	**Śrī**	**Bhairava**	**Bhairava**
1.1	Mālavī	Madhyamādī	Vangalī
1.2	Trivanī	Bhairavī	Guṇakarī
1.3	Gauḍī	Vangālī	Madhyamādi
1.4	Kedārī	Varāṭikā	Vasanta
1.5	Madhumādhavī	Saindhavī	Dhanaśrī
1.6	Pāhāḍī	-	-
2.	**Vasanta**	**Mālakauśika**	**Pañcama**
2.1	Deśī	Toḍī	Lalita
2.2	Devagirī	Khambāvatī	Gurjarī
2.3	Varātī	Gaurī	Deśrī
2.4	Toḍī	Gunakarī	Varāṭī
2.5	Lalitā	Kakubhā	Rāmakṛt
2.6	Hindolī	-	-
3.	**Bhairava**	**Hiṇḍola**	**Nāṭa**
3.1	Bhairavī	Velāvalī	Nāṭanārāyaṇa
3.2	Gurjarī	Rāmakarī	Gāndhāra
3.3	Reva	Deśā	Sālaga
3.4	Guṇakarī	Paṭamanjarī	Kedāra
3.5	Vāngālī	Lalitā	Karṇāṭa
3.6	Bahulā	-	-

4.	**Pañcama**	**Dīpaka**	**Mallāra**
4.1	Vibhāṣā	Kedārī	Meghamallārikā
4.2	Bhupālī	Karṇāta	Mālakauśika
4.3	karṇātī	Deśī	Paṭamañjarī
4.4	Paṭahaṁsika	Kāmodī	Asāvarī
4.5	Mālaśrī	Nāṭikā	-
4.6	Paṭamañjarī	-	-
5.	**Megha**	**Śrī**	**Gauḍa**
5.1	Mallārī	Vasantī	Hiṇḍola
5.2	Soraṭhī	Mālavī	Trivaṇā
5.3	Sāverī	Mālaśrī	Andhārī
5.4	Kauśikī	Dhanāśrī	Gauḍī
5.5	Gāndhārī	Āsāvarī	Paḍahamsikā
5.6	Haraśṛṅgāra	-	-
6.	**Naṭanārāyana**	**Megharāga**	**Deśa**
6.1	Kamodī	Mallārī	Bhūpālī
6.2	Kalyāṇī	Deśikārī	Kūḍāī
6.3	Ābhīrī	Bhūpālī	Kamodī
6.4	Nāṭikā	Gurjarī	Naṭṭikā
6.5	Sālaṅgī	Ṭakkā	Velāvalī
6.6	Naṭahambīra	-	-

The *Saṅgītadarpaṇa* (SD), written by Dāmodara circa 1625, is certainly the source of the most well-known rāga dhyānas. Dāmodara presents three different rāga-rāgiṇī systems (see table 15), according to Someśvara (SD 2.14-20), the Hanumān system (SD 2.32-38), and the Rāgarṇava system (SD 2.39-45). Yet, the SD dhyānas are organized in conformity to the Hanumān system. The *Catvāriṁśacchatarāganirūpaṇa*, attributed to Nārada, was written by the 16th or 17th century, and consists mostly of dhyānas.

The *Rāgavibodha* (RV) – written by Somanātha in 1609, Andhra – classifies the described rāgas into 23 melas. It also gives notated examples to be played on the vīṇā (see Nijenhuis 1976), and establishes a theory of ornamentation. The dhyānas are justified in terms of nāyaka-nāyikā themes of Sanskrit dramaturgy. The middle-East influence in Hindustani music can be attested by rāgas with Persian names such as husseini, navroj, zīluf, and irakh (Bhātkhaṇḍe 1990: 88). This is also found in the *Rāgataraṅginī* – written by Locana, c. 1675, eastern Ganges valley – as the rāgas imam and farodast (Bhātkhaṇḍe 1990: 13). Locana combines the rāga-rāgiṇī system with the 12 melas: bhairavī, toḍī, gaurī, karṇaṭa, kedāra, imana, sāranga, megha, dhanaśrī, pūrva, mukharī, dīpaka (ibid. 16-20). According to Jhairazbhoy, among the eleven melas specified by Locana, there are eight that correspond to contemporary Hindustani pitch sets, most under different denominations, except for imana, which corresponds to yaman, or kalyāṇ (1971: 92-93).

Deification of Rāgas

The association of rāgas with deities found in the SR evolved in the rāga-rāgiṇī systems as the development of meaning in terms of personification of musical structures, and as a theory of performance and interpretation, in which the rāga only represents its object properly if its meaning incarnates the musical form. There are two systems of rāga personification. One is based on Tantric conceptions and imagery, and can be called deification. The other derives from classical Sanskrit poetics and dramaturgy, and can be referred to as nāyaka-nāyikā bheda (hero-heroine themes). The rāga-rāgiṇī systems often present traces of one concept within the other. Gangoly writes: 'It is believed that each rāga, or rāgiṇī has its peculiar psychic form, corresponding to its sonal body over which the former presides as the nymph, deity, or the devatā (presiding genious or god) of that particular melody' (1989: 96). As noted before, when the meaning of rāgas is conceived as a peculiar psychic form, then the focus of the representation narrows. In such cases, individuality and specificity are the norm, rather than the broad scope of signification offered by jātis and grāmarāgas, which are employed or conceived as carrying a wider range of rasas or dramatic elements in the Sanskrit theater. Rāgas and rāgiṇīs, after the 13th century, become independent, particularized semiotic entities. This holds true in both the Tantric and the nāyaka-nāyikā traditions. Therefore, the psychic form of a rāga, on either a religious or mythological basis, or as theatrical or poetical paradigms, constitutes a definite object and an interpretant to be expressed, perceived and enjoyed.

The relation between the musical materiality of a rāga sign and the object to be interpreted and ultimately enjoyed as rasa, is explained in the RV in terms of rūpa (form), which has a double sense: 'That is called rūpa which by being embellished with sweet flourishes of svaras brings a rāga vividly before one's mind. It is of two kinds – *Nādātma* (one whose soul or essence is sound), and *Devamaya* (= *devatā-dehamayaṁ*, one whose soul, or essence is an image incarnating the deity), of which the former has many phases, and the latter has only one' (RV 5.11 in Gangoly 1989: 96-97). Therefore, Somanātha states that the sound form of a rāga, which is constituted by ornamented and malleable melodic phrases that are open to various manifestations, represents an essentially individual object, its signification goal, which is the embodiment of a general idea, such as a deity or a type of theater character.

In this context, rāgas and rāgiṇīs were described in the treatises in both forms: *nādamaya rūpa* and *devatāmaya rūpa*. The description of the sound form follows the tradition of stating the rāga lakṣaṇas, such as aṁśa, graha, nyāsa, altered and omitted svaras, etc. The reference to the personality of the rāga, however, is more than a mere portrayal of its attributes; it has recourse to the dhyānas, which are meditation formulas used to invoke the deities in religious rituals in India. The musician is expected not only to perform the music correctly, but by concentrating on the rāga dhyāna to bring forth the deep meaning of a rāga. Thus 'the spirit or ethos of a rāga or rāgiṇī can be induced to come down and incarnate (*avatīrṇa* – lit. "made to descend") in its physical sound-form (nāda-maya-rūpa). If the presiding spirit cannot be induced "to descend", the rendering, or interpreting of that particular melody cannot be pronounced to have been successfully achieved' (Gangoly 1989: 97). A number of legends narrate how Nārada, the mythical sage and musician, deformed several devatā forms of rāgas by performing them incorrectly. A detailed source of those stories can be found in the *Bṛhaddharma Purāṇa* (30.44.16-101; see Ramalakshmi 1993: 38-44), according to which, at the end of the episode, it is Śiva himself that demonstrates to Nārada how the rāgas should be performed in order to successfully manifest their devatās. On such an occasion, 'rasa is, as it were, seen in flesh and blood' (ibid.). The idea in this myth is that effective musical creation, accomplished in the act of performing a rāga, equates to the cosmogonic creation of Śiva, the emblem of which is the sound of the damaru drum. The diagrammatic sign is operating here.

Dhyāna is a technical term borrowed from yoga. It is one of the highest levels of the eight progressive steps established by Patañjali in the *Yogasūtras: yama* (abstention), *niyama* (observance), *āsana* (postures), *prāṇāyāma* (breath control), *pratyāhāra* (withdrawal of the senses), *dhāraṇa* (concentration), *dhyāna* (contemplation or meditation), and *samādhi* (absorption). Some of these steps – for example, breath control and concentration – are clearly related to musical practice, especially singing. The rāga dhyānas found in treatises of this period suggest that music was viewed as a kind of yoga, a concept deeply rooted in the idea of sound (nāda) as an essential and pervading element in the cosmos, which grounds the power of Vedic chants, and is also expressed richly in the Tantric texts. However, music has a special aim, rasa, absorption in aesthetic bliss: 'The objective of the rāga is the rasa – the aesthetic emotion, the theme, the subject-matter, – the motif of the melody. As the soul must inhabit a body, so every rasa is incarnated in the rūpa (form) of a particular rāga or rāgiṇī. To invoke the rasa, one must meditate upon the rūpa' (Gangoly 1989: 98-99). Rasa, the musical samādhi, is equated by some aestheticians (Abhinavagupta) with absorption into Brahman, which is essentially the paradoxical, unstruck sound called anāhatanāda.

Tantric dhyānas

The personification of rāgas in terms of deities is based in the philosophical and yogic discipline of Tantra. Often misconceived as a reaction to traditional vedic knowledge and rituals (see Goudriaan in Gupta et al. 1979: 18 ff.), Tantra is a complex combination of Indian beliefs rooted both in Aryan and non-Aryan traditions. The treatises and practices that formed the core of Tantra developed during the second half of the first millennium and can be traced to several religions: Buddhism, Jainism and Hinduism; the latter, in still more specific cults such as Śakta (the cult to Devī, or the goddess), Śaiva (the cult of Śiva) and Vaiṣṇava (the cult of Viṣṇu). The earliest evidence for a Tantric view of music comes from the BD, at the opening of the chapter on deśīrāgas:

> I make obeisance to the Devī who bears a red hue like that of the *bandhūka* (flower), has three eyes, wears a crest of the *kalā* (part) of the one having rays of *amṛa* (nectar) (crescent moon), wears red cloths, is bent with the weight of breasts that are becoming plump and elevated, is conventionally associated with the beginning of youth, is adorned with all ornaments, has abode in the lotus, whose body bears association with the citron fruit, whose (two) hands hold the snare (*pāśa*) (and) hook (*aṅkuśa*) (and the other two) hands are held in the *abhaya* (granting of freedom from fear) and *vara* (granting of boons) gestures and who is the *yoni* of the universe. (BD 5.345)

This is the *maṅgalācaraṇa śloka*, the auspicious introductory stanza for the deśīrāgas chapter. The goddess, here conceived as the yoni (vagina) of the universe, and clearly bearing Śaiva symbols, such as the three eyes and the crescent moon, is certainly Pārvatī, the wife or śakti of Śiva. The greatness of this reverence to the Devī suggests that the BD chapter on deśīrāgas was strongly conceived in Tantric terms and possibly included dhyānas for the rāgas. It is well known, however, that only a few verses of this chapter survived. Besides those first lines, there is no evidence in the text itself for rāga dhyānas. Yet, P.L. Sharma argues that 'from indirect evidence [it was] clear that deśīraga-s were not strictly associated with drama as the grāmarāga-s were. The system of rāga dhyāna-s seems to have developed in the context of deśīrāga-s and the roots of this tradition could be traced back to Mataṅga' (1970: 60). The oldest source of Tantric rāga dhyānas are the 14th century Jain treatise, *Saṅgītopaniṣatsāroddhāra*; and the 15th century *Saṅgītarāja*. The latter includes the references to Mataṅga that led Sharma to her contention (1970: 61).

Hindu Tantrism is present in most of the rāgamālā treatises (even those based on nāyaka-nāyikā themes) in the relation between rāga bhairava and rāgiṇī bhairavī, representing forms of Śiva and Pārvatī. The SD explains the origin of the six main rāgas as born from the copulation of the divine couple:

> By the union of Śiva and Śakti the birth of rāgas came about. From Pancāsya (Śiva) five rāgas sprang, the sixth from the mouth of Girijā (Pārvatī). Śrīrāga from Śiva in his form of Sadya, vasanta from him as Vāmadeva, from him as Aghora the rāga bhairava, and as Tatpuruṣa the rāga pañcama; megharāga sprang from Śiva in his form of Īśāna, in the beginning of nāṭya (dance). The rāga naṭanārāyaṇa came from the mouth of Girijā, when she was performing lāsya (women's dance). (SD 2.9-12)

The six main rāgas, as offspring of Śiva and Pārvatī, show how classical Indian music is interlaced with Hindu cosmology. Rāgas emerged from the ontological combination of male and female principles, and their sonic character may be linked to the importance of sound, breath and voice production, as expressed in the concepts of nāda, prāṇa and mantra. The act of singing corresponds to the diagrammatic representation of the creation and dissolution of the universe.[28] Rāga bhairava, which in the SR was associated with Brahmā via its parent rāga bhinnaṣaḍja, gained importance when it became a representation of Śiva. At the time of SD it is already considered the foremost rāga: '*bhairavaḥ ādirāgaḥ,*' bhairava is the first rāga (SD 2.48). Its alliance with rāgiṇī bhairavī completes the Tantric unity of Śiva and Śakti.

Several factors apparently link together the Bhairavas, the ancient Indian tribe, their possible influence on Tantrism and the mythology of Śiva, and eventually the rāga bhairava. One feature of Bhairava, the terrible form of Śiva, is his color: Bhairava or Kāla Bhairava is black, as is his śakti, Kālī. A dark complexion was a distinctive mark of aboriginal people in India, though evidence suggests that it was despised by the Aryans (see Lannoy 1971: 178). Besides, there is reference to the fierceness of tribal people, as well as their rituals, which sometimes included human sacrifice (Bashan 1954: 199). Furthermore, tribal, non-Aryan cultures have contributed elements to Śaktism and Tantrism, some of which were later absorbed into Hinduism (Goudriaan in Gupta et al. 1979: 36-37). Thus, it is possible that the conception of Bhairava as a form of Śiva, and Kālī as his śakti, has its roots in the aboriginal culture of the Bhairavas. Musically, it seems that, at first, there was simply an ethnic absorption of musical features, such as the pentatonic bhairava presented in the SR; later, the rāga bhairava was associated with the

[28]This is a very important subject that I have to leave aside in this section on rasa. See 2.3.2; and Rowell 1992: 38-41 and 151.

developing Tantric ideas, as well as explicitly related to Śiva. An early dhyāna of rāga bhairava, from the *Rāgasāgara*, still depicts fearsome elements, such as the body smeared with ashes and adorned with skulls as ornaments:

> The sea of notes and microtones, with the nectar of all varieties of rhythms and time-measures, the fulfillment of the desire of the worship of Śiva, with the body always besmeared with ashes, decked with matted locks, with the shine of young moon on the head, with skulls as decorations, I adore Bhairava, the skillful Dancer. (in Gangoly 1989: 107-08)

Later, the rāga bhairava seems to have lost its relation to the fearsome Bhairava and was described rather in terms of a meditating Śiva, as in this dhyāna from the Meṣakarṇa's *Rāgamālā* (1509 A.D.):

> White in complexion, clad in white, carrying the crescent, and the horn and wearing a garland, Bhairava is born from the mouth of Śiva, and carries the poison on his neck and his eyes are red. He (also) carries the trident, the skull, and the lotus, and wears jeweled pendants on his two-ears and matted locks. This (melody) is sung by the gods in the autumn. (in Gangoly 1989: 111).

The well-known dhyāna of bhairava in the SD adds the river Gangā springing from the yogi's matted hair, completing Śiva's munificent picture, instead of the fierce Bhairava. In fact, in the verses relating the birth of the six rāgas in this treatise, bhairava springs from Śiva's face, named Aghora, which means 'the non-terrible one'. Here is a beautiful translation of SD's bhairava dhyāna by Alain Daniélou:

> Upholding Gangā, the crescent moon upon his brow, three-eyed, wrapped in the skin of an elephant and adorned with snakes, his scarf white, his garland of human skulls, armed with a burning trident – so triumphs Bhairava, the first of rāga-s. (SD 2.48, in Daniélou 1991: 125)

Almost all attributes here come from the myth of Śiva's dancing in the pine forest and destroying the demons (cobra, elephant) sent against him by the enraged sages. There is nearly nothing left of Bhairava imagery, such as the black color, hair in flames, long teeth, the skull of Brahmā (which he had cut off) attached to his left hand, and the dog as his vehicle. This is even more clear in the rāgamālā miniature paintings, which depict neither the malevolent Bhairava nor his śakti. Thus, it is no surprise that the rasas of rāga bhairava have little to do with bhayānaka, bībhatsa, raudra or adbhuta, but rather express śānta, in his yogic posture and/or śṛṅgāra, and for his Tantric feature as the erotic and ascetic God (see O'Flaherty 1973). It is peculiar that, as a designation, the fiery Bhairava assumed the main aspects of Śiva musically, while his other, mild and protective forms, such as kedāra, śankara (causer of tranquillity, auspicious), and śankarābharaṇa (the ornament of Śiva), only appear as rāgiṇīs or putrās and never as a main rāga. In the end, it is the paradoxical duality of Śiva – ascetic-erotic, creative-destructive, good-evil – that reflects the real character of the deity, and consequently its musical representation.

Another side of the Tantra conception of rāgas and rāgiṇīs is the relation between male and female musical forms, in the sense of a rāgiṇī being the śakti of a rāga. Bhairavī is certainly the musical śakti of bhairava, but there are other important devīs among the rāgiṇīs, such as lalitā (the playful one), gaurī (the fair one, or Pārvatī), kedārī (the lady from Mount Kedāra), haraśṛṅgārā (Śiva's eroticism), śrīkaṇṭhī (the beautiful throated), and the like. The Vaiṣṇava Tantrism is also represented with the female forms of śrī (Lakṣmī), such as mālaśrī, dhanāśrī; and śyāmā, the consort of Kṛṣṇa (as Śyāma, the dark one), that is, Rādhā. The dhyāna of bhairavī in the SD still bears some Tantric features:

> Seated in the lovely top of Kailāsa on a stool ornamented with rock crystal and leaves of radiant lotuses, singing the praise of Śiva with the instrument of heavenly hosts in hand, of yellow complexion, and with oval-shaped eyes, is bhairavī, the wife of bhairava, as described by the clever poets. (SD 2.52)

Thus, bhairavī is depicted as a gaurī lady ('yellow complexion', another name for the Devī), sitting atop Mount Kailāsa, Śiva's dwelling place in the Himālaya. Several rāgamālā paintings portray bhairavī worshipping Śiva's liṅga in a shrine (see Ebeling 1973: 33, 35). A very interesting Devī in the form of a rāgiṇī is lalitā, which as a goddess is also called Tripurāsundarī, the beauty of three cities. She represents love and sexuality while Kālī represents death. Somanātha conceives a dhyāna of lalitā in which she is performing pūjā with lamps: 'At dawn lalitā uninterruptedly illuminates Umā's Lord [Śiva] with lamps. She is decorated with various ornaments, clad in white and has a fair complexion' (RV 5.172 in Nijenhuis 1976: 47). In the *Rāgaratnākara* by Deo-kavi (1673-1745), a longer description of lalitā is given, first as a couplet and then as a quatrain:

> Lalita is of delicate frame of golden complexion, she wears ornaments and robes made of gold; coming out of her chamber on a spring morning, she waits, her mind full of the expectation of her lover.
>
> Dressed in yellow, she carries a garland of fresh *campaka* flowers, mingled with blossoms of mango and *aśoka*; she has decked her complexion of gold with ornaments of gold, her voice is mistaken for the song of the cuckoo on spring mornings. The Moon leaving the celestial abode (and assuming the form of her face) has secured a rare ambrosia of her sweet and juicy lips. Lalita is seeking union with her beloved and coming out of her abode is looking out for him. (in Gangoly 1989: 124)

Lalitā here presents Tantric elements in a poetic way. The dhyāna is also based on the dramatic and passionate mistress, a nāyikā. But it is precisely her eroticism, or śṛṅgāra, that secures connection with Lalitā as Śakti. This corresponds to the conception of Devī as a voluptuous young woman, whose emblems are the Śrī yantra (a cosmological diagram formed by nine interlocking triangles); five flowery arrows and the sugar-cane bow, representing the five senses and the mind (as well as the weapons of Kāma); and the three fortified cities (Tripurā) are the fire (Agni), the moon (Soma), and the sun (Ravi). Furthermore, Lalitā as Tripurasundarī is more than a passionate lady, for the three cities stand for a cosmological unity of Śiva, Śakti and nāda (creative sound, or oṁ). This triadic relation, as much as any genuine semiosis, has the generative power described by Hoens as 'the creative union of the primeval parental pair; a pulsating cosmic atom with two nuclei graphically represented by a white and a red dot which automatically produce a third point of gravity. This situation is often represented graphically as a triangle' (in Gupta et al. 1979: 95). The white and red dots (the *bindu* usually marked on the forehead in any Hindu ritual) suggest the sperm and the ovule as the two essential creative elements, which generate a third, in this case, nāda, the subtle sonic energy that pervades the universe and gives its life. In the dhyāna above there is an interesting double meaning in the last line, where *'Cāhati hai* ***dha ni saṅgama*** *ko lalitā gṛhatain cali tāhi vilokai'* can be read either as 'lalitā is seeking union with her beloved', or she seeks the notes D, N, S, G and M. The double reading is meaningful in this context, since the musical notes are icons for nāda, the cosmogonic sound. Rāgiṇī lalitā is also presented in a dramatic situation in which, after a night of love, the day eventually comes, interrupting the lovers. Dāmodara writes in the SD: 'Lalitā is described as a young woman, wearing a crown of seven full-grown leaves, a goddess Śrī in beauty, with brightly shining eyes, whose husband sighs at daybreak at the cruelty of fate' (SD 2.82). In Tantric terms, what is born after the union of Śiva (as Agni) with Śakti (as Soma) is Sūrya, the sun (Hoens in Gupta et al. 1979: 94). Thus, lalitā, her lover and the sun are the triadic elements constituting a cosmogonic unity.

Rāgas and the Six Indian Seasons

The six male rāgas that comprise the head of six families of rāga-rāgiṇīs have a natural relationship with the six seasons of the Indian subcontinent. The reference is based not only on natural events, such as the rāga vasanta for spring and rāga megha (cloud) for the rains, but also grounded in rituals related to the seasons and the agricultural cycle during the year, as well as the appropriate time for each stage of work in the fields. Thus, the myth of five rāgas springing forth from the mouths of Śiva's five heads and the sixth from Pārvatī's may also represent the birth of a new year with its six seasons. In this sense, the birth of six rāgas is similar in some respects to the myth of Skanda, the six-headed son of Śiva and Devī.

Skanda's origin is sometimes narrated as an indirect insemination of Śiva's golden semen, through Agni, into the wives of six sages, the Kṛttikās or Pleiades. Although in the developed form of the myth Skanda is the god who led the war against the demon Tāraka, there is a related, ancient myth, in which the birth of Skanda can be interpreted as the beginning of the new year, and his six heads are representations of the six seasons (see O'Flaherty 1973: 100).

The SD quotes a passage of the *Mānasollāsa*, or *Abhilāṣartha Cintāmaṇi* written by Someśvara (c. 1131) in which the six seasons are clearly related to the six head rāgas (SD 2.29-31; Gangoly 1989: 82; Bhandyopadhyaya 1977: 30-31):

1. Vasanta (and rāgiṇīs): *vasanta* (spring), Caitra and Vaiśākha (March/April/May);

2. Bhairava (and rāgiṇīs): *grīṣma* (summer), Jyaiṣṭha and Āṣāḍha (May/June/July);

3. Megha (and rāgiṇīs): *varṣā* (monsoon), Śrāvaṇa and Bhādrapada (July/Aug./Sep.);

4. Pañcama (and rāgiṇīs): *śārada* (autumn), Āśvina and Kārttika (Sep./Oct./Nov.);

5. Naṭanārāyaṇa (and rāgiṇīs): *hemanta* (cool season), Āgrahāyaṇa and Pauṣa (Nov./Dec./Jan.);

6. Śrī (and rāgiṇīs): *śiśira* (winter), Māgha and Phālguna (Jan./Feb./March).

Some of these associations are explicit and can be connected to popular festivals currently held at the pertinent season in India. Certain kinds of folk songs are performed at those occasions, but there seems to be no evidence of a musical connection or similarity between them and the classical rāgas as performed today. It should be remembered, however, that the relation between folk and classical music is still a largely unexplored field.

Vasanta represents the beginning of the new Hindu year, and its first day is the culmination of Holī, the spring festival. The Holī celebrations actually start during śiśira, on a holiday called Vasanta Pañcamī (the fifth of spring). It lasts the whole month of Phālguna, when the weather warms up, and finally has its apotheosis on the eve (when the Holī fire is lit) and the first day of spring proper. The rāga of spring is represented in the following terms by Dāmodara:

> Vasanta is sportive, with a body dark like the blue lotus, and a tuft of hair bound together with many feathers from the peacock's tail, having made earrings of beautiful mango sprouts, lovely by the bees around him. (SD 2.98)

Vasanta is here identified both with Kṛṣṇa and Kāma; the dark blue is a feature of the former, and the peacock feathers are a clear sign of the god of love. In fact, Holī is the celebration of fertility. Formerly, the spring festival was held in honor of Kāma, in a sort of event wherein caste restrictions were somewhat relaxed (Bashan 1954: 209). There remains some trace of this event in today's Holī, in the form of merrymaking, water battles, throwing of dye powders, and singing of obscene songs – the phaguās – performed by men in the streets or in gatherings (see Henry 1988: 121-33). The connection of summertime with rāga bhairava may have its roots in traditions that have disappeared or changed. Nowadays, there seems to be no outstanding celebration connected with Śiva during the summer. His main festival is the Mahāśivarātri, the great night of Śiva, held in February or March. In Varanasi, Bhairava, the terrible form of Śiva, is celebrated at the beginning of hemanta, the cool season (Eck 1983: 366).

The varṣā season is so quintessentially Indian that its association with rāga megha (and several other rāgas) is taken to be 'natural'. One ancient festival of this season is the Nāga Pañcamī, the serpents' fifth. The connection of snakes with certain rāgas or rāgiṇīs is represented in several miniature paintings of rāgamālās. In the dhyāna of rāga megha, the Indians' expectancy of the rains is expressed by the image of thirsty birds. The rāga is described as a swarthy young man among the dark, rainy clouds:

> Having a body like the blue lotus, with garments like the moon, dressed in yellow,, implored by the thirsty *cātaka* birds (who drink only raindrops), with a smile sweet like nectar, in the midst of clouds, radiated among the heroes, rāga megha, the youth. (SD 2.109)

The main celebration of autumn is the Navarātra, the nine nights of the Devī. This is certainly related to Śiva, since most of the devīs are also his śakti, but at this time it is Durgā who is worshipped (Durgā pūjā or śāradīyā pūjā, i.e., autumnal celebration). The relation of rāga Pañcama to autumn is again unclear. The upaṅga rāga Pañcamaṣaḍava is not related to this season in the SR (2.2.88), nor are the later rāgamālā interpretations, which favor the nāyaka-nāyikā concepts. Similarly, Naṭanārāyaṇa, the dancing Viṣṇu, seems to be unrelated to hemanta in any meaningful respect. But Śrī, or Lakṣmī, the goddess of fortune, and the consort of Viṣṇu, is clearly an agricultural deity:

> Śrī-rāga (lit. meaning Lakṣmī, beauty, riches, the presiding deity of the harvest) may easily be connected with the harvesting season in the winter when the crop is cut, raised, and garnered. In most places in Northern India, the worship of Lakṣmī (Śrī) is timed to synchronize with the collection of the harvest in early winter. Śrī-rāga may, therefore, have been the 'proper melody' associated with the harvest festivals in winter. (Gangoly 1989: 81)

Yet, the worship of Lakṣmī also happens during other seasons. Divālī, a major autumnal festival, is also dedicated to her. Rāgas associated with agricultural rituals, such as preparations for planting, prayers for a good crop, and harvest celebrations, are grounded on the idea that music is above all auspicious (*maṅgala*). In the *Kālikāpurāṇa* there is a detailed prescription for the ritual of bathing and consecrating the new shoot, *nava-patrikā*. This is again connected with the autumnal festival (śāradīyā-pūjā). In the text, bathing the shoot is to be done with eight jars filled with water drawn from eight different sources. But, above all, a rāga and a drum accompaniment are prescribed for each stage. The rāgas mentioned are: (1) mālava, (2) lalita, (3) vibhāsa, (4) bhairava, (5) kedāra, (6) varāḍi, (7) vasanta, and (8) dhannāśrī (see Gangoly 1989: 27-28; Ramalakshmi 1993: 44-46). The multiplicity of festivals in India cannot offer a constant rule by which rāgas may be associated with them. There are regional variations, such as ceremonies which are held at different times of year and at various places in India. If, on one hand, the relation of rāgas with some of the six Indian seasons is not always consistent, on the other, there is also evidence that rāgas were, and still are, related to the yearly cycle.

Nāyaka-nāyikā Bheda Dhyānas

Despite the importance of Tantric and seasonal views of rāgas and rāgiṇīs, treatises from the 16th century onwards construct most of the dhyānas on the nāyaka-nāyikā-bheda, the classification of dramatic and poetic themes in terms of hero-heroine types. This is certainly not a novelty in Sanskrit literature, for the classification is as old as the NŚ at least, and probably originated in the ancient art of traveling minstrels (*bhanakāvi*). There are eight basic heroines, or better, 'charming mistresses' as Srinivasan contends, writing that 'the term "heroine" is inadequate, even misleading' (1985: 7). In the NŚ they are listed as follows:

> In this connection heroines (nāyikā) are known to be of eight kinds such as, 'one dressed up for union' (*vāsakasajjā*), 'one distressed by separation' (*virahotkaṇṭhitā*), 'one having her husband in subjection' (*svādhīnabhartṛkā*), 'one separated [from her lover] by a quarrel' (*kalahāntaritā*), 'one enraged with her lover' (*khaṇḍitā*), 'one deceived by her lover' (*vipralabdhā*), 'one with a sojourning husband' (*proṣitabhartṛka*) and 'one who moves [to her lover]' (*abhisārikā*). (NŚ 24.210-11)

The basic division of the eight types of nāyikās is made according to the two varieties of śṛṅgāra rasa, sambhoga and vipralambha. Therefore:

Table 16

Nāyikās

Sambhoga:	
Abhisārikā	the nāyikā who is adventurous in love
Vāsakasajjā	the nāyikā who is adorned to meet her lover
Svādhīnabhartṛkā	'happy, proud wife', or the nāyikā who holds her lover in subjection
Vipralambha:	
Proṣitabhartṛka	the nāyikā whose lover is away on travel
Vipralabdhā	the nāyikā who is deceived, her lover failing the appointment with her
Virahotkaṇṭhitā	the nāyikā who is distressed in solitude
Kalahāntaritā	the nāyikā who is separated by a quarrel with her lover
Khaṇḍitā	the nāyikā who is reproving her lover, who has another woman

Later authors further divided the themes into sub-species with more specific dramatic ideas. The proṣitabhartṛka, for instance, can be a *pravatsyat-patikā*, 'a mistress whose lover is about to leave on a journey;' or a *vigalita-prasthāna-patikā*, a lady whose 'man cancels his trip on seeing her anguish'. The vāsakasajjā can be an *avasita-pravasa-patikā*, the 'girl whose lover is returning from abroad', and so she prepares herself carefully to receive him (Srinivasan 1985: 10). In the *Śṛṅgāra Prakaśā*, Bhoja classifies minutely the nāyakas and nāyikās and relates them to his theory of rasa (see Table 9 in 3.2). By the time of rāgamālā treatises, the nāyaka-nāyikā bheda had grown enormously in the number of subvarieties and in the particularity of themes.

The dhyānas of nāyaka-nāyikā types are not static images of standard characters, but rather dynamic representations of gallant love, as devised by Indian dramatists. The personified rāgas and rāgiṇīs are placed in a situation, so as to act out a role in which at least one more character is implied. However, the male and female types do not correspond to each other unequivocally.

I will analyze only the eight classical nāyikās and nāyakas in relation to some rāgas and rāgiṇīs. An author who has himself classified the rāga dhyānas in terms of dramatic types was Somanātha, in the RV. Although Somanātha is usually considered a Karnatic music scholar, it is clear that many of the rāgas and rāgiṇīs he discusses are closer to the Hindustani tradition than the Southern one. Somanātha, who worked in the Andhra region, can be included among the scholars who described the usage of rāgas in different areas. He was in part influenced by the work of Puṇḍarīka Viṭṭhāla (see Nijenhuis 1976: 3), who was also combining South and North Indian traditions. The pitch sets of the examples below come from the RV, and I compare the dhyānas from this treatise with those similarly found in the SD.

Two rāgiṇīs are marked out as the daring nāyikā, or abhisārikā nāyikā, the mistress who takes the lead and goes to meet her lover: bahulī and saurāṣṭrī. Somanātha writes:

> Saurāṣṭrī is wearing clothes of various colours and has a very fair complexion. Her busts are covered with a dark-blue bodice. She has red teeth, a face like the moon, and being afflicted by love's passion, she goes [to see her lover]. (RV 5.192 in Nijenhuis 1976: 75)

The dhyāna offered by Dāmodara is similar to the one above:

> With a pearl necklace enhancing her beauty, and with a full and heavy bosom, her attention turned to the sound of the bees, humming round the lotus behind the ear, she goes to meet her lover, her arms hanging down listlessly, she, the girl from Saurāṣṭra (Kathiawar), beautiful like the embodiment of the God of love. (SD 2.128)

Rāgiṇī saurāṣṭrī is described by Somanātha as heptatonic, with S as aṁśa, graha, and nyāsa, and it should be performed at the evening (Ex. 29). According to Dāmodara, the rāgiṇī is hexatonic, lacking R, and has P performing all functions, but he acknowledges the former features (SD 2.127). It belongs to the family of megha, in Someśvara's classification.

Example 29

Rāgiṇī saurāṣṭrī (RV 4.41)

The nāyikā prepared or preparing herself to receive her lover, the vāsakasajjikā nāyikā , is represented musically by bhūpālī and toḍī in the RV. The dhyāna reads:

> Bhūpālī, staying in a groove and moving hither and thither like a swing, while her bracelets are shaking, is adorning herself. She is much attached to her lover. Being overwhelmed by love she is pale like saffron. (RV 5.171 in Nijenhuis 1976: 20)

Yet, the same bhūpālī in the SD represents another dramatic situation, the girl suffering in vipralambha. Thus, it should be noted that, as much as the musical features of rāgas and rāgiṇīs vary from one author to another, in respect to period and region, the significations do not always correspond to each other. At any rate, it is not difficult to classify Dāmodara's bhūpālī as the nāyikā whose husband is traveling.

> Bhūpālī, belonging to the quiescent mood, a woman in the splendour of beauty, lovely, with a face beautiful like the moon, and a full bosom, her

> body anointed with saffron, pained by the separation, remembers her husband. (SD 2.115)

Scholars have quite different opinions as to the musical properties of this rāga, which may justify the differences in meaning. Somanātha states that bhūpālī is a pentatonic rāgiṇī, and that G has the main modal functions (Ex. 30). According to Dāmodara, bhūpālī is located in the family of megha, with S operating as aṁśa, graha and nyāsa, and it is heptatonic. In the case of a pentatonic version, R and P should be omitted instead (SD 2.114). This is a rather ancient conception of this rāgiṇī. Somanātha's view comes very close to the contemporary Hindustani bhūp.

Example 30

Rāgiṇī bhūpālī (RV 4.36)

Several rāgiṇīs represent the svādhīnabhartṛkā nāyikā, the secure lady who has her lover under her spell: mālāśrī, trāvaṇikā, rāmakṛti, jaitāśrī, and pūrvī. Mālāśrī is present in both RV and SD.

> Slender Mālāśrī is walking under a mango tree, singing a melodious song and smiling to her own husband. She is brilliant, has eyes like a dear, is holding a lotus flower in her hand and is wearing a garland. (RV 5.210 in Nijenhuis 1976: 49)

> Having taken a red lotus flower in her hand[,] showing her body, slender like a liana, reclining at the foot of a mango tree, smiling a little, that is mālāvaśrī. (SD 2.102)

According to Nijenhuis, the flower in nāyikās' hand is a symbol (actually an iconic legisign, in Peircean terms) of the fixed relationship with her lover (1976: 49). Dāmodara mentions explicitly the rasa śṛṅgāra, and places the rāgiṇī as a wife of rāga śrī. Mālāśrī or mālāvaśrī is, according to Somanātha (Ex. 31), a heptatonic rāgiṇī whose R and D svaras are to be played scarcely (*alpatva*). Predominant, initial and final functions are all carried out by the first degree S, which can be performed at any time.

Example 31

Rāgiṇī mālāśrī or mālāvaśrī (RV 4.30)

The most common dramatic situation for vipralambha is when the nāyaka is traveling for business or military reasons, and the nāyikā suffers because of the separation. This is the proṣitabhartṛka nāyikā, and Somanātha indicates dhanaśrī and kāmodī in this category.

> With a complexion like *dūrvā* grass, incapable of enduring the separation, dhanāśrī is drawing a picture of her husband, her breasts being wetted by her weeping. She has white cheeks and fixed, braided hair. (RV 5.177 in Nijenhuis 1976: 30)

The dhyāna mentioned by Dāmodara represents precisely the same rasa:

> Dhanāśrī, whose bosom is washed by streams of tears, with a tear still on her white cheeks, pained by separation, with a complexion dark like a blade of dūrvā grass, charming, is busy painting the portrait of her lover. (SD 2.104)

Somanātha classifies dhanāśrī as being in the same mela as mālāśrī. Dāmodara accordingly places this rāgiṇī as a wife of śrī. Both authors refer to this as a hexatonic rāgiṇī, for the R should be omitted. Again, S has all the important modal functions (Ex. 32). It should be performed in the morning.

Example 32
Rāgiṇī dhanāśrī (RV 4.31)

In the RV, rāgiṇīs varāṭī and velāvalī represent the vipralabdhā nāyikā, the deceived lady whose lover has failed to honor the meeting, because he was spending time with another woman. Somanātha sets the nāyikā as hopelessly seeking her lover in a wood where they were supposed to meet:

> Varāṭī is a young lady of fair complexion, who is piteously searching for her lord in the wood. She wears dark blue clothes and her beauty is enhanced by flowers of the 'tree of the gods' [*mandara*]. (RV 5.187 in Nijenhuis 1976: 84)

Dāmodara, however, presents varāṭī as the irritated nāyikā (a predictable aftermath of the above situation!), which must be classified as a different type, the khaṇḍitā. She rejects her lover with a *caṁvarī*, the fly whisk.

> A beautiful woman, with lovely locks, beautiful bracelets in a flower of the *sūra* tree in her ear, pushing back her lover with a movement of her *chowree*, such is described varāṭī. (SD 2.55)

Somanātha describes varāṭī as a heptatonic rāgiṇī, in which the main modal functions center on S (Ex. 33). It is to be performed by midday.

Example 33

Rāgiṇī varāṭī (RV 3.46)

The mistress unable to bear separation from her lover, the virahotkaṇṭhika nāyikā, is represented by several rāgiṇīs in the RV: mukharī, pauravi and turuṣkatoḍī. None of them is mentioned in the SD. Turuṣkatoḍī, an ancient variety of toḍī, is a deśīrāga that came originally from Turkestan or Turuṣkadeśa (Gangoly 1989: 22 n.), depicted in the RV as a Moghul woman, by her clothes and physique:

> Wearing a long, dark-blue outer garment, a rosary in her hands, turuṣkatoḍī, whispers the name of her husband, distressed by the separation. She is tall, has a fair complexion and wears her hair in long plaits. (RV 5.181 in Nijenhuis 1976: 82)

This rāga was probably obsolete at the time of Somanātha, for his descriptions are imprecise. He counts this rāga among the Persian modes (Nijenhuis 1976: 81). Turuṣkatoḍī does not relate in meaning to rāgiṇī toḍī. An example of the virahotkaṇṭhika nāyikā in the SD is the rāgiṇī paṭamanjarī, in a dramatic scene where the *sakhī*, the mistress's confidant, gives comfort to the nāyikā:

> A fair woman, separated from her beloved, her body tormented by love, withered, wearing a garland on her beautiful body, her limbs gray like dust, but being comforted by her beloved girlfriend – that is paṭamanjarī. (SD 2.80)

According to Dāmodara, paṭamanjarī is heptatonic and has P for aṁśa, graha and nyāsa (Ex. 34).

Example 34

Rāgiṇī paṭamanjarī (SD 2.79)

Rāgiṇī saindhavī is depicted in the RV as the kalahāntaritā nāyikā, the mistress who has separated from her lover because of a quarrel.

> Saindhavī, who is very slender but developed in her hips, wears red cloths. Her symbol is the trident. She has a fair complexion and an elephantine (i.e. stately) gait. She is very angry because of a fight with her lover. (RV 5.215 in Nijenhuis 1976: 70)

There are some Tantric traces in this dhyāna, which are very clear in Dāmodara's version:

> With a trident in hand, glowing with devotion for Śiva, dressed in red, carrying a *bandhujīva* flower, in fiery anger, inspired by the heroic sentiment, is saindhavī, the rāgiṇī of bhairava. (SD 2.58)

The trident and the fierceness relate clearly to Bhairava. This seems to be a case where an originally Tantric dhyāna was transformed into a form of nāyaka-nāyikā bheda. Dāmodara's dhyāna, therefore, comes from an older source than Somanātha's, although the RV precedes the Saṅgitadarpaṇa by about 16 years. The rasa mentioned in the SD was vīra, but Somanātha transformed the heroic anger into a form of vipralambha śṛṅgāra marked by peevishness. He describes the musical features of this rāgiṇī as belonging to the śuddhasvara mela, that is, a mode with all natural degrees. This, in his time, corresponds to the scale of ṣaḍjagrāma. S is aṁśa as well as the other functions. Saindhavī is pentatonic, omitting G and D (Ex. 35).

Example 35

Rāgiṇī saindhavī (RV 4.33)

Somanātha designates no rāgiṇī for the role of khaṇḍitā, the admonishing mistress. It would be interesting to find an instance of that. But here, I have to distinguish clearly a dhyāna according to the refined differences which characterize the nāyaka-nāyikā classification. Both kalahāntaritā and khaṇḍitā are enraged at their lovers. The khaṇḍitā, however, has her lover close by, and rejects him for his fault. That is the case with Dāmodara's varāṭī, and also rāmakarī, according to the following dhyāna:

> Golden in hue and with shining jewels, arrayed in a garment of blue – though besought by her prostrated lover, obdurate she remains. Such is said to be Rāmakarī. (in Ebeling 1973: 122).

The dhyāna is illustrated with a miniature painting from a rāgamālā in Gujarat style, ca. 1575 (Ebeling 1973: 53). Somanātha's conception of this rāgiṇī, spelled as rāmakṛtī, hardly conveys the idea of khaṇḍitā nāyikā:

> Rāmakṛtī, who has a golden complexion, extremely glittering ornaments, bluish-black clothes, is very charming and has beautiful teeth. She speaks delicately, while her beloved is in her neighborhood. (RV 5.213 in Nijenhuis 1976: 17)

This is clearly a case of sambhoga śṛṅgāra, and the nāyikā is the svādhīnabhartṛkā, the happy mistress. However, Dāmodara gives an intriguing dhyāna for Rāmakarī:

> Rāmakarī is to be imagined as being in high spirits, as the beloved is near, with a charming voice, shining like gold, with brilliant ornaments, but wearing a dark veil over her beauty. (SD 2.76)

Although the lady is apparently happy about her nearby lover, she wears a dark veil, which seems to indicate the nāyikā as being in a capricious mood. In fact, Dāmodara mentions the rasa karuṇa in connection with this rāgiṇī (SD 2.75). Therefore, Rāmakarī may represent a subtle case of khaṇḍitā nāyikā, classified as *dhīrādhīrā* – a jealous woman who alternately expresses and suppresses her jealousy.

The description of the musical features of rāmakarī varies among the authors of this period. Dāmodara states it can be either pentatonic, hexatonic or heptatonic. He agrees with Somanātha as to aṁśa and the other functions, which are exerted by S (Ex. 36). The rāmakarī can be performed at any time.

Example 36

Rāgiṇī rāmakṛtī (RV 4.20)

The nāyakas are only four in the NŚ: 'the self-controlled and vehement (*dhīroddhata*), the self-controlled and light-hearted (*dhīralalita*), the self-controlled and exalted (*dhīrodātta*) and self-controlled and calm (*dhīrapraśānta*)' (NŚ 34.18-19). These are related to the three kinds of vīra, namely: dānavīra (munificence), dharmavīra (following the right at all costs), and yuddhavīra (martial heroism) (NŚ 6.79). Later dramatists added to those the *śṛṅgāranāyakas*, which correspond to the situations represented by the nāyikās, as described above, in four types: *anukūla*, the kind husband or lover; *dakṣiṇa*, the clever, dexterous lover; *dhṛṣṭa*, the daring, audacious lover; and *śaṭha*, the wicked lover (*Sahityadarpaṇa* 3.35 in Shukla 1994: 1.218). Therefore, there are basically two groups of nāyakas, one concerned with vīra and related rasas, and another related to śṛṅgāra. One could add an extra hero to the first group, the *dhīrośṇin* or battle hero, which represents the yuddhavīra rasa. The nine nāyakas are displayed in the following table.[29]

[29] This is not an exhaustive classification, however.

Table 17
Nāyakas

Vīra:	
dhīrodātta	brave and noble-minded
dhīroddhata	brave but haughty
dhīrośṇin	brave and fiery
dhīraśānta	brave and calm
dhīralalita	brave, but reckless and sportive
Śṛṅgāra:	
anukūla	the kind husband or lover
dakṣiṇa	the clever, dexterous lover
dhṛṣṭa	the audacious lover
śaṭha	the wicked lover

The nāyakas are not represented in music as neatly as are the nāyikās. A simple reason for this is the obvious fact that in the rāga-rāgiṇī systems, such as those mentioned by Dāmodara, there are only six male rāgas and a number of 30 or 36 rāgiṇīs. Yet, other systems include the sons, or putrās, and therefore, the number of rāgas is even bigger than the rāgiṇīs. Another fact that dismisses any kinds of perfect correspondence between the character types and the musical structures is a certain inconsistency in the dhyānas, whether they are male or female. Dāmodara sometimes gives a male dhyāna where a female one was supposed to be; for instance, the rāga deśa as a wife of hiṇḍola (SD 2.78). In treatises not organized by rāga-rāgiṇī families, such as Somanātha's RV, occasionally a female and male form of a similar name appear, not always with clearly distinct musical features.

The dhīrodātta, brave and noble-minded hero, can be represented by the rāga kalyāṇa. This is a royal character, described in battle, or at his palace chewing betel leaves:

> Kalyāṇa, who is being protected by parasol and fly whisk, has a complexion white as crystal and is chewing betel leaf. He is wearing a crown and a string of pearls, is dressed in white like a king and seated on a royal throne. (RV 5.200 in Nijenhuis 1976: 39)

> Kalyāṇanāṭa is described by the wisest of the wise as being of red colour, clad in gold, with a mark in his forehead, smiling, and strong, engaged in a battle with sword in hand. (SD 2.121)

Somanātha's kalyāṇa is a heptatonic rāga of the bitonal type: the aṁśa is the minor third, G; and the nyāsa is S (Ex. 37). The rāga is to be performed in the afternoon (or evening, according to other authors).

Example 37
Rāga kalyāṇa (RV 4.33)

There is no clear dhīroddhata, the brave but arrogant and disdainful hero, among Somanātha's or Dāmodāra's rāgas. The chāyānāṭa dhyāna below could possibly represent such a character, but it also fits as a yuddhavīra nāyaka.

> Varṇanāta, who is also named chāyānāṭa, has a fair complexion and red eyes. He is wearing a necklace, a garment white as snow and a transparent pale red turban. He is a passionate warrior. (RV 5.206 in Nijenhuis 1976: 23)

Chāyānāṭā is, according to Somanātha, a heptatonic rāga, in which S actualizes the main modal functions (Ex. 38). It has to be performed at evening.

Example 38
Rāga chāyānāṭā (RV 4.44)

The dhīrośṇin nāyaka, the brave and fiery hero, is embedded in yuddhavīra, martial heroism. Rāga nāṭa is a representation of this type. Somanātha and Dāmodara agree in all essential ideas about this dhyāna:

> Nāṭa is described as having the appearance of the *muṇi* Śṛṅga, going round the battlefield, vexed, his body red with blood, shining like gold, his arms hanging round the shoulder of a horse. SD 2.94

> Nāṭa, who is holding shield and sword, terrifies his enemies in a fight. He has red eyes, a yellow complexion, is wearing a necklace, rides a horse and is courageous in battle. (RV 5.198 in Nijenhuis 1976: 60)

The rāga musical features according to Somanātha are notated in Ex. 39. This type of scale, with an augmented second and sixth, was retained in contemporary Karnatic music, but not in the North. The central note is S, and the rāga is prescribed for the evening.

Example 39

Rāga nāṭa (RV 4.45)

There seems to be no better rāga than śrī to represent the dhīrapraśānta nāyaka, the self-controlled and calm hero. Śrī personifies temporal power, such as that of a lord or a rāja. In several rāga-rāgiṇī systems, śrī is one of the head rāgas, related to five or six wives. Moreover, in the myth of Śiva and Pārvatī conceiving the six main rāgas, śrī is the first mentioned, despite the fact that many authors assign the first rāga position to bhairava.

> Siting under a golden parasol, the fine cloth of which is moving, śrīrāga is riding on an elephant. He is splendid, has all enjoyments, and wears a garland of lotus flowers on his head. (RV 5.201 in Nijenhuis 1976: 77)

Dāmodara's dhyāna for śrī depicts a lad of rather high position, instead of a patriarchal ruler; nevertheless, he is compared to a king. Remarkably, this rāga is described as being a proficient musician, of whom the svaras, or notes, are servants.

> Having the appearance of one beloved by the god of love, eighteen years old, with ever fresh young leaves stuck behind the ears, dressed in ruddy clothes, to whom ṣaḍja and the other notes are servants, looking like a king. [...] That is rāga śrī. (SD 2.96)

In the RV, śrī is a bitonal rāga, with the functions of aṁśa and nyāsa attributed to different svaras: R to the former, and S to the latter (Ex. 40). Śrī is to be performed at evenings.

Example 40

Rāga śrī (RV 4.30)

The self-controlled and light-hearted hero, or dhīralalita, could be represented by hammīrā, a new rāga in this period, mentioned for the first time by Puṇḍarīka Viṭṭhāla and Somanātha. The dhyāna portraying hammīrā gives clear signs of his sportiveness, such as curiosity, the ball and stick, and his fondness for betel.

> Hammīrā is a young man of taste. He is smiling, and showing curiosity. He is clad in red and carries ball and stick. He is a beautiful and fair hero, fond of betel leaves. (RV 5.204 in Nijenhuis 1976: 35)

Somanātha describes rāga hammīrā's musical features as a heptatonic scale with P as modal center (Ex. 41). It should be performed in the evening.

Example 41
Rāga hammīrā (RV 4.25)

The first śṛṅgāranāyaka is anukūla, the kind lover or husband. This is certainly a dramatic situation of sambhoga. Rāga mālava, representing a king in love, is the personification of the anukūla nāyaka.

> His mouth being kissed by his beloved, while his crown is moving, mālava, who is wearing ear-rings and has the colour of a parrot, enters the dancing hall. He is wearing a garland and is deeply in love. (RV 5.202 in Nijenhuis 1976: 51)

> The rāga mālavī [sic], of pure beauty, wearing a garland, and earrings, deeply in love, enters the meeting place at night fall, (where) his face (is) kissed by a lovely woman. (SD 2.100)

This is also an instance of unclear gender in the SD. Dāmodara classifies mālavī as a rāgiṇī of śrī, but the dhyāna in question instead suggests the male mālava. In fact, there should be a correspondence among the situations characterized by the nāyaka-nāyikā bheda. Some of the nāyakas are indeed related to some of the nāyikās, but there is no strict causal relation between the two groups. In general terms, the anukūla nāyaka corresponds to the svādhīnabhartṛkā nāyikā.

Rāga mālava is described by Somanātha as a bitonal structure; N is aṁśa and S is nyāsa (Ex. 42). The svaras G and D can be dropped. Mālava's performing time is the evening.

Example 42
Rāga mālava (RV 4.15)

The dakṣiṇa nāyaka, the able or dexterous hero, is the *polyamorous* character who knows how to conduct a love affair without hurting the feelings of the involved ladies. He is, therefore, 'the impartial man, who is kind while loving another woman' (Nihenjuis 1976: 37). Rāga hiṇḍola is the musical structure pointed out by Somanātha as representing the dakṣiṇa nāyaka.

> Wearing a garland of red, yellow and pink lotus flowers, hiṇḍola is decorated and has a fair complexion. He is swinging on a swing pushed by his girlfriends. (RV 5.174 in Nijenhuis 1976: 37)

> Hiṇḍola – thus say the wise – accompanied by the god of love whose beauty is enhanced by small doves, enjoys the pleasure of the play on a swing, which is brought into soft motion by a beautiful woman. (SD 2.72)

Hiṇḍola, which Dāmodara classifies as the head of a rāga-rāgiṇī group, is a rāga connected to the spring and the Indian swing festivals. The beautiful women surrounding hiṇḍola make evident his succeśs as an ingenious lover.

Example 43
Rāga hiṇḍola (RV 4.14)

The dhṛṣṭa nāyaka, the audacious lover, could be represented by rāga aḍḍāṇa:

> Aḍḍāṇa, who is beautiful with a garland of *kuṭaja* flowers, whose emblem is the delphin (*makara*), who has a dark complexion, enjoys the battle of love, which uses *ketakī* flowers as arrows. (RV 5.205 in Nijenhuis 1976: 13)

In this dhyāna, aḍḍāṇa incarnates Kāma, who is certainly a daring deity, not hesitating to draw back his bow and to shoot his own father, Brahmā, and other gods with his flowery arrows. The makara, a sea monster that could be a shark, dolphin or crocodile, is also a sign of intrepid attitude. Aḍḍāṇa is a heptatonic bitonal rāga, according to Somanātha. The aṁśa is rendered by D and nyāsa by S (Ex. 44). This rāga should be performed at night.

Example 44
Rāga aḍḍāṇa (RV 4.42)

Finally, the śaṭha nāyaka is the dishonest husband or lover, who pretends affection for one lady while his heart is fixed on another. Lalita represents such a character, whose wife is the khaṇḍitā nāyikā:

> Lalita is a dishonest, charming young man, who is returning in the morning. Concealing the signs of his dalliance with another [lady] he

pretends to be very decent and cunningly speaks sweet words to his depressed wife. (RV 5.175 in Nijenhuis 1976: 46)

Somanātha distinguishes the rāga lalita from lalitā, which has a Tantric dhyāna and different musical features. Lalita is also a bitonal rāga; the aṁśa is D and nyāsa S (Ex. 45). It can be performed at any time.

Example 45

Rāga lalita (RV 4.28)

All these interpretations of rāgas and rāgiṇīs in terms of Tantric, seasonal or theatrical conceptions are easily understood as mythological, religious or cultural symbols of India, and it is not surprising that music, literature and painting come into agreement and support each other in their representations. Still, it is possible to reach further conclusions, as P.L. Sharma does, by virtue of her triple authority as Indian native, musician and scholar:

> The significance of this tradition can be definitely associated with the spiritual basis of musical culture in India. Tantra is the technique of spiritual culture and the musical system based on spiritual cultures or forming part of the same could logically transfer to itself the system of dhyāna-s of Devī-s and Deva-s. Naturally, this tradition could originate and evolve only in rāga-s independent of drama. In a period of decadence of this tradition, another stream of visual contemplation appeared[,] viz. the system of rāga-dhyāna based on nāyaka-bheda. This system could be reasonably justified by the fact that the detachment of music from drama did leave a vacuum[;] as the background of dramatic representation was lacking, a visual rāga-dhyāna-s filled up the void by supplying a visual correlate for aesthetic contemplation, mainly on the part of the musician and to some extent on the part of the listener. Both modern physics and our traditional metaphysics of sound uphold that the objects of visual and auditory perception are not basically different, but are mutually convertible. It is common experience that hearing and seeing are not only mutually supplementary or complementary, but also capable of replacing each other to a considerable extent. The tradition of rāga-dhyāna was, therefore, nothing far-fetched or fantastic; it was a realistic approach to artistic imagery. (Sharma 1970: 61)

3.3.5 Rāga and Rasa in Contemporary Music

Besides the oral traditions, of which there are no records, rāga dhyānas and rāgamālā miniatures seem to have been the primary means for transmitting the aesthetical features of rāgas and rāgiṇīs from the 15th to the 19th century. Hindi and Persian translations of those poems multiplied and to some extent popularized knowledge that had previously been confined to the Sanskrit scholarly milieu. Even so, the diffusion was limited. Just as the hand-copied treatises, the Hindi dhyāna books and rāgamālās were commissioned by aristocrats and rich persons in India. The vernacular version of the *Saṅgītadarpaṇa*, translated by Harivallabha (c. 1625-1643), exists in four manuscripts; one of them, 'a magnificent *editio princeps*' dated 1798 A.D., was written to the order of Babu Meghrāj, from Murshidabad. In that text, 'the poet does not slavishly follow the original Sanskrit verses, but gives an amplified and original version of the "picture" of each rāga' (Gangoly 1989: 121). Although few could afford to own Hindi translations of a Sanskrit saṅgītaśāstra or a rāgamālā miniature album, it is probable that, in the 18th and 19th centuries, rāga dhyānas were widely known via oral transmission among musicians and listeners in North India.

The first treatise leading to modern Hindustani music theory was the *Saṅgītapārijāta*, written by Ahobala-paṇḍita in the 17th century, and translated into Persian in 1724. A remarkable feature of this work is that, although the pitch sets are based on the 22 śrutis, and Ahobala specifies no less than 29 *svarasthānas* (pitch positions), it is clear from his descriptions of rāgas, in terms of string length, that only 12 pitches were used in practice (see Bhātkhaṇḍe 1990: 33). Another fundamental change in the rāga system was the simplification of modal functions, such as aṁśa and nyāsa, now subsumed by the system tonic S (Bhātkhaṇḍe 1990: 36). Ahobala classifies the rāgas in a system of six melas. This treatise seems to have been quite influential, for later authors quoted or based new works on it (Nihenhuis 1977: 28-29). That is the case with two other 17th-century works, the *Rāgatattvavibodha* by Śrīnivāsa, and the *Hṛdayaprakaśa*, written by Hṛdayanarāyana in Jabalpūr (central India).

The *Saṅgītsār* – commissioned by the Mahārāja of Jaipur, Pratāp Singh (ruled between 1779-1804), Rajasthan – is a rāga-rāgiṇī treatise, which uses the classification system of Hanumān. New rāgas were included as putrās, with a total of eight for each main rāga. In the early 19th century, a work in Persian introduced what is now considered the natural pitch set in Hindustani music. This is the *Naghmāt-i-āsafi*, written by Muḥammad Reza in 1813 (Patna). The basic scale corresponds to rāga bilāval, which has all the śuddha svaras. In the late 19th century the *Saṅgītasārasaṅgraha* and a number of short works were written by Rāja S.M. Tagore, all of which show clearly the influence of rāga dhyānas. Some of these books, written in English, contain rāgas and songs transcribed into Western staff notation (see Tagore 1990a [1877] and 1990b [1892]).

In the early 20th century a number of music treatises were published in North India. Representing the traditional scholarly view, and linking Hindustani music with past treatises, the *Rāgakalpadruma* was written in Hindi by Kṛṣṇānanda Vyāsa (alias Appa Tulasī), was initially printed by lithograph, from 1842 to 1849, for subscribing patrons, and eventually saw publication in 1914-6. This work is a huge compilation of compositions, along with a description of 120 rāgas. It, too, was influenced by rāga dhyānas, which are quoted from the SD (P.L. Sharma 1969: 110). Also in this period came the first works written in Sanskrit by V.N. Bhātkhaṇḍe (1860-1936), a scholar who is nowadays passionately defended by his followers and criticized by his detractors, with both sides showing equal enthusiasm. Bhātkhaṇḍe was one of the organizers of the first All-India Music Conference in Baroda (1916). His contribution was to recognize the incommensurability of the contemporary music system with those of authors who wrote during the first and early second millennium. He developed the system of ten ṭhāṭs, into which rāgas were classified. Bhātkhaṇḍe's two main works are the *Saṅgītaśāstra* (1956-7) and the *Hindustānī Saṅgīt-Paddhati Kramik Pustak Mālikā* (1923 [KPM]). The latter, designed as a series of six textbooks for a seven-year course in classical music, is widely used in music colleges in North India.

Omkarnāth Ṭhākur (1897-1967), a renowned singer and scholar, believed that the great variety of Hindustani rāgas could not be dealt with in reductive classification systems. His *Saṅgītañjalī* (1938-62 [SA]) describes rāgas both individually and in their relationships to other rāgas. Ṭhākur gives great attention to the rāga's particular qualities and to the rasas they represent. The *Saṅgītañjalī* is the main source for the semiotic analysis of rāgas in this chapter.

Rāgas and Rasas according to Contemporary Scholars

In the 20th century there has been a clear disintegration of the rāga dhyāna representational universe. The work of Bhātkhaṇḍe, for instance, contains no systematic reference to the objects that rāgas represent. For many contemporary musicians, rāgas no longer represent a single rasa, but are thought to be capable of evoking a group of rasas, as a kind of aesthetic range (see several rāga descriptions in Khan and Ruckert 1991). Such references may be considered as inconsistent, for conflicting rasas are often mentioned in association with the same rāga. A few rāgas are more strongly connected with a particular rasa, as is the case with the seasonal rāgas such as vasant and malhār. A great number of rāgas are related by the musicians to śānta or bhakti, as an expression of their religious beliefs, but this has little to do with classical aesthetics.

According to P.L. Sharma, there are three points to be considered with regard to rasa in contemporary music. First, classical music in North India is completely independent of drama. In this sense, the ancient references found in the NŚ, BD and SR, which relate musical structures to conventional situations in a play, are as far from contemporary music significations as is the music of that period. Second, the tradition of rāga dhyānas is 'completely lost and if some stray remnants are rarely found here and there, they are most arbitrary and there is no established norm for the guidance of the musician and the listener.' Finally, she remarks the inefficacy of lyrics in vocal music: 'the verbal element in music, which is the only means for suggesting a situation of life for aesthetic contemplation, is either very brief and hence ineffective, or unrelated to the aesthetic potentiality of the particular rāga, or it is totally absent as, for example, in instrumental music' (Sharma 1970: 61-62).

There is not much to add to Sharma's first point. Although Indian music is usually viewed as an uninterrupted musical tradition, its roots run back to a past that is distant from nowadays in both time and practice. As for the rāga dhyānas, they never constituted a unified system, even in their most highly developed forms. Comparison of the several systems shows that often the same rāgas are described in dhyānas that exhibit different features and aesthetical qualities. Rāga dhyānas were, however, a powerful and efficient means for preserving and divulging the musical qualities of rāgas; and they were probably transmitted orally from musician to musician, if only in outline form. Still, as Sharma notes, what survived of that tradition cannot serve as a representation system in contemporary music. Finally, in relation to vocal music, it seems to me that lyrics have long been and remain an effective way of extending and making explicit the aesthetic significations in Indian music, even if only very short phrases or single words are used. This much becomes clear if one pays close attention to how the best dhrupad, khayāl or ṭhumrī singers expressively use a word or short sentence in their bolbāṅṭ and bolbanānā, so as to emphasize and develop the aesthetic and musical expression of a rāga. But once again, Sharma is keen to point out that sometimes the text is, in principle, unrelated to the general aesthetic core of the rāga. In reference to the absence of lyrics in instrumental music, there are cases in which musicians play a well-known tune, which conveys the same scope of meanings – as if it had words – to listeners who recall the original lyrics.

Further, Sharma deals with the nine classical rasas and the pertinence of their qualities in contemporary music. She argues that hāsya, raudra, bhayānaka, and bībhatsa cannot be represented musically beyond the dramatic context. 'Adbhuta can be identified with all levels of virtuosity' (Sharma 1970: 62-63). In fact, both hāsya and bībhatsa are already bereft of rāga dhyānas. Raudra can be related to the yuddhavīra nāyaka, and bhayānaka can be represented by rāgas related to the vipralabdhā nāyikā, the lady wandering alone in a dark forest, as suggested by the dhyāna of kamodī (SD 2.92). However, in the case of contemporary music, these rasas are not represented as often as the others are. It seems that, as early as the 17th century, musicians and composers were already not interested in some rasas, since they are scarcely found in the music of that time. But I do not think that music itself lacks the means to represent the nine or more rasas. When Sharma relates adbhuta to musical virtuosity, however, she is not taking the concept of rasa in the strict sense. For adbhuta, as a rasa, is a generic aesthetic experience, which exists apart from the mere surprise or admiration aroused by the technical abilities of a performer.

Thus, according to P.L. Sharma, there are only four significant rasas in contemporary Hindustani music: śṛṅgāra, karuṇa, vīra, and śānta. This view is supported by a number of authors and musicians. Sharma, then, seeks to reduce the effective remaining rasas to the concept of *guṇas*, as three emotional qualities.[30]

> For the remaining four[,] viz. śānta, śṛṅgāra, karuṇa and vīra, the concept of three guṇa-s is very apt for their description. *Druti* (melting) and *dīpti* (incitement) of the citta [mind] are two basic categories in which the variety of the aesthetic effect of any art can be broadly condensed. Druti is associated with *mādhurya* guṇa and it is brought about by śānta, śṛṅgāra and karuṇa rasa-s[;] and dīpti is associated with *ojas* guṇa and goes well with vīra rasa. These two broad categories can logically encompass the aesthetic effects of all rāga-s. The third guṇa[,] viz. *prasāda* implies the direct, straight or absorbing appeal of a rāga, which can be equally compatible with mādhurya or ojas. In my humble opinion, the vagueness and abstract nature of musical representation can very well be covered logically by these three terms. The fact that the names of rasa-s are very loosely used in the context of present day music, lends support to this opinion. (Sharma 1970: 63)

The concepts of mādhurya (sweetness), ojas (vigorous, emphatic expression) and prasāda (brightness, clearness of style) are related to the rasas in Ānandavardhana's *Dhvanyāloka*. Śṛṅgāra in both its forms, as well as karuṇa, is qualified as possessing mādhurya; and raudra and other related rasas contain ojas (DL 2.7-10). However, if for Ānandhavardhana the guṇas are properties of the rasas, for Abhinavagupta they are merely qualities of the words in a poem (see Masson & Patwardhan 1969: 71 and notes). In both cases, it seems to me reductive to subsume the rasas to these three guṇas. As a pair, mādhurya and ojas could describe some

---

30 Ṭhākur J. Singh also proposed a similar view; see Singh 1970: 28.

characteristic of rāgas, but these concepts are so vague that they cannot distinguish more specific qualities of feeling, such as the fundamental difference between sambhoga and vipralambha rasas, both loosely related to mādhurya. Finally, these three guṇas do not seem to be a consistent set of categories, for prasāda does not relate on the same conceptual level with mādhurya and ojas. This is clear in the way Sharma rationalizes prasāda, as the 'straight or absorbing appeal of a rāga' that indiscriminately refers to the other two guṇas. Further, to replace the rasas with the guṇas would deprive Indian music of a great variety of significations, finely illustrated by the nāyaka-nāyikā bheda, and perhaps push it into a somewhat puritanical or even abstract conception of music, which is totally alien to Indian aesthetics. Besides, the power of rasa theory is not merely classificatory; it is also a theory of aesthetic perception, to which the next chapter will be devoted.

Apart from the purely aesthetic views of Sharma (and Singh), some authors have contended for an acoustic basis as supporting the representation of rasas in music. This is the case with Bhātkhaṇḍe, G.H. Ranade, and O. Ṭhākur, among others. Bhātkhaṇḍe, too, accepted only śṛṅgāra, karuṇa, vīra and śānta rasas as meaningful in Hindustani contemporary music. For him, the expression of rasa depends on the following pitch rules (apud Nayar 1989: 156):

1. *Sandhi prakāś* rāgas, that is, rāgas which are prescribed to be performed at sunrise or sunset, having (komal) R and (komal) D, represent śānta and karuṇa. Bhairav, lalit and pūrvī would be some rāgas that conform to these rules.

2. Rāgas with śuddh R, G and D represent śṛṅgāra. A number of rāgas, such as bilāval, bhūpālī, kāmod, khamāj, etc. would fit in this class.

3. Rāgas with (komal) G and (komal) N represent vīra. Here one would recall kāfī, bhīmpalāsī, darbārī kānhḍā, etc.

In this way, Bhātkhaṇḍe seems to have tried to link his time-theory of performance with that of rasa. In the first group, it should be noticed that most sandhi prakāś rāgas have a (tīvra) M, i.e., an augmented forth, in their structure. Bhātkhaṇḍe does not distinguish this feature as being significant, though. Yamankalyāṇ, for instance, is a sunset rāga with śuddh R, G and D, but it also has both śuddh and (tīvra) M. Thus, yamankalyāṇ has at the same time elements of rules one and two, and does not fit easily into this schedule. In fact, there would be many exceptions to those rules (it suffices to consult the rāga and rasa tables below). It seems, however, that Bhātkhaṇḍe was postulating a hypothesis rather than a complete theory, and he left this research for 'future generations' (Nayar 1989: 156).

G.H. Ranade combined aesthetics and acoustics in a much more detailed way. For him, 'the Physical appeal of a note is pleasant (bright) or unpleasant (dull or jarring) according as a note is a consonance or a dissonance' (1951: 131). Therefore, his aesthetics depends on factors such as consonance and dissonance, not on all intervals in a performance, but on the particular relations established by the vādī and saṁvādī degrees. In this sense, Ranade returns to the basic assumption as that found in the NŚ, namely, that the aṁśa – the predominant degree, called usually vādī in contemporary music – determines the representational qualities of a rāga. Ranade states that music, on one hand, 'employs consonances for a pleasing and hence bright effect;' and on the other, 'dissonances for an unpleasant or a dull effect' (ibid.). For this author, absolute consonances are the unison or perfect octave; a perfect consonance is that of a perfect fifth or fourth; a medial consonance consists in a major or minor third; the major second and sixth are imperfect dissonances; and finally, perfect dissonances are any minor second or sixth, major seventh, or augmented forth. Then Ranade specifies the minor seventh, which in Indian music is a medial consonance if associated with the fifth; otherwise it is an imperfect dissonance (1951: 132). However, this classification does not imply a general idea of interval, which could be applied to any circumstance of melodic movement, but rather a more static view, in which the role of vādī is determinant: 'The Vādī note therefore serves as an index, as it were, of the kind of appeal a Rāga may put forth' (1951: 133).

If such a theory is to be constructed, one has to start with the most basic element in Indian music. And that is the tonic, or ṣaḍja, to which tambūrās are always tuned, reinforced usually by the fifth or fourth and sometimes other degrees (such as the major seventh), depending on the rāga to be performed. Prajñānānanda writes that the svara S 'creates a fundamental sentiment for generating mood or moods. Almost all the melodies (rāgas) start from the tonic, so the tonic (ṣaḍja) is recognized as the basic note or tone which can be said to be the musical symbol of mental unity and tranquil peace' (1973: 239). Indeed, the tonic can stand for śānta in Indian music. In this case, the representation is based on an iconic sign, such that a deviation from the tonic causes tension, and no deviation at all maintains the rasa of tranquillity. It is inaccurate, however, to state that all rāgas start on the tonic. Many rāgas, such as mārvā and pūriyā, avoid the tonic (and the fifth), although the svara S is present in the drone, and a performer should eventually lead the melodic resolutions to S in those ragas.

There is, in general, some common sense in Ranade's psycho-acoustic ideas. However, he defends a sort of acoustic aesthetics that is hardly consistent with Hindustani music. There are rāgas that use an augmented fourth or a minor second and yet do not produce a sad or dull effect. Rāga bhairav, for instance, has (komal) D as vādī and (komal) R as samvādī; in that case, both minor sixth and second should imply an unpleasant effect, which is not at all the general aesthetic idea of bhairav. Rāgas employing an augmented fourth abound in Indian music, but there is no sense in attributing any unpleasantly dissonant effect to this interval in India. It seems that Ranade is applying a Western traditional view of consonance and dissonance to Hindustani music, which can only be misleading. Eventually, he rejects a whole field of significations in Indian music as 'obscene', and concludes that, of the nine rasas, only śānta has a place in music (1951: 157).

This view, also expressed by other Indian authors, seems to reflect the puritanical attitude taken by scholars and musicians in their attempts to defend and preserve classical music, particularly during the first half of this century. It might be related to an effort to prove the respectability of Indian classical music at a time when the courts had been dismantled, and when the survival of classical music depended on its acceptance by the emerging state, by the broadcasting media, and by the Indian middle class. The repression of the institution of *ṭawā'ifs*, accomplished music and dance mistresses (see Manuel 1986: 473-79; 1989: 57-58; and Kippen 1988: 42-45), may also have influenced that puritanical attitude, which is still found in the work of some Indian scholars. It seems to me, however, that such an attitude is no longer justifiable. Eroticism, an important subject in Indian arts, does not merely relate to the ancient tradition of dancing girls (a socio-cultural institution that has disappeared in this century), but also to a whole conceptual universe as found in the Śaiva and Vaiṣṇava religions. (See O'Flaherty's *Śiva: The Erotic Ascetic* [1973]; or the classic poetry of Jayadeva's *Gītagovinda*, [1977]; not to speak of Śaktism and the several forms of Tantrism [see Gupta et al. 1979]). Although nowadays most of those mythological, religious and philosophical ideas are invoked in an euphemistic way, it would be a great loss to empty Indian music of śṛṅgāra, which, after all, represents the basic creative force of this planet, and certainly one of the highest forms of semiosis.

Omkarnāth Ṭhākur presents basically a psycho-acoustic theory, but, because of the great singer and scholar he was, it is quite precise, and takes into account several levels of musical organization and utterance in the representation of rasas. Ṭhākur, in his performances, was also engaged in demonstrating the traditional system of musical signification. He used to lecture shortly about the rāga he was going to perform and about its related meanings, in an attempt to enliven the association between rāga and rasa for the general public. In this way, O. Ṭhākur consistently furnished orientation in regard to the rasa and other significations associated with a rāga (Rao 1992: 38). He claimed that lyrics were not determinant in this sense, and that, even in situations where there is no meaningful text, such as instrumental music or the dhrupad ālāp, the purely musical forms alone can characterize a rasa (Ṭhākur's *Rāg ane Ras*; 1952: 44-49, in Rao 1992: 40). He also makes clear that contemporary music practice was the source of his ideas on rāga and the represented rasas.

According to Ṭhākur, the signification of a rāga does not depend merely on the svaras, but also on several other factors such as tempo (laya), the registers in which a rāga typically develops (saptak), articulation (kāku), ornamentation (gamak), and so forth. Thus, rāgas as aḍāṇa, when moving predominantly in the high octaves, express emotions like anger, excitement and enthusiasm; this situation is described by the word *cañcal*. Rāgas with an emphasis on M in a perfect fourth relation to S, such as kedār and mālkauṅs, are tranquil and mature; these are described with the Hindi word *gambhīr*, or are said to represent śānta. Further, Ṭhākur writes that the rāgas of the khamāj group and those that do not have a very definite mode of movement, such as jhiṅjhoṭī, pahāḍī and māṅḍ, are erotic and lighter in vein, and thus represent śṛṅgāra. Those with (komal) R and (komal) D, and śuddh M, such as jogiyā and gaurī, develop essentially the karuṇa rasa. And rāgas with (komal) R, (komal) D and (tīvra) M̄, such as śrī and pūriyā dhanāśrī, represent tiredness or lack of enthusiasm (apud Deva and Virmani 1968: 55; and Rao 1992: 39).

Among the rāga qualities described by Ṭhākur in the SA, two immediately catch one's attention: the pair of gambhīr (deep, serious, solemn) and cañcal (restless, moving, active, flirtatious, volatile). Powers points out that 'a pseudo-ethic contrast of serious and stately (gambhīr) versus playful and wild (cañcal) in darbārī versus aḍāṇa is a reflection of the rather faster than average performing tradition of aḍāṇa as well as of its characteristic emphasis on a higher tessitura' (1980b: 433). This is clearly a case of iconic representation, in which the fast tempo and melodic development centered in the tār saptak are qualities similar to those of a restless and enthusiastic youth, or in more formal terms, the energetic disposition necessary as the sthāyibhāva of vīra, represented by rāgas such as aḍāṇa and śaṅkarā. Hypoicons of this kind are often found in several descriptions of rāgas in the SA and in the writings of other authors as well.

Another interesting point in Ṭhākur's theory is that śānta may be represented by the perfect fourth in rāgas that have śuddh M as vādī (or aṁśa, as he prefers to call the main modal function). The relative harmonic stability of the interval S-M could be iconic in relation to the śānta or gambhīr ascribed to those kind of rāgas. This is especially true when the tambūrā is tuned to M (M S S Ṣ), as in rāga mālkauṅs. But the fourth is less stable when the singer has to produce a perfect fourth against a drone reinforcing P (P S S Ṣ), as in the case of rāgas kedār or bhairav. In that case, the singer has to take extra care in the intonation of M, so as not to sing it too high.[31] It is remarkable, however, that the fourth was the interval upon which this representation consolidated,

[31] According to Wim van der Meer, personal communication.

instead of the fifth, for instance, which is a closer partial to the tonic in its harmonic series, and thus more stable. The emphasis on S-M in some rāgas could be an indexical feature of the ancient plagal character of the jātis and grāmarāgas of long ago, as found in the NŚ, BD and SR.

Rāgas and Represented Rasa in Contemporary Music

There are a few hundred rāgas in Hindustani contemporary music. There are rāgas employed only in one or two genres, semi-classical rāgas, old rāgas, popular rāgas, imported rāgas, rare rāgas, brand new rāgas, and so on. as well as a number of mixed rāgas. Yet few of those hundreds of rāgas are regularly performed. I have explored the idea that rāgas, as symbols, have their own life (see 2.3.1 and 2.3.2). Some rāgas are obsolete and no longer performed, while others are old and rarely performed, and still other rāgas are preferred by musicians and listeners during a certain period of time. It would not be wrong to say that some rāgas are in fashion, and others have their respected, classical niche, and thus are well assured of a place in the repertoire. The rāgas in current usage in North Indian music may be divided into two classes: first, the established rāgas, those which are often performed; second, those less regulary performed. In these two classes, two specifications are necessary. First, among the well-established and regularly performed rāgas, there is a subgroup constituted by what could be called the 'great rāgas'. Similarly, in the second class, there are minor rāgas. Therefore, three groups are the most significant: (1) great rāgas, (2) known rāgas, and (3) less-known rāgas (including some minor and rare ones). This triple division, and the rāgas which constitute these groups, was suggested by Wim van der Meer, who said that, although not formalized, these groups represent an approximate consensus among contemporary musicians.[32] It is necessary to make clear that I have adopted this division as a practical device for the study of signification that follows. The three groups do not represent an absolute classification, nor are they intended to rank rāgas according to aesthetic, social or ideological values.

The tables below display the rāgas of these three groups and the rasas and/or other meanings and related qualities for which they stand. I have collected information on the rāga's rasas and other meanings from different authors, the references to which are in the standard abbreviated format for treatises, except those quoted from Ali Akbar Khan and G. Ruckert's book (1991), which I have abbreviated as K&R. It is also necessary to assess the opinion of each author who refers to the signification of rāgas. It seems to me that the most dependable information comes from O. Ṭhākur's *Saṅgītañjalī* (SA), where the rasas and the character of the rāgas are carefully analyzed in relation to their

[32] Personal communication.

musical materiality. Even so, there are instances when Ṭhākur's opinion is disputable; for instance, his attribution of bhayānaka to śrī rāga. Vināyak Rāv Paṭvardhan's ***Rāgavijñāna*** (RVJ) comes next, and since Paṭvardhan and Ṭhākur were both disciples of Viṣṇu Digambar Paluskar, one might suppose that their opinions would agree, which is not always the case. The least accurate information comes, of course, from Western authors. In each table, I present the rāgas in alphabetical order, thus ignoring the fact there are borderline rāgas, that is, rāgas which could instead be situated in between the two groups. A few rāgas among the known group, and many more in the less-known group, have no special attribution of meaning in the works I have studied. This is probably because, on one hand, the meaning of some well-known rāgas were so obvious for a particular audience or readership that the author did not feel the need to specify them; on the other, it is likely that some rāgas that are not really independent may have meanings that are connected to the rāga they come from (but, again, this is not a rule). Most rāgas, especially the minor ones, simply do not refer to any particular non-acoustic object. Nevertheless, the tables below have retained the rāgas that do not have a distinctive meaning, for that in itself is a significant fact.

It is beyond the scope of this work to present detailed musical descriptions of all listed rāgas. The musical examples that follow rather serve as reminders, merely displaying the āroha and avaroha and some basic motifs and melodic movements, as well as essential ornamentation. The complete description of musical features of contemporary Hindustani rāgas can be found in the works referenced.

Before considering the great, the known and less-known rāgas, it is first necessary to introduce another, explanatory, table. Indian contemporary scholars and musicians have employed a whole special vocabulary to describe the qualities of the rāgas, their *prakṛti* (character or the way they used to be performed), and to explain the rasas they traditionally represent. Often, no rasa is directly indicated, but only referred to in terms such as *cañcal, taral, gambhīr* or *madhur.* The table below translates most of those words as found in O. Ṭhākur's *Saṅgītāñjalī* and other authors' works. Some of them may be directly related to rasa theory, such as *śok*, of which the Sanskrit form śoka is the sthāyibhāva of karuṇa. Yet, most of the words in the list below are merely terms employed in everyday Hindi life.

Table 18

Terms in Hindi Used as Reference to Musical Meaning

atmanivedan	self-sacrifice
cañcal	restless, moving, active, flirtatious, volatile
capal	tremulous, volatile
dainya	wretchedness, miserable
dhīr	resolute, constant, self-controlled, solemn
gambhīr	deep serious, solemn
klant	tired, wearied, languid
madhur	sweet, gentle
mugdha	fascinating, enchanting, charming
mṛdu	soft, tender
prauṛh	adult, mature
rat	love, to fall in love
saral	direct, simple
śok	sorrow
śramit	tired
taral	tremulous, glittering, sparkling, volatile
tīkhā	sharp, smart, spritly
tyāg	renunciation
uddām	unrestrained, self-willed
ugra	fierce, over-powering
utsāhaprad	enthusiasm
uttejanā	excitement
vātsalya	parental love
vedanā	pain, suffering
viraha	separation
yuvā	youth

Great Rāgas

Great rāgas are not merely those that are most performed; they also represent in general a certain majestic, dignified character. The exceptions are rāga khamāj, which is used mainly in light classical music, as ṭhumrī; and rāga deś. Rāga pūrvī, although serious and certainly great, is a rāga that has lost popularity of late, and is nowadays seldom performed. There are also some rāgas that exhibit a balance, on several levels, between deep seriousness and lightness, such as mārvā, multānī, sāraṅg and siṅdūrā. Bhairavī affords a variety of meanings. Besides these, however, most of the other rāgas in this group are quiet, but deeply affecting, and often characterized as gambhīr.

Table 19

Great Rāgas and Their Signification

Great rāgas:	**rasas**	**other meanings or related qualities**	**references**
Alhaiyā Bilāval		not gambhīr, but another kind of seriousness	SA 3.12
	śṛṅgāra, karuṇa		K&R 1991: 82
		peaceful repose	Kaufmann 1993: 119
Āsāvarī (śuddh re āsāvarī = jaunpurī)	*tender* śṛṅgāra	positive self-sacrifice	SA 3.82
	śṛṅgāra, karuṇa	tyāg	K&R 1991: 69-70
		quiet, gentle	Kaufmann 1993: 463
Bāgeśrī	vipralambha	sensitive feelings, pangs of separation, love	SA 2.67
		serious and great	Kaufmann 1993: 382
Bhairav	raudra	mature gambhīr	SA 3.158
	śānta, bhakti	very appealing in the morning	RN 1.75
	śānta, bhakti, vīra, karuṇa	gambhīr	K&R 1991: 32
		awesome grandeur, horror, fright, melancholy, tender adoration	Kaufmann 1993:233-34

Bhairavī	śṛṅgāra, karuṇa, bhakti	vātsalya	SA 2.150
	bhakti	madhur, gambhīr, fascination	RVJ 3.128
	bhakti, śānta, śṛṅgāra, karuṇa	compassion	K&R 1991: 47-48
		peaceful, serious, sad mood	Kaufmann 1993: 533
Bhīmpalāsī	śānta	gambhīr	SA 2.42
		quiet, peaceful, tender	Kaufmann 1993: 362
Bhūpālī (= bhūp)		gambhīr	SA 1.10
		royal, courtly character	Kaufmann 1993:66
Bihāg	vipralambha	mugdha	SA 2.2
	śṛṅgāra		RN 1.111
		loving, thoughtful longing, gentle anxiety	Kaufmann 1993: 133
Darbārī kānhḍā		gambhīr	SA 5.121
		very gambhīr, madhur, delightful	RVJ 1.15
	śānta	gambhīr, majesty	RN 2.47-48
		majestic, dignified, slow manner	Kaufmann 1993: 499
Deś		self-sacrifice, in light-classical music enchantment	SA 1.85
		madhur	RVJ 1.180
Deśī (deśī toḍī)	śṛṅgāra	madhur	SA 6.15
		attractive and pleasing to the ear	RVJ 5.2
		serious	Kaufmann 1993: 478
Kedār	śānta	gambhīr	SA 3.50

Khamāj	śṛṅgāra		SA 1.73
	śṛṅgāra		RVJ 1.166
	śṛṅgāra		RN 3.40
	śṛṅgāra, karuṇa		K&R 1991:136
		flirtatious	Kaufmann 1993: 205
Lalit	śānta	madhur, gambhīr	SA 6.139-40
	bhakti		RVJ 3.62
		pleasing	RN 3.78
Mālkauṅs	śānta	gambhīr	SA 3.129
	vīra	gambhīr, wise	RVJ 3.208
		very serious	Kaufmann 1993: 535
Mārvā		mid taral, 'unlike pūriyā, it is not gambhīr'	SA 4.134
	karuṇa, vīra, bhakti		K&R 1991: 194
		Quiet, tender love; or anxiety and solemn expectation	Kaufmann 1993: 315-56
Multānī		dhīr becoming taral	SA 4.69
	karuṇa-śṛṅgāra		RVJ 2.126
		quiet, loving contemplation	Kaufmann 1993: 554
Miyāṁ kī malhār (Tānsenī malhār)		mid gambhīr	SA 5.60
	karuṇa, vipralambha	gambhīr	RVJ 3.2
Miyāṁ kī toḍī (Tānsenī toḍī)	bhakti		RVJ 2.74
	bhakti		RN 4.184
	śṛṅgāra, karuṇa, bhakti		K&R 1991: 96
		gentle, loving, delighted adoration	Kaufmann 1993: 551

Pūriyā		gambhīr (in the slow, mandra ālāp)	SA 4.109
	vipralambha		RVJ 2.113
		gambhīr	RN 3.229
		quiet, peace, love	Kaufmann 1993: 318
Pūrvī		fatigue, lack of energy, initial feeling of wretchedness	SA 6.54
		gambhīr	RN 3.237
		deep serious, quiet, mysterious	Kaufmann 1993: 277
Sāraṅg (biṅdrābanī sāraṅg)		neither taral nor gambhīr	SA 1.39
		quiet and tender	Kaufmann 1993: 449
Siṅdūrā	śṛṅgāra		RVJ 3.52
		either serious or joyful	Kaufmann 1993: 374
Śrī	śānta, bhayānaka	klant (tiredness)	SA 6.68
		gambhīr, ascetic feelings	RVJ 2.28
		gentle, mysterious, love, nostalgic and prayerful	Kaufmann 1991: 133
Yamankalyāṇ		madhur, 'the feeling of awakening, out from that of sleepiness,' śuddha M evokes a tender feeling	SA 2.123
	bhakti, śānta, śṛṅgāra, karuṇa		K&R 1991: 160
		blessing, soothing	Kaufmann 1993: 62

Musical genre is, in fact, the first parameter for understanding the signification of several rāgas. Among the three main genres current in Hindustani music – dhrupad, khayāl and ṭhumrī – a sub-genre of dhrupad, the dhamār, refers particularly to themes of the Holī festival; and the ṭhumrī is also specialized, in that its songs are invariably related to all forms of śṛṅgāra and are presented in a very ornamented style. Thus, rāgas connected to these two particular genres represent rasas pertaining to their referential range. But the topic is not that simple, for many of the ṭhumrī rāgas are also employed in dhrupad, with a totally different treatment and signifying tendency. Thus, the same rāgas used in dhrupad have a different signification when used in ṭhumrī. Among the great rāgas, bhairavī, khamāj and siṅdūrā are also ṭhumrī rāgas. Other rāgas used in ṭhumrī are pīlū, kāfī, jogiyā, jhiṅjhoṭī, sohinī, kāliṅgaḍā, tilak kāmod, deś, bihārī and māṅḍ (Powers 1980a: 117; Manuel 1989: 195-221). Most of those are listed in the second group. The signification mode of a rāga, when associated with a genre, is indexical, for its use and context establishes the ground of representation.

Besides genre, other musical features, such as tempo and tessitura, are significant. Seriousness is a character of many rāgas, and the expressed rasa is certainly śānta. The rāgas in the first group, whose nature is unmistakably gambhīr, are as follows: bhairav, bhīmpalāsī, bhūpālī, darbārī kānhḍā, kedār, mālkauṅs, miyāṁ kī malhār, pūriyā, and pūrvī (see Ex. 46). They are usually performed in a slow tempo[33]. As noted by Powers, some of these rāgas have melodic developments centered in the mandra and madhya saptaks. This attribute identifies bhūpālī, darbārī, miyāṁ kī malhār and pūriyā. The low tessitura and slow tempo of these rāgas iconically represent gambhīr. This can be justified in terms of rāga personification. In India, a serious and wise person has the demeanor of a senior patriarch, whose movements are controlled and solemn. This is also represented by the extensive use of mīṅḍ (a glissando connecting two or more notes) instead of direct attacks. A special ornament, the āndolan (a slow and deep oscillation), is another important feature of some of the gambhīr rāgas. Bhairav, bhīmpalāsī, darbārī, mālkauṅs and miyāṁ kī malhār all require the āndolan on a certain svara. But this usage is not uniform; for instance, the āndolan on (komal) G̱ and (komal) Ḏ in darbārī kānhḍā is the most typical and compulsory; whereas the lighter āndolan on (komal) G̱ in mālkauṅs is a matter left to the musicians' discretion. There seems to be no iconic or indexical ground for the use of āndolan in gambhīr rāgas, which is thus a matter of habit; in other words, the āndolan is a legisign. If this oscillation is regarded as indicating the character of a rāga as gambhīr, then it can be more precisely classified as a dicent indexical legisign; for, being a rule (e.g., in darbārī), it gives positive information about the rāga expressing seriousness, which is its dynamical object.

[33] It should be noted, however, that musicians do not always follow the indications found in treatises such as the SA or KPM. There are performances of rāga darbārī kānhḍā in a fast tempo, and at least one compostion in drut ektāl is found in RVJ (1.34-5).

Example 46
Gambhīr rāgas

A feature, recognized by Ṭhākur, of rāgas representing śānta and gambhīr is the perfect fourth in relation to the tonic. Śuddh M is an important svara in kedār and mālkauṅs. Describing kedār, Ṭhākur writes that S-M is the 'rāga determining interval' (SA 3.50). Besides, he points to M as the aṁśa[34] of kedār. This perfect fourth relation may represent śānta on an iconic basis, as I have stated above. Kedār has preserved the meaning ascribed to this rāga in the dhyānas of the 17th century. Other

---

[34] Omkarnāth Ṭhākur prefers the term aṁśa to designate the function that most contemporary Hindustani scholars call vādī.

rāgas, however, have had their meanings changed in the last centuries. Mālkauṅs, for instance, has almost lost its association with vīra; only a few musicians still mention this rasa in mālkauṅs (as does Paṭvardhan, RVJ 3.208).

In general, the serene, slow and deep melodic features of these rāgas represent śānta on an iconic basis. The only clear contradiction in the rāgas I have pointed to as gambhīr is the furious rasa, raudra, attributed by Ṭhākur to the rāga bhairav (SA 3.158). This seems to be a personal interpretation in which Ṭhākur recalls the idea of Śiva as the terrible deity. But this view is difficult to support in the light of music history: According to the SR, the ancient rāga bhairav was to be sung as a prayer (SR 2.2.82b). Later, the rāga dhyānas of bhairav depicts an ascetic. Finally, in contemporary practice, bhairav is conceived as representing śānta, the morning invocation to the universe when sun rises (see Saxena 1992: 9). Therefore, historically and in live practice, the prevailing conception and performance of rāga bhairav signifying śānta or bhakti does not match with raudra.

Before I discuss the rāgas referred to as cañcal and taral, which will lead this study into the second and third groups, some observations on rāga bhairavī are necessary. Bhairavī is a very popular rāga (Ex. 47), employed widely in all genres (except khayāl), and having great structural flexibility. In bhairavī the musician is allowed to introduce almost all chromatic notes, which do not destroy the essential qualities of the rāga. This is an interesting point that could explain the variety of representations possible in this rāga. O. Ṭhākur writes:

> In the several usages of bhairavī, the distinct circumstances and expressions of the nāyikā rouse different affections. Sometimes fascinated, sometimes in the form of a newly wed girl, or a mature [woman], the abhisārikā or the proṣitabhartṛka, bhairavī gives to the listeners divergent possibilities. On occasion [bhairavī expresses] *samyoga*-śṛṅgāra, or the karuṇa of separation, now and then self-sacrifice, parental affection or abundant bhakti; from all those emotions, the inner-outer unseen atmosphere becomes – in the sensitive heart – the purging flow of various rasas. (SA 2.150)

Example 47

Rāga bhairavī

A survey of the songs in bhairavī, as presented by Bhātkhaṇḍe (KPM 2.394-428), confirms the view of Ṭhākur. The lyrics display a great variety of themes: the complaints of one of the gopīs about Kṛṣṇa's mischievous deeds (KPM 2.394-95); a dhrupad in jhaptāl about Sarasvatī (KPM 2.413-14); another about Durgā, the goddess who destroyed the Mahiṣāsur demon (KPM 2.415-16); Śiva described in grand terms in a four-section dhrupad in cautāl (KPM 2.417-20); the fascinated nāyikā, imploring her lover to turn up (KPM 2.424-25); or Kṛṣṇa playing Holī with his girlfriend (KPM 2.426); and the disappointed lady (KPM 2.427-28). Similar diversity is also found in Paṭvardhan (RVJ 3.131-46).

Rāga śrī is another great rāga deserving special attention. Ṭhākur proposes that this rāga could represent bhayānaka, although it is usually performed at sunset, which in general relates to śānta. His reasoning is that the beginning of the evening is the time when Śiva's *gaṇas*, his assistant demons are released (their leader is Gaṇeśa, who not only removes obstacles but also poses them). Also, it is the time when the *tāṇḍava* dance, Śiva's dance of death and destruction, was performed. Therefore, the rasa aroused by these circumstances would be bhayānaka (SA 6.70). Still, śrī should have some special features to represent bhayānaka, in contradistinction to all other sunset rāgas that do not have the same meaning. Śrī is indeed one of the most difficult rāgas. There are complex melodic movements, especially in the avaroha, which is very oblique (Ex. 48). Śrī also involves disjunct intervals, long mīṇḍs and gamaks. There is a mysterious, perhaps ascetic, quality of feeling in śrī, as writes Paṭvardhan (RVJ 2.28). But, in the tradition of rāga dhyānas, śrī is represented as the dhīrapraśānta nāyaka, the self-controlled and calm hero, in the form of a royal character. There were considerable changes in the musical structure of śrī, from the way it was presented in the 17th century treatises and as it is performed nowadays. Yet, it is less likely that its meaning would have changed from śānta to bhayānaka.

Example 48

Rāga śrī

Known Rāgas

The rāgas representing qualities opposite to gambhīr are described as taral or cañcal. These two terms are almost synonymous, and an apt translation for both is 'volatile'. Rāgas of this kind are found in the two other groups, the known and less-known rāgas. In the former, aḍāṇa, hamīr, haṅsadhvāni, śaṅkarā, tilak kāmod and tilaṅg are cañcal or taral; whereas in the latter, deśkār and śyām kalyāṇ are such (Ex. 49). The musical feature that grounds the representation of these young, moving rāgas is basically a high tessitura, with melodic movements centered in the madhya and tār saptaks, and a tendency toward medium and fast tempos. Thus, the basis of representation is iconic. The volatile character of these rāgas is signified by fast movements and high tessitura. In terms of personification, taral and cañcal rāgas are young and energetic. Aḍāṇa, hamīr and śaṅkarā represent vīra, but this is not the only rasa expressed by cañcal and taral rāgas (see the tables). Haṅsadhvani and deśkār are pentatonic, tilak kāmod and śyām kalyāṇ are pentatonic in the āroha and heptatonic in the avaroha. Although pentatonicism is not a determining feature of cañcal rāgas, it somehow gives a forward movement, specially in the āroha. Rāga tilaṅg is mainly used in dhamār and ṭhumrī; and tilak kāmod is also a ṭhumrī rāga, often employed in lighter genres such as dādrā and ghazal. Therefore, they represent their objects on both an iconic and indexical basis.

Example 49

Taral or cañcal rāgas

Interesting musical correspondences exist between certain gambhīr and cañcal rāgas. Aḍāṇa is usually thought of as the fast version of darbārī kānhḍā, and both rāgas share the same pitch set and some melodic motifs, such as the cadence GMRS. Similarly, hamīr is the young form of kedār; deśkār the light form of bhūpālī; kāliṅgaḍā corresponds to bhairav; and bahār, a spring rāga, corresponds to miyāṁ kī malhār, the rainy season rāga. This last pair presents an engaging case of signification. Although many rāgas connected to varṣā represent forms of śṛṅgāra, miyāṁ kī malhār represents śānta, 'a sage in meditation', as Dilip Chandra Vedi used to say (Meer 1980: 17). Rainy season rāgas represent śṛṅgāra indexically, for they are related to cultural life in India during the rains. Gangoly writes on rāga megha: 'the advent of rains, – with all the exuberance of desire and opportunity for enjoyment' (1989: 100-01). But śānta is part of Indian customs, too, for the wandering ascetics do not travel during this season, but instead stay in *aśrams* (see Eck 1983: 60). Bahār, on the other hand, literally means spring, flourishing, blossoming, delight. It is not historically an old rāga, and very often is mixed with other rāgas, such as hiṇḍolabahār, bhairavabahār, or even vasantabahār. In general, the dual form of rāgas, one being gambhīr and the other cañcal, is more than a simple coincidence, and may throw light on the evolutionary process of rāgas. One such process might be that of a rāga being transformed into another one, with its own aesthetic character, by merely a change in aspects of tempo and compass.

Table 20

Known Rāgas and Their Signification

Known rāgas:	**rasas**	**other meanings or related qualities**	**references**
Aḍāṇa		taral, young	SA 3.70
	vīra		RN 1.7
		it is the light counterpart of darbārī kānhḍā	Kaufmann 1993: 133
Ahīr Bhairav		gambhīr	RVJ 5.193
Āsāvarī (komal re)		mṛdu gambhīr	SA 6.1
	karuṇa, śṛṅgāra		RVJ 5.30
Bahār		utsāha, young, enthusiastic	SA 3.107
Candrakauṅs			
Chāyānaṭ	śṛṅgāra		SA 5.27

Durgā		neither very gambhīr nor very cañcal	SA 1.31
		pleasant, friendly, but by no means light-hearted	Kaufmann 1993: 183
Gauḍ malhār (śuddh)	śṛṅgāra, viraha	deep thought	SA 4.33
	śṛṅgāra		RVJ 3.25
		very serious, dignity	Kaufmann 1993: 404-5
Gauḍ sāraṅg		mid young, gambhīr (in vilambit)	SA 4.17
	śṛṅgāra		RVJ 3.37
Gurjarī toḍī	karuṇa	intolerable suffering of separation	SA 6.31
	bhakti		RVJ 5.223
Hamīr		taral, unrestrained behavior, full of excitement	SA 2.15
		serious, bellicose	Kaufmann 1993: 133
Haṅsadhvāni		cañcal, but saral	SA 1.21
Hiṇḍol	vīra, raudra, adbhuta	ugratā; 'the vīra of Hiṇḍol is of a particular nature'	SA 2.137
		gambhīr	RN 2.129
		quiet, dignified joy	Kaufmann 1993: 116
Jayjayvantī		deep thought and self-sacrifice	SA 3.31
	śṛṅgāra	madhur	RVJ 2.96
		friendly, romantic	Kaufmann 1993: 228
Jogī (= jogiyā)	excessive karuṇa		SA 5.167
	karuṇa-śṛṅgāra, bhakti		RVJ 3.74
		quiet contemplation and adoration, serious	Kaufmann 1993: 241

Kāfī	prema-śṛṅgāra, or bhakti	very madhur, 'delicate feelings of the heart,' somehow gambhīr in a dhāmar, related to Holī	SA 1.97
	śṛṅgāra, karuṇa		K&R 1991: 110
Kāmod		a bit gambhīr, a bit taral	SA 5.45
Mārūbihāg		mixed prauṛh and taral	SA 5.15
	śṛṅgāra		RVJ 5.250
Nāyak kānhḍā			
Paṭdīp		(komal) G and śuddh M gambhīr, śuddh N taral	SA 4.52
Pīlū	karuṇa-śṛṅgāra		RVJ 3.221
	karuṇa	śok (semi-classical music)	RN 3.228
Pūriyā dhanāśrī		gambhīr, tiredness	SA 4.153
	śṛṅgāra, karuṇa, bhakti	gambhīr	K&R 1991: 181-82
Pūriyākalyāṇ		(gambhīr)	
Rāgeśrī		'not only dhīr and gambhīr, but a mixture of śānta and cañcalya'	SA 2.82
		serious	Kaufmann 1993: 216
Rāmkalī	vipralambha		SA 4.1
Śaṅkarā		taral and self-willed	SA 2.30
		serious and dignified	Kaufmann 1993: 130
Śuddh sāraṅg			
Sohinī		auspicious, wedding	RN 4.148
		tender, loving	Kaufmann 1993: 321
Sūrmalhār	bhakti		RVJ 4.51
Tilak kāmod		young, taral	SA 3.1
		light	Kaufmann 1993: 208
Tilaṅg	śṛṅgāra	cañcal (semi-classical)	SA 1.50
		light	Kaufmann 1993: 207

Vasant (= Basant)	vipralambha	sometimes cañcal sometimes gambhīr	SA 6.111
		gentle loveliness and quiet joy	Kaufmann 1993: 285
Vilāskhānī toḍī			

The two forms of śṛṅgāra, sambhoga and vipralambha, constitute a major field of musical representation. Karuṇa is often expressed in the domain of vipralambha śṛṅgāra. A number of rāgas can signify equally well these two fundamentally different qualities of feeling. In fact, it is often difficult to state confidently and in general terms whether a rāga represents sambhoga or vipralambha. The distinction is crucial, but it is to be found in more concrete situations of musical semiosis, when the musician's interpretation tempers the musical form, with or without the collaboration of the lyrics of a composition. Rāga bhairavī was already pointed out as a case in which a diversity of themes can appear. This is also true of rāga miyāṁ kī toḍī (Ex. 50). The khayāl '*Deu daras mere pyāre*' ('Oh, my beloved, please appear before me'; KPM 2.442) is an instance of vipralambha, as is '*Ab more Rām, Rām*' ('Rām, you are my only Rām'; KPM 2.446-47).[35] Songs like '*Tum samā na na dūjo*' ('There is no one like you'; KPM 2.473-74), however, instead bring qualities of feeling related to sambhoga. But it is necessary to realize that other subjects are also represented in rāga toḍī, such as devotional songs to Kṛṣṇa (KPM 2.434-35) or a solemn dhrupad to Śiva (RVJ 2.77-78).

Example 50

Rāga miyāṁ kī toḍī

Two other rāgas that can represent equally well sambhoga or vipralambha are komal re āsāvarī and pīlū (Ex. 51). Whereas this kind of āsāvarī has features highlighted by Ṭhākur as signifying karuṇa ([komal] R and [komal] D, śuddha M), there are other compositions which clearly express sambhoga, as occurs in Tānsen's dhrupad '*Ānā sunāī, bāṁsurī Kānhā*' ('Come and listen to Kṛṣṇa playing the flute'). Pīlū is a rāga employed in ṭhumrī, a genre that involves both kinds of śṛṅgāra. Similarly to bhairavī, foreign svaras can be freely introduced into the basic structure of pīlū.

---

[35] See Example 72, in chapter 3.4.

Example 51

Rāgas komal re āsāvarī and pīlū

Some rāgas have a tendency to express sambhoga śṛṅgāra. Khamāj is certainly such a rāga, as well as chāyānaṭ, deśī, kāfī (Ex. 52) and tilaṅg. Tilaṅg was referred to above as a cañcal rāga. The other four rāgas hardly have any musical feature in common, except perhaps a special descending mīṇḍ. This ornament characterizes khamāj (from D to M), chāyānaṭ (from P to R), and deśī (from [tār] Ṡ to P). Still, this is an inconclusive musical feature for the representation of śṛṅgāra. All these rāgas have particular melodic motifs; therefore, Ṭhākur's assertion that rāgas without clear melodic movements represent śṛṅgāra seems not to be applicable here.

Example 52

Rāgas khamāj, chāyānaṭ, deśī, and kāfī

Rāgas with a disposition for representing vipralambha are śuddh re āsāvarī (jaunpurī), bāgeśrī, bihāg, gauḍ malhār, rāmkālī and vasant (see Ex. 53). Āsāvarī, also known as jaunpurī, has āndolan on (komal) D and (komal) G, and its pitch set is similar to darbārī kānhḍā, but the motifs are clearly different and the two rāgas have their own distinct character. Thus, the mere disposition of pitches is insufficient to classify rāgas in terms of represented rasa. In some cases it does indicate a rasa; for example, rāmkālī and vasant which have (komal) R and (komal) D, and śuddh M plus (tīvra) M. The rare chromatic motif typical of vasant, MMM, is a sign of vipralambha for Ṭhākur (SA 6.111). However, rāgas bihāg and gauḍ malhār have none of those features, and yet they can equally signify vipralambha.

Example 53

Rāgas śuddh re āsāvarī (jaunpurī), bāgeśrī, bihāg, gauḍ malhār, rāmkālī, and vasant

Two rāgas pointed out by Ṭhākur as representing extreme karuṇa are jogiyā and gurjarī toḍī. These two rāgas all include (komal) R and (komal) D in their structure (Ex. 54). Jogiyā, characterized by Ṭhākur as signifying 'excessive karuṇa' (SA 5.167), is mainly used in ṭhumrī. Gurjarī toḍī, representing an 'intolerable suffering of separation' (SA 6.31), is a raga to be developed mainly in the mandra and madhya registers. A descending mīṅḍ between (tīvra) M and (komal) R is a typical motif of gurjarī toḍī. The extremely pathetic character attributed by Ṭhākur to this rāga derives from the distended effect produced by (tīvra) M. The reason seems to be that a rāga with R and D represents karuṇa, but a rāga with those pitches, but including (tīvra) M instead of śuddha M, represents a stupendous level of that rasa.

Example 54

Rāgas jogiyā and gurjarī toḍī

Another example of the crucial signification function accomplished by the augmented fourth, according to Omkarnāth Ṭhākur, is that of hiṇḍol, and its contrary case, bhinnaṣaḍja. He writes that (tīvra) M in hiṇḍol conveys tīvratā (intensity, ardor, impetuosity), while, a rāga with same svaras, but having śuddh M instead of tīvra, brings forward mṛidutva (softness, gentleness, tenderness), which is the character of bhinnaṣaḍja (Ṭhākur's Pravnabharati, 1956: 51; in Rao 1992: 39). In Ex. 55, the structure of these two rāgas shows they have basically the same pitch set, except for M, tīvra in hiṇḍol and śuddh in bhinnaṣaḍja. Ṭhākur writes: 'If tīvra ma is introduced in bhinnaṣaḍja, the śānta and gambhīr bhāvas would be destroyed, and instead, a sharp and fierce bhāva would come forth' (SA 1.61). The energetic character of hiṇḍol obtains also in focusing a performance in the madhya and tār saptaks. In fact, since N is avoided in āroha, the only four svaras left allow a fiery ascending movement. Conversely, bhinnaṣaḍja should be presented in a slow and solemn motion, proper of a gambhīr rāga. This is a relatively new rāga in Hindustani music, and it does not relate to the ancient grāmarāga bearing the same name. In fact, bhinnaṣaḍja can also be called hiṇḍolī, hiṇḍolīkā or kauśik dhvani; hence, in the former two alternative names, its correspondence with hiṇḍol becomes even more clear.

Example 55

Rāga hiṇḍol and bhinnaṣaḍja

Table 21
Less-Known Rāgas and Their Signification

Less Known rāgas:	**rasas**	**other meanings or related qualities**	**references**
Abhogī	bhakti	gambhīr	RVJ 6.85
Ānand bhairav	(śānta)	the peacefulness of bhakti	RVJ 5.203
Baṅgāl bhairav			
Baivā			
Bhaṭiyār			
Bhinnaṣaḍja	śānta	gambhīr	SA 1.61
Bhūpāl toḍī		bhakti	RVJ 5.232
Bihāgḍā		dhīrā (madhya laya)	SA 5.1
	śṛṅgāra		RVJ 5.263
Deśkār		taral	SA 5.82
	bhakti		RVJ 3.78
Devgirī bilāval			
Dhānī			
Gārā			
Gaurī			
Gorakh kalyāṇ			
Guṇkalī	śānta	gambhīr	RVJ 7.16
Jait			
Jait kalyāṇ			
Jaitśrī			
Jhiṅjhoṭī		taral	SA 5.162
	śṛṅgāra		RVJ 3.99
	śṛṅgāra		RN 2.169
Kāliṅgaḍā		capal, young	SA 5.172
	bhakti		RVJ 2.92
		light and flirtatious	Kaufmann 1993: 246-48
Kukubh bilāval			
Lalitāgaurī			
Madhmād sāraṅg	śṛṅgāra, karuṇa		RVJ 6.41

Madhuvantī	śṛṅgāra	karuṇa	RVJ 6.41
Māṅḍ		light, folksy	Kaufmann 1993: 147
Megh malhār			
Naṭ			
Sāvanī			
Śivmat bhairav	bhakti		RVJ 5.107
Śuddh kalyāṇ			
Śukla bilāval			
Śyām kalyāṇ		taral, excited youth	SA 4.92
Suhā kānhḍā			
Vibhās (= bibhās)		progressively from dhīr to taral	SA 5.103
	bhakti	gambhīr	RVJ 3.91
		neither light nor serious	Kaufmann 1993: 248
Yamanībilāval			

The survey presented in the tables above seems to affirm that only four rasas are represented by contemporary Hindustani rāgas: śṛṅgāra (in both its forms, of sambhoga and vipralambha), karuṇa, vīra and śānta. It would be a mistake, however, to infer that those rasas define strictly the scope of Hindustani music capacity for signification. There are two factors that refute this proposition. First, vocal music is a special art, in the sense that the combination of music and words can represent any of the classical nine or ten rasas, as well as other qualities of feeling not covered by rasa theory. Besides, even in a pure ālāp, a master singer can make use of several musical resources, vocal inflections and ornaments, which also permits great flexibility in the qualitative possibilities of the feelings expressed. Secondly, the studies presented in chapter 3.3 and its subdivisions are not so much about what Hindustani music can represent, but about what representations are preferred during each period. Music has great powers of signification, and this is not limited to the rasas. Musical signification, as I have demonstrated in section 2, allows a variety of interpretants, from mere quality of feelings to the rāgabhāva, from non-acoustic objects to musical metalanguage, and so on. In relation to the capacity of musical representation of rasas, it seems to me that raudra, bhayānaka, bībhatsa, hāsya and adbhuta can be as effectively represented as any of the other four or five rasas, if bhakti is added to the list. In fact, the case of bhakti rasa is exemplary, for this rasa is not mentioned in

Indian aesthetics before the 15th century. It was out of necessity, triggered by the springing forth of devotional movements in India, that a whole religious aesthetics was created. Thus, if on one hand Abhinavagupta defended the inclusion of śānta in the 10th century, and Caitanya later argued for bhakti, on the other, some rasas tended to be abandoned. These changes in the aesthetic palette are not related to the rasas themselves or to the means employed in their representation, but probably due to circumstantial factors; such as the views of the patrons, or what repertoire attracted their attention during a certain period. Musicians long had to organize the content of their performances in accordance with court and temple interests. If four or five rasas are predominant today, this does not mean that Hindustani classical music can only represent this limited scope of significations.

3.4 Aesthetic Rapture: A Semiotic Analysis

Rakti (charm) is an inherent characteristic of music, vocal and instrumental, and dance. (SD 1.6)

Just as a tree grows from a seed, and from the tree come flowers; and from flowers fruit, so also rasas are the root, and from them are all bhāvas derived. (NŚ 6.38)

Thus the rasa existing in the poet is like the seed which is the root (i.e. the cause) (of a tree). For the poet is just as the spectator. (...) The tree stands for poetry. Flowers, etc., stand for such activities of the actor as abhinaya, etc. Fruit stands for the aesthetic enjoyment of the spectator. Thus the whole world is made of rasa! (Abhinavagupta's commentary on the above verse of the NŚ, in Masson & Patwardhan 1969: 52-54 n.5)

The Palimpsest of Rasa

The previous chapters tried to detail some of the multifarious forms and concepts that Hindustani music has embodied during its millennia-long generation of musical life and musical entities (rāgas, tālas, instruments, forms, styles, and the like). When viewed from the contemporary vantage point, that panoply of forms and concepts may evoke the idea of a palimpsest, to which Nehru once likened Indian culture: 'She was like some ancient palimpsest on which layer upon layer of thought and reverie had been inscribed, and yet no succeeding layer had completely hidden or erased what had been written previously' (1964: 60). In some respects, what Lannoy says about the Indians – that they have an 'instinct for borrowing and at the same time conserving, for clinging to everything and never rejecting what is outworn or outmoded' (1971: xvi) – also holds true for music theory. Contemporary scholars hold paradoxical views regarding issues of rāga and rasa in Hindustani music. Some of them, although recognizing the difficulties of applying rasa theory to music, still think that the idea of rasa, in itself, has deep significance for music and cannot be abandoned. On the other hand, as concerns music itself, it is clear that musical structures have changed over the centuries, resulting in a palimpsest that is even more complex than the theoretical one; for the description of rāgas, tālas and forms in the treatises are mere traces of oral traditions that have disappeared or mutated along with the generations of musicians. Thus, one finds puzzling, in several ways, the relation of contemporary, living musical practices to their earlier forms as described in the saṅgīta śāstras.

Recognized as a leading authority in this field, P.L. Sharma is one of the authors who have questioned the validity of rasa theory as applied to Hindustani music. She writes: 'we need not expect the whole paraphernalia of the rasa theory that developed in the context of drama, to be directly presentable in our music' (1970: 63). Sharma is referring not only to the technicalities of the theory, such as the several kinds of bhāvas and their relations with theater techniques (abhinaya), but also the lack of signification of some of the nine rasas in relation to music, as I have already discussed (see 3.3.5). Still, she believes that 'Rasa in its essential form of aesthetic delight is undoubtedly present in music' (Sharma 1970: 63). In fact, the theory of rasa appeared in connection with the jāti system and the Sanskrit drama as exposed in the NŚ. One might see the development of the rāga system, in which musical structures evolved more and more as individual entities, to be in conflict with the generality of the rasas, as Widdess indicates: 'In the aesthetic sense, the rāga of each song or mode is unique, whereas the rasas are very broad categories of feeling. Similarly, each musical rāga, in the technical sense, is unique, and precisely defined, whereas the jātis are comparatively broad modal categories' (1995: 40). Thus, one may conclude that the rasas were appropriate categories when applied to the jātis, but not so in relation to rāgas, which are more singular melodic structures. Nevertheless, later treatises persisted in assigning rasas to rāgas, in a continuous tradition of scholarship that extends into the present day.

Another skeptical view on the subject of rāga and rasa grounds its argument on personal and socio-cultural factors of listening. S.S. Rao claims that 'in the light of subjectivity involved in rāga-performance, listeners and performers; changed socio-cultural values and aesthetic norms, the specificity attached to rāga-rasa relation has become a questionable issue. Hence, the musicians seem to be hesitant in accepting the idea of associating a rāga with a specific rasa' (1992: 3). Still, and similarly to Sharma's view, Rao defends the notion that rāgas produce some sort of 'unique aesthetic atmosphere' (ibid.). In opposition to the subjective factor, there are authors who defend the application of rasa theory to music, contending that aesthetical experience is instead based on 'disinterested or impersonal pleasure and enjoyment of bliss (ānanda)', as Prajñānānanda writes. He continues: 'We know that the poetic or musical sentiment (rasa) is peculiar in its nature, and it is, no doubt, a fact of one's own consciousness, but it is essentially universal and impersonal in nature, being common to all readers, artists and audiences, and possessing no significance to their personal relations and interests. The rasa in this sense is alaukika or supernormal' (1973: 246). The basis of Prajñānānanda's argument is that rasa is not merely unworldly (alaukika) but transcendental: 'Rasa or aesthetic sentiment is the medium for appreciation of the Supreme Ānanda' (1973: 237).

Conversely, Saxena defends the idea that the musical aesthetic experience is rational, and rasa is not excluded from it: 'the pervasive charm of a rāga is always, in part, intellectual' (1991a: 35). Further, he refuses mere sensation as the basis of appreciating rasa: 'Even the rasika's experience, as he feels captivated by a rāga's variform beauty, is no mere abandonment to a quite nebulous relish, as when we give ourselves up to the taste of a richly spiced delicacy the constituent flavors of which we may not be able to distinguish' (ibid.). In this way, Saxena does not interpret the NŚ (6.31-33) metaphor for rasa as literally 'tasting'. The true enjoyment of rāga is not only sensuous, but involves the understanding of a rāga's intellectual construction. Thus, the rasa a musician projects 'is no mere emotion conveyed by, or expressed through the form of the rāga; it is the feeling appearance of the rāga-rūpa itself, provided this form has been evoked by means of an apt selection of the elements and their proper integration' (Saxena 1991a: 42). Thus, the rasa of a rāga for Saxena is neither a subjective emotion nor a transcendent mystical state, but a concrete enjoyment of musical structures and their qualities.

These are some of the elements on the palimpsest of music and rasa at the end of the 20th century. In fact, since its origin and development, the several aspects of rasa theory itself – the multiplication of hypotheses and opinions, discussions of rasa in academic debates, especially during the second half of the first millennium – have collaborated in sustaining a variety of points of view, to which no agreement can be expected among scholars of today. Nevertheless, it seems to me that the theory of rasa remains significant to Hindustani music, as long as the aesthetic experience and concept of rasa are understood as being interrelated with the total musical universe, and not limited to a single item of its theoretical aspects. I will propose a semiotic interpretation for such interrelations, despite the risk of introducing more elements onto this already cluttered palimpsest. I believe that a semiotic view can serve as a map or diagram of how the appreciation of Indian music may be conceived in terms of rasa.

Triadic Unity of Aesthetic Experience: Rāga-Bhāva-Rasa

Whatever kind of experience aesthetic enjoyment may be, it must take place by means of semiosis. I take semiosis here in a broad sense, in which not only forms of genuine thirdness are involved, but also secondness and firstness. In 2.3.3.1 I discussed the Peircean theory of perception, and explained how firstness and secondness are necessary elements in the generation of perceptive judgments and subsequent semiosis. On one hand, from a strict point of view, even the most immediate of perceptions is mediated at least by the percipuum; and, on the other, from a broad point of view, semiosis can determine interpretants the nature of which is of secondness and firstness rather than genuine thirdness (CP 8.332).

The semiotic unity of Indian music, aesthetically speaking, is constituted by three relata: rāga, bhāva and rasa. These terms engage in semiosis in a triadic way. Rāga is a first, that is, the musical sign, the entity that represents an object. The object is a second, and can be called bhāva; thus, a rāga stands for its object – bhāva – and determines an interpretant, a third, which is the rasa. Rāga, bhāva and rasa are signs themselves, involved in a complex web of signification, and their main relationships have to be made clear. Rāga, as a musical sign in itself, is less problematic. Its musical materiality can be described accurately in terms of qualisigns, sinsigns and legisigns (see 2.3.1). Many descriptions of rāgas have been advanced, running from the early Sanskrit treatises up to contemporary textbooks, the interrelations of which are no simple matter. Yet, contemporary rāgas can be clearly described and analyzed by drawing from current traditions (bānīs and gharānās). The objects for which rāgas stand, however, present some difficulty. Chapters 2.3 and 3.3 discussed some of the possible objects represented by Hindustani music, but my study was not exhaustive.[1] In order to understand the object of the rāga-sign, it is necessary to consider the nature and relations of immediate and dynamical objects (see 2.2). The immediate object is the object as represented by the sign. Thus, it is necessarily an acoustic entity, if the sign is a rāga in its musical materiality (and not a musical instrument or the body of a musician). There is one modality of semiosis in which the dynamical and immediate object of a rāga-sign are the same, and that is when music is interpreted as representing nothing other than its musical capacities. In that case, a rāga is an icon of its musical materiality, for the object is also a musical object. In this situation the sign is the musical form or rāgarūpa, and the dynamic object is constituted by the rāgabhāva. If an interpretant (dynamical) is limited to the reference of the rāga-sign as rāgabhāva, it is likely to develop thought-signs related only to the musical materiality, its qualities, the particular way musical legisigns actualize as sinsigns, and so on. Thus, the aesthetic experience is basically intellectual in nature, as Saxena says, and the rasa interpretant would be a musical quality of feeling. However, the nature of the dynamical object of a rāga is such that it can be of an enormous variety of acoustic and non-acoustic qualities, existents and thoughts. A rāga may refer to contexts of history, region, culture, myth, religion, literature and drama, as well as to individuals (composers, musicians, rulers), ideas, facts, qualities, and many other things. All those function as dynamical objects in the web of musical semiosis, in which rāga-signs may refer in different modes

[1] An exhaustive study of objects represented by Indian music would be an impossibility, not only in face of the complexity of this culture, but also in the sense that it is changing and evolving continuously.

(generally, they can be iconic, indexical and symbolic; see 2.3.2), affording great possibilities of different interpretants. The rasa interpretant here would be some kind of very refined quality of feeling, related to its object by the mediation of the sign. It is useless to proceed in such general terms, however, so I will make use of two rāgas, which have been related to different kinds of śṛṅgāra, as concrete examples: hiṇḍola and toḍī. I will first discuss the musical materiality of these rāgas; secondly, their scope of reference; and thirdly, their interpretants, in the broad context of the aesthetic experience as conceived by Abhinavagupta.

Rāga hiṇḍola (or hiṇḍol)

Hiṇḍola is one of the oldest rāgas, and it represents very well the aspects of continuity and change in Indian music. As early as the first appearance (in the BD) of the concept of rāga in musical scholarship, rāga hiṇḍola was listed and described as being among the 33 main grāmarāgas. It had and still has a pentatonic structure. In the early hiṇḍola, the second and sixth degrees are omitted. The two main modal functions – aṁśa (predominant) and nyāsa (final) – coincide with the first degree **s** (BD 3.325). The scale of hiṇḍola can be approximately notated as in Ex. 56. This pitch set was still the basis of hiṇḍola as practiced some five hundred years later, for the same structure is given in the SR (2.2.93c-93a). Śārṅgadeva presents, in addition to verbal descriptions, notated songs for each of the main rāgas. Śārṅgadeva wrote a song in rāga hiṇḍola as well, which is transnotated in Ex. 57 (SR 2.2.93c-93a ff.). In this song, not only is the pitch set clear, but more importantly, some melodic motifs can be sorted out; these are marked in brackets on the staff, identified as A, B, C, and D. It is obvious that, in this example, the rāga was conceived as structure, a script for improvisation and/or composition (as Rowell writes, 1992: 81-82).

Treatises written after the 16th century present disparate conceptions of rāga hiṇḍola. This may be explained by the incursion of foreign musical elements, which Indian music received on several occasions, especially from the time of Śārṅgadeva onwards, when new rāgas, forms and instruments appeared as the result of influences from the middle East and central Asia. In addition, the regional traditions in India were far from being uniform. Puṇḍarīka Viṭṭhāla, a scholar who worked for several patrons in North and South India, presented two versions of hiṇḍola (Ex. 58; according to Bhātkhaṇḍe 1990: 49, 58). The major difference in relation to BD and SR hiṇḍola is the omission of the fifth degree, instead of the sixth, and this is specified as a minor sixth.

Example 56

Rāga hiṇḍola (BD, SR)

Example 57

Rāga hiṇḍola (SR)

Example 58

Rāga hiṇḍola (Puṇḍarīka Viṭṭhāla)

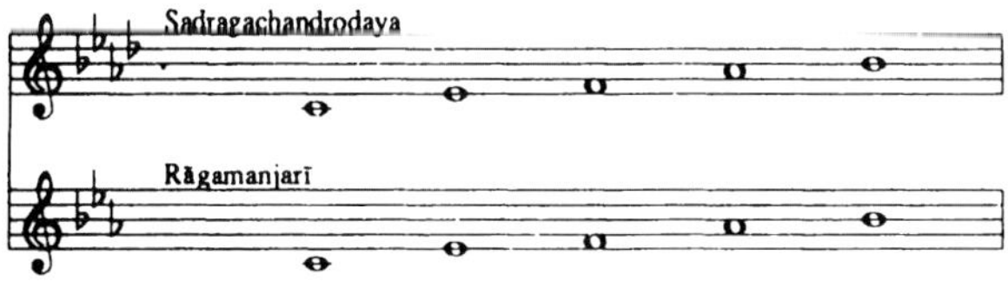

According to Somanātha, in his RV, hiṇḍola had a totally different scale (Ex. 59), featuring at that time a major third. Somanātha left written compositions for the vīṇā with precise notations for the ornaments. I have adapted a transnotation from Nijenhuis (1976: 2.75) in Ex. 60. It seems that this rāga was evolving in a certain direction, but the old form of hiṇḍola was still mentioned by Dāmodara, in the SD, who gave the same scale for hiṇḍola as one finds in the earliest sources (Ex. 61). Another work of the 17th century, the *Saṅgītapārijāta* by Ahobala-paṇḍita, describes hiṇḍola as a structure similar to Puṇḍarīka Viṭṭhāla's *Rāgamanjarī*, as Ex. 62 makes clear.

Example 59
Rāga hiṇḍola (RV)

Example 60
Rāga hiṇḍola, composition (RV)

Example 61
Rāga hiṇḍola (SD)

Example 62
Rāga hiṇḍola (Ahobala-paṇḍita)

The contemporary Hindustani conception of hiṇḍola appears in the *Saṅgītsār* (according to Nijenhuis 1976: 36), a treatise commissioned by the Mahārāja of Jaipur, Pratāp Singh in the late 18th century. The distinctive marks of contemporary hiṇḍola are the major third and the augmented fourth (Ex. 63). The vādī is D, and saṁvādī is G. It is considered an uttaraṅga rāga, because the predominant degree is in the upper tetrachord; thus, the rāga tends to move in the upper registers. Some typical melodic movements are presented in Ex. 64, according to contemporary authors. Notice that the seventh is avoided in approaching the high tonic in an upwards movement; a curved motif (vakra) based on D is applied instead (as in Ex. 64, A). This musical material is used for improvisations, either in ālāps or bandiśes, set in particular forms and tālas. A dhamār composed by Viṣṇu Digaṁbar Paluskar is presented in Ex. 67.

Example 63

Rāga hiṇḍola (Hindustani contemporary)

Example 64

Rāga hiṇḍola (KPM, RVJ, SA)

I have been focusing on hiṇḍola's aspects of legisign, that is, the rāga as a musical habit or law, and how it has changed during its life of more than 12 centuries. There are at least two other relevant semiotic features of hiṇḍola. Prior to its character as a legisign, hiṇḍola is an existent, a sinsign; and prior to its character as sinsign, hiṇḍola is a qualisign, a complex of musical qualities. In fact, hiṇḍola only has actuality when all three features manifest. In Hindustani music theory this is called svarūp: form, nature, or the essential properties. Powers describes it as the gestalt of a rāga (1970: 45-46).

The dynamical object of a rāga may be understood as purely musical structures, as I have been exploring in relation to hiṇḍola. Yet, rāgas are also able to function as signs referring to other kinds of objects. It is well known that the word hiṇḍola means 'swing'. Swings in India have great importance. They are used by tribal mystics to attain contact with deities, and enjoyed in themselves as entertainment in villages and cities. In this latter sense, swings may be understood as symbols of a good time, of leisure and sensual games. Swinging is often connected with songs that have an erotic content. There are two seasons particularly suitable to playing on swings, spring and monsoon, both of which are special times of year in India. Rāga hiṇḍola has long been associated with springtime, but at least one old reference connects it to the monsoon festival. According to Bhoja's *Śṛṅgāra Prakaśā*, rāgiṇī hiṇḍola is mentioned in the context of a rains festival called Āndolanacaturthī, or Hiṇḍolakrīḍā, which consists in playing on the swing. Bhoja also explains that this was not a religious festival, but rather a secular, romantic occasion (in Raghavan 1978: 635).

Besides swinging, hiṇḍola refers to the awakening of nature in spring. The Indian calendar begins with vasanta,[2] and its advent is celebrated with the Holī festival (which, as a festive period, starts some weeks before). This festival is connected with ancient fertility rites held in honor of Kāma, the god of erotic love (see Bashan 1954: 209). Nowadays, it refers to another folk form of this deity, usually a lewd demon whose effigy may be burned on the Holī pyre at the culmination of the festival (O'Flaherty 1973: 160).[3] The relation of Holī to springtime and fertility is an obvious one, and its animated and, at the same time, erotic character still manifests in today's Holī, in the form of merrymaking and the singing of obscene songs – the *phaguās* (see Henry 1988: 121-33). According to Kane:

> The *Kāmasūtra* and *Bhaviṣyottara* connect it [Holī] with spring and it was performed at the end of the year (on Pūrṇimānta reckoning). Therefore, the bonfire represents the expiration of the season of frost and cold and heralds the warmth and love-making of spring. The ribald songs, dance and music are further accretions due to the joy felt on the advent of spring. The sprinkling of coloured water and powder is an additional item in the celebration of the delights of spring. (1974: 240-41)

---

[2] Depending on the means of calculation, vasanta starts on the first day of the dark half of the Caitra month (by Pūrṇimānta reckoning), as indicated in most Indian calendars; or on the fifth day of the bright half of the Māgha month (following Nirṇayāmṛta), also called Vasantapañcamī (see Kane 1974: 403-04).

Swinging is not an activity directly connected with Holī, although people may play on swings in spring. However, in West Bengal, a religious swing festival called Dolotsava or Dolayātrā is held during the spring in honor of Kṛṣṇa and his lover Rādhā, when statues of the divine couple are put on a swing and worshipped (see Kane 1974: 239-40).

Varśa, or the rainy season, is doubly important, both as an agricultural need and as refreshment after the dry Indian summer. It is culturally thought of as a season for amusement and romance, for most travelers and workers return to their home-place shortly before the rains. Couples who have been apart for almost one year meet again. On the other hand, there is also the habit of married women going to visit their parents in this season. In this case, there is the feeling of separation, the longing for the company of their husbands, which is intensified by the pleasantness of the season. The signs of nature, such as the heavy clouds, bird songs, the cry of peacocks (the vehicle of Kāma), are all symbols of love in India. Varśa is a season when swinging is important. In the states of Uttar Pradeś and Bihar swinging is accompanied by folk songs called *kajalī*, which are erotic in content (Henry 1988: 133-39). Although hiṇḍola is not usually considered a rāga related to the rains, it can refer narratively to the high spirits and pleasantness of that season, especially when performed in seasons other than spring.

As early as its first available description, rāga hiṇḍola is said to represent śṛṅgāra rasa, the erotic sentiment. Both varieties of śṛṅgāra – sambhoga, or love in union; and vipralambha, or love in separation – are meaningful in songs, dances and plays related to spring and rains. In the BD's description of hiṇḍola, one reads: 'Its application is prescribed in sambhoga-śṛṅgāra' (BD 3.anu.198). In the SR, hiṇḍola is explicitly related to the god of eroticism: hiṇḍola is 'employed in the context of [the] enjoyment of erotic love to the endearment of Kāma;' moreover, Śārṅgadeva writes that hiṇḍola's proper season is spring, and also that it has to be performed in the fourth quarter of the day (SR 2.2.93c-96a). The lyrics of the song, transcribed in Ex. 57. associate hiṇḍola with the Śaiva universe, to which Kāma relates in a number of ancient myths. This song refers to the burning of Kāma by Śiva's third eye. The lyrics translate as: 'I bow down to Śiva who has satisfied the wishes of all people who have taken refuge in him, and who, accompanied by his consort, is the destroyer of the body of Kāma' (SR ibid.).

Between the 14th and 17th centuries, in the rāga-rāgiṇī systems (see 3.3.4), hiṇḍola appears as a male rāga in schemes by Meṣakarṇa, Viṭṭhāla and Hanumān; and as a rāgiṇī in classifications by Someśvara and Rāgarṇava (see Tables 13 and 14 in 3.3.4). The dynamical objects to

---

[3] O'Flaherty calls attention to the significant parallel between burning the Holī pyre and the myth of the burning of Kāma by Śiva (ibid.)

which rāgas and rāgiṇīs referred were described in poems (dhyāna) and miniature paintings. In the SD (2.72) and RV (5.174), hiṇḍola is portrayed as a handsome man, enjoying the pleasure of playing on a swing pushed by beautiful women (see 3.3.4). In this context, hiṇḍola is described as one of the theater characters, which may be classified as the dakṣiṇa nāyaka: a hero, of high rank, who is kind and impartial, while loving another woman.

The *Rāgasāgara*, written in this same period, presents a female form of hiṇḍola. She worships Kṛṣṇa and Kamalā,[4] who sit on a swing:

> From my heart I pray to hiṇḍola, fair-bodied and dressed in variegated patterned [sic] apparel. Adorned with ornaments and precious gems, fond of music of the murali [flute], she devoutly worships Lord Kṛṣṇa, sitting with Kamalā on a golden swing supported by braided fibres of the fig tree. (*Rāgasāgara* 3.61 in Kaufmann 1993: 114)

Here Kṛṣṇa takes the place of the classical Sanskrit theater hero of older texts, and hiṇḍola is one of his devotees. But the Vaiśnava absorption is smooth, for Kṛṣṇa is also the god of love. But now, the love is that of a devotee for a deity, as well as conversely. A miniature painting from the 17th century, in the style of Marwar, represents rāga hiṇḍola. It shows Kṛṣṇa and his lover sitting on a large swing, assisted by two other women and musicians. Kṛṣṇa himself is grasping a vīṇā, while his other hand holds his girlfriend's hand. Peacocks and dark clouds seem to refer to the rainy season (see Ebeling 1973: 57). Both the dhyāna and paintings may also be understood as references to the Dolotsava festival in Bengal. Several other miniatures of hiṇḍola (always in the context of a swing) depict musicians and instruments, indicating that music, in general, is a sign of good times.

A dhrupad attributed to Tānsen represents very well all these features – the enjoyment of springtime with music and romantic feelings. In this composition (translated by Delvoye 1994b: 7), Tānsen is probably addressing his patron, Emperor Akbar, to whom the attention of lovely ladies is directed, although 'the Lord of Tānsen' may also be interpreted as a deity.

> Let us play together in different ways,
> Now the Spring season has come!
> Among the young woman, O my friend,
> One is laughing while beating time,
> Another is playing the lute kinara,
> A third sports a diadem [of flowers].
> A woman is singing, another plays the drum mṛdaṅga,
> A third one applies perfume to her body.
> All together with their sakhīs, all exhilarated,
> They surrender to the Lord of Tānsen.

[4] Another name of Kṛṣṇa's consort.

Although hiṇḍola's sign, in its musical materiality, has varied and changed during the centuries, there is a remarkable agreement in its scope of meaning, that is, the objects to which hiṇḍola refers, which could be interpreted in general terms as the rasa śṛṅgāra. At the end of the last century, a Hindi treatise written by Appa Tulasī describes hiṇḍola in terms similar to those in the older sources: 'The sages say that hiṇḍola rāga, gleaming with the radiance of innumerable doves flying in the sky, is highly amorous and moves to and fro in a slow moving swing in the company of women with well-shaped hips' (*Rāgakalapadruma* 20, in Kaufmann 1993: 114).

However, contemporary hiṇḍola is not as clearly associated with śṛṅgāra as its earlier forms were. In fact, although its scalar structure is still pentatonic, it differs notably from the pitch set ascribed to hiṇḍola in BD or in Ahobala's *Saṅgītapārijāta*. One may ask if the contemporary hiṇḍola still represents the same dynamic objects as its older conceptions. The answer to this question is complex, involving not only the musical features and references of hiṇḍola, but also the possible interpretants it may generate. Considering the musical materiality of this rāga, and given the lack of evidence in the musical treatises of a gradual change from old to contemporary forms of hiṇḍola, some authors tried to find direct connections explaining its musical changes. Powers argues that BD's hiṇḍola and its contemporary Hindustani form are similar in their scalar configuration (1970: 15-16), which becomes apparent if one of them is shifted (or loosely transposed) a fourth in relation to the other, as in Ex. 65. The pattern of intervals in both scales is similar, but they do not correspond perfectly. Powers's justification is that rotations of basic scales were an important way of deriving rāgas, and in this sense, contemporary hiṇḍola has features that have persisted since the earliest forms (1970: 16), such as the pattern of a minor third, major second, (major or minor) second, major third and (major or minor) second.

Example 65

The relations between early and contemporary hiṇḍola (according to Powers)

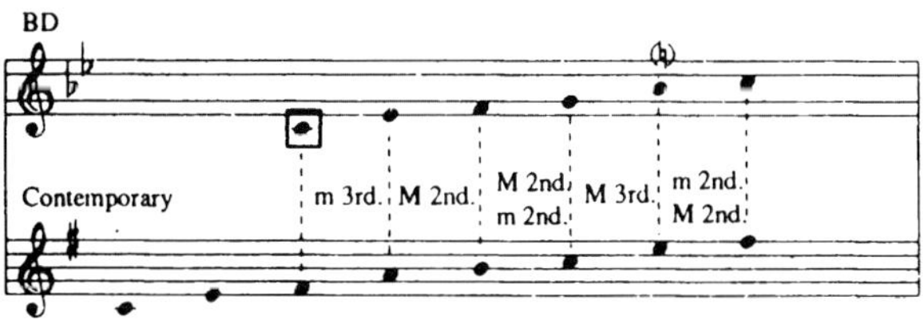

Another explanation is offered by Jairazbhoy, on different grounds. He suggests that, since hiṇḍola, according to the *Saṅgītapārijāta*, has all variable degrees in directly opposite forms in relation to the contemporary form of this rāga (that is, S, G, M, D, N, contrasted to S, G, M, D, N), what could have happened was a semitonal shift of the tonic (1971: 101). Lowering the pitch of S by one semitone, while keeping the pitches of the other svaras, indeed produces, in a single move, the contemporary hiṇḍola (Ex. 66). Although both Power's and Jairazbhoy's hypotheses are theoretically correct, the direct derivation of a contemporary rāga from structures that were in practice hundreds, or even more than a thousand years ago, is not totally convincing.

Example 66

Semitonal shift in hiṇḍola (according to Jairazbhoy)

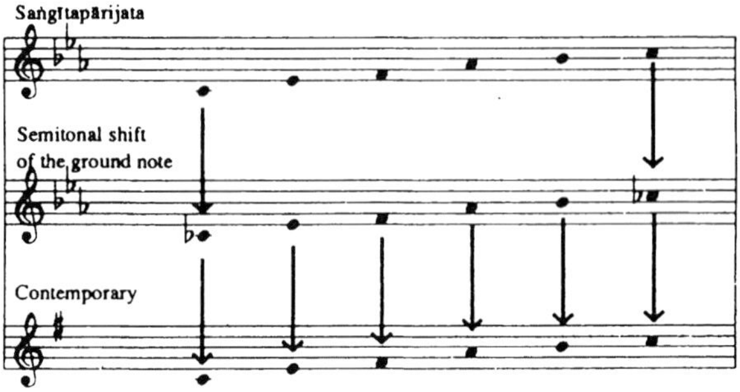

As to the meanings of hiṇḍola, there is some disagreement among contemporary authors. Rao states hiṇḍola signifies gambhīr (RN 2.129), whereas Kaufmann mentions a quiet, dignified joy (1993:116). According to Ṭhākur, hiṇḍola has tīvratā – intensity, ardor, impetuosity. He even mentions vīra, specifying that 'the vīra of hiṇḍola is of a particular nature' (SA 2.138). Ṭhākur argues that it is the augmented fourth and the predominant melodic movement in the high registers that produce the tīvratā of hiṇḍola. Ṭhākur's specification of hiṇḍola as having tīvratā seems to indicate that contemporary hiṇḍola not only has a distinct pitch set, but it also refers to other dynamical objects than did its earlier forms. Ṭhākur even mentions the NŚ rule (SA 2.137). The latter states that jātis with S or R as aṁśa express vīra, adbhuta and raudra, which would apply to the early forms of hiṇḍola in regard to S. This line of argument proves unfruitful, however, for the NŚ rule for the rasas represented by the jātis of early music cannot be applied to different musical systems, such as that of the contemporary Hindustani rāga.

The bandiśes in hiṇḍola, as presented in the main contemporary treatises, constitute another source of reference to the meanings possibly represented by this rāga. It is clear that most of the compositions are not related to the heroic rasa, but strongly connected to themes of spring, the Holī festival, the rainy season, and the nāyaka-nāyikā bheda. The typical subjects of poems related to vasant and Holī are referred to in the following compositions: *Khelata phaga unmaṁga saba Brija sundara ḍhora mila āī* (RVJ 1.96), 'Playing Holī, full of joy, the beauties of Braj have come together'; *Horī khelata hai Giridhāri* (RVJ 1.103), 'The Mountain-holder [Kṛṣṇa] plays Holī'; *Karale picakārī kesara bhara abīla gulāl uḍhaye khele* (RVJ 1.99, KPM 4.184), 'Fill your pipettes, [take] the yellow and red powders – let us play, sprinkling [the water] and casting [the dyes]'; *Khelata basanta rājādhirāja dekhata nabha kautuka sura samāja khelata* (RVJ 1.100), 'In the sky, the assembly of gods, with curious gaze, looks on: Spring, the king of kings, is playing'. These are all themes of spring and the Holī festival, but also the rainy season and the month of Sāvan is represented in the following khayāl: *Koyaliyā bole bana meṁ ḍāre ḍāre* (KPM 4.179, and a similar composition in SA 2.141-43), 'In the forest sing the cuckoos from every branch'. Here, although the composition is set in hiṇḍola, a spring rāga, the topic refers narratively to the rainy season and to the song of the cuckoo bird. None of those compositions refers to forms of vīra, but rather point to the range of meanings represented by the older forms of hiṇḍola. Thus, it seems to me that, on one hand, if the musical features of hiṇḍola have changed sharply during the several periods, on the other, its meanings have remained consistent.

Ṭhākur is also right about hiṇḍola's tīvratā. In contemporary Hindustani music the rasa represented by the latter has a special character: an energetic and intense quality, not incompatible with the springtime imagery of blossoms shooting forth. Similarly, there are forms of intense śṛṅgāra. Reflecting this idea of impetuous love are the lyrics in Ex. 67 (RVJ 1.95-96), which are those of a dhamār, a genre of composition particularly related to themes of the Holī festival. The song tells of Śyāmā, a mistress of Kṛṣṇa (who is also called Śyāma, the dark one). She wants anxiously to play Holī with Kṛṣṇa, beseeching him with the traditional gesture of folded hands.[5] She is not supposed to go out, however, because of her duties at home. Yet she finds an excuse to slip away and deceive her in-laws. Śyāmā, in this context, may be thought of as the daring girl, or abhisārikā nāyikā:[6]

---

[5] A literal translation of the second verse refers to the gesture of bowing down and touching the feet of an elder person or the guru's feet, as a sign of respect. In this case, an iconic sign might be seen in the descending line of the melody for the words *pā lāgo*.

[6] My translation.

Please, enjoy [yourself] playing Holī with me [O, Śyāma],
Śyāmā implores with folded hands.
I [have to] go out to tend the little cows,
Leaving behind my mother-in-law and my sister-in-law.[7]

Example 67

Rāga hiṇḍola, dhamār, *Śyāmā Moso Khelonā Horī* (RVJ 1.95-96)

I have hence added yet another semiotic dimension to the study of rāga hiṇḍola: the objects which it may stand for. Bhāva, or the semiotic complex that a rāga represents, includes the acoustical and non-acoustical objects of a rāga. The svarūp, or the rāga's gestalt, refers to a musical object that may be called rāgabhāva, the tonal complex of a rāga and its particular atmosphere, that is, the totality of qualisigns, sinsigns, and legisigns that characterize a rāga as an individual. Yet, the word bhāva means not only being, existence, disposition, temperament; it also denotes the 'outward indication of emotion or meaning' (McGregor 1995). Therefore, besides the rāgabhāva, which is a rāga's immediate object, the bhāva of a rāga includes its entire scope of representation as a complex sign, referring to dynamical objects both acoustic and non-acoustic in nature. In the case of hiṇḍola, its dynamical object is the Indian springtime and its cultural elements.

Peirce thought the relation of a sign to its object to be of three kinds: icon, index and symbol (see 2.2). As a symbol, hiṇḍola refers to śṛṅgāra,

[7] This composition does not readily lend itself for a clear translation. The first line is problematic in relation to the third and fourth lines, for the addresser and addressee cannot be easily identified. Delvoye, in a personal communication, remarks that this is a typical problem of oral transmission, where a single corrupted word (such as Śyāma or Śyāmā) can make the meanings of a poem indefinite.

and is grounded on a habit of interpretation. If one relates rāga hiṇḍola to the idea of swings and their connection with spring or rains in India, then it is operating as an indexical sign. If qualities belonging to the sign itself somehow recall qualities of a swing or the act of swinging, then the sign is an iconic sign. For instance, the oscillations of a swing can be represented by waves of melodic movement, or tāns, improvised by the soloist. However, this kind of melodic curve abounds in any rāga and is not a particular feature of hiṇḍola. In fact, icons cannot assure anything, for qualities are only appearances. Still, this does not invalidate the iconic mode of reference; rather, its decoding is left to the interpreters, that is, to both musicians and listeners. The more one finds significations in a rāga, the more s/he will enjoy it. But to talk about enjoyment is already a discussion of interpretants.

Toḍī

Contrasting with hiṇḍola, rāga toḍī may represent vipralambha, or in extreme cases, karuṇa. The evolution of toḍī and its varieties seems as complex as that of hiṇḍola, and several authors have tried to trace the musical features of toḍī through the centuries (see Powers 1970: 17-27; Jairazbhoy 1971: 94-99; Manuel 1985). In the SR, toḍī is related to grāmarāga ṣāḍava, from which it derives its early musical and representational features. Ṣāḍava is a heptatonic rāga, has weak G and P, employs antara-ga, and has kākali-ni as an ascending leading tone (SR 2.74-76; see Widdess 1995: 296, 389-90). All modal functions are centered on M, and it represents śṛṅgāra and hāsya. Toḍī has similar features, except that all svaras have equal status, except M, toḍī's aṁśa, and P, which is to be ornamented with shakes. Toḍī is considered a deśī rāga, and signifies harṣa (excitement or delight) (SR 2.76d-77). Its scale is displayed in Ex. 68. Two upaṅgas ragas are derived from it, chāyātoḍī and turuskatoḍī: 'Toḍī, when devoid of ṛṣabha and pañcama[,] is known as chāyātoḍī. Toḍī with ahata gamakas and having a weak gāndhāra and a profusion of niṣāda and dhaivata (becomes) turuṣkatoḍī' (SR 2.134). Chāyātoḍī is thus a pentatonic rāga, lacking R and P, and turuṣkatoḍī is heptatonic, but performed with a scarcity of G and a profusion of N and D (see Ex. 69). According to Gangoly (1989: 22 n.), Turuṣkatoḍī was probably imported from central Asia (Turuṣka-deśa = Turkestan), brought by the Kuṣāṇas, who invaded India early in the first century A.D. Later, this rāga was associated indexically with the Moghuls, but with a different pitch set and referential scope.

Example 68
Rāgiṇī toḍī (SR)

Example 69
Chāyātoḍī and turuskatoḍī (SR)

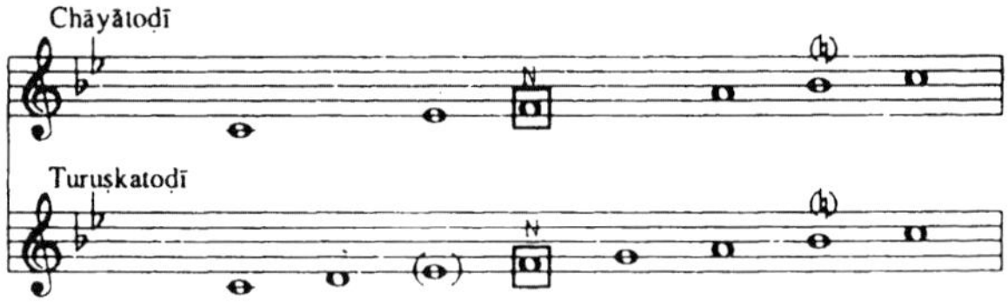

Somanātha classifies turuṣkatoḍī in the RV into two different varieties, one in the mukhārī mela (S R̲ R M P D̲ D Ṡ)[8] and the other in the toḍī mela (S R̲ G̲ M P D̲ N̲ Ṡ). In any case, turuṣkatoḍī has G as aṁśa. Its dhyāna personifies the rāgiṇī as a Moghul lady, wearing a *burka* (a typical Moghul dress). She is very distressed at being separated from her husband, and is referred to by Somanātha as kāntavioygapīḍitā, 'the lady who is incapable of bearing the separation from her lover'; that is, a viharotkaṇṭhitā nāyikā (RV 5.181 in Nijenhuis 1976: 82; see also 3.3.4, above).

Toḍī, the main rāga of this mela, has G as aṁśa (see Ex. 70); it is conceived as a lonely lady wandering in the fields, playing an instrument and charming deer or other wild animals with her music: 'Toḍī is standing in a grove, carrying a vipañcī (vīṇā), while a deer is caressed by her. She is wearing red clothes, has a pale complexion, white cosmetics being applied to her body. She has a soft voice and is decorated' (RV 5.180 in Nijenhuis 1976: 78).

Example 70
Rāgiṇī toḍī (RV)

The several dhyānas and miniatures of toḍī are very consistent, although the musical features change from one treatise to the other. In the

[8] Equivalent Hindustani svaras.

SD, toḍī is heptatonic with M as aṁśa, graha and nyāsa, and belongs to mālavakauśika's family, in Hanumān's rāga-rāgiṇī system. Yet, Dāmodara gives a dhyāna with the same aesthetical objects as Somanātha's: 'The slender body with fresh jasmines shining, anointed with camphor from Kashmir her limbs, pushing back a deer at the edge of a forest glade, holding a vīṇā, shines ṭoḍī' (SD 2.62). Gangoly, who considers this rāga as 'the surrender of animal life to the magic and enchantment of the beauty of nature' (1989: 101), has an ingenious explanation for its origin:

> Possibly the melody came originally from the peasant's field. Very probably, it was a melody sung by the wife or daughter of the peasant who watched the padded fields, (as they still do today, from sunrise to sunset, perched on a bamboo frame), chiding away the deer, and other animals which strayed into the fields, in groups, to eat up the standing crop, before it was ready to be shorn. Perhaps, the farmer's daughter weaned away the encroaching depredator [sic], by the music of her primitive lute, which attracted the deer, and kept them away from mischief. (Gangoly 1989: 152)

Toḍī is indeed mentioned in the SR as a deśī rāga, yet the possibility that it was formerly a worksong later adapted into the classical system is difficult to prove. Nevertheless, the poetical idea of a lonely lady and her enchanting music, powerful enough to charm deer, but still unable to soften her lover's heart, is certainly the aesthetical object which toḍī represents.

The evolution of toḍī into contemporary Hindustani forms – such as miyāṁ kī toḍī, vilaskhānī toḍī, bhūpāl toḍī and gurjarī toḍī – implies several generations of mutating rāga legisigns, which evolved from a pitch set similar to Somanātha's toḍī mela, into the current miyāṁ kī toḍī, which, notwithstanding the reference to Tānsen, is a recent development. Jairazbhoy summarizes the evolution of toḍī since the 17th century in four stages (see Ex. 71, after Jairazbhoy 1971: 98-99).

Example 71

The evolution of toḍī

Example 72

Vilambit khayāl in toḍī, *Ab More Rām-Rām* (KPM 2.446-7)

A vilambit khayāl in toḍī, *Ab More Rām-Rām* (KPM 2.446-7), aptly depicts the sufferings of vipralambha śṛṅgāra (see Ex. 72). The lyrics translate as follows:

Rām, you are my only Rām,
My resting place, Rām.
I call you day and night,
My mind colored [by desire].
I am your servant, you are the dark Rām,
My resting place, Rām.[9]

The song may be understood in religious terms – the devotee's yearning that can only be consummated in the divinity – and also in reference to the heroine whose lover has left her. In the *Rāmāyaṇa* there are certain situations of vipralambha that relate to this khayāl. For instance, when Sītā was separated from Rām when she was abducted by

[9] My translation.

Rāvaṇ, or later, when she was abandoned in the forest because of Rām's doubt about her chastity. In both of those situations, Sītā remained faithful to Rām, in spite of her intense emotional distress, which could rise vipralambha to the high pitch of karuṇa. In terms of nāyaka-nāyikā bheda, the heroine of this composition may not necessarily be Sītā. Her despair is nevertheless utter, not only because of the continuous romantic (and erotic) expectation, but also because the nāyikā has such high esteem for her lover, comparing him to the god Rām, who is also a symbol of the ideal husband. Thus, she can be classified either as the virahotkhaṇṭhitā or as the vipralabdhā nāyikā, and one could easily imagine this lady as the lonely toḍī depicted in the miniatures. The representation, in this case, is much more conventional than hiṇḍola, which has several possibilities of indexical reference. Toḍī is rather likely to be understood as a symbol, and its dynamical object is a poetical idea, that is, another symbol.

According to Ṭhākur, a rāga with (komal) R and (komal) D signifies vipralambha or karuṇa (see 3.3.5). However, (tīvra) M has a special function in this kind of rāga, operating independently of hiṇḍola. In the case of sorrowful rāgas, M acts to intensify the feeling of separation. A very high pitch of vipralambha is represented by gurjarī toḍī. This rāga, similarly to toḍī, has a pitch set constituted by the combination of R, D and M; however, it is a hexatonic rāga, omitting P. The lack of a perfect fifth in relation to the tonic is not a significant factor in the representation of vipralambha in this rāga. According to Jairazbhoy, the lack of P in gurjarī toḍī instead reestablishes harmonic balance between the two tetrachords (1971: 84-85). Thus, the character of gurjarī toḍī as representing intolerable suffering of separation (SA 6.31) is grounded not on individual pitch relations but on the totality of the rāga as a symbol.

Musical Experience as a Double Spiral

The aesthetic experience obviously commences with perception, which should be understood as a dialogical process of semiosis. The performance of a rāga consists in the dynamical causation of sounds by the musicians, who act according to the principle of final causation; that is, the physical aspect of music is controlled by the teleological aspect of mental design. Thus, musicians playing rāga hiṇḍola or toḍī, for instance, will coordinate their physical actions in such a way that the resulting svaras and vistārs actualize the legisigns which those rāgas represent. On the other hand, musical perception is the result of the physical impact of acoustical percepts upon the sense of hearing, the aspect of secondness of which is clear from the fact that the sounds reaching one's ears act independently of the will of the hearer. As long as the listener stays in the concert hall, the music will manifest to the ears. Yet, perception is not merely dyadic, although this relation is undeniably present. Perception obtains in the generation of dynamical interpretants in the listener's mind, which range from the emotional and energetic to the logical. These dynamical interpretants are not generated randomly, but in accordance with a tendency related to the sign's capacity of significations, or final interpretant. This tendency is not deterministic, however, for a substantial margin of chance and iconic relations may lead interpretants to other directions of meaning. Therefore, on one hand, from the purely musical point of view, the final interpretant of a rāga constitutes the tendency for realizing its rāgabhāva; and, on the other, from the broader field of aesthetic experience, the tendency for realizing its rasa, say, sambhoga in the case of hiṇḍola, or vipralambha in the case of toḍī.

Listeners do not passively receive the music, but interact with the musicians, either physically (as when the audience of an Indian music concert utter words of appreciation), or psychically (which is not as empirically evident, but possible in view of the idea of a collective mind shared by musicians and listeners during an inspired performance).[10] Thus, a concert can be said to function as a dialogical form of semiosis, which may be described as a double spiral. The performance constitutes the outward spiral, and perception the inward spiral; these are the philosophical-musical correlations referred to by Rowell: 'The metaphor works in both directions: the way of action (the *karmamārga*) radiates outward from the center, whereas the way of perception and of knowledge (the *jñānamārga*) proceeds in the opposite direction' (1992: 33). The image of 'musical sound as an emanation along an outward spiral pathway' is a typical one in Indian thought, and may be found in a variety of forms in both musical and philosophical literature; for example: 'the concentric ripples produced by a stone dropped into a pool of water' (Rowell 1992: 33); the process of sound causation by the will of the mind, which impels prāṇa, or vital force, to gradually manifest nāda, rising upwards in the human body from the root of the navel to heart, throat, and finally resonating audibly in the mouth (SR 1.3.3-4); or the progressive development of nāda into letters, words, sentences, language and all the 'business of life' (SR 1.2.2). Conversely, the inward spiral signifies 'a process of increasing focus, distillation, and concentration of energies, leading to a great purity, understanding, and eventual detachment of the phenomenal world' (Rowell 1992: 33). The two kinds of spiral, which I would specify as semiotic spirals, function simultaneously and in a double direction, from the perspectives of both the musicians and the listeners.

This image of musical-dialogical semiosis seems especially relevant to Indian music. Spirals imply continuity and dynamic evolution, which are obvious features of Indian music. Continuity is apparent in the sound of the omnipresent drone of a tambūrā (or any other instrument with similar function). The performance of a rāga can be described as a cumulative process. Progressively, around the drone, the tonal and rhythmic

---

10 The idea of collective mind in musical performance will be explained in detail below.

materials evolve in a spiral-like, non-linear development. Both vocal and instrumental music in India follow a general improvisation form that arises from the unmetered presentation of a rāga's melodic characteristics, and develops into a melodic composition set to a rhythmic structure (tāla). This can be illustrated with the sequence of ālāp, joṛ, jhālā, gat,[11] which is a traditional form rendered in instrumental music, especially on string instruments such as the rudrāvīṇā, sitār and sarod. In the ālāp, the unmetered opening section, notes are presented almost one by one, in a progressive display of the scope of musical qualities, which emphasizes the different qualities of feeling of the intervallic relations typical of that rāga. Later, the other two sections, joṛ and jhālā, establish progressively a pulse for the development of melodic motifs, which are brought to a musical climax in the jhālā. These sections can be thought of as an intermediate state between the liquid nature of ālāp and the cyclic aspect of tāla. When the gat is presented, according to the tāla cycle, and the mukhṛā, or chief melodic phrase, is repeated after each round of improvisation, the musical spiral becomes even more distinct. During the performance the musicians employ several resources for the amplification of aesthetic enjoyment, such as the creation of expectations, their evasion, their partial or total fulfillment, and so forth. These techniques are also employed in a progressive way. Therefore (in a condensed exposition), this constitutes the outward spiral of musical performance.

From the perceptual point of view, the continuity of a drone provides a source of constant focus, which helps the listener to concentrate and to immerse her or himself totally in the perception of a rāga. As the several musical elements are gradually introduced, the listener more and more realizes the totality of feeling of the rāga, that is, its rāgabhāva. The ālāp section is crucial in signifying the rāga's profundity. According to Saxena, 'The true aesthetic warrant of ālāpa, I believe, is its unmatched power to produce such effects as those of grandeur, serenity, seamlessness and infinity; and to evoke an intense yet identifiable rāga-atmosphere' (1992: 6). As the performance evolves, musical elements are more and more clearly articulated, and the perception of musical continua is modulated by the recognition of musical patterns, as Lannoy points out: 'The audience at a recital of Indian classical music becomes physically engrossed by the agile patterns and counter-patterns, responding with unfailing and instinctive kinaesthetic accuracy to the terminal beat in each tāla' (1971: 277).

Thus, it is by progressive realization and empathy that the musical-aesthetic impression is relished. This process can be described as *circumaudition*, as Rowell proposes: 'In the case of music, the required mode of perception might be described as *circumaudition:* just as we

---

[11] This sequence derives from the basic form of dhrupad: ālāp, nom-tom ālāp, bandiś (composition), which progresses from slow to fast tempo. A similar arrangement is present in the sequence of vilambit khayāl, and drut khayāl.

come to know a temple by circumambulating it, in the same way we come to know a musical event by a process of gradual discovery' (1992: 228). In the process of circumaudition, all the modes of semiosis and inference may be used. The features of musical appearance, or qualisigns, are assimilated by the listener contiguously with the identification of sinsigns and legisigns. In 2.3.3 I explored the role of the three modes of inference – abduction, induction and deduction – in the musical cognition process. However, this active intellectual form of listening neither precludes the consciousness of musical experience as the actual performance develops, nor the quality of feelings which necessarily come before, and follows along with all forms of semiosis.

The Aesthetic Process as Sign Interpretation

Circumaudition – a complex form of musical semiosis – is, thus, the process by which the ultimate experience of rasa is to be achieved. However, the listener who wishes to relish rasa must be prepared and must actively adjust her/his consciousness in a particular way. The Indian aestheticians believe that the highest levels of the aesthetic experience are only enjoyed by connoisseurs (rasika, in Sanskrit). Such a listener has the capacity to relish musical qualities in themselves and, having enjoyed a number of different performances, is able to recognize the different forms: thus, the rasika, reacting from a solid base of musical knowledge, values accordingly the accomplishments of the musicians. These three features – sensitivity, experience and knowledge – should not identify the rasika as an 'ideal listener', but rather characterize the aesthetic capacities that are present in different degrees and proportions in every attentive listener. In fact, the most important aptitude of a rasika is that of empathy. Abhinavagupta designates the spectator (or reader) who has this capacity as sahṛdaya, the possessed of heart: 'Those people who are capable of identifying with the subject matter; as the mirror of their hearts has been polished through constant repetition and study of poetry, and who sympathetically respond in their own hearts – those (people) are what are known as sensitive readers' (in Masson & Patwardhan 1969: 78 n.4). Thus, the level of empathy with the musical signs depends on the polishing of the sahṛdaya's mirror of her/his heart. This polishing involves not only education and training, but also an attitude concerning the circumstances of aesthetic experience, as Abhinavagupta writes:

> When we go to the theater (*nāṭye*) we do not have any inclination to think (*abhisandhisaṁskāra*): 'Today I will have to accomplish something real (*pāramārthikam*).' Rather we feel: 'I will listen to and see something beyond my everyday experience (*lokottara*), something worthy (of my attention), whose innermost essence is pure joy (from beginning) to end (reading: *āparyanta samādaraṇīya*). I will share this experience with the whole audience (*sarvapariṣatsādhāraṇa*).' One's heart becomes like a spotless mirror (i.e. able to reflect without distortion), for all of one's preoccupations (*sāṁsārikabhāva*) have been completely forgotten, and

> one is lost in aesthetic rapture (*carvaṇā*), listening to the singing and fine music. (in Masson & Patwardhan 1970: 33)

In this way, the sahṛdaya sets her/his mind to a state of availability to the musical (or dramatic) performance, and also exerts detachment from all obstructions that could limit one's capacity for sign interpretation. In other words, the sahṛdaya approaches the temple of music humbly, with heart open to the qualities, forms and meanings to be absorbed and relished, and by means of circumaudition, attains deeper and deeper involvement with the rāga being performed. The sahṛdaya is able to reflect on her/his mind, a spotless mirror, the essential elements that will lead to the experience of rasa. In the case of music, the realization of the rāgabhāva is the first step that supports a broader field of bhāva, to be inferred and developed in the imagination, and from which rasa can be relished.

Now, it is no simple matter to keep the mirror of the mind as clear as it must be to enjoy the purified feeling of rasa. The aesthetic experience always faces obstacles that limit or totally block the enjoyment of its higher levels. Obstacles, or *vighnas*, may appear on both sides of a concert – in the spirals of both musical performance spiral and perception. Abhinavagupta listed the obstacles limiting the aesthetic experience in the theater, which may also apply to the musical situation:

> Now, the obstacles to the perception in question are – a) the unsuitability, that is to say, the lack of verisimilitude; b) the immersion in temporal and spatial determinations perceived as exclusively one's own or exclusively those of another; c) the fact of being at the mercy of our own sensations of pleasure, etc., d) the defective state of the means of perception; e) the lack of evidence; f) the lack of some predominant factor; g) and the presence of doubt. (in Gnoli 1985: 62-63)

Just as the musicians must be accomplished performers, because any lack of musical competence will present obstacles to the musical appreciation, the listeners are equally supposed to be able to draw fine musical distinctions of what is performed. This concerns the intellectual interpretation of musical signs. The practical conditions for a musical performance and its enjoyment must also be arranged so that they will not become obtrusions to the music itself. If any circumstantial incident by chance appears in the performance, musicians and listeners should not let themselves be disturbed. Further, when the rāgabhāva and sthāyibhāva is already inferred, and the listener concentrates deeply on the presented qualities of feeling, s/he must overcome the tendency to identify the bhāvas with personal emotions. Indeed, Abhinavagupta states that:

> One of the principal obstacles regularly occurs when the spectator is at the mercy of the tasting of pleasures, pains, etc., inhering in his own person. This obstacle consists in the appearance of other forms of consciousness, due variously to the fear of being abandoned by the sensations of pleasure, etc., to concern for their preservation, to a desire to

procure other similar sensations, to the desire to get rid of them, give them openly [sic] expression, hide them, etc. (in Gnoli 1985: 64).

For instance, if the listener is feeling gloomy because of something that happened in her/his personal life, and tends to identify the bhāva of rāga toḍī with those feelings, s/he will not be able to experience the rasa of vipralambha śṛṅgāra, which requires aesthetic distance from everyday life, because rasa is a kind of very refined and impersonal quality of feeling. Therefore, once the sahṛdaya is detached from the surrounding conditions of the performance and also uninvolved with her/his own personal emotions, the experience of rasa can be achieved.

This experience of rasa, however, is not merely the cognition of presented signs and their objects. Abhinavagupta 'recognizes the aesthetic object to be only a medium and not the object of aesthetic experience' (Pandey 1950: 124-25). In semiotic terms, the musical qualities and structures of a rāga are signs that, in subsequent layers of interpretants, will eventually constitute rasa, the ultimate object of aesthetic experience. Thus, the appreciation of the materiality of music is not rasa, but its indispensable groundwork. The first stages of aesthetic experience are necessarily related to the perception and cognition of the presented signs. There is comprehension involved in rāgabhāva and in recognizing the general bhāvas, the inferential results of which are called sthāyibhāva. Thus, all these phases are clearly bound to processes of reasoning. Abhinavagupta writes, 'it is legitimate to say that the perception of a permanent mental state consists in a inference; but we certainly cannot rightly say that Rasa is also of this nature' (in Gnoli 1985: 80). As the aesthetic process develops, the logical links of reasoning become more and more focused on aspects of their emotional interpretants. Indeed, as Peirce theorized, logical interpretants necessarily encompass their peculiar qualities of feelings (see 2.2). Although the inferential interpretants are not rasa, they are aesthetically necessary steps in that direction. It is the quality of feelings of those logical representations which, after the distillation process that constitutes the aesthetic experience as conceived in India, will eventually unveil rasa. Peirce recognized that the aesthetic sign obtains in a simultaneity of feeling and reason:

> It is esthetic enjoyment which concerns us; and ignorant as I am of Art, I have a fair share of capacity for esthetic enjoyment; and it seems to me that while in esthetic enjoyment we attend to the totality of Feeling – and especially to the total resultant Quality of Feeling presented in the work of art we are contemplating – yet it is a sort of intellectual sympathy, a sense that here is a Feeling that one can comprehend, a reasonable Feeling. I do not succeed in saying exactly what it is, but it is a consciousness belonging to the category of Representation, though representing something in the Category of Quality of Feeling. (CP 5.113)

This artistic representation that refers to a quality of feeling, which in turn attracts the intellectual sympathy of the interpreter, is the semiotic description of the sthāyibhāva, a sign of general character that signifies a quality of feeling.

The realization of the sthāyibhāva, the permanent state of mind, which constitutes the intermediate emotional platform in the aesthetic experience, is accomplished by a combination of suggestions (the possible action of several kinds of sign references present in the music performed) with the imaginative interpretants generated in the mind of the listener. The perception of musical signs is not limited to the level of sensation, but it is rather prone to generate further interpretants. Thus, musical semiosis is suggestive (*abhivyajyante*, in Abhinavagupta's terminology), and its interpretants are developed imaginatively by the listener, who inserts the perceived signs into the web of her/his own mind. The unfolding of imagination depends on the accrued, collateral experiences of the interpreter (see CP 8.178, 8.183, 8.314). In the case of rāga hiṇḍola, for instance, the idea of springtime may be expanded by the listener's imagination, as a result of the cognition of musical signs (as the energetic and intense character of hiṇḍola's pentatonic scale) combined with her/his collateral observation of a blossoming spring and the qualities of feeling the interpreter usually associates with it. Thus, the listener is left to complete the image of the aesthetical content, which a rāga offers only in vague contours. The role of iconic representation here is crucial, for the icon favors the most suggestive forms of semiosis. Peirce writes: 'The value of an icon consists in its exhibiting the features of a state of things regarded as if it were purely imaginary' (CP 4.448).[12] The suggestive power of art is itself the core of dhvani theory as it is presented in Ānandavardhana's poetics (see DL 1.13, and 3.2). In this sense, music is extremely suggestive when the legisigns of musical structure are interpreted not purely in their conventional capacities, but as iconic signs open to a multiplication of possible interpretants.

The sthāyibhāva does not merely appear from inferences, suggestions and their imaginative interpretants. The principle which grounds the consciousness of the sthāyibhāva is inherent in the interpreter's mind in the form of latent impressions, the instinctual set of habits of feeling and action that are common to humanity. This is referred to in Indian philosophies as saṁskāra or vāsanā, which can be traditionally understood as the residual substance of all experiences one has gone through in the innumerable cycles of existence (saṁsāra). Contemporary scholars have associated saṁskāra variously with the Freudian unconscious (Masson & Patwardhan 1969: 48; Pandey 1950: 129) and with instinct (Gnoli 1985: xv; Raghavan 1975: 17; see also 3.1, above); the Jungian idea of the collective unconscious may be pertinent here as well. Whatever the nature of saṁskāra may be, the web of perceived signs and their interpreted suggestions is modulated by it, and a general quality of feeling may be grasped in the form of a universalized interpretant, which is the

[12] See also CP 2.92, 2.444 and 7.555.

sthāyibhāva. Thus, although the listener may have never experienced to call day and night for her/his lover, s/he will be able to appreciate the general aesthetic state of mind implied in a situation of vipralambha as represented by the khayāl *Ab More Rām-Rām* in rāga toḍī. Saṁskāra, in this case, means the instinctual tendency to grieve when parted from one's beloved. The aesthetic contemplation of this situation is a universalized feeling, that is, a feeling not related to the interpreter's own emotional life, nor to that of the musician or the composer.[13] It is not an actual ordinary emotion, but rather a meta-feeling, as Masson and Patwardhan put it: 'Abhinava[gupta] distinguishes between conceiving an emotion and actually having one. In the theatre we are at one removed from real emotions, we are "meta-feeling" as it were, feeling about emotions rather than directly experiencing them' (1970: 35). The instinctual basis of saṁskāra, underlying the meta-feeling of sthāyibhāva, is the factor in art that makes representations impersonal, and whose universality Abhinavagupta refers to as *sādhāraṇīkaraṇa*.

Since the sahṛdaya interprets the aesthetic signs in a universal way, a special kind of mental state arises, distinct from ordinary forms of cognition, and not particularized as representing any actual instance of life, but rather constituting a general state of feeling that promotes the enjoyment of its essence, or rasa. Abhinavagupta illustrates how an inferred idea of fear established as the sthāyibhāva bhaya leads to the bhayānaka rasa:

> This perception of fear is different from ordinary perceptions ('I am afraid, he – my enemy, my friend, anybody – is afraid'); for these are necessarily affected by the appearance of fresh mental movements (of shunning, etc.), consisting of pleasure, pain, etc., and just for this reason are full of obstacles (vighna). The sensation of fear mentioned above, on the contrary, is the matter of cognition by a perception devoid of obstacles (*nirvighna*), and may be said to enter directly (*niviś*) into our hearts, to dance (*viparivṛt*) before our eyes: this is the terrible Rasa. In such a fear, one's own self is neither completely immersed (*tiraskṛ*) [mystical cognition] nor in a state of particular emergence (*ullikh*) [ordinary discursive cognition], and the same thing happens with the other selves. As a result of this, the state of generality involved is not limited (*parimita*), but extended (*vitata*) – as happens at the moment in which is formed the idea of the invariable concomitance (*vyāpti*) between smoke and fire or, in fact, between trembling and fear. (in Gnoli 1985: 55-56)

The idea of generality implied here is similar to a deduction, in which the first clause represents a general law. The sthāyibhāva of fear is inferred from the trembling of the actor, and it is neither apprehended as a real instance (for it is an extra-worldly state, or *alaukikāvasthā*), nor as an ordinary statement, but is assimilated by virtue of the spectators'

---

[13] According to Indian aestheticians, the development of an emotion based on any of those cases would give rise to obstacles impeding the development of further aesthetic experience.

receptivity, a state of mind free of obstacles, and is apt to be relished as rasa, when an emotion dances before the interpreter's eyes.

The bhayānaka rasa, as referred to above, brings the discussion of aesthetics to the question of whether such a feeling can be relished; that is, if the terrible and the odious rasas may be considered aesthetically good, or more naively, if there is any beauty in them. The semiotic answer to this question displaces the focus of inquiry from the questionable idea of the beautiful to that of admirability. Peirce reflects on this issue in the following terms:

> In the light of the doctrine of categories I should say that an object, to be esthetically good, must have a multitude of parts so related to one another as to impart a positive simple immediate quality to their totality; and whatever does this is, in so far, esthetically good, no matter what the particular quality of the total may be. If that quality be such as to nauseate us, to scare us, or otherwise to disturb us to the point of throwing us out of the mood of esthetic enjoyment, out of the mood of simply contemplating the embodiment of the quality – just, for example, as the Alps affected the people of old times, when the state of civilization was such that an impression of great power was inseparably associated with lively apprehension and terror – then the object remains none the less esthetically good, although people in our condition are incapacitated from a calm esthetic contemplation of it. (CP 5.131)

Although Peirce considered himself ignorant in matters of art, his keen conclusion is a negation of the (Western) classical theory of beauty: 'This suggestion must go for what it may be worth, which I dare say may be very little. If it be correct, it will follow that there is no such thing as positive esthetic badness; and since by goodness we chiefly in this discussion mean merely the absence of badness, or faultlessness, there will be no such thing as esthetic goodness. All there will be will be various esthetic qualities' (CP 5.132). That is, all qualities may be valuable aesthetically. The feeling of disgust that in real life may disturb the consciousness, when aesthetically represented does not result in personal affect, but rather the contemplation of its qualities. This has been a clear point since the earliest forms of the theory of rasa.

As impersonal as it should be, the sthāyibhāva is only effective if the interpreter sympathizes with the represented situation, or more concretely in drama, if the spectator sympathizes with the nāyaka or nāyikā.[14] At this point, the sahṛdaya is reflecting in the mirror of her/his mind an iconic form of the qualities of feelings represented by the artistic resources. This is the sympathetic response that Abhinavagupta calls *hṛdayasaṁvāda*, which, again, is not the personal sympathy of the interpreter, but a sort of universal sense of kinship. Thus, both interpreter and sign are generalities. Yet, the sthāyibhāva at this stage is not a feeble feeling, but rather an emotion developed at a high pitch. The relishing of the

[14] Sympathy is also a necessary condition for the aesthetic experience, which otherwise would be disrupted by all kinds of vighnas.

sthāyibhāva is rasa, and it is as intense as fire on dry wood, as Bharata writes: 'the tasting of that which finds the consent of the heart arouses the Rasa. The body is pervaded by it, as dry wood by fire' (NŚ 7.7).[15]

Therefore, rasa is a kind of feeling arising from a complex semiotic process, and although it is conceived as essence, its distillation implies previously elaborated mental preparations, inferences and interpretations. The aesthetic experience starts with the perceptive cognition and evolves into the general representation of instinctual feelings. This whole process does not happen spontaneously, but only with the diligent effort of a mind trained in experiencing aesthetically as an art form, such as rāga music. The goal of the aesthetic experience is the contemplation of a highly intense and pure quality of feeling. Peirce, discussing the role of icons in the processes of contemplation and fixation of the attention, discusses the matter in a way that recalls several aspects of rasa theory:

> there are certain combinations of feelings which are specially interesting. These are those which tend toward a reaction between mind and body, whether in sense, in the action of the glands, in contractions of involuntary muscles, in coördinated voluntary deeds, or, finally, in discharges of an extraordinary kind of one part of the nerves upon another. Interesting combinations of ideas are more active than others, both in the way of suggestion, and in the way of subjective intensity. The action of thought is all the time going on, not merely in that part of consciousness which thrusts itself on the attention, and which is the most under discipline, but also in its deeply shaded parts, of which we are in some measure conscious but not sufficiently so to be strongly affected by what is there. But when in the uncontrolled play of that part of thought, an interesting combination occurs, its subjective intensity increases for a short time with great rapidity. This is what constitutes the fixation of the attention. Contemplation consists in using our self-control to remove us from the forcible intrusion of other thoughts, and in considering the interesting bearings of what may lie hidden in the icon, so as to cause the subjective intensity of it to increase. (CP 7.555)

Abhinavagupta recognizes that rasa is not necessarily mental, but may involve forms of reaction in both mind and body. When defining *camatkāra*, the delight or wonder which the experience of rasa is, Abhinavagupta also refers to the bodily effects of this state of mind: 'This (form of) consciousness without obstacles is called camatkāra; the physical effects of it, that is to say, trembling, horripilation [sic], joyful motions of limbs (*ullukasana*), etc., are also called camatkāra'; and further, 'The mental movements, which are phenomena of consciousness, are also transmitted to the body and pervade it' (in Gnoli 1985: 59). In the quote above, Peirce refers to the issue of suggestion and the influence of ideas arising in the unconscious. Contemplation can be thought of as a similar process of setting the conditions for relishing rasa. The outstanding semiotic character of this kind of mental state is certainly iconic, as the metaphor of the spotless mirror suggests.

---

15 Translation according to Gnoli 1985: XLIII-XLIV n.1.

Abhinavagupta refers to the experience of rasa on two levels. According to Pandey:

> In the case of the first level, in which the universalized basic mental state is realized objectively as it were by the universalized subject, Rasa means 'The object of relish' (*Rasyate iti Rasaḥ*): because it is the basic mental state that is relished and, therefore, it is Rasa. In the case of the second level, in which the basic mental state sinks into the sub-conscious, and there is the experience of the Ānanda aspect of the Self consisting in its introversion and, therefore, rest within itself, (*Niravacchinna svātma parāmarśa; Svātma viśrānti*). Rasa means the act of relishing (*Rasanam Rasaḥ*). (1950: 130)

The first level, rasa as the object of relish, implies a generalized interpreter of a qualisign, the rasa, which is the interpretant of the sthāyibhāva (an iconic legisign). Since interpreter and sign are general ideas (universalized subject and universalized aesthetic object), the semiotic configuration is such that both are legisigns of a degenerated kind, whose outstanding character is that of a quality of feeling. Pandey explains this level of aesthetic enjoyment in these terms: 'though there is duality, though the object shines as distinct from the subject, yet both are free of all elements of individuality, both are universals. Here universalized subject experiences universalized object. Here the process of universalization of subject and object is complete. Here the object is apprehended but not determined. Here the cognizing subject is not conscious of "not this" ' (1950: 139-40). Therefore, rasa is understood here as consciousness of a quality of feeling distilled from a general emotion (the sthāyibhāva), but there still is a distinct conscience and a distinct object, and so the firstness of a rasa is still mediated. Rasa may be visualized as the loose part of a link still connected by other parts of the triadic relation to the web of musical semiosis; a form of highly degenerated thirdness, protruding, as it were, from the web (see Figure 17).

Furthermore, the aesthetic experience manifesting at this level is fundamentally emotional, for all the logical interpretants grounding the semiosic process have been disregarded. The semiosis of this meta-feeling is grounded in a pure icon, the essence of a feeling: 'The essence of rasa is aesthetic delight (camatkāra) and it is found in all the rasas' (*Sāhityadarpaṇa* 3.3, Masson & Patwardhan 1970: 18). Abhinavagupta also refers to it as camatkāra, the wonder that arises when a rasa dances before the spectators eyes, which is a form of aesthetic relish: 'The word camatkāra, indeed, properly means the action being done by a tasting subject (*camataḥ karaṇam*), in other words, by the enjoying subject, he who is immersed in the vibrations (*spanda*) of a marvelous enjoyment (*adbhutabhoga*)' (in Gnoli 1985: 59-60). In camatkāra, the interpreter experiences 'a seizure by joy (*bhogāveśa*), unbroken (*avicchinna*), and continuous satisfaction (*atṛptivyatireka*)' (in Masson & Patwardhan 1969:

46). Yet, the rasika still has another, even higher degree available for enjoyment.

The ultimate level of rasa is accomplished by *tanmayībhavana*, the identification of subject and aesthetic object. This is defined in Abhinavagupta's *Tantrāloka* as one's identification with the object of contemplation, the merging of mind and body in that object: 'identification is the attainment of one's highest Self. It is the highest stage of fulfillment, and there can be no further fruit after that'[16] (in Masson & Patwardhan 1969: 49). Rasa, in this sense, is the highest stage the sahṛdaya may reach, a level on which the spectators attain themselves, and therefore have nothing further to desire. Rasa is defined here as the act of relishing, that is, *relishing* itself. The last level of rasa is the timeless present of a consciousness filled by a pure quality of feeling, or genuine firstness. Peirce writes: 'A Firstness is exemplified in every quality of a total feeling. It is perfectly simple and without parts' (CP 1.531). This rasa is not the consciousness of a cognized external quality, but the inner quality of the self, which according to Indian philosophy is ānanda, sheer bliss. This consciousness is not conscious of anything else, and the very idea of self is extraneous to it, for there is no consciousness of ego and non-ego. Self here is self in itself, and therefore, self and rasa become one, a monad of bliss. At this point, the rasika reaches the epicenter of the perceptual spiral.

The experience of rasa in its ultimate level is related to the category of firstness in several respects. Abhinavagupta writes that rasa, as a mental form of a pure quality of feeling, 'is not something that is objectively existent (*siddhasvabhāva*) (for) it exists only for the duration of aesthetic relish (*tātkālika eva*) and does not persist for any time after the aesthetic emotion' (in Masson & Patwardhan 1970: 27). Thus, rasa is a matter of immediate present, and so is firstness. Besides, rasa is sheer feeling, which Peirce regularly connects with firstness: 'Feeling is the momentarily present contents of consciousness taken in its pristine simplicity, apart from anything else. It is consciousness in its first state, and might be called ***primisense***. (...) Feeling, or ***primisense***, is the consciousness of firstness' (CP 7.551). The immediate (and volatile) character of rasa is compared by Abhinavagupta – in a passage where aesthetics is conflated with poetry itself – with the appearance of a magic flower: 'In literature the aesthetic relish (of the suggested sense) through the verbal paraphernalia (of a drama) is like (the blossoming) of a magic flower; it is essentially a thing of the present moment which does not depend on past or future time' (in Masson & Patwardhan 1970: 17-18). No wonder rasa is thought of as camatkāra, wonder, when the ordinary historical world, regulated by saṁsāra, is replaced by another dimension of reality. 'Aesthetic sensibility, as Abhinava says, is nothing but a

[16] Notice the rich metaphoric implications of *fruit* with rasa, as juice.

capacity of wonder more elevated than the ordinary one' (Gnoli 1985: xlv-xlvi).

Rasa appears to the interpreter who moves into this last phase of aesthetic experience by the power of revelation, or *bhāvanā*. The main capacity of bhāvanā consists in untying the 'hard knot of "selfness" ' (Masson & Patwardhan 1969: vii), and the consequences of this selfless state brings the aesthetic experience to the same field that is usually only attained by the yogis, and that is communion with Brahman, which is part of all beings, things and ideas in the universe. According to Abhinavagupta:

> Rasa is revealed (*bhāvyamāna*) by a special power assumed by the words in poetry and drama, the power of revelation (*bhāvanā*) – to be distinguished from the power of denotation (*abhidhā*) – consisting of the reaction of generalized vibhāvas, etc. This power has the faculty of suppressing the thick layer of mental stupor (*moha*) occupying our own consciousness: in poetry it is characterized by the absence of defects (*doṣa*) and the presence of qualities (*guṇa*) and ornaments (*alaṁkāra*); in drama by the four kinds of representation. Rasa, revealed by this power, is then enjoyed (*bhuj*) with a kind of enjoyment (*bhoga*), different from direct experience, memory, etc. This enjoyment, by virtue of different forms of contact between *sattva* and *rajaḥ* and *tamaḥ*, consisting of the states of fluidity[,] (*druti*) enlargement (*vistāra*) and expansion (*vikāsa*), is characterized by a resting (*viśrāntī*) on one's own consciousness (*samvit*), which due to the emergent state of *sattva*, is pervaded by beatitude (*ānanda*) and light (*prakāśa*), and it is similar to the tasting (*āsvāda*) of the supreme *brahmaṇ*. (in Gnoli 1985: 45-48)

This is *ānandaikaghana*, a mental experience on such a deep level that one realizes the unity of universe (Brahman) existing in the self (ātman). Abhinavagupta maintains that the pure aspect of rasa is similar to the samādhi, the highest state of absorption sought by the yogi. Both forms of experience, the aesthetic and the yogic, indeed share several common elements and similar phases. For example, music and dance are considered preparations for its achievement. Obstacles must be removed; that is, a consciousness free of interference is a necessary condition to attain the bliss of rasa or samādhi. Both involve no material gain. In such an experience, the consciousness of time and space disappears, and therefore it is non worldly, or alaukika. The spectator and the yogi forget the self, and this forgetfulness extends to the point where the distance between object and subject is removed, and thus the idea of self is transcended. Total immersion in this state leads to ānandaikaghna, where everything is blissful, for the innermost essence has been attained. 'In both cases, what appears is not something that is "created" anew, but something that is "manifested," or "suggested." Rasa is not "produced", it is "suggested"' (Masson & Patwardhan 1969: 161). However, the two forms are still distinguishable, for the aesthetic experience depends on the medium of artistic language, and the enjoyment of its supreme bliss is not as permanent as that of the yogic experience. Still, the true aesthetic experience is always transformational, for the aesthete does not return to the everyday world unchanged.

Furthermore, the transformational aspect of art is not necessarily individual, for the whole community of enjoyers is affected synergetically. According to Sāṅkhya philosophy, consciousness is conditioned by three guṇas, or qualities of mental substance: sattva, rajas and tamas. Sattva is the principle of pleasure and light; rajas, that of pain and activity; and tamas, the principle of passivity and negativity. These three elements are simultaneously in conflict and in cooperation. They determine certain states of consciousness identified as expansion (vikāsa), incited by a total prevalence of sattva; fluidity (druti), which comes by a combination of sattva with rajas; and dilatation (vistara) resulting from an association of sattva with tamas. The aesthetic enjoyment is characterized by the combined effects of these three mental actions: 'It is when rajaḥ is in fluidity, tamaḥ in dilatation, and sattva in full expansion that fruition is realized' (*Māṇikyacandra* 74, in Gnoli 1985: 46 n.1). Yet, the expansion of consciousness, which occurs when rasa is enjoyed, does not only manifest in the individual mind of each spectator, but, according to Abhinavagupta, has the tendency to overflow, and thus the whole audience is involved collectively in the experience of rasa. As he writes in the *Tantrāloka* (28.373):

> The consciousness, which consists of, and is animated by, all things, on account of the difference of the bodies, enters into a state of contraction. But, in public celebrations, it returns to a state of expansion – since all the components are reflected in each other. The radiance of one's own consciousness in ebullition (i.e. when it is tending to pour out of itself) is reflected in the consciousness of all the bystanders, as if in so many mirrors, and, inflamed by these, it abandons without effort its state of individual contraction. For this very reason, in meetings of many people (at a performance of dancers, singers, etc.), fullness of joy occurs when every bystander, not only one of them, is identified with the spectacle. The consciousness, which, considered separately also, is innately made up of beatitude, attains, in these circumstances – during the execution of dances, etc. – a state of unity, and so enters into a state of beatitude which is full and perfect. In virtue of the absence of any cause of contraction, jealousy, envy, etc. the consciousness finds itself, in these circumstances, in a state of expansion, free of obstacles, and pervaded of beatitude. When, on the other hand, [if] even one only of the bystanders does not concentrate on the spectacle he is looking at, and does not share, therefore, the form of consciousness in which the others spectators are immersed, this consciousness is disturbed, as at the touch of an uneven surface. (in Gnoli 1985: XXXVIII)

The overflow and blend of minds in the enjoyment of rasa is certainly the highest possible realization of aesthetic experience. As passages like this are often understood in the domain of the transcendental, it seems unlikely that any logical interpretation could throw light on it. However,

Abhinavagupta was not a fictionist, and his theories are quite likely constructions based on Tantric techniques whose results were experimentally known. The extended concept of mind such as that developed by Peirce may clarify, at least hypothetically, how the communion of minds is possible. The starting point of this argument is that, according to Peirce, a person is not an absolute individual, and a community may be conceptualized as a loosely compacted person (CP 5.421). He writes:

> But are we shut up in a box of flesh and blood? When I communicate my thought and my sentiments to a friend with whom I am in full sympathy, so that my feelings pass into him and I am conscious of what he feels, do I not live in his brain as well as in my own – most literally? True, my animal life is not there but my soul, my feeling thought attention are. (...) Each man has an identity which far transcends the mere animal; – an essence, a ***meaning*** subtile [sic] as it may be. He cannot know his own essential significance; of his eye it is eyebeam. But that he truly has this outreaching identity – such as a word has – is the true and exact expression of the fact of sympathy, fellow feeling – together with all unselfish interests – and all that makes us feel that he has an absolute worth. (CP 7.591)

Although the organism constitutes a biological boundary, by means of several forms of human interaction, such as conversation and sympathy, the limits of a single self may be extended, so that a mind *outreaches* and merges in some respect with other minds. Peirce's conclusion is that 'A person is, in truth, like a cluster of stars, which appears to be one star when viewed with the naked eye, but which scanned with the telescope of scientific psychology is found on the one hand, to be multiple within itself, and on the other hand to have no absolute demarcation from a neighboring condensation' (Peirce MS 403). Therefore, the expansion of consciousnesses and the overflow of the spectators' minds in the course of relishing the highly intense and pervasive feeling which rasa is, can be understood semiotically as the communion of minds in their collective galaxy. Furthermore, the metaphor of a person as a cluster of stars brings up another topic of Indian philosophy, which can be only mentioned here, namely, that mind is self-luminous, or prakāśa. And both light and bliss are its innermost essence, or rasa.

Recapitulation

The above interpretation of the aesthetic experience from a semiotic perspective has had, necessarily, to criss-cross several layers of the palimpsest of rasa and Indian philosophies. In the process, the connection of rasa with musical matters may have become too faint. As compensation, a synthetic view of the topic is graphically represented in Figure 17.

Figure 17
Aesthetic Rapture as the Spiral of Interpretants

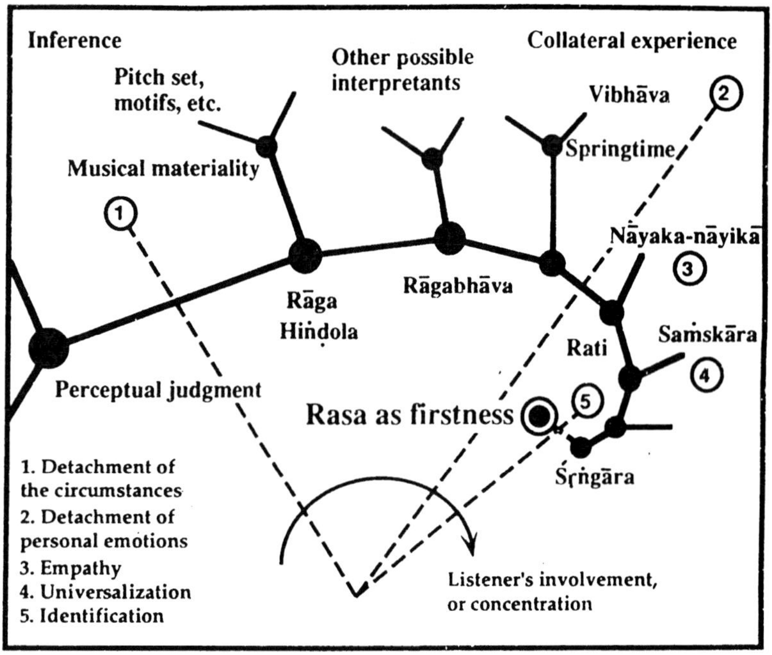

Aesthetic enjoyment starts with a concert, where the audience ponders what rāga is being performed. The listener hypothesizes, by means of abductive reasoning, and starts comparing the svaras and melodic motives heard to those of her/his knowledge. This actually takes places as series of deductive and inductive inquiries. In this way, anyone with enough ear-training and reasonable experience with Hindustani rāgas will recognize what is performed. An experienced listener may take only a few seconds to recognize the rāga. This is accomplished by training (or trained instincts, as Peirce would say), but, irrespective of how fast a listener figures out the rāga, the recognition of musical aspects is a kind of inference that is always mediated and of an intellectual nature. In addition to this ongoing reasoning, the process described up to this point does not exclude the emotional and the energetic interpretants, which will lead the listener to experience qualities of feelings and/or physical reactions. Thus, on one hand, each svara, in combination with the sound of the tambūrā, has its peculiar quality of feeling, as do all the other musical elements, such as the rāgarūpa, tāla and musical form. On the other hand, the interpretant of a rāga can trigger psychic or physical reactions, such as verbal statements of approval, which at Indian concerts are quite common and appreciated by the musicians.

Assume that a listener identifies the rāga in, say, the dhamār *Śyāmā Moso Khelonā Horī*, as hiṇḍola (Ex. 67). As the concert goes on, the interpretant of hiṇḍola develops in the listener's mind, becoming more and more clear as the music continues. After the listener has enjoyed the music awhile, the interpretant presents itself as an iconic sign, which has its own formal wholeness, and therefore the rāgabhāva or the gestalt (as Powers says) of hiṇḍola pervades her/his consciousness. At this point, there is a communion of qualities of feeling and form between the performer and the sahṛdaya, the receptive and skilled listener. The musician must also have the rāgabhāva of hiṇḍola in mind, in order to play or sing it properly. S/he is able to translate all technical and aesthetical resources into musical strategies, such as tirobhāva and avīrbhāva as well as several forms of reference (see 2.3, above), thereby enriching and heightening the enjoyment of the performance.

This is the level of aesthetic experience that Abhinavagupta describes as conceivable by inference. Besides the musical features of this rāga, other ideas form part of the interpretants evolving in a listener's mind that is properly attuned to the performance; these would include its level of inner signification, other technical features of performance (such as the variations presented during each round of improvisation, or the patterns played by the drummer), and the objects hiṇḍola stands for in its cultural position as a symbol. In that case, the ancient habit of associating this rāga with springtime will take hold on the mind, bringing forth recollections of Holī, for instance; especially if the rāga is actually being played during the spring, as prescribed. Other ideas can be similarly related to this rāga, such as the swing festival. These thoughts, cultural signs that have been learned (i.e., symbols), could combine with the listener's present interpretations of hiṇḍola so as to generate further an interpretant in the form of the dramatic sthāyibhāva of rati (love). An Indian listener might also interpret this sign (the rāga hiṇḍola) as an index or indexical sign, which may bring to mind personal experiences with those seasons, their festivals and qualities of feeling, and/or a particular event that actually happened at that time. To the extent that the listener merely reinforces the general aesthetic idea of rati with vague feelings derived from her/his personal life, there would be no obstruction to the development of the aesthetic experience.

In this way, from the rāgabhāva of hiṇḍola and the bhāvas of the song's lyrics, the sthāyibhāva of rati emerges. Both hiṇḍola and rati are symbols, but a special kind of symbol whose main character is a quality. If certain conditions are met, the formal aspect of the signs can be abstracted and only their qualities of feeling remain: the śṛṅgāra rasa. This is a special skill of the cognizing mind. As Abhinavagupta wrote, the spectator's consciousness must be free of obstacles such as one's attention straying from the performance, confusing or conflating the sthāyibhāva of the rāga with one's own feelings or moods, and so on. A spectator with the ability to overcome those faults and to reach the rasa level is really a connoisseur, a sahṛdaya, one whose heart stays fixed on the artistic performance. Such a listener can concentrate on it to the point that a sympathetic mental response, that is, an iconic interpretant, is generated during this inner dialogue with the performance. But to reach the rasa level, more is required than sympathetic response. Identification is necessary. When the listener concentrates so deeply on the rāgabhāva that the whole of her/his consciousness is only the quality of feeling of rati, and when all the technical and musical features of the performance are present to the consciousness yet are somehow abstracted – only then, by a process which Abhinavagupta called revelation, would śṛṅgāra (or another rasa, depending on the case) manifest itself. In this state of mind, there is no difference between sign and object, and therefore the interpretant is a pure icon. Further, when a mind is flooded by this qualisign to such a degree that there is no distinction between ego and non-ego, no consciousness of the flow of time, but only a continuous present, the highest level of rasa is reached. That level can only be understood semiotically as a peculiar state of firstness, whose character is purely that of śṛṅgāra, a brilliant state of bliss.

Therefore, the aesthetic experience as conceived in India is a semiotic process during which an elaborate intellectual scaffolding arises, one based on a multitude of signs of several kinds, and interpreted in a highly conventional way, but whose final tendency or telos is merely a quality of feeling. Although the nine rasas are formal categories, their final experience is a tremendous semiotic abstraction, in which all triadic and dyadic relations are reduced to the monadic state of firstness. However, the firstness of a rasa is not related to the indeterminacy and freedom of possibility with which firstnesses are usually identified. Thanks to all previous intellectual and artistic developments, the sahṛdaya is able to concentrate on the firstness that the musician presents for enjoyment. And then, the essential flavor, the rasa of a rāga, artificially selected, amplified and prolonged, intense as fire on dry wood, pervading not only one consciousness but spreading among the audience, flows out as a collective mind in aesthetic rapture.

Conclusion

In view of the richness of musical meaning in Hindustani music, as explored in the previous section, there is no evidence for any conception of it as being absolute. Deshpande, however, seems to take an absolutist position, when he discusses mediate and immediate signification in music: 'The literary meaning thus having no purpose to fulfill in music, "things," "objects," "scenes," etc., have no place in it. Music, in other words, is not descriptive of the "traffic of the world". There is a region, beyond verbal meaning, into which music directly and immediately transports us. One can say that the impact of the "word" is mediate, while that of music is immediate' (1987: 26). The possibility of an immediate interpretation of music, a form of musical consciousness in firstness, is not at all inconceivable, as I have demonstrated in 2.1 and 3.4. Nevertheless, music cannot be considered devoid of mediation, for semiosis is the agency of all forms of interpretants. The mediation might be more or less diaphanous, and music is prone to constitute very thin representamens. Hindustani music, however, is lodged in a web of significations with which it is factually and culturally related, and thus it mediates a variety of possible objects, some of which Deshpande lists as disconnected from music.

It is true that most forms of drumming in India generate interpretants that tend to purely intrinsic musical signification. However, one can hardly say the same with regard to any of the great and known rāgas, all of them being filled with symbolic potential for interpretation. They can obviously be listened to as pure music, but in the mind of any interpreter that has minimal acquaintance with Indian culture, the purely musical signs are apt to generate a fertile web of significations. What would lead an Indian scholar to claim that music is non-referential? It seems to me that the influence of certain Western conceptions of music, such as Stravinsky's *Poetics of Music* (translated into Marathi by A. Ranade) and Aaron Copland's *Music and Imagination* (also translated into Marathi, by S.H. Deshpande) might have led some Indian scholars to adopt musical views that are utterly foreign to Indian traditions. Stravinsky's ideas are certainly valuable, but they refer to his own conception of composition, and thus cannot be extended to all musics in the world, including Indian music. It is sufficient to examine how Indian music has always been conceived as representational, in early treatises such as the NŚ, BD, SR, RD, RV, and in this century, in RN, RVJ and SA.

Therefore, one may conclude that Western approaches to Indian music will likely fail to understand its essence. It seems to me, however, that a semiotic approach can succeed, while maintaining fidelity to the traditional view of Indian music, for it is not biased toward particular aesthetic preconceptions. Rather, semiotics consists in a system of logic dedicated to the problem of the nature of signs, their modes of operation, and their forms of interpretation; and sign here is understood as any possible quality, thing or idea, such as the timbre of a tambūrā, the DNA of any being, or the theory of Quanta. This refers especially to the semiotics developed by Peirce, a theory that does not privilege linguistic concepts (another source of bias), but starts from the logic of relatives, which, being mathematically devised, is much less prone to cultural and representational biases. Music is sign, and its form of action is semiosis. Musical signs vary in all cultures in all respects, and their study must be contextualized. The rationales behind the music of Pierre Boulez, or the music of Yanomami aborigines in the Amazon forest, or the renditions of rāga vilāskhānī toḍī by Sulochana Brahaspati are all incommensurable among themselves, except for the fact that all involve some form of semiosis and musical signs.

This Peirce-based semiotic theory of music, when applied to Hindustani music, has had as its main goal the understanding of music in its own web of significations. If, in this respect, any distortion has appeared in this study, it should not be credited to the theory itself, but rather to my inability to translate and analyze the meanings of those significations. Any systematic study leaves room for error. Peirce was well aware of this, to the point of incorporating a theory of fallibilism into his own philosophy of science (see 1.3). In this connection, he wrote: In those sciences of measurement which are the least subject to error – metrology, geodesy, and metrical astronomy – no man of self-respect ever now states his result, without affixing to it its probable error; and if this practice is not followed in other sciences it is because in those the probable errors are too vast to be estimated' (CP 1.9). Thus, not underestimating the margins of fallibilism that pervade all sciences, the main achievements of this study may be summarized as follows.

My purpose in the first section was to demonstrate the need for a semiotic theory of music, and this was accomplished by study of the anthropological views of Blacking and Merriam, as well as the unified-field theory of C. Seeger. All those authors pointed to the complexity of music in its relation to the cultural universe from which it springs. However, their theories, though addressing some problems of signification, are not specific enough to clarify the essential problem of musical meaning, namely, semiosis. Theories of musical semiotics were intended to engage with this problem directly. Yet several of the proposed systems, while addressing a particular aspect of musical signification, sometimes disregard the very question of semiosis. It seems to me that, if a theory sets aside essential features of musical semiosis, then it can neither maintain consistency, nor claim to be a complete system. This is the case with Nattiez's theory, when he states that semiology 'is not the science of communication' (1990: 16). Conversely, I hold that a semiotic theory of music based on the Peircean general theory of the signs can cope, in an integrated way, with the fundamental aspects of musical semiosis. Such a theory has the power to generate understandings of inner signification, reference, perception and performance (or communication, better understood as dialogical semiosis), composition, and so on – and to do so with pertinence and great capacity for theoretical translation. Initially, the application of Peirce's theory to musical matters was very fragmentary. A few scholars have more recently begun to understand how Peirce's ideas of semiosis can engage music. Nevertheless, the potentiality of Peircean semiotics, in its broad heuristic, analytic and methodological capacities, remains largely unexplored. Above, I situated musical studies within Peirce's architecture of the sciences, a classification system in which the humanities and sciences are conceived as complementary. I did so mainly in order to determine the implications and the main fields of inquiry pertinent to an applied or descriptive musical semiotics in relation to its general, formal or pure semiotics (the science Peirce actually developed as one of the branches of philosophy). The conclusion was that there are three relevant fields of inquiry in musical semiosis: (1) Intrinsic Musical Signification; (2) Musical Reference; and (3) Musical Interpretation. They are not isolated spheres, but rather overlap each other according to a certain logic, such that the second and the third encompass, cumulatively, the previous field or fields.

The second section consisted in the expansion and initial exploration of those three fields in regard to their theoretical bases and their applications to aspects of Hindustani music. Since Peirce's phaneroscopy is the basis of all philosophical inquiry, its study constitutes a necessary premiss for a Peircean semiotic theory of music. Thus, the comprehension of the musical phenomenon in its mere appearance was the subject of the first chapter of that section. There followed a study of musical semiosis and an explanation of the main tool for its analysis, which is the classification of signs. The core of the second section was the study of each field of musical inquiry. Intrinsic musical signification starts with the essential problem of musical qualities. Indeed, quality is the necessary aspect of existence, and the foremost element in musical semiosis. This seems to be a clear point in Indian musical philosophy, where several classical authors maintain that sound is not only the basis of music and dance, but the ultimate component of the universe. The structural organization of Indian music was then analyzed in terms of the relationship of sinsigns, as actualized musical forms of legisigns. The analyses showed that great flexibility exists in the replications of Hindustani music legisigns, especially the concept of rāga; and such suppleness results in a rich and vibrantly alive musical system. The characterization of rāgas as euphorganisms, as proposed by Saxena, was justified analytically by the idea of the generative power of legisigns, which manifest on all other levels of musical signification.

The study of musical reference on a Peircean basis (which encompasses intrinsic musical signification) points up the misguidedness of disputes between a view of music as pure and 'non-referential' and the opposite conception, of music as representational – for both are possible forms of semiosis. Here one may situate the question of Indian music as consisting in the pure musical significations of a rāga, or as referring to a broad universe of cultural forms, existents and ideas, evident since the earliest Indian treatises. The solution depends on whether the object to which a musical sign refers is acoustical or otherwise. Thus, there is a mode of musical reference that generates pure icons, and these are likely to be interpreted as pure music. Conversely, music has enormous power for iconic reference, and Indian music is no exception. Peirce divided iconic signs, or hypoicons, into images, diagrams and metaphors, and above I explored their musical manifestations in early Indian and contemporary Hindustani music. I concluded that images consist in the musical representation of acoustic qualities of the object; that musical diagrams represent likenesses of movement qualities and of formal qualities; and that metaphors concern musical metalanguage, proposing the division of these last into paraphrase, quotation, and allegorical reference. Because praxis is the essential reality of music, it follows that a web of infinite determinations can provide an equally infinite capacity for musical indexicality. This refers not only to musical existents (actual indices), but also to musical representations, which may function as indexical signs in a variety of forms. The most outstanding cases in Hindustani music were analyzed. The question of symbolic representation in Hindustani music is an aspect of rāgas, in their capacity of generating music and musical meaning. This chapter did not attempt to describe exhaustively the objects to which Hindustani music may refer, but rather its modes and strategies of reference.

The field of musical interpretation, encompassing the former two, is the most complex and lengthy, because it deals with musical semiosis in actuality. I divided interpretation into three domains: (1) Musical Perception, (2) Musical Performance, and (3) a double third, consisting of Musical Intelligence and Musical Composition. Peirce offers a theory of perception that conforms perfectly to his semiotics. From evidence found in Indian music theory and practice, I was able to discern three kinds of interpretants that musical perception can generate: (1) emotive listening, (2) energetic listening, and (3) rational listening. Musical performance, a necessary counterpart of perception, is essential to Indian music, not only to perpetuate it, but because musical structures and representations are produced at the very moment in which the music is actualized. In this sense, performance and composition are very closely related in this tradition. My three modes of performance were classified according to (1) the musical, (2) the functional, and (3) the representational features of a performance. Musical intelligence, as a form of generating interpretants about music, has long been a concern in India. Musical intelligence forms the object of several kinds of scholarship: (1) musical aesthetics (including the theory of rasa), (2) musical pragmatics, and (3) musical semiotics. All of them have been explored for millennia by Indian scholars. Finally, musical composition, which depends on all the above fields, their branches and their subdivisions, can be understood as the creation of (1) absolute music, (2) functional music, and (3) representational music. In the Hindustani tradition, the first kind is found mostly in drumming, the second in dance and educational music; the third covers most Hindustani music, with its variety of musical, existential and aesthetical representations. My evidence for this idea was presented in a study, if brief, of some outstanding composers of Hindustani music and their work.

An investigation of semiosis in Hindustani music could not be satisfactory if its universe of representations were not considered. The third section of my study explored this subject in the light of the classical Indian aesthetic theory of rasa and in view of Peircean semiotics. The first two chapters of section three explained the fundamentals and the subsequent development of rasa theory, especially as presented originally by Bharata and later expanded by Abhinavagupta. There followed an historical inquiry into how rāgas were conceived as representing rasas and other aesthetical objects, and the correlation of those objects with their musical structures. It was concluded that, although both musical structures and meanings have varied according to time and place in India, there has been remarkable continuity as well as expansion of representations, especially in the domain of rāga, some of which are still found in contemporary music. This semiotic universe cannot be disregarded by listeners, musicians, scholars, critics, or anyone who thinks seriously about Indian music. Those representations refer to the very core of Indian culture, in its polysemous and multifaceted forms. The last chapter of the third section consisted in a semiotic analysis of the aesthetical experience of Hindustani music. It proved that rasa theory is not merely a classification of general categories of aesthetic feelings, but a true theory of aesthetical perception, representation and interpretation. My contention is that aesthetic problems are also semiotic. A semiotic theory of music, when applied, with all its power of inner, referential and interpretative analysis, to cases as complex as semiosis in Hindustani music, can bring significant and clear understandings; and it can do this without conflicting with the traditional view of rasa theory. Therefore, the value of Peircean semiotics can be appreciated for its capacity to approach the phenomena of Hindustani music in terms that *clarify* the traditional view, instead of replacing it with a superstructure that is disengaged from Indian qualities of feeling, facts and thought.

In this last chapter, I must consider the practical possibilities of a semiotic theory of music. Peirce, in regard to logic as a theory, writes:

> Begin, if you will, by calling logic the theory of the conditions which determine reasonings to be secure. (...) Logic, then, is a theory. The end of any theory is to furnish a rational account of its object. (...) A theory directly aims at nothing but knowing. Maybe, if it be sound, it is likely, some day, to prove useful. Still, fairness forbids our making utility the criterion of the excellence of the theory. One must acknowledge that such a way of thinking would not abase logic, as it does the generality of sciences. To judge of logic by its applications would only be to judge of it by how far it does, or does not in a [certain] manner, help us to understand things. Clearly, it is the proper aim of any theory to do that. (CP 2.1)

Logic, or 'semeiotic', conceived by Peirce as one of the highest heuretical sciences, has its practical value in the way it promotes understanding of its subject matter. The heuristic capacity of semiotics can also be understood in the same terms by which Peirce explained the usefulness of his existential graphs: 'Its true utility is in the assistance it renders – the support to the mind, by furnishing concrete diagrams upon which to experiment – in the solution of the most difficult problems of logical theory' (CP 4.571). Similarly, a semiotic theory of music may be thought of as a diagram that aids not only the comprehension of musical phenomena in their different cultural conceptions, but also the construction or assembling of performances and compositions, both traditional and innovative.

Even the most theoretical discipline has a practical side, which helps not only the academicians, but everyone to understand the world that surrounds them or the world of interiority and introspection. A semiotic theory of music helps the comprehension of musical semiosis in all its features and varieties, implying a connectedness between questions that are apparently separated: How does music convey feelings, which can be as immediate (just what it apparently is) as the quality of the sitār's timbre? By what means does a certain musical sequence remind the listeners of the gait of a charming lady? Why (and how) is it possible to recognize in a recording the identity of a singer or the style of a particular composer? How can a rāga flood Indian listeners with a distinctive rasa, while producing totally different feelings in a foreign audience? Answers to these questions will help composers, musicians and listeners, as well as scholars, critics and teachers, to comprehend music better and to 'do' it better.

It is also true, however, that a semiotic theory of music is unimportant for most people. Even some musicians would find it worthless; i.e., those who practice music in an instinctive way. Fishermen do not need semiotics to pull their nets to the rhythm of a worksong. Neither do Indian musicians, who were born listening to rāgas brimming with meanings, and who received their training right from the beginning in this semiotic environment. Peirce was well aware of this situation. He thought, 'In particular, applications of theories would be worse than useless where they would interfere with the operation of trained instincts.

Who could play billiards by analytic mechanics?' (CP 2.3) However, music is not confined to trained instincts. Anyone intending to analyze any kind of music needs theoretical tools. If the analysis evolves into problems of signification, a semiotic theory of music has to be considered. Any musician or conductor who feels the need to understand deeply what s/he plays in order to perform it correctly, will recognize the usefulness of musical semiotics. If the composition belongs to a tradition in which expression is important, it is fundamental for that performer and/or conductor to be conscious of the semiotic means employed in that piece. Every composer who wants to convey an idea (even a purely musical one) with her/his work deals with semiotic questions; this is certainly the case with composers of music for film, theater, dance, advertising, and the like – hence the need for a powerful semiotic theory of music.

It seems to me that semiotics will become more and more a major discipline in musical scholarship, not only dealing with all questions directly related to musical semiosis, but also as a necessary complement to established musical disciplines, in their systematic, historical, or ethnomusicological aspects. Musical semiotics perfuses all their domains, from acoustics to perception, from scales and modes to harmony, from musical forms to orchestration, from rituals to aesthetics. Furthermore, semiotic analysis can clarify interrelations among the several arts in forms such as song, dance, theater, dance dramas, cinema, video, and computerized multimedia; and by means of semiotic analysis, new forms of intersemiosis may be devised.

Any art with roots in a distant past, especially one as old as that of Indian music, has plenty to offer the music semiotician. The music of India, a complex sign-form, is generous in producing interpretants. From the materiality of rāga and tāla, to facts of Indian clime and culture, and the richness of their aesthetic representations based on millennia of artistic and philosophical activities, the interpretation of this music requires that musicians, listeners, and scholars consider not only the diversity of musical signs themselves, but also the referential universe they stand for. Interpreters are invited to be as generous in their interpretations as this exuberant music is in its aural and mental enticements. Just as the final interpretant of rāgas, tālas, forms and musical styles is the totality of significations that Indian culture can generate, its potential to generate wonder is equally infinite.

Bibliography[1]

ADLER, Guido (1981). The Scope, Method, and Aim of Musicology, trans. by Erica Mugglestone. *Yearbook for Traditional Music* 13, 5-21.

ĀNANDAVARDHANA (1982). *Dhvanyāloka* [The Light of Suggestion], 2nd. ed., trans. by K. Krishnamoorth. Delhi: Motilal Bararsidass.

ARNOLD, W.J. (1984). Playing with Intonation. *ISTAR - Newsletter* 3-4, 60-62. New Delhi: International Society for Traditional Arts Research.

ASHIRWADAM, P.D. (1990). *Raigarh Darbar.* Delhi: Agamkala Prakashan.

BAKE, Arnold A. (1930). *Bijdrage tot de kennis der Voor-Indische muziek.* Paris: Paul Geuthner.

– (1964). The Aesthetics of Indian Music. *British Journal of Aesthetics* 4, 47-57.

BAKHŚŪ, Nāyak (1972). *Sahasarasa, ke dhrupaddoṃ kā saṅgrah* [The Thousand Delights, dhrupads of Nāyak Bakhśū], Prem Lata Sharma (ed.). New Delhi: Sangeet Natak Akademi.

BANDYOPADHYAYA, S. (1977). *The Origin of Rāga,* 2nd ed. New Delhi: Munshiram Manoharlal.

– (1988). *Techniques of Sitar.* Delhi: B.R.

BASHAM, A.L. (1954). *The Wonder that India Was.* New Delhi: Rupa.

BEL, Bernard (1992). Modeling improvisational and compositional processes. *Languages of Design* 1, 11-26.

BERNETT, Elise B. (1970). Special Bibliography: Art Music of India. *Ethnomusicology* 14(2), 278-312.

BERNSTEIN, Richard J. (1964). Peirce's Theory of Perception. In *Studies in the Philosophy of Charles Sanders Peirce,* E.C. Moore and R.S. Robin (eds.), 165-189. Amherst: The University of Massachusetts Press.

BHARATA (1967). *The Nāṭyaśāstra* [Dramaturgy], 2 vols., 2nd. ed., trans. by Manomohan Ghosh. Calcutta: Manisha Granthalaya.

BHATTACHARYA, Shashthi Prasad (1976). *Śānta Rasa and Its Scope in Literature.* Calcutta: Sanskrit College.

BHAṬṬ, Śaśimohan (1967). *Sitār-praveś* [Introduction to the Sitar]. Agra: Mehara Aphaset Press.

BHĀTKHAṆḌE, V.N. (1939). *Hindusthānī Saṅgīta Paddhati-Krāmika Pustaka Mākikā* [Hindustani Music Treatise, Progressive Book Series], vol. 4. Bombay: Kulkarni.

[1] References to all multi-volume works will be given as [volume number].[paragraph number], [volume number].[page number], or [chapter number].[verse number], and the like, preceded by either an abbreviation code or by the author's name.

– (1990-1993). *Hindusthānī Saṅgīta Paddhati - Krāmika Pustaka Mālikā* [Hindustani Music Treatise, Progressive Book Series], 6 vols. Hāthras: Saṅgīt Kāryālay.

– (1990). *A Comparative Study of Some of the Leading Musical Systems of the 15th, 16th, 17th 18th Centuries*, reprint. New Delhi: Low Price.

BLACKING, John (1973). *How Musical is Man?* Seattle: University of Washington Press.

BOILES, Charles L. (1973). *Sémiotique de l'ethnomusicologie*. Musique en Jeu 10, 34-41.

BOR, Joep (1984). Raga Sketches. *Istar Newsletter* 2, 21-23.

– (1986-1987). The Voice of the Sarangi. *NCPA Quarterly* 15(3/4)-16(1).

– (1988) The Rise of Ethnomusicology: Sources on Indian Music c. 1780 – c. 1890. *Yearbook for Traditional Music* 20, 51-73.

BOR, Joep & MOTT, Issaro (1984-5). Notating Hindustani Music. *Istar Newsletter* 3/4, 29-42.

BOULEZ, Pierre (1986). *Orientations*, trans. by M. Cooper, J.J. Nattiez (ed.). Cambridge: Harvard Univeresity Press.

BRAHASPATI, K.C.D. (1979). Tānsen. In *Composers* (= Cultural Leaders of India), V. RAGHAVAN (ed.), 75-88. New Delhi: Ministry of Information and Broadcasting.

– (1983). Mussalmans and Indian Music. In *Studies in Musicology*, R.C. Mehta (ed.). Baroda: Indian Musicological Society, 57-79.

– (1989). *Saṅgīt Cintāmaṇi* [The Thought Jewel of Music]. Hathras: Sangita Karyalay.

BRENT, Joseph (1993). *Charles Sanders Peirce: A Life*. Bloomington: Indiana University Press.

BURKS, A. (1949). *Icon, Index, and Symbol*. Philosophy and Phenomenological Research 9(4), 673-689.

CAGE, John (1961). *Silence*. Middletown: Wesleyan University Press.

CAGE, John & CHARLES, Daniel (1981). *For the Birds*, trans. by Richard Gardner. Boston, London: Marion Boyars.

CHAITANYA, K. (ed.) (1983). *Aestheticians* (= Cultural Leaders of India), V. RAGHAVAN (ed.). New Delhi: Ministry of Information and Broadcasting.

CHANDOLA, Anoop (1988). *Music as Speech: An Ethnomusicolinguistic Study of India*. New Delhi: Navrang.

CHATTERJEE, Satischandra & DATTA, Dhirendra Mohan (1984). *An Introduction to Indian Philosophy*, 8th ed. Calcutta: University of Calcutta.

CHENNAKESAVAN, Sarasvati (1991). *Concept of Mind in Indian Philosophy*. Delhi: Motilal Banarsidass.

CLOUGH, John; DOUTHETT, Jack; RAMANATHAN, R.; ROWELL, Lewis (1993). Early Indian Heptatonic Scales and recent Diatonic Theory. *Music Theory Spectrum* 15(1), 36-58.

COKER, Wilson (1972). *Music and Meaning*. New York: Free Press.

COOMARASWAMY, Anand (1991). *The Dance of Shiva*, 3rd ed. New Delhi: Munshiram Manoharlal.

DANIÉLOU, Alain (1991). *The Rāga-s of Northern Indian Music*, 2 ed. New Delhi: Munshiram Manoharlal.

DATTILA (1988). *Dattilam*, trans. by Mukund Lath. New Delhi: IGNCA & Motilal Banarsidass.

DELVOYE, Françoise 'Nalini' (1986-95). Bibliography on Dhrupad. *Dhrupad Annual* 1-10.

– (1990a). Tānsen at la tradition des chants dhrupad en langue braj, du XVIe siecle a nos jours [Tānsen and the tradition of dhrupad singing in Braj language, from the 16th century to contemporaneity]. Unpublished doctoral dissertation. Paris: Universite de la Sorbonne Nouvelle.

– (1990b). The Verbal Content of Dhrupad Songs from the Earliest Collections: 1. The Hazar Dhrupad or Sahasras, a collection of 1004 dhrupads attributed to Nāyak Bakhśū. *Dhrupad Annual* 5, 93-108.

– (1992). The Verbal Content of Dhrupad Songs from the Earliest Collections: 2. Kitāb-i-nauras (part 1). *Dhrupad Annual* 6, 38-54.

– (1993). The Verbal Content of Dhrupad Songs from the Earliest Collections: 2. Kitāb-i-nauras (part 2). *Dhrupad Annual* 8, 1-23.

– (1994a). The Thematic Range of Dhrupad Songs Attributed to Tānsen, Foremost Court Musician of the Mughal Emperor Akbar. In *South Asian Devotional Literature*, Alan W. Entwistie and Françoise Mallison (eds.), 406-429. New Delhi: Manohar.

– (1994b). The Verbal Content of Dhrupad Songs from the Earliest Collections: 3. Dhrupad Songs Attributed to Tānsen in Court-musicians' Repertoires. *Dhrupad Annual* 9, 1-12.

– (1994c). Indo-Persian Literature on Art-Music: Some Historical and Technical Aspects. In *Confluence of Cultures – French Contributions to Indo-Persian Studies*, F. Delvoye (ed.), 130-147. New Delhi: Manohar.

DĀMODARA (1930). *Saṅgītadarpaṇa* [The Mirror of Music] (= Bake 1930), trans. by A. Bake. Paris: Geuthner.

DESAI, Chaitanya P. (1979). Amir Khusrau. In *Composers* (= Cultural Leaders of India), V. Raghavan (ed.), 66-74. New Delhi: Ministry of Information and Broadcasting

DESHPANDE, Vamanrao H. (1987). *Indian Musical Traditions*, 2nd ed., trans. by S.H. Deshpande, V.C. Devadhar. Bombay: Popular Prakasham.

DEVA, B. Chaitanya (1981). *The Music of India: A Scientific Study*. New Delhi: Munshiram Manoharlal.

DEVA, B.C. & VIRMANI, K.C. (1968). Meaning of Music, an empirical study of psychological responses to Indian music. *Sangeet Natak Academi* (journal) 10, 54-93.

DIMOCK, Edward C. Jr.; GEROW, Edwin; NAIM, C.M.; RAMANUJAM, A.K.; ROADARMEL, Gordon; van BUITENEN, J.A.B (1974). *The Literatures of India: An Introduction*. Chicago: University of Chicago Press.

DOUGHERTY, William P. (1992). What is a Musical Sign? A Guess at the Riddle. Paper Presented at the Third International Congress of Musical Signification, Edimburg (forthcoming).

– (1993). The Play of Interpretants: A Peircean Approach to Beethoven's Lieder. In *The Peirce Seminar Papers: An Annual of Semiotic Analysis* 1, M. Haley (ed.), 67-95. Oxford: Berg.

– (1994). The quest for interpretants: Toward a Peircean paradigm for musical semiotics. *Semiotica* 99(1/2), 163-184.

EBELING, Klaus (1973). *Ragamala Painting*. New Delhi: Ravi Kumar.

ECK, Diana L. (1983). *Banaras: City of Light*. New Delhi: Penguin.

ERDMAN, Joan L. (1982). The Empty Beat: Khālī as a Sign of Time. *American Journal of Semiotics* 1(4), 21-45.

FEYERABEND, Paul (1975). *Against Method*. London: NBL.

FISCH, Max H. (1986). *Peirce, Semeiotic and Pragmatism*, Kenneth L. Ketner and Christian J.W. Kloesel (eds.). Bloomington: Indiana University Press.

FISCH, Max, KETNER, Kenneth L., KLOESEL, Christian J.W. (1979). The New Tools of Peirce Scholarship, with Particular Reference to Semiotic. *Peirce Studies* 1, 1-17.

FISHER, G. R. (1985). How Music Communicates. *Semiotica* 53(1/3), 131-144.

GANGOLY, O.C. (1989). *Rāgas & Rāginīs*, reprint (first edition 1935). New Delhi: Munshiram Manoharlal.

GEROW, Edwin (1977). Indian Poetics. In *A History of Indian Literature* 5(3), Jan Gonda (ed.). Wiesbaden: Otto Harrassowitz.

GHOSH, Manamohan (1967). Introduction. In *Nāṭyaśāstra*, 2 vols., 2nd. ed. Calcutta: Manisha Granthalaya.

GNOLI, Raniero (1985). *The Aesthetic Experience According to Abhinavagupta* (= Chowkhamba Sanskrit Studies 62), 3rd. ed. Varanasi: Chowkhamba.

GOSWAMI, Roshmi (1995). *Meaning in Music*. Shimla: Indian Institute of Advanced Studies.

GOTTLIEB, Robert (1981). Symbolisms Underlying Improvisatory Practices in Indian Music. *Journal of the Indian Musicological Society* 12(3/4), 23-36.

– (1993). *Solo Tabla Drumming of North India*. Delhi: Motilal Banarsidass.

GUPTA, Sanjukta, HOENS, Dirk Jan and GOUDRIAAN, Teun (1979). *Hindu Tantrism* (= Handbuch Der Orientalistik 2.4.2), J. Gonda (ed.). Leiden: Brill.

GUTZWILLER, (1984). The Shakuhachi of the Fuke-Sect: Instrument of Zen. *The World of Music* 26(3), 53-65.

HATTEN, Robert (1980). Nattiez's Semiology of Music: Flaws in the New Science. *Semiotica* 31(1/2), 139-155.

– (1994a). *Musical Meaning in Beethoven: Markedness, Correlation and Interpretation*. Bloomington: Indiana University Press.

– (1994b). A Peircean Perspective on the Growth of Markedness and Musical Meaning, In *Peirce and Value Theory* (= Semiotic Crossroads 6), H. Parret (ed.), 349-358. Amsterdam, Philadelphia: John Benjamins.

HATTEN, Robert & HENROTTE, Gayle A. (1988). Recent Perspectives on Musical Semiotics. In *The Semiotic Web 1987* (= Approaches to Semiotics 81), T.A. Sebeok & J. Umiker-Sebeok (eds.), 421-463. Amsterdam, Berlin, New York: Mouton de Gruyter.

HENRY, Edward O. (1988). *Chant the Names of God*. San Diego: San Diego State University Press.

HIRIYANNA, M. (1993). *Outlines of Indian Philosophy*. Delhi: Motilal Banarsidass.

HOLYOAK, Keith & THAGARD, Paul (1995). *Mental Leaps: Analogy in Creative Thought*. Cambridge, London: MIT Press.

HOOD, Mantle (1971). *The Ethnomusicologist*. New York: McGraw-Hill.

HOUSER, N. (1990). O escopo da semiótica peirceana (= The Scope of Peircean Semiotics, paper presented in the C.S. Peirce Sesquicentennial International Congress, Harvard, 1989), trans. by L. Santaella. *Face* 3(2), 207-215.

IMAM, Hakim Mohammad Karam (1959). Effect of Ragas and Mannerism in Singing, trans. by Govind Vidyarthi. *Sangeet Natak Academi Bulletin* 13-14, 6-14.

JAIRAZBHOY, Nazir Ali (1971). *The Rāgs of North Indian Music: Their Structure and Evolution.* Middletown: Wesleyan University Press.

– (1975). An Interpretation of the 22 Śrutis. *Asian Music* 6(1/2), 38-59.

– (1980). India, Ṭhumrī and Ghazal (part III). In *The New Grove Dictionary of Music and Musicians*, vol.9, Stanley Sadie (ed.), 141-143. London: Macmillan.

– (1993). South Asia (1. India; 2. Pakistan). In *Ethnomusicology: Historical and Regional Studies*, Helen Myers (ed.), 274-296. London: Macmillan.

JAMES, William (1985). *The Varieties of Religious Experience.* Cambridge: Harvard University Press.

JAYADEVA (1977). *The Gitagovinda of Jayadeva*, trans. by Barbara Stoler Miller. Delhi: Motilal Banarsidass.

JOHANSEN, Jørgen Dines (1985). Prolegomena to Semiotic Theory of Text Interpretation. Semiotica 57(3/4), 225-288.

– (1993). *Dialogic Semiosis.* Bloomington: Indiana University Press.

JONES, Sir William (1990 [1784]). On the musical modes of the Hindoos. In *Hindu Music*, Sourindro Mohun Tagore (ed.), 125-160. Delhi: Low Price.

KANE, Padurang Vaman (1974). *History of Dharmaśāstra*, vol. 5, part 1, 2nd. edition. Poona: Bhandarkar Oriental Research Institute.

KARBUSICKY, Vladimir (1987). The Index Sign in Music. *Semiotica* 66(1/3), 23-35.

KAUFMANN Walter (1965). Rasa, Rāga-mālā and performance times in North Indian Rāgas. *Ethnomusicology* 9(3), 272-291.

– (1993). *The Rāga-s of North India.* New Delhi: Oxford & IBH.

KAUMUDI (1950). Mingling of Islamic and Indigenous Traditions in Indian Music. *The Indian Historical Quarterly* 26(2), 129-137.

KENT, Beverley (1987). *Charles S. Peirce: Logic and the Classification of the Sciences.* Kingston and Montreal: McGill Queen's University Press.

KETNER, Kenneth L. (1988). Toward an Understanding of Peirce's Master Argument. *Cruzeiro Semiótico* 8, 57-66.

KEVELSON, Roberta (1985). Riddles, legal decisions, and Peirce's Existential Graphs. *Semiotica* 57(3/4), 197 223.

KHAN, Ali Akbar (ed.) & RUCKERT, George (1991). *The Classical Music of North India: The Music of the Baba Allauddin Gharana as Taught by Ali Akbar Khan.* Saint Louis: East Bay Books.

KHAN, Mobarak Hossain (1992). *Islamic Contribution to South Asia's Classical Music.* New Delhi: Sterling.

KIPPEN, James (1988). *The Tabla of Lucknow* (= Cambridge Studies in Ethnomusicology), John Blacking (ed.). New Delhi: Cambridge & Manohar.

– (1992a). Tabla Drumming and the Human-Computer Interaction. The *World of Music* 34(3), 72-98

– (1992b). Where does the End Begin? Problems in Musico-Cognitive Modeling. *Minds and Machines* 2(4), 329-344.

KOSTELANETZ, Richard (1988). *Conversing with John Cage*. New York: Limelight.

KUHN, Thomas S. (1967). *The Structure of Scientific Revolutions*. Chicago: University of Chicago Press.

LANNOY , Richard (1971). *The Speaking Tree*. Oxford: Oxford University Press.

LATH, Mukund (1978). *A Study of Dattilam*. New Delhi: Impex.

– (1988a). Commentary on the Text. In *Dattilam*, New Delhi, Delhi: Indira Gandhi National Centre for the Arts and Motilal Banarsidass.

– (1988b). The "Modern", the "Traditional", and Criticism in the Indian Musical Tradition. *Sangeet Natak Academi* (journal) 89-90, 5-15.

LIDOV, David (1986). Music. In *Encyclopedic Dictionary of Semiotics*, T. Sebeok (ed.), 577-587. Amsterdam, Berlin, New York: Mouton de Gruyter.

– (1987). Mind and Body in Music. *Semiotica* 66(1/3), 69-97.

MACHADO, Arlindo (1984). *A Ilusão Especular* [The Specular Illusion]. São Paulo: Brasiliense.

MANUEL, Peter (1985). The Evolution of Toḍī Rāg-s in Indian Music. *Journal of the Indian Musicological Society* 16(2), 14-30.

– (1986). The Evolution of Modern Ṭhumrī *Ethnomusicology* 30(3), 470-490.

– (1989). *Ṭhumrī in Historical and Stylistic Perspectives*. Delhi: Motilal Banarsidass.

– (1990). Legitimate and Illegitimate Variation in Raga Interpretation. *Sangeet Natak Academi* (journal) 96, 19-27.

MARTINEZ, José Luiz (1991). Música & Semiótica: Um Estudo Sobre a Questão da Representação na Linguagem Musical [Music & Semiotics: a Study on Musical Representation]. Unpublished master's thesis, Pontifícia Universidade Católica de São Paulo.

– (1994). Practicing Musical Semiotics. *Musiikkitiede* 1-2, 158-163.

– (1996a). Icons in Music: a Peircean Rationale. *Semiotica* 110(1/2), 57-86.

– (1996b). Musical Semiosis and the Rasa Theory. In *Musical Semiotics in Growth* (= Acta Semiotica Fennica 4), Eero Tarasti (ed.), 99-125. Bloomington, Imatra: Indiana University Press, International Semiotics Institute.

MASSON, J.L. & PATWARDHAN, M.V. (1969). *Śāntarasa and Abhinavagupta 's Philosophy of Aesthetics* (= Bhandarkar Oriental Series 9). Poona: Bhandarkar Oriental Research Institute.

– (1970). Aesthetic Rapture, 2 vols. Poona: Deccan College.

MATAṄGA (1992-1994). *Bṛhaddeśī* [The Greatness of Regional Music] , trans. by Prem Lata Sharma and A.B. Beohar, 2 vols. New Delhi, Delhi: Indira Gandhi National Centre for the Arts and Motilal Banarsidass.

McGREGOR, R.S. (1995). *Hindi-English Dictionary*, reprint. Delhi: Oxford.

MEER, Wim van der (1980). Hindustani Music in the 20th Century. The Hague: Martinus Nijhoff.

MEHTA, R.C. (ed.) (1983). *Studies in Musicology*. Bombay: Indian Musicological Society.

MENON, Narayana (1982). *The Language of Music*. The World of Music 24(1), 3-29.

MERRIAM, Alan P. (1964). *The Anthropology of Music*. Evanston: Northwestern University Press.

MEYER, Leonard B. (1956). *Emotion and Meaning in Music*. Chicago, London: University of Chicago Press.

MIŚR, Vidyāvās (1989). *Sāhityak Brajabhaṣā Koś* [Braj-Hindī Dictionary]. Agra: Hindī Saṁsthān.

MILLER, Barbara Stoler (1977). Introduction. In *The Gitagovinda of Jayadeva* (= Jayadeva 1977). Delhi: Motilal Banarsidass.

MOLINO, Jean (1990). Musical Fact and the Semiology of Music, trans. by J.A. Underwood. *Music Analysis* 9(2), 113-156.

MONELLE, Raymond (1991). Music and the Peircean Trichotomies. *IRASM* 22(1), 99-108.

– (1992). *Linguistics and Semiotics in Music*. Chur: Harwood.

MONIER-WILLIAMS, M. (1994). *Sanskrit English Dictionary*. New Delhi: Munshiram Manoharlal.

MONTAUT, Annie (1987). Dhrupad de l'Inde et musiques répétitives d'Occident. *Semiotica* 66(1/3), 315-330.

MORAES, J. Jota (1983). *O que é Música* [What is Music]. São Paulo: Brasiliense.

MOSLEY, DAVID L. (1995). Peirce's 'Ground' and the 19th Century Lieder. In *Musical Signification*, Eero Tarasti (ed.), 413-421. Berlin, New York: Mouton de Gruyter.

MOUTAL, Patrick (1991). *Hindustāni Rāga-s Index*. New Delhi: Munshiram Manoharlal.

MUGGLESTONE, Erica (1981). Guido Adler's 'The Scope, Method, and Aim of Musicology' (1885): an English Translation with an Historico-Analytical Commentary. *Yearbook for Traditional Music* 13, 1-5.

NANDIKEŚVARA (1970). *The Mirror of Gesture*, 2nd. edition, trans. by A. Coomaraswamy & G.K. Duggirala. New Delhi: Munshiram Manoharlal.

NATTIEZ, Jean-Jacques (1975). *Fondements d'une sémiologie de la musique*. Paris: Union Générale d'éditions.

– (1990). *Music and Discourse: Towards a Semiology of Music*, trans. by C. Abbate. Princeton: Princeton University Press.

NAYAR, Sobhana (1989). *Bhatkhande's Contribution to Music*. Bombay: Popular Prakashan.

NEHRU, Jawaharlal (1966). *The Discovery of India*, reprint. Bombay: Asia Publishing House.

NETTL, Bruno (1983). *The Study of Ethnomusicology*. Urbana: University of Illinois Press.

NEUMAN, Daniel M. (1990). *The Life of Music in North India*. Chicago: University of Chicago Press.

NIJENHUIS, Emmie Te (1974). *Indian Music: History and Structure* (= Handbuch der Orientalistik 2[6]), Jan GONDA (ed.). Leiden: Brill.

– (1976). *The Rāgas of Somanātha* (= Orientalia Rheno-Traiectina), 2vols., J. Gonda and H.W. Obbink (eds.). Leiden: Brill.

– (1977). *Musicological Literature* (= A History of Indian Literature 6[1]), Jan GONDA (ed.). Wiesbaden: Otto Harrassowitz.

– (1992). Introduction. In *Saṅgītaśiromaṇi: a medieval handbook of Indian music* (= *Saṅgītaśiromaṇi* 1992). Leiden: Brill.

NYLUND, H. (1983). Syntactic Structures of North Indian Rāgas. The *World of Music* 25(2), 47-57.

O'FLAHERTY, Wendy Doniger (1973). *Śiva: The Erotic Ascetic*. Oxford: Oxford University Press.

OLIVEIRA, Willy C. de (1979). *Beethoven: Proprietário de Um Cérebro* [Beethoven: Owner of a Brain]. São Paulo: Perspectiva.

PANDEY, Kanti Chandra (1950). *Comparative Aesthetics*, vol. 1, Indian Aesthetics. Varanasi: Chowkhamba.

– (1972). *Comparative Aesthetics*, vol. 2, Western Aesthetics, 2nd ed. Varanasi: Chowkhamba.

– (1983). Abhinavagupta. In *Aestheticians* (= Cultural Leaders of India), V. Raghavan, 56-65. New Delhi: Ministry of Information and Broadcasting.

PARPOLA, Asko (1994). *Deciphering the Indus Script*. Cambridge: Cambridge University Press.

PARRET, Herman (1994). Peircean Fragments on the Aesthetical Experience. In *Peirce and Value Theory* (= Semiotic Crossroads 6), H. Parret (ed.), 179-190. Amsterdam, Philadelphia: John Benjamins.

PATANJALI (1976). *The Yogasūtra*, trans. by Bangali Baba. Delhi: Motilal Banarsidass.

PAṬVARDHAN, Vinayak Rao (1982). *Rāga Vijñāna* [The Knowledge of Rāga], 7 vols., 10th ed. Poona: Saṅgīt Gaurav Granthmālā.

PEIRCE, Charles S. (1902). Manuscript L75, (Application to the Carnegie Institution for support for his Research in Logic), J. Ransdell (ed.). [Text available in electronic format at 'gopher://gopher.ttu.edu:70/11/Pubs/peirce/OnLine%20Library/Peirce%27s%20Writings', or at Arisbe, the WWW home of Charles S. Peirce, 'http://www.door.net/arisbe/menu/library/bycsp/bycsp.htm'.]

– (1938-1956). *The Collected Papers*, 8 vols., Charles Hartshorne, Paul Weiss, and Arthur W. Burks (eds.). Cambridge: Harvard University Press.

– (1982-). *Writings of Charles Peirce: A Chronological Edition*, M.H. Fisch, E.C. More, C.J.W. Kloesel (eds.). Bloomington: Indiana University Press.

– (1983). A Brief Intellectual Autobiography by Charles Sanders Peirce [Manuscripts L107, and 914], Kenneth L. Ketner (ed.), *American Journal of Semiotics* 2(1/2), 61-83.

– (1992). *The Essential Peirce*, vol. 1, Nathan Houser and Christian Kloesel (eds.). Bloomington: Indiana University Press.

PERERA, E.S. (1994). *The Origin and Development of Dhrupad and its Bearing on Instrumental Music*. Calcutta: Bagchi.

PIATIGORSKY, A.M. & ZILBERMAN, D.B. (1976). The Emergence of Semiotics in India. *Semiotica* 17(3), 255-265.

POWERS, Harold (1965). Indian Music and the English Language: a Review Essay. *Ethnomusicology* 9(1), 1-12.

– (1970). An historical and comparative approach to the classification of ragas (with an appendix on ancient Indian tunings). *Selected Reports in Ethnomusicology* 1(3), 2-78.

– (1976). The Structure of Musical Meaning: a View from Banaras. *Perspectives of New Music* 14(2)-15(1), 308-334.

– (1980a). India (parts I and II). In *The New Grove Dictionary of Music and Musicians*, vol.9, Stanley Sadie (ed.), 69-141. London: Macmillan.

– (1980b). Mode. In *The New Grove Dictionary of Music and Musicians*, vol.12, Stanley Sadie (ed.), 376-450. London: Macmillan.

PRAJÑĀNĀNANDA, Swāmī (1961) Aryan and Non-Aryan Origin of Some Indian Rāgas. *Nāda Rūpa* 1(1), 49-57.

– (1973). *Historical Development of Indian Music*, 2nd ed. Calcutta: Firma KLM.

PRIGOGINE, Ilya & STENGERS, Isabelle (1984). *Order Out of Chaos*. Boulder: Shambhala.

QURESHI, Regula Burckhardt (1980). India: Chanted poetry; Popular Religious Music, Muslim (part IV, V, 2). In *The New Grove Dictionary of Music and Musicians*, vol.9, Stanley Sadie (ed.), 143-147. London: Macmillan.

– (1986). *Sufi Music of India and Pakistan*. Calcutta: Seagull & Cambridge.

RADHAKRISHNAN, S. (1994).. *The Principal Upaniṣads*. New Delhi: Indus.

RAGHAVAN, V. (1956). Some Names in Early Sangita Literature. *Sangeet Natak Academi Bulletin* 5, 19-28.

– (1957). Some Names In Early Sangeet Literature. *Sangeet Natak Academi Bulletin* 6, 23-30.

– (1960), Later Sangita Literature. *Sangeet Natak Academi Bulletin* 17, 1-24.

– (1961). Later Sangita Literature. *Sangeet Natak Academi Bulletin* 18, 1-18.

– (1975). *The Number of Rasa-s*, 3rd ed. Madras: Adyar Library and Research Centre.

– (1978), *Bhoja's Śṛṅgāra Prakāśa*, 3rd ed. Madras: Vasanta Press.

– (1981). *Abhinavagupta and His Works* (= Chaukhambha Oriental Research Studies 20). Varanasi: Chaukhambha.

RAGHAVAN, V. (ed.) (1979). *Composers* (= Cultural Leaders of India). New Delhi: Ministry of Information and Broadcasting.

RAJA, K. Kunjunni (1977). *Indian Theories of Meaning*. Madras: Adyar Library and Research Centre.

RAMALAKSHMI, T. Seetha (1993). *References to Music in Non-Sangitha Literature*. Bangalore: Vedasruthi.

RANADE, Ashok Damodar (1992). Rāgamālā Paintings: A Musicological Perspective. *Sangeet Natak Academi* (journal) 103, 3-11.

RANADE, G.H. (1951). *Hindustani Music: Its Physics and Aesthetics*, 2nd. ed. Bombay: Popular Prakashan.

RANSDELL, Joseph (1966). Charles Peirce: the Idea of Representation. Unpublished Ph.D. dissertation. New York: Columbia University.

– (1979). The Epistemic Function of Iconicity in Perception. *Peirce Studies* 1, 51-66.

– (1977). Some Leading Ideas in Peirce's Semiotics. *Semiotica* 19(3/4), 157-178.

– (1986). Peirce, Charles Sanders. In *Encyclopedical Dictionary of Semiotics*, Thomas A. Sebeok (ed.), 673-695. Berlin: Mouton de Grutyer.

RAO, B. Subba (1965). *Raganidhi: A Comparative Study of Hindustani and Karnatak Ragas*, 4 vols. Madras: The Music Academy.

RAO, Survanalata S. (1992). Acoustical Perspective on Raga-Rasa Theory. Unpublished doctoral dissertation. Bombay: S.N.D.T. Women's University.

RAY, Sitansu (1991). Tagore-Music: Composition Span and Perspectives. *Journal of the Indian Musicological Society* 22, 101-130.

– (1992). Tagore and Music Research. *Journal of the Indian Musicological Society* 23, 70-73.

ṚGVEDA (1951). *Der Rig-Veda, Aus Dem Sanskrit ins Deutsche Übersetzt* (= The Harvard Oriental Series 35), trans. by K.F. Geldner. Cambridge: Harvard University Press.

RICHMOND, Farley P.; SWANN, Darius L.; ZARRILLI, Phillip B. (eds.) (1993). *Indian Theatre* (= Performing Arts Series 1), Farley P. Richmond (general ed.). Delhi: Motilal Banarsidass.

ROBERTS, Don D. (1973). *The Existential Graphs of Charles S. Peirce*. The Hague, Paris: Mouton de Grutyer.

ROWELL, Lewis (1983). *Thinking About Music: An Introduction to the Philosophy of Music*. Amherst: University of Massachusetts Press.

– (1987). Stasis in Music. *Semiotica* 66(1/3), 181-195.

– (1988). The Idea of Music in India and the Ancient West. In *Essays on the Philosophy of Music* (= Acta Semiotica Fennica 43), V. Rantala, L. Rowell, and E. Tarasti (eds.), 323-342. Helsinki: Societas Philosophica Fennica.

– (1992). *Music and Musical Thought in Early India*. Chicago: University of Chicago Press.

SAṄGĪTAŚIROMAṆI (1992). *Saṅgītaśiromaṇi* [The Paragon Jewel of Music]: *A Medieval Handbook of Indian music* (= Brill's Indological Library), trans. by E.T. Nijenhuis, Johannes Bronkhorst (ed.). Leiden: Brill.

SANTAELLA, Lúcia (1983). *O que é Semiótica* [What is Semiotics]. São Paulo: Brasiliense.

– (1988). For a Classification of Visual Signs. *Semiotica*: 70(1/2), 59-78.

– (1989). From Pure Icon to Metaphor: Six Degrees of Iconicity, paper presented in the C.S. Peirce Sesquicentennial International Congress, Harvard (forthcoming).

– (1991). Instinct, logic, or the logic of instinct? *Semiotica* 83(1/2), 123-141.

– (1992). *A Assinatura das Coisas: Peirce e a Literatura* [Things' Signature: Peirce and Literary Studies]. Rio de Janeiro: Imago.

– (1993a). *A Percepção: uma teoria semiótica* [Perception: A Semiotic Theory]. São Paulo: Experimento.

– (1993b). Difficulties and strategies in applying Peirce's semiotics. *Semiotica* 97(3/4), 401-410.

– (1994a). *Estética: de Platão a Peirce* [Aesthetics, from Plato to Peirce]. São Paulo: Experimento.

– (1994b). Peirce's Broad Concept of Mind. *S* (European Journal for Semiotic Studies) 6(3/4), 399-411.

– (1995). *A Teoria Geral dos Signos: Semiose e Autogeração* [The General Theory of Signs: Semiosis and Self-generation]. São Paulo: Ática.

SANYAL, Ritwik (1986). The Dagar Tradition. *Dhrupad Annual* 1, 43-47.

– (1987). *Philosophy of Music*. Bombay: Somaiya.

– (1989). The Dagar Tradition: Voice and Tone. *Dhrupad Annual* 4, 91-94.

– (1990). The Dagar Tradition: Characteristics of Ālāpa. *Dhrupad Annual* 5, 64-67.

– (1993). The Dagar Tradition: Characteristics of Tāla. *Dhrupad Annual* 8, 30-33.

– (1995). The Pada in the Dagar Tradition. *Dhrupad Annual* 10, 113-116.

SANYAL, Ritwik & WIDDESS, Richard (1994). Some Techniques of Laykārī in the Dagar Tradition. *Dhrupad Annual* 9, 19-27.

SARMADEE, Shahab (1984-1985). Mankutuhal and Rag Darpan – Reflections on a Great Seventeenth Century Scholar-Musician. *ISTAR Newsletter* 3-4, 18-26.

ŚĀRṄGADEVA (1978-1989). *Saṅgītaratnākara of Śārṅgadeva* [The Mine of Musical Jewels], 2 vols., trans. by R.K. Shringy (under the supervision of Prem Lata Sharma). New Delhi: Munshiram Manoharlal.

SAXENA, S. K. (1973). Aesthetics of Hindustani Music. *Sangeet Natak Academi* (journal) 28, 5-23.

– (1979). *The Winged Form: Aesthetical Essays on Hindustani Rhythm*. New Delhi: Sangeet Natak Akademi.

– (1989a). The Rasa Theory: An Essay in Understanding. *Sangeet Natak Academi* (journal) 91, 3-30.

– (1989b). 'Philosophy of Music' by Ritwik Sanyal (Book Review). *Sangeet Natak Academi* (journal) 91, 60-66.

– (1990). Hindustani Rhythm and John Dewey's Aesthetics. *Sangeet Natak Academi* (journal) 95, 3-25.

– (1991a). The Concept of Raga: An Essay In Understanding. *Sangeet Natak Academi* (journal) 101-102, 32-46

– (1991b). *Swinging Syllables: Aesthetics of Kathak Dance*. New Delhi: Sangeet Natak Akademy.

– (1992). Hindustani Music and the Philosophy of Art. *Sangeet Natak Academi* (journal) 105-106, 3-23.

SEBEOK, Thomas (1981). *The Play of Musement*. Bloomington: Indiana University Press.

SEEGER, Charles (1977). *Studies in Musicology 1935-1975*. Berkeley, Los Angeles: University of California Press.

SEN, Sharmistha (1988). *The String Instruments of North India*, 2 vols. Delhi: Eastern Books Linkers.

SHAEFFER, Pierre (1952). *A lá Recherche d'une Musique Concréte*. Paris: Seuil.

– (1988). *Tratado de los Objetos Musicales*, trans. by Araceli C. de Diego. Madrid: Alianza.

SHAKUNTALA, K.V. (1968). Martial Musical Instruments of Ancient India. *Sangeet Natak Academi* (journal) 10, 5-11.

SHANKAR, Ravi (1969). *My Music, My Life*. New Delhi: Vikas.

SHARMA, Amal Das (1993). *Musicians of India – Past and Present: Gharanas of Hindustani Music and Genealogies*. Calcutta: Naya Prokash.

SHARMA, Prem Lata (1961). Indian Aesthetics or Rasaśāstra as Applied to Music: an Introduction. *Nāda Rūpa* 1(1), 167-168.

– (1963a). Unique and Unrivaled Characteristics of the Art and Science of Indian Music. *Nāda Rūpa* 2(2), 1-9.

– (1963b). Śrīkaṇṭha's Rasakaumudī. *Nāda Rūpa* 2(2), 10-38.

– (1963c). European Aesthetics of Music and Indian Saṅgīta Śāstra. *Nāda Rūpa* 2(2), 39-90.

– (1969). Ragakalpadruma (synopsis of treatise). *Indian Music Journal* 2(10), 108-112.

– (1970). Rasa Theory and Indian Music. *Sangeet Natak Academi* (journal) 16, 57-64.

– (1972-74). Sahasarasa – A Compilation of Dhrupad Texts Ascribed to Bakshoo (synopsis of treatise). *Indian Music Journal* 8(1/2), 9(1/2), 10(1/2), 41-48.

SHORT, Thomas L. (1982). Life Among the Legisigns. *Transactions of the Charles S. Peirce Society* 18(4), 285-310.

– (1988). The Growth of Symbols. *Cruzeiro Semiótico* 8, 81-87.

SHUKLA, H.L. (1994). *Semiotica Indica: Encyclopaedic Dictionary of Body-Language in Indian Art & Culture*, 2 vols. New Delhi: Aryan Books International.

SIMON, Robert (1980). India: Religious Music, Hindu (part V, 1). In *The New Grove Dictionary of Music and Musicians*, vol.9, Stanley Sadie (ed.), 144-145. London: Macmillan.

SINGER, Milton (1984). *Man's Glassy Essence* – Explorations in Semiotic Anthropology. Bloomington: Indiana University Press.

SINGH, Thakur Jaideva (1970). Aesthetics of Hindustani Musical Forms. *Sangeet Natak Academi* (journal) 16, 23-32.

SINHA, Jadunath Sinha (1986). *Indian Psychology*, 3 vol. (Volume 1: Cognition; volume 2: Emotion and Will; volume 3: Epistemology of Perception). Delhi: Motilal Banarsidass.

SMALL, Edward S. (1987). Semiotic Referentiality: Saussure's Sign and the Sanskrit Nama-Rupa. *American Journal of Semiotics* 5(3), 447-459.

SPINKS, C.W. (1991). *Peirce and Triadomania: A Walk in the Semiotic Wilderness*. Berlin: Mouton de Gruyter.

SRINIVASAN, K.S. (1985). The Nayikas of Indian Classics. *Sangeet Natak Academi* (journal) 75, 7-13.

SRIVASTAVA, Indurama (1980). *Dhrupada: A Study of its Origin, Historical Development, Structure and Present State*. Delhi: Motilal Banarsidass.

SRIVASTAVA, R.N. & KAPOOR, K. (1988). Semiotics in India, in *The Semiotic Web 1987* (= Approaches to Semiotics 81), T. Sebeok & J. Umiker-Sebeok (eds.), 271-265. Berlin, Amsterdam, New York: Mouton de Gruyter.

STRANGWAYS, A.H. Fox (1995). *The Music of Hindustan*, reprint. New Delhi: Mittal.

TAGORE, Rabindranath (1961). *Art & Aesthetics*. Calcutta: Orient Longmans.

– (1991). *My Reminiscences*. London: Papermac.

TAGORE, Sourindro Mohan (1990a). *Six Principal Ragas*, reprint. Delhi: Low Price.

– (1990b). *The Seven Principal Notes of the Hindus*, reprint. Delhi: Low Price.

– (1990c). *Hindu Music*, reprint. Delhi: Low Price.

TARASTI, Eero (1978). *Myth and Music* (= Acta Musicologica Fennica 11). Helsinki: Suomen Musiikkitieteellinen Seura.

– (1985). Music as Sign and Process. *Analytica* (Studies in the Description and Analysis in Honour of Ingmar Bergtsson) 47, 97-115. Stockholm: The Royal Swedish Academy of Music.

– (1986). Musical Models Through Ages: A Semiotic Interpretation. *International Review of the Aesthetics and Sociology of Music* 17(1), 22-32.

– (1987). Some Peircean and Greimasian Concepts as Applied to Music. In *The Semiotic Web 1986*, Thomas A. Sebeok and Jean Umiker-Sebeok (eds.), 445-459. Amsterdam, Berlin, New York: Mouton de Gruyter.

– (1994a). *A Theory of Musical Semiotics*. Bloomington: Indiana University Press.

– (1994b). Can Peirce be Applied to Music? In *Peirce and Value Theory: On Peircean Ethics and Aesthetics* (= Semiotic Crossroads 6), Herman Parret (ed.), 335-348. Amsterdam, Philadelphia: John Benjamins.

– (1994c). From Mastersingers to Bororo Indians – on the Semiosis of Improvisation. In *Improvisation* 2, 62-81. Frankfurt: Amadeus Verlag.

THAGARD, Paul (1988). *Computational Philosophy of Science*. Cambridge, London: MIT Press.

ṬHĀKUR, Omkārnāth (1955-1975). *Saṅgītāñjali* [Music Offering], 6 vols. (1. Pratham bhāg, pratham puṣp, pratham kalī [1959]; 2. Pratham puṣp, dvitīya kalī [1975]; 3. Dvitīya puṣp, pratham kalī [1955]; 4. Caturth bhāg, dvitīya puṣp, dvitīya kalī [1957]; 5. Pañcam bhāg, dvitīya puṣp, pratham kalī [1957]; 6. Ṣaṣṭ bhāg, tṛtīya puṣp, dvitīya kalī [1962]). Hathras: Saṅgīt Karyālay.

VĀLMĪKI (1990). *Rāmāyaṇa*, trans. by Kamala Subramaniam, 5th ed. Bombay: Bharatya Vidya Bhavan.

VATSYAYAN, Kapila (1980). India: Dance (part VII). In *The New Grove Dictionary of Music and Musicians*, vol.9, Stanley Sadie (ed.), 158-166. London: Macmillan.

– (1992). *Indian Classical Dance*, 2nd. ed. New Delhi: Ministry of Information and Broadcasting.

VENKATACHAKAM, V. (1983). Bhoja. In *Aestheticians* (= Cultural Leaders of India), K. Chaitanya (ed.), 86-109. New Delhi: Ministry of Information and Broadcasting.

VIRMANI, K.G. (1970). Experimental Psychology and Indian Music. *Sangeet Natak Academi* (journal) 16, 45-56

VYĀSA (1990). *Mahābhārata*, trans. by Kamala Subramaniam, 8th ed. Bombay: Bharatya Vidya Bhavan.

WADE, Bonnie C. (1971). Khyāl: a Study in Hindustani Classical Vocal Music, 2 vols., doctoral dissertation. Los Angeles, University of California: UMI.

– (1980). India: Folk Music (part VI). In The New Grove Dictionary of Music and Musicians, vol.9, Stanley Sadie (ed.), 147-158. London: Macmillan.

– (1984). *Khyāl: Creativity within North India's classical Music Tradition*. Cambridge: Cambridge University Press.

– (1987). *Music in India: The Classical Traditions*. New Delhi: Manohar.

– (1990). The Meeting of Musical Cultures in the 16th-Century Court of the Mughal Akbar. *The World of Music* 32(2), 3-24.

WATSON, Francis (1974). *A Concise History of India*. London: Thames and Hudson.

WIDDESS, Richard (1994). Involving the Performers in Transcription and Analysis: A Collaborative Approach to Dhrupad. *Ethnomusicology* 38(1), 59-79.

– (1995). *The Rāgas of Early Indian Music*. Oxford: Clarendon.

– (1996). The Oral in Writing: Early Indian Musical Notations. *Early Music* 24(3), 391-405.

WILLARD, N. Augustus (1990 [1834]). A Treatise on the Music of Hindoostan. In *Hindu Music*, Tagore, Sourindro Mohun (ed.), 1-122. Delhi: Low Price.

YĀDAV, P.B.E. (1992). *Tablā Prakāś* [Splendor of the Tablā], 3 vols. Īlāhābād: Saṅgīta Sadan.

Index